Volume 3 carries the story of the XIV Reserve Corps thr█████████████████
the Somme and into 1917, a period of transition for the █████████████████
and strategy of trench warfare would undergo great changes as the German Army was
transformed from a military force rooted in the 19th Century into a modern 20th Century
fighting force with new strategies and tactics. The concept of a continuous trench system
was being transformed into a defense in depth as a direct result of a shortage of men in
the German Army. The reader will experience the withdrawal to the Siegfried Stellung
(Hindenburg Line) and the subsequent fighting by Arras and trench warfare by Verdun and
in the Champagne. What was not known to the rank and file during this time were the
difficulties facing the German High Command in regard to manpower problems, and the
huge consumption of critical resources resulting from fighting on numerous battle fronts. It
was a time when Germany began to realize that something needed to change otherwise the
war could be lost. It was a time for bold ideas and new strategies, tactics and weapons that
could sustain the German Army as the war entered its third year. The reader will follow the
men of the XIV Reserve Corps in their own words as they experienced the transformation
of the German Army through Feldpost letters and previously unseen first-hand accounts.
They will also see how the Allies changed the way they fought the war as new weapons and
tactics appeared on the battlefield.

It would be a volatile period during the war that became the basis for the final act of the
war, the preparation and execution of the German offensives of 1918 and the eventual end
of the war that will be covered in the fourth and final volume of this series.

Ralph Whitehead is a graduate of C.W. Post College in Greenvale, New York where he concentrated his studies in 19th and 20th Century American and 20th Century European history. He is currently the head of a Fraud Investigative unit for a national insurance carrier and has enjoyed a 34-year career in the insurance field.

He has been actively studying the Great War for many decades and has established himself as an expert on the German Army of 1914-1918 with a special interest in German casualties.

He has been a member of several well-known Great War groups including the Western Front Association, The Imperial German Military Collector's Association and is a member of the Great War Archaeological Group 'No Man's Land'.

He has been a contributor to numerous Great War books including the Pals series and the Battleground Europe series. Ralph was an historic advisor to YAP Films on their series Finding the Fallen that involved Great War archaeology.

He currently resides with his wife in the small village of Fayetteville located in the historic Central New York region. The village was named in honor of the Marquis de Lafayette following the War of American Independence.

THE OTHER SIDE OF THE WIRE VOLUME 3

With the XIV Reserve Corps
The Period of Transition
2 July 1916-August 1917

Ralph J. Whitehead

Helion & Company

Helion & Company Limited
Unit 8 Amherst Business Centre
Budbrooke Road
Warwick
CV34 5WE
England
Tel. 01926 499 619
Email: info@helion.co.uk
Website: www.helion.co.uk
Twitter: @helionbooks
Visit our blog http://blog.helion.co.uk/

Published by Helion & Company 2018. Reprinted in paperback 2023
Designed and typeset by Farr out Publications, Wokingham, Berkshire
Cover designed by Farr out Publications, Wokingham, Berkshire

Every reasonable effort has been made to trace copyright holders and to obtain their permission for the use of copyright material. The author and publisher apologize for any errors or omissions in this work, and would be grateful if notified of any corrections that should be incorporated in future reprints or editions of this book.

ISBN 978-1-804513-80-4

British Library Cataloguing-in-Publication Data.
A catalogue record for this book is available from the British Library.

For details of other military history titles published by Helion & Company Limited contact the above address, or visit our website: http://www.helion.co.uk.

We always welcome receiving book proposals from prospective authors.

Contents

List of Illustrations

List of Maps

Preface

The creation of the final two volumes of my series of books on the XIV Reserve Corps has been the most difficult of them all. This instalment of the series took far longer than I had expected, in part due to the need to accumulate and then translate all of the materials that were necessary for the narrative, in part due to unexpected outside factors that are beyond our control. Finally, after a great deal of time and effort I have finally reached the point where I am pleased with the results of my writing. I feel that the last two books have remained true to my original efforts to restore the humanity of the people behind the historic facts and not just to provide places and dates and troop movements. When I had completed the original third volume I found that it was almost 500,000 words. When adding maps, illustrations and appendices the book would reach approximately 1,000 pages, far too large for a single volume, and as a result the manuscript was divided into two volumes.

Volume 3 carries the story of the XIV Reserve Corps through the momentous Battle of the Somme and into 1917, a period of transition for the German Army. The old tactics and strategy of trench warfare would undergo great changes as the German Army was transformed from a military force rooted in the 19th Century into a modern 20th Century fighting force with new strategies and tactics.

Acknowledgments

As I had originally planned on a single volume about the XIV Reserve Corps from the period of late September 1914 through 30 June 1916 I was not prepared to expand this single volume into what would become four books that would cover the XIV Reserve Corps through the end of the war and in the decades that followed.

Much of the time working on the final books was spent in translating the hundreds of pages of German documents needed to complete the books and reviewing thousands of original records from various national archives for any mention of the XIV Reserve Corps. Fortunately I had most of the books I needed in my collection as well as having unprecedented access to on-line archive materials, something that has only increased in scope since I started the first volume.

It seems that with the publication of each volume I receive more and more inquiries from fellow enthusiasts as well as people with family connections to the men of the XIV Reserve Corps. In this last category, I am extremely grateful to everyone who has shared their family history with me and who have a similar interest in history, especially when it involves the XIV Reserve Corps.

I am very grateful to the assistance of Felix Fregin from the Netherlands. Felix has been extremely helpful in translating the *Sütterlin* script on postcards, letters and other documents that sometimes defied every attempt to make sense of the old German writing. Felix has also opened his vast and fascinating collection and allowed me to use items for this series of books. While we have never met in person, I feel a close personal friendship with Felix and his lovely family.

I am grateful to the foresight of many national archives that have been placing their collections into digital form on-line where you can access the documents while sitting at your computer instead of having to travel vast distances. I would also like to extend my thanks to Major Chris Buckham of the Canadian Army for his assistance in completing this volume and his overall support.

I suppose it would not be a Whitehead production without at least one apology. I mentioned that Chris Jordan had helped me on Volume 2 and I had mentioned he was from Virginia. Chris very politely pointed out that he actually resides in West Virginia, sorry about that Chris.

German Army Organization and Rank Comparison

I n order for the reader to better understand the military terms and ranks mentioned in this book I have prepared a basic breakdown of the formation of the German army and the comparison of ranks between the German Army and the British Army. The German Army consisted of several parts including Active regiments, Reserve regiments, *Landwehr* regiments and *Landsturm* units. All qualified German males would be required to serve 2 years in the Active Army starting at age 20. 4-5 years in the Reserve, 11 years in the *Landwehr* and 7 years in the *Landsturm* 2nd Ban followed this.

The basic infantry regiment consisted of three battalions of infantry, designated I, II and III. Each battalion consisted of four companies (1-4, 5-8 and 9-12 respectively) that were further broken down into three platoons (*Zug*) and then into sections or *Gruppe* that consisted of 1 Non-Commissioned Officer and 8 men. Each soldier in a reserve regiment would have been armed with the M98 Mauser rifle or the M88 rifle. Each regiment would normally contain one Machine Gun Company armed with six MG08 heavy machine guns and one spare gun. The average strength of the regiment would have been 83 officers and 3,204 men.

The XIV Reserve Corps that was presented in Volume 2 has been restored to include the two original divisions, the 26th (Württemberg) and 28th (Baden) Reserve Divisions. The different divisions contained men from one active regiment as well as reserve regiments. The men who fought on the German side could range in age from their late teens to a few in their 50s and 60s. The field artillery was normally established into three sections or *Abteilung*. The I and II *Abteilung* consisted of 3 batteries each of M96 7.7cm field guns while the III *Abteilung* consisted of 3 batteries of M98.09 10.5cm light field howitzers.

As in most cases there were always exceptions to the rules. RIR 99 was one of the regiments in the army that had 4 battalions (I, II, III, IV) instead of the normal 3 and therefore had 16 companies of infantry at the start of the war. The 27th RFAR assigned to the 28th Reserve Division consisted of two *Abteilung* (I and II) and was not equipped with the light field howitzers, something not uncommon in reserve units.

Abbreviations used to designate the different military units found in this book:
RIR 99 Reserve Infantry Regiment Nr. 99
IR 180 Infantry Regiment Nr. 180
II/RFAR 26 II *Abteilung* Reserve Field Artillery Regiment Nr. 26
4/R109 4th Company Reserve Infantry Regiment Nr. 109
III/R111 III Battalion Reserve Infantry Regiment Nr. 111
9/180 9th Company Infantry Regiment Nr. 180
III(F)/FAR 12 III *Abteilung*, (howitzers), Field Artillery Regiment Nr. 12
1R/*Pionier* Bn 13 1st Reserve Company 13th *Pionier* Battalion

Rank Comparison

Grenadier }	Ranks equivalent to a Private Soldier. The different terms were
Musketier }	due to the type of unit the soldier belonged to, the military
Füsilier }	class of the soldier or from tradition.
Jäger }	
Wehrmann }	
Landsturmmann }	
Landsturmpflichtiger }	
Reservist}	
Infanterist }	
Soldat }	
Ersatz-Reservist}	
Schütze}	(Normally associated with Machine Gun troops)
Einjährig Freiwilliger	One Year Volunteer
Kriegsfreiwilliger	War Volunteer
Kanonier	Gunner
Radfahrer	Cyclist
Pionier	Sapper
Fahrer	Driver
Hornist	Trumpeter
Tambour	Drummer
Krankenträger	Stretcher-bearer
Gefreiter	Lance Corporal
Oberjäger	Corporal (*Jäger* units)
Unteroffizier	Corporal
Sergeant	Sergeant
Vizefeldwebel	Staff Sergeant
Vizewachtmeister	Staff Sergeant (Cavalry, artillery, train)
Feldwebel	Sergeant Major
Wachtmeister	Sergeant Major (Cavalry, artillery)
Fähnrich	Officer Cadet
Offizier Stellvertreter	Acting officer
Feldwebelleutnant	Sergeant Major Lieutenant
Leutnant	Second Lieutenant
Oberleutnant	Lieutenant
Rittmeister	Captain (Mounted unit, Transport)
Hauptmann	Captain
Major	Major
Oberstleutnant	Lieutenant Colonel
Oberst	Colonel
Generalmajor	Major General
Generalleutnant	Lieutenant General
General der Artillerie	General of Artillery
General der Infanterie	General of Infantry
General der Kavallerie	General of Cavalry

Medical Staff

Sanitäter	Medical Assistant
Assistentzarzt	Second Lieutenant
Oberarzt	Lieutenant
Stabsarzt	Captain
Oberstabsarzt	Major or higher

Chaplains
Pfarrer Padre

One final point regarding terminology used in the Great War. The reader will note the use of terms such as shrapnel and shellfire. These represent two different types of ammunition used during the war. High explosive shells formed fragments or splinters when exploding and were set off by impact fuzes. Shrapnel shells were basically large shotgun shells. Each shrapnel shell was filled with numerous lead balls that were expelled by an explosive charge inside the shell casing. This was accomplished with the use of a time fuze so that the shell would burst at an appropriate height above enemy troops scattering the lead balls over a wide area. The term shrapnel only applies to the latter type of shell and should not be confused with the modern version of this term.

Introduction

The fighting on 1 July 1916 was over, the long awaited battle had finally started but no one could know just how long the massive series of battles would last and how many hundreds of thousands of men on both sides of the wire would be killed, wounded or missing. Over the next five months the men on both sides of the wire faced one another in almost daily onslaughts as the Allies still hoped to break through the German lines, while the defenders did everything in their power to stop them.

What was not known to the rank and file were the problems facing the German High Command in regard to manpower problems, and the huge consumption of critical resources resulting from fighting on numerous battle fronts. It was a time when Germany began to realize that something needed to change otherwise the war could be lost. It was a time for bold ideas and new strategies and tactics that could sustain the German Army as the war entered its third year.

While the men of the XIV Reserve Corps were unaware of these issues, they would experience the transformation of the German Army first hand. They would see how the Allies also changed the way the war was fought as new weapons and tactics appeared on the battlefield. However, the current situation the men faced on 2 July 1916 was still the main focus of the soldiers as the Battle of the Somme continued to rage along the front of the XIV Reserve Corps.

1

26th Reserve Division
The Battle of the Somme, 2 July to August 1916

The result of the fighting on 1 July 1916 north of the Bapaume-Albert road was seen as a brilliant victory by the German Army commanders. It was estimated that in front of the 26th Reserve Division alone there were up to 10,000 enemy dead, especially before the front of RIR 99 by Thiepval.

While heavy fighting was still taking place along the front of the 26th Reserve Division near Thiepval and Ovillers on 2 July, the German command realized that General Haig was concentrating his efforts in the areas where the most gains had been made on 1 July; south of the Bapaume-Albert road, the sectors held by the 28th Reserve Division and 12th Infantry Division. Even here, where the British and French had been able to make significant headway into the German positions, they had not been able to achieve a breakthrough of the German defenses and this too was considered a victory.

There was little happening along the front north of the Ancre. Here, where the enemy had been repulsed at every point, the German lines were mainly kept under persistent artillery fire. It was generally accepted that at some point, the enemy would turn his attention to this portion of the Somme front, but not at this moment in time. However, with the overall reduction in fighting north of the Ancre there was the opportunity of shifting troops to the threatened sectors further south; just what the Allies had hoped to avoid.

In the days following 1 July, RIR 121 completed the task of clearing the last enemy soldiers from its position and spent the next 10 days attempting to remove all of the dead from inside the trenches as well as from the areas just in front of the forward most fire trench. Nothing at all was occurring on the front held by RIR 119 just north of the Ancre with the exception of the artillery fire raids. These raids would occasionally increase in strength, only to subside once more a short time later. These harassing tactics continued throughout 2 July without any infantry attacks taking place.

In addition to being able to transfer existing troops from one portion of the Somme front to the threatened areas, reinforcements had also been sent to the Somme when the enemy attack became expected. Among the first troops to arrive on the Somme was the 185th Infantry Division that came from Tahure on the Champagne front, which had received orders to move to the Somme on 30 June. This division would provide critical reinforcements to the regiments that had faced the Allied attack on 1 July and that would most likely face renewed enemy onslaughts.

One regiment from the 185th Infantry Division, IR 186, knew it was heading to a dangerous sector just from the level of artillery fire it experienced far behind the front lines as the regiment approached the battle zone. At 10 p.m. on 30 June, the regiment came under fire from 38cm shells, which literally caused the ground to quiver and shake under the feet of the men.

1 July 1916. Refugees coming out of Bapaume. Strong drum fire at the front. Continuous traffic on the large road back and forth. All rumors. We stand and lie idly around. 10 o'clock roll call for iron rations. French women with whom I talked, praise the German soldiers because of their politeness and order. Shortly before 2 o'clock alarm. 2.15 p.m. march to Bihucourt, terribly hot. A long stop in B, first between hedges, then on the way. Heavy shells, numerous duds. 9 p.m. further. 2 hours without resting. Everyone believes they will all fall down. Cursing and swearing. Hellish concert. Through grain fields and high grass. Finally rest. Want to unpack our blankets now, because it became cold, and because they were much needed: further! Marched until 4 a.m. and are stuffed into an arbitrary dugout, which we respectively tumble down. 6 o'clock further forward. Deep water in the trench, we sink until to the body. Many dead lie around. [1]

On the morning of 1 July, IR 186 lost the first of many men who would be killed or wounded on the Somme. A heavy shell fell on the quarters of the 3/186 and destroyed it. One man was killed and eight others were buried in the rubble and had to be sent to the nearby military hospital for treatment.

Like many of the units that were being transferred to the Somme, IR 186 would not fight as a unified regiment. Instead, the companies and battalions would be inserted at locations of the front where they were needed most. As such, the I/186 was alarmed at 11 p.m. on 1 July and marched toward the front lines through the night.

Following orders received from the 26th Reserve Division, three companies from the I/186 were assigned to support RIR 119 north of the Ancre while the fourth company became subordinate to RIR 99 south of the Ancre. At 4 a.m. on 2 July the three companies assigned to RIR 119 marched from Miraumont along the Miraumont-Beaucourt railway

Artist's impression of the fighting on the Somme. (Author's collection)

embankment and after two hours reached the village of Beaucourt. The companies then followed the heights south of the Beaucourt-Beaumont road where the 1st and 2/186 were positioned in *Beaumont-Nord*, the 3/186 in *Beaumont-Süd* and the 4/186 in the mined tunnel located by St. Pierre-Division.

The 1/186 relieved the 9/R119 in Sector B1 in *Beaumont-Nord*, the company that had suffered numerous losses from the mine explosion detonated at 7.20 a.m. on 1 July. One platoon from the 3/186 occupied the third trench of *Beaumont-Süd* while the rest of the company remained further in the rear as the sector reserve. The I/186 Battalion staff moved into the battle headquarters of RIR 119 in *Beaumont-Süd*.

Later in the evening, three platoons of the 4/186 were sent into the front lines. Platoon Neubronner was inserted into Sector C1 with the 12/R99. Platoon Schaper occupied the third line, the *Kirchen Stellung*, and Platoon Pvesve reinforced the 2/8th Bavarian RIR in the second trench of Sector C2.

The II/186 became subordinate to the 52nd Infantry Division and began to march toward the front. The battalion did not get any further than Bihucourt when it was ordered to stop and set up camp in the nearby open fields. Apparently the situation at the front was still unclear and until additional details could be obtained, the battalion was ordered to remain at its current location.

While the men waited in their camp, new orders were received and then almost immediately rescinded. This sequence of events occurred several times further until finally, at 7.30 p.m., orders arrived from the 52nd Division that the II/186 was to be placed in possession of the 51st Reserve Infantry Brigade from the 26th Reserve Division. The battalion was assembled and marched to the hollow north of Beauregard. At 8.30 p.m. the men were marched across open fields as all of the roads were under constant enemy observation by aircraft and covered with shell fire. The men followed the path between Achiet-le-Grand and Miraumont where it then turned into the hollow south of Puisieux toward the village of Serre.

Finally, the battalion arrived at the Puisieux-Miraumont road and after a short wait the commander of RIR 121 arrived at 11.30 p.m. and guided the battalion into the front line trenches. In spite of almost constant artillery fire and the difficulties encountered while walking through the communication trenches that were filled with deep mud, the battalion reached the *Zwischenstellung* in the sector held by RIR 121 by 4 a.m. on 2 July with remarkably few losses.

The men in the II/186 noted that the overall mood of the men in RIR 121 was quite good despite the heavy fighting that had occurred the previous day. Not only had the men of RIR 121 repulsed a large-scale enemy attack, they had also captured a considerable number of prisoners and equipment. Since a resumption of the enemy attack was expected at any time, the companies from the II/186 remained on alert in the event they were needed to help defend the position.

The II/186 occupied the *Zwischenstellung* and found that it was fully equipped for any contingency. There were stockpiles of hand grenades, machine gun and rifle ammunition, food, water and a large quantity of wire obstacles that were destined for the front line. Some of the men in the battalion were assigned to carry the supplies to the front. Others had the less enviable assignment of carrying the dead to a nearby mass grave or carrying the wounded to the main dressing station located further to the rear. When it was decided that the neighboring RIR 119 required more support, the 8/186 was sent to provide assistance.

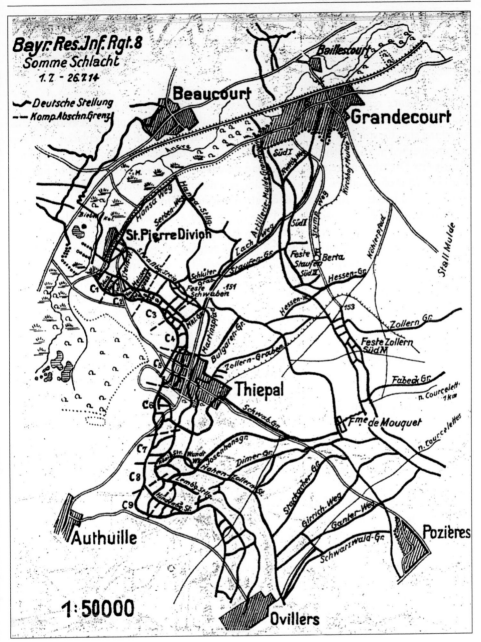

Thiepval Sector

Once the company arrived, one platoon reinforced the 3/R119 while the other two platoons relieved the 11/R119 in Sector B3.

2nd July. Spent the morning until 12 noon in a beautiful dugout with friendly Württembergers, who gave us coffee, bread and bacon. Then out and back again in the same, because only 80 of our company were required at the front. No success for the Englishmen. In the afternoon more drum fire. At 11 p.m. we became fetched to the front by *Unteroffizier* Steinkrug. Dugout overcrowded, Knopp and Knott arrived at the camp where I was located.[2]

Intelligence reports compiled from observers in the trenches, observation balloons and aircraft as well as identification of prisoners and enemy dead provided evidence that following the disaster of 1 July, many of the British divisions had been replaced. This was not unexpected as the 26th Reserve Division estimated that from the 9,000 men of the British 8th Division; more than 5,000 had become casualties in a single day of fighting. With this level of casualties, the 8th Division was no longer considered capable of offensive action until it had time to rest and to obtain replacements for the men lost.

The Thiepval Sector had always been recognized as a critical point in the German defenses. The position had been occupied by RIR 99 with the support of the 8th Bavarian RIR during the fighting on 1 July. The overall defense of the Thiepval sector had been considered successful with the exception of two portions of the front line; part of Sectors C2 and C3, known as the *Meisennest* which had been occupied by the 9th and 10/R99, and the *Granatloch* at the tip of Sector C9. Both areas had been captured and held by British troops following the fighting on 1 July. Both sectors needed to be recaptured as quickly as possible.

The two regiments that had defended the Thiepval sector had suffered numerous losses and it was decided that additional forces were needed, both to defend the sector and hopefully to recapture the lost positions. A second regiment from the 185th Division was assigned to the Thiepval Sector, IR 185. Two of the three battalions of IR 185 were assigned to the 26th Reserve Division on 1 July.

At noon, on the previous day, the I/185 under *Hauptmann* Leonhard and a Machine Gun Company marched to Courcelette where they were placed in possession of the 52nd Reserve Infantry Brigade. The II/185 along with Machine Gun *Zug* 311 and Machine Gun *Zug* 559 were placed in possession of the 26th Reserve Division and took up positions in the hollow east of Pys.

At 7.30 p.m. on 1 July the I/185 was ordered to provide support for the 8th Bavarian RIR and the battalion occupied the second line from *Feste Zollern* to Mouquet farm by 10 p.m. The II/185 minus the two machine gun *Zug* occupied the position vacated by the I/185 by Courcelette. At 11 p.m. the I Battalion advanced into the second line with the right wing at the *Lach Weg* and the left wing at the *Hessen Weg* with the intent of supporting the counterattack to recapture *Feste Schwaben*.

When it was determined that this strongpoint had already been recaptured, the II/185 was moved once more into the second line, from the *Hessen Weg* up to the Albert–Bapaume road. The two machine gun platoons, 311 and 559, were transferred north of the Ancre into the sector of the 51st Reserve Infantry Brigade in Sectors *Nord-I* through *Nord-IV* where the machine guns would provide valuable support in the event of an enemy attack.

Following the intense fighting on 1 July, the regimental staff of the 8th Bavarian RIR was located in *Feste Staufen,* on the stairs of a dugout filled with wounded men. The regimental commander, *Oberstleutnant* Bram, along with his indispensable adjutant, *Oberleutnant* Grabinger, worked non-stop until well after midnight. The two officers were engaged with receiving and writing messages and orders, fulfilling with the urgent cries for water, food, ammunition, close combat methods and the seemingly constant requests for additional men. Finding the necessary number of men required as reinforcements for the front line was perhaps the most difficult to comply with.

The request for reinforcements by the weak garrison of *Feste Schwaben* and the adjoining trenches was partially met when the 52nd Reserve Infantry Brigade sent the I/185 under *Hauptmann der Reserve* Leonhard to help the Bavarians while *Oberstleutnant* Krause, IR 185, took over the command in the second defensive position of the 52nd Reserve Infantry Brigade.

Just after midnight on 2 July the 3/185 arrived at *Feste Schwaben* and was then placed in possession of *Hauptmann* Wurm, where they were greeted quite happily by Wurm when they arrived. The 4/185 followed a short time later along with the rest of the I/185. The majority of the I/185 reinforced the 8th Bavarian RIR in *Feste Schwaben*. Half of the 2/185 was inserted into the *Martinspfad*, half of the 4/185 in C4 and C3, the rest were placed in *Feste Schwaben*. Later, the 3/185 was moved into the *Strassburger Steig*.

The entire battalion from IR 185 could have easily become used in the defense of *Feste Schwaben* and *Thiepval-Nord*, but, as reinforcements were desperately needed at several key positions, *Oberstleutnant* Bram allowed the 1/185 to be taken to the *Wundtwerk* by Thiepval, guided by an *Unteroffizier* from RIR 99. Numerous requests for help had also arrived at the regimental headquarters from the garrison of *Thiepval-Süd*. The 1/185 would later become involved in the fierce fighting south of Thiepval in the *Hindenburg Stellung* with the 9/8th Bavarian RIR by the *Granatloch*.

Additional reinforcements under *Leutnant der Reserve* Höffken, 4/186, arrived in the tunnel of St. Pierre-Divion in the early morning of 2 July. The platoon of *Leutnant* Neubronner was inserted by the 12/R99 south of the village. Now, in the midst of the multitude of duties that small Bavarian headquarters staff was attempting to accomplish in the chaos following the recapture of *Feste Schwaben*, *Oberstleutnant* Bram, assigned *Hauptmann* Wurm to clear the enemy from the group of trenches located in the second trench of Sectors C2 and C3, the portion of the front line that contained the *Meisennest*.

Hauptmann Wurm completed his plans for the recapture of Sectors C2 and C3 during the early morning hours of 2 July. At 6.30 a.m. Wurm proceeded to Sector C4 with assault troops from the 4/185 under *Leutnant der Landwehr* Scheidt and a number of his own men, especially *Unteroffiziers* Siegmann of the 3rd and Zahn of the 12/8th Bavarian RIR who had stood out in the fighting of 1 July. *Pioniers* of the 4/*Pionier* Battalion 13 would provide the infantry with ammunition and hand grenades.

While Wurm and Scheidt guided the men through the maze of damaged trenches and shell craters, two machine guns from Machine Gun Marksman Detachment 89 arrived at *Feste Schwaben* at 7 a.m. These guns were a very welcome sight and with their arrival, *Hauptmann* Wurm now had more than six machine guns at his disposal for his attack.

Wurm and his detachment reached Sector C4 that was being held by the survivors of the 7/R99 under *Leutnant der Reserve* Schmidt. According to reports from this company, men from the 8th Bavarian RIR ho had been captured by the British the previous day had been disarmed and robbed of their money, their rings and watches by their captors. Other than to possibly stir up a greater dislike of the enemy the men were soon to face, this report had no real military value of any kind.

Detachment Wurm began to clear the former 2nd trench of Sector C3 in the morning hours of 2 July, advancing from Sector C4, while the enemy still held the foremost trench

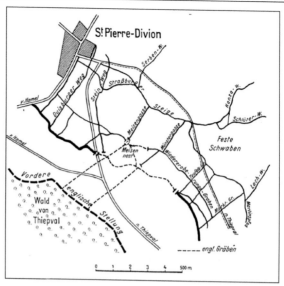

Meisennest 2–5.7.1916

of this sector. The existing crater-field in C4 barely allowed the old trenches to still be recognized. At first, the advance went smoothly using hand grenades to clear out each traverse as Wurm and his men moved quickly through the terrain. In the beginning, there was very little British artillery fire to disrupt the advance. However, the enemy fire soon increased in volume as the British garrison sent reports back to the artillery in the rear. As more and more shells fell around the German bombing parties, larger intervals between groups gradually had to be taken to avoid heavy losses.

Soon, the momentum of the attack was lost and the bombing parties came to a standstill. In part this was caused by increased enemy fire and resistance and in part it was that the men were exhausted. Both bombing party leaders, Siegmann and Zahn, among others, were also wounded by the enemy shell fire.

During this counterattack, other portions of the front by St. Pierre-Divion were being reorganized. This was necessary because so many men had become separated from their companies following the fighting on 1 July. Time was needed to get everything back into order and for the company, battalion and regimental commanders to know exactly where their men were positioned.

2nd July. 6 a.m., a different day, I raised myself from my bed, i.e. from on a piece of board, on which I had placed my gas mask as a pillow. A day so splendid and beautiful like yesterday. At that hour the firing was somewhat more subdued. I awakened the company leader and asked if I should possibly look for the dispersed men. He said no and advised me to first question all men passing by. He was dreadfully weakened and severely ill besides. My inquiries had success so that I confirmed the location of part of the company that was actually in Grandcourt, and Schmeisser as well as Kamm were with the remaining part in the sector of the second trench specified for the company. However, where was this sector? I offered to look for both. Meanwhile *Leutnant* Barz prohibited it, because it was however pointless and with the heavy fire that lay on that position, I would die unnecessarily. *Feldwebel* and *Offizier Stellvertreter* Stahlhofer, 2/8th Bavarian RIR.[3]

While Wurm's counterattack was taking place, the rest of the 6th and 7/8th Bavarian RIR arrived at *Feste Schwaben* with *Oberleutnant* Illig. The companies had arrived at the command post of the regiment at 7.30 the previous evening and had then become ordered forward to command post Wurm. Similarly, *Oberleutnant* Hartmann, who had been sick on 1 July, was now found back with his 5th Company.

Following the failure of Detachment Wurm recapturing all of the lost trenches, *Hauptmann* Wurm proceeded to St. Pierre-Division in the afternoon under heavy British shell fire, to discuss a mutual undertaking to take place later in the night with *Hauptmann* Mandel, commander of the III/R99. According to the plan worked out, several detachments would proceed from both sides of the enemy occupied trenches at midnight. They were expected to close the gap in the second trench by C2 and C4.

While the men assigned for this undertaking were moving into their positions, the British continued to apply pressure to expand their gains by C2 and C3. At 5 p.m., approximately 100 British troops began to advance through the damaged trenches. The defending Germans managed to stop the British from making any headway in this attack through short, but effective advances by assault troops under the command of the platoon leaders of the 4/186. The British were prevented from rolling up the left wing of the sector any further.

A brigade order arrived at 7.30 p.m., transferring command over all troops in Sectors C1 up to C4 and behind these sectors to *Oberstleutnant* Bram. Bram was now in charge of Group Prager, named after the commander of the I/8th Bavarian RIR, at St. Pierre-Division and Group Wurm, named after the commander of the III/8th Bavarian RIR, at *Feste Schwaben*. Both Groups consisted of portions of different regiments, RIR 99, 8th Bavarian RIR, IR 185 and IR 186.

The regimental staff of the 8th Bavarian RIR found a very hospitable reception in the dugout of Artillery Group Berta located in the *Stump Weg* where the new headquarters was set up. Telephone communications were quickly established with *Feste Schwaben* and at 8.45 p.m. *Hauptmann* Wurm reported significant attack preparations being made by the British were observed in front of C4. The artillery fire that was immediately directed against the enemy troop concentrations was not as effective as hoped for, probably because of inadequate direct observation of the enemy position and too few guns. Fortunately for Wurm, the attack was not directed against his sector.

Even though the enemy was not directly attacking the positions near St. Pierre-Division, the ever present enemy artillery fire was causing a number of losses among the men and continued to damage the makeshift trenches. The undertaking planned by Wurm for midnight never occurred, since before the plan could be put into motion a number of key officers were wounded by shell fire. The officer assigned the task of leading the attack, *Oberleutnant* Illig, 7/8th Bavarian RIR had been wounded. His replacement, *Leutnant der Reserve* Bickel, also became wounded a short time later as well as *Feldwebel Leutnant* Hussong. With the officers placed out of action, and numerous Other Ranks killed or wounded, the attack was called off for the present. The large losses prompted *Major* Prager to request further support.

The reorganization within Sector *Thiepval-Nord* continued throughout the remainder of 2 July. As part of this, the staff of the I/8th Bavarian RIR was transferred to St. Pierre Divion in the night.

Towards evening we wanted to go together on the search and then during the night to direct the dispersed small groups back. About midday we found a nearby destroyed vehicle with food; now perhaps the men in the position have nothing to eat, so as far as it was possible Hanauer and I would get some food and then take it into the position. The British, who maintained active fire on the road, drove quite a wind at us. So we quickly hurried and gathered together what was still there – together we brought approximately 5 full sandbags – so fierce was the fire placed here by us that I am still surprised today, how we got away. The return route was not a hair more pleasant. The shrapnel always burst above our heads and the scattered its load in front of our noses, while the shells drove into the hillside beside us. Completely open and without the least cover, we ran as swiftly as our legs would carry us to only just reach the tunnels. I carried two sandbags with preserved meat. Hanauer had three with bread. I advanced slightly swifter and was already close to the dugout, when Hanauer, who was perhaps 20 meters behind, shouted: 'Herr Feldwebel, I can't any longer!' I immediately hurried back, to take part of it from him. He gave me one bag and now went further. Finally we were there. However although we had gone back at most perhaps 1,000 meters, we were worn out and laid down exhausted on the ground.

It had become evening and we left, Wilhelm carried one sack, Hanauer two, I two. Barz went ahead. The shells howled, striking on the right and on the left. Tired, we dragged ourselves forward, for the poetry of the evening was missing at every glance. All at once I heard a whistling coming forth out of the howling; only an instant. Instinctively I pressed myself against the trench wall. Splash, the ground erupted over me; I stood up, crawled out, saw that the person in front of me was also covered. I still did not know if it was Hanauer or Wilhelm. I grabbed him on the projecting shoulder, he doesn't move. Meanwhile Barz and Wilhelm, who were directly curved around a corner, turned around. William grabbed the one protruding rifle – Hanauer carried two – the man doesn't respond. All in vain, he is dead. A couple of hours before the arrival of his 25th Birthday, a noble chap, gallant and self-sacrificing. I thought of the small Stanzas that had often sung in Prémont in the barroom of my quarters ...

Now he was dead, not a foot in front of me, brushed by death, who came to collect him. How did I look, I was not white, but the humor had deserted me. Barz and Wilhelm were also deathly pale. Death had visibly waved the scythe. We went further. We met men from our company, who wandered around aimlessly. They didn't know about Schmeisser and Kamm, it was believed they were prisoners. We pressed on further. There we were summoned by *Major* Prager and *Leutnant der Reserve* Sundhaussen. Prager's stare promised nothing good. He grabbed Barz harshly, what was going on. After Barz finished his report, he said: 'Message upon message comes to the battalion. Barz and Stahlhofer are missing, Schmeisser and Kamm had fallen prey to the British all around and in the meantime *Leutnant* Barz and *Offizier Stellvertreter* Stahlhofer were wandering around behind and looking like scattered chickens. I want to trust that you and the company will soon be together and everything spotless! These words were more than clear. You understandably do not also have the responsibility that weighed on the battalion commander. The assumption, we were shirking, was offensive. Nonetheless it raged in me. Going on further. The trench was still possibly churned up from yesterday. We reached something like a junction to a trench. The wood support still lay beside it. *'Meisengasse'* was on it. It was already almost dark, dense fog; a number of shells scattered behind us; I was behind Barz. The shrapnel burst with dense hail. We curved into the *Meisengasse*, maybe we would find our company there, because yesterday we stormed up to the *Meisengasse*. It did not go long like this. It shimmered something like a line in the churned up chalk floor; a shrapnel bursting quite close illuminated it. Still a few more steps, then we had the trench. Putsch, Putsch, flashed up the sparks flying in front of the eyes. British! Still a few salvos! Back like the devil and with it so tired that the bones creaked. Now where? We a reached a dugout. Men from the 8th Company. Where is the Second Company? 'We don't have any idea!' the dugout of *Leutnant* Rentrop from the 1st Company is very close by. A man directed us. Finally, we are there. I realize that I had lost one sandbag with bread. No matter. 'Yes, where actually is the 2nd Company?' said Rentrop, 'I do not know. Anyway they must be directly in front of me, if they are still there. The trench is no longer recognizable. Wait, I will give you two men from RIR 99, who must know it.

However, the two ninety niners also lost their way. Now we encountered one man from Schmeisser, who was getting water. He should lead us, but he is also lost himself. Now *Leutnant* Barz is back again, looking painstakingly for the dugout of *Leutnant* Rentrop and from there we now grope helplessly to the front. Slow, appallingly slow; well, at least we are certain, the company is still there. Finally we meet *Unteroffizier* Wolf. 'Where is Schmeisser?' Just keep going, *Herr Leutnant*! So there we are. Heinlein joyfully greets me and tells us that among others today that Infantryman Rehm was killed in the hand grenade fighting.

A very cold-blooded, always silent, pale individual, also an old Bavarian. Schmeisser is heartily glad to have Barz again. We crawled into the buried dugout on our stomachs. Two severely wounded British lie underneath and cry for water. I unstrapped my canteen and gave it to them. They give it back to me empty. Now if we could only lie down, how good that would be. However still no rest, first the rest of the company must be in position. Therefore I went to Barz and said: '*Herr Leutnant*, now I must go and collect the dispersed men.' He looked at me so and replied; 'In the condition that you are now in, I could not ask for that strain from you. Should we send down an *Unteroffizier*?' 'That is exactly so like the dog I am,' was my answer, 'the men must go up in any event and soon, otherwise it becomes bright and then it is too late. Perhaps I could have just one man who knows something of the position otherwise we might end up with the British.' 'Well, so you go in God's name.' Wilhelm, the servant of *Leutnant* Barz accompanied me. A young chap, who claimed to know the position, was made the leader. He leaves like a weasel, gets lost, runs back, like that five, six times. Pitch black. The shrapnel above the head. Now I could scream, the life had been taken from the chap in the next shell hole.

I advanced, still lost a few more times; finally I had the right road. Finally, the road goes away over the corpse of Hanauer, on which was now terrifying fire. My companion urged: 'we must run, *Herr Feldwebel*, otherwise all three of us will be *kaput*.' A feeling of great indifference was in me; I walked at a calm step, I still think about the encounter with Prager and grind my teeth from rage. The speed of the others became always swifter, until there are only three of us left that went out. In the vicinity of Grandcourt the fire became more moderate; we went at a walk again. I sent both into the hole, to retrieve everything I left. Into the dugout, where we had still been on 1st July. I kept going ready to fall over from exhaustion; severe thirst closed my throat together. Now everything was the same. I went to the nearby situated medical dugout. Maybe I would find something drinkable there. I entered quietly, a pot of warm milk stood on a stove; I took it and drank it half empty. I managed as I had come, I disappeared again. Then I drummed the men out. They came sleepily. The heaviest fire lay on the forward most position, I heard it quite clearly. One thinks we should wait, until it was convenient. I wanted to leave; I risked as much as that there. There however I saw the dense fog sink lower, I waited. The fire really lessens shortly. So we therefore set off. A part had already advanced, I sent my men under leadership of *Gefreiter* Burger, who also knew the path, and I searched through the trench again, where I caught four men and sent them after them. I had placed my beautiful new cap in my belt and also four hand grenades. Unfortunately it was the last walk with my beautiful cap; I now lost it on the path. Later I found an Other Rank cap that I wore up to my being wounded. Again I went up to the tiresome well-known *Hansa Graben*. Now I climbed over the body of Hanauer. I saw in the brightness that the top of his skull had been torn off. Finally I curved again in the third trench and then in the *Stein Weg*, three men in front of me. However I believed we were going in the wrong direction, hurried back at full speed, leaving the three behind. However, it turned out that I was going correctly. There they called to me: '*Herr Feldwebel*, watch out, a pilot.' I saw in the heights and noticed how further on the left an Englishman, pursued by a German, sank lower. That was likely from his part. Only a few more jumps over the corpses of Englishmen and finally at the goal. *Unteroffizier* Göbel, also coming out with the dispersed men, reported to me, all of the troops that preceded me, had arrived. So I gladly stepped in front of *Leutnant* Barz with the report: 'All dispersed in position!' He thanked me, and I asked what I could do now. There I would get the answer: 'Now you place yourself there and sleep!' An order that I executed with commendable strictness. So, as I was, with the helmet on the head, I stretched myself out and slept. It was likely 6 o'clock. About 11.30 p.m. I woke up; however, I did not get up. 'Ah now he becomes alive again,' I heard Schmeisser say. 'He is solidly contented' replied Barz. 'That is true,' I heard Schmeisser say. I heard them speak of Heinlein, who this morning, armed with hand grenades had dared to go alone in the trench piece occupied by the British on the left of us and has still not come back. He never came again; he is certainly dead, even if he has also been reported as missing. A heavy loss because he was worth five others. *Feldwebel* and *Offizier Stellvertreter* Stahlhofer, 2/8th Bavarian RIR. [4]

On the far left wing of the Thiepval Sector, where the British had managed to capture and occupy the *Granatloch* in Sector C9, the fighting had never fully ceased during the night of 1/2 July. During the hours of darkness, British sappers had created a communication trench running from the main British trench up to the *Granatloch* where the 17th Highlander Battalion (97th Brigade) along with parts of the 2nd Manchester and the 15th Highlander Battalions (14th Brigade) occupied the small chalk pit, the *Granatloch*, located at the tip of C9.

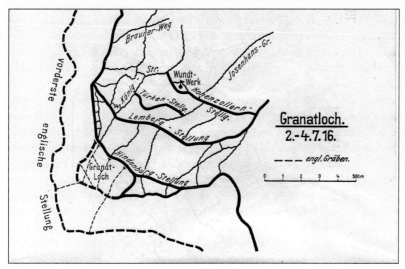

Granatloch 2–4.7.16

The British attempted to completely capture Hill 141 by the *Granatloch* with all means available and maintained a constant pressure on the shrinking German garrison holding them back, including part of IR 180 which had blocked off its right wing facing the *Granatloch*. *Leutnant der Reserve* Meister, located in the *Wundtwerk,* received orders from the commander of RIR 99, *Major* von Fabeck, to attack the *Granatloch* with his 9/8th Bavarian RIR. However, the surprise attack devised by Meister failed due to the alertness of the enemy sentries. The men of the 9th Company did manage to come quite close to the enemy position following a very long, bloody hand grenade battle, during which many of the Bavarian assault troops had become killed or wounded.

It is 3.45 a.m. the first grey of day appears to the east. *Leutnant* Meister stands in front of me with *Unteroffizier* Weindel close by. I wake up Walcher and we four once again go over the details, fetch our men and stand to. Four o'clock! *Leutnant* Meister nods and everyone leaves the trench. At my side is *Gefreiter* Kneller with a sack of hand grenades, and Guth, my orderly. We stumble through the barbed wire and shell holes in the half light, right into the enemy's attentive sentries which immediately sound the alarm with hand grenades and rifle fire. already the attack is not going as I had imagined it, but we throw ourselves hard at the English. 'Hand grenades!' I shout, and Kneller begins lobbing them forward. 'Bravo Kneller, they are landing in their trench!' I can hear our comrades on the right and left going about their work. A sharp fight rages all around us. hand grenades fly in both directions, accompanied by vicious rifle fire. it is the heaviest on the left. Has Welcher found some strong resistance?

Kneller is growing tired but continues to fling hand grenades. Then, in front of us, a machine gun is shoved over the enemy's parapet. 'Everyone on the machine gun!' our men fired like madmen. We throw more hand grenades. In vain! Tack-tack-tack and bullets fly over our heads. The same hammering also resounds on the right. The first casualties lie next to me. Several men groan in pain. Over on the other side loud screams and shouting can also be heard. Our hand grenades are almost gone, but who can get back through this hail of lead for more? Everyone hesitates, so I go back myself. Jumping, running and crawling through the rain of bullets I somehow make my way back to the barricade where *Leutnant* Meister greets me. I quickly procure a new supply of hand grenades and return forward with these in sandbags, accompanied by two other carriers.

Kneller has just thrown his last hand grenade when we arrive. The enemy machine gun continues chattering away. If we can knock it out the trench will be ours. Suddenly, Kneller cries out. A bullet has hit him in the chest while a second has torn away his lower jaw. He is dead in a second or two. Guth and I lay him at the bottom of our crater and close his sightless eyes. Sleep well, valiant comrade. Your artistic career which held such promise is now at an end. The English machine gun has not stopped firing. We throw more hand grenades. Then Guth's head jerks downward and blood covers his face. I order him off to the rear and look around. I cannot see anyone. Where are the others? It is quiet on the right and nothing can be seen of Weindel's platoon. Rearward on the left I hear rifle fire. I am down to my last hand grenade. I let it fly toward the enemy machine gun. When it explodes I jump out of the crater and run back for all I am worth. There I find the company's reserve sorely pressed on both flanks in the Hindenburg Stellung. At the barricade, men of the 3rd Platoon are firing shoulder to shoulder with a section from IR 185.

'Where is the *Leutnant*?' I ask. Someone points toward a nearby shell hole. There is *Leutnant* Meister, calmly aiming and firing a rifle. From hole to hole I crawl and roll over to him and report the attack's failure. He nods to me sadly, then motions to a corpse lying behind us. From the new sash (*Portepee*) at the dead man's side, I realize it is *Vizefeldwebel* Walther. 'Where is Walcher?' I want to know. 'Dead' replies *Leutnant* Meister. 'Weindel?' 'Also dead'. Now the stillness on either side of me out in front made sense. The poor fellows!

But this is no time for mourning. The demands of the fighting seize us. The English intend to come here. *Leutnant* Meister points right, telling me to take over the platoon there and move to the threatened *Hindenburgeck*. At the barricade a stiff fight is still in progress, but our men and the dependable 185ers are holding their own. Tommy will not get through here.

Just then, from the left, a shout: 'Company commander wounded!' I shout 'Company listen for commands from Conrad'. I look for *Leutnant* Meister. He has already gone back with a shot in the right arm. I am given his map case with the position's sketches and orders and while they accept me, I also physically feel that a heavy responsibility now rests on me for the lives of so many men and for the good reputation and the honor of our regiment. Now we will also still do our duty!

The firing grows weaker as the enemy withdraws. The attack has stopped. We lay exhausted some 20 meters behind the *Hindenburg Stellung*. 'Everyone dig in! We will hold this position!' it is my first order. Soon the craters have been connected with a knee-deep trench. A radiating morning sun promises another hot summer day. *Vizefeldwebel der Reserve* Heinrich Conrad, 9/8th Bavarian RIR. [5]

Conrad and his men did the best they could under the circumstances. They had not expected that the enemy would also suddenly advance on the *Josenhans Graben*. Fortunately a supporting platoon and one Group of the 1/185 had arrived in the position behind the right wing of the *Hindenburg Stellung* during the fire fight. The new trench created by Conrad's men behind the *Hindenburg Stellung* was thinly occupied, but still had enough men to keep the enemy at bay. The 9/8th Bavarian RIR had started the battle with more than 200 men. By the afternoon of 2 July it numbered only 73 men, the rest had been either killed or wounded.

About 9.00 a.m. the sector commander, *Major* von Hüllesem, arrived. I report. He looked over our position and was pleased. His praise lifts our spirits. We dig further, each man carving out a splinter proof niche in the forward wall of the deepened trench. The sentries keep a sharp lookout. The enemy is concentrating his artillery fire on the *König Strasse*, interfering with contact to the battalion. And, his planes drone overhead unmolested.

During a quiet spell in the afternoon I take stock of the company's remaining battle strength. I can write down only seventy-three names. The rest have been wounded, or are dead. For more than one and-a-half years most of them had been with the company, spending many happy hours together. The splendid fellows! It is so sad. I will especially miss my good-natured friend Ludwig Walcher. Badly wounded in our counterattack, he was carried to a dressing station in the *Wundtwerk* where he died a short time later. And the efficient, conscientious Weindel. I had learned to appreciate him as the best Group commander ... .. He was due soon for a furlough to visit his wife, children and home along the Rhine. One of his daughters, only several months old, he had never seen.

In the evening I stood by the parapet chatting with *Leutnant* Kleudgen (3/R99). We spoke about our former positions. I held the map, showing him and explaining our beautiful position by Soyécourt, which we transformed into a first rank earthen position through our tireless entrenching work. We did not pay any attention to the individual shells exploding in our vicinity. Then one whizzed quite close by and before I knew it, I feel something hit and through my cap sprays a spurt of blood. The strategic discussion suddenly ended. A good Württemberger bandaged me. I remained with the company.

The uncertainty of the situation over on the left still concerns me greatly. After dusk I moved through a shallow communication trench that ran from the *Lemberg Stellung* parallel to the *König Strasse* with several men to investigate the situation, but we were received by enemy machine gun fire at the approximate height of our position. We must turn back, especially as the night could still bring all sorts of surprises. To prevent this I sent four men back to the communication trench to block it as a security measure. I also ordered *Vizefeldwebel* Albrecht, the last remaining sabre rank, to organize the company's left flank for defense against being outflanked.

The commander of the neighboring platoon on our right came over to visit. 'Where is the enemy?' he asks excitedly, taking off for the *Hindenburgeck* without waiting for a reply. 'Be careful, *Herr Leutnant*!' I call to him, but the warning comes too late. Pffffft! The bullet striking him is followed by a shriek. He falls backward into my arms, blood spurting from his neck. I cover the hole with my hand to try to stem the flow and yell for the stretcher bearers. However, I know it is no use. He is already dead. I stood over the body, my uniform and hands covered with his blood.

An hour before midnight the enemy opens up on our position with heavy

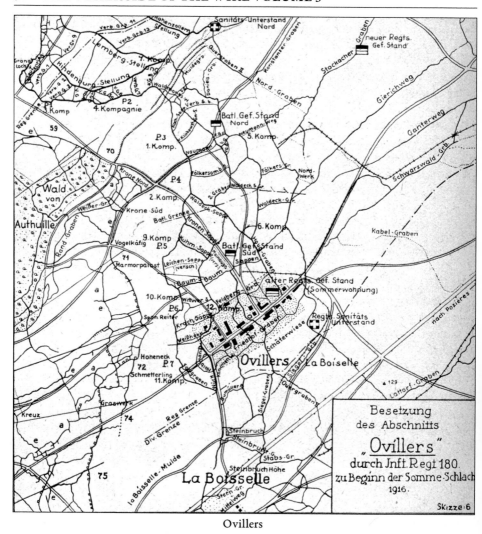

Ovillers

shell fire. Albrecht is badly wounded and the four men sent back to the barricade the communication trench are missing. It is clear the English will be coming over again after this artillery preparation. So we remain awake, watching. If they come we will give them a taste of what they received the day before. *Vizefeldwebel der Reserve* Heinrich Conrad, 9/8th Bavarian RIR. [6]

Vizefeldwebel Conrad tirelessly attempted to improve his new position, to secure it from all sides and to maintain the connection to the neighboring units. The few men left under his command managed to achieve remarkable success in being able to prevent the British from any further advances.

Further south, in the Ovillers Sector, where some of the heaviest fighting had taken place on 1 July, and, where some of the worst losses were suffered by the British during their attack, remained active. While the men of IR 180 and the neighboring RIR 110 had suffered relatively few losses in comparison to the British casualties on 1 July, the loss of even a small number of men reduced the overall effectiveness of the German defenses.

There were few reinforcements at hand on 1 July and, given the disaster that was developing further to the south by La Boisselle, Fricourt, Mametz and Montauban, the availability of reinforcements for the men of IR 180 was a problem. Fortunately, two battalions from IR 186 (185th Division) had arrived in the Ovillers Sector in the night of 1/2 July and were placed in possession of the 51st Reserve Infantry Brigade. This support could prove to be critical as new enemy attacks were expected at any time. In addition, the II/185 was also ordered to proceed to the Ovillers Sector where it arrived at 2.30 a.m. on 3 July and it was immediately assigned to the I/180 in *Ovillers-Nord*.

While reinforcements were at hand, the situation facing the left wing of IR 180 was becoming a serious threat to the overall defense of the German front line. The left neighboring regiment, RIR 110, from the 28th Reserve Division, which was holding La Boisselle, was growing weaker with each enemy thrust. The village of La Boisselle was being lost piece by piece as the fighting surged back and forth between RIR 110 and the British. Fricourt had already ended up in the possession of the enemy and under these circumstances the flank and the rear of Ovillers were seriously threatened.

Despite the events taking place in the neighboring sectors held by the 28th Reserve Division, a confident mood prevailed in the 26th Reserve Division. The division headquarters sent the following telephone message to IR 180 at 5 p.m.: 'RIR 110 goes back above La Boisselle. IR 180 is to hold Ovillers up to the last man.'

Simultaneously, an orderly officer from division was sent to IR 180 who was to personally bring back news about the situation at the right wing of the division. The same officer carried a letter to the commander of IR 180 from General von Stein, commander of the 26th Reserve Division, who said that 'everything now depended on IR 180. It was a matter of honor for the regiment to hold Ovillers under all circumstances.' Despite the heavy fighting still taking place by La Boisselle, a slim connection was continuously preserved with the neighboring RIR 110 through runners. The enemy had failed to drive a wedge between the two divisions and was unable to force a breakthrough on this portion of the line.

At 3.50 a.m. RIR 99 sent a report to IR 180 that one company was moving up to C9 via the *Lemberg Stellung*, which was supposed to take over the portion of the regimental front line that had been occupied by IR 180 since 1 July. However, this company had still not arrived by 5 a.m. It was considered to be critical that the platoon of the 7/180 occupying the front line trench on the left wing of the regimental sector of RIR 99 with only 80 rifles become relieved as the men were exhausted and very short of ammunition and supplies. Finally, with no relief in sight, the platoon was ordered to withdraw from its position and once back in the right wing sector of IR 180, the trenches leading toward the *Granatloch* were blocked off to prevent the enemy from penetrating the regimental flank.

At daybreak on 2 July, it was revealed that the enemy had created a communication trench between target sector 58 in the British lines and C9 in the German lines over night. IR 180 quickly came to the conclusion that the enemy would undoubtedly use the trench and the portion of C9 they had captured for the start of further actions against the German defenses. It therefore became urgent to clear the trenches that were occupied by the British. However, this was also seen by IR 180 as being the responsibility of RIR 99 as the captured portions of the line were in its regimental sector.

The activity of the enemy artillery had become noticeably weaker towards morning. Then, during the day they only fired individual shrapnel shells on the sector *Ovillers-Nord*. For the most part there was conspicuous silence when compared to the previous week. IR 180 assumed that the opposing enemy leadership had come to the conclusion that their detailed planned breakthrough attempt against the German position had failed miserably and was reevaluating their plans. However, while the enemy artillery was minimal, enemy aerial activity was quite lively.

At 8.50 a.m. a counterattack in *Thiepval-Süd* by RIR 99 against the British who had advanced into the *Hindenburg Stellung* and up to the *Josenhans Graben* did not take place as planned. As a result of this, the I/180 in *Ovillers-Nord* received orders, to block off Sector P1 to the right, something already accomplished. The first trench of P1 was now occupied by 80 men; the second trench was occupied by 140 men during the day. At night, the first trench was occupied by 94 men, the second trench by 120 men, and *Verbindungs Graben 3* by ten men.

When it became evident that Sector C9 was not going to be cleared from the enemy any time soon by the neighboring regiment, IR 180 saw the need to create a new communication trench in P1 from the northern end of *Verbindungs Graben 3* running in a southeasterly direction towards the border of P1 and P2. This new trench would allow IR 180 to prevent any British encroachment into the Ovillers Sector from the north in the event the enemy was successful in penetrating deeper into the neighboring trenches.

After a small British advance had been repulsed in the morning, one Group each from the 3rd and 7/180 occupied the new barricades at the right wing sector of their regiment. The barricade came under the command of *Oberleutnant der Reserve* Vogler, who would hold the position the rest of the day. It was not long before the British tried to force their way further to the right once more and ran into Vogler's men where a bitter hand grenade fight began, which lasted until the evening, causing a number of losses on both sides.

At 8 p.m. *Oberleutnant der Reserve* Vogler took over the leadership of all the parts of the regiment on the right of the hollow running between Ovillers and Thiepval. The sector now under his command included the front trench of P1, *Verbindungs Graben 3* and the *Hindenburg Stellung*, which ran across the regimental sector from the *Granatloch*.

The night of 1/2 July was restless in Sector *Ovillers-Süd;* all connecting routes to the rear of IR 180 were held under heavy enemy artillery fire. The huge number of British wounded lying in the foreground from 1 July attempted to crawl back into their trenches; in addition, the enemy had sent out strong patrols into no man's land. At 2.35 a.m. on 2 July one patrol from the 11/180 ran into one of the British patrols and in the ensuing hand grenade battle, drove the enemy back to their lines.

By daybreak of 2 July, *Ovillers-Süd* grew very quiet, with little enemy activity. This all changed at 12 noon when the British placed heavy artillery fire on the front line trench, which increased in intensity at 5 p.m., especially on Sector P7.

At 6.15 p.m. the following message from the neighboring RIR 110 arrived: 'Because the enemy has had some success at the left wing of the regiment and by the subsequent regiments, the reserves are to be moved from the right to the left wing. The right wing is no longer in a position to hold back a strong attack. Regiment 110 asks Regiment 180, to protect the Ovillers position by staggering the reserves behind the left wing, with the goal of possibly interfering in the fighting by 110.'

IR 180 had few reserves available for such a task but did everything they could to comply with the request. The 12/180 was placed in the *Schäferwiese* and in the *Bumiller Dorf* in a staggered formation behind the left wing of the sector. No other men were available as the brigade could not provide any additional troops to the regiment. The 5/180 was also shifted further to the right to provide some additional support. In response to the situation, the staff of the II/180 under *Major* Keerl moved from Le Sars to the unfinished regimental battle headquarters in the *Stockacher Graben*.

As each new message arrived from the neighboring RIR 110, it was clear that the situation at the left wing of the regiment was becoming increasingly serious. At 8 p.m. the following message from RIR 110 arrived: 'RIR 110 has been given orders for the preparation of a withdrawal into the second position of Pozières. The time of the withdrawal was not ordered yet.'

After IR 180 passed along this report to division headquarters, a machine gun company from IR 186 was ordered to proceed to IR 180 as quickly as possible. Some good news was received at 10 p.m. when a report arrived that RIR 110 was being reinforced by IR 190 which had the ultimate goal of replacing the badly damaged Baden regiment. Later in the evening, two officer's patrols from IR 185 under *Leutnants* Ehrhardt and Sturzebecher were sent out to clarify the situation by Contalmaison and La Boisselle. At 11 p.m. the 8/185 was assigned to IR 180 where it was placed in the front line by Ovillers-La Boisselle for further protection of the threatened left flank of IR 180.

While two battalions from IR 186 had been assigned to assist the 26th Reserve Division, the third, the III/186, had been sent to assist RIR 111 near Fricourt while the remaining regiment of the 185th Division, IR 190, had been sent to assist RIR 110 in La Boisselle. Considering the events taking place south of the 26th Reserve Division, these reinforcements would be critical if the left flank of the Württemberg division was to hold.

The losses of IR 180 on 2 July reflected the reduction in the fighting when comparing it to the previous day. On 2 July, the entire regiment had suffered losses of 16 men killed, 29 men wounded and 3 men missing. This was far lower than the losses suffered on the previous day of 4 officers, 79 men killed, 3 officers, 181 men wounded and 13 men missing.

The III/186 received orders on the evening of 2 July, to relieve RIR 111 from the position along the Fricourt-Contalmaison farm road up to the flank by Mametz. Shortly after 12 midnight (2/3 July) the III/186 marched from Flers in the order 11th, 12th, 9th, 10th Companies. A spacing of 20-25 meters existed between the individual companies and platoons as a precaution against enemy shell fire.

We marched a while on the road to Bazentin while a Battalion from IR 190 was on the left next to us that then later turned off to the right and separated a part of the 9th Coy from us. The road to Bazentin was scattered about with shells by the British.

The marching in the growing darkness and completely shot up wood was very difficult. In Bazentin we became led to the division battle Head Quarters, the companies received hand grenades here, most of which were without detonators. Complete obscurity about the situation at the front prevailed in the division battle Head Quarters and with the commander of RIR 111. *Hauptmann* Kade gave the following orders after having found the map: 11th Coy placed in the first line on the right connecting to IR 190 here, the 12th Coy first line in the middle, 9th Coy first line on the left connecting to the left here, 10th Coy to the possession of the battalion commander in the second line in the *Nestlerhöhlen. Feld Machine Gun Zug* 312 placed all guns in the front line, Platoon Henrart to the possession of the battalion commander.

During the march to the front the connection between the 11th and 12th Coy was disrupted very badly, because we could only reach the road through a narrow hole in a hedge. I assembled the 12th Coy again at Mametz Wood by a shot up battery position. The entire area became scattered about by the English artillery. We went through a communication trench and bumped into the 11th Coy in it again; then it went a stretch through an occupied second line further into a communication trench that however was almost completely shot up. It partly led along to a completely destroyed piece of forest. Finally we went over open fields in the hollow and in this we hurried to the west until by a Medical dugout. Here lay the 11th Coy, which however was soon led further westward. In one of the dugouts I found an officer, who said to me, the company must go further to the right. I began to start, when it came from behind: we were going the wrong way; we must go further on the left. I went back and became directed to another officer, who pointed out that we were to be in at another trench, then admonished me at the rush and then disappeared. A *Vizefeldwebel* of the M.G. Coy R111 then inadequately informed me about the position and wanted to take his machine gun out of the position. I said to him, he should wait, until our machine guns came. He claimed to have orders to move off immediately and furthermore that the machine gun had already moved away. On the right from me was Ravoth with his platoon, he had gone as far to the right, as the trench reached. Furthermore at the right angle to our trench it revealed the British, which however were driven back by our rifle fire. Connection to the 11th or 9th Coy could not be established, because the trench had completely ceased, it was at most 30 centimeters deep. Further to the left came Rauch, then Gallbach and Gebhardt. *Leutnant* Gallbach was wounded very early on the shoulder, he went away to be bandaged and on orders of the doctor remained in the dugout. On the left of the company was a platoon from RIR 111 that was still not relieved.

I went to the battalion dugout, to render my report to *Hauptmann* Kade. He now conferred with the battalion leader of RIR 111 because of the surrender of the position. *Leutnant* Quietmeyer, adjutant III/186, became sent out to get reports from the 11th and 9th Coy, because certainly nothing remained known about them. The 111er on the left of me became relieved through a platoon from the 10th Coy. When I came up out of the dugout, to regulate this, *Feldwebel* Freund came with one platoon from the 10th Coy with him the machine gun of *Leutnant* Freise. I allowed the 10th Coy to go into position and to bring the machine gun in position with help from *Leutnant* Freise. *Leutnant der Reserve* Ballheimer, 12/186. [7]

The second day of the battle was now over and the entire position of the 26th Reserve Division had remained in the hands of the defenders, with the exception of the *Granatloch* and the *Meisennest*. The situation facing the neighboring 28th Reserve Division was far worse. RIR 110 was gradually being forced out of La Boisselle, step by step. IR 190 was approaching the besieged village but would not arrive until 3 July at the earliest.

With the events taking place at La Boisselle and Fricourt, the concerns about the left flank of the 26th Reserve Division grew. Still, the men in the 26th Reserve Division became encouraged by the rumors that numerous men from different regiments were scattered around aimlessly in the rear and drifted around Pozières without leadership and these men were being assembled and provided further support to the exposed flank.

While this news sounded good, IR 180 immediately took the sharpest measures at the left flank of the division to provide as much security as possible. By the evening the division commander reported to His Majesty, the King: 'Attack victoriously repulsed. The entire position is intact in our hands.'

3 July

In the early morning hours of 3 July, drum fire of unheard force shrouded the positions of the 52nd and consequently the 56th Reserve Infantry Brigades in dense smoke and fumes. Phosgene shells and smoke bombs were mixed into the destructive fire and gas clouds formed by the enemy trenches that slowly rolled toward the German lines at several locations. Finally, in the pre-dawn darkness, immense masses of enemy infantry climbed out of the Ancre ground up toward St. Pierre-Division, they rushed out of Thiepval Wood against the ruins of the village of Thiepval and broke forth out of Authuille Wood against the hill by the *Granatloch*. More enemy troops advanced over the ridge of Aveluy toward Ovillers, against the badly damaged trenches at La Boisselle and to the east of the village. The enemy attacks to the south, along the National road, appeared to be designed to widen and deepen the successful gains made by the British on the previous days.

In the sector by St. Pierre-Division, *Major* Prager's request for additional support had been routed to IR 186, where on the morning of 3 July, instructions from the 51st Reserve Infantry Brigade arrived at the headquarters of the I/186 to send the 3/186 to Battalion Prager (I/8th Bavarian RIR) in the sector *Thiepval-Nord*. Before the 3/186 was able to arrive at the designated location, the existing garrison of men from RIR 99 and the 8th Bavarian RIR had already refused the attack and inflicted heavy losses on the enemy assault waves. The forward most positions at and south of St. Pierre-Division had held, while west of *Feste Schwaben*, the former German front line at the *Meisennest* was still in enemy hands.

At 3 a.m. on the morning of 3 July enemy drum fire fell on Thiepval and the positions south of the village that were being held by RIR 99 and the 8th Bavarian RIR, especially on Sector C9. Everything appeared to indicate a renewal of the enemy attacks at these locations. The possibility of an attack on the sector *Thiepval-Süd* had worried *Hauptmann* Wurm a great deal. He was concerned that the British were going to attempt to break through the German defenses where the front was being held only with weak forces. Such an attack could easily shatter the fragile defenses and destroy the men who had performed so well on 1 July.

Major von Fabeck had asked for support from the Bavarians in the early morning hours. Despite the losses already suffered by the regiment, the 8th Bavarian RIR could still provide some assistance in the defense against the enemy attack by *Thiepval-Süd*. *Vizefeldwebel der Reserve* Stolz, 3/8th Bavarian RIR, was in charge of the only available support troops in the vicinity and he was immediately sent to aid the men of RIR 99 in response to von Fabeck's request. When Stolz arrived at the regimental command post with his 55 men they were immediately ordered forward to Thiepval.

Stolz needed to hurry as RIR 99 expected an enemy attack at any moment. Powerful barrage fire fell on all of the access roads. Stolz and his men worked through the heavy fire as quickly as possible, and, eventually reached Thiepval with the men being worn out and totally exhausted from their tedious journey. A few men had been killed or wounded during

In the fire trench by Thiepval. Still deep and formidable despite
the heavy bombardment. (Author's collection)

the journey, mostly from being buried by shell impacts. However, Stolz's detachment did reach Thiepval in time to decisively interfere in the fighting. This small group then formed the backbone of the defense of Thiepval in the days following.

In front of Thiepval dense waves of men from the 11th Cheshire, 2nd South Lancaster and 8th Border Battalions (75th Brigade, 25th Division) swarmed out of the Park of Thiepval and attacked the foremost position. Parts of these battalions penetrated the German line between the 1st and 2/R99 north of the *Granatloch*. 'Praise God', was all Wurm could say when he saw that the British were only attacking Sectors C4 and C9; while also placing severe artillery fire on the *Strassburger Steig*.

The situation was becoming critical where the British troops had broken into the German defenses and where additional enemy detachments were close at hand to exploit their success. Fortunately, most of the remaining attacking troops had been forced back with heavy losses from infantry fire along with supporting artillery fire. The men of RIR 99 reported that the subsequent British assault waves had begun to panic and withdrew in great haste in the face of such concentrated fire.

Something needed to be done about the enemy troops still inside the German trenches in order to restore the situation. The I/R99 had no more reserves at hand. Now, with the arrival of Stolz and his men, the British troops inside the German lines could be attacked from three sides, by the 1/R99, mainly by the Platoon of *Leutnant der Reserve* Schreiner, the platoon of *Leutnant der Reserve* Hein, 2/R99, as well as from part of the 16/R99 under *Oberleutnant der Reserve* Andreé. Detachment Stolz added its firepower to the other units and provided the extra force that was needed to expel the enemy troops.

Further south, by Sector C9, the enemy had brought forward two battalions of the 14th Brigade with an abundant number of machine guns into the *Granatloch* area under cover of darkness. The entire sector then came under extraordinarily heavy artillery fire starting at 4 a.m. The British apparently wanted to enlarge their gains on the right and on the left through hand grenade fighting. Three enemy attacks came out from the *Granatloch*. Each one became refused outright through the fire from the 9/8th Bavarian RIR and part of the 1/185.

3rd July: Morning dawns. Our eyelids are heavy with fatigue, but we must stay alert. Sooner than expected the enemy resumes his attack. Tommies climb out of their trench and advance at a trot. The order to fire is unnecessary. Everyone knows what is at stake. After a few bursts of rifle fire the assault is stopped. Is that all? No, it is only the beginning. The enemy is using the same tactics as yesterday. The Tommies run forward a short distance, drop into shell holes, then jump up again to repeat the performance, always moving closer. However, we are on our guard. Whenever an Englishman shows himself he is greeted with a volley of shots. But there are far more of the enemy than us, and suddenly they jump out of the craters en masse to attack again.

Once more our rifles crack is salvos. Several nimble Tommies run up in a quick rush – and are shot dead within a few meters of our trench. The *Hindenburgeck* is dangerously pressed, but the company's most dependable men are posted there. Among them are *Unteroffizier* Büttner, the III Battalion's old flag carrier, then *Unteroffizier* Hörning who came over to us as a volunteer from the Train by Wytschaete, further, the *Reservists* Karl Bergmann and Eduard Ballweg. With them is a small *Unteroffizier* from IR 185 with his Group, honest, tough *Swabians*.

Once again Tommy is 'greased', though following a short pause he tries a third time. He receives the same reception. With this attempt, however, it appears he has had enough. The survivors flee back toward their own trench. In astonishment I hear *Unteroffizier* Hopf yell, 'Everyone, let's go!' With hand grenades in hand, his Group climbs out of the trench and is followed by others. In an instant the *Hindenburg Stellung* is occupied by Germans again. *Reservist* Leimeister picks up an English machine gun and Hopf links up with the 180th Regiment. The approach trenches are blocked off and two dugouts are still found intact. In one of these we find two wounded comrades. They whimper and cry for joy. Piles of English hand grenades have been left behind. They are distributed among the men along with quick instructions on their use. If the enemy comes back again we will give him a greeting he won't forget. Some of the men discover English knapsacks lying about. They are instantly searched for food. Even the crumbs taste delicious after our past two day fast. I immediately report our success to Battalion, whose commander sends back his appreciation in a simple note: 'Of course, the Bavarians!'[8]

At 7.20 a.m., when Hill 141 was being attacked, the men defending the trench and the barricade on the right of IR 180 came under heavy enemy fire. Even though the men defending the *Granatloch* had their hands full fending off several British attacks, one small platoon was sent to offer help to the men in IR 180. However, as soon as the platoon had arrived, the Sector commander said: 'Children, I thank you. However, do not stay and go back and report to the comrades next door: the Ovillers Sector is firmly in our hands!' When this story was passed along to the regimental commander, it was reported that his

Schmidt (Paul)
Leutnant d. R. i. Inf.-Regt. 180,
gefallen bei Ovillers la Boiffelle
am 3. Juli 1916

Leutenant der Reserve Paul Schmidt (*Kriegstagebuch aus Schwaben*)

eyes lit up. His young adjutant shouted boisterously: 'That was an unforgettably proud minute. I would not have changed places with a prince!'

About 8.30 a.m. fierce hand grenade fighting took place in the first trench of P1 and in the *Hindenburg Stellung*. Company Vogler had received additional support through the 4/180 together with a large reserve of hand grenades just prior to the enemy attack. When *Unteroffizier* Hopf entered the *Hindenburg Stellung* he joined up with parts of the 3rd and 7/180 under *Oberleutnant der Reserve* Vogler whose men had also attacked the British from the east. The fighting in the trenches at the barricade at the right wing of the regiment was severe; there was also an advance by the enemy over the open ground from the front that had to be dealt with. Luckily, the British assault waves were cut down in the heavy defensive fire, much as they had been on 1 July and the attack was bloodily refused.

While the *Hindenburg Stellung* was being cleared, *Leutnant der Reserve* Kleudgen, RIR 99, captured an additional enemy machine gun. Also, a wounded Captain and a few Scotsmen from the 15th Highland Light Infantry were brought in. The 5/185 was then ordered to relieve parts of the I/R99 north of the *Granatloch*, whose four companies, in part consisting of only 30 men, had been combined together to form a single company.

In the further course of the fighting Vogler succeeded in expelling the enemy completely out of the *Hindenburg Stellung* and established a connection with RIR 99 and his men eventually recaptured 100 meters of the former sector of RIR 99. The fighting finally died down towards midday at the right wing of IR 180. The position was now occupied by Bavarians, men from RIR 99, IR 185 and IR 180. The victory was not without losses on the German side. Numerous men had been killed or wounded during the fighting; including *Leutnant der Reserve* Paul Schmidt and *Leutnant der Reserve* Alber from IR 180 who were both wounded. The former died of his injuries the same evening.

During the British attacks and German counterattack, the reserves further back in the rear did not know what was taking place at the front. Because of the lack of information *Hauptmann* Heyberger sent three Groups of the 5/180 into the *Lemberg Stellung* as support, which quickly became involved in the defense of the position. Without the arrival of these men, it was very possible that the British could have expanded their gains by the *Granatloch*. While the British were once more prevented from capturing further ground, the small numbers of defenders and weak reserves meant that the *Granatloch* could not be cleared from enemy troops.

In order to prevent the possibility of an enemy breakthrough by Thiepval, *Hauptmann* Wurm also sent out the 2/185 with two machine guns into the *Auwärter Weg* as reinforcement for the 3/8th Bavarian RIR, who had suffered heavy losses there. The German defenses were already stretched very thin and with each casualty it became harder to hold on to every sector of the front line. Still, the remaining survivors continued to hold out in spite of every hardship.

Perhaps the greatest threat facing the 26th Reserve Division occurred when the British attempted to capture the village of Ovillers and the Sector *Ovillers-Süd*. During the night of 2/3 July the enemy was actively working in his first trench, while the connecting routes leading to the rear of IR 180 came under the heaviest artillery fire. At 3 a.m. fierce drum fire from guns of every caliber and heavy mines began to fall upon the first and second trench in the Ovillers Sector, reportedly to be substantially more violent than the bombardment experienced on 1 July.

At 4.15 a.m. the British attacked the III/180 (*Major* Scupin) in *Ovillers-Süd*. Bombing parties formed the first wave, which were followed closely by waves of skirmishers. Behind them came columns of infantry, supposedly with officers mounted on horseback. In addition to the heavy enemy artillery fire, the trenches and craters occupied by the men of IR 180 were being strafed by enemy aircraft. The enemy pilots were even reported to be firing on medical dugouts.

Using the few existing intact telephone lines and red flares, the German artillery was signaled to open fire, which was promptly employed. Artillery Group Pys provided the majority of defensive artillery fire for this sector however, the large numbers of guns already lost in the previous days had caused significant gaps in the wall of defensive barrage fire. This was most evident in front of Sector P5 held by men of the 9/180. Most of the batteries assigned to protect this portion of the line had been destroyed. Also, the enemy fire had leveled most of the front line trench in P5, badly damaged the wire entanglements and buried most of the dugout entrances. Because of these conditions, the enemy was able to penetrate the German line here and continue to advance toward the next series of trenches.

On 1 July the 2/180 in Sector P4 was able to take the enemy advancing against P5 under very effective flanking fire. However, today this was impossible, because P4 was continuously under the heaviest enemy artillery fire. Parts of the 6th Royal West Kent and the 6th Queen's West Surrey Battalions from the 37th Brigade poured through the gaps in the defensive fire and inexorably advanced, penetrating the German front line.

The fortunes of war were arbitrary; while the British had been able to reach the second trench in P5, the 10/180 in P6 completely refused the repeated enemy advances. The wire entanglements in front of P6 were damaged the least of any sector in front of Ovillers. Also, fewer dugout entrances had been destroyed or buried in the preparation fire, allowing the company to man the positions inside the trench and successfully refuse repeated enemy attacks. Once the 6th Royal West Kent and the 6th Queen's West Surrey Battalions had breached the German line at P5, bombing parties on both sides of the enemy break-in location immediately blocked off the first trench and prevented the position from being

8th *Korporalschaft*, 4th Zug, 8/180. The men marked 1, 2, 3, 5, 7 and 8 in
the left hand photo were all killed on 3 July 1916. (Felix Fregin)

rolled up.

Cut off from any possible support, the British troops inside the German line by P5 could now be eliminated. Groups from the 2nd, 9th and 10/180 attacked the West Kent and West Surrey Battalions inside the German position, bringing any further enemy advance to a halt. Three groups of the 6/180, as well as one platoon from the 8/180 from in the *Harrer Graben* as well as support from Groups of the 9th and 10/180, which were in the *Kuhm* and *Baum* saps, then began a counterattack that was designed to completely eliminate the threat within Sector P6.

In addition, bombing parties of the 2/180 went forward in a counterattack in P5 and helped to destroy all of the enemy troops who had penetrated the German line. At 5.45 a.m., after almost two hours of trench fighting, the position of the 9/180 in P5 was firmly in German hands again.

At the same time Sector P5 had been breached, parts of the 7th Suffolk and the 5th Royal Berkshire Battalions (35th Brigade) advancing on the Albert-Ovillers road poured over the totally leveled first trench of the 11/180 west of Ovillers. Within a short time, at least 300 British soldiers were inside the village ruins.

The men of the 11/180 under *Oberleutnant der Reserve* Knapp had finally succeeded in becoming freed from the buried dugouts and received the second British assault wave with devastating infantry and machine gun fire, forcing them back. *Gefreiter* Pfeil from the machine gun company had been recommended for an award for his bravery on this day. He operated his machine gun completely alone with a serious wound; the middle of his hand had been shot through early in the fighting. During the initial enemy attack, Pfeil, while ignoring his painful wound, became angry when his gun jammed and unable to fire as a result of the thick mud in the *Zuführer.*[9]

While Pfeil was attempting to clear the jammed machine gun, the British troops continued to advance toward his position. He cursed at the weapon and tried everything he could think of to clear the jam. Finally, after wiping the mud from the firing mechanism and cartridge belt, hitting the gun with his hand and trying to knock any additional mud from the *Zuführer* he looked up and saw several British soldiers standing directly in front of the machine gun, making their way toward him.

Pfeil quickly cocked the machine gun and pressed the firing levers. His efforts were successful and the machine gun began to fire once more. The cone of bullets poured into the oncoming British troops at point blank range and proved to be devastating as men fell by the dozens. The attack hesitated and then, suddenly, the British troops turned around and made their way back toward the British trenches. Pfeil remained at his gun until the situation appeared to be well in hand. Then he finally went to the rear and stood at attention while he reported to his company commander. Once finished, he was sent to the medical dugout where his shattered hand could be cleaned and dressed. The fire from Pfeil's machine gun was considered to be an integral part of the success in stopping the subsequent enemy waves of infantry from penetrating the German line at Ovillers.[10]

The British troops that had made their way into Ovillers had also managed to bring up two machine guns and place them in position at the church. Faced with this threat, the regiment immediately made arrangements to move the last two platoons of the 8/180 under the leadership of *Oberleutnant* Dettling closer to the village. *Hauptmann* Heyberger placed both last platoons of the 5/180 and a bombing party from the 2/180 to the possession of the endangered Battalion Scupin.

First of all the different groups must clear a path to the village through the heavy fire. The two British machine guns that were in position immediately fired on the defending companies from the rear, causing many losses among the *Württembergers.* These guns needed to be placed out of action as quickly as possible.

In a short time, all available men were in position to attack and eliminate the enemy threat. Groups located in the third trench from the 6th and 12/180 as well as the two platoons of the 8/180 attacked from the right, while simultaneously Groups of the 12/180 situated in the *Bumiller Dorf* and *Schäferwiese* lying eastward of Ovillers attacked from the left.

The British troops inside Ovillers put up a stout defense and both enemy machine guns continued to fire until the very last. The men of IR 180 moved through the trenches and ruins of the village, eliminating one enemy pocket of resistance after the other. The ring of German troops slowly closed in upon the shrinking number of defenders and destroyed the largest part in close combat. The corpses piled up six deep in some places, one on top of another as the brutal fighting continued to rage; no one escaped. Finally, the small numbers of enemy troops that were still holding out were forced to surrender or become destroyed and the threat had been eliminated.

Artist's impression of the capture of the Church of Ovillers, 3
July 1916. *(Illustrierte Geschichte des Weltkrieges 1914/16)*

The two enemy machine guns had proved to be the most difficult to eliminate. Four men from IR 180 took on both machine guns and their crews as their targets during the counterattack. Each machine gun was operated by a gun crew and infantry support, reported to total 16 men for each weapon. During the attack by the four man assault team, one machine gun became vulnerable to being captured following a strong hand grenade attack. Before the Germans could capture the gun, the crew tossed it down a well near the church.

The enemy attempted to carry the second machine gun to the well, to keep it from falling into German hands but was prevented with well-thrown hand grenades that began to explode around the men. Finally, after holding out for an additional 30 minutes, the surviving enemy soldiers surrendered to the four German bombers who brought back the second machine gun and 36 prisoners, of which one was a Captain. *Gefreiter* Bäder, one of the four men who had taken on the enemy machine guns, had his small sense of revenge on the enemy officer who he forced to carry the heavy machine gun back to the company headquarters.

Once the fighting was over, *Oberleutnant* Dettling occupied positions in P7 west of Ovillers with his platoons from the 8/180, while *Leutnant der Reserve* Kupferschmid, with two platoons of the 5/180 occupied the *Bumiller Dorf* and *Schäferwiese*. By 6.50 a.m. the entire Sector *Ovillers-Süd* was already firmly in the possession of the Württembergers again.

Hecht
Leutnant d. R. i. Inf.-Regt. 180,
gefallen bei Ovillers la Boisselle
am 3. Juli 1916

Hahn (friedrich)
Leutnant im Infanterie-Regt. 180,
gefallen bei Ovillers la Boisselle
am 3. Juli 1916

Leutnant der Reserve Hecht and *Leutnant* Friedrich Hahn (*Kriegstagebuch aus Schwaben*)

At 7 a.m. a report was sent to the division: 'Ovillers is free from the enemy'.

IR 180 had suffered numerous losses, both during the bombardment and initial enemy attack as well as during the counterattacks held to clear the enemy from inside the German positions. Among the fatal casualties was the leader of the 12/180, *Oberleutnant* Kraut, *Leutnant der Reserve* Hecht, *Leutnant der Reserve* Paul Schmid and *Leutnant* Friedrich Hahn. The leader of the 11/180, *Oberleutnant der Landwehr* Knapp, *Leutnant* Speer and *Leutnant der Reserve* Fechter were severely wounded; *Leutnant der Reserve* Gussmann and *Leutnant* Alber were slightly wounded. In addition, 85 Other Ranks were killed, 160 Other Ranks were wounded (amongst them one man was buried); 13 Other Ranks were missing.

Transporting the severely wounded to the rear had proven to be very difficult in the constant British artillery fire. Until the heavy fire died down the men would have to wait patiently. There were 60 severely wounded men alone, all awaiting transportation to the rear, in the densely crowded small medical dugout of the I/180, where Dr. Speich worked tirelessly. For some, the wait would prove to be too long.

In the fighting around Ovillers a total of 3 British officers and 120 men were taken prisoner. Both in and in front of the position lay an estimated 1,500 enemy dead and numerous wounded men. The loss of officers was especially large in the British ranks from what the men of IR 180 could determine.

According to statements from prisoners, from pieces of captured equipment and insignia it was established that two English Brigades, the 35th and 37th, had undertaken the attack on *Ovillers-Süd*. Orders for the attack upon Ovillers were found on a captive English officer, in which they had expressly ordered that the village must be taken under all circumstances. Heavy fighting by Ovillers continued in the next days, demonstrating to the German command the high value that the British commander-in-chief placed on this part of the German line for his future plans.

The 8/185 that arrived at 7.30 a.m. from the brigade as reinforcements was placed in the front line in the sector *Ovillers-Süd*, the same sector as the recently arrived Machine Gun

Transporting the wounded on the Somme. (Author's collection)

Company/186. This welcome addition to the defense of the Ovillers Sector also became positioned at the left wing of the sector *Ovillers-Süd*. Two machine guns were placed at the left wing of P7, with one machine gun in the *Bumiller Dorf* and one machine gun in the *Schäferwiese*. Two machine guns remained as the sector reserve by the regimental command post. During the afternoon the Sector *Ovillers-Süd* only received weak artillery fire.

In the afternoon, an Orderly Officer of the division delivered the following hand written letter from His *Excellenz* von Soden, the Division Commander to *Oberstleutnant* Vischer, IR 180:

> I send my greetings to Regiment 180. The regiment has performed very well, but this was also not any different than what was expected, it could be proud of its performance. I hope, the regiment will soon be allowed to be reinforced, also to be able to be replaced in the foreseeable time.
>
> However, as long as this is not possible, the regiment must endure and become, according to God's will, also refuse further attacks with its own power. It must be clear to every *Musketier* that the decision of the war depends upon our endurance. Intimate connections should be made with IR 190. Also if this regiment should go back further, IR 180 will hold its position and will not go back. The situation will improve. Therefore fresh courage, keep your heads up! I send my best wishes and greetings. Signed: *Frhr.* von Soden. [11]

In the division daily orders from 4 July; 3 July 1916 was described as a day of honor in the history of IR 180.

> The IR 180 has bloodily refused multiple English attacks yesterday in the Sector Ovillers. The enemy that advanced into the village up to the church was surrounded and destroyed. Our position was completely held. The 3rd of July would remain a

day of fame in the history of Regiment 180, to which I voice my congratulations to the same.

On the same day had RIR 99 under heavy casualties refused superior attacks by the Englishmen on the village of Thiepval and about Hill 141. Through the tenacity and bravery of the good regiment the enemy onrush has failed. Thiepval and Hill 141 remained completely in our possession. I speak of my fullest acknowledgement to the regiment for this excellent performance. *Von* Soden. [12]

Following the intense enemy attacks, much work was required to restore the Ovillers position and to ensure that the ability to maintain command and control continued to be uninterrupted. In order to accomplish in the face of the most recent enemy attack, the battle headquarters of IR 180 needed to be moved to a safer location, further to the rear.

When about midday of this day the tactical situation was assessed as far as it was allowed, a repetition of the attack was no longer to be expected, so I decided to exchange the battle command position of the regiment that, how already mentioned, lay too near behind the front and the left wing of the Regimental Sector, and move to the new position, although still unfinished regimental battle headquarters in the *Stockacher Graben*. Swiftly the necessary preparations were made, the orderly officer with 2 Telephonists remained back for a long time, until the new dugout had been reached, and went on the journey in small parties. The 2 kilometer long route through the *Haug Graben*, third trench, *Fölkersamb* Sap (*Nordwerk*) and *Stockacher Graben* became accomplished without incident and a look into the dreadful devastation work of the last ten days. Duds, blow outs (shrapnel cases), fuses, pieces of explosive, infantry cartridges, pieces of equipment of all types lay everywhere on the routes, now and then a dead person between them, and through the air screamed and whistled the projectiles heavier and lighter caliber, while the round circle of shells and shrapnel bursts formed the basis for this hellish concert. Entirely leveled positions must naturally be crossed by jumping over long shadowy trench walls, until the frightening journey was past. So everyone went safely and with ease one climbed down the stairway shaft that would serve us for that next time as a work place and habitation. In the three different stairway shafts fixed themselves the Telephonists, clerks, orderlies, servants and cooks. *Major* Keerl, who until now had inhabited the tunnels with his staff, fortified us still with a strong tinned soup, before he himself went to work on the so-called 'Badger-construction', a dugout on the Pozières-Thiepval road, there where the road from Mouquet farm flowed into it. After telephone connections with all command position had been established, they now tackled the equipment in the tunnel. From the bottom tread out approximately three steps straight out further were still mined, but the walls still uncovered. The water dripped down from the chalk rock, collected on the ground in small puddles of water. That was our sleeping area. In the part under the stairway became the telephone, further up to fixed on some treads the writing room and the upper part of the stairway up to the entrance served during the day as the residential and dining room. The food sequence was very simple, bread covered with meat and vegetable preserves from the iron rations, served in a single cooking cover that was passed from one man to the other. Nevertheless, however, it tasted excellent to us, especially as the question of the relief and so that the outlook for better times always moved closer. So passed the so eventful day without further incident and in the night heavy artillery fire lay again, as usual, upon all rearward connections.[13]

At 10 a.m. General von Soden promised additional reinforcements for the hard-pressed troops, which in view of the situation by Thiepval and Ovillers was so desperately needed. By late morning on 3 July, reinforcements had begun to arrive and were inserted at key points in the line. Among the reinforcements were units from the 2nd Guard Reserve Division that had fought at Gommécourt on 1 July. While it had been the intention of the British to prevent these units from being used further south where the main fighting was taking place, it was very obvious that they had completely failed.

In the afternoon the 6/185 arrived and was placed in possession of IR 180, as well as the Recruit Company 180 (Friedrich). The 6/185 became accommodated in part at the left wing of the third trench of *Ovillers-Süd*, in part in the *Nordwerk*. The Recruit Company 180 (Friedrich) occupied the Intermediate position between Mouquet farm and the *Schwarzwald Graben*, with one platoon in the battery positions by the *Schwarzwald Graben*.

In the course of the evening the I/R15 under *Hauptmann Frhr.* von Forstner from the 2nd Guard Reserve Division and the I/*Garde Füsiliers* under *Major* von Delius from the 3rd Guard Infantry Division became assigned to support the 52nd Reserve Infantry Brigade, von Auwärter. The former battalion relieved the II/R99 in *Thiepval-Mitte*, the latter battalion relieved part of the I/R99 and 5/185 at the *Granatloch*. The remaining battalions of the *Garde Füsilier* Regiment were approaching the front, coming from the village of Warlencourt. By the evening of 3 July, General von Auwärter had two battalions from IR 185, two battalions from RIR 15 and the I/*Garde Füsilier* Regiment besides the regiments RIR 99, IR 180 and the 8th Bavarian RIR. Two battalions from IR 186 had also been assigned to the 51st Reserve Infantry Brigade.

The Second Line by Thiepval and Ovillers had received considerable reinforcements, substantially reducing any chances of an enemy breakthrough. *Oberstleutnant* Krause was located in *Feste Zollern; Süd I* and *II* by Grandcourt were under the command of *Leutnant* Mauch with the 6/Reserve *Pionier* Battalion 13, 2nd Recruit Coy/180, two machine guns from Machine Gun Marksman Detachment 45; *Süd-III* and *Feste Staufen* were commanded by *Leutnant* Klug with a combined company from the 8th Bavarian RIR, one machine gun from the 8th Bavarian RIR, four machine guns from Machine Gun Marksman Detachment 45; *Süd-IV* and *Feste Zollern* up to *Süd-VI* were under *Hauptmann* Josephson (subsequently under *Oberleutnant* von Mücke) with the 5th, 6th, 7th, and a MG Coy/185. The II/R99 occupied the second line of *Süd-IV* while the 5/185 was placed in the second trench south of Thiepval.

The 1st Recruit Coy/180 arrived in the second position for the protection of the left flank and occupied the left wing from *Süd-VI*; after, the 6/185 moved to the left and occupied the right wing of *Süd-VI*. At 10 a.m. the 5/185 moved to the *Wundtwerk*, relieving parts of the 8th Bavarian RIR and 1/R99 subsequently on the right of the 1/185 in the front line at C8. One half of the 2/185, which was located in *Feste Schwaben*, now occupied the *Auwärter Weg*. In the afternoon the 6/185 moved to *Ovillers-Süd*, with one half reinforcing the 11/180, the other half became the battalion reserve and at night was placed in position to help protect the flank facing La Boisselle. The 7/185 moved forward to Thiepval to reinforce RIR 99 (one fourth in C6, one fourth in the *Martinspfad*, one half in the *Kanonen Weg*; The Staff of the II/185 went back to Warlencourt and was the possession of IR 180. Later, in the second position, part of the 1st Recruit Coy/180 extended further to the right, the MG Coy/185 further to the left. One platoon from Machine Gun *Zug* 311 and 559 was located in *Feste Staufen*.

The defensive fighting on 3 July had relied heavily on infantry and machine gun fire along with some additional supporting artillery fire. Artillery Group Berta, located in the neighboring sector, had performed splendidly in the morning. When the batteries ran out of high explosive and shrapnel ammunition, they fired as long as possible into the woods opposite Thiepval with gas shells, until 10.15 a.m. when the replacement ammunition requested only one hour earlier, had arrived.

The German artillery regiments were facing a serious situation. The batteries providing the most effective defensive fire belonged to the 26th Reserve Field Artillery Brigade under General von Maur. The 28th Reserve Field Artillery Brigade had very few guns still capable of action. The Württemberg II/RFAR 29 under *Major* Hartenstein had been badly damaged in the disaster that had befallen most of the batteries of the 28th Reserve Division and now consisted of only two batteries, which were virtually worn down.

Batteries from the 52nd Infantry Division had provided support for both the 26th and 28th Reserve Divisions on 3 July. Additional batteries had been quickly brought up during the day and were placed in position under the cover of darkness, including the 1st, 2nd, 3rd, 7th (F) and 8 (F)/RFAR 11 from the 11th Reserve Division that were placed by at Martinpuich, Foureaux Wood and Delville Wood. While these batteries were a valuable addition to the overall German defenses, they were not yet familiar with the present configuration of the battlefield. Until this was accomplished, and they had accurate firing maps they were unable to effectively interfere in the fighting.

While the British were making every attempt to expand their gains along the front of the 26th Reserve Division, the fighting by the 28th Reserve Division also continued unabated. RIR 110 was still barely holding on to La Boisselle at the start of 3 July. The desperately needed reinforcements had not arrived until approximately 2 a.m. During the entire time the men of RIR 110 held on to the village, they were under strict orders not to give up a single foot of ground without a fight.

The long awaited reinforcements from IR 190 had been steadily moving toward La Boisselle for some time. The regiment had advanced in three columns from Flers. The right hand column, the II/190 without the 5/190, with three machine guns from *Ergänzung* Platoon 582 under *Hauptmann der Reserve* Blume advanced to the north past Pozières through the *Schwarzwald Graben*. The I/190 with four machine guns from *Ergänzung* Platoon 316 formed the middle column under *Hauptmann* Kuntze. The battalion marched south of Pozières through the *Lattorf Graben*; while the left column, the III/190, and the 5/190, with six machine guns from the Machine Gun Company under *Hauptmann der Reserve* Vaske moved through the *Grossherzog Graben* past Contalmaison.

The three columns from IR 190 had suffered their first losses when they came under increasingly heavy British artillery fire that was falling on the Second Position. A number of officers and men were wounded and forced to return to the rear for treatment. A few, like Battalion Adjutant, *Leutnant der Reserve* Bindel, who was wounded on the knee by shell splinters, remained with the men. The remainder continued to advance as they knew that their arrival could mean the difference between success and disaster for the German front line.

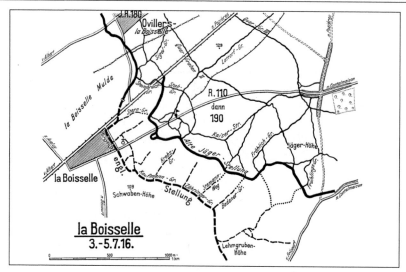

La Boisselle

The men of IR 190 advanced very slowly in the darkness in the marshy communication trenches. At times the columns were forced to stop until the guides could determine where they were and what routes they needed to take. All of this caused delays and confusion among the ranks. Several companies from the II/190 lost contact with the column and eventually ended up in the rear, northeast of Pozières.

The lead elements of IR 190 finally arrived in La Boisselle just after the 8th North Staffordshire and 10th Worcester Battalion (57th Brigade, 19th Division) had attacked. The British had managed to advance up to the *Steinbruch Graben* and *Kaiser Strasse*. The fresh troops from the I/190 managed to halt the enemy advance and recapture several positions at the northern and eastern edge of the village and push the enemy back to the *Kirch Stellung*.

During the advance, the I/190 managed to liberate the 11/R110 that had already been surrounded by the enemy. The fresh troops continued to press forward into the *Grenz Graben* and soon became embroiled in a hand grenade battle that lasted several hours. Losses were heavy on both sides and included the commanders of the 8th North Staffordshire and 10th Worcester Battalions, Colonel Wedgewood and Colonel Piggot. When the fighting finally died down, the 3rd, 4th and 2/190 with elements of RIR 110 held the positions roughly east of La Boisselle on both sides of the national road. The 1/190 lay further to the rear in reserve.

Only a few groups of the 8/190 with the staff of the II/190 managed to reach the front line north of the national road. Here they cleared the left wing of the sector from the enemy in a fierce hand grenade battle. Still, this position was quite threatened; the enemy occupied the front line German trenches in the neighboring sector and only a barricade separated the men from both sides.

The situation at the right wing of the 28th Reserve Division was still dangerous and new reinforcements were needed for the front line. *Gefreiter* Bent, 6/190, a runner from the battalion staff, succeeded in guiding the companies of the regiment that had remained behind to the threatened position. The troops advanced in thin waves through the enemy barrage fire by Pozières, then advanced to the north and finally through the smashed *Schwarzwald Graben*. By the afternoon two thirds of the 6th and 7/190 occupied the right wing of the front line sector, one third of the 6th and 8/190 were located in the second line. The machine guns from *Landwehr Brigade Ersatz Battalion 55* were relieved by the machine guns from the *Ergänzung* Platoon 582 under *Leutnant der Reserve* Hansen.

The III/190 and 5/190 were at the fork in the road northeast of Contalmaison when they received news about a breakthrough by the adversary at La Boisselle. By now, the enemy could be advancing upon Contalmaison. With this possibility in mind, the 9th, 10th and 12/190 continued to move forward, swarming out along the Contalmaison-Pozières road in order to reach the front line and possibly block any further enemy advance. Two thirds of the 11/190 occupied the position in front of the southwestern edge of Contalmaison. The other part of the 11/190 was advancing on both sides of the Contalmaison-La Boisselle road.

In the morning, when it was possible to survey the situation at the front in daylight, it was discovered that the reports about the enemy breakthrough at La Boisselle were not accurate. Consequently, the 12th, 9th and 5/190 received orders to occupy the *Alt Jäger Stellung*. The entire 11/190 was then reassembled at the southwestern edge of Contalmaison. In the confusion of the previous evening, many of the men had lost contact with their companies. Some had become casualties in the constant enemy shelling while others had simply become lost in the unfamiliar terrain.

Only little by little did the men locate their companies in the new positions. A connection was then established with the I/190. Subsequently on the left of the 11/190 were parts of the 9/186, on the right, the 10/190 north of the Contalmaison-La Boisselle road and in the copse 200 meters west of Contalmaison. The machine guns of the regiment under *Leutnant von der* Heyden-Linden, had positioned four machine guns in the line and held two in reserve. The I and III/190 had already suffered heavy losses on the first days of their deployment, because only few mined dugouts were available in the trenches, which for the most part were leveled. The situation by the II/190 was more favorable. This battalion had a number of shell proof dugouts that offered ample protection against the murderous artillery fire.

With the situation by Ovillers being under control for the time being, it was now the turn of the Germans to attack. At 10 a.m. on the morning of 3 July, the 3/186 that was subordinate to Battalion Prager (I/8th Bavarian RIR) in Sector *Thiepval-Nord* was ordered to take part in an assault to recapture the *Meisennest*. The company leader, *Leutnant der Landwehr I* Moehl, knew that with the men he had available in his company, he would not be able to recapture the entire position that had been assigned to him. Instead, he decided to perform a detailed reconnaissance of the target position in order to determine just where the enemy was at his weakest. He was determined to capture as much lost ground as possible by using his resources to the fullest.

Moehl and several orderlies made their way across the Ancre and found a position on the northern bank where they could overlook the enemy occupied trenches in C2 and C3. The small group made the journey to the observation point under enemy artillery fire the entire way without suffering any losses. Once safely in position in the heights in *Beaumont-Süd*, Moehl used his binoculars to scan the entire British position. He was able to quickly determine which trench sections were occupied by British troops, what main routes led to these points in the line, how the trench sections were occupied, where sandbag barricades had been erected and where machine guns had been installed.

While Moehl scanned the enemy position, his orderlies took down everything he said and marked it on the maps they carried. With the possession of this important information, Moehl made the final plans for his attack. He was going to direct his men at the various points in the enemy position where the enemy position was at its weakest. If everything went as planned, even his small company could clear a substantial portion of the former German line.

The time set for the attack was 12 midnight. The password provided to the men for the attack was 'Schnapps.' Six assault detachments consisting of especially good hand grenade throwers and resolute Other Ranks were formed from the men of the 3/186. The assault detachments would be supported by bearer troops that carried ammunition, hand grenades and other supplies needed in the advance.

The first detachment of assault troops under *Leutnant der Reserve* Volk, received orders to advance from sector C1 into the foremost battle trench and then if possible move to the left up to the St. Pierre-Divion – *Thiepval-Nord* road. The second detachment of assault troops under *Vizefeldwebel der Reserve* Landau, would advance through the first battle trench and once there, establish a connection with the first detachment.

The advance of the first section under *Leutnant der Reserve* Volk succeeded completely because of the previous precautions taken by *Leutnant* Moehl: the enemy garrison located in the dugouts were taken completely by surprise and after a short fight, and were rendered harmless. Similarly the crews of two enemy machine guns were so surprised by the sudden attack that they were not able to fire a single shot. Parts of the 8/8th Bavarian RIR which were advancing through the *Meisengasse* to support the attack were unable to make any headway at all because of the heavy fire of a British machine gun located in the *Meisennest*.

The advance of the second detachment of assault troops under *Vizefeldwebel* Landau also succeeded completely. As a result of this well-coordinated attack, the K1 trench up to the St. Pierre-Divion – Thiepval road had been recaptured. A part of the second trench up to the barrier at the *Meisengasse* had also been recaptured. The spoils taken in the attack consisted of two machine guns, one *Minenwerfer*, one *Granatwerfer*, eight prisoners, of which four had been wounded. After *Leutnant* Volk's men had re-captured approximately 200 meters of the enemy position, Volk sent a message back to the company leader, who, upon receiving it sent both remaining platoons of his company (Bleyer and Skiba) forward in order to relieve the assault units and blocked off the captured trench.

4 July

Despite Moehl's success the strongly occupied British nests remaining in the *Meisennest* that were connected with the main British position through communication trenches continued to threaten the troops in *Thiepval-Nord*. If the enemy eventually succeeded in gaining any more ground, then the positions by St. Pierre-Divion could be jeopardized. The loss of this key location could then threaten the entire position of the 26th Reserve Division. While the enemy held portion of the old front line was being held under almost constant artillery fire, it would be necessary to use infantry to finally expel the British once and for all.

New preparations were being made for the total elimination of the British nest on 4 July. It would take time to obtain information about the location and strength of each unit located in *Thiepval-Nord* and to make arrangements for additional support from the artillery in the rear, arrange for fresh supplies of ammunition, food and water before any attack had the slightest chance of success. The officers and their staff worked tirelessly on these problems.

Their task was made that much more difficult in the constant heavy British artillery fire. Any movement through the badly damaged positions drew enemy fire and areas once crossed in a matter of minutes now took hours in some cases. Also, heavy cloud bursts and a severe thunderstorm in the afternoon made the trenches look like rivers of mud; filled the craters and many of the dugouts with a mixture of water and thick, sticky clay almost one meter deep. These conditions almost resulted in all movement within the position coming to a halt. In addition to the constant shell fire, the enemy conducted a night attack against the garrisons of the barricades; he was repulsed with the assistance of the 1st and 5/185.

Despite the difficulties making preparations for the new attack and the horrible condition of the ground, bombing parties from Battle Group Wurm west of *Feste Schwaben* advanced against the enemy. The attack by Wurm and his men was made even more difficult when immediately after the commencement of the assault the alert British artillery placed drum fire on the German positions. The enemy fire only gradually decreased in strength following the request that the German batteries reduce their level of fire. Once the perceived threat had disappeared, the British guns fell silent. During the heavy bombardment falling on the German lines at the commencement of the attack, a shell fatally wounded *Leutnant der Landwehr* Meye, leader of the 6/8th Bavarian RIR, inside *Feste Schwaben*. When his men ran over to help him, he said: Leave me, help those who are there in the front. I will soon be out of it.!'

Despite some losses, Wurm's Group succeeded in capturing about 200 meters of the second trench of Sector C3 between the *Meisengasse* and the *Münstergasse* then closed off the trench through a barricade. The occupation of the newly captured trench was taken on by parts of the 4/185 under *Leutnant der Reserve* Riemann, and the 5th, 7th and 11/8th Bavarian RIR.

The much needed relief for all of the men who had been in the thick of the fighting since 24 June was still not possible, despite the arrival of fresh reinforcements. The need for men to hold the front line in the 26th Reserve Division far exceeded the availability of new units. Other portions of the front were facing even stiffer enemy attacks and also desperately required reinforcements. The men in the 26th Reserve Division used all of their available strength to improve the defensive capabilities of their sector as best they could.

While the men stood watch in their mud filled trenches or sat inside the damp, musty, mud filled dugouts with water dripping down from the ceiling above, the most nauseating odor spread throughout the sector coming from the numerous corpses and body parts that were lying around everywhere. Notwithstanding hunger and particularly despite the burning thirst and lack of water at the front, the men reassured their regimental commanders who visited the front that they were in the best mood. Considering life in the front line by St. Pierre-Divion the optimistic attitude presented to *Oberstleutnant* Bram seems implausible.

> After all it was not bad on the right wing, because they came very thinly and quickly disappeared again, different than on the left wing, where Barz and Schmeisser were. There they always came in masses and were hard to expel. In the afternoon the cry resounded again: 'British!' This time it was not very harmless. Not because of the British, they soon disappeared; however large and heavy German shells roared into

our trench and brought the most considerable bewilderment among our men, who could barely withstand it any more. It also rained in torrents, in which one could sink deeply into the soil and could barely see. It was especially bad for me because of my eyeglasses. On the left wing however, the hand grenades continued to crash until it became dark. Finally the noise subsided. *Leutnant* Schmeisser came to us and said: 'We have beaten them up severely today, but they also us.' Generally everything was well, if I only had something to smoke. However the last cigar, the last cigarette had been smoked. Meanwhile I wanted to attempt, even if I did not get hold of anything else, to obtain the necessarily needed hand grenades. So I went to the company leader. I got cigars, but no hand grenades. Barz had personally gone to the battalion however, as he had the means to get them, accordingly you had to scan all of the lost trenches, because otherwise you would not know in whose possession they stood. That was disagreeable. I went back again. After some time Kamm called for Barz. I waited; he didn't come, it became 1 o'clock at night, he still didn't come. *Feldwebel* and *Offizier Stellvertreter* Stahlhofer, 2/8th Bavarian RIR. [14]

The commander in St. Pierre-Divion, *Major* Prager, and his mixed garrison of men from RIR 119, RIR 99 and the 8th Bavarian RIR was constantly struggling to maintain a firm connection with *Hauptmann* Wurm. On one occasion, when *Leutnant* Mehl, RIR 119 and a few of his men attempted to reach *Hauptmann* Wurm, they sprinted across the battlefield, running from St. Pierre-Divion to *Feste Schwaben* as fast as they could. The ground they covered was littered with numerous corpses, most of which were quite young soldiers according to Mehl. The ground was also covered with numerous weapons and scattered pieces of equipment left behind by the enemy during his attacks.

During the journey, Mehl and his men came across a soldier from RIR 99 who was unable to move due to the wounds he suffered on 1 July. He told Mehl that he had been without food or water for the past three days and had waited in vain for rescue. No one could apparently hear his weak cries for help amidst all of the noise of the battle. Mehl and his companions managed to save the unfortunate man and carried him with them to the dressing station by *Feste Staufen* where he could receive treatment.

Oberstleutnant Bram trudged through water filled trenches and holes to the dugout of Artillery Group Berta in the firm belief that his men would stand their ground despite the adverse conditions. He was confident that the position still held by the enemy by the *Meisennest* would be cleared and, he was informed that the connections between the various groups manning the defenses of *Thiepval-Nord* had been firmly established. With communications restored between the different Groups, numerous requests for food, water and ammunition began to arrive at headquarters where hopefully steps could be taken to supply all of the appeals.

The German defenses were strengthened with the arrival of machine Gun Marksman Detachment 89 under the command of *Leutnant* Zimmermann, the former adjutant of Group Wurm by *Feste Staufen*. Zimmermann's guns would relieve the 1MG/8th Bavarian RIR, commanded by *Leutnant der Reserve* Fischer. While the Bavarian machine gun company was able to be relieved, the same could not be said for the infantry of the 8th Bavarian RIR.

Further troop shifts were made on 4 July in order to ensure the best possible coverage of the front lines. In the Sector *Thiepval-Mitte*, C5 to C7, the I/R15 from the 2nd Guard

MG 08s used in anti-aircraft role, RIR 99. (Author's collection)

Reserve Division relieved the II/R99 in the early morning hours of 4 July. The II/R99 then moved into the second position at *Süd-IV* and *Süd-V.* The 5/185 was relieved by one company of the *Garde Füsiliers* from the second trench in C7.

In Sector *Thiepval-Süd* the *Garde Füsilier* Regiment from the 3rd Guard Infantry Division relieved the I/R99 and part of IR 180. In the time from 4 July to 6 July the regimental staff, the III and IV/R99 were also replaced through parts of RIR 15, IR 185 and IR 186 which would mean that the entire RIR 99 would have been withdrawn in order to rest and refit. The exhausted men of RIR 99 were first sent to Bapaume, and soon afterward into billets in Graincourt, southwest of Cambrai. On 5 July the commander of IR 185, *Oberstleutnant* Krause, took over command of the sector that had formerly been held by RIR 99.

RIR 99 had fought well in the battle at Thiepval. It had fully justified the trust placed in the regiment in holding such a key position in the German defenses. Despite the enemy penetration into *Feste Schwaben* and the *Granatloch* on 1 July, almost the entire position had become recaptured and held against repeated British attacks.

Much of the credit given for the successful defense by RIR 99 was given to the hard work in creating deep, mined dugouts before the attack began and which had been promoted with vigor on the entire regimental front by *Major* von Fabeck. The large tunnel complexes constructed under the direction of *Hauptmann* Leiling on the St. Pierre-Divion-Hamel road was also a key factor in the successful defense of the sectors by St. Pierre-Divion. Not only could his tunnel complex could accommodate 1,000 men, it was also used for storage of critical equipment, ammunition, food and water along with medical facilities and was shell proof. In the same vein was the large, deep tunnel facility under Mouquet farm where the regimental battle headquarters was located. Despite coming under fire from the heaviest enemy shells, the tunnel complex remained intact. All of the hard work performed by RIR 99 had made Thiepval into an 'earthen pillar of the defensive front'.

The British never appeared to tire of attacking the German lines by Thiepval. During the day, the enemy attempted several enemy hand grenade attacks in order to expand their gains. All were successfully repulsed by the 1st and 4/185, the latter in *Thiepval-Nord*. In the evening of 4 July, Machine Gun *Zug* 559, now reinforced through one machine gun from *Feld* Machine Gun *Zug* 311, occupied the *Zwischenstellung* in front of Pozières. The rest of Feld Machine Gun *Zug* 311 was moved to *Nord IV* by the Ancre as anti-aircraft defenses for the artillery battery positions.

By 4 July most of the troops in the *Granatloch* who had been fighting since 1 July had reached a point of exhaustion that would render them almost useless in defending the position. Then, almost miraculously, the possibility of being relieved looked as if it might take place.

We anticipate waking on the new day, 4 July. Who could describe my astonishment, when I went through the position on the morning and directly saw the 'New'! It is *Unteroffizier* Kurz, the same who I 'trained' under in Zweibrücken. We shake hands, laughing. 'Why have you not immediately called out your name this night?' Oh Herr *Feldwebel*, like they I whistled, so all of my courage did not leave me.' And now for a questions about the friends at home and I was doubly pleased, to have him here. He himself, maybe less.

Between 9 and 10 o'clock it becomes lively in the *König Strasse*. Oho! What is this? Relief? Prussians! Guard! Two officers advance! A platoon followed. 'Where are the Bavarians?' already calls the one in front from far off. I jump up and report that I am the leader. There I now find out that he, *Leutnant* Klotz is with the 4/*Garde Füsilier* Regiment; a platoon from his company would be put in at the left wing of our position, while we had to close it off to the right.

I explain the situation to the newcomers and give them all of the information on the position. They come from Russia and were unceremoniously startled by the thunder of the Somme Battle out of idyllic summer freshness at Valenciennes. 'Some mess, we had 4 more weeks relaxation due to us,' I hear one say to Büttner. Yes, rest! So that it is now over. It is simply unfortunate that the people do not seem to believe it. They have no idea of such position warfare. If only the cost of the lesson does not become too high!

The company leader and I go from the left wing back to the *König Strasse*. The two groups of recruits have now vanished. We shed no tears for them. 'Herr *Leutnant*, my people have already had no rest the 4 days. They are completely exhausted.' 'You will become relieved tonight through Platoon Hoffmann,' he said and goes back to his two other platoons, which were in large dugouts in the *König Strasse* and *Türken Stellung*, the present third trench.

I share the news of the pending relief with my company and new hope animates the tired faces. Since Sunday afternoon, it is now Wednesday, always on their feet, affected by the numerous attacks, the annoying artillery fires, the flooding of the trench, inadequate and always cold food, which reduces the battle strength more and more. Only sometimes being able to have a good sleep! Then it goes further. *Feldwebel* Hoffmann came in the afternoon and was introduced to the position by me. In the dusk he goes back to get his platoon. I advise to him not to come too early, so that that enemy does not notice any movement.

Night falls. We wait, and wait. In vain. Platoon Hoffmann had not appeared. I went back, asked and heard: *Feldwebel* Hoffmann is not coming back any longer. An enemy bullet had made his life a target.

There is considerable commotion by the *Garde Füsiliers*. The I/*Garde Füsilier* Regiment, *Major* Delius, has taken over the headquarters in the *Wundtwerk*. He has ordered an immediate attack. *Leutnant* Klotz is at the battalion. First of all, there was no thought of being relieved. This news doesn't have a cheering effect on the men. However they know: it cannot be changed. The Prussians soon move up. Everything was made ready. However they carry everything out with considerable noise, despite our most forceful warnings. 'The British will certainly open their eyes, when they see our newly scrubbed *Garde Litzen*,' remarked one. 'Or you will, when the dance starts," replied one of ours. In the meantime, the artillery was employed and after moderate fire the order for the attack became given. The attack fails. The '*Maikäfer*' [cockchafers] return back into the trench after suffering heavy losses. Their preparations had taken too long and had been too noisy. The men had no idea of idea about the conduct of the war in the west, and still knew nothing about how tough the British could be. The Guard now remained in front and we received orders to go back into the *Türken Stellung*; there, where a platoon of the Guard was until now. With forceful warnings for the greatest caution and vigilance, especially at the sap which turned out to be more and more as a place to penetrate, we pushed on. And now finally the *Hindenburgeck*! Now it goes back into the *Türken Stellung, König Strasse* how much they have changed! We trudged back through collapsed trench parts, through puddles of water, almost knee deep through muck and morass. Suddenly the platoon hesitated. We stand before a trench piece almost completely filled in with this dirty clay soup. Should we climb out of the trench and run across the open ground? That means certain wounding, if not more. The grey of an early dawn is breaking and there over there; lurked the English machine guns. Therefore through! The first one hesitantly climbs in, vanishes inside until up to the chest. The most flattering words are not now what was expected at the '*König Strasse*'. However as everything disagreeable disappears, also this water hole is behind us and soon we branch off to the right in a similarly swampy trench: the *Türken Stellung. Vizefeldwebel der Reserve* Heinrich Conrad, 9/8th Bavarian RIR.[15]

The attack against the British in the *Granatloch* by the *Garde Füsiliers* failed, primarily as a result of the enemy barrage fire and the soggy ground; the attackers could only make slow progress in the thick mud. Still, the 2/*Garde Füsiliers* almost reached the British obstacles but no matter how much effort went in to the attack it was no match against the enemy machine gun and rifle fire. The *Garde Füsiliers* had finally been forced to turn back with heavy losses.

4 July was comparatively quiet after the intense fighting of the previous three days in the Sector *Ovillers-Süd*. In Sector *Ovillers-Nord*, the fighting against the enemy nest in the *Granatloch* continued to rage. The flanking companies of IR 180 were a great help to the units in the *Hindenburg Stellung* by preventing the enemy from expanding his gains toward Ovillers.

The men of IR 180 were also happy to see new reinforcements arrive in their sector to help keep the enemy at bay. Two companies of the *Garde Füsiliers* arrived in the morning, with one company being placed in possession of Sector *Ovillers-Nord* and given accommodations inside dugouts located in the *Lemberg Stellung* and in the third trench. The other company was placed in possession of Sector *Ovillers-Süd* and was put into the *Bumiller Dorf* and *Schäferwiese*. With the arrival of these companies, it was possible to maintain a continuous connection with IR 190 on the left of IR 180 by La Boiselle.

The telephone connection with Artillery Group Cäsar, commanded by *Hauptmann* Jäckh, which was assigned to provide defensive artillery fire for the regimental sector, had been destroyed so thoroughly that any thought of quickly restoring the service was impossible. Until the telephone lines could be repaired or replaced, the connection from IR 180 to Artillery Group Cäsar had to be conducted with signal flags and light signals. *Oberleutnant der Reserve* Lang, leaders of the 6/180, supplied the men responsible for the signal flag service in *Ovillers-Süd*.

The signal flag service had worked splendidly in the heavy fighting and every request for barrage fire or support from the artillery was immediately responded to without any delays. The success of this manner of communication was not only due to the efforts of the 6/180 but also by the hard work of the gunners and observers in Artillery Group Cäsar. The artillery fire provided by this group had been prompt, accurate and, in the enemy's view, deadly. IR 180 had been fortunate that Artillery Group Cäsar had supported the regiment in such an outstanding manner since the start of the battle.

The support provided was even more impressive when you consider that many of the German batteries had suffered losses in guns and personnel as a result of the concentrated enemy artillery fire that had been directed against them since 24 June. On 4 July, a direct telephone connection with Group Cäsar was successfully established, which from this time on, remained intact despite the hundreds of enemy shells falling on the sector each day. With the restoration of direct communication to the rear, requests for artillery assistance could be answered almost instantaneously as each battery had precise coordinates of every possible target in range of the guns.

Then as if the conditions facing the men of IR 180 could not get any worse, cloud bursts occurred in the afternoon and the rain soaked ground soon turned into a thick morass. The devastation of the positions caused by the enemy artillery fire increased as the trench walls began to crumble even faster from the rain. Still, there was a silver lining of sorts. While it made life in the German trenches miserable, the enemy was no better off and in the case of an enemy attack, the opposing troops would have to cross open ground with even greater difficulty as they advanced through the muddy terrain.

In the course of 4 and 5 July the II and III/*Garde Füsilier* Regiment under *Major* von Ammon arrived by Ovillers. These battalions were initially placed in the *Zwischenstellung* to bolster the defenses of the sector because the situation at La Boiselle had become increasingly dangerous. In addition to the numerous reinforcements streaming toward the Somme, individual officers also returned to their commands. The regimental adjutant of IR 180, *Oberleutnant* Liebfried, was among those who returned to his regiment on this day.

Hearing about the Somme battle taking place, he cut short his furlough and returned as quickly as he could. Now *Oberleutnant* Guth, the commander of the 1st Machine Gun Company could return to his guns; Guth had been acting as the adjutant in place of Liebfried in his absence. The day ended with slight losses in IR 180. *Leutnant der Reserve*

Deiß (Wilhelm)
Leutnant d. R. i. Inf.-Regt. 180,
gefallen bei Ovillers la Boiffelle
am 4. Juli 1916

(*Kriegstagebuch aus Schwaben*)

Deiss was killed by artillery fire; three men were also killed; 26 men wounded from which one man had been injured after being buried; 1 man was missing.

All across the front held by the 26th Reserve Division, the troops that had been fighting had become completely mixed together little by little. Group Prager lay south of the Ancre up to the *Münstergasse* and consisted of the remnants of the 10th, 11th and 12/R99, the remnants of the 1st, 2nd, 3rd, 4th and 8/8th Bavarian RIR, 3rd and 4/186 and 3/185. Subsequently, in Sector *Thiepval-Nord;* Group Wurm consisted of the remnants of the 7/R99, 5th, 6th, 7th and 9/8th Bavarian RIR, 2nd and 4/185. Group Forstner occupied *Thiepval-Mitte* and *Thiepval-Süd* in Sectors Fabeck and Delius which held the 4th, 3rd and 2/R15, 1/*Garde Füsiliers*, 1/185 and 4/*Garde Füsiliers*. The rear positions of Sectors Bram and Fabeck were occupied by Recruit Companies from RIR 99 and IR 180, 6/*Pionier* Battalion 13, 11th and 12/8th Bavarian RIR, 1/R15, 5th and 7/185, 10/8th Bavarian RIR, 1/R99, Machine Gun Marksman Detachment 45, MG Coy/185. The III/R99 would remain in the position up to 6 July when it was moved to Bapaume.

4 July was an important date in the conduct of the fighting and would have a major impact on how the battle was fought from then on. General von Below issued an order that would have far reaching effects. This infamous order was probably designed to instill an iron will into the men in order to withstand the overpowering enemy pressure. Instead, it probably resulted in higher casualties for the British and French troops as well as the German defenders.

> I forbid the voluntary withdrawal from positions. Every leader is responsible that every man in the army becomes familiar with this unfaltering fighting will. The enemy will only find his way forward over corpses. Von Below. [16]

This order was carried out verbatim in many instances when a small withdrawal or strategic movement could have saved men's lives and not radically changed the course of the fighting. Now, as the defenders literally fought to the bitter end, the losses on both sides increased rapidly. If this order had been in place on 1 July then most likely RIR 109, RIR 110 and RIR 111 would have ceased to exist as fighting units.

The fighting on 4 July had gone on throughout the day and it was apparently still not finished in the late evening when at 11.15 p.m. bombing parties from Battle Group Wurm attempted to clear the *Meisennest* in the first trench of C2, forward of *Feste Schwaben*. The bombing parties advanced through the *Meisengasse*, the men attempting to move through the bottomless mud filled trenches. The attackers quickly became fired upon from three British machine guns and were forced to turn back again, empty handed once again.

5 July

The fighting by the *Meisennest* continued to rage during the early morning hours of 5 July when heavy drum fire began to fall upon the German lines by St. Pierre-Divion and the *Meisennest* at 1 a.m. This was followed at 5 a.m. with an attack by two companies of the 5th Yorkshire Battalion (148th Brigade, 49th Division) north of Thiepval, under the command of a Captain. The attack did not only approach from the front, but also out of the left flank. The attack struck the men of the 2/8th Bavarian RIR in the first and second trenches of C2. The Yorkshiremen managed to reach the German positions despite heavy defensive fire and broke through the first line by the 1/8th Bavarian RIR that had been leveled by the intense artillery fire.

Once inside the German position, the British attempted to push along the front

Jakob Huber, killed by an artillery projectile. (Author's collection)

line toward the large tunnel complex by St. Pierre-Divion where the sector reserves were positioned. The British were able to attack the rear of Platoons Skiba and Bleyer, 3/186 and both units quickly suffered heavy losses. The platoon of *Leutnant* Neubronner, 4/186, swarmed in to close the gap in the line. *Leutnant* Bleyer, 3/186, immediately counterattacked, whereupon the British detachment, including the leader, was almost completely destroyed. Blocked from retreating through the shallow trenches, the fleeing British were showered with a hail of bullets as they crossed the open terrain so that only a few escaped. Apparently only ten men managed to reach the British lines. The enemy had been thrown back in stubborn fighting along with the help of the 2/8th Bavarian RIR, whose leader, *Leutnant der Reserve Schmeisser*, was killed.

> *Unteroffizier* Ködel ran breathless and reported: A shell has smashed, straight into the group in there. I believe both officers are dead. 'Well,' I said, 'what is going on with Forster?' 'I do not know,' was the answer. 'Then I must look there,' I said. There *Unteroffizier* Goebel hurled toward us already and shouted: '*Leutnant* Schmeisser has fallen, of Forster and Barz we know nothing. The British are clearly coming and have surprised us.' 'Kamm' I said, 'be so good and look, so that we do not end up like the brother down here', I looked up a bit now. 'And Goebel, you go to the battalion, if you could maybe ask for barrage fire by telephone, if no more telephones existed, then by firing the light balls see if we could get that down upon our own backs.' Then I went, still cursing the men if they were not at the right place. I call to the wounded coming towards us: 'Is *Leutnant* Barz above?' Always the reply: 'No'. Now I was sure that I was the company leader. I tore a paper out of the notebook: 'Company taken over. Urgent; hand grenades, reinforcements or relief necessary. *Leutnant* Schmeisser dead, *Leutnant* Barz missing.' I gave the paper to the next wounded man. Further. I saw him lying dead, something which shocked me. New *Waffenrock* and pants, a small moustache on the lip was there on his face. I wanted to go past, but it was something like a fever in the legs, because I saw the shoulder-pieces and the bag with the binoculars. It was Schmeisser. I heard always more violent growling therefore at the place where the fire was, it was already close. A wounded man came towards me. 'Where were the chaps really?' Directly around the traverses here about.' Was the reply. All around, still nothing. *Feldwebel* and *Offizier Stellvertreter* Stahlhofer, 2/8th Bavarian RIR. [17]

The officer in command of the attack, a Captain, had shot down several men in the 3/186 with his pistol during the fighting. He was eventually wounded and taken prisoner. The capture of this officer provided valuable intelligence, as it established that new enemy units had been assigned to this portion of the front and when the officer was searched, valuable papers and maps were found in his possession; however, he would not make any statements. On the other hand, other prisoners captured with the officer provided information to the Germans that the 49th Division had relieved the 36th Division in front of Thiepval.

The 1st, 2nd and 8/8th Bavarian RIR had suffered considerable losses during the attack. The losses of the 3/186 during the defense of the British attack on 5 July amounted to: 16 dead, 9 wounded. Later on the same day, Platoons Bleyer and Skiba, 3/186, became relieved by two platoons from the 4/186 and were sent into the St. Pierre-Divion tunnel as reserves.

During the close combat in *Thiepval-Nord*, *Gefreiter* Georg Maier and *Gefreiter* Ludwig Scharl, 2/8th Bavarian RIR, were both awarded the Bavarian Silver Medal for Bravery for their part in the fighting on this day. During the British attack, a portion of the German front line near the Ancre had been captured. *Gefreiters* Maier and Scharl, along with a small group of men from the 2/8th Bavarian RIR successfully stopped the superior enemy forces from advancing any further and prevented the trench from being rolled up from the flank.

The men under Maier and Scharl then forced the enemy back into his position with both *Gefreiters* prominently at the head of the counterattack, providing their comrades outstanding examples of bravery and tenacity during the close combat. When the two men had used up their own hand grenades, they took British hand grenades found lying around and hurled them against the enemy.

Unlike the British, the Germans holding the front line had received only a small number of reinforcements, battalions at times or, as in many cases, individual companies or platoons. The limited number of reinforcements meant that units were constantly being shifted around the front line where they were needed the most. However, in *Thiepval-Nord*, it was expected that by 6 July or the following day at the latest the occupation of the sector should have sufficient reinforcements so that only one company of IR 186 had to remain there.

At the opposite end of the Thiepval Sector the situation at the *Granatloch* remained tense, despite the arrival of fresh troops. Shortly after dawn, the enemy artillery opened fire on the German positions near the *Granatloch*. It was evident that an attack would follow as the British continued their attempts to expand their earlier gains. At 8.30 a.m. the 1st Wiltshire Battalion (75th Brigade, 25th Division) attacked, but they were met with intense infantry and artillery fire almost from the start of the advance and the attack failed.

After a short period of drum fire another strong attack followed at approximately 8.30 a.m. by the *Granatloch*. While the 1/*Garde Füsiliers* and 1/185 drove the enemy back north of the *Granatloch*, the British were successful in penetrating the badly damaged, mud filled *Hindenburg Stellung* that was occupied by the 4/*Garde Füsiliers*.

Troops supporting the 4/*Garde Füsiliers* immediately launched counterattacks from their positions in the *Lemberg Stellung*. When the fighting finally died down, the British had retained a foothold in the German lines by occupying a portion of the *Hindenburg Stellung* approximately 70 meters wide. During the close fighting, *Leutnant Frhr.* von Salmuth and 23 *Garde Füsiliers* were killed. In addition, the 1st and 4/*Garde Füsiliers* lost 85 men wounded, amongst them two officers. According to statements from prisoners taken in the fighting, the British 48th Division had been moved from in front of the 52nd Infantry Division, and was now being used against the 26th Reserve Division.

It is 3 o'clock Thursday morning when we arrive there [*Turken Stellung*]. The 'entire company' found room in two dugouts. They are well built and remarkably dry. With the feeling that a great weight has been lifted from our backs, we pull off our boots, become provided as far as possible with fresh underwear, wrap ourselves in our overcoats and slept, slept, slept. Only the sentries at the entrance remain awake. Around noon, the sentry comes down the stairway. 'Is the 9th Company here?' They are food bearers, who have found us only after a long search. They are greeted with joy. And when they go again, we sleep again. In the evening I go to the nearby *Wundtwerk*. We are all curious, how does it look at the front. Is everything still in order? Did the enemy no longer attack? I went to the other dugout, chat with the men and issue safety orders for the night. On the return route, I became called from 'above'. It is *Leutnant* Klotz. 'Conrad, we both have no luck with each other!' 'Why not, *Herr Leutnant*?' 'Since 8.30 p.m. those chaps sit in the middle of my company! In a width of approximately 3 Groups. It is simply frightful. The best men had already fallen last night. And now still this! 'That is very serious. Yes, there must be an immediate intervention in order to avoid anything worse, the battalion has ordered an immediate counterattack, which should take place at 10.00 p.m. now in any case you will occupy the *Lemberg Stellung* with your Bavarians. This is the battalion order I had to deliver to you.' with that, he disappears. We go forth, no more than 20 men strong, and occupied the approach leading to the *Lemberg Stellung*. It crashes in the front, was the Guard successful in clearing the nest? Then *Leutnant* Koch of the 4/*Garde Füsiliers* appears and brings the order to return to the *Turkenstellung*. The attack by the 4/*Garde Füsiliers* and parts of Platoon Gassert, 5/185 that became undertaken, has failed. How long will the *Hindenburg Stellung* hold now? At 11.45 p.m. we are in the *Turken Stellung* again. We find the other dugout occupied by the 8/195. My men beg about relief. Also, what could such a small group of men still do? And top of all, completely exhausted! I sent urgent pleas about relief to the battalion, in vain. *Vizefeldwebel der Reserve* Heinrich Conrad, 9/8th Bavarian RIR.[18]

All available troops continued to be shifted across the front lines where they were needed most. The men, though exhausted, would need to hold on a bit longer until fresh divisions could arrive. At 4 p.m. *Oberstleutnant* Krause, IR 185, moved into the battle headquarters at Mouquet farm and took command of Sector *Thiepval-Mitte,* Sectors C5 until C7 as well as *Thiepval-Süd*, Sectors C8 until C9. The units were distributed as follows: *Thiepval-Mitte*: I/R15 (*Hauptmann* von Forstner), 5th and 7/185, part of the 8th Bavarian RIR. *Thiepval-Süd*: one half of the I/*Garde Füsiliers* (*Major* von Delius), 1/185, part of the 8th Bavarian RIR. *Zwischenstellung* and Mouquet Farm: IV/R99 and 2nd Recruit Company/R99. Second defensive position: II/R99, 6/185, MG Coy/185. The command over the *Zwischenstellung* and second position was undertaken by *Hauptmann* Josephson. In *Thiepval-Nord* was the 3/185 in the *Strassburger Steig* that had suffered heavily under artillery fire, which then became reinforced by three quarters of the 2/185.

At 8.15 p.m. the enemy attempted a sudden attack upon C9 and C8 after a short period of artillery preparation. The connections between the companies of RIR 99 in the *Hindenburg Stellung* were repeatedly disrupted; however, they were re-established over and over with great effort. Finally, when the attack died down, the enemy continued to hold a small stretch of the *Hindenburg Stellung* in Sector C9 under hand grenade fire from positions in *Verbindungs Graben* 1. In order to determine which portions of the trenches were held by the enemy, RIR 99 sent a request to headquarters asking to be allowed to send out patrols in order to clarify the situation.

By Ovillers, the morning of 5 July in Sector *Ovillers-Nord* proceeded quietly. The enemy artillery fired relatively few shots at the sector and did not become more active until noon. Some of the men in IR 180 believed that some enemy batteries were only firing with 2-3 guns. Either this was the result of the other guns breaking down from constant use, or some guns had been moved away from this part of the line. IR 180 took full advantage of the reduced enemy artillery fire to work on the defenses. The 2/*Garde Füsiliers* arrived in the Intermediate position between Mouquet Farm and the *Schwarzwald Graben*, while one battalion of the *Garde Füsiliers* occupied the Sectors *Süd V* and *Süd VI*. The losses suffered by IR 180 on this day were: *Leutnant der Reserve* Mebold severely wounded; two men dead six men wounded and one man missing.

In Sector *Ovillers-Süd*, the 6th and 8/185 were relieved from the sector in the morning and were replaced by 5th and 8/*Garde Füsiliers*, which had arrived at Mouquet Farm at 10 p.m. and which were placed in possession of IR 180. Now, with new troops available changes could be made in the occupation of the front line. Shortly afterward, the companies in Sector P5 become replaced by the 5/*Garde Füsiliers* and Company Dettling in P7 became replaced by the 8/*Garde Füsiliers*. Company Kurz was assigned to take over the third trench and *Harrer Graben* north of the *Feldberg Graben*, and Company Dettling took over the third trench and the *Harrer Graben* south of the *Feldberg Graben*.

The *Garde Füsiliers* then became moved forward to the *König Strasse* (C9) at midnight because the Englishmen penetrated into C9 after a strong attack a short time earlier upon Sectors C8 and C9. While immediate local counterattacks had almost completely expelled the enemy, additional troops were still required to hold the position. One half of the 5/185 located in trench K2 in Sector C7 then occupied the *Lemberg Stellung*.

6 July

The front by the *Meisennest* was relatively quiet on 6 July with the exception of an early morning attack by bombing parties from the 1/5 King's Own Yorkshire Light Infantry (1/5 KOYLI). The attacking force consisting of 7 officers, 80 Other Ranks were divided into five bombing parties. The 1/5 KOYLI had expected to rely upon the 1/4 KOYLI for assistance until it was discovered that the 1/4 KOYLI had been attacked during the night and had run out of hand grenades and its hold on the trenches was considered 'precarious'.

So, without support, the five bombing parties moved off at 8 a.m., two on the right, two on the left and one in reserve. The right hand bombing parties quickly ran into a German trench barricade and became involved in a fierce hand grenade battle with the German defenders. As reported in the battalion war diary: 'finally last man came back when last bomb had been thrown.'

The two left hand bombing parties ran into stiff German resistance as well and were unable to make any progress at all. The situation became critical when the men were faced with a German counterattack and were forced to defend the position instead of pressing the Germans back. Lieutenant-Colonel Rendell, who was commanding the attack, had been wounded early in the fighting and had been taken to a nearby German dugout for safety. Finally, German pressure became so great that the survivors of the British bombing parties were forced to evacuate their position and return to the starting point across open ground.

Under these circumstances it was found to be impossible to transport Lieutenant-Colonel Rendell to the rear and he was forced to remain inside the dugout. Of the 7 officers and 80 Other Ranks which had started out in the morning, only 22 Other Ranks returned. All of the officers had become casualties in the fighting. Upon review of the reports from the survivors the reasons given for the failure of the attack included the unexpected occurrence of turning an attacking force into a defensive force; good German sniping; the German bombers out throwing the British due to a lighter bomb; running out of the supply of bombs because the communication trench used to bring new supplies to the *Meisennest* was too shallow and German support fire that effectively closed off this source of supply.

The companies of IR 186 that were still in the position were scheduled to be replaced by the III/R15 under *Hauptmann* von Wedekind, who was scheduled to assume command over the sector. The III/R15 arrived in the morning of 6 July and was made subordinate to the 8th Bavarian RIR. The 9th and 11/R15 reached the *Artilleriemulde* Grandcourt in the morning while the 10th and 12/R15 occupied the Second Line between the Ancre and the *Staufen Graben*. At noon, the 9/R15 moved forward into *Feste Schwaben*.

With the arrival of fresh troops, the 9/8th Bavarian RIR under *Leutnant* Bruckmann and the 11/8th Bavarian RIR became sent to *Feste Schwaben*. This allowed the 6/8th Bavarian RIR to become relieved and the 7/R99 in Sector C4 could be replaced; then the 7/R99 along with the 3/185 withdrew from Sector Wurm. The 10th and 12/185 were sent to St Pierre-Divion because of repeated urgent requests for support had been received from there.

On the morning of 6 July the 1st and 2/186 reported nothing unusual was taking place on their portion of the front, other than the normal heavy artillery and mine fire. Both companies spent the day trying to restore the position they occupied to a defensible state, especially installing new wire entanglements under the difficult circumstances. Later in the day, *Leutnant der Reserve* Volk, along with bombing parties from RIR 119, moved through the first trench on the St. Pierre-Divion – Thiepval road in order to reconnoiter the enemy positions. In the evening, *Leutnant* Bleyer from the 3/186 along with three Groups cleared the *Hansa Weg* from enemy troops and reconnoitered towards the *Meisennest*. All of these patrol actions were designed to provide intelligence for the attack that was in the planning stages.

On 6 July the 26th Reserve Division had ordered a new undertaking against the *Meisennest*. The attack was under the leadership of *Major* Prager and *Hauptmann* Wurm and would be supported by batteries from Artillery Group Pys. The attack was to take place in the evening of 6 July following a short period of artillery preparation fire. It was hoped that one more attack with sufficient force would finally expel the British from the *Meisennest*.

The plan called for a three prong approach, with the enemy position being attacked simultaneously from both flanks and taken under fire from the rear. Assault troops from the 5th, 7th, 8/8th Bavarian RIR, 11/R15 and 4/185 would participate in the attack. The III/R15 under *Hauptmann* von Wedekind had recently arrived in the sector and was inserted into the second position early on 6 July between the *Stump Weg* and *Artillerie Mulde*.

The 9/R15 discovered that no dugouts existed in the second position where the company was located. To remain in such an exposed position would only result in unnecessary losses from the constant enemy fire. Between noon and 1 p.m. the 9/R15 was ordered to move forward up to *Feste Schwaben* and once there, look for any available dugouts. The men did locate a number of dugouts that could accommodate most of the company however, first they had to clear them of the bodies of the former defenders of *Feste Schwaben*. It was evident that some of these men had been severely wounded in the earlier fighting and had either crawled down or been carried down into the dugouts where they eventually succumbed to their wounds. It was an extremely grisly task to carry the bodies to the surface and place them in nearby shell craters in makeshift graves or simply covered with a few shovels full of dirt. After the grim work was completed, the 1st and 2nd platoons could be pressed into the dugouts. The 3rd platoon was forced to create *Karnickelhöhlen* or 'rabbit holes' in the trench wall in order to find any protection at all from the British fire.

Heavy fire of varying strength fell constantly on the artillery positions in front of and behind the second position as well as on the trenches where the men of the III/R15 were accommodated. At 11.40 a.m. another company from the battalion was ordered to immediately move forward to *Feste Schwaben*, where it would join the attack to throw the enemy out of the first trench and the *Meisengasse*. The men of RIR 15 would be subordinate to the I/8th Bavarian RIR under the command of *Major* Prager who was in charge of the attack.

The plan called for one company from IR 185 to advance from the south, one company from RIR 15 from the north. *Oberstleutnant* von Bram, had contacted the III/R15 and requested the assistance of only one company, and as a result, the 11/R15 had been chosen. Everything appeared to be ready for the attack when it was suddenly called off because of the shortness of the preparation time. Not every unit involved had been able to reach their designated locations. Instead, the assault would take place at 4 a.m. on 7 July so that the artillery had time to prepare for the attack and the troops could all be moved into position in order to start the advance at the appointed time. The 11/R15 was then ordered back to Grandcourt where the men were provided with a warm meal. After a short rest, the men were moved forward once more and took up their positions.

While the preparations continued for the attack against the *Meisennest* the situation by the *Granatloch* had not changed substantially on this day. There were constant hand grenade battles as the British continued the attempts to expand their foothold in the German lines. Before additional infantry reinforcements could arrive to help contain the enemy by the *Granatloch* , a platoon of *Musketen*, ten weapons and crews, arrived in the *Zwischenstellung* which provided a substantial increase in firepower that would be helpful in keeping the British from advancing any deeper into the German lines. More troops did arrive later in the day when in the afternoon, the staff II/185 moved into the *Wundtwerk* for orientation about the overall situation.

The situation facing the men from IR 180 was finally looking brighter when orders arrived for the regiment to be relieved. IR 180 had withstood the week long preparation bombardment at the end of June and had been constantly fighting for nearly one week and the men were worn out. On the night of 6/7 July IR 180 was expecting to be relieved; only two Recruit Companies from the regiment would remain behind for the time being. The regiment was to be withdrawn into rest quarters on 7 July in Bapaume. By the end of the 6th all of the surviving men from RIR 99 had also been successfully relieved from the front lines and sent to the rear.

7 July

At 1.30 a.m. on 7 July the German field guns, Light field howitzers and *Minenwerfer* opened fire on the trenches occupied by the British around the *Meisennest*. The battalion war diary of the 1/5 KOYLI provided a clear picture of the German bombardment.

> 12.30 a.m. Enemy opened intense bombardment of original British front line. This continued till 2.15 a.m. our artillery replying effectively. The bombardment was turned on to the 'A' line till 2.50 a.m. when it was turned again on to the communication trenches and lines behind. Enemy bombers advanced down the trench towards A.18 & A.16 and across the open to A.17 a furious fight with bombs ensued lasting till 6.30 a.m. [British time, 1 hour earlier than German time]. [19]

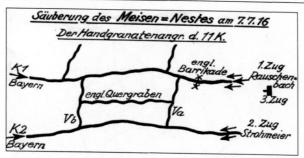

Attack on the Meisennest by RIR 15

The German bombing parties moved quickly through the old first and second German trenches on both flanks of the *Meisennest* as well as across the open ground.

The first and second trenches at the left wing of IR 186 in conjunction with a *Sturm Trupp* from the 8th Bavarian RIR were to be cleared. Our 11th Coy attacked from the right, the Bavarians attacked from the left. The 1st Platoon, reinforced by the *Sturm Trupp* of the 3rd, would capture battle trench 1, the 2nd Platoon, battle trench 2, the 3rd Platoon would initially carry hand grenades, ammunition and material.

After two minutes of drum fire the storm would begin from all sides. The *Sturm Trupp* of the 2nd Platoon jumped over the English barricade, after it had rendered the garrison harmless through hand grenades, pressed further forward and took one machine gun, which was immediately placed in activity by *Vizefeldwebel* Strohmeier behind the escaping British. For the wounded *Feldwebels* Strohmeier and Brandt, *Unteroffizier* Weber took over the platoon and distinguished himself very much. The entrance to Va was occupied by sentries and K2 until Vb were cleared. The second machine gun was captured here and the remnants of the British garrison taken prisoner. In Vb the third machine gun was taken, then through the *Quergraben* Va until Vb that had already been constructed by the enemy, we cleared Va and the fourth machine gun was captured. The 2nd Platoon now made contact with the 1st. They advanced upon a strong barricade, the garrison became pressed back. The platoon now received machine gun fire out of the communication trench leading to the English position, L1, and lively rifle fire out of Va. It was forced to go back behind the barricade. *Vizefeldwebel* Vietmeyer took over the 1st Platoon for *Leutnant* Rauschenbach who had fallen at the head of the *Sturm Trupp* and he stood out through bold advances. One group stormed on the right of the trench, two stormed on the left of it, one advanced in the trench. The last three carried hand grenades behind them. The enemy defended himself tenaciously, however he had to yield. There, when our heavy artillery placed three direct hits among the *Sturm Trupp* and with it also wounded the company leader, the enemy was able to advance again; however, he was soon stopped. A further advance was currently not possible because of a lack of hand grenades. Therefore *Vizefeldwebel* Vietmeyer allowed a barricade to be constructed and furnished the men for defense, until new hand grenades could be brought to the position and the artillery fire had been transferred. Then he arranged for the decisive thrust. The British became driven toward the Bavarians. When they ended up in their fire, they began their retreat into their old position. Artillery and

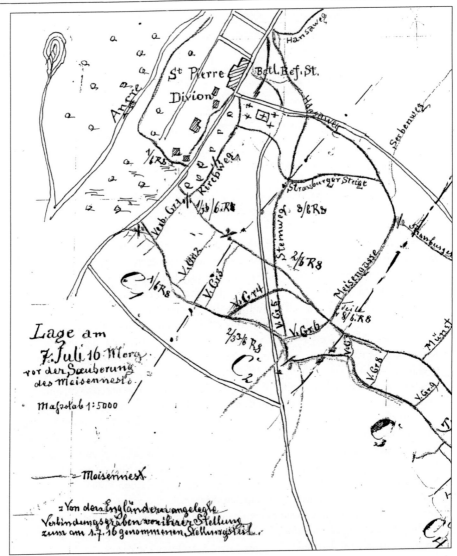

Positions of the 8th Bavarian RIR on 7 July 1916

infantry opened rapid fire upon the fleeing enemy. Only a few of his men escaped. Immediate connections with the Bavarians were established. Several requests for support remained unfulfilled. At 9.00 a.m. it was all free from the enemy. We had 10 dead, 55 wounded, 3 missing. *Leutnant* Hartwig, RIR 15. [20]

While the men from RIR 15 attacked the *Meisennest* from the north, the 8th Bavarian RIR, IR 185 and IR 186 attacked from the south. At the appointed time, the men from Groups Prager and Wurm began their advance. *Leutnant der Reserve* Volk and *Vizefeldwebel* Landau and several other men from the 3/186 volunteered as guides for the *Sturm Trupp*. Following the assault, the 3/186 and one platoon of the 4/186 would work to rebuild the captured position.

Bombing parties from the 5th and 7/8th Bavarian RIR in Group Wurm under *Vizefeldwebels* Gerber and Grobholz, together with bombing parties from the 2nd and 4/185 advanced into the second trench in the vicinity of the *Meisengasse* without meeting much opposition. The bombers soon met up with the troops from the 8th and 11/185 from Group Prager.

Once the two groups had united, they advanced further through *Verbindungs Graben* Nr. 6 and 7 against the enemy garrison holding the first trench. *Vizefeldwebel* Gerber was wounded early in the fighting and *Unteroffiziers* Reichert and Beckert of the 7/8th Bavarian RIR and Rückert and Stock of the 5/8th Bavarian RIR took command of the situation. During the advance, *Unteroffizier* Stock captured a British Lewis Gun and within minutes he was operating it against its former owners. At 4.40 a.m. the enemy artillery replied to the German fire, though no one in Groups Prager or Wurm seemed to be particularly disturbed by it.

The British inside the *Meisennest* fought back vigorously, however supplies of hand grenades were being consumed far faster than they could be replaced. Many of the British defenders were being shot down by German snipers who were particularly effective.

Numerous casualties were incurred both from bombs and enemy snipers, who were lying out in the open and who shot down our men as they fired and threw bombs out of the trench. *Major* H. Moorehouse, D.S.O. in command of the sector was wounded in the arm by a sniper about 4.00 a.m., but remained in command till 5.30 a.m. when forced through loss of blood to go to the Dressing Station. Capt. W.M. Williamson, Commanding 'Z' Company and 2/Lts. Carter, Massin, Mackay, De Jonquet and Huntington were also wounded. Capt. H.G. Fraser took command and continued the fight till 6.30 a.m. when he ran out of bombs and was forced to retire down the communication trench to the original British front line which he held along with the 4th and 5th Y & L Regt. already there with the 35 men remaining out of the two companies ... [21]

During the fighting, the 4/185 helped recapture part of Sector C3 and because of the higher than expected casualties, it became reinforced through one fourth of the 2/185 located in the *Martinspfad*. With the new reinforcements, the 4/185 continued to advance deeper into the British line and eventually drove the enemy out. In the course of the fighting, *Landwehrmann* Kehl, 4/185, particularly stood out from the other men. After the fighting was over, the 3/185, which had been greatly weakened by enemy fire, was taken back to *Feste Zollern*.

Starting from 6 a.m. *Hauptmann* Wurm was in the middle of his men at the front when his strained activity at the command post would permit it, regulating the occupation of the newly recaptured trenches, the substitution of the hand grenade throwers, the distribution and use of the giant quantities of English hand grenades and also provided the drive for further advances against the British, who still desperately fought back in the first trench with one machine gun. However, their opposition gradually weakened. Once they finally flooded over the open terrain, *Unteroffizier* Rückert with 6 men from the 5th Company jumped up on the rear defenses in the

Killed by an artillery projectile while on sentry duty. (Author's collection)

trench and took them under powerful persecution fire; men of the 7th Company broke the last opposition with hand grenades. The English Machine Gun *Lieutenant* Lewis H. Neville Grenher (1/5 York Lancaster Regiment) ended up with the machine gun that had been rendered unserviceable in the hands of *Hauptmann* Wurm; he made those present in the trench aware of the wounded English Lieutenant-Colonel F.H.S. Rendall, who was brought back by our stretcher bearers. Now the last trench piece lost by the Reserve Regiment 99 on 1 July was in German possession again, so that the untiring and active on the 1 July begins and untiring and active work was fully carrier out. [22]

During the fighting, a request was sent back by the British defenders for more bombs to be brought forward. B Company, 1/5 KOYLI was sent forward to the *Meisennest* with 100 boxes of bombs but found the task almost impossible to accomplish. The communication trench was too shallow to provide any real protection and was under constant shrapnel fire throughout the fighting. The trench was also extremely congested with the bodies of men who had been killed or wounded who had tried to make the journey previously as well as numerous boxes of hand grenades and other supplies that these men had been carrying. In the end, the ammunition boxes were passed to the front from man to man and in this manner only a few reached their destination. It was simply not enough to help stem the German advance.

During the attack, the British machine guns located in the German 'A' line [old

German front line] were unable to provide any support as the gunners reported that the British and German troops were all mixed together and there was no clear target. Eventually several machine guns were repositioned into a communication trench and were able to fire on the German bombing parties from the 8th Bavarian RIR. The fire helped to suppress the German snipers and cover the withdrawal of the surviving British troops. Later, when the position inside the German lines was being abandoned, the two machine guns were lost. One was blown up using a hand grenade, the other was disabled and the lock and spare parts were carried back to the old British front line by the gun crew.

When the fighting had died down, it was time for both sides to take stock of what had occurred and to evaluate the losses suffered during the attack. At least two men taking part in the attack from the 8th Bavarian RIR were recognized for their acts of bravery and were awarded medals. 31 year old *Unteroffizier* Georg Rees, 7/8th Bavarian RIR, was presented with the Gold Medal for bravery:

> When the 7th Company was involved in recapturing the lost piece of trench by St. Pierre-Divion by the Ancre on 7 July 1916, Rees jumped into the position of his wounded company leader. He quickly fetched hand grenades here and pelted the British at the next shell crater for a long time with the rest of his men, who had been reduced from 20 down to 6, until they gave up their opposition. He pursued the enemy, continuously throwing hand grenades, seized an enemy machine gun and finally reached the rear of the enemy, so that they also avoided them here. Then, when the company received some reinforcements, he was soon able to deal with the British. He was able to deliver one wounded enemy officer and five Englishmen as prisoners. [23]

29 year old *Vizefeldwebel der Landwehr* August Rückert, 5/8th Bavarian RIR, was presented with the Silver Medal for Bravery for his action on 7 July:

> During the Somme battle on 7th July 1916 during the clearing of the *Meisengasse* the attack hesitated, because the British, protected by a traverse, stubbornly defended themselves. In the knowledge that the British would not come out from the bottom of the trench, Rückert jumped up on the traverse upon a highly situated part of the trench, accompanied by a few brave comrades. From there he gave lively rifle fire down upon the British, despite strong machine gun fire. The British were forced to yield to the rear under the effect of this fire so that the further clearing of the trench with hand grenades could be successfully accomplished. [24]

In addition to the men already mentioned who had been singled out for their bravery and resolve in the fierce fighting, *Leutnant der Landwehr* Scheid, 4/185; *Leutnant der Reserve* Rauschenbach who had fallen in the fighting, *Vizefeldwebels* Strohmeier and Brandt (both wounded), *Vizefeldwebel* Vietmeier and *Unteroffizier* Weber, 11/R15; *Vizefeldwebel* Gerber (wounded), *Unteroffiziers* Reicherd and Becker, 7/8th Bavarian RIR were all recognized for their actions on 7 July.

By 9 a.m. the entire position was free from the enemy. There was a joyous and confident mood among the German assault troops when the last trench piece occupied by the British had been taken accompanied by cheers. With the *Meisennest* back in German hands, the threat of the British expanding further into the German defenses by the Ancre was eliminated. This portion of the German front by St. Pierre-Division was to remain in German hands for many months to come.

The adversaries had defended themselves with extraordinary tenacity and bravery in the opinion of the Bavarians. The Bavarians had captured three machine guns and numerous other weapons and ammunition as well as one Lieutenant-Colonel, one Captain and 24 men from the 5th Yorkshire Battalion, 148th Brigade, 49th Division, as well as a Non-Commissioned officer of the 1st West Riding Field Company Royal Engineers.

The Captain who had been captured by the Bavarians gave the losses of his division at 25 to 30% and in addition mentioned that the 36th (Ulster) Division was virtually worn out. Statements from other prisoners indicated that the British garrison of the *Meisennest* had consisted of two companies with two machine guns from the Yorkshire and York and Lancaster Territorial Regiments, which until the previous evening consisted of 120 men who had been combined together. At the end of the fighting, they were apparently quite worn down; they had not had any food for three days and were starving. The total number of prisoners taken in this action: 1 Lieutenant-Colonel, 3 Captains, 1 Lieutenant approximately 135 men. Also captured were one mine thrower and three British machine guns while three German machine guns had been recovered.

With success also came losses; casualties among the officers and senior non commissioned officers involved in the successful attack were a serious blow to the different regiments. These were men, whose knowledge and experience would be difficult to replace Among them were the leader of the 11/R15, *Leutnant* Kaiser, who become severely wounded in the heavy fighting. He succumbed to his wounds in a *Feldlazarett* on 16 July. *Leutnant* Neubronner, 4/185, took over command of the leaderless company.

> Among the dead were found two extraordinarily popular, efficient officers: Fred Rauschenbach, who told me of his premonition of his death before in the tranquility of the Logeast wood, and sent his regards to his girlfriend, and the Kaiser. On the 10th he came back. Two bullets have wounded him in the head. Enthusiastically, he tells of the storm. His eyes shine. Then he becomes mute and thoughtful. He thinks about the heavy losses of his company and his friend Fred. Suddenly he gets a raging headache. His eyes burned. He suspects that he is severely hit. On the 16th our good comrade died in the military hospital at Vélu. With him the battalion loses a model officer, one always ready to help, a cheerful comrade, a ray of sunshine. *Leutnant* Petersen, RIR 15. [25]

Intelligence being gathered from numerous sources that included the statements made by some prisoners, uniform insignia indicating the regimental designation, pay books, letters, maps, orders, etc. taken off of the dead and wounded and prisoners provided valuable information to both sides in the fighting. In the case of the 1/5 York and Lancaster Battalion, many losses during this period were the result of German bombardments of Aveluy Wood, a location that had not been actively shelled by the Germans up until this time. Now, all of the assembly trenches were accurately bombarded with high explosives, shrapnel and lachrymatory shells. It was suspected that the Germans had utilized both statements from prisoners and captured maps to provide target coordinates for the artillery. In the present day, such intelligence information could be useless within hours of when it was obtained. While the fighting on the Somme by the Ancre was almost stationary and intelligence information could be useful for days, weeks or even months following the date it was acquired.

Early on 7 July *Generalmajor* Burkhardt, 10th Bavarian Infantry Division, took command over the sector south of the Ancre. *General der Infanterie Frhr.* von Soden only retained command of the sector north of the river. With the successful fighting by St. Pierre-Divion Von Soden was able to report the total ejection of the enemy foothold in Sector *Thiepval-Nord* when His *Excellenz* handed over the southern part of the sector to *Generalmajor* Burkhardt. Von Soden was reportedly delighted that he was able to give Burkhardt this parting gift.

Even with the changes being made in the command over the different sectors, the staff of the 52nd Reserve Infantry Brigade would remain in its current position for the time being. *Generalmajor* Burkhardt had *Generalmajor* Langhäuser at his disposal with the Staff of the Bavarian 10th Field Artillery Brigade, which now included Artillery Group Pys, *Major* Reiniger: RFAR 27. Under-Groups Berta, *Hauptmann Graf* von Preysing: II/RFAR 26, Zollern, *Hauptmann* Wiedtemann: I/RFAR 27, and Cäsar, *Hauptmann* Jäckh: II (F)/RFAR 27.

8 July

On 8 July the 3/186 and Platoon Neubronner from the 4/186 were relieved by RIR 15 and received quarters in the tunnel by St. Pierre-Divion. The commander of the I/8th Bavarian RIR, *Major* Prager, had directed the following letter to *Hauptmann* Rhein, the battalion commander of I/186:

> I am urged to inform your Excellency that the companies of the I/186 fighting in my group have done their full duty. The achievements of the 3/186 were quite outstanding. The company leader who was animated through an iron sense of duty, who also did not fail in the most difficult circumstances, supported through similarly excellent under leaders, has afforded me invaluable services. I can only congratulate the commander for such an outstanding unit.[26]

Because of the exceptional behavior in the fighting at St. Pierre-Divion the following men received the Iron Cross I Class: *Leutnant der Landwehr I* Moehl, *Leutnant der Reserve* Volk, *Leutnant* Bleyer, *Vizefeldwebel* Landau, *Wehrmann* Hogen, all from the 3/186.

On 8 July the German defenses at Thiepval and the *Granatloch* were still occupied by bits and pieces of several divisions; the men being scattered throughout the sector. Some effort was needed to determine just what forces were still available and where they were positioned if there was to be any sort of coordinated defense of the Thiepval Sector.

The staff of the II/R15, 6th, 7th and 8/R15 had moved into the Second Position between the Recruit Company/R119 and the 5/R15. In the afternoon the 1st and 4/*Garde Füsiliers* became extracted from their positions by Hill 141. *Major* von Delius, I/*Garde Füsiliers*, was relieved by *Hauptmann der Landwehr* Josephson, II/185. The 7/186 was inserted into the *König Strasse*, *Lemberg Stellung*, *Türken Stellung* and in the *Wundtwerk*, the 8/186 was inserted into *Thiepval-Mitte*. Machine Gun Company/185 had replaced four machine guns from a MG Coy/R99 in *Thiepval-Mitte* and *Thiepval-Süd*. The remnants of the 1st and 4/*Garde Füsiliers* that had already lost 5 officers and 170 Other Ranks, were combined into one company and located at Mouquet farm under *Leutnant Frhr.* von

Esebeck. The 3/185, which from 2 until 6 July had been in the *Strassburger Steige*, then in *Feste Zollern*, which also had large losses, now occupied the *Zwischenstellung*. The 2nd and 4/185 became withdrawn to the *Meisennest* in the *Auwärter Weg* and to Mouquet farm after heavy losses. In Sector *Thiepval-Mitte* under *Hauptmann Frhr.* von Forstner, whose Battle Headquarters was in southern corner of Thiepval, along with the 4/R15, 8/186 and 1/R15. The 2/R15, 7/186, 7th, 1st, 8th, 5th and 6/185 were in Sector *Thiepval-Süd* under *Hauptmann der Landwehr* Josephson, with the Battle Headquarters in the *Wundtwerk*. Machine guns from a MG Coy/R15 and MG Coy/185 were distributed throughout Sector Krause under *Oberleutnant* von Mücke, IR 185. The 2nd, 4th, 3rd and two machine guns from IR 185 under *Hauptmann van* Vaernewyck, I/185, replaced two additional machine guns from RIR 99 positioned in the *Zwischenstellung* by Mouquet Farm and took over the operation of three captured machine guns in Thiepval, with the Battle Headquarters at Mouquet farm. [27]

The number of different regiments and divisions represented above provides clear evidence of the problems associated with command and control of such a varied force. While it was important to know where the different companies were located, it did not provide any details on the condition of the men. Just what were the conditions faced by the average infantryman?

> We sit deep in the mud. In the valley moved a flock of casualties, proceeding with Red Cross flags. Pulled on other stockings. I poured water out of the boots. No food, no coffee. 9.00 p.m. marched into the front line. Further through mud and water. What was half dry is completely wet again. Relieve Bavarians. One of them says: 'Here no one comes back, except wounded or dead.' Dugouts good, however overcrowded. Poor Knott had to go back immediately again through the mud to get food. No one was able to sleep, but all eyes were closing. [27]

It was not any different in the neighboring Ovillers Sector. At the end of 7 July the men in IR 180 were in poor shape; partly because of fatigue, partly due to the lack of food and water and in part due to the considerable number of men who were reporting sick. With no signs of the promised relief, the regimental headquarters applied for an allocation of *Schnapps* from the division. It was hoped that the stimulant would revive the flagging spirits of the men somewhat.

On the early morning of 8 July two large casks arrived at regimental headquarters. The *Schnapps* they contained was immediately decanted into bottles and quickly sent up to the battalions. While the liquor helped to warm up the men's insides and revive their sinking spirits, it was only a temporary solution. General von Soden visited the regiment in the muddy trenches on the 8th and encouraged the men to hold on as he moved through the position.

After many anxious hours, the men from IR 180 were finally given the news that the regiment would be moving to the rear in the late afternoon. The relief of the regiment was able to take place because the rest of the 183rd Infantry Division had arrived on the Somme as reinforcements. Under the cover of darkness the companies marched to Bapaume and on the next morning the regiment moved into rest quarters south of Cambrai, the regimental staff located in Masnieres. The men of IR 180 left their position with the awareness of having fully performed their duty.

The fighting from the Ancre to the Somme was obviously drawing in more and more reinforcements, many of them from the sectors north of the Somme front. These included additional men from the 2nd Guard Reserve Division. On 7 July the II/R15 received orders to move south of the Ancre. The 5/R15 arrived first at 7.30 p.m. on 7 July, the 5/R15 at 2.30 a.m. on 8 July, the 8/R15 at 3.20 a.m. and the battalion staff, 6th and 7/R15 arrived at 3.40 a.m. The companies were placed in a switch line to act as a barrier against any possible enemy breakthrough where they waited for orders.

Previous reports had indicated that several companies of IR 186 were supposed to arrive at 2.30 a.m. on 7 July; however the 7/186 did not arrive until 5 a.m. on 8 July. The leader of the 8/186 reported one hour later: 'His men could do no more! They were underway for 20 hours! The 7/186 occupied the dugouts that had been designated for the 8/186 and did not vacate them!' There was no thought of any actions being taken against the men of the 7/186 under these circumstances and everything possible was being done to look after the men who were half dead from marching.

The II/R15 was extracted out of the trenches of IR 170 south of Gommécourt on 7 and 8 July and moved south until they were in the Second Position south of the Ancre. The overtired men were provided with poor accommodations here and then, despite the fire, sank into the deep mud to rest. Soon after midday the order came that two companies were to be inserted into the Sector von Amann: 'Uff! Orders are orders. The soldier has no permanent quarters on earth!' However *Oberstleutnant* Schwartz had also built a few. He had hardly obtained any clarity in the occupation of the Second position, because it was downright looted by the troops: The *Wachtkommando* went back to Miraumont, the 10th and 11th Coy becomes subordinate to Regiment von Bram, the Recruit Companies are released to Pys, the II Battalion goes to the front! And no one knows, if Contalmaison was still held. At least two Bavarian Recruit Companies under *Rittmeister* Baumann from the 5th *Chevauleger* arrive; ... these became summoned to the front on the following day. At 10.30 IR 183 wants the *Quergraben III* taken again. More confused battle noise penetrates across out of the vicinity of Ovillers. In this direction our II Battalion now moves forward.

Ovillers lay close behind the front line as a quadrilateral block and was already ploughed up stone houses. It was strongly fortified and surrounded by trenches: In the north with the *Friedhof*, in the east with the *Haug Graben* that according to the map continued to the national road in a *Riegelstellung* and out of that to the often called *Schwarzwald Graben* (abbreviated as: *Quergraben I* or QI respectively) which led to Pozières. It, like the parallel running approach routes: *Ganter* and *Gierig Weg, Stockacher, Fabeck* and *Zollern Graben*, became familiar to us. However, the *Quergraben* I, II, and III ran through Ovillers from north to south, leading past the western edge, through the middle and the eastern tip. Previously they had the front toward the enemy. Now they already led toward him. Q I is lost, Q II and III were blocked off through the *Sigel Graben*. Finally the *Kabel* leaves the *Schwarzwald Graben* approximately 200 meters east of Ovillers and goes over into the *Röder Graben* that lead parallel to the national road on the western tip of Pozières and here merged into the outflanking trench of Pozières. *Major* Kiesel, II/R15 [28]

In order to guarantee sufficient food and water, *Major* Kiesel ordered *Leutnant*

Engelken proceed to Courcelette where he and the *Verpflegungs* Officer set up a provisions warehouse. This was a necessary function considering the huge influx of men arriving at such a small area of the front. While officers poured over maps and made decisions based upon assumptions of unit strength and condition, the reality was quite different. The men who comprised the markings on the maps marched with heavy packs and equipment in an unfamiliar terrain that was under enemy fire.

> *'Die Schweinerei'*, ['The mess'], no one should shudder about this soldierly crudeness – begins with the forward march. At 2.30 p.m. the staff breaks off the 6th and 8th Companies and the Machine Gun *Ergänzung* Platoon 662 under *Vizefeldwebel* Grauert via Mouquet farm, to occupy the *Riegel Stellung* by the eastern tip of Ovillers up to the national road. Three English aircraft accompanied the gray snake and they fired from only 200 meters high. Rifle fire at least forces the impudent pilots to climb higher. However, the 8th Company had barely left the approach road by the farm, when barrage fire was employed. In the quick march it succeeds in reaching the *Stockacher Graben* through the hollow. The 6th Coy however become separated, loses their brilliant and trusted leader, *Leutnant* Drewell and 9 men. They become detained over a half hour and could follow only in small squads. The aircraft directs the fire from over there. Therefore the march is at first a death walk. And because of the mud filled trench for the already strongly tired, deficiently fed troops, was extraordinarily difficult. A number of men remained lying down. About 5 o'clock the staff and the 8th Company reached Ovillers and found the *Riegel Stellung* after a long search, also with general disappointment to find only 100-150 meters of trench from 40-80 centimeters deep, lying under heavy fire, almost leveled. In the report *Major* Jiesel does not avoid the powerful reply: 'Herein to also be able to place just one company was irresponsible, because they would never be able to fulfill the task of the *Riegel.*' The brigade received the reply from him. So the companies only occupied the eastern edge of Ovillers and Q III. The situation is completely unclear. The *Röder* and *Kabel Graben* were held, the terrain up to the Ovillers-Pozières road was already dominated by the enemy. Meanwhile the 7th Company receives orders to move at 6.30 in the evening. (We join the battalion battle headquarters with the last officers of the 7th Company, *Leutnant* Meyerhoff. Both were somewhat reduced. Neither the 8th nor the 6th Company was forwarding reports, probably because of the leaders being wounded. The 5th Company fought with the III Battalion and was dealt with there. What however the 5th Company suffered through that also that all others suffered through, only that they had the luck not to become isolated like the 8th and 7th Coy. *Major* Kiesel, II/R15 [29]

The men remained with their packs, hand grenades, rifles and large entrenching tools stuck in the deep mud. In the *Stockacher Graben* it was held for a longer time, because as a result of an attack in the front strong fire lay on the trench crossings. The leaders broke down completely, so that the company did not arrive at the battle headquarters of the II Battalion *Garde Füsilier* Regiment until after midnight. The company relieved the exhausted Recruit Coy IR 180 and with two platoons occupying the *Friedhof Graben* between the 4th Company IR 183 and the medical dugout, in which the 8th Coy lay. The perpendicular trench proceeding to the front as an old approach route had no dugouts. Therefore the dugout in the *Wasserwerk* was provided for the 1st Platoon, the medical dugout for the 2nd and the former reserve battle headquarters for the 3rd, the *'Sommerwohnung.'* Because this dugout was 500 meters distant, the 3rd Platoon became the reserve. Whoever was able to, laid himself there and slept, no matter if it was on a stairway or in craters. A direct hit from the heaviest caliber struck through one of the three entrances of the *Sommerwohnung* at midday and buried 4 men, who could not be rescued. *Leutnant* Meyerhoff, RIR 15 [30]

In the period following the relief of IR 180, both regiments of the 26th Reserve Division that had been fighting south of the Ancre had been relieved. The remaining two, RIR 119 and RIR 121, still occupied the trenches north of the Ancre while the batteries of the 26th Reserve Field Artillery Brigade would continue to participate in the fighting uninterrupted for some time to come. South of the Ancre, one of the few units from the division still in action was the 6/*Pionier* Battalion 13, which was actively involved in the fighting by Ovillers.

With the *Meisennest* recaptured, with no major attacks against the *Granatloch*, the only portion of the line once held by the 26th Reserve Division that was still active was the Ovillers Sector. For purposes of continuity of the narrative, the events taking place by Ovillers and Thiepval during this period of time will be included in the narrative, which will hopefully help the reader in making sense of the often confusing series of events that occurred a century ago.

9 July

At 2 a.m. on 9 July the parts of the 5th and 7/185 still found in *Thiepval-Mitte* were moved to *Thiepval-Süd*. The staff of the II/185 took on this sub-sector and with it the entire regiment was employed on the Somme. With most of the troops from the 26th Reserve Division already relieved from the front lines, the defense of positions by Thiepval and Ovillers became assumed by portions of several different divisions.

On 9 July the commander of the 52nd Reserve Infantry Brigade, *Generalleutnant* von Auwärter, turned over command of the Ancre-Ovillers sector to the commander of the 20th Bavarian Infantry Brigade, *Generalmajor* Rauchenberger. *Von* Auwärter's staff was then withdrawn in to Bapaume, later to Beugny. While the infantry regiments were being relieved along the front line of the 26th Reserve Division the division artillery remained in Sector Burkhardt. General von Maur remained as the Artillery Commander for the 10th Bavarian Division and the 26th Reserve Division simultaneously. The division headquarters of the 10th Bavarian Infantry Division was transferred to Bancourt.

With the conclusion of this period of the fighting, the division commander spoke to all of the troops and staff of his thanks and his acknowledgment of their dedication to duty in a subsequent daily order.

Daily order from the 26th Reserve Division 8 July 1916:
After I had turned over the command over the sector south of the Ancre yesterday to the commander of the 10th Bavarian ID, I felt a need, to express my heartfelt thanks and my fullest appreciation to all those staff and units of the 26th Reserve Division, which so effectively supported me on the southern Ancre shore. It is in this manner successful, in the hitherto existing fighting, to firmly hold the overall division sector from Serre to La Boisselle in our hands and deliver intact after clearing the last nest

of Englishmen in C3 through the dashing undertaking by Group Bram in the night from the 6th July.

Frhr. von Soden. [31]

While the men from IR 180 and RIR 99 had been sent to the rear the fighting had never ceased and the situation by Thiepval and Ovillers, while not critical, was still uncertain and required constant attention by army commanders. Even the badly tired and worn out men from the regiments relieved knew they would probably be back in the thick of things before too long.

On the 9th, 5 p.m., orders from the Bavarian 20th Infantry Brigade: III Battalion 15 to relieve Bavarian RIR 8 ... ... from this comes nothing. Instead the 10th and 11th Companies from 10 o'clock entrenched at a *Riegel Stellung* from Thiepval to Pozières ... .. Then the Battalion should again replace the II Battalion Bavarian RIR 8. However: 'Counter orders come again! Instead of that the second position, Sector *Süd*, is to be occupied and to leave behind only one Group at each machine gun for protection. The 11th Company reached 400 meters north of the national road. In connection to Grenadier Regiment 9, the 10th Company moved forward with the right wing at the Mouquet farm-Courcelette road. The march in the strong artillery fire, often in trenches filled a meter high with water was very exhausting. *Hauptmann* von Widekind, RIR 15. [32]

Georg Köglmeier, killed by an artillery projectile. (Author's collection)

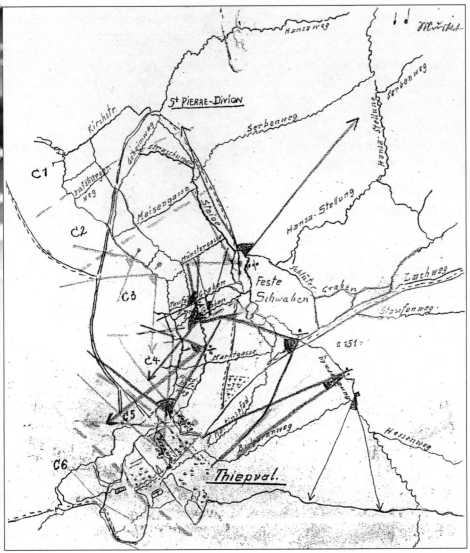

Fields of fire for the machine guns of the 8th Bavarian RIR.

The nerves of the men were quickly frayed in the constant enemy fire. At 12.30 a.m. on 9 July reports start to come in across the front: 'The enemy was mining!' All of the companies of RIR 15 report again and again that the men heard subterranean sounds and the men were growing concerned. If they did nothing, it would only be a matter of time when the ground beneath their feet would blow up. The regimental headquarters called in *pioniers* who were most familiar with the signs of mining. The *pioniers* listen for the tell-tale sounds of enemy tunneling, the sounds created by 'hammering, chopping, drilling and rolling masses of rocks,' turned out to be the impacts of the numerous shells that caused the ground to tremble.

In the early afternoon hours of 9 July conspicuous movement could be seen on the road to Pozières and in the nearby hollow. Without knowing the enemy's intentions, the main trench remained occupied by two platoons from RIR 15 during the day that were then exposed to the enemy artillery fire, which brought considerable losses: 8 killed including *Vizefeldwebel* Denkhaus, 11 wounded on the first day. For the next few days the pattern would remain the same, heavy artillery fire during the day and enemy patrol undertakings at night.

10 July

Daily orders from the 26th Reserve Division continued to praise the men of the division for their efforts in the fighting. On 10 July the following statement was issued:

> The first onrush of the English offensive against our positions appears at an end. That everything, including Serre was held, can be credited in the first line by the great courage of our brave troops and their leaders, not at least also to the intimate relationship between infantry and artillery. However, it is especially also to the credit of the brigade and regimental commanders. The same for the past 1 ½ years in faithful hard work have encouraged the expansion of our positions. You have according to arrangements properly prepared the troops for the big day of the enemy attack and instilled the spirit that has led to victory. It is my desire, to speak of my warmest thanks to the brigade and regimental commanders and their staff for this, as well as for their vigorous support during the last days of fighting.[33]

While it was all said and good in praising the officers and staff for the success achieved by the division at the start of the powerful enemy offensive, the actual resistance was being offered by the rank and file occupying the muddy trenches. Fortunately the men the individual soldiers also received kind words of praise in a telegram from the King of Württemberg. 'His Majesty expressed his special appreciation to the 26th Reserve Division that in several days of hot wrestling had repulsed the onrush of an overly powerful enemy and congratulated the brave troops for these successes.'

While the front north of the Ancre was relatively peaceful, apart from almost continuous artillery fire and aerial combat, the enemy continued his tactics of piecemeal destruction south of the Ancre, especially between Ovillers and the Somme. It was the tenth day of the enemy offensive; the enemy had made significant headway into the German positions south of La Boisselle and was applying constant pressure to the Ovillers Sector. In many instances, the exact location of friend and foe was not known and this uncertainty needed to be resolved if the German forces had any hope of providing a firm defense against future enemy attacks. As such, the front line units were ordered to send out patrols along the front line to locate the enemy positions.

In the night of 9/10 July, patrols from the 6th and 8/R15 had firmly established that *Quergraben III* was unoccupied by the enemy up to the National road, and reported that they were not showered with hand grenades until well beyond this road. Then, at 4.30 a.m. sentries inside listening posts sounded the alarm: 'Approximately 150 British were advancing, going through *Quergraben III* against the eastern edge of Ovillers!' The sap heads and *Riegel Stellung* were quickly occupied and the approaching enemy troops were forced to withdraw under heavy losses through infantry fire and hand grenades. Something new appeared during this attack, the fleeing enemy troops received support from a pilot who flew at an altitude of 200 meters and fired into the German trenches. This close aerial support allowed many of the retreating troops to make it safely back to their own lines. While not a common occurrence, it was a portent of things to come.

The men from IR 180 were enjoying their time in rest quarters where many of the soldiers wrote to their families for the first time since the start of the offensive on 1 July. To some, such as *Unteroffizier* Nuding, their survival in the heavy fighting was most likely the result of divine intervention.

Unteroffizier Otto Nuding, IR 180 2nd Comp. 26 Res. Div. 14 RAK,
July 10, 1916
Dear parents, brothers and sisters! Now I'm sitting here in a village near Cambrai. The last period of time is almost like a dream to me. I have had terrible times behind me in which one was often almost desperate. I survived the seven-day bombardment as well as yet another seven days of the attack. My heart is full of gratitude to God who has protected me in these thousands of dangers and has always given me the necessary peace. The strain on the nerves of such a struggle is almost indescribable and unbelievable, but also indescribable are the days of being connected to and being sheltered by God that I have experienced. I have had days of fighting that I can say I have felt God's protection directly. You then feel that this time it does not apply to you, you still escape one more time. Therefore, my beloved, if I still now live, it can be seen as a gift from God. Give thanks to him and do not stop there every day to praise him again. It may be unbelievable for some that when it rains down iron splinters that he would make any exception for what they now kill. Even in such a shelling God's will protected, which I have not believed, but especially in one of my people from my group whom I've known from the Tübingen E.S.V. He is now a vicar, as he did the exam during leave a quarter year ago. He felt so protected that he even once said that the bullet has not yet been cast that will hit him. Although physically difficult, he has performed immensely in the days of battle, of course, precisely through this alone. This was often more exciting for the spectators if he does not go away when one shell struck after the other. I hope to write you a full report in the next few days. My address is the same old. The Training Company in Bapaume had been cancelled right at the beginning of the French English offensive. I have already written you everything about that but I do not know if you received it. Since yesterday we received mail again, but I have received no mail from you. I greet you in love from my heart. Otto. [35]

The thoughts about God and religion were not restricted to the men behind the lines. Great effort was made to provide whatever comfort possible to the men at the front. On Sunday, 10 July the Catholic Division *Pfarrer*, Dr. Brem, visited *Feste Schwaben* and held religious services. Because of the constant enemy artillery and mine fire, the service had to be held inside one of the nearby mined dugouts where Dr. Brem and his congregation could remain safe from the bursting shells. Several large, thick boards were set up to act as a makeshift altar. The boards were covered with a dirty, grey coat to serve as the altar cloth.

While Dr. Brem held the religious service, the altar and surrounding room was filled with men wearing filthy, mud and clay covered uniforms, sporting unruly beards after weeks of not being able to shave or wash properly. The men were tanned from the hot July sun as they knelt or stood about stirring during the sermon and the sacrament. To some it reminded them of stories of the first Christians who stood together in the catacombs under the earth in order to hold church services.

Others also made the comparison that the dangers they faced in 1916 were very similar to those far back in early history. With the fighting raging on the earth's surface, they did not know if they would become torn apart into thousands of pieces from the hundreds of bursting projectiles, almost in the same manner as the early Christians who faced persecution and possible death in the arena by being torn apart by wild animals.

Outside, in the trenches, the situation by Ovillers had become very serious. On 10 July, the last well located at the northeastern edge of the village was destroyed by shell fire. All water and coffee had to be carried up from the rear and because of the heavy British fire these critical commodities rarely succeeded in making it to the men at the front and only under heavy losses for the carrying parties.

> In the morning no coffee, but mail. Thereby the mood lifts. Newspapers clarify the situation at the front for us. Attempted to clean my muddy boots. 10.00 p.m., while receiving food from the rear, we become severely bombarded. To my great sorrow I hear that our good *Unteroffizier* Schnupp has fallen. In the communication trench I become completely wet and muddy again. At night work.[36]

Ovillers was being smothered by hundreds upon hundreds of high explosive and shrapnel shells almost daily. 13 British observation balloons could be seen just across the lines from which every movement made inside the German positions could be seen and relayed to the gunners, providing them with specific targets to destroy. The neighboring sectors were also under intense fire, in one afternoon at least 100 heavy shells fell on Thiepval alone. One *Leutnant* predicted that all of these signs pointed to it becoming a 'hot' day. A large enemy attack was fully expected to occur in the morning.

Even troops stationed further to the rear were not safe from enemy fire. A bombing attack was made on the rest quarters of IR 180 where some of the first replacements for the regiment had arrived six days earlier. The air raid resulted in 8 men killed and 4 men wounded. These losses and some of the ones suffered earlier in the fighting were made up when later on the same day 2 officers and 137 men arrived as replacements for IR 180.

Still, for most of 10 July the Ovillers-Thiepval sectors were quiet, the enemy artillery fire, while heavy, was less than usual and there was no attack as many had expected. Then, when night fell, the British became active once again and the artillery fire increased accompanied by a great deal of commotion inside the British trenches which meant the defenders would get little sleep this night. One man in RIR 15 described the experience: 'The impacts heard in the distance were like reclining on a bed of planks that millions upon millions of growling ocean waves smashed to pieces.'

While most of the troops that had fought south of the Ancre on 1 July had been replaced over time, the number of men across the critical front were simply too few to properly defend the position. The troops that were available were all posted in the front lines, distributed in three lines of trenches and shell crater positions. However, the backbone of the defense by Ovillers consisted of ten carefully concealed machine guns staggered throughout the position which would provide the highest level of defensive fire across the front. The machine guns that had been in position until 8 July under *Hauptmann* von Babo, RIR 99, had finally been replaced by a machine gun company from RIR 15 under

Rittmeister von Mücke[37] whose guns had taken over the empty emplacements on this date.

With the extreme shortage of men all carrying parties were discontinued in the night of 10/11 July, instead, these men were used to create a new trench. The last reserves available between the front line troops and Thiepval consisted of the 1/R15 with 80 rifles and the 8/186 with 60 rifles. The former carrying parties, nine Groups of men from the 7/186 along with 60 *pioniers,* were now busy entrenching. This small detachment of men had orders to produce an outline of an entire second trench in the night of 10 July at any cost which turned out to be quite small; the loss of two *pioniers* from shell fire.

The situation facing the defenders of Ovillers was confusing. Reports and messages provided conflicting details of the location of friendly troops and in particular, where the enemy was actually located at any given time. While *Quergraben III* had been reported to be clear of British troop until well past the National road, it was not the same situation in *Quergraben II.*

On the evening of 10 July *Major* von Delius, I/*Garde Füsiliers* reported to RIR 15 that *Quergraben* II up to the National road was occupied by German troops. However, patrols sent out toward the British lines had already received fire when in the *Sigel Graben* and firmly established that *Quergraben* II was occupied or controlled by the British up to the *Friedhof Graben.* This level of uncertainty was not restricted to the Ovillers-Thiepval Sector; it was quite common throughout the fighting.

It was suspected even at this stage of the battle that the staff located in the rear had no real idea of what was taking place at the front at times or in some cases, accurately knowing where the front was located. On the other hand, the men located at the front did not fully realize the pressures placed on the different commands to maintain control over the situation. The stresses being placed on the different command levels is described in the regimental history of RIR 15: 'The tenseness of the situation, the worry by the regiment and brigade about the position of their trenches, the screams for help from all sides, destitute of reserves, therefore the great preoccupation with the troops and their superlative spirit in that they willingly fulfill every tough demand, are appreciated. War history is not always spicy.'[38]

10th July. Still the reserve! The fighting activity in front is less today. However in the evening red light ball climb up with pearl beads: Attack! Already the order comes: '10th and 11th Company move to *Feste Zollern.* Leaders by the 11th Company are to maintain the connection.' However the 11th moves off. There we stand, without any idea where *Feste Zollern* was! Because we do not possess maps. We moved along the trench, going at random. It becomes darker, the terrain impassable. Finally we meet a Bavarian sentry. We were naturally going the wrong way, heading to *Feste Schwaben*! The route that was now described to us, leads back into our trench. It is depressing! We let the company rest. *Leutnant* Loof and I look further. After many mistakes we find the regimental battle headquarters. I summon the company after. A shell hits; one man remains lying, bleeding. The next scoops out the grave. At home it is soon described as: 'Missing!' Gone, with the misty thought! The same waits for 100 faithful soldiers. The new orderly also leads us crisscrossing. 4.00 a.m. Before us is Ovillers. Now we know we are still not out of the artillery fire and let the company swarm out into craters to look for cover. Then Hübner and I look for a guide. We had luck and a cyclist arrives, who intended to go the regiment and knows the route. We were released from our dubious situation. To be sure, artillery fire remains our constant companion, but about 5 a.m. we reach *Feste Zollern* and received our trench. There are no dugouts. My 5th Group received a direct hit that killed one man, wounded two. Up to 6 a.m. we have to dig our camp bed holes and fall into a death like sleep out of which we are torn out by an alarm at 10 o'clock. We shall occupy the *Schwarzwald Graben*. If it is still in our possession, no one knows ... .. *Leutnant* Petersen, RIR 15. [39]

11 July

The British continued to repeat the same tactics used the previous day, a period of heavy shelling that was not followed by an infantry attack. At 4 a.m. the German front line was heavily bombarded, which gave every indication of an imminent infantry attack; then nothing happened. The garrison had been alarmed and the defenses were manned but all it did was to tire the men out even more than they had been before or to bring the men into the open where they could be taken under fire, resulting in heavier losses.

During 11 July the 6th and 8/R15 suffered substantial losses through enemy drum fire falling on the entire sector. With the growing threat to the left flank by Ovillers, the *Garde Füsilier* Regiment ordered the II/R15 to construct a *Riegel Stellung* between Battery positions 763 and 743 that could be used as a main defensive line if needed. In addition, the 6/R15 would occupy the *Schwarzwald Graben* from Artillery position 763 until Ovillers. However, the 6/R15 consisted of only 75 rifles. It was soon discovered that the extremely weakened II/R15 could only be expected to complete a small part of the tasks assigned to the battalion; there were simply too few men left to make any real progress on the new position.

The new *Riegel Stellung* was going to be 500 meters long while the *Schwarzwald Graben* was already 800 meters in length. The *Garde Füsilier* Regiment then decided to follow a suggestion by *Major* Kiesel that the work on the *Riegel Stellung* should be considered secondary and that the II/R15 would work on the position as best it could under the circumstances. There was also the possibility that the II/R15 might receive support through one company from the *Garde Füsiliers,* something that would be very appreciated if it came about. Until that time, the enemy continued to harass the small number of German defenders.

> At 6.40 p.m. the enemy repeated his tactics of heavy fire without the subsequent infantry attack. Once more, the exhausted garrison was alarmed and manned the defenses, peering into the foreground, straining to see the enemy advance. It was simply designed to keep the German garrison from getting any rest. Then, starting from 9.00 p.m. on the night of 11/12 July, heavy fire once more; still, no attack. 'Oh, that the enemy would finally come however, so that one could pay him back!' However no attack follows. [40]

By the evening of 11 July, the 6/R15 became reinforced through two machine guns in the *Riegel Stellung* and then moved into the *Schwarzwald Graben* where the company discovered that the position was already occupied up to Battery position 763 by the 10th and 11/R15. The 6/R15 was unable to find any protection against neither inclement weather nor artillery fire in the *Schwarzwald Graben* where the last 150 meters of the trench until Ovillers was completely leveled.

Leutn. d. R. Lämmle
gef. bei Pozières 11. 7. 1916

Leutnant der Reserve Lämmle, RFAR 26, KIA 11 July 1916. (*Das Württembergisches Reserve-Feldartillerie-Regiment Nr.26 im Weltkrieg 1914-1918*)

Much of the confusion in the front line was the result of communication problems. Telephone connections with Ovillers and the Battle Headquarters of the *Garde Füsilier* Regiment had been established, however the lines worked for only a short period of time until they were destroyed once again in the heavy fire. Runners now had to be relied upon to carry messages between the various units.

With the troops becoming fatigued under the constant strain of waiting for the enemy to attack and the increasing number of losses due to enemy fire, the need to replace some units reached a critical stage. On 11 July the 5/185 located in the *Lemberg Stellung* was relieved by the 6/185. Once relieved, the 5th Company was ordered to occupy the *Türken Stellung*. While not in the front line the company was still in the thick of things and could be called forward at any moment. For additional support, the 4/185 became moved closer to the front and place in the *Wundtwerk*.

Of course, under the circumstances facing the men, not every casualty was the result of enemy activity. Considering the conditions where the men lived, amidst the filth where it would not be unusual for men to become ill from polluted water, contaminated food or diseases carried by the thousands of flies that were a constant presence. The men also lived and fought alongside piles of ammunition and high explosives in the form of hand grenades and *Minenwerfer* shells; accidents were bound to happen.

We are all full of the runs. Nothing helps against this terrible nuisance. Knott was extremely annoyed about the propagation of the lice: 'If one becomes born in the morning, by the evening they are already a grandmother.' At 6 o'clock I sit on one step of the dugouts, under me Josbächer, beneath him Schulz, who had undressed himself and was delousing. When he got dressed again, the fuze string of a hand grenade was hanging on the haversack strap, which was sets off and ignited others that were standing piled on the stair tread. Schulz's hand and thigh were torn open, nothing happened to the others of us. IR 186. [41]

12 July

The situation by the *Granatloch* had never died down completely and small actions were a common event. At 2 a.m. on 12 July the British staged a hand grenade attack, which effectively prevented a German attack that had been planned against the *Hindenburg Stellung;* the enemy bombing parties were repulsed by the 7/185. Further attacks followed after 11 a.m. which were also repulsed, however despite successfully defending the position the losses in the 7/185 continued to increase. While the fighting continued by the *Granatloch*, the III/185 spent the rest of the day and the following day entrenching in the *Grosser Riegel Stellung.*

The situation at Ovillers continued to grow worse as the enemy encroached on the German trenches. Already on the evening of 11/12 July the *Kabel Graben* and *Röder Graben* had been evacuated by the neighboring units, so that the *Schwarzwald Graben* now became known as the front line. At 1 a.m. there was an attack against the 8/R15 and against the sap head in *Quergraben* III, both of which were bloodily refused.

One good aspect of this day was the misty weather. For once the enemy pilots were forced to stay away from the front and the men enjoyed the opportunity to move about in the open without the danger of being observed. The men of the 8th Bavarian RIR were still in the thick of the fighting and had been since 24 June. Finally, there were signs that the badly worn regiment might be relieved from the front lines the first signs of this happening occurred when in the night from 12/13 July the 3/8th Bavarian RIR moved from *Feste Schwaben* to St. Pierre-Divion and returned to the formation of the I/8th Bavarian RIR.

13 July

While the fighting raged along the Somme front, IR 180 still enjoyed the time spent in the rear. The regimental losses were slowly being replaced. On 13 July IR 180 received a new draft of replacements, 7 officers, 9 *Unteroffiziere* and 486 Other Ranks, which were then distributed among the different battalions as needed. While the regiment was being restored to full strength, the quality of the new arrivals left much to be desired. Of the 502 replacements received on 13 July, not one had ever thrown a hand grenade. There would be much to do before these men were ready for the style of warfare being fought on the Somme.

These skills would be needed before too long as the men who had replaced IR 180 were slowly being destroyed under constant enemy shelling and infantry attacks. Early on 13 July a message arrived that the 3/*Garde Füsiliers* in the *Schäferwiese* on the right beside the 3/183 could no longer hold the position against non-stop enemy bombing attacks from three different sides. *Leutnant* Meyerhoff, RIR 15, travelled to the threatened location to see the situation first hand. Apparently the sap in *Quergraben* II had been lost during the night when the 3/*Garde Füsiliers* began to run out of ammunition and hand grenades and supplies of both would not be forthcoming for some hours.

So it came that about 4 a.m. the 3/*Garde Füsiliers*, exhausted from the attacks by parts of the 2nd South Lancaster and the 19th Lancaster Battalions (75th and 14th Brigades), was pressed back into the *Friedhof Graben* and the southeastern edge of the village despite the most extreme resistance. The brave company still fought back desperately up to the early afternoon until the men were at the end of their strength. Part of the company became cut off with the well-liked leader, *Leutnant der Reserve* Hasselmann; only a few came back, the remaining covered the battle field.

Also the remnants of the 4/183 located on the left of the 3/*Garde Füsiliers* had to give up their position in the *Friedhof Graben*, and then the right wing of the 7/R15 also yielded to the rear. The *Feldberg Graben* with its few dugouts was inadequate for a lasting defense; it was especially exposed to the British artillery fire. All of these movements were, of course, in direct violation of the orders to hold each position until killed that was issued only a short time earlier by General von Below. Through prolonged heavy fire and repeated enemy advances the defenders of Ovillers were seriously weakened. Inadequate supplies of food and water made their condition worse, so that before too long serious resistance in Ovillers could hardly still be expected.

In this critical situation *General Major* Burkhardt ordered the employment of two companies from the I/R77, the 1st and 2/R77 under *Major* Wambold had been moved from the Pozières position and directed to hold the small *Riegelstellung* north of Ovillers under all circumstances. Both companies from RIR 77 were supported by four machine guns and two platoons from the 2/*Musketen* Battalion 2, a substantial amount of firepower. It was already light before the two companies were in position; it was a well-built trench, only the wire obstacles were still missing.

The greatest part of the '*Grosse Riegel*' which ran in the line southern edge of Thiepval - *Josenhans-Graben* – Thiepval – Pozières road up to the *Stockacher Graben* – north of this road – westward of the northwestern tip of Pozières until the *Schwarzwald Graben* was already defensible. The 6/*Pionier* Battalion 13 had worked diligently on this *Riegel* for support of the III/185. With the imminent loss of Ovillers, measures were being taken to destroy any facilities the enemy might make use of. For blowing up the dugouts in Ovillers, squads from the 1/Bavarian *Pionier* Regiment were held ready while other detachments of the 1/Bavarian *Pionier* Regiment occupied key locations in the positions surrounding Ovillers.

In the afternoon the remnants of the 3/*Garde Füsiliers* and 4/183 became replaced by the 1/*Garde Füsiliers* in the *Feldberg Graben* between half of the 2/*Garde Füsiliers* and 4/183. At this time advancing English bombing parties attacked through the *Friedhof Graben* at the right wing of the 7/R15. Every available soldier manned the parapet while German bombing parties, including one from the 3/*Chevauxleger* 5 which had just arrived there, drove the enemy back until he was in *Quergraben* II.

It was a text book defense: two to three men threw hand grenades; those behind handed fuzed hand grenades up to the throwers. Whenever a thrower became tired, his relief jumped forth and took his place. In this manner the enemy was held down in *Quergraben* II. During this dashingly led attack, where *Unteroffizier* Bode especially stood out, *Vizefeldwebel* Schlink and five other men were killed, 16 men were wounded. *Quergraben II* and the *Friedhof Graben* were then blocked off with a trench barricade.

During this time the connection to the right was established once more and the neighboring company was asked if it did not want to push the position forward again. This request was apparently declined and the companies remained in their new trenches. It had become obvious that the companies lacked the strength to take on such a task.

After the trench was cleared from the material that the British had brought up in large quantities including spades, rifles, ammunition and large quantities of hand grenades, the garrison went back behind the new barricades. The enemy made no further attempts to roll up the trench. Instead, during the night the British constructed a barricade 30 meters in front of the German barricade and installed machine guns and used mirrors to observe the German positions.

Georg Vogler. (Author's collection)

At the onset of darkness the second half of the 2/*Garde Füsiliers* relieved the 1/*Garde Füsiliers,* which then took on the sector for the 4/183 that only numbered three Groups. The III/*Garde Füsiliers* had occupied the line that was expected to be the right wing of the future front line. Now, the position was occupied in part by Half Battalion Wambold up to the Battery position 763. There were only dugouts in Battery positions 743, 734 and 763, in which the companies and machine guns were able to find some protection against the devastating British artillery fire.

Despite the heavy enemy fire, the extension of the position still had to take place. In connection to the small *Riegelstellung,* the line Battery 763 – *Schwarzwald Graben* – Western edge of Pozières up to 50 meters west of the National road was maintained in Sector Schwartz. The Bavarian 10th Field Artillery Brigade provided support in Sector Amann, by blocking off Ovillers on all sides by barrage fire and providing continuous barrage fire against the new southern front of Division Burkhardt. In addition a few batteries held the Albert-La Boisselle road under fire.

The western front of the division from St. Pierre-Divion up to the *Hindenburg Stellung* by Hill 141 south of Thiepval was held by the troops that were subordinate to *Oberstleutnants* Bram and Krause and consisted of the 8th Bavarian RIR, 8th and 12/R15, 3rd and 4/186, I and II/185, I/R15, 7th and 8/186 with their machine guns. The 183rd Infantry Division had been ordered to be relieved and had essentially proceeded without interruptions. In the morning the II/27 under *Hauptmann* Lyons, with two machine guns from the *Feld* Machine Gun Zug 125 were in the Pozières position; then in the old Second Line up to Bazentin le Petit wood was the 5th and 7/R77 with three machine guns from the 9th Grenadier Regiment; the I/184 under *Major* Otto, with one machine gun from IR 184, six *Musketen* from the 1/*Musketen* Battalion 2 and two machine guns from the 9th Grenadier Regiment; then the III/165 (without the 10/165) under *Hauptmann* Walter, with Machine Gun Marksman Detachment 171. The 6/R77 and 10/165 were located at Martinpuich, the III/184 was in Eaucourt l'Abbaye with six machine guns from IR 183, the I and III/27 were in Ligny-Thilloy, the I and II/165 were in Geuedecourt.

The commanders of IR 27 and IR 165 had taken over command of their regimental sectors in Martinpuich in filthy gas filled mined dugouts located in the middle of the village ruins. IR 183 had gone back to Barastre along with the rest of the 183rd Infantry Division. The Saxon regiment had lost 122 killed, 848 wounded and 5 men missing. The I/*Lehr* Infantry Regiment, which had joined the fighting on 3 July with 14 officers, 863 *Unteroffiziere* and Other Ranks, left early on 13 July with 4 officers, 100 *Unteroffiziere* and Other Ranks.

14 July

A large-scale attack, apparently in honor of the French national holiday, Bastille Day, took place on 14 July on the front from Longueval to Bazentin while simultaneous demonstrations were made against the remaining front from Gommécourt to the Somme. The villages of Bazentin le Grand, Bazentin le Petit and the largest part of Longueval all fell into the hands of the British on this date.

14 July was also the same day that a new command structure was put into place on the Somme in the hope of improving the administration of the extensive battle front. The sector of Group Stein, XIV Reserve Corps that was being managed with increasing difficulty from one command position, was divided into two parts. The northern half of the sector, up to the National Road was taken over by Group Stein with the 2nd Guard Reserve Division, 52nd Infantry Division and 26th Reserve Division with the headquarters located in Louverval. The command over the southern half of the sector was transferred to *General der Infanterie* Sixt von Armin with the IV Army Corps, 7th and 8th Infantry Divisions, with the headquarters located in Havrincourt.

The men of the 8th Bavarian RIR in Sector C4, C5 and C6 by Thiepval fully expected an attack on 14 July because of the substantial artillery fire the enemy was employing on these areas. While close watch was made on the opposing trenches, no attack took place. It was later determined that it had been a diversion to the main attack held further south. .

The position of the 7th and 8/186 also came under strong enemy drum fire for 45 minutes in the early morning hours of 14 July. Unlike the sectors being held by the Bavarians, the bombardment of the two companies from IR 186 was soon followed by a British attack on the 7/185, which connected on the left of the 7/186. The 7/185 eventually successfully repulsed three British attacks; however, the company could no longer defend the communication trench it occupied because of heavy losses and the consumption of all close combat supplies. The enemy had overrun the barricade in the *König Strasse* Sap. However, before the British could advance any further they became shattered through devastating fire of the machine guns located in the *Privat Weg* under *Leutnant* Ziehe. Parts of the 7th and 8/185 then cleared the position completely with the help of three Groups of the 7/186, which brought up hand grenades to the left and drove the enemy back out of the communication trench. When these hand grenades had also been used up, the British managed to storm the left Barricade II and the communication trench following a strong defense by the 5/185, while the right Barricade II was still held by three men from the 7/185.

Other men from the 7/185 who were retreating from the communication trench were detained near the company leader's dugout by *Leutnant der Reserve* Weber, 7/186 and *Leutnant* Markmann and, reinforced by two additional Groups and provided with a fresh supply of hand grenades, were led back again into the abandoned position.

The men occupied the communication trench once more and had come just at the right time to prevent the further advance by the enemy over the right barricade. Meanwhile, the newly deployed reserves of IR 185 had thrown back the British that were advancing through the *König Strasse* and *Privat Weg* and which had almost surrounded the 3rd Platoon of the 7/186. *Musketier* Lorey, 7/186, had fought bravely against the uneven odds until he was killed by an enemy hand grenade. After a brief fight, the position was firmly in German hands once again. The parts of the 7/186 that had been sent to assist in the defense were relieved by IR 185 and returned to their company sector.

> 14 July. At 3 a.m. drum-fire again! After 15 minutes artificial fog rises up, the full moon in the grey overcast was a magical sight. 'Red Light balls high! 'The artillery is on alert and is employed instantaneously. Our men and a few machine guns fire slowly. After one and a half hours it becomes quiet. *Leutnant* Jakobsen was now in front. He says that the men make a magnificent impression: everyone at the parapet are in feverish expectation, with brilliant eyes, a dozen hand grenades alongside them for the reception of Tommy, with the only wish that he came! However he only comes on the left, throws bombs in the dugouts there, becomes engaged with the 185er in close fighting and thrown out by them after a bloody struggle. By us a falls a battle orderly, an excellent man. The 7/186 loses 2 dead, 5 wounded through a direct hit. The remains now amount to 160 men, of them 35 are sick. The wire obstacles were shredded again, an omen ... ... We have few reserves ... Yesterday we learned a bit about the last 2,000 captives from Verdun! [42]

The 2/185 became moved forward for the occupation of the *Türken Stellung* and *König Strasse* north of the *Privat Weg*, while the weakened 1/185 was taken back to Mouquet farm. In the evening the III/185 located in Ligny-Thilloy was moved forward and was positioned as follows: the 9/185 in the *Lemberg Stellung*, the battalion staff in *Feste Zollern*, the 10th, 11th (temporarily in Courcelette), 12/185 in the Second position *Süd IV* with Group Schwartz from RIR 15, one platoon of the 10/185 was later placed with the 5/27 in front of Pozières.

One of the participants in the fighting, *Leutnant* Markmann, sent a letter home in which he described the fighting by the barricades.

> Dear parents!
> As I now have some time, I want to write a short letter to you, of what we have undergone since Vouziers. We embarked early on Friday. The journey went via Hirson to Cambrai, from there after a short stay, to Fremicourt, east of Bapaume. Already soon after, the individual battalions became distributed in the northern sector, in order to reinforce the regiments of that place. The I and II Battalions became inserted on both sides of Beaumont, where we, in union with Württembergers, repulsed several mass attacks by the enemy, in the largest part in close combat. All of the troops of sector there behaved

superbly. No trench piece was lost. The losses of the English were horrendous, our own were very low. Here the Englishmen did not attack then again. After a few days would parts of both battalions, therefore our company, be thrown on the left wing of the line Ovillers-Thiepval. Therefore here, everything was held. Already across, on the left from us would be the Guard that held quite heroically, being repressed little by little (8-10 attacks a day). Also by us at least one attack almost daily became refused. The losses of the Englishmen were very severe, but ours were also. Horrible hand grenade fighting and close combat with spades, picks and daggers! Our people fought quite wonderfully against the superior strength. One man from my company, who stood directly in front of me, fought against seven Englishmen during the defense of the barricade, of which he killed four. I could only shoot down one, because I had enough to do. The two that remained of them, overpowered the hero and struck him dead. The one, which hit me on the head with a rifle butt (I had one of the new German steel helmets on that repeatedly saved my life) I ran at, sinking the dagger into his abdomen, the other fell from his own hand grenade that happily did not affect me. I recovered quickly. This most terrible attack had been refused, the Englishmen yielded back. However worse than all of this fighting, were the effects of all of the artillery and mine fire that were obvious in this battle. Three weeks as wandering lumps of clay. You could not conceive at all what that means. One's living flesh almost decayed from the muck and vermin. I don't want glory for myself, but Germany doesn't know what it has to thank to the fighters in the battle on the Somme. In the night from Thursday to Friday we were relieved. The rest of the regiment assembled by Bapaume, we in Biefvillers. Finally one could clean himself, others to put on clean laundry, the joy could not be described! One could sleep, even if it was also on straw. *Leutnant* Markmann. Walincourt 23 July 1916.[43]

The numerous British attacks against the defenders of Ovillers mentioned in Markmann's letter were being repulsed but with each attack came more losses. On 14 July heavy infantry fire had already started at 1 a.m., and towards dawn the enemy attacked by Ovillers. Masses of British infantry advanced through the wide hollow between Ovillers and the National road while using the protection offered by *Quergraben II* and *Quergraben III* to develop their lines and then attacked at several positions. The companies of RIR 15 had been reduced to barely 40 rifles. Still, rifle and machine gun fire and parties of individual hand grenade throwers prevented any enemy success. The attacking waves were able to approach to within 30 to 40 meters from the main defensive line despite the heavy fire but could go no further. Once the attacks had stopped, the enemy artillery fire fell continuously across the lines for the remainder of the day and the following day.

15 July

At 2.30 a.m. on 15 July Division Burkhardt began to take immediate measures to protect the left flank of the division following the receipt of a report about an enemy breakthrough between Bazentin le Petit and Longueval. At 5 a.m. IR 62 from the 12th Infantry Division, which was located in Irles, was alarmed and moved toward Martinpuich, between Courcelette and Le Sars. The 10th and 11/185 from the III/185 under *Major zur* Nedden which were positioned northeast of Courcelette, as well as the 2MG/8th Bavarian RIR were ordered into *Feste Zollern* and in the second line behind the left wing of the division.

The 12/185 was positioned in *Süd-IV* in the second line and the 9/185 was placed in the *Lemberg Stellung.*

While measures were being taken to bolster the increasingly vulnerable left flank in the Ovillers-Pozières line, the vicious close fighting by the *Granatloch* continued. At 5 a.m. several *Sturm Trupp* from the 7th and 9/185, reinforced with machine guns, *Flammenwerfer* and *pioniers*, attempted to capture the *Hindenburg Stellung*. After an initial success, the undertaking failed, reportedly due to a lack of cooperation between the infantry and *pionier* troops operating the *Flammenwerfer*. The problem apparently involved the *Flammenwerfer,* which had broken down soon after the start of the attack. The only success achieved from the undertaking was the destruction of a British trench block by the *Sturm Abteilung.*

An extremely fierce battle also began by a barricade occupied by men from IR 185. The trench garrison barely managed to hold out against repeated British advances but in the end still held the position. During the fighting *Leutnants der Reserve* Ficken, Ehrhardt, Sturzebecker (wounded) and *Vizefeldwebels* Reichmann and Ehlers (both killed), from IR 185, as well as the parts of the 9th, 10th and 11/*Garde Füsiliers* under *Leutnant der Reserve* Küsters were particularly singled out for their actions that day. When the fighting eventually died down, it was found that the losses to these companies were considerable.

With losses mounting, the available companies needed to be shifted from position to position in order to provide an adequate defense. In the afternoon the 7/185 was relieved by the 6/185 and then occupied the *Wundtwerk*. The 2/185 was moved forward into the *Lemberg Stellung*, the 4/185 was taken back to Mouquet farm. The 9/185, reinforced with one fourth of the 8/185, occupied *Kampf Graben* 2 in Sector C8, and part of the *Wundtwerk.*

In the morning of 15 July strong drum fire lay on Pozières that was followed by a large British attack against Bazentin le Petit Wood and the area between Ovillers and Pozières. The men of RIR 15 took some enjoyment watching how smoke began to pour out of British aircraft that had been caused by anti-aircraft machine gun fire. However, despite these successes there were always numerous enemy aircraft that quickly took their place.

It was not long before the British turned their attention back to Ovillers. At 3.45 a.m. strong enemy bombing parties advanced upon four locations in *Ovillers-Süd* following a short period of drum fire; they were all driven back. Then at 5 a.m. the 1st Dorsets from the 14th Brigade, 32nd Division, attacked the positions by Ovillers four times. Each time they were thrown back, in part following severe hand to hand fighting where losses were heavy on both sides.

There was further heavy fighting by Pozières in the night of 15 July where the II/27 was located. Constant heavy artillery fire followed almost constantly by enemy attacks was slowly eating away at the strength of the battalion. The positions occupied by IR 27 had not been developed and the men were unable to find any shelter against the high explosive and shrapnel shells. With each enemy attack, the number of defenders grew smaller.

The losses in the companies of the II/R77 and I/84 which had been inserted into the front line were just as heavy as those in the II/27. It was becoming evident that under the constant British shell and shrapnel fire the physical and spiritual attitude and the morale of the troops, who had held out under similar circumstances in the past, had finally broken. *Major* Otto, I/184, had serious doubts that his battalion could hold its position any further under such circumstances as his battalion now only numbered 300 men. The battalion staff now consisted of *Major* Otto, his adjutant, *Leutnant* Werner, and two other men. All of the other members of the staff of the I/184 were dead, buried or severely wounded. In spite of

Zur Erinnerung im hl. Gebete
an den tugendsamen Jüngling

Max Kerler

Soldat beim 8. bayr. Ref.-Inf.-Reg.,
Maschinengewehr-Kompagnie.

Geb. den 24. Juli 1895 in Hiltenfingen.
Gest. den Heldentod fürs Vaterland auf dem
Felde der Ehre am 15. Juli 1916.

Treu hast Du gekämpft fürs Vaterland,
Hast geopfert Dein junges Leben;
Und gibt auch die Welt Dir nur Undank als Lohn,
Gott wird ihn im Himmel Dir geben.
Nun ruhe sanft in fremder Erden,
Bis wir einst ewig mit Dir vereinigt werden.

R. I. P.

Druck von A. Barthlme, Schwabmünchen.

Max Kerler. (Author's collection)

the circumstances, the men were simply told they had to continue to occupy their positions and hold out.

The successful advances by the British along the left flank of the Thiepval Sector in the past two weeks had become a growing concern for the German commanders. The deeper the enemy penetrated into the German lines, the more vulnerable Thiepval became from being attacked in the rear.

The units that had fought in the Ovillers Sector had become worn down and in some cases almost completely destroyed. The Germans were still defending the area with makeshift units that had been assembled from several different divisions in accordance with the demands of the situation. There were no readily available reinforcements and the men still occupying the trenches and shell craters would simply have to wait until their relief arrived.

In the night an infantry mass storm took place. We now have 32 rifles in the trench because of bloody losses and sickness and no *Portepeeträger* as platoon leaders any more. The regular messages sent that we needed support continued to remain unanswered. The men's condition became grave. In part they lie there apathetically in the strongest drum fire. However the attacks stir them up. Firing standing upright, most of them from on the parapet, and mutually jeering and yelling to spur them on. All the more notable then is the relaxation on the next day. Because they were still exhausted from what they had done on the previous day, fewer stood at the parapet, unable to shoot, but willingly, to be there. The fighting capability of the 8th Company

Zur frommen Erinnerung

an unsern innigstgeliebten
Gatten und Vater
Wehrmann Georg Ritter
Res.-Inf.-Reg. 119, 7. Komp.
Geboren 11. Dezember 1885. Er starb
den Heldentod fürs Vaterland den
15. Juli 1916 bei Miraumont.

___

O, Gattin und Kind mein
Ich kehre nicht mehr zu Euch heim.
Der letzte Gedanke, letzte Blick,
Der eilte noch zu Euch zurück,
Als ich starb im Feindesland,
Reichte niemand mir die Hand,
Doch eh' mein Auge war gebrochen,
Sah ich schon den Himmel offen.

im heiligen Gebete

an unsern lieben Sohn und Bruder
Hornist Gefreiter
Wilhelm Ritter
Inf.-Reg. 122, 7. Komp.
Geboren 4. März 1895. Er starb den
Heldentod fürs Vaterland den
3. August 1916 bei Arleux.

___

Ich hab mein Blut, ich hab mein Leben
Fürs Vaterland dahin gegeben,
Ich hab mir nun den Sieg errungen
Denn Gott hat mich zu sich genommen!
Er tröst nun auch die lieben Meinen,
Die schmerzerfüllt um mich jetzt weinen!

___

Vater unser. Gegrüsset seist Du Maria.

Wehrmann Georg Ritter. Died from gas poisoning. (Author's collection)

was totally exhausted because of lack of food and rest at night. The enemy attempted an advance upon the 6th Company through the *Kabel Graben*. He is driven back also here and pursued. In the *Kabel Graben* alone two officers and 14 dead Englishmen were counted. 15 July. Still in the night the *Schwarzwald Graben* becomes closed off through a barricade in the vicinity of *Kabel Graben*. In the early morning hours the enemy has already approached and was refused by the 8th Company with hand grenades. He leaves behind here one officer, 15 men dead, two *Musketen*, 20 rifles and much ammunition. Stronger fire then lies on the 7th and 8th Companies.[44]

It was very hard for us to succeed in repulsing the attack in the night to the 16th up to the end. It was the strongest of all. Only through shifting by individuals to many different positions and work of the greatest exertion of the last men who were battle capable did it succeed. However, it succeeds completely. The foreground is scattered with corpses. The enemy was able to drag the wounded into the hollow. One prisoner from the 10th Cheshire Regiment carried upside down bullets on him.[45] At dawn, an attack the left wing of the 6th Company became taken under heavy fire. The machine gun moved forward doesn't fire, because the leader and crew had fallen. Meanwhile it becomes active again at the barricade. It had been in the last two days since a mine thrower was installed opposite the barricade that pelted us with medium mines the day over and during the night before the attack. During the day the men succeed in avoiding them; the night brought new losses. Today he covered the entire length of the trench with fire, while we are at repair work. There, drum fire with mines began at noon. 6, 7 mine throwers were now observed. In minutes the trench was leveled, the barricade swept away and disappeared, the depot with the last hand grenades, with light and *Musketen* ammunition flies into the air. With still one *Unteroffizier* and three men, who had endured at the barricade to the last, I moved back to the right to the 1st Company *Garde Füsiliers* that a few days before relieved the 4th Company IR 183 and who already had to evacuate 100 meters of their trench. At the moment the mine fire grew silent the enemy pushed forward and penetrated through the *Friedhof Graben* up against to the *Haug Graben*. Too few men are available for an immediate counterattack. Also they are too weak. Also no hand grenades. Also the lost trench was immediately covered with machine guns, so that the dashing bombing party of *Chevauxleger* could not even think about advancing. With the 1st Company *Garde Füsiliers* a barricade was built, a position was laid out and occupied. Reinforcements from RIR 77 were pushed into different companies of the *Garde Füsiliers*. The connection with the 8th Company was lost. In the night it was good to observe how the Englishmen joined together northeast of the village behind the northeastern edge through the *Kabel Graben* and shot up Q III. After the bloody losses came the sick, initially feet, then stomach and intestinal illnesses. Many have blood in their stool. Both *Musketen* that had proven to be so good in the first night, broke down in the second, went back in the third, because the men, according to declarations of the leaders, could no longer, turn out. There the order to move out to Courcelette comes towards 10 o'clock. This command came too late!! *Oberstleutnant* Graf von der Schulenberg, the returning commander of the *Garde Füsilier* Regiment has his work cut out for him, because he considers the situation in the projecting angle of Ovillers to be untenable. There, in Ovillers, fighting in part for 13 days was the I and II/*Garde Füsiliers*, parts of Regiments 183 and 184, the 8th Bavarian RIR, the 6/*Pionier* Battalion 13 and the 3/*Chevauxleger* 5, finally our three companies. All were spent. There was no warm food there, only bread and cold canned meat. Already on the 10th the last well at the northeastern edge was destroyed. So water and coffee was sent for from behind that only rarely succeeded in making it and also then only under heavy losses. Therefore the fighters suffered horribly under hunger and thirst. *Oberstleutnant* von Stosch, RIR 15.[46]

For the survivors of IR 190, the regiment that had originally relived RIR 110 in La Boisselle, the prospect of being relieved came true during the night of 15 July when the regiment moved to the rear by Bertincourt and Vélu. During the 14 days the regiment had fought on the Somme it had suffered losses of 10 officers, 190 Other Ranks killed, 20 officers, 798 Other Ranks wounded and 16 officers, 914 Other Ranks missing, a total of 46 officers and 1,902 Other Ranks, or two thirds of the regiment.

16 July
The fighting by Ovillers continued unabated on 16 July the following day, it was also the day that the rest of Ovillers was lost to the enemy after a valiant fight by the *Garde Füsiliers*. As a result of their impressive endurance, the defenders of Ovillers from RIR 15 and the *Garde Füsilier* Regiment that were taken prisoner were given military honors by the British as they were being led away to captivity, not something often seen in this battle or in the

war for that fact.

The strength of our 6th Company had weakened: At daybreak of the 16th the sentries at the *Kabel Graben* barricade were pressed back. Reinforcements expelled the enemy, who lost eight dead and one prisoner. About 11 in the evening one more attack finally becomes refused. Then the survivors assembled together on the left. A rescue attempt by the 4/R77 from the direction of artillery position 743 failed. The enemy floods through the small Groups and the corpse filled trench between the 8th and 6th Companies. Quite correctly, *Major* Kiesel says that our own heroic spirit and unswerving will for victory has given a breath to his II Battalion: The breakthrough could be detained no longer, because no more men were available. The battle strength of the three companies amounted to only 65 men! And moreover fate also approached here from the right, from the west. Here the enemy penetrated over the corpses of the 5th Company of the *Garde Füsiliers* between the *Leichen* and *Baum* saps and already stand in the rear of the of our 7th Company and subsequent 2/*Garde Füsiliers*, 2/R77 and 1/*Garde Füsiliers*, Ovillers was Hell for days. So Ovillers with the survivors of four companies are lost. Favored by misty weather, but also as a price for that trusted bravery the enemy only timidly had learned to feel their way forward, reached the ruins in the small switch line position on both sides behind artillery positions 743 and 763 that had the connection to our III Battalion and in which are fresher troops. At 2.30 this movement was executed. At 3.00 in the afternoon our 6th Company also receives instructions to take evasive action in the second position by *Feste Zollern*. Still in the course of the evening a few men of the 7th and 8th Company find themselves here. The enemy is able to state, says *Major* Kiesel, approximately 40-50 men and two machine guns have fallen into their hands. The 7th and 8th Companies have afforded splendid service, inflicted the heaviest losses to the enemy – one estimates his dead at 500 – and that they were released from their long duty, to hold Ovillers up to the very last, six days. His *Excellenz. Frhr.* von Süsskind has written the words among the account of *Leutnant* Meyerhof: With admiration to acknowledge of the persistent bravery the cheerful sacrifice of the 7th Company. *Generalmajor* Burkhardt, the commander of the Bavarian 10 Infantry Division, who since the 8th commanded the sector Ovillers-Pozières, concluded his report to the Army Group of who was well known by us since Hulluch, General Sixt von Armin: I bow before the tenacious bravery and the self-sacrifice of the heroes of Ovillers. The history of the war hands them the deserved laurels. RIR 15 [47]

The I/*Garde Füsiliers* came back with 175 men, the II/*Garde Füsiliers* with 160 men; the II/R15 (without the 5th Company) came back with 65 men. 80 severely wounded men had remained behind in Ovillers with a stretcher bearer. 'According to later reports they became well provided by English doctors.' We know that the British in front of the 124 prisoners from the *Garde Füsiliers* and RIR 15 presented their rifles. They were also not a little impressed with the proud manner, with which *Hauptmann* Settekorn assessed the enemy, the monocle in his eye, the gaze rigid and directed straight out. The deepest sense of this heroism might be understood by our grandsons: Rougher to them than the enemy! Only through pride and stronger will is one able to break the will of the enemy, who have killed our dearest comrades! RIR 15 [48]

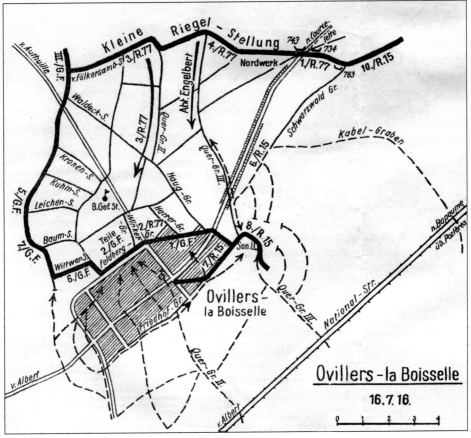

Ovillers-la Boiselle 16.7.1916

The praise given to the defenders of Ovillers by the enemy was considered to be proof of the determination and bravery of the small garrison who had held out far longer than had been expected. Apparently this news spread across the planet and was reported in the foreign press of numerous countries:

> Sir Douglas Haig said on the evening of the 17th: Important successes achieved. On our left flank we took in Ovillers La Boisselle, where since 7th July continuous close combat was found, the extant that remained of the enemy (!) was two officers and 124 men of the Guard, which formed the remains of the brave garrison. RIR 15 [49]

While the heavy fighting continued by Ovillers and Pozières there was little going on by Thiepval between 16 and 21 July. There were no enemy attacks; the artillery fire had died down and all that occurred was an occasional sentry skirmish. With the reduction in fighting by Thiepval there was an opportunity to reorganize the overall defenses in consideration of the loss of Ovillers. On this day, three fourths of the 9/185 was taken back to Mouquet farm. The 11th and 12/185 occupied the *Kleine Riegelstellung* north of Ovillers and were subordinate to the *Garde Füsilier* Regiment This position became the new front line.

17 July

17 July was a quiet day in the Thiepval Sector with the exception of one small incident that occurred near the Ancre. A small British raiding party had attacked the right wing of the 1/8th Bavarian RIR. The enemy had made some progress during the attack but was eventually stopped when additional reinforcements arrived to assist the Bavarian company. As a result of this minor action, one man was singled out for his bravery during the fighting and was appropriately rewarded.

> Eberhardt, Philipp, *Unteroffizier der Reserve*, 4th Company, 8th Bavarian RIR, born 11 February 1888 at Medard (Prussia). Awarded with the Silver medal for bravery:
> When on 17 July the British by Thiepval at that Ancre looked to advance against the right wing of the 1st Company, Eberhardt with his Group threw themselves against them and erected a sandbag barrier in the course of the fighting, from where he was able to refuse further attacks by the enemy with hand grenades. [50]

18 July

Reorganization of the different units holding the Thiepval Sector continued on 18 July. The 9th and 12/R15 as well as the 3rd and 4/186 separated from the 8th Bavarian RIR on 18 July and returned to their units. The Bavarians expressed their gratitude to their departing comrades for all of their help in the heavy days of fighting. The gaps created in the defenses in the *Hindenburg Stellung* with the loss of these companies were made up when the 9/8th Bavarian RIR took over the positions after a few days of rest in Warlencourt. *Hauptmann* Schmidt, the leader of the 8/8th *Bavarian* RIR was appointed as the commander of the III Battalion in place of the fallen *Major* Beyerköhler.

The remnants of the II/R15 were assembled and accommodated in the Courcelette-Pys sunken road on 18 July. The survivors of the II Battalion then moved to Ligny-Thilloy during the night, under cover of darkness. The staff, the 6th and 7/R15 were accommodated in Bihucourt, with the 5/R15 in Béhagnies, the 8/R15 in Sapignies. Now a determination could be made of the heavy losses suffered by the II/R15 in the recent fighting. The II Battalion still possessed the battle strength of 14 officers and 416 men. However, the II Battalion had altogether lost 8 officers and 613 men, of which 126 were killed, 367 wounded and 128 were missing.

At 1 a.m. the staff I, 1st, 3rd, 4th and 3/4 of the 9/185 became relieved by the 3rd and 4/186. Later, the staff of the III/185 moved to Mouquet farm. More troops from the 2nd Guard Reserve Division were moving down to the Thiepval Sector. RIR 91, without the I/R91 was transferred to Division Burkhardt on 16 July to be used to gradually relieve the jaded troops in the sector of the *Garde Füsilier* Regiment. Because of the arrival of this new regiment, the I/R77 became replaced in the night of 17/18 July in the *Kleine Riegelstellung* north of Ovillers by the 10th and 11/R91 along with eight machine guns. The 12th and 9/R91 were held back by Mouquet farm and in the *Stockacher Graben* as a reserve. The remnants of the I and II/*Garde Füsiliers* went back to Warlencourt, while the remnants of the I/R77 were in reserve trenches by Courcelette.

Given the numbers of men lost in the constant fighting, the overall mood of many of the defenders was poor. However, the morale of the defenders was raised when reports

Die Kämpfe um Thiepval.
Jm Zollerngraben, kurze Ruhe nach schwerem Kampf.

A short rest in the *Zollern Graben* after heavy fighting. (Author's collection)

circulated about statements made from some of the numerous enemy prisoners that had been captured in the last few weeks of fighting. The prisoners spoke of their huge losses, the bravery of their officers, but also of their tactical incompetence. They admired the bravery of the Germans who stood openly on the parapet with rifles and hand grenades refusing the attacks. One prisoner mentioned that he and his comrades had been told they would only find corpses in the 1st and 2nd trenches and further behind only weak opposition.

Both officers and Other Ranks were full of praise and gratitude for the kind treatment they had received after their capture, also for the compassionate treatment of their wounded and the food and water provided to all. Apparently, this reception had many of them perplexed; their newspapers had led them to expect the direct opposite. The compassionate treatment of enemy prisoners was no surprise to the men defending the Thiepval Sector, especially with respect to the wounded. It was something that they would have done under any circumstances.

While it was basically quiet by Thiepval, the attacks by the enemy against the sector south of the 10th Bavarian Infantry Division were repeated daily with increasingly larger masses of troops following the heaviest artillery preparation fire. These attacks only increased concern for the left flank of the division; therefore the reserves were ordered to develop a new trench from the *Schwaben Graben* to the *Zollern Graben* as a *Riegel Stellung*.

At 2 a.m. on 18 July a British attack took place against the southwest corner of Pozières. At most locations, the enemy had been repulsed before reaching the German lines. The only enemy success was in a small portion of a trench in front of the *Schwarzwald Graben* where approximately 80 British soldiers had become firmly seated. This small breach of the defensive line was quickly eliminated through a counterattack by *Leutnant* Petersen, 10/R15, with a few of his men through two strong counter thrusts. At 4 a.m. strong enemy reconnaissance detachments coming from Ovillers attacked the left wing of the III/*Garde Füsiliers* as well as the 11th and 12/185; it was reported that the enemy detachment was easily refused.

19 July

Significant changes were made in the army leadership once again on 19 July. The sector of the former 2nd Army had become too large and could no longer manage the battle from one command position. Therefore on 19 July a new First Army was created out of the northern half of the former 2nd Army. This was taken on as commander-in-chief by the hitherto existing commander-in-chief of the 2nd Army, *General der Infanterie* Fritz von Below, his Chief of the General-Staff would be *Oberst* von Lossberg, the former Chief of Staff of the XIII Army Corps.

The southern part south of the Somme, respectively the *Colognebachs* moved under the new 2nd Army, commanded by *General der Artillerie* von Gallwitz. Together, both the 1st and 2nd Armies were under the commander-in-chief of Army Group Gallwitz with the headquarters in St. Quentin.

This new organization of the higher commands had initially proven to work well; however, it was only to last slightly more than one month. The dissolution of the new command structure took place on 25 August, in part influenced by the many personal differences between the army commanders. Afterward General von Below remained the Army Commander-in-chief for the 26th Reserve Division, for which little had changed since the start of the battle because of the existing defensive situation. One point that General von Below wanted to make sure everyone in the army understood was his order prohibiting the voluntary evacuation of positions and that every leader was made responsible that every man in the army understood and obeyed this order.

With the arrival of fresh troops, the relief of the tattered front line units continued. In the morning the 11th and 12/185 were relieved by the II/R91; the staff of the III/185 moved back later in the afternoon. The 6th and one fourth of the 9/185 were relieved in the evening by the 4/186. The 7th and 8/186 by Thiepval were relieved in the night from 20/21 July by IR 22. The individual Groups from the two companies assembled in Pys and after being provided with plentiful food and drink, were marched further to Biefvillers, where they were given poor accommodations according to the men.

20 July

There were new enemy attacks against the line Martinpuich – Foureaux Wald – Delville Wald northeastern Longueval – Guillemont on 20 July. Up to 20 July the III/R15 had been working on the rearward positions. At midday this day battalion received orders, with the assigned Machine Gun *Ersatz* Company to be ready to provide protection at positions northeast of Irles. Part of the battalion moved forward in the night for the occupation of the position 300 meters south of Pys, while one company was sent to *Feste Zollern* for entrenching under the control of *Major* Glette, commander of the III/69.

The short period of time IR 180 had been allowed to rest and refit behind the front ended on 20 July. Orders had arrived that the regiment was being moved forward to the front lines once more.

21 July

RIR 99, which had been withdrawn from the front between 4 and 6 July, became moved forward once more on 12 July. The understrength regiment was positioned by Flers where it came under the command of the 3rd Guard Infantry Division. RIR 99 was still not in any shape to become involved in heavy fighting but it was needed to occupy the Flers and Foureaux *Riegels*. The regiment became shattered in the constant shell fire on this position and on 21 July, with the exception of the IV/R99, which had become the division reserve of the 26th Reserve Division in Grévillers, the regiment was withdrawn to Inchy-Sains lez Marquion. From there it was made available the 26th Reserve Division again as soon as 28 July, when it would became used to garrison the rear support positions on the southern side of the Ancre.

The relief that had been dangling in front of the men's eyes in the II/R15 for the past few days had disappeared. Instead, at 12.30 a.m. on 21 July orders arrived that the battalion would immediately move via the *Köhler Pfad* to the *Hessen Graben*. Then, at 1.30 a.m. the order to be ready to march became rescinded. Then a new order arrived at 2.40 a.m.: 'Leaders expected at the exit of Miraumont to Pozières!' Apparently the British had penetrated the German positions by RIR 28 and were to be thrown out again in a counterattack. At 3.15 a.m. the II/R15 was at the exit to Miraumont where the battalion finally received orders to march via the *Hessen Graben* and *Bulgaren Graben* to the *Wundtwerk*. *Major* Kiesel had proceeded in advance with his staff in order to receive instructions in *Feste Staufen*.

Major Kiesel received his orders: 'The 8th and 5/R28 are to be relieved in the *Hindenburg Stellung*. The gap between the 5th and 2/R28 that has emerged through the retreat of the 9th Company, is to be closed through a further company. The last company comes into the *Hohenzollern Stellung*.'

The II/R15 did not reach the *Wundtwerk* until daylight where it was advised by the commander of the II/R28 that any relief during daylight was impossible; 'it had the same meaning as suicide.' However, the commander of RIR 28, knowing what he asked was tantamount to madness, urged that an attempt be made to reinforce the 5/R28 and to close an existing gap by this company. Following this request, the 6/R15 became accommodated in the *Hohenzollern Stellung*, the 8/R15 in Thiepval. The attempt to relieve the 5/R28 was made and failed as expected, not as a result of enemy fire, but rather because the sector held by the 5/R28 was already occupied by the British. The 5/R15 paid a high price for this attempt, losing the company leader, *Leutnant* Schürmann, one additional officer, 3 *Vizefeldwebel* and 30 men. The 7th and 8/R15 had followed the 5th Coy in support, taking intervals while advancing because the open terrain was obstructed through artillery and machine gun fire. These companies were to be accommodated in the sector of the 3rd and 4/R28.

Major Kiesel gave orders in the *Wundtwerk*: 'The 5th Coy is to fill the gap existing on the left of the 5/R28. The both following companies would relieve the 5th and 8/28. The last company of the II Battalion remained in my possession in the *Wundtwerk*.'

There, as the approach route to the position of the II/28 only existed out of craters, my 5th Company, proceeding in broad daylight, was covered with heavy caliber shells by the enemy and torn apart. Only a part of the 1st platoon under *Leutnant* Müller and I arrived in the front. It proved impossible to determine the width of the gap by day. Furthermore we had to discover also that unfortunately the rest of the 5th and 8/28 had lost the connection to the right. If the runners with the corresponding message reached here from each of the Battalions, I know not.

In the meantime the few men become distributed in the line. In the course of the early afternoon the enemy attacked after short, but very severe drum fire on the thin line. He immediately penetrated by the 8/R28 out of a sap head only 10 meters distant. *Leutnant* Müller and I became severely wounded. Heavy losses occurred through flanking machine guns. The survivors finally ended up in captivity.

Meanwhile, in the communication trench the leader of the 3rd platoon, *Leutnant* Kölin, fell out through being wounded. *Vizefeldwebel* Lückebergfeld and another, whose name escapes me, attempted to establish the connection to the front and ended up in captivity. From the 1st platoon *Vizefeldwebel* Rübsamen also ended up in captivity. So the 5th Coy, after *Feldwebel Leutnant* Brenner had also already fallen out, lost on this one day all *Portepeeträger*.[51]

Our II Battalion lost by this adventure the first officer that had come to the battalion, *Leutnant* Rütgers, 2 *Unteroffiziere* and 29 men. Furthermore would *Leutnants* Engelken and Kölln, 9 *Unteroffiziere* and 112 men become wounded and finally *Leutnants* Schürmann and Müller, 7 *Unteroffiziere* and 36 men were missing. That is 5 officers and 195 *Unteroffiziere* and men lost in total. With it the losses of the II/R15 since the beginning of the battle climbed to 15 officers and 806 Other Ranks, virtually the entire combat strength of the battalion. *Leutnant* Schürmann RIR 15. [52]

It was evident that all further troop movements would have to take place at night. At 7 p.m. the brigade order went out that the staff and 2/R86 were placed in possession of RIR 15 for the relief of the I/R86. With this it became agreed with the I/R86 that the 6th and 8/R15 should be inserted at 12.30 at night on 22 July. These two companies did not reach their goal until after a journey of 5 and 7 hours respectively because the guides ended up being lost after becoming wounded. Once found, the position existed only out of shell craters. There were two dugouts on the right for the 8/R15 that could hold about 80 men. On the right by the 6/R15 there was only one dugout available, which could hold 60 men.

The position was a shambles, all wire obstacles were missing. While the connection on the right to the 2/R28 was successfully established, on the left was a gap 300 meters wide that remained unoccupied during the day because of strong enemy fire. Further on the right it appeared that RIR 28 apparently no longer held the *Hindenburg Stellung* and that the 3rd and 4/R86, consisted of only 35 to 40 rifles. When the two companies from RIR 86 reported that they were no longer capable of fighting the men were placed in the old medical dugout, in which the 2nd platoon of the 8/R15 also found shelter.

Mulde Graben and *Daniels Graben* were no longer recognizable and were useless as communication trenches. Since it was impossible to maintain or establish a telephone connection with the rear a relay post consisting of 1 *Unteroffizier* and 8 men was established. The runners performed quite well under the difficult circumstances but all too often the men never made it to the rear or if they did, were unable to return with new orders. Carrying parties also suffered in the heavy enemy fire. Of 60 carriers from the I/R86 only 13 arrived at the front line in the night of 22/23 July; soon they were all missing.

Confusion over the situation at the front line reigned on 21 July. Most orders that were issued were just as quickly rescinded; a pattern that was repeated numerous times. Finally, when one order was given at 7.30 p.m. the companies of the III/R15 moved forward via

Feste Zollern into the *Hessen Graben*. The machine guns assigned to the battalion followed on the next day. However, by the early morning, at 2 a.m., the situation at the front was already different again.

The alarm that had been expected for a long time had arrived. The Battalion assembled in a sunken road at Grévillers, where the packs remained behind under guard. At 3.00 p.m. we moved to the front, very cautiously because of the poor visibility from the weather. Our 10th wound its way forward in Groups. In front of Irles the companies assembled again at the hillsides of a hollow and waited for the night to start. At 9.00 o'clock we were entrenching on the road to Mouquet farm. That said enough! There was bitter fighting at the farm in the last days. Still our brave men held. One could read about it in every army report. The leaders came to Pys. Losses occurred already in the 3rd position. Finally we reached our own sector. How the trench looked! Crater next to crater. Every moment we bumped upon dead: Food haulers or material bearers that had been caught at night. 'Chaps! Make sure that you get into the earth, before the shooting begins!' In whatever you could create there. Towards morning our work place was under drum fire. Even *Leutnant* Hepp was fatally wounded coming to the company. I bound his upper arm up and had him carried back. He died in Essen. My platoon lost 16 men, of which two were dead. On the evening of the 21st powerful shooting began: Major attack by Thiepval! The enemy has success. We should throw him back. In the succession of the 9th, 10th, 11th, 12th we receive hand grenades and ammunition in the *Stahl Mulde*. Then forward until in a hollow in front of Grandcourt, out of which the mortars strike at the farm. The connection to the 9th was torn away. Fortunately it acquired a battery. Connection with the battalion in Pys. New leaders became promised. The 11th and 12th arrived. We finally got further to *Feste Schwaben*. Many drops of perspiration trickled down. A sector is assigned to us. However, we have hardly become distributed and assigned sentries, when a runner calls the company leaders to the front. *Leutnant* Ohlberger and I, have to report to *Major* Castenholz in *Thiepval-Süd*. Now we know what caused the delay!

Tommy controls the tempo because he holds all roads under fire. The roads are dreadful. Of trenches often no trace. Then through the Hell of Thiepval. There is an explosion and the falling and noise of tree trunks and the last wall remnants. Is there anything spookier than a walk at the night through a shot up village? *Leutnant* Loof gets a bullet in the back. 4.00 a.m. I am in the Battle headquarters of the I/R28. A trench 250 meters in length was lost, an immediate counterattack follows. 'Do you have any more questions?' *Major* Castenholz turns to us. 'A counterattack must be considered to be hopeless. After all, we do not know the terrain.' The *Major* wants to explain it to me on the map. I said: 'The trench no longer exists, and in the dark the map is of no use.' 'Then I will give you my orderly officer.' However, I am fully responsible that the undertaking is still executed before daybreak. Before the companies learn of this information. Their attack would be supported through flanking fire. We go. The orderly officer also has no idea of the terrain. 'I only came into the position yesterday ... however, if you proceed in a southeastern direction, you will hit the relevant trench ... .' He could not give any better clues. It becomes brighter and brighter. If it does not take place during darkness, we are lost. The *Major* sends the message again, I should begin immediately. I divide [my men] into three waves for the advance, with protection to the right. The 9th is on the left. Now with the compass in hand and come on! Thank God the artillery fire is tolerable. Seemingly the enemy suspects nothing. 5 o'clock. The morning fog becomes our ally. Slowly and surely we push forth. The enemy should still be 500 meters distant, uphill. There on the hill a strong position is revealed to our gaze. There he must sit! Hand grenade salvos! Our protection troops have contact. Quickly I let the waves close up and lay down on the hillside. Then I hurry to those in the fighting. However what is this? They are Germans in the trench! They have considered us to be Tommies and received us accordingly. Unfortunately it has produced wounded on both sides. We thrust on a sap, while the enemy sits in a trench on the right. I let them swarm out on the right. In front the British have their machine guns ready to fire, the first hand grenades fly at them in the face! A short flicker and Tack-tack. 30 captives are ours. Whoever doesn't yield or hurries to save himself, is dealt with. We smoked the dugouts out with their gas bombs. At 9.00 o'clock I can fire off three yellow light balls: 'Goal reached!' We have many losses to mourn. *Leutnant* Zech is wounded. The brave Ohlberger has a stomach shot and died. However the hardest part should still come. The fog has lifted. The pilots are nearby. Then the enemy opened a raging fire. Also mines from the smallest up to largest caliber rained down. The hurricane became always wilder. We fight off three counter thrusts. Then the fire begins anew. Furthermore rifle grenades directed at us cause great mischief. The number of fighters shrinks together from 200 to 50. And it is only midday. After I allowed our old position to be blocked off through three barricades, I evacuate the largest part of the captured trench. I send the *Major* a message and request close combat means and water. At night the answer comes: '*Leutnant* Lindau will reinforce!'[54]

22 July

After being alerted, IR 180 finally received instructions on 22 July that the regiment would take over the sector between the Ancre by St. Pierre-Divion up to and including Thiepval. This task of holding this critical sector was becoming increasingly difficult due to the British gains to the south of Thiepval. Holding the Thiepval Sector had become regarded by the regiment as a matter of honor. IR 180 had captured the position in September 1914 and had fought in and around the village nearly two years. In the opinion of General von Soden, IR 180 was a proven regiment and would perform this important duty to the end.

On 22 July I received the news that the regiment would probably be put in to the sector south of the Ancre – right wing the Ancre, left wing Thiepval. That is the sector north of Ovillers and the same that the regiment snatched from the French late in the year 1914 and had then developed for defense. The possession of Thiepval was of the greatest importance for the Englishmen, and one had to safely calculate that they would utilize all of their efforts to obtain this sector in their hands. An enormously serious task stood before the regiment that every individual in the regiment was aware of; however nonetheless, everyone was firmly determined, now as at Ovillers, to endure unwavering and defend the sector, so long as this was humanly possible. This sector from the right wing of the Ancre until Thiepval, the latter exclusive, was occupied by the 8th Bavarian RIR and Thiepval was occupied by parts of RIR 22. IR 180. [54]

The inexorable British advance deeper into the German lines south of Thiepval continued. The preparations made by the enemy for the attack against Pozières offered a particularly gruesome sight in the night from 22 to 23 July as the full weight of the enemy artillery pulverized what little remained of the village and surrounding terrain. The shells could be observed falling upon the village from the arc caused by the burning fuzes and the never ending rumble filled the air from the huge fountains of earth that were thrown up by the heavy shells while the skies were filled with the small clouds of exploding shrapnel shells. Little by little the entire village came under the control of the enemy.

Along with the capture of Pozières the enemy continued to make headway in the *Gierichweg* and *Bayern Riegel*, and other positions located on the left flank of the new regimental sector. Mingled in with the discouraging reports of the enemy advance on the left wing of the 8th Bavarian RIR there was also joyful news. A message was delivered to the Bavarians by an orderly officer from IR 180 on the evening of 22 July: 'His regiment would begin the replacement of ours tomorrow evening.'

In the late evening of 21 July the men of IR 185 also received some very welcome news. The infantry and regimental staff were to become relieved by RIR 22. The infantry and machine gun sections were relieved from their positions between 21 and 23 July and arrived at Vélu after first being accommodated in intermediate quarters in Ligny-Thilloy, Flesquieres and Esnes. The regiment was then moved further to the rear for a well-deserved rest.

On 23 July the 117th Infantry Division under *General der Infanterie* Kuntze took over control of the sector of the 10th Bavarian Infantry Division with the exception of Sectors C1 up to C6, which had come under the control of the 26th Reserve Division once again. On 23 July the official order to assume control over the Thiepval Sector arrived at the headquarters of IR 180. As the entire sector had a frontage of at least 2,500 meters, all three battalions of the regiment would have to be put into the front line to ensure it was properly defended.

While the Thiepval Sector was well known to many of the officers and men in IR 180 from late 1914, much had changed since those early days. There was ample evidence of the intensity of the fighting that had raged there since the beginning of July along the route to the battle headquarters that moved through Miraumont. Most of the buildings in the once bucolic village had been destroyed or badly damaged. There was a large gaping hole in the roof of the church where a direct hit by a British shell had almost completely destroyed the interior of the structure.

There were only a few houses that had remained relatively intact and did not reflect massive structural damage. The home of Notary Turlot, where the officers of the regiment had once been quartered was a ruined and desolate place. In addition to scattered bodies of soldiers who had been caught by the enemy fire there were also many of the owners of the houses, who lay buried under the ruins of their homes. Notary Turlot was among the unfortunate villagers whose body lay in his cellar, buried by the first shell that struck his home. Grandcourt looked even worse than Miraumont with evidence of the destructive enemy shelling evident everywhere one looked. The doctor and his staff were left behind in Grandcourt when the regiment took over the Thiepval Sector. His task was to locate a suitable dugout that could accommodate his staff and equipment. This dugout would then be the collection point for wounded which were expected to be received in large numbers before too long.

The neighboring village Ovillers had fallen into enemy hands weeks earlier; because it had been considered untenable following the enemy advance east of the Albert-Bapaume National road. This was a rather 'generous' explanation. Ovillers had fallen because the men assigned to hold the village had simply been overwhelmed by superior enemy forces.

As each part of the old German front line fell into enemy hands, the neighboring sectors became increasingly vulnerable to enemy advances from the front as well as the flank at the same time. The projecting corner between Ovillers and Thiepval, the *Granatloch*, which had threatened the right wing of IR 180 when occupying Ovillers, now, threatened the left wing of the regiment holding Thiepval.

24 July

In the sector north of the Ancre the 5th, 6th and *Pionier* Coy/186 became relieved in the night from 23/24 July from the positions by RIR 119 and arrived in Le Cateau on 26 July. Even in a sector that saw no heavy fighting the losses in the three companies of IR 186 proved to be fairly high, mainly due to the constant shell and mine fire. Between 1 and 24 July the companies had suffered losses of 24 killed, 104 wounded, of which 14 men had remained with the regiment, and 2 men missing.

The commander of Württemberg RIR 119 sent the following correspondence to the commander of IR 186 on 24 July:

> I speak of my warmest thanks to IR 186 for the brave, conscientious attitude by the leaders and Other Ranks of the parts of IR 186 which were placed in the area of the regiment, and for all of the excellent support of the regiment afforded by them in the Sector *Beaumont-Nord* and *Beaumont-Süd*. *Frhr*. von Ziegesar, *Oberst*. [55]

For many of the regiments that were thrown into the fighting in early July, the time was rapidly approaching where they would finally be relieved from the front line and allowed a period of rest and recuperation. For the men of RIR 15 who had been fighting almost continuously since 1 July, this time had not arrived soon enough.

The units from RIR 15 holding positions near Mouquet Farm lay scattered throughout the terrain in sectors far too large for a single company. In part, this prevented too many men from becoming casualties in the constant British artillery fire because of the huge spaces between each man. However, it also meant that if the enemy made a concerted attack in this sector, he would probably succeed. The 6/R15 was scheduled for relief in the night of 24/25 July. While waiting for their replacements, the men of the 6/R15 could observe the enemy advance on Mouquet farm, but did not become directly involved in the attacks. However, the 8/R15 had been less fortunate and had been attacked almost on a daily basis.

Enemy hand grenade attacks made by strong patrols were almost a daily routine, all of which were repulsed. Seemingly the hand grenade attacks were only aimed at forcing the garrison to occupy the trenches and to tempt the reserves forward, so that they could all be annihilated with shell fire. Within moments of the last shell falling in the newest assault, the enemy attacked the front from the *Lemberg Stellung* up to the 8/R15. This attack also failed in the heavy infantry and machine gun fire of the defenders.

From 3.30 to 4.30 a.m. on 24 July the British directed well-aimed fire on the tunnel entrances by Mouquet Farm followed by several waves of infantry which surged forward against the German trenches. The British were able to penetrate the line held by the 8/R15 until a short round from the German guns struck a sap head, allowing the enemy infantry to enter the nearby trench. Nevertheless, after a vicious fight the enemy was repulsed along the entire line, and the attackers disappeared into the numerous shell craters and waited for night before crawling back to the British trenches.

The 2/R15 that was located in the *Hessen Graben* by Mouquet Farm was finally relieved and the men were quite pleased to leave Thiepval far behind. For other companies in the regiment the time had still not come. The 1/R15 became sent forward once more and established a connection on the left to the 8/R15; however the right wing had no connecting troops and hung in the air.

Then finally, relief! In the night the II/*Garde* Grenadier Regiment 5 arrived and took over the positions once held by the men of RIR 15. The companies were relieved in part through the badly damaged trenches, in part over open fields. While the relief took place enemy barrage fire began, which caused heavy losses to the fresh *Garde* Companies. Despite the intense shelling the relief was successful, with each company leaving behind one officer and one *Unteroffizier* and 6 men to act as guides and to introduce the Grenadiers to the sector. The guides were assembled at the exit of Miraumont which led to Irles, where the field kitchens and wagons carrying the knapsacks had been ordered to assemble. At 11 p.m. RIR 15 moved to Avesnes by Bapaume, then motor lorries brought the men to Moeuvres, and Boursies, where excellent provisions were provided for them.

> The Supply Officer had learned of the large numbers approaching from the Town Major's office. However, he had the orders from the Corps Headquarters that only the best should be provided for the troops coming out of the abrasive fighting. The men of the columns moved into the modest barns and left their spacious housing for the front fighters. Officers and Other Ranks had grateful feelings for this order and viewed it as an acknowledgment of their performance.[56]

While it is easy to write that one regiment relieved another or that individual battalions or companies were moved from one sector to another, the reality of the situation requires a more realistic description. In the example of when the 5th and 7/R15 had relieved the 5th, 9th and 1/R28 in the *Hindenburg Stellung* the official account was:

> They attempted to relieve the 5th and 9/R28 at the fall of darkness. The execution was however impossible, because that sector was already strongly occupied by the British with infantry and machine guns! [57]

The senior leadership had misjudged the effect of modern weapons and the massive enemy firepower directed on the troops being relieved; in this instance the men from RIR 28. The army commanders continued to demand that untenable sections of trench be held, without truly understanding what the men were experiencing. In this case, the men of RIR 28 had already taken action on their own initiative: the last of the men had silently evacuated the position before the relief had arrived without reporting this to higher authorities.

It was also often very possible that no more men existed to make such a report. It was even quite common that the company leaders had no idea where they were actually located in the field of craters where the positions were so badly damaged and the ground so physically changed that no one knew anymore where he was. Also, no one possessed maps so that none could fall into the enemy hands.

Sometimes the message of the loss of a few thousand craters was omitted – out of self-preservation, in order to save the Sector commander or regimental commander issuing orders: 'to have them taken again!' At this stage of the fighting the higher placed officers rarely came to the front as they had once done in quiet times.

As such, the companies picked out a series of craters that could reasonably be recognized as being where a trench had once run through, and described them as an 'extended *Lemberg Stellung*'. They would often yield so far out of the 'position' that the drum fire that had fallen on them the day before, preferably did not fall on their heads the next day.

Then, as if a miracle, rumors spread about a pending relief and on occasion this was followed by the rumored orders. Then the waiting game started, would the men still be alive when the relief actually arrived.

> We remain awake through the night in nervous tension. Tommy should not be able to surprise us. Will the relief come? It has the look as if they failed to appear, because it already becomes light. We become worried. Then it spreads like wild fire: 'The relief is here!' One company from *Garde* Grenadier Regiment 5. I met our *Oberstleutnant* in Miraumont. He reports everything accurately and does for us what is in his power to do. The 10th Coy numbered only 20 men. It has lost three officers and 77 men, of them 20 were dead. (10/R15) [58]

26 July

On this day IR 180 would report to the commander of the 52nd Reserve Infantry Brigade, *Generalleutnant* von Auwärter, who, at that time, was the commander of the Army Group reserve in Beugny. The division battle headquarters located in Irles was placed in possession of *Von* Auwärter and was to be used as the brigade battle headquarters. This well-constructed dugout proved to be invaluable for control and command in the upcoming fighting.

The III/180 occupied the right wing from the *Biber Kolonie* along the Ancre to St. Pierre-Divion, the I/180 occupied the middle sector from St. Pierre-Divion up to Thiepval and the II/180 occupied Thiepval. All three battalions were able to move into the new positions without any interference from the enemy. The 8th Bavarian RIR staff remained in the position until 7 a.m. on 26 July when the regimental commander of IR 180 formally took over command of the sector.

The regimental battle headquarters was located in the upper portion of the shallow, road like end of the *Stumpweg*, together with the command post of Artillery Group Berta. This arrangement would prove to be invaluable in the coming days by ensuring close cooperation between both branches of the army.

> When the artillery commander was informed by one of us at any time that our main battle front was being threatened, he could almost always direct the fire of his batteries on the critical sector. The artillery fire was able to protect the left flank of the position at the *Stockacher Graben*, Pozières, Windmill hill and Mouquet farm. The guns could even direct their fire further to the rear and impede the enemy advance most effectively. [59]

The situation now facing IR 180 brought little joy to the officers or men of the regiment.

The large expanse required to be covered by the regiment did not allow for any substantial reserves to be available in the event of a crisis. There was a complete lack of any defense in depth, which had previously existed on 1 July. While the sector had remained almost unchanged from the beginning of the month, the defensive positions had been very badly damaged from the initial enemy attack, numerous counterattacks and almost non-stop shelling.

For support IR 180 relied upon the 4th *Schützen* Squadron of the Württemberg Reserve Dragoon Regiment and Reserve *Uhlan* Regiment 2, which occupied a second position by Grandcourt. The 4th *Schützen* Squadron remained only a short time until it was replaced on 29 July through the III/R99. The Reserve Dragoon Regiment had become recalled and was being transferred to a different theatre of war.

The Württemberg Reserve Dragoon Regiment had been part of the 26th Reserve Division since the beginning of the war. The regiment had served in the Vosges fighting and the autumn battles of 1914 in northern France where it acquired a share of the glory in the position warfare in the Artois as well as in the battle on the Somme, 'both on horse and on foot, with the lance and the carbine'. The division commander spoke of his thanks to the regiment when it was being transported into the column area. The Württemberg Reserve Dragoon Regiment now became used to protect the border between Belgium and Holland. As replacements, the division was assigned the 2nd Squadron *Ulan* Regiment 20 under *Hauptmann Frhr.* von Bautz.

On 23 July, when the neighboring Division Burkhardt was replaced by the 117th Infantry Division, the numerous batteries belonging to the 26th Reserve Division that had been fighting under Division Burkhardt were returned to the association of the division. The artillery of the 26th Reserve Division had to bear the heavy weight of the increasing isolation of the position. At this time the division had an average of 19 field and 12 heavy batteries. They had operated continuously in the left neighboring sector and had been involved in the fighting about the Windmill of Pozières. Once back in the division association the batteries became effectively supported by the artillery of the 52nd Infantry Division located on the right wing, the fruits of the hard lessons learned in the fighting by Serre in June 1915.

Then, on 28 July, there was a reorganization of the artillery resources. All of the heavy artillery batteries under direct orders of Group Stein were placed under a special Artillery commander, Bavarian *Major Frhr.* von Botzheim. This was not seen as a positive move as it would drastically reduce the unified control and employment of these key defensive weapons at a critical time. Even the smallest delay in deploying defensive artillery fire could mean the difference between success and failure. The new distribution of command and control was viewed by many as a disaster waiting to happen.

Once in the new sector, any restoration work or attempt to extend the position by the men of IR 180 was increasingly impeded by the enemy artillery and mine fire, which fell night and day. The British also utilized gas in every form, from gas clouds to gas shells and mines, which continued to erode the German defensive capabilities more and more.

The constant bombardment of every path or trench used to carry up critical materials to the front at night and the deeper enemy penetration on the left flank of the regiment created even greater hardships in trying to keep the front line adequately supplied. In order to bring up construction materials, food, water and ammunition the routes became lengthy and meandered through the shattered terrain so much that the time needed to bring up a

Ewige Ruhe und Frieden
finde bei dir und deinen lieben heiligen
dein treuer Diener, unfer lieber Sohn u. Bruder

Ludwig Kathan

Erf.-Ref. im württemb. Ref.-Inf.-Regt. Nr. 121
geboren den 23. August 1886 in Metzlers
gefallen auf dem felde der Ehre
am 28. Juli 1916 in frankreich.

Zu früh bist du von uns geschieden,
Du liebes, gutes, treues Herz,
Dir sei der letzte Gruß beschieden,
Schwer tragen wir den bittern Schmerz,
Ja über d. in so frühes Scheiden
Könnt' brechen fast das Elternherz.
Auch die Geschwister müssen weinen,
Ueber das so früh entschlafene Bruderherz,
Drum laßt uns schauen himmelan,
Was Gott tut, das ist wohlgetan.
Im Grab ist Ruh. Im stillen Todesschmerz,
Da schlummert sanft des tapferen Helden Herz.

Barmherzigster Jesus, gib ihm die ewige Ruhe!
(7 Jahr und 7 Quadrag. Ablaß)

Ludwig Kathan. (Author's collection)

single load of supplies to Thiepval required one hour just to reach the village. New routes needed to be found on a regular basis as the paths taken by the carrying parties stood out prominently in the aerial photographs taken by the British observation aircraft each day.

The heavy strain placed on the troops could also be seen from the number of men who reported sick on a daily basis, which increased from one day to the next. No one was immune from illness; the regiment had barely moved into the Thiepval position when the leader of the I/180, *Hauptmann* Heyberger, became ill and was sent into the military hospital. His illness became so severe that he was eventually transferred to a hospital in Germany. A few days after *Hauptmann* Heyberger left the regiment, his successor, *Major* Majer, the former commander of the *Feldeisenbahnwesen* arrived. He immediately devoted his full energies into the improvement of his sector and in particular in the extension of *Feste Schwaben*.

From the very beginning the regiment expected that an attack would take place against Thiepval sooner or later and as a result of this the men worked feverishly on the construction of the position in spite of the enemy fire and growing numbers of sick. The men also concentrated their efforts on preparing the *Zollern Graben* for defense against attacks that increasingly threatened to come from the south. Mined dugouts were non-existent in the position and there was a concerted effort to create as many dugouts as possible in the fastest time. The remaining time was used to repair what the British had weakened with the constant shell fire.

The attempts to restore the position and create new defenses grew more and more difficult as the enemy continued to advance via Pozières in the direction of Courcelette, threatening the left flank of Thiepval. The effective enemy bombardments against the regimental sector, particularly against Sector C3 and *Feste Schwaben*, increased in severity and numbers of heavy caliber guns as well as mines from day to day.

Even with the hard work and constant enemy fire the men were not in a sector that was under direct attack and had the luxury of writing home when off duty.

Unteroffizier Otto Nuding, IR 180, 2. Komp. 26. Res. Div. 14 R.AK, July 27, 1916
Dear parents, brothers and sisters!
My most heartfelt thanks for all your lovely birthday greetings which pleased me greatly and made my heart warm. As soon as I have more time, I will take a closer look at your lovely letters. Because I'm already back in position and there is always a lot of work, especially in the beginning, especially when it's all shot up, as here. I'm lying just to the left of the Ancre brook on the slope up to the village of Thiepval. So we are temporarily out of the direct attack zone, but being as quiet as before, of course, there is no question. What you see in the newspapers, the attacks go on with unabated violence and I guess it will go on for at least 14 days as such. I greet you, trusting in God, Your Otto.

As soon as possible please send me cards and stationary. For stationary could you send the good government writing paper. These cut and fold. I quite like this, you can also write very well on it with a pencil.[60]

30 July

The positions of the 26th Reserve Division north of the Ancre, while not under direct attack, still required constant alertness. The British had continued to mine under the positions held by the men of RIR 119 and RIR 121, who were vigilant in listening for the signs that a mine was about to be detonated. The time of greatest concern was when the sounds of mining stopped. During these pauses, the defenders listened intently and nervously for any indication that the mine chamber was being loaded with explosives and never knew from one moment to the next if the ground would simply explode under their feet as it had done under the 9/R119 on 1 July. The men were far happier when they detected the distant sounds of the British miners, as they worked deep under the ground. This meant the mine was still being excavated and there was little concern about a mine detonation.

In the weeks following the British attack on 1 July, the men in RIR 121 and RIR 119 often had the impression that the British were going to repeat their disastrous attack of 1 July once again. At times, the enemy artillery fire increased to the level of drum fire and artificial smoke and fog were generated. At these times, the men of both regiments opened fire with rifles and machine guns and supporting artillery batteries opened up barrage fire into the opaque cloud on the suspected enemy attack, but no attack ever took place.

Eventually, the men Württembergers came to the conclusion that the British were attempting to disrupt the connections from the German front lines to the rear and destroy the work being performed on the trenches on a daily basis. It was also suspected that the bombardments and gas were a ruse, designed to prevent any men from the regiments from being sent further south to where the heavy fighting was taking place.

Over time, the men of RIR 121 and RIR 119 grew accustomed to the enemy fire and accepted the British actions as being normal. While there was no need for either regiment

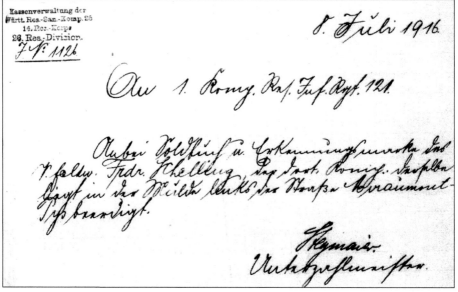

Inventory for deceased Reservist Sailer. (*Landesarchiv Baden-Württemberg, Hauptstaatsarchiv Stuttgart*)

to be moved to the south, the German reaction to the constant enemy disturbance fire probably had the opposite effect of what the British had desired. After undergoing numerous fire raids, the longer the enemy disturbance fire lasted, the calmer the German soldiers became, 'because everyone knew that everything was only a bluff.'

In addition to the normal trench routine and constant enemy disturbance fire RIR 119 and RIR 121 were occupied with preparing detailed reports on the men who had been killed, wounded or listed as missing as well as a mountain of documents relating to the men who had reported sick or suffered minor injuries during the fighting. Over time, as these reports filtered back to the rear, they would be incorporated into the official records of each soldier as well as to the families and eventually printed in the *Verlustlisten*.[61]

The reports, while just a part of the official paperwork required by the German Army on a normal basis, also reveals small personal details on the life and in some cases, death of a soldier.

Reserve Infantry Regiment No. 121
5th Company   4th July 1916
Objects of the estate of the deceased Reservist Sailer 1/R121
Fallen on 1 July 1916 at 8.45 a.m. from an artillery shell wound of the chest
    1 watch with chain
    1 wallet with *Soldbuch*
    Money and other objects were not found as Sailer had received a direct hit
    Stammrolle entry: Reservist Karl Sailer, Kleinbottwar, Marbach, Struck in chest
by mine fragments at 8.45 a.m.

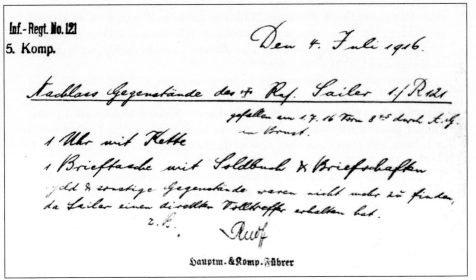

Inventory and burial notice for deceased Reservist Sailer. (*Landesarchiv Baden-Württemberg, Hauptstaatsarchiv Stuttgart*)

Kassenverwaltung (Paymaster's Office) der Württemberg Reserve *Sanitäts* Company 26, 14th Reserve Corps, 26th Reserve Division
8 July 1916
To the 1st Company Reserve Infantry Regiment 121
Enclosed *Soldbuch* (Pay book) and *Erkennungsmarke* (Identity Disc) of *Vizefeldwebel* Friedrich Schelling, the same who the company buried in the hollow on the left of the Miraumont-Pys road.

Stammrolle entry: Schelling, Friedrich *Vizefeldwebel, Offiz. Asp.* 1/R121 Waiblingen. KIA 8.45 a.m., struck in head and back by artillery projectile, buried in Miraumont by Reserve *Sanitäts* Company 26

Stammrolle entry: *Unteroffizier* Karl Eisele, 29, Married, 2 children, Typesetter from Sindelfingen, Böblingen, Killed in action at 9 a.m. from an infantry projectile to the head. Inventory of possessions: Money and chest wallet with 66.36 *Marks* and 1 wedding ring, 1 pocket knife, 1 watch chain, 1 handkerchief, 1 calendar and 2 notebooks. Sent to the Finance Section of the Intendance I/R121 on 18 July 1916

Stammrolle entry: *Reservist* Friedrich Munz, 28, Single, Tailor from Pfedelbach, Oehringen, Killed in action, struck in head by artillery projectile. Inventory of possessions: 1 purse with 23.02 Marks, 1 wallet, 1 watch with chain, 3 pocket knives, 4 thimbles, snuff tobacco tin and letters. Sent to the Finance Section of the Intendance I/R121 on 18 July 1916

Stammrolle entry: *Landsturmmann* Johannes Holz, 38, Married, 5 children, Day Laborer from Reichenbach, Gmünd. Killed in action at 10 a.m. from an infantry projectile to the head. Inventory of possessions: 1 Purse with 20.70 Marks, 1 watch with chain, 1 letter pad with letters, 1 pocket torch and 1 pocket knife. Sent to the Finance Section of the Intendance I/R121 on 18 July 1916

Stammrolle entry: *Landsturmmann* Kaspar Jäger, 38, Married, 1 child, Farmer from Unterschneitheim, Ellwangen. Killed in action at 10 a.m. from an infantry projectile to the head. Inventory of possessions: 1 Wallet and 1 Purse with 32.53 Marks, 1 Rosary, 1 pocket knife and 1 handkerchief. Sent to the Finance Section of the Intendance I/R121 on 18 July 1916

Stammrolle entry: *Leutnant der Reserve* Erich Rapp, 21, Single, Student from Ulm a.D. Killed in action at 9 a.m. from an infantry projectile to the head. Inventory of possessions: 1 Purse with 100.00 Marks, 1 breast pocket with contents, 1 pocket knife, 1 pair of glasses with case, 1 matchbox, 1 pair of binoculars, 1 wristwatch, 1 purse with 5.55 Marks and 1 key. Sent to the Finance Section of the Intendance I/R121 on 18 July 1916

Stammrolle entry: *Gefreiter der Reserve* Heinrich Holzwarth, 29, Single, Brick Worker from Ossweil, Ludwigsburg. Killed in action at 9 a.m. from an infantry projectile to the head. Inventory of possessions: 1 Purse with 6.56 Marks, 1 watch with chain, 1 wallet with letters and note paper, 1 pocket knife and 1 Iron Cross ribbon. Sent to the Finance Section of the Intendance I/R121 on 18 July 1916

Stammrolle entry: *Landwehrmann* Johannes Müller, 33, Single, Laborer from Birkmannsweiler, Waiblingen. Killed in action at 10 a.m. from an infantry projectile to the head. Inventory of possessions: Money and personal possessions were taken away by the English.

This work went on for most of the day as each company completed the necessary paperwork for the men who were casualties of the recent fighting. All of the possessions would eventually be returned to the men's families, seemingly insignificant items that were all that was left of the life of a loved one.

While paperwork was a constant presence in the lives of a soldier, the men at the front had far more to worry about than filling out a form. The British opposite RIR 119 and RIR 121 continued to do was to tirelessly push their positions forward by sapping closer and closer to the German lines. The British had recognized that trying to cross 300-400 meters of open ground in order just to reach the first German trench had resulted in devastating losses. It had become all too obvious that the assault distance was too far. By sapping, the British had advanced their trenches much closer to the German lines. By Beaumont, the British trenches eventually absorbed the sunken road, the scene of numerous patrol fights in the years past. The enemy eliminated the exposed corner by the road to Auchonvillers, created a maze of new trenches in the vicinity of the ravine that moved closer and closer to the German lines each week.

New enemy saps ascended the slope in front of Hamel from their former positions. The saps were driven forward and then the sap heads were connected with one another to form a new trench and in this manner the British moved up the undulating terrain, on which the I/R119 was positioned.

The artillery, infantry and machine guns in RIR 119 attempted to prevent the British from approaching the German trenches using all means possible. Patrols watched the nightly entrenching by the enemy, reported their findings and the artillery opened fire with severe fire raids. While the enemy fire raids had been considered a bluff, there was now as no doubt in anyone's mind that the enemy was making preparations for new attacks north of the Ancre. The only unanswered questions were when and where these attacks would take place?

Men from RIR 119 in the trenches. (Author's collection)

There were other indications that an attack would take place at some point when it was observed that gas cylinders had been installed inside one of the new trenches. This discovery was repeatedly confirmed after the suspect trench was bombarded by *Minenwerfer* and the resulting heavy discharge of gas was noted. Despite this setback, the destroyed gas cylinders were quickly replaced and the enemy continued to push his trenches closer to the German lines. It seemed as if nothing could slow them down. The British were considered a brave and tough adversary and had to be kept under close scrutiny in order to prevent a surprise attack in the future.

The German artillery battery positions north of the Ancre had also been systematically bombarded by British guns under the direct control of enemy observation aircraft. This counter-battery work was also being employed on German batteries located in the left neighboring Sector Burkhardt, as well as the sector of the 183rd Infantry Division Schüssler.

Despite the British counterbattery work, the batteries of the 26th Reserve Division on the north side of the Ancre were very useful in the fighting taking place south of the river. The division artillery had provided effective support during the defense of Ovillers and Pozières before these villages were overrun by the enemy. All throughout July the artillery of the 26th Reserve Division had remained battle capable. As each gun became disabled through enemy fire or from mechanical breakdown, it was almost immediately repaired or replaced and the firepower of the batteries remained intact.

Up until the end of July the artillery of the 26th Reserve Division could proudly state

Popular pose with dud shells, IR 180. (Felix Fregin)

that the division did not have a single gun captured by the enemy. The ammunition supply to each battery was handled efficiently by the ammunition columns and no battery ever experienced a shortage of ammunition. The ammunition columns which transported their volatile cargo over rough roads that were under direct enemy fire never failed to reach their assigned battery positions with fresh supplies. There were inevitable losses of horses and men under such conditions but there were always new replacements to step in and complete the task.

The extremely successful use of the batteries of the 26th Reserve Division was mainly thanks to the efficient organization of *Generalmajor* von Maur who was the Artillery Brigade Commander. The individual artillery regiments also deserved great praise for their tenacious opposition to the enemy on both sides of the National road. As the front of Sector Burkhardt gradually crumbled under the constant enemy pressure, the batteries located by the left wing of the 26th Reserve Division were transferred into new positions further in the rear. The II/RFAR 27 under *Hauptmann* Jäckh was particularly commended for its outstanding performances in the defensive fighting.

The intelligence service was able to keep track of enemy troop movements and when opposing divisions were being replaced through a variety of means. Patrols were sent out each night in every sector to observe enemy activities, bring in any part of a uniform that

Same shells as previous picture being used for a photo
op, men from RIR 99. (Author's collection)

could be used to identify the particular enemy regiment. Maps, documents and letters taken from enemy dead that were scattered throughout no man's land were also a valuable source of intelligence. As such, on 27 July the presence of the 25th British Division was established through the discovery of a dead body from this division by a patrol from RIR 119.

Each regiment was also encouraged to hold raids against the enemy lines in order to take prisoners where afterward, the interrogation of the prisoners could provide valuable intelligence. On 27 July a patrol from the II/R119 under *Leutnant* Dippon broke into one of the new British trenches and blew it up using *Erdmörser* ammunition; while an impressive feat, it did nothing to slow down the relentless enemy advance.

The British had also been very active and not about to give the German garrison a minute's rest. In addition to the constant fire raids there were numerous smoke and gas attacks that alternated with nightly patrol attacks and raids. On 3 July, IR 186 repulsed a raid against *Beaumont-Nord* and took several enemy prisoners. On 13 July the enemy attacked *Beaumont-Süd* behind gas clouds. On 18 July enemy raiding parties attempted to break into the German lines at *Beaumont-Süd* once again. In these instances, the British were prevented from entering the German lines and were forced to withdraw leaving behind a number of casualties.

While most accounts of the fighting on the Somme focus on the front line troops, supplying and distributing food to the thousands of men across the front of the 26th Reserve

Division was a daunting task when even there was no fighting. Now, with daily skirmishes, enemy attacks and constant artillery and mine fire, it appeared almost impossible at times. This important job was under the guidance of *Feldintendantur* Klaus whose men performed this critical task with untiring diligence. Klaus was dedicated in providing the front line troops with adequate food under any circumstance as well as providing supply depots at critical locations in and behind the front line.

Just as important as the food service was the medical service, which were under the guidance of the Division *Arzt, Generaloberarzt* Dr. Bihler. The medical service had performed superbly in the month of July, especially the services rendered by Reserve *Sanitäts* Company 26 under *Stabsarzt* Dr. Rall. The main division dressing station in the *Sanitäts Mulde* south of Miraumont deserved special praise for the untiring efforts of the medical staff in helping to save lives of men who had been wounded. The activities of the Württemberg Reserve *Feldlazarette* had also been exceptional and as a result, men who might have died from their wounds survived, and in many cases the same men would eventually return to their regiments.

One constant of the fighting throughout July was the enemy superiority in the air. Even before the start of the battle on 1 July, the British had demonstrated aerial dominance over the German pilots. Despite this inequality, both in aircraft and observation balloons, the German pilots still succeeded in bringing down numerous British pilots in air combat and in doing so, helped in the fight against the German artillery batteries by protecting them against aerial observation. To the ground troops however, enemy aircraft were a constant sight while few German planes were ever seen.

The regiments of the 26th Reserve Division continued to work diligently on restoring and expanding the defensive positions. Artillery and mine fire had been eroding the once powerful defenses and before the end of the month heavy rainstorms added to the rapidly deteriorating conditions. Much of the effort by the 26th Reserve Division was being directed toward the construction of new switch lines and blocking positions as the direction of the front changed from the west to the south. New defensive lines, such as the Beaucourt, Grandcourt, Staufen, Gallwitz and Mouquet *Riegels* quickly began to take shape. Their value would not be fully appreciated by the men until sometime later in the fighting.

There was also a need to create a third position in the event of further enemy advances. All available resources were deployed in the creation of these new trench systems. At parts of the front, there were troops that were technically considered to be resting but as every man was needed, more often than not, the men were put to work each night to entrench. Mining activities had not ceased and in some areas continued at the same pace as before the enemy offensive, especially at the *Heidenkopf.*

From the heavy fighting at the beginning of the month and the daily losses from enemy action and illnesses, all of the regiments of the 26th Reserve Division had required replacement troops. The adequate supply of replacement troops was considered to be of the highest importance and there were numerous visits in the positions and discussions with the different commanders by the division commander on this subject. The replenishment of IR 180 and RIR 99 was carried out under the leadership of the commander of the 185th Infantry Division, *Generalmajor* von Uthmann.

The Recruit Depot of the 26th Reserve Division was located at Hermies-Inchy and the training of new replacements that arrived at the depot was the responsibility of von

Uthmann. His task was made far easier when the Replacement Battalions in Germany were sending out men who were comparatively well trained. These young recruits represented a valuable resource for the division and in some cases the recruits were thrown into action before they had received all of their training as on 1 July. Fortunately, the training of these men did not take very long, and the new troops could be integrated into the regiments at the front in the fastest possible time.

The battle on the Somme raged further to the left of the 26th Reserve Division in undiminished intensity. The rolling thunder of artillery fire could be heard almost continuously, the men located north of the Ancre could also see the massive impacts on the hills by Thiepval, the shrapnel clouds that appeared in the sky and the ever-present tethered observation balloons, up to 40 in number. The colored light balls that were fired into the sky at night gave the appearance of fireworks and the flash of the firing of the guns and the arc of the comet tail of the burning fuse, by which the path of the projectile could be followed, combined with the fire glow of the bursting projectiles were frighteningly beautiful.

As soon as there was a major day of battle south of the Ancre the regiments of the 26th Reserve Division also received their share of artillery and mine fire. Similarly the enemy artillery facing the regiment fired overhead in the direction of Courcelette and the division artillery returned fire and took part in the fighting. Even though the regiments were not being attacked directly, they were being drawn in detrimentally. Constant orders from higher commands: 'Elevated battle readiness, or great attention, or an enemy attack is certainly expected!' did not bring any reassurance to the troops.

The overall situation on 30 July can be represented in the following Daily Orders of Army Group Gallwitz:

> Severe attacks are to be expected by the enemy in the next period of time. The decision of the war is being fought on the fields of the Somme. It must be made clear to all officers and Other Ranks up until the front line, what the stakes are here for our Fatherland. The greatest attention and self-sacrificing bravery will still prevent the enemy from winning any ground. His onrush must be smashed to pieces against the wall of German men. *Oberbefehlshaber* von Gallwitz. [62]

August 1916

Fighting raged on the Somme throughout the month of August with massive British attacks and tenacious resistance by the German defenders. During this time, the 26th Reserve Division was still not directly involved in the fighting. The focus of the British attacks continued to be east of the National Road, where the enemy pushed deeper and deeper into the German defenses south of the Thiepval Sector. The British seemed to be determined to direct the main pressure of their attacks against the line: Martinpuich-Longueval-Guillemont-Maurepas and if successful, to capture the high ridge formed by these villages and use it as a springboard for attacks to the north. From all indications it appeared as if the enemy's intention was to eventually attack Thiepval from the south and roll up the German line from the flank.

On 5 August the hill where the windmill of Pozières once stood had been captured by the British. Immediate counterattacks by the IX Reserve Corps von Böhn had all failed and had not been able to retake this key position. The windmill was the same one that had been visited by His Majesty the King of Württemberg who had climbed it in April 1915

  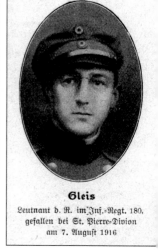

Schefold

Oberleuta. i. d. 6. Pion.-Komp. im II. Württ. Pion.-Batl. 13, gefallen bei Miraumont am 4. August 1916

Wurster

Leutnant d. R. im Inf.-Regt. 180, gefallen bei Thiepval am 6. August 1916

Gleis

Leutnant d. R. im Inf.-Regt. 180, gefallen bei St. Pierre-Divion am 7. August 1916

(Kriegstagebuch aus Schwaben)

with the entourage of the division commander in order to obtain an overview of the 26th Reserve Division sector.

With the capture of the windmill position, the enemy now had unrestricted observation of the area from Martinpuich to Courcelette and the German artillery positions located there could be identified and subsequently destroyed. In order to prevent this from happening, many of the batteries had to be quickly relocated. Then, following the British success by Pozières, the main focus of the British offensive was directed against Delville Wood northeast of Longueval and the villages of Ginchy and Guillemont where active Württemberg regiments were heavily engaged in the fighting.

Further British attacks eventually took place against positions near Thiepval with the enemy working ever closer in the direction of Mouquet farm and the *Wundtwerk*. However despite every effort, the British had failed to capture the farm or what once remained of the farm. There was virtually nothing left above ground other than a few damaged bricks However, the nearby *Stockacher Graben* and *Konstanzer Graben* both fell. As the British advanced deeper into the German positions the headquarters in the rear areas in Grévillers, Avesnes and Bapaume were under increasing bombardment by heavy guns. The village of Thiepval now received enemy fire from three directions and what remnants were left of the small village were gradually turned into a pile of dust, and it became difficult to recognize that a village had once stood there.

Now, with attacks being made along the left flank of the Thiepval Sector, the 26th Reserve Division became increasingly threatened by being encompassed on the left flank and in the rear. The two parts of the division most impacted by these recent events were IR 180 and the artillery units, all of which had to bear the brunt of the increasing isolation of the division sector south of the Ancre.

Because of the increased enemy bombardment of Grévillers, the staff of the 26th Reserve Field Artillery Brigade was relocated to Favreuil on 5 August. The staff headquarters of the heavy artillery was also relocated to Favreuil where there were two beautiful château available to use as quarters by the artillery staff. With the gradual encroachment of the enemy artillery batteries on the left flank, the German batteries on left wing of the 26th Reserve Division had to take actions that would have been considered impossible during peacetime. Many of the guns were forced to traverse at angles up to 270 degrees in order to fire at the enemy who pressed further and further into the rear of the division sector.

Generalleutnant von Auwärter had taken over the sector south of the Ancre on 5 August and he immediately moved his battle headquarters to Irles. The new headquarters had been prepared in advance, using all of the lessons learned so far from the fighting on the Somme. Of the troops available to von Auwärter, in the first line from St. Pierre-Divion up to and including Thiepval was IR 180. RIR 99 stood in the second line and occupied the second position as well as the blocking positions with three of its four battalions, which served as rear support. The regimental staff of RIR 99 under *Major* von Fabeck took up its battle headquarters south of Miraumont at the eastern road leading to Courcelette.

While the divisions of Group Stein had remained in position week after week since the start of the Allied offensive, the troops on the left of the 26th Reserve Division were being rotated on a regular basis. Group Sixt von Armin, which had been in position since 24 July, was replaced with Group Böhn, IX Army Corps. Group Böhn became replaced on 11 August through Group Lassert, XIX Army Corps, and Group Lassert was replaced on 28 August by Group Marschall (Guard Reserve Corps).

The 117th Infantry Division was positioned on the left flank of the 26th Reserve Division since 20 July. This division was replaced on 11 August through the 16th Infantry Division from Group Böhn. The 16th Infantry Division was then replaced on 25 August through the 4th Guard Infantry Division from Group Marschall. The divisions on the left flank of the 26th Reserve Division spent no longer than three weeks in the front lines during periods of major fighting. Only the 51st Reserve Infantry Brigade and the artillery of the 26th Reserve Division remained in their positions, unrelieved month after month.

RIR 99 had been given the task to develop the rear positions and the *Riegelstellungen*, in particular the *Zollerngraben*, the *Staufen Riegel* and *Grandcourt Riegel* and to equip them with dugouts. The regiment had the well-earned reputation of being the master of dugout construction. However, the regiment no longer had the luxury of time needed to create large, mined dugouts as they had in the months preceding the Somme battle. The effort of the men was also severely hampered by the non-stop enemy artillery fire that fell on the position day and night. More importantly, the regiment was not at full strength as a result of severe stomach and intestinal disorders. The latter significantly reduced the trench strength of the regiment. Eventually, it was decided to replace RIR 99 in the position and by the end of August IR 66 from the 52nd Infantry Division had relieved the regiment.

The 26th Reserve Division headquarters located in the Château Biefvillers, was a scene of intense activity. While large portions of the division sector were not directly under attack, there always seemed to be a myriad of work to perform. The General Staff Officer, *Major* Fischer, and his assistants, worked day and night in order to meet all of the responsibilities they were given.

Some of the work performed by the division was to oversee the placement and construction of new defensive positions. Foreign units were provided to Group Stein for the construction of the Third position and switch lines. Among these was the already familiar *Landwehr Brigade Ersatz Battalion* 55 that had been heavily involved in the fighting on 1 July. These men continued to afford valuable services to the 26th Reserve Division.

The important work of the artillery was refined and supported with fire exercises in

Men from IR 180 in the trenches. (Author's collection)

conjunction with the neighboring sectors under the guidance of the artillery commander and in with the use of artillery flights. The Communication Section held Light signal practice and improved the connection between infantry and pilots where the ground troops would use ground cloths to relay specific messages to the observation pilots who in turn could relay the message to headquarters or the artillery. Familiarity with the use of messenger pigeons was practiced, because a Messenger pigeon station had been assigned to the division. Pigeons were brought up to the commander of Thiepval, where they should soon prove their worth. The *Pioniers* practiced using the *Flammenwerfer* to clear trenches.

The small numbers of reserves available to the division were barely able to find any rest. If they were not being used for labor and position construction during the night, they were being constantly pushed into threatened points when enemy attacks were expected. In order to disconcert the enemy, a gas mine undertaking against the Wood of Thiepval was being prepared with the code name '*Britentod*' ['British-death'] under the leadership of the Prussian *Pionier Major* Biermann. Volunteer patrols, which would advance in connection with the gas firing, and who would take prisoners, were practiced behind the lines. When it became time to implement *Britentod*, in late August, the winds were unfavorable and the attack was postponed until the wind direction had changed.

Everything possible was being done to maintain the morale of the men and to keep their spirits up during the period of time of great tension and stress. General von Stein visited the positions of the front line troops almost daily and established close, personal connections with the commanders of the neighboring sectors. Special orders commending the men on the stalwart defense of their positions, the higher losses inflicted on the enemy troops and similar methods used to maintain morale were issued on a regular basis.

Numerous visits from envoys sent from home also became welcomed in this period in the division headquarters and were taken on tours in the less dangerous positions. Much had changed since the relatively peaceful days in 1914 and 1915 when such visits were discouraged as often as possible. Now, the visits from home were seen as distractions that kept the men's minds occupied with thoughts other than their imminent destruction in the Battle of the Somme.

Special awards given out to the men for bravery during a raid or patrol were also seen as ways of maintaining morale. The special award given to the Commander of the 4th Army, Duke Albrecht von Württemberg that took place at the beginning of August when he was appointed *Generalfeldmarschall* was also seen as giving a boost to the overall morale of the army.

The battle front moved closer behind the left rear of IR 180, almost with each passing day. In the middle of August there was already fighting about the former regimental battle headquarters at Mouquet farm and the Courcelette sugar factory, so that the position of the division from Serre via Beaumont to Thiepval formed a peninsula and the situation became increasingly dangerous.

Enemy artillery activity continued to increase more and more during the month and enemy aircraft appeared more frequently and in larger numbers. Squadrons with 25 aircraft were no longer a rarity. British aircraft had always been a thorn in the side of the German Army on the Somme since before the battle had even started. Enemy pilots directed the artillery fire with great accuracy as well as dropping bombs while flying over the German positions. The increase of enemy aircraft and the increasing boldness demonstrated by the pilots as they flew lower and lower above the German lines was becoming insufferable. The enemy aircraft strafed the German troops in the front lines on a regular basis and dropped bombs on the billets in the rear. *Hauptmann* Oswald Böelcke's squadron was active in this sector and his pilots were successful in shooting down many of the British aircraft, but there always seemed more to take their place and the enemy maintained superiority in the air.

Up through late August, the British had focused their attacks south of Thiepval. The

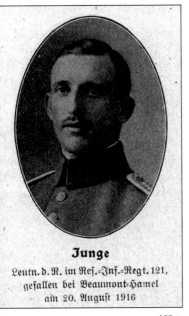

Junge

Leutn. b. R. im Ref.-Inf.-Regt. 121,
gefallen bei Beaumont-Hamel
am 20. August 1916

Beck

Leutnant b. R. im Inf.-Regt. 180,
gefallen bei Thiepval
am 26. August 1916

(*Kriegstagebuch aus Schwaben*)

village of Thiepval stood like a rock at the left wing of the British penetration into the German lines. Now, at the end of August, new plans were being prepared by the British to capture Pozières and Grandcourt Ridge; hopefully by the end of the month. The plan also called for an attack north of the Ancre in order to prevent the Germans from sending any reinforcements south to help in the fighting on the southern bank of the river, similar to the reasons for the attack made against Gommécourt on 1 July. On 24 August plans were made for an attack astride the Ancre, which would take place on 30 August. However, there were repeated postponements, mainly due to weather, until finally the date set for the attack was 3 September.

While the Allies formulated their plans for the attack, the German Army was also making major changes in the way in which the battle was being conducted. On 25 August Army Group Gallwitz was disbanded. Starting from 28 August Crown Prince Rupprecht of Bavaria assumed the supreme command over a new Army Group, consisting of the 6th 1st and 2nd German Armies. *General der Infanterie Frhr.* von Falkenhausen became the commander of the 6th Army. The XIV Reserve Corps, with the 26th Reserve Division remained in the 1st Army under General Fritz von Below, while *General der Artillerie* von Gallwitz assumed command over the 2nd Army.

With these changes, it was hoped that the overall command and control of the fighting on the Somme could be managed more efficiently as it was still proving to be very difficult for a single headquarters to monitor and control the actions of so many different units support troops, artillery, etc. across such a wide front.

The German sectors north of the Ancre were becoming increasingly active. The sector of RIR 119 was under constant alert as the enemy systematically sapped closer and closer to the regimental position. By the start of August the British were located directly in front of *Beaumont-Süd*, barely 100 meters distant from the first German trench. The enemy had reduced the storm distance by about 500 to 600 meters and from all indications they were systematically preparing for a new attack north of the Ancre.

Enemy raids had increased in numbers and size during the latter half of August another sign that the British were up to something. The British attempted a number of large-scale raids against RIR 119 at *Beaumont-Süd* in August; on the 11th, 15th, 22nd and 26th; all of which failed to break into the German trenches. It should also be noted that at this point in the fighting RIR 119 had been in its position for 16 months and had never been relieved during this time and the men were becoming worn down.

In the middle of August the British artillery fire on *Beaumont-Süd* increased in severity. Flanking batteries systematically fired on the position from the north. The trenches on the Ancre became badly damaged without being able to effectively fight back. On 17 August the British artillery wreaked devastation on the German position without one shot being fired in retaliation. The positions of RIR 119 slowly began to crumble under the weight of fire, including the well-liked small porches attached to the dugouts that had been driven deep into the steep slopes of the position.

The lack of a German response to the artillery fire was the result of a lack of sufficient ammunition supplies once again and the infantry paid a heavy price for this. There were huge masses of enemy torpedo mines, the same type that had smashed the positions of the 9/R119 in June. On 22 August the bombardment of the staff headquarters in the *Kolonie* began. On 23 August a direct hit penetrated a dugout in the Ancre ground killing 10 men and wounding 7 others from RIR 119.

Enjoying the dugout porch in quieter times, RIR 99. (Author's collection)

The situation in the neighboring sector of RIR 121 was slightly more bearable. While not under the same level of artillery and mine fire as the neighboring RIR 119, the British were also sapping closer to the regimental trenches. RIR 121 was also constantly being ordered to maintain heightened battle readiness in the event of an infantry attack, which helped to deprive the infantry of any chance of rest.

During this period of unrest a disturbing report arrived along with the numerous official reports, letters and other documents generated by the unprecedented losses from 1 July 1916. The document was created on 17 August 1916 at the Reserve Hospital II, Ludwigsburg by *Unteroffizier der Landwehr* Albert Danner 3/R121. Danner was severely wounded on 1 July 1916 when he was struck on the left shoulder, head, back and numerous other body parts by mine and hand grenade splinters.

According to Danner, *Landwehrmann* Wilhelm Peterhans, 3/R121, who was originally listed as missing in action was in fact dead. Danner stated that Peterhans was wounded in the stomach by an infantry projectile, taken prisoner and dragged back to the enemy wire, placed inside a shell crater and then killed by a bayonet thrust.

Nothing further was mentioned on the *Stammrolle* entry for Wilhelm Peterhans. This was the only record of any supposed atrocity entered in the records for RIR 121. There are some issues connected to such a report that places doubt on its accuracy. The time of day when both men became wounded was not listed so it is impossible to know if Danner had already been wounded when this act allegedly occurred.

Danner had suffered severe wounds which would have made it impossible for him to observe such an event unless it had occurred within his field of vision. Finally, it is doubtful Danner could have accurately observed an event which allegedly took place directly in front of the British wire when the distance between the opposing trenches was quite considerable, making observation without field glasses impossible. Based on the lack of any corroborating evidence and the conditions that existed at that time I feel that the affidavit is partially

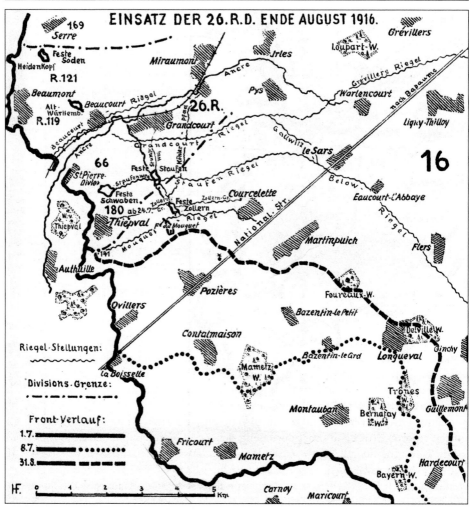

Position of the 26th Reserve Division at the end of August 1916.

inaccurate. It is very possible Peterhans had been shot in the stomach and also dragged back to the British lines but it is much more likely he died on the way or shortly after arriving at the British lines from his original wounds as there was no reason to make the effort to bring back a German prisoner to the British lines only to kill him once there.

British artillery fire against the German positions increased in intensity from day to day. In addition to the large number of high explosive shells and shrapnel, the bombardments included an increasing number of gas shells. At first, the bombardment fell primarily on the right flank of the 52nd Reserve Infantry Brigade, therefore Sectors C2 and C3. Within a short time most of the trenches in these sectors had been leveled, the wire obstacles almost completely destroyed, especially in front of C2 and many of the existing dugouts were crushed in.

Major Majer was untiringly active as he oversaw the transformation of the Thiepval position into a virtual fortress once again. Then, on the afternoon of 27 August, Majer was

Majer

Major und Bataillonskommandeur, gestorben am
27. Sept. 1916 an den bei Thiepval erhalt. Wunden

(*Kriegstagebuch aus Schwaben*)

accompanied by the communication trench-officer, *Leutnant der Reserve* Peyn while on an inspection trip to the *Artillerie Mulde* to inspect the work at the Medical dugout. During the trip he was severely wounded in the back of the head by a splinter from a shell that had exploded a considerable distance away.

He never regained consciousness, and a few days later Majer died quietly from his wound. A new, 'Special Commander' then became appointed to hold Thiepval. The first officer to assume this role was *Major* Keerl, II/180. His instructions were short and to the point; 'Thiepval would be held to the last man.' *Hauptmann* Schaal, former leader of the 10th Company, then assumed the leadership of the II/180.

With the enemy attack apparently imminent, Crown Prince Rupprecht requested additional troops to be inserted into the endangered sectors. He knew all too well that *Feste Schwaben* and Thiepval Ridge must be held, otherwise the German lines to the north and south could be seriously threatened. All means available would need to be used to keep this key sector in German hands.

IR 66, from the 52nd Division, located directly north of the 26th Reserve Division, was also well aware of the approaching attack. From its position near Serre, the men of IR 66 could see how vulnerable the Thiepval Sector and the left flank of the 26th Reserve Division had become with the constant enemy advances in the neighboring sectors further south. Orders soon arrived at the regimental headquarters that IR 66 would reinforce the right wing of IR 180 in the Thiepval Sector. With the addition of these reinforcements, the front line could be held in greater strength and each regiment could rotate one battalion to

Zur frommen Erinnerung an

O Herr   Und
gib   das
ihm   ewige
die   Licht
ewige   leuchte
Ruhe !   ihm !

Rudolf Baur
Musketier im Inf.-Reg. Nr. 180, 10. Komp.
geboren den 10. April 1895 in Wendelsheim
gestorben den Heldentod fürs Vaterland
am 31. August 1916 bei Thiepval.

Gebet.
Allmächtiger, barmherziger Gott,
der Du in Deiner anbetungswürdigen
Vorsehung uns den Augenblick des
Todes bestimmt hast, wir bitten Dich
aus vertrauensvollem und ergebenem
Herzen: siehe gnädig auf die Seele
dieses gefallenen Soldaten, nimm den
in treuer Pflichterfüllung erlittenen
Tod als vollgültige Buße an und
führe sie nach den Schrecknissen des
Krieges in Deinen ewigen Frieden.
Amen. Vater unser.

(Author's collection)

the second line to rest. Prior to this, the manpower requirements of each regiment and the size of the sectors they controlled prevented any portion of the regiment from being able to leave the front line.

By the end of August, work in the trenches after the early morning hours was impossible and the traffic in the trench had to be restricted to a minimum. Even though Thiepval was not the focus of the enemy attacks during this time, it was quite close to the fighting along the left flank of the position and losses occurred on a daily basis from mine and artillery fire. The losses in IR 180 from the end of July through the beginning of September were: 4 officers, 108 Other Ranks killed with 6 officers, 370 Other Ranks wounded; all without a single enemy attack.

Notes

1.   Neubronn, *Leutnant* Dr. Carl & Pfeffer, *Leutnant d. R.* Dr. Georg, *Geschichte des Infanterie-Regiments 186,* p. 251.

2.   IBID.

3.   Wurmb, Herbert Ritter von, *Das K. B. Reserve-Infanterie-Regiment Nr. 8,*pp. 153-154.

4.   *Wurmb,* op. cit., pp. 154-156.

5.   *Wurmb,* op. cit., pp. 165-166.

6.   *Wurmb,* op. cit., pp. 166-168.

7.   *Neubronn,* op. cit., pp. 67-69.

8.   *Wurmb,* op. cit., pp. 168-169.

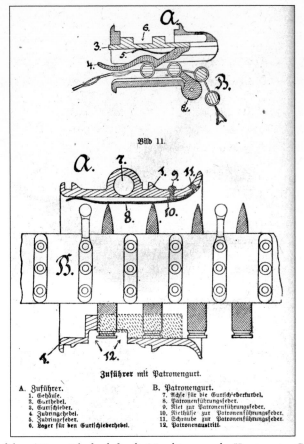

Bild 11.

Zuführer mit Patronengurt.

A. Zuführer.
1. Gehäuse.
2. Gurthebel.
3. Gurtschieber.
4. Zubringehebel.
5. Zubringefeder.
6. Lager für den Gurtschieberhebel.

B. Patronengurt.
7. Achse für die Gurtschieberkurbel.
8. Patronenführungsfeder.
9. Niet zur Patronenführungsfeder.
10. Niethülse zur Patronenführungsfeder.
11. Schraube zur Patronenführungsfeder.
12. Patronenaustritt.

Zuführer (Unterrichtsbuch für die Maschinengewehr-Kompagnien Gerät 08)

9.   *Zufuhrer – feed mechanism for the MG 08,* where the belted ammunition entered the machine gun.

10. Kalkschmidt, Eugen, Schwäbisches, *Kriegstagebuch aus Schwaben*, Band 3, Stuttgart, 1914-1919, p. 1341.

11. Vischer, *Oberstleutnant* Alfred, *Das 10. Württembergische Infanterie-Regiment Nr. 180 im Weltkrieg, 1914-1918,* p. 40.

12. Soden, *General der Infanterie* a.D. *Freiherr* von, *Die 26.(Württembergische) Reserve-Division im Weltkrieg 1914-1918,*p. 115.

13. Vischer, op. cit., p. 41.

14. Wurmb, op. cit., p. 157.

15. Wurm, op. cit., pp. 171-173.

16. Soden, op. cit., p. 115.

17. Wurmb, op. cit., pp. 157-158.

18. Wurmb, op. cit., p. 173.

19. Battalion War Diary, 1/4 KOYLI.

20. Forstner, *Major* a.D. Kurt *Freiherr* von, *Das Königlich-Preussische Reserve-Infanterie-Regiment Nr. 15,* p. 313.

21. Battalion War Diary, 1/4 KOYLI.

22. Wurmb, op. cit., p. 77.

23. Wurmb, op. cit., p. 207.
24. Wurmb, op. cit., p. 206.
25. Forstner, op. cit., pp. 313-314.
26. Neubronn, op. cit., p. 64.
27. Stosch, *Oberstleutnant* a.D. Albrecht von, *Somme-Nord I.Teil: Die Brennpunkte der Schlacht im Juli 1916,* pp. 149-155.
28. Neubronn, op. cit., p. 252.
29. Forstner, op. cit., pp. 320-321.
30. Forstner, op. cit., pp. 321-322.
31. Forstner, op. cit., p. 322.
32. Soden, op. cit., p. 118.
33. Forstner, op. cit., p. 315.
34. Soden, op. cit., pp. 118-119.
35. Feldpost letter, courtesy of Felix Freegin.
36. Neubronn, op. cit., p. 252.
37. The brother of the 1st Officer of the German Light Cruiser SMS Emden and the Captain of the sail boat SMS Ayesha.
38. Forstner, op. cit., p. 316.
39. Forstner, op. cit., p. 315.
40. Forstner, op. cit., p. 314.
41. Neubronn, op. cit., p. 252.
42. Forstner, op. cit., pp. 318-319.
43. Neubronn, op. cit., p. 232.
44. Forstner, op. cit., p. 315.
45. While not actually a dum-dum bullet, by reversing the bullet you would get greater penetrating power as well as rotation of the bullet, which could result in terrible wounds.
46. Forstner, op. cit., pp. 325-326.
47. Forstner, op. cit., pp. 326-327.
48. Forstner, op. cit., p. 327.
49. IBID.
50. Wurmb, op. cit., p. 205.
51. Forstner, op. cit., p. 353.
52. Forstner, op. cit., p. 356.
53. Forstner, op. cit., pp. 357-359.
54. Vischer, op. cit., p. 47.
55. Neubronn, op. cit., p. 67.
56. Forstner, op. cit., p. 355.
57. IBID.
58. Forstner, op. cit., p. 359.
59. Vischer, op. cit., p. 47.
60. Feldpost letter, courtesy of Felix Freegin.
61. The *Verlustlisten* entries for RIR 119 and RIR 121 were not printed until 4 August, 23 August, 5 September and 18 September 1916.
62. Soden, op. cit., pp. 122-123.

Chapter 2

26th Reserve Division

The Somme – September 1916

September had arrived, the third month of the great battle. The final plans for the British advance on 3 September had been finalized and called for the Anzac Corps and part of the British II Corps to form the right wing of the attack. This portion of the assault would have limited objectives. The left wing of the II Corps, 49th Division, located in Thiepval Wood, was supposed to take two German trench lines on a front of 1,000 yards. On the next day, 4 September, the division would capture St. Pierre-Divion and the Strassburg Line (*Strassburger Steige*) that connected this village with *Feste Schwaben* from where further advances could be made against the Schwaben Redoubt and Thiepval.

The 39th Division (V Corps) on the northern bank of the Ancre was supposed to take three German trench lines on the spur south of Beaumont and then advance up the river valley in order to protect the left flank of the 49th Division. The preparations being made for this attack, which included heavy bombardments of the overall objectives, gave irrefutable evidence to the German regiments holding the Thiepval and Beaumont Sectors that a major enemy attack was going to take place soon.

> From the beginning we expected an attack on Thiepval and therefore we worked feverishly with all strength on the construction of the position and on the facilities of the *Zollern Graben* to defend against an attack threatening from the south. The creation of mined dugouts that were completely lacking, and repairing what the English had weakened, but their advance via Pozières in the direction of Courcelette threatened Thiepval more and more. Their scheduled effective bombardment against the regimental sector, namely against the middle, therefore C3 and *Feste Schwaben*, increased in severity and numbers of heavy calibers as well as mines from day to day.[1]

When IR 180 found out that the St. Pierre-Divion and the middle sector that included *Feste Schwaben* the regiment had been holding would now pass to IR 66, the men were genuinely relieved. IR 180 would now be concerned only with the defense of the village of Thiepval and the neighboring sector to the north up to the *Markt Graben*. It was now possible for IR 180 to place a full battalion as reserve in the II Line.

North of the Ancre, at the beginning of September, RIR 119 reported that Sector *Beaumont-Süd* was ripe for an attack, while almost complete silence prevailed in *Beaumont-Nord*. The border of the two sectors was clearly going to be the delineation of the enemy attack according to German intelligence reports. The only unknown factor in the upcoming British attack was the actual date it would begin.

In order to move IR 66 to the Thiepval Sector, the regiment had to be replaced in its current sector and on 1 September, IR 66 was relieved by parts of RIR 99. The I/R55 from the 2nd Guard Reserve Division, the division that had successfully defended Gommécourt

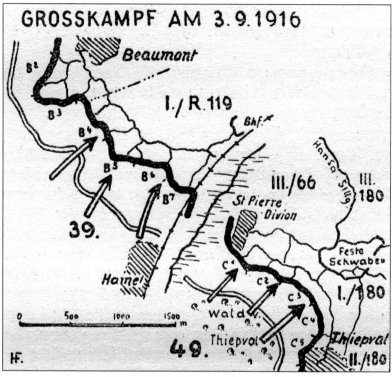

British attacks by the Ancre 3 September 1916.

on 1 July 1916, was also relieved from its position and transferred closer to Thiepval where it would become the reserve for Army Group Stein. The III/R55 moved closer to the threatened front and was positioned in the rear between Miraumont and Grandcourt.

Because the British were behaving so quietly in the afternoon and evening hours of 2 September, the 52nd Reserve Infantry Brigade conducted the long planned relief of the front line troops. In the night from 2/3 September the III/180 located in St. Pierre-Division and Sectors C1 and C2 was relieved by the III/66. The III/66 left Achiet le Petit in the darkness and marched the short distance to the new sector where the battalion would be under the command of IR 180. IR 66 also relieved the III/R99 located in the *Hansa Stellung* and *Süd I-III*. The exchange of troops was carried out without incident.

IR 66 and IR 180 now formed the 52nd Reserve Infantry Brigade, and came under the control of the 26th Reserve Division. The I/66 received billets in Irles, with the 4/66 located in Miraumont. The III/66 was allowed to rest in Achiet le Petit. On the northern bank of the Ancre, RIR 119 placed the last of its reserves, three machine guns, into positions in *Beaumont-Süd* on 2 September.

During the takeover of the new position by St. Pierre-Division, the III/66 reported no losses despite strong enemy artillery fire falling on the position. This was even more remarkable as Grandcourt was also being smothered under strong gas shell fire as well. The remainder of the evening continued to be quiet as the III/66 settled in to its new positions. Early on 3 September the staff of the III/180, which was still in the battle headquarters in St. Pierre-Division in the process of handing over the sector, was eager to complete the transfer and begin the journey to the rear into the II Position.

Upon entering the front lines, the men from IR 66 found an appalling sight. Very little remained of the once powerful defenses, most of the front line consisted of very shallow trenches or in most cases, shell craters. All of the underground telephone wires had been destroyed in the recent bombardment. Communications to the rear were established using freshly laid wires that had been strung on poles above ground. Apparently these wires were found to have a higher survivability rate during bombardments thus ensuring that a secure connection with headquarters in the rear remained intact for longer periods of time. Additionally, the new telephone lines took much less effort and manpower to put into place and maintain than traditional buried cables..

The British artillery opened fire early in the morning of 3 September as it had done on previous days, reaching its crescendo at 5 a.m. According to German records, the 39th Division attacked north of the Ancre about 5.10 a.m. while the 49th Division attacked south of the Ancre at 5.13 a.m. Just prior to the attack the British artillery pounded the German front lines and rear areas with high explosives, gas and Ammonal bombs that continued to fall at the same time the British troops began their advance across no man's land.

Dense waves of enemy soldiers climbed out of their trenches and quickly moved toward the German trenches. The attacks by the British 116th and 117th Infantry Brigades were made against the I/R119, located directly north of the Ancre. The men of RIR 119, who had been in this sector since May 1915 without ever being fully relieved, knew every inch of the terrain in and around their sector. Most of the men in the regiment had fought on the first day of the battle and the relative quiet of the night preceding the attack on 3 September reminded them of the night before 1 July. This peaceful time was used by the men of RIR 119 to take stock of their situation, much as they had done on the night of 30 June.

The 6/R119 was located in Sector B5, the 4/R119 in B6 and the 1/R119 in B7 in the foremost trench. The 7th, 3rd and 2/R119 occupied the second and third trench lines in support. At exactly 5 a.m. powerful drum fire of all calibers fell upon the three companies holding the front line, while the neighboring sector, *Beaumont-Nord* was being covered with shrapnel fire. The bombardment had already cut all of the telephone cables running from the front lines to the rear. However, in accordance with standing orders, the German batteries protecting the Beaumont Sector opened barrage fire on pre-set target areas very punctually and with considerable force.

At approximately 5.10 a.m. the British artillery transferred its destructive fire to the rear as dense waves of rifleman climbed out of the enemy trenches and advanced. In front of B6 and B7 the British were protected by the early morning darkness and could organize their ranks in a hollow before making their final advance.

Much of the barbed wire obstacles that had been protecting Sectors B6 and B7 had been destroyed or badly damaged in the heavy bombardment; however, at the left wing of the 6/R119 in B5 the wire obstacles were still partially intact. At this stage of the fighting on the Somme, the Germans had found it almost impossible to create the dense belts of barbed wire entanglements, with tightly stretched wire attached to numerous stakes pounded or screwed deep into the ground. Instead, the Germans had begun to use large coils of loose wire that could be quickly deployed along the front.

The Germans discovered that the new type of wire entanglements not only could be erected quickly and with little loss of life, but was also much more difficult to cut using artillery fire. Since the explosions merely tossed the loose wire coils about they tended to create an even more effective barrier to the attacking troops.

The remnants of barbed wire that still protected the 6/R119 had given most of the trench garrison enough time to man their defenses and open fire into the mass of British troops, most likely the right wing of the 117th Brigade, who was approaching their trenches and shell crater position. The heavy rifle and machine gun fire was able to stop most of the British troops before they could reach the German trenches; the attackers were only able to penetrate the German front line at a few locations.

On the right, British troops succeeded in penetrating into the German front line where the wire entanglements had been almost completely destroyed. There were simply too few obstacles in place to prevent the British from reaching the German trenches even in the face of machine gun and rifle fire combined with defensive German artillery fire. Once inside the German front lines, small groups of British soldiers made valiant attempts to advance toward the second and third German trench lines.

The small groups of British soldiers from the 117th Brigade did not get very far however. Some men from the 6/R119 had taken cover in shell craters located just behind the front line trench in order to avoid the enemy who had penetrated into the neighboring Sector B6; others had moved further to the right or left of their sector, whichever proved to be the safest. When the British attempted to advance beyond the captured front line trench, many of them were cut down by the defenders firing from the second trench where several groups of the 7/R119 were located. Still, despite all the odds against them, a few of the British troops managed to penetrate into the second trench at several locations.

At one spot where the British managed to enter the German front line in B5, a platoon leader of the 6/R119, was trapped with his men when their dugout entrance was destroyed. The presence of the British outside of the collapsed entrance prevented his soldiers from reopening the entrance. The platoon leader remained calm under these difficult circumstances and simply telephoned the neighboring platoon that was about 100 meters to his left, for help. While the telephone connections to the rear had been destroyed, the lines connecting the different sectors of the front line had remained intact. In a short time, a bombing party approached the dugout and quickly ejected the enemy using hand grenades. Once the enemy had been thrown out of the trench, the platoon leader and his men were freed from the dugout and joined the fighting.

Many of the men in the 6/R119 who had been forced to move further right or left in order to evade the British now quickly regrouped. They then advanced in an organized counterattack from the right and out of the shell holes behind the front line trench. Bitter close fighting arose in the trenches, primarily with the use of hand grenades on both sides. The individual German groups quickly gained the upper hand and simply overwhelmed the British. While the 6/R119 swept down along the trench from the north, parts of the 7/R119 stormed out of the second trench, helped by men from the 4/R119. Faced with such overwhelming odds, the British were forced back from the second trench and the position was eventually cleared.

Within 30 minutes of the opening attack, the assault groups and bombing parties from RIR 119 had recaptured their entire trench system in B5. A number of men from RIR 119 stood out from their comrades in this counterattack and were officially recognized for their efforts: *Vizefeldwebel* Traub, *Unteroffizier* Hilligard, *Gefreiter* Kuno Müller and the *Reservists* Klaiber and Speidel.

The main enemy thrust had been directed against the two southern most sectors, B6 and B7. The enemy troops followed closely behind the bombardment and when the fire was lifted off of the German front line, the British troops were literally standing at the edge of the German trench. Much of the front line in B6 and B7 was therefore quickly captured; only a few scattered groups of defenders were able to avoid being overwhelmed.

One of these small groups included *Leutnant der Reserve* Beisswenger, a teacher in civilian life, and eight of his men. They were able to hold their portion of the German trench and prevented the British from expanding their gains to the right. In the heavy close quarters fighting, Beisswenger's small group managed to drive the British back down the trench using hand grenades. When the hand grenades ran out, Beisswenger ordered the trench blocked off and sent men back for additional supplies of this critical close combat weapon.

The right wing of the 4/R119 in B6 was also able to stand firm and prevent the British from reaching the first trench. However at the *Junker Graben*, the British were able to penetrate into the first trench and quickly push forward against the second trench. The momentum of the attack continued and the British made it all of the way to the third German trench until, exhausted, with much of the impetus lost and casualties increasing by the minute, they were finally stopped.

By the sector near the Ancre, B7, the British had reached a position in front of the third German trench. They were being prevented from completely taking this trench by the company leader, *Oberleutnant* Schafferdt, 1/R119, along with one Group from the company. Reserves from the *Kolonie* were quickly sent to help Schafferdt's men. The 11/R119 was moving up from Beaucourt to offer assistance and most importantly, brought additional supplies of hand grenades to the front. When they arrived, the men of the 11th Coy would join the counterattacks being undertaken. In the meantime, the German artillery placed a dense wall of fire in front of the position to prevent any further enemy advance. Every machine gun in the area also directed its fire on any enemy target that appeared in its sites.

Württemberg *Hauptmann* Taute, from the General Staff of Group Stein had also arrived in the third trench in B7. Taute had been going home on leave when the attack began. Instead of heading home, he hurried to the battle front and formed a small company with men from the 3/R119. He personally led his composite company in a counterattack and helped to destroy the British troops that had reached the third trench. At the same time Platoon Malblanc counterattacked the British troops located in the second trench and in close fighting he was able to capture one machine gun. Shortly after 9 a.m. the two rear trenches were in German hands again.

The men from the 1/R119 holding the center of B7 had been able to prevent the British from taking their portion of the front line trench while British troops could be seen streaming past on their right and left. Some of the British troops had stopped and took up a position in an unfinished front line trench, from which they took the remnants of the 1/R119 under severe close range machine gun fire.

The surrounded German garrison acted quickly and counterattacked to the right and managed to push the British back a short distance. The counterattack faltered as there were far too many enemy troops holding long stretches of the front line on both sides of the small group from the 1/R119. In addition, no connections could be established with the rest of the 1st Coy on either flank.

At the left wing of the *Berg Stellung* the entrances of most of the dugouts had been buried as a result of the enemy drum fire. Before the garrison could dig out from below, the

British were already standing in front of the dugouts. Any men who managed to exit the shelters were killed in close combat. When it had become evident that no one could survive if they tried to leave the safety of the shelters the garrison fought back from inside the tunnels as best they could, mainly by firing up the stairway from the bottom of the dugout at any targets that appeared silhouetted at the entrance.

All attempts by the British to extend to the right had failed because of the resolute garrison holding the center of B7. Fierce fighting was taking place inside the German trench system at the hillside sloping down toward the Ancre valley. Platoon Weitz was located inside the *Tunnel Stollen,* a large dugout driven deep into the hillside that was named the *Schleusingerhauses.*

When the enemy attack began, the men of Platoon Weitz swarmed out into the trenches, however the British had already entered the German trenches and a severe hand grenade battle broke out between the opposing sides, from one traverse to the next. Platoon Weitz suffered numerous losses in the fighting and the survivors were forced to withdraw back into the *Schleusingerhauses* where they could still effectively prevent the enemy from advancing any further up the valley.

The garrison of the *Schleusingerhauses* continued to hold out against all attempts by the British to capture this key position. The occupants of the tunnel covered the entire embankment with their fire, ensuring certain death for anyone to move in the open. In addition to the fire from the tunnel, a nearby *Priester Granatwerfer* [2] effectively fired on the advancing British troops; each fragmentation shell bringing new losses to the attackers.

At 7 a.m. *Oberleutnant* Schafferdt, 1/R119, went forward into the first trench of B7, in order to personally determine the exact situation facing his company. While Schafferdt and his staff were on reconnaissance another enemy advance occurred. The new waves of British troops broke down completely under the rifle and machine gun fire coming from the men of RIR 119. Unfortunately, *Oberleutnant* Schafferdt was killed by a shot to the head while fighting next to his personal orderly, Ulrich Bauer. *Leutnant der Reserve* Mörk, who had already behaved splendidly in the earlier hand grenade battle, assumed command of the company. A half hour later he was also killed while performing a reconnaissance toward the location of the British penetration. Observation on both sides was difficult due to the mist as well as the smoke and dust raised by the heavy shelling. It was often very difficult to know just where the opposing side was, hence the need for personal reconnaissance by the company leaders.

Repeated British attacks did not result in any expansion of the captured terrain. After hours of combat, at 10 a.m., there was a pause in the fighting. Once the advance had commenced, , the British commanders in the rear knew very little about what was happening in the German trenches. Heavy fire swept across no man's land making it almost impossible for runners to make the journey to the British trenches. The mist and smoke made all signaling attempts useless. The men who had made it across no man's land to the German lines were effectively on their own.

The British troops in the German trenches now worked with all haste to prepare the captured trenches for defense. However, the men of RIR 119 were not going to allow the British the luxury of the time that they would need to complete their work. The I/R119 received assistance from Beaumont, where the 11/R119 had arrived just after 10 a.m.

Now, with fresh troops and most importantly, new supplies of hand grenades, the German counterattacks would have a better chance of succeeding. All previous attempts to recapture the lost trenches had had failed until now, mainly because the hand grenades had run out before the enemy resistance could be broken.

The British attacked the 1st and 4/R119 shortly before 12 noon in large masses, without success. The barrage fire from the supporting artillery shattered the attack waves. Once this attack failed, *Leutnant der Reserve* Beisswenger, gathered together his eight men, armed with as many hand grenades as they could carry and prepared for a counterattack. The men with Beisswenger were *Pionier Gefreiter* Finkbeiner, an *Unteroffizier* from the *Minenwerfer* Company, *Unteroffiziers* Schick and Fröhlich and *Landwehrmann* Glück, Mauser, Fiedler and Kotz.

Not far from Beisswenger and his men, the British had already brought a machine gun and a mine thrower into position. The enemy still held a section of trench 150 meters in length and it needed to be recaptured as quickly as possible. *Leutnant* Beisswenger quickly advanced toward the enemy held trench and stood up on top of a traverse and demanded the British surrender. According to Beisswenger, there were over 400 British troops densely crowded inside the trench. When no one came forth following his request, Beisswenger raised his hand as if on the practice field, giving the signal for the attack to begin.

Almost instantly, numerous German hand grenades flew into the adjoining trench pieces, where they exploded with a crash. The British replied to the attack by throwing hand grenades in the direction of Beisswenger's position; however the Germans were so close that the British hand grenades flew far behind the small group. Wasting no time, the German assault group sprang over the traverse with a cheer and fell on the machine gun and the mine thrower. *Pionier Gefreiter* Finkbeiner quickly grabbed the captured machine gun, a Lewis Gun, and then fired it into the surprised British troops packed inside the trench, who quickly retreated in the face of this sudden turn of events.

As the British troops were pressed back through the badly damaged trench the men began to bunch up in the confined space. More and more men tried to escape the German assault but were running out places to go. Beisswenger and his eight men quickly followed on their heels, moving from one traverse to another, all the while continuing to throw their hand grenades into the large mass of men in front of them. As the *Stielhandgranaten* exploded in the close confines of the trench the hand grenade splinters and concussion caused terrible wounds to anyone in their vicinity.

The British troops who were uninjured continued to flood down the trench as Finkbeiner took up a position and fired his captured machine gun down the length of the trench, into the rear of the fleeing men. At the same time machine gun fire from the right, left and rear in the German trenches struck both flanks of the retreating British troops. In just a few minutes not only was the entire trench cleared but also a communication trench leading to the rear was successfully stormed by Beisswenger's group. Most, if not all of the surviving British troops who tried to flee across the open ground were cut down in the fire from flanking machine guns. Miraculously, Beisswenger and his eight men had not suffered a single casualty during their attack.

When the attack was over, the captured position was a scene out of Hell with bodies lying everywhere, piled one on top of another, nearly 100 British dead lay inside it. 20 unwounded prisoners were taken in the surprise assault and ten men from RIR 119 were released from captivity (they had been held inside of a dugout as prisoners). The Württembergers had been surprised by the British at the start of the attack and had quickly surrendered. Unfortunately, after being taken inside a nearby dugout, the prisoners could

Prisoners and machine guns captured by RIR 119 on 3
September by RIR 119. (Author's collection)

only sit by and watch as their guards happily consume the supplies stored there of meat, tinned food, water and cigars.

The captives from RIR 119 observed how their guards appeared quite pleased to be safe inside the deep dugout rather than out in the close combat that was clearly audible to the men under the ground. After being held as prisoners for some time, they suddenly heard the crash of hand grenades and recognized them as being German, help was apparently coming. The former prisoners confidently stood up and strapped on their leather equipment again, motioning to their captors that their roles had now become reversed. The British guards apparently recognizing the futility of any opposition in that situation, un-strapped their equipment and surrendered.

Shortly before 1 p.m. the main position was back in German possession again. The British still sat in the unfinished front line trench where they had dug in. The men of RIR 119 could see their bayonets flashing in the light and fully expected a further attack. Shortly after, the British artillery fire increased once again with enemy pilots directing the fire using horns and klaxon signals. The last mass enemy attack against the 1/R119 commenced at 1.30 p.m. It was met with fierce infantry and machine gun fire as well as well-placed German barrage fire. The German shells were very accurate and so destructive that after a few minutes the attackers were flooding to the rear.

RIR 119 reported four further attacks against their front line, all of which were completely repulsed.. The first, about 12.15 p.m., succeeded in reaching the first trench again. Once more, bombing parties threw the adversary back. Two further advances at 12.30 and 2 p.m. were immediately blocked by defensive fire. At 2.30 in the afternoon one final British attack was repulsed and soon after the artillery fire died down. Finally, at 3 p.m. it grew silent along the front of RIR 119 and the regiment could report that it had held the entire position. The spoils and prisoners taken by RIR 119 during the fighting amounted

Same prisoners as in the previous illustration taken from a different angle.
This photo is the one I have seen most duplicated. (*Das Württembergische
Reserve-Infanterie-Regiment Nr. 119 im Weltkrieg 1914-1918*)

to: 3 officers and approximately 100 men, 3 mine throwers, 5 machine guns, 9 Lewis Guns, 2 telephone apparatus and numerous weapons and ammunition.

RIR 119 did not come out of the fighting unscathed; the regiment had lost 3 officers killed and 8 officers wounded;107 men killed and 191 men wounded. One other notable casualty was *Hauptmann* Taute. After participating in the fighting instead of heading home on leave, he had been called back to the General Staff of the Corps by telephone in the early evening. As he was about to make the trip to the rear he was killed while taking a final look at the regimental position that had been recaptured.

From captured orders and statements made by British prisoners, the 26th Reserve Division was able to piece together the goal and strength of the attack of 3 September. The goal was apparently the capture of the three southern company sectors, in order to obtain observation and flanking positions for an attack upon Thiepval (occurring on the same day south of the Ancre). The 26th Reserve Division came to the conclusion that an entire brigade, the 117th Infantry Brigade from the British 39th Division, had attacked three companies of RIR 119. What they apparently had missed was that both brigades of the 39th Division were involved in the attack; however, only one had managed to make any headway into the German lines.

Documents taken off prisoners also contained the final order of the day given to the men of the 117th Brigade by the commanding officer, Brigadier-General R.D.F. Oldman: 'I wish that all ranks up to the last man are notified that we are participating in a clash of considerable size. Not only is our own division attacking, but also the 5th Army and the army to our right. Our brigade has the honor to attack on the wing farthest on the left of the British troops engaged, to take and to hold.'[3]

As a result of the attack north of the Ancre, the enemy had been repulsed and had suffered enormous losses. According to statements from the prisoners their losses were estimated at 2,000 men. The intermediate terrain looked terrible, it was covered with dead and wounded British soldiers. The trenches, in which close combat had raged, were literally filled with dead and wounded men. 400 British dead alone were counted in front of the 6/ R119 on 4 September. In another section of trench lay 40 British corpses.

The men from RIR 119 felt a certain pride in that they had once again managed to defeat a major enemy attack against their position, in a manner very reminiscent of 1 July 1916. An officer in RIR 119 noted that the British soldiers always came on in dense, open waves and the bravery with which they attacked, deserved honest admiration. While the German artillery fire was effective, individual detachments of enemy troops had still managed to reach the German lines. However, all of them finally succumbed to the German defensive fire. The fighting surged back and forth all morning, in all, almost ten separate attacks had been attempted and all had failed.

The success achieved by RIR 119 was all the more significant as many of the officers and men were in poor health as a result of the continuous stress that they had been under since 24 June when the battle began. The toll that stress had taken on the men had been incredibly debilitating, with many men reporting sick. However, despite this, many of the men wanted to be back with their comrades at such difficult times.

> Walincourt 7 September 1916
> Dear Johanna!
> Yesterday such a lovely letter came to me in my remote location with such a lovely picture of you so that I was very pleased. You have my heartfelt thanks for that! Forgive me that I have not thanked you for your 2 packets before my illness. But all the time since 24 June has been a terrible physical and mental effort, day and night, there was almost no rest and then the great responsibility and the pain of all the good comrades, who were taken sequentially. And yet I would give so much if I could be with my company instead of having to sit here while my regiment had further particularly hot fighting again (3 Sept.). The packet unfortunately came this day in a completely crushed and compressed condition. If Karl comes to the 180th in the field, then he would be in my division and there exists a possibility that we could meet at times. The 180th was lately beside us at Thiepval and surely needs to come back for replacements after the recent heavy fighting. But I wish for you and him, from the heart, that he may remain at home as long as possible, because during the war he can probably come a long time into next year. I am now back to such an extent that the actual stomach and intestinal problems no longer exist. So if you want to send a packet, everything (for example Zwieback and pickles) are equally welcome. It is going on midnight, putting an end to my letter. Many greetings to you and my dear aunt. Your faithful Albert. Within 8-10 days I'm probably with my company again. [4]

South of the Ancre, the fighting was no less severe than what the men of RIR 119 were experiencing. The attack against the St. Pierre-Divion – Thiepval front was being undertaken by the British 49th Division, consisting of the 146th Brigade on the left and the 147th Brigade on the right.

The advance by the 146th Brigade was directed against the men of IR 66 who had only just taken over the new sector (C1, C2 and C3) a few hours before the attack began. At 4.15 a.m. IR 66 reported that the entire regimental sector was covered under heavy enemy drum fire. It was considered to be particularly strong on the first and second trenches in Sector C2. Within an hour, enemy attack columns could be observed emerging from the British front line trench along the Thiepval-Hamel road opposite the regiment. Dense waves of enemy troops poured out of Thiepval Wood and advanced closely behind the barrage fire.

The attackers were being opposed by the men of the 11th and 10/66 who immediately opened fire into the massed ranks approaching them. The batteries in the rear formed a protective wall of fire in front of the German lines. The 10/66 was fortunate in that there were still machine guns from RIR 99 in positions where they were able to provide much needed support against the attack. The machine guns were the last unit in RIR 99 scheduled to be relieved and had remained in place in order to give IR 66 time to set its guns up.

> When I was in the tunnel and arrived at the first trench, one heard the cry: "They come, they are already here!" The Englishmen knocked at the castle gate of our bulwark with hand grenades and bayonets! The machine gun of the 2nd Machine Gun Company, RIR 99 that I should replace, was already firing, because the guns had already been brought into position in the preparation fire. However the machine gun had a jam after 100 shots, so that my machine gun under *Unteroffizier* Horn and *Gefreiter* Müller could be moved for better use. Because, as correctly recognized, the adversary followed on foot immediately behind the last impact of his shrapnel. We found orders with the Englishmen that losses are only reduced, the closer each man remains connected with their own rolling fire. The dead that lay 15 steps in front of the trench, proved how far the attack by the enemy had already come. Close in front of my dugout lay a dead English officer. My Gun Captain, *Unteroffizier* Horn, my *Richtschütze* and two other *Schützen* were wounded at the same time. In the defensive in the great battle one is entirely employed with the defense. In the first line one has to look out for the enemy, because there is no time to help a severely wounded comrade. Our *Gefreiter* Müller had a leg shot off by a shell; a doctor could have probably helped him, if one had been there. So he must die in the dugout. My machine gun fired further half-left, where the enemy had already penetrated into the first trench, and stopped the enemy pressing after in masses. Meanwhile a ghastlier close combat played out by the 9/66 with hand grenades in the trench, about 50 meters to the left of me. With it the good 9/66 had lost two third of its men, of which I knew many. Many *Unteroffizieren* lay there, torn apart in pieces, and with smashed skulls. It is simply impossible to take away the corpses, amongst them also many Englishmen, because the rear terrain was under the most severe fire. Our wounded had to lie here a long time, until a doctor was able to be brought here. Their moans and whimpers had an effect on us; it also did not especially cheer us up. About 30 Englishmen who were in the trench by the 9th Company, had found the garrison in the dugouts and had thrown hand grenades into these. *Leutnant* Kusel was partially blocked off by frames and became freed when the Englishmen were expelled through a counterattack out of the second trench, during which *Leutnant der Reserve* Bötticher and *Leutnant* Hädrich fell. The trenches were completely leveled and only the dugout entrances were open, everything else was a

field of craters. *Leutnant* Meyer, Platoon leader 3rd MG Coy/66 [5]

Flanking machine guns, *Minenwerfer* and *Erdmörser* poured fire into the flanks of the enemy attack, especially from a projecting portion of the German line the British called 'The Pope's Nose.[6] The fire enfiladed the attackers, causing numerous losses. The men in C2 and C3 poured a devastating fire and threw hand grenades directly into the advancing British waves but nothing seemed to stop the approaching enemy troops. The fighting continued with great intensity as the opposing waves came closer and closer to the German trenches. However, the German fire was wreaking havoc in the British ranks and the attack began to falter.

The strong German defensive artillery fire caused many of the men in the subsequent waves to turn around and make their way back to the British lines. Still, despite the heavy German fire, men in the first wave of the 147th Brigade managed to reach and enter the first line trench occupied by the 9/66. This was possible in part because the wire entanglements were lacking in front of the 9th Company. Also, the British fire had already resulted in a high number of losses in the 9/66 with numerous men becoming trapped inside their dugouts when the entrances collapsed under the weight of artillery fire.

The survivors of the 9/66 who managed to exit their dugouts quickly joined together and started small counterattacks against the enemy who was already in the process of creating barricades inside the German front line. The Magdeburg troops knew that a rapid counterattack would prevent the enemy from becoming oriented inside the German trenches and prevent the British from creating a viable defensive position. The fighting quickly became man against man as both sides fought savagely to secure the trench. Knives, pistols, trench shovels, rifles and hand grenades were used freely and losses on both sides rose quickly.

The company leader of the 9/66, *Leutnant der Reserve* Bötticher, was in the second trench of Sector C2 when the attack occurred. When he observed that the British had penetrated into his first trench, he assembled a group of men from his company and attacked the first trench across the open ground. During the subsequent close fighting, Bötticher was killed when he was struck in the head by a fragment from an enemy hand grenade. A number of his men also became killed or wounded during this attack including another officer in the 9/66, *Leutnant der Reserve* Kröplin, who was wounded.

Seeing how bad the situation was becoming by the 9/66, *Oberleutnant* Hermens, the leader of the neighboring 10/66, gathered together all available men and hurried to help the 9th Company. This counterattack by Hermens was undertaken in darkness in a position that was entirely unfamiliar to the men of the 10/66. Despite this daunting situation the counterattack was a great success.

Many of the British troops who remained inside the German trenches were shot down, while others, recognizing that the fight was lost, fled back to the British lines. That the 10/66 was even able to help fend off the enemy attack against the 9/66 was due to *Leutnant der Reserve* Mewes. Mewes was a platoon leader in the 10/66 which was located in the first trench and he had immediately recognized when the enemy artillery fire was transferred to the rear. He instantly ordered the men in his platoon to man their positions and open fire against the approaching enemy troops with devastating effect.

By 8.30 a.m. the III/66 could report that their position was free from the enemy. In addition to the two officers mentioned above from the 10/66 *Unteroffizier* Nonnemann drew special attention to himself, especially in the close combat. After he had helped in the fighting by the 9/66, he then hurried with his Group to the neighboring 4/180 to help expel the British from the trench where they had also become firmly established.

All telephone communications to the rear had been destroyed in the British fire. Reports took far too long to reach even the nearby 52nd Reserve Infantry Brigade headquarters so, during the fighting, the brigade turned over command of the sector from Thiepval to the Ancre to *Oberstleutnant* Vischer, commander of IR 180. During the course of the fighting south of the Ancre additional reserves were also moved forward in the event they were required. The III/R55 was made available to *Oberstleutnant* Vischer as well the I/66 under *Hauptmann* Niemeyer, which was placed on alert.

The men of the I/66 were equipped with hand grenades and moved forward into the *Hansa Stellung* where the 2nd, 3rd and 4/66 occupied *Süd-1, Süd-2* and *Feste Staufen*. The insertion of these companies into the front lines had proven to be extremely difficult, because it took place during daylight and the Miraumont-Grandcourt road was constantly under concentrated enemy artillery fire. The II/66 was replaced in the Sector *Mitte* in its former position north of Serre by the III/R99 and then moved south to Irles and Miraumont. When the fighting was finally finished, the men from IR 66 took stock of their losses and determined that they had suffered casualties of 2 officers and 37 men killed, 1 officer and 133 men wounded.

The trenches occupied by the neighboring IR 180 also came under the British drum fire at 5 a.m. The fire appeared to be falling mainly on Sectors C2 and C3. In C3 the second trench had already been completely leveled through the systematic bombardment of the previous few days. Almost all of the wire entanglements had been destroyed or badly damaged and numerous dugouts in the first and second trench had collapsed. On 3 September the enemy artillery fire on the forward most trenches consisted almost exclusively of shrapnel shells, while the rear areas and communication trenches were bombarded with heavy shells and numerous gas shells.

The German artillery immediately employed blocking barrage fire when the British attack started, which effectively protected the positions of IR 180. However, due to the close proximity of the enemy trenches the adversaries were successful in penetrating into C3 with strong forces where the 4/180 was positioned. The commander of the 4/180 sent a report to headquarters by runner about the enemy penetration. Immediately after the battalion received this report the 10th and 12/180 were placed in possession of the Sector Commander of *Feste Schwaben, Hauptmann* Scharl, I/180. Within a short time the British had become firmly established in the first trench of C3 and smaller groups had advanced deeper into the German lines specifically the second trench between the *Münstergasse* and *Teufels Graben*.

Bombing parties from the 10th and 12/180 along with the 2nd and 4/180 advanced down the trenches to where the enemy was located and quickly drove them out of the second trench. The Württemberg troops were assisted by a platoon from the 12/66 that joined in the counterattack from the right flank. The bombing parties continued to advance toward the first trench and also quickly forced the British back into their start lines. Starting from 7 a.m., individual Englishmen, then entire groups came out of the sectors of the 3rd, 7th and 5/180 by C3 and could be seen going back to the British front lines.

The fleeing men were effectively fired upon with infantry and machine gun fire, as well as with devastating *Erdmörser, Minenwerfer* and flanking machine gun fire from Thiepval.

'Rest in Peace', Notice of death, 3 September 1916. IR 180 (Author's collection)

In order to further intensify the effectiveness of the fire a machine gun that was located in the *Auwärter Weg* was moved forward into the Sector of the 3/180 to provide flanking fire. Shortly after 10.35 a.m. a report was sent to division headquarters by carrier pigeon: 'In C2 and C3 the invading adversary was thrown out, the regimental sector is in our hands.'

Following the failure of the morning attack, the British placed heavy drum fire upon Sectors C1 to C4, but especially on C3, for the entire afternoon. The fire was so heavy there could be no thought of occupying this sector. In order to prevent the British from penetrating the German front line again, the gap was closed off with artillery barrage fire and the corresponding occupation of the right wing of C3 and the *Burk Graben*. Furthermore, three machine guns were brought into position at the western part of *Feste Schwaben*, which assured the possibility of strong flanking fire on any enemy attack in that sector.

The British attempted one further attack around noon but heavy German artillery fire smashed the attack before it could advance very far beyond the enemy lines. The survivors quickly withdrew into the safety of their trenches.

With the onset of darkness the gap at C3 was occupied by infantry and a connection with the III/66 was established. Afterward, the enemy artillery fire died down considerably. In the night, the 9th and 11/180 were moved closer to *Feste Schwaben* and into the *Strassburger Steige* as reinforcements.

The events of this day were summed up by *Leutnant der Reserve* Matthias Gerster, RIR 119:

Like in the first day of the Somme battle the leaders in the front line said that the enemy should be quickly attacked with strength. The counter thrust became carefully prepared. The 10th and 12th Companies of IR 180 pushed forward from the *Schwaben Feste*, covered the break in position with powerful mine fire and prevented a supply route of reserves through machine gun fire. Then the storm troops fell about the Englishmen here and threw them back. In the flanking fire of the machine guns and *Erdmörser* out of Thiepval and the prosecution fire of the storm troops the escaping Englishmen melted together into a small remnant that made it back safely. At 10.40 a.m. the entire position was German again. One attack planned against the village did not come to development at all in the barrage fire. However the Englishmen still gave us no rest. Already at 11 o'clock their artillery and their mine throwers began to pound again. After one hour they believed that the position was ripe for the new storm. New masses wanted to storm forward again; however, they broke together in the German artillery fire. 2 officers and 30 men of which 8 were wounded, and 15 Lewis Guns remained in our hands. In front of and in the break in position was a further 500 English corpses. [7]

The British failure on 3 September was not for the lack of trying. Perhaps the most disturbing aspect of the research into this action came in the British Official History when explaining the failure of the attacks against *Feste Schwaben*:

There was little fault to find with the artillery preparation and support; but a frontal attack, with no attempt at surprise, upon this portion of the original German defenses, commanded as it was by Schwaben Redoubt, seems to have offered very little chance of success. Moreover, the troops were very tired, and in the attacking battalions were many partially trained reinforcements posted from many different regiments. These men displayed a certain apathy and lack of determination, in sharp contrast to the devotion of the platoon leaders *who died with their usual gallantry, and to the splendid resolution of the older soldier.* [Author's italics] [8]

Numerous rifles, hand grenades, ammunition and other pieces of equipment were salvaged by the Germans. The prisoner's uniform insignia and other documents indicated that the attack against the regimental sector, including the III/66 by St. Pierre-Divion had been executed by the 146th and 147th Brigades, therefore from the 49th (West Riding) Division. In addition to the estimated 500 enemy dead lying in no man's land, there were numerous men who were wounded, many of them severely. Many of these unfortunate men were trapped between the opposing lines and had to wait hours for help to arrive, if it arrived at all. One piece of new intelligence obtained from statements made by the British prisoners indicated that the British Guards Division was supposedly marching from Albert to Thiepval in order to take part in the fighting on the Somme front.

The losses to IR 180 on this day consisted of: 1 officer (*Leutnant der Reserve* Schölhammer) and 47 men killed; 5 officers (*Leutnant* Hoch and *Leutnant der Reserve* Sauer severely, *Leutnant* Ehemann, *Leutnant der Reserve* Teuffel and *Leutnant* Hagenmeyer slightly) wounded; 110 men wounded, 16 men missing.

Even though the danger of an enemy breakthrough had been avoided early in the fighting the reinforcements requested in the morning were still sent forward. *Leutnant*

Schöllhammer
Leutnant d. R. im Jnf.-Regt. 180
gefallen bei Thiepval
am 3. September 1916

(*Kriegstagebuch aus Schwaben*)

Keiser from the III/R55 arrived at 8.30 a.m. with the 10/R55 and was ordered to occupy Sector *Süd-I*, south of Grandcourt where it remained at the disposal of IR 180. At 10 a.m. the 9/R55 occupied *Feste Staufen*.

At 10.45 a.m. the battalion staff of the III/R55, commanded by *Major* Tauscher, came under the control of the 52nd Reserve Infantry Brigade. 30 minutes later, Tauscher travelled to Miraumont to the telephone exchange of IR 180. A short time later, *Hauptmann* Winkelmann, commander of the 12/R55 moved forward to the Miraumont-Grandcourt road with the 11th and 12/R55. He was directed to occupy a support position there.

By 12.40 p.m. the III/R55 battalion staff had reached the battle headquarters of IR 180 where reports from the 9th and 10/R55 arrived: 'The Sectors *Süd-I* and *Süd-II* were occupied.' At 3.45 p.m. *Hauptmann* Winkelmann reported that the 11th and 12/R55 stood at the western exit of Petit Miraumont, 500 meters west of the village exit. Winkelmann made his headquarters in the dugout of the carrying troops for IR 180 where he was joined by *Major* Tauscher and the battalion staff at 4.30 p.m.

The fighting had ceased along the entire front line and at 8.50 p.m., when this became evident, the 52nd Reserve Infantry Brigade ordered the men from RIR 55 to take up nearby reserve positions. In the evening of 3 September the II/R55 also arrived behind the sector and was sent to Beauregard Farm north of the Ancre. The battalion took up positions in order to provide support for the 51st Reserve Infantry Brigade: the 6th Coy – from Ancre Shore to the *Mühlen Graben*, the 8th Coy – from the *Mühlen Graben* to the *Fischer Graben*, the 5th Coy – from the *Fischer Graben* to the *Soden Graben*, the 7th Coy – from the *Soden Graben* to the division border.

While not needed to take part in the fighting of 3 September, the arrival of RIR 55 would enable other troops to be relieved from the front lines. After manning the same

(Author's collection)

trenches since May 1915 without a break, something needed to be done to provide relief for RIR119. The men were overtired and with the conclusion of this latest fighting, it was time to replace the regiment. There was a grave concern that 'Trench madness' threatened to infect the officers and Other Ranks; the men desperately needed to rest. Subsequently, orders soon came through with the good news that the regiment was to be relieved by RIR 55.

The XIV Reserve Corps had once again demonstrated the ability to repulse enemy attacks carried out by superior numbers, utilizing an enormous amount of light and heavy guns, mine throwers and almost complete mastery of the air. In recognition of these spectacular achievements, General von Stein was presented with the Order *Pour le Merité* on 4 September; a number of Prussian awards were also conferred on other Württemberg officers.

All through the night of 3/4 September the German heavy artillery batteries fired gas shells on all known enemy approach routes. The shells made a distinctive sound as they shrieked overhead but there was no resulting explosion or flash of light when they impacted. Instead, they simply discharged their lethal contents almost silently.

On 4 September the regimental commander of IR 180 passed along the following document to his men: 'His *Excellenz* the Division Commander as well as the Brigade Commander wanted to speak to the regiment, especially above all to the attacked I Battalion, of their congratulations for heroically holding the position and the vigorous defense against the English attacks, supported through energetic counter-thrusts. So as with Ovillers, the regiment carried out its task brilliantly and they know it will also do so in the future.'

On the same day, Sector C2 and the northern half of C3 experienced a very strong fire raid in the late morning hours. Observers in IR 180 also noted what appeared to be attack movements threatening the boundary between C2 and C3. When the first wave of British climbed up over the breastworks, they were instantly engaged and shot down by the German infantry while the artillery observers immediately called for barrage fire in order to block the suspected attack. Because of the fire from the German artillery and the British battery fire falling short upon the following wave, no more enemy troops dared to come out of the trench. The defensive fire was deemed to be effective as only a few enemy troops were seen leaving their trench.

On 4 September, the relief of the rest of IR 66 continued. On this day the regimental staff in Sector '*Mitte*'was relieved and the commander of IR 66 took over Sector Grandcourt. The I/66 relieved the I/180 in C3 and C4 and in *Feste Schwaben*. The I/180 moved into positions north and east of Thiepval. The III/180 was transferred into the II position and *Feste Staufen*. The II/66 was also moved close behind the front line where the men could be deployed quickly if the need arose.

After the relief was completed on 4 September Grandcourt Sector was occupied as follows: C1 and C2 by the 11/66, 9/66, 12/66 and 10/66. The portion of the *Strassburger Steige* behind these sectors by the 6/66 and the 1st MG/66. C3 and C4 were occupied by the 1st and 2/66, the *Strassburger Steige* to the rear of these sectors by the 3/66 and 2nd MG/66. *Feste Schwaben* and the *Schwaben Riegel* were occupied by the 4/66 and the Reserve Battalion was the II/66. The 8/66 occupied the *Hansa Stellung, Süd-I* by the 5th and 7/66.

Throughout the period needed for the relief to be completed, C1 and C2 were under strong enemy fire. The trenches were in poor condition following the attack of the previous day and could only be cleared with considerable difficulty. Due to a lack of manpower, it was impossible to transport all of the wounded from the fighting on 3 September to the rear. It was not until the following day, 5 September, when the bulk of the wounded could be brought to the *Feldlazarett* located in the rear areas. While the wounded were slowly being cared for, no one had any time to be concerned about the numerous dead lying everywhere.

The 9th and 12/66 were so intermingled they were combined to form one company, Company Pitschke. Great effort was used in rebuilding the wire entanglements, clearing the trenches of debris and creating defensible positions where the trenches had been leveled by enemy fire. There was so much to do that the men had to work throughout the day without any protection against enemy observation balloons, aircraft and infantry observers; shrapnel and high explosive shells were constantly being fired on the positions and losses occurred daily.

The men especially worked on repairing the crushed entrances to the mined dugouts where some protection from the enemy fire could be found. Performing all of the work required placed great demands on the troops and little sleep was allowed until the tasks were finished. The men understood this as they were being subjected to constant artillery and mine fire and continued to work diligently as shells up to 28cm in caliber smashed along the front line and *Feste Schwaben*.

However, much of the hard work performed by the men was destroyed over and over again by the heavy fire. Despite their efforts, large numbers of dugouts were being destroyed one after the other. IR 66 asked for help in restoring the position. A request was sent to the 52nd Reserve Infantry Brigade for *pioniers* to be sent up to help increase the number of useable dugouts. Unfortunately this request was denied due to a lack of *pioniers*.

There was also a great shortage of men in the rear critical to the resupply of the front lines. Carrying food and *pionier* materials required an immense amount of effort as everything

The much feared 2-inch trench mortar shell, identified in this
instance as a gas bomb. (Author's collection)

needed to be brought up by hand. The field railway had been destroyed and there was no safe method of transporting supplies by horse and wagon past Grandcourt. Even getting supplies as far as Grandcourt required considerable effort, with numerous horses being lost each day. However, through ingenuity and superhuman effort provision of critical supplies to the front lines was managed.

Anything and everything needed at the front had to be carried over the cratered terrain at night in order to avoid being observed by the enemy. Despite this precaution the tracks made on the ground by the numerous carrying parties were clearly visible in aerial photographs taken by British pilots. This information would then be passed to the artillery that would randomly open fire on these paths during the hours of darkness in the hopes of catching one of the carrying parties out in the open. Fortunately, there was comparative silence in the early morning hours during which both sides transported their wounded to the rear.

Whenever the wire entanglements had been restored somewhat in front of the regimental sector, the enemy mine throwers became very active and destroyed them once again. Above all, Company Pitschke and the 10/66 suffered extensively under the ball mines, the 2-inch trench mortar shells, commonly known as 'Plum Puddings' by the British troops. As the days passed, the strain on the nerves of the men only increased at every level of the regiment.

The 4/66 arrived in *Feste Schwaben* during thick fog. We come through a section of trench newly created in the night, in part only knee deep, parts chest deep, anyway however, only a single, hastily and meager night's work. Here we were now in a completely simple, zig-zag communication trench without any dugouts or other cover, without any obstacles in front of the position, totally unshielded in the open trench, and that called itself *Feste Schwaben*. We are all of the opinion that we could not remain here, because however that meant certain death in the shell fire. Then our battalion commander, *Hauptmann* Niemeyer, came and urged fast entrenching, because as soon as the fog lifts, the enemy fire began upon the new trench. So we remained because there was nothing else to do, as we dug in and waited for the things that should come there. Everyone worked at his position now, two by two where possible in all haste, deeper into the trench. Slowly the fog dissipates and the sun breaks through. Then, suddenly, a veritable rain of shells and shrapnel. We ducked into our holes, in which we were soon literally virtually leveled. One after the other escaped out of this miserable piece of trench, soon it is entirely abandoned. To remain was simply impossible or however, certain destruction. When this crazy shooting ceased, the leaders assembled their men together again and occupied the unlucky trench once more. As good as it goes the holes are uncovered again and enlarged, however the Englishmen have us keenly in their sights and attack us anew with a hail of fire and iron. In an instant everyone are in the holes or else disappeared somewhere, until the raid is past. The entire day we have suffered heavily under the continuous fire over events and nevertheless we have almost no losses. Finally it became evening and the adversary was quiet, however by us remained immense work. Wood became brought into the position and a series of dugout frameworks, one after the other, brought us deeper into the earth, step by step, up to the bright morning, without rest. Everyone works with their utmost strength. The company leader relieved the *Musketier* and the *Musketier* the platoon leader with pickaxes and spades. *Vizefeldwebel* Collet 4/66.[9]

Now in their new positions, the men of IR 66 came to the conclusion that they had not done as much physical labor in the entire war as they did from 5 to 13 September. They were holding a position that consisted of nothing more than thousands of shell holes; *Feste Schwaben*. To the men it was literally hell;

In which the men worked as if possessed from the evening up to the morning and from the morning until to the evening shells were scattered about us, in which one could despair. The worst was when we were allowed to go out during the bombardment and when our work on the new dugouts was discovered, despite using all possible precaution, to remain concealed. The English shells were placed on our heads at a slow rate, in order to bury us in our holes or crush us. Shells with time-fuses: that generally punched 2-3 meters deep in the earth and had an effect of crushing everything in the vicinity. I was with approximately 20 men upon the steps of a newly started dugout, one pressed against the other like herring. We had approximately 6 meters of ground above us. Light shells and shrapnel tore and yapped at the surface of the earth like angry dogs, however, nothing that could do any harm to us. In-between we heard a heavy discharge from a further distance; then an utterly dangerous roaring in the air that degenerated into a gurgling noise as it came closer. Everyone knows the noise, like a monster coming directly at us. Everyone listened, was anxious; there, a dull blow, we jerk together, a short earthquake like jolt follows it in which all of the joints of the wooden framework about us creak, a groan is wrested from the chest then, it is quiet, except for the barking dogs above. Now everyone breathes in and out, in the distance however a new launching, anxious seconds, the nerves are extremely tense, it rustles and gargles here, a dull blow, everything twitches, a huge jolt, our stairway makes a rocking movement, as if it wanted to collapse, resisting the terrifying pressure of the explosion. Now, one of these monsters follows the other in endless succession, hour after hour up to the night. Then it becomes quiet, even the frenzied dogs above there are silent. The soldiers crawl up to the earth's surface on all fours, stiff limbs and tired, half unconscious from the hours of horror. The cool evening air slowly restores the consciousness again, and then we are concerned with work anew again, deeper under the earth. So, passed the days in pain and horror and the nights in endless work. A true Hell, this *Feste Schwaben*. [10]

It seemed amazing to many of the men in the 4/66 that their company had managed to survive the time in *Feste Schwaben* from the 5th to 14th September. In part, it was from a strong sense of duty to their officers; one in particular who provided an exemplary model for the men to follow.

Here the old saying has proven itself: 'Actions speak louder than words.' Here our battalion commander gave an example to his loyal soldiers, who sought to emulate him. Day and night he was in the middle among us in the shell holes of *Feste Schwaben* that was consumed by fire and iron; he endured here at the hottest position when everyone else's nerves gave way. If *Feste Schwaben* remained occupied in these days, then it was to the credit of our battalion commander, *Hauptmann* Niemeyer. I still remember well today, how he lay more than once in his very cramped area alone, above there in his hole, because everyone around him around had fled. If the fire died down somewhat, we soldiers have stealthy moved back here so that he should not realize it: he has honestly embarrassed us. In these days the trust of the soldiers to their leader became unlimited. [10]

The leader of the 3/66, *Leutnant der Reserve* Heine, described the effects of the enemy artillery fire on the *Strassburger Steige*:

I reported to the commander of a Guard Regiment in *Feste Staufen*. On the next day, about midday, I received an order, to move with the company through the *Lach Weg* into *Feste Schwaben* and there to relieve Regt. 180. The trench in parts there was completely smashed in, so our route took us along above. It was a moment that all of us will never forget. The enemy showered us formally with shells, the company, 270 men strong, was torn apart, and a herd looked to find a way to the front on its own initiative. The roaring down of the heavy 38cm English shells here was completely dreadful. It was a sign of excellent discipline that the company found itself together at *Feste Schwaben* again. We had to mourn the loss of two men. Both brave men were found in shell craters by the evening during a walk around, without any injuries; however the lower side of the body was blue. Comrades saw how both bodies flew through the air from the enormous breeze of a descending enemy 38er shell. The company lay in three dugouts. I had with me about 130 men packed into a 10 meter deep tunnel. We were above on the hill of *Feste Schwaben* in the third trench behind

C4 and had the task, during an eventual English attack, to serve as support for the first line. The continuous hand grenades explosions in front necessitated the strictest alertness from us. The heavy enemy artillery had systematically taken our dugouts under fire. The trenches were so badly shot up that the dugout entrances could only be barely kept open. Numerous enemy aircraft observed the effect on our dugouts. The Englishmen were quite familiar with the dugouts, because they had already been in possession of *Feste Schwaben* on the 1st of July for a short time. During the entire day we covered the entrances with a tarpaulin and by the break of darkness we dared to come out. Then moderate movement became possible in the trench again and the entrances were uncovered. However the big English shells did not remain completely without effect. Different individual frameworks squealed as if breaking, and so it was necessary, to get and install new props and iron cleats for the further security of the dugout and its many occupants. They were bitter days to experience; day out, day in a tunnel, densely herded together, the earth constantly trembling from the heavy impacts. Then one day the worst happened: A direct hit by a 38cm shell had struck and completely destroyed the entrance of the dugout approximately 10 meters on the right of us. Now it was right to quickly bring help to our 38 comrades, who had been trapped there. First and foremost *Leutnant der Reserve* Mau who, in disregard of his own life, repeatedly attempted to work himself through the cave in to the trapped men. However the falling masses of earth hindered him and his trusted men from saving their comrades. [12]

North of the Ancre, the situation appeared far brighter for the men of RIR 119. On 5 September the relief of RIR 119 began when the III/R55 took over *Beaumont-Süd* in the night from 5/6 September and came under the command of the 26th Reserve Division. It would take three days before the regiment, battalion by battalion, could be relieved from the front lines. Finally, as the men from RIR 119, were leaving Beaucourt behind, the troops could breathe a sigh of relief.

The men marched past once familiar locations with wide eyed astonishment of what they saw. Baillescourt, where the regimental headquarters was located, was almost completely destroyed. Miraumont, where the men had once spent their days at rest was entirely burned out; every building was destroyed and deserted. When the regiment reached Achiet le Petit the men were loaded on to motor lorries and the I Battalion was brought to Moeuvres, the II Battalion to Pronville, the regimental staff with the III Battalion to Inchy, all far behind the front line. Instead of experiencing almost constant enemy fire, the clamor of the fighting was far in the distance, sounding like a dull thunderstorm.

For the men at the front, the necessity of patrols remained a daily occurrence despite the intensive fighting taking place across the Somme. It was still one of the best methods to keep an eye on nocturnal enemy activities as well as to serve as an early warning system in the event of a sudden enemy raid or attack.

A patrol from the 3/180 proceeded towards the British lines from C4 in the early morning hours of 6 September under cover of the morning fog. The patrol returned with rather grisly news. They had firmly established that there were still approximately 300 British bodies lying in front of Sector C3 from the fighting on 3 September. The patrol also reported that some of the men they encountered were severely wounded but there was little they could do to help them. Upon returning to the German lines, the patrol members

Patrol *Britentod*, Gas mine undertaking, 7 September 1916. (*Die 26. Reserve Division 1914-1918*)

brought along with them some very useful items; three Lewis Guns along with a great deal of ammunition. This brought the total number of captured Lewis Guns to 18.

In addition to normal regimental patrols, the concept of the trench raid had also not disappeared from the Somme. A large raid, that had been planned since the end of August and was now about to take place was intended to help relieve enemy pressure at the left wing of the 1st Army. The raid, code named '*Britentod*' was being directed against Thiepval Wood would include gas shells.

In order to provide a sufficient number of gas shells, 70 medium and heavy *Minenwerfer* had been assembled in the Thiepval Sector close to Thiepval Wood under the technical guidance of *Major* Biermann. It had been originally planned for late August but was postponed numerous times due to unfavorable wind direction. Finally, everything appeared to be in order and the gas mine undertaking was set to take place in the early morning hours of 7 September.

Raids had been fairly commonplace occurrence for some time along the entire Western Front amongst both the German and Allied forces.. While they might differ in size, goals and methods used; for the most part they involved volunteers from the different companies of a particular regiment under the direction of several officers, and often accompanied by *pioniers*. Within the German Army however, doctrinal development and experimentation had resulted in the creation of units whose sole purpose was to execute these specialized raids and attacks against the enemy.

Instead of volunteers from each regiment, a new structure was being developed that created specialized units that would be formed from picked men under leaders who had shown a particular knack for the type of work. These new units, from the smaller *Sturm Trupp* to the much larger *Sturm Bataillon* began to appear in the different armies, corps and divisions in the German Army. *Sturm Bataillon* Rohr was the first to be created as an actual assault battalion, equipped with various purpose-built weaponry, from *Flammenwerfer* to small assault guns that could be manhandled into action. Another early example of a *Sturm Bataillon* was the 3rd *Jäger Bataillon*, which on 4 August 1916 was designated as the 3rd *Jäger Sturm Bataillon*.

While the concept of well trained, physically fit and aggressive soldiers would prove useful, it also had an unforeseen detrimental effect on the German Army over time. In the process of transforming the 3rd *Jäger Bataillon* into a *Sturm Bataillon*, 500 men of the original battalion were transferred to other units as they were not deemed physically fit enough to withstand the intensive training required. These men were replaced with younger soldiers taken from a large number of other units. The process of concentrating the fittest soldiers in specialized units provided a powerful force that could be used in critical situations. However, it also took the very best from the basic infantry units and left them with men who were not of the same caliber. This practice, taken cumulatively, would eventually cause problems over the next few years.

On 6 September, the I/R55 continued the process of relief in the Beaumont sector by replacing the II/R119 in *Beaumont-Mitte*. In addition to relieving a portion of RIR 119, the I/R55 was ordered to form a *Sturm Bataillon* for Army Group Stein. *Leutnant* Kröger, 7/R55, would be the new adjutant for *Sturm Abteilung* Stein. The *Sturm Trupp* leader was assigned to *Leutnant* Scharlemann, 12/R55. Other members of the new unit included *Leutnants* Köhler, Schmitz, Weinberg, *Unteroffizier* and *Ausbildungsoffizier* Kleinberg among others. The men needed for this new specialized detachment were to be drawn from the best troops in the regiment.

It is most likely that the orders issued to create this *Sturm Bataillon* were a direct result of an incident that had taken place a short time earlier. While the concept of a specialized *Sturm Abteilung* had been in existence since 1915, it had not become standardized in the German army and few of these units existed into 1916.

Expansion of this concept was slow at first. On 15 May 1916, General Falkenhayn ordered each division to send two officers and four non-commissioned officers to visit *Sturm Bataillon* Rohr, where they would attend a two week instructional course. They would observe the training and tactics being used by Rohr's men and then take this knowledge back to their divisions. The information would then be passed along to the units of the division. This makeshift approach did not lead to any well-organized structure of *Sturm Abteilung* in the army.

Then, on 29 August 1916, General Erich von Ludendorff assumed supreme command over the German armies in the west. In early September Ludendorff visited the headquarters of the German Crown Prince Wilhelm in Montmedy and while there he reviewed a company from *Sturm Bataillon* Rohr that had formed an honor guard. He was quite impressed with what he saw in these men and after a few days he was convinced that the structure of the *Sturm Bataillon* could and should be used as a model for the rest of the German infantry. It is probably not a coincidence that within a few days of these events the orders came to have RIR 55 form a *Sturm Bataillon* for Army Group Stein.[13]

On the following day, the II/R55 relieved the II/R119 in *Beaumont-Nord*. The 5/R55 took over Sector B1, the 6/R55 Sector B2, the 7/R55 Sector B3 and the 8/R55 was in reserve. The 2MG/R55 relieved a machine gun coy in RIR 119 in the northern part of the sector. Five machine guns were positioned in the first trench, two machine guns

Dieter
Leutnant d. R. im Inf.-Regt. 180
gefallen bei Thiepval
am 7. September 1916

Leutnant der Reserve Dieter (*Kriegstagebuch aus Schwaben*)

in the second trench, two machine guns in the third trench and one machine gun was held in reserve. When the II/R55 arrived, the battalion was able to recover 11 British wounded from the front lines near the III/R55 and transport them to the *Verbandplatz* for treatment. On the following day *Oberstleutnant* von Laue, RIR 55, assumed command over the Beaumont Sector.

The date had arrived to execute the raid against Thiepval Wood. At 12.30 a.m. on 7 September the 70 *Minenwerfer* in the Thiepval Sector opened fire on the British lines in Thiepval Wood. The *Minenwerfer* would eventually fire 12,000 gas mines, (the new *Grünkreuz* [14] ammunition), into the British line, accompanied by shell and shrapnel fire from German batteries located further in the rear. The old method of using volunteers for a raid was still in use as the *Sturm Abteilung* had not yet been completely formed or trained at this time.

The raiding parties were comprised of personnel from three regiments, IR 180, RIR 99 and RIR 119. The men and officers, all volunteers, had practiced the raid at a nearby location where the enemy trenches had been re-created thereby ensuring that each man would know precisely what was expected from them as well as the overall plan. If the officers fell, leadership of the raid would fall to the NCO's. The three raiding parties advanced toward the gas saturated British trenches at 3.30 a.m. as planned, but then something went wrong.

Instead of facing badly gassed enemy troops, the Germans were suddenly confronted with artillery barrage fire and heavy infantry fire, almost as soon as they had left the German lines. Not one of the three raiding parties managed to enter the British lines at any location and after a short fire fight they were forced to return to the German lines having suffered a number of losses, including *Leutnant der Reserve* Dieter from IR 180, a well-liked and competent officer.

After the raid was over, the 26th Reserve Division undertook an after action analysis seeking to determine the reasons for the failure. After interviewing the men in the raiding parties the division came to the conclusion that the British front line had simply not been gassed sufficiently.

British artillery fire continued to fall across the entire Thiepval Sector without interruption, day and night. The defenses suffered considerably under the weight of fire and losses were a daily occurrence. The days when the deep, mined dugouts were strong enough to stop even the heaviest enemy shell were long past. The newer dugouts were shallower in depth as a result of not having sufficient time and resources to create mined tunnels equal to those created from 1915 and the first half of 1916.

On 9 September a British heavy shell penetrated the battle headquarters of the I/180 resulting in battalion leader, *Hauptmann* Schaal, and the communication trench-officer *Leutnant der Reserve* Peyn, being slightly wounded. Since the regiment had taken over the Thiepval Sector it was the third commander of the I Battalion to be lost to enemy fire. The I/180 would not be leaderless for long however; early on 10 September a new commander arrived, *Major* Weeber, from *Landwehr* IR 125. He immediately took command of the battalion and quickly assessed the situation facing his men.

The last steps required in the relief of RIR 119 were finally being completed. The Staff of the 51st Reserve Infantry Brigade was relieved on 10 September by the Staff of the 26th Reserve Infantry Brigade. The companies of the I/R55 took up their positions in Sectors B4, B5 and the *Leiling Schlucht* (Y Ravine). The companies of the II/R55 took over Sectors B6 and B7. Because of the recent enemy attacks, five machine guns of the 1MG/R55 were placed in the first trench, two machine guns were in the second trench, two machine guns in the third trench and one machine gun was held in reserve in the *Kolonie*.

In a much safer location behind the Somme front, the men of RIR 119 were fully enjoying their well-deserved rest. The regiment received a note from *General der Infanterie* von Soden in which he praised the performance of the regiment in glowing terms.

> After 16 full months in position, uninterrupted and without relief since May 1915, RIR 119 has brilliantly defended the position during which they victoriously repelled three large enemy attacks. Afterward, the celebrated regiment could now, for the first time, become secluded, to become restored, it is necessary for me to speak to the same of my special thanks for its tough time holding out and my wishes for the best good fortune. It was a great performance, which was rightly assessed and will remain remembered in future history. *General der Infanterie* von Soden. [15]

Generalleutnant von Stein also visited the regiment and personally gave his warmest thanks to the regiment for its bravery, and steadfast behavior in very difficult situations. He felt that the regiment should be proud of its accomplishments.

Speeches were a fine thing; however, for the men it was the enjoyment of comfortable quarters and to be able to rest without any concern of being attacked or performing strenuous fatigues. They could still hear the sounds from the battle in the distance. Despite being far behind the front lines, they were constantly reminded of their situation as the men watched air combat taking place overhead or when the occasional bomb was dropped in their vicinity. However, these events did little to dampen their enthusiasm. They could take baths in hot water, get rid of the extremely annoying lice even if for only a few days, sightsee in Cambrai, visit shops, cafes and *Estaminets* and enjoy good food and drink. They all knew that with the battle on the Somme being in its third month, it was only a matter of time before they would be sent back into the fight.

The scene facing the men from RIR 55 was daunting. The once powerfully constructed position was badly damaged from months of enemy artillery and mine fire. The enemy trenches, once hundreds of meters in the distance, had slowly moved forward by extending saps and then creating new trenches until they were 100 meters or closer in some locations to the German positions. There would no longer be the luxury of extra minutes to prepare a defense in the time needed for the enemy to cross no man's land. Now, the distance could be crossed in mere seconds.

Because of eight days of artillery fire prior to the attack on 3 September, the overall position required extensive restoration. At the left wing of B4 and in B5 the trenches were virtually leveled. The battle trench in *Beaumont-Süd* consisted only of individual shell craters, some joined together, some not. The Intermediate line by *Feste Alt Württemberg* had for the most part been completely destroyed. The communication trenches were unusable by day and many of the dugouts were collapsed in. Numerous dugouts in the *Kolonie* were also destroyed, as well as the field railway in the Ancre valley.

The regimental headquarters was located *Feste Alt Württemberg*. The Under Staff in dugouts by Mill of Miraumont, and the houses of Favreuil. Ever since 8 September the regiment officially belonged to 51st Reserve Infantry Brigade. Along with them were the 2nd Recruit Coy/R121, *Radfahrer* Coy/R121 and *Festungs Machine Gun Abteilung* Fassbender. The mobile field kitchens were replaced by kitchens set up in shell proof dugouts driven into the slopes of the Beaumont *Schlucht* the entire way up to the railway station.

The highest point of the sector was at the left wing of B5 which was held by the I/R55. From this location, a man could see all around the position and far into the enemy rear. While the positions of the I Battalion in B5 and B4 proceeded in a northerly direction, the mouth of the *Leiling Schlucht* extended out on the right wing of the B ravine sharply to the west toward the enemy, and then, proceeding more to the north again in the neighboring sector. The projecting part provided the 1/R55 an excellent flanking position of the entire hollow that would prove to be very useful on 13 November during a British attack.

Overall, sector B ravine had a good field of fire; however, in front of B4 and B5 the field of fire was very short at individual positions. The most threatened sector was B6, where the enemy position had advanced to within 80 meters. The field of fire and view into the enemy position was completely lacking. On the other hand, the enemy could see into the German trenches from the raised southern bank of the Ancre – (the heights by Thiepval).

Even in its damaged condition, the three parallel trench lines provided a solid defense in the Beaumont Sector. They were equipped with numerous communication and approach trenches that allowed traffic to move throughout the sector quickly (once free of mud and debris). While some dugouts had been damaged or destroyed, the deep mined dugouts were mostly still intact and had several exits. The deep tunnel of the *Leiling Stollen* in B4 reached from the first trench until the third trench. Inside of it was the company leader and part of the 4/R55, and as it was also being utilized as a medical dugout by the medical officers Dr. Paulsen and *Feldunterarzt* Schlarb as well as by *Minenwerfer* crews. However, it was also considered to be uncomfortably close to the firing line and therefore extremely vulnerable to an enemy attack.

To the east was the *Kolonie Mulde*, which ran from the railway station Beaucourt on the Ancre to the village of Beaumont. In the *Kolonie* was the battalion staff of the I and III Battalions, the reserves of the III Battalion, the telephone exchange, medical dugout, depots, and kitchens, the latter being of great value for the overall health and morale of the troops.

More troops were needed to replace the tired and worn out battalions that had been defending the Thiepval Sector. IR 180 had been in the front lines since 25 July and had been involved in the opening fighting of the battle on 1 July and the days following. IR 66 and RIR 55 had already been brought up; the next would be men from RIR 77, from the 2nd Guard Reserve Division.

On the morning of 10 September, the baggage section of the train of RIR 77 was inspected in Ervillers by *Oberleutnant* Voigt. On this occasion the officers who were present were told by the regimental commander that the I/R77 would leave Courcelles on 11 September and that it was being deployed to Thiepval. The particular details of the order came at noon. One battalion from IR 180 by Thiepval was eagerly waiting to be relieved. The relief was designed to give every battalion of IR 180 eight days of rest. In accordance with these requirements, the I/R77 would be placed under the command of IR 180 for the period 12 September to 5th October.

As the I/R77 would be under the control of the 26th Reserve Division, the I/R77 leader, *Hauptmann* von Heugel, immediately went to the 26th Reserve Division headquarters on the same afternoons where he received his instructions. The relief of the I/180 was scheduled to take place in the night from 11 to 12 September.

In preparation for the changes being made at the front, the III/180 was moved to the rear support position of *Feste Staufen,* at St. Pierre-Divion, while the I/180 took on the southern front of Thiepval. From there, it was replaced on the night of 11/12 September by the I/R77. The men from IR 180 marched to Achiet le Petit and from there they were transported by motor lorries into rest quarters in Marquion.

The I/R77 provided support for IR 180, while the battalion staff moved its battle headquarters by *Feste Schwaben*. One company occupied the sector north of Thiepval and three companies were positioned at the southeast and eastern edge of Thiepval. The entire regimental sector was divides into the sub sectors *Thiepval-Nord* and *Thiepval-Mitte*. On the left of the 26th Reserve Division was originally the 4th Guard Division and since 11 September, the 89th Reserve Infantry Brigade from the 207th Infantry Division.

The relief was completed in Sector *Thiepval-Nord* as follows: Sector commander, *Major* Weeber, I/180, was replaced by *Hauptmann* von Heugel, I/R77. In C4: the 3/IR 180 was replaced by the 4/RIR 77; in the *Bulgaren Weg*: the 4/180 through the 1/R77. In Sector *Thiepval-Mitte*: In T2: the 1/180 through the 3/R77; In T3: the 2/180 through the 2/R77. The orderly rooms remained in Courcelles and one detachment from each company remained behind to work on the expansion of the quarters.

The I/R77 marched at 2 a.m., 12 September, from Courcelles to Grandcourt where they were expected to arrive at 6 a.m. The I/R77 staff moved to Grandcourt at 8 a.m. and from there went to the regimental battle headquarters of IR 180 in the *Stumpf Weg*. After reporting to the regimental commander, *Oberstleutnant* Fischer, the I/R77 staff went to the battle headquarters in the *Lach Weg* in *Thiepval-Nord*.

Further details of the relief were arranged with *Major* Weeber and the orders issued for the individual companies of RIR 77. Starting from 5 p.m., at intervals of half an hour the

Die Württemberger bei Thiepval!

Artist's impression of a Württemberg *Musketen* crew by Thiepval. (Author's collection)

companies would move from Courcelles to Grandcourt in the sequence: 3rd, 2nd, 4th and 1/R77. From Grandcourt the companies would be brought into the position by the company leaders. The relief went as expected, smoothly and without losses. It was completed at 3.25 a.m. the following day. The strength of the I/R77 was: 1/R77 and battalion staff: 6 officers 167 men, 2/R77: 3 officers 178 men, 3/R77: 3 officers 158 men, 4/R77: 3 officers 155 men. In total: 15 officers, 658 men.

As of 12 September Sector *Thiepval-Nord* was under the command of *Hauptmann* von Heugel. Under him the 4/R77 was in C4 in the front line, the 1/R77 was in the *Bulgaren Weg* and the 9/IR 180 was in the *Auwärter Weg*. Furthermore, 4 machine guns, 2 *Minenwerfer* and 2 *Musketen* were distributed in the sector. To ensure the cooperation between the artillery and infantry, an *Artillerie Verbindungs Offizier* (AVO) was also attached to the battalion staff. When the I/R77 was inserted into the position, the 2nd and 3/R77 were moved under the command of *Major* Kerl, II/180 in *Thiepval-Mitte*.

The quality of the positions taken over by the companies from RIR 77 varied greatly. The front line of C4 was well developed. The existing dugouts furnished secure quarters for all of the men. The mined dugouts were consistently deep, the wire obstacles were intact and quite wide; the trenches were passable and well-furnished for defense.

On the other hand, the remaining communication trenches leading to the rear left very much to be desired. In part these trenches were badly damaged by shell fire and at other locations, filled with mud. There were almost no completed dugouts in the communication trenches, only tunnel entrances ranging from 3 to 5 meters deep and providing little in the way of protection against enemy artillery fire. These tunnel entrances were where the support companies were accommodated.

For communications, telephone lines still existed and functioned on a regular basis, thanks to the hard work of the Telephone Troops from IR 180 and RIR 77. The telephone

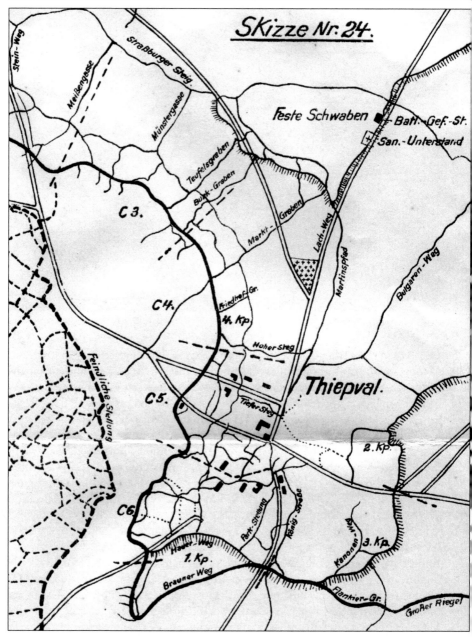

Positions of the I/R77 by Thiepval.

wires were still being shattered at least 10-12 times each day because of the ongoing heavy artillery fire. The repairmen were constantly heading out into the heavy fire looking for breaks in the lines and restoring the damaged wires. Thanks to their untiring activity the telephones were generally back in service in a comparatively short time.

In addition there were runner stations and carrier pigeons that carried messages to the rear when needed. The carrier pigeon station was located at the battalion battle headquarters. The messages were written on very thin paper and placed in a small aluminum capsule. The capsules were then placed on the legs of the birds with small clips. As a precaution, two pigeons were always released carrying the same message in the event one became lost. The birds followed the route from Thiepval to Biefvillers, a straight line distance of 11.5 kilometers, and made the journey in 6 to 10 minutes. This traditional method of sending messages had proven to be very reliable as there was no record of the birds missing their goal.

Sufficient material was at hand in the front line for the extension of the position, thanks to the nightly efforts of carrying parties who hauled heavy loads up to the front. Only duckboards were lacking, therefore the men of the baggage section of the train of the battalion were directed to make them.

The men from RIR 77 were not unfamiliar with the rolling terrain, crisscrossed with a few hollows. In July they had been only a few hundred meters further to the south in the *Stockacher Graben* by Mouquet farm. The once pleasant village of Thiepval no longer existed. Only a few ruined houses were the only indication that a village had ever existed there. Thiepval wood could not still be considered as such; only a few splintered tree stumps rose up from the ground.

The men from RIR 77 were dismayed to find that enemy pilots were still as numerous and annoying as ever. Additionally, the enemy artillery seemed to be even more intense than even several months earlier. On the first day in the new trenches the sector received about 500 shrapnel shells and 80 heavy shells in the morning smashing the trenches in at many places. The enemy continued to fire in the afternoon; covering the front line of C4 with about 600 shrapnel shells and 150 heavy shells. Finally, the fire stopped, only to be resumed close to midnight.

On 13 September the 26th Reserve Division lost several invaluable officers but not due to combat. First was *Major* Bornemann, who had commanded the I *Abteilung* RFAR 26 since the commencement of the war. Bornemann knew the Thiepval and Beaucourt Sectors like the back of his hand. During the opening phases of the Battle of the Somme he directed the fire from his batteries as the commander of Group Adolf. He was now being transferred to become the commander of Prussian Field Artillery Regiment 274.[16] Changes were also made on the division staff. The second adjutant, *Rittmeister* von Bülow who had been with the division staff since the start of the war, was being replaced by *Hauptmann* Kurt Rupff, formerly an officer with RIR 121.

While the opposing enemy infantry had remained quiet ever since the attack on 3 September, the British artillery never seemed to rest. The front and rear trenches of the sectors on both sides of the Ancre were systematically shelled day and night. Despite this fire, German night patrols were very active regardless of the strains placed on the men during the day. It is possible that patrolling no man's land was safer than being inside a trench as less fire was dropped on the terrain between the opposing armies than on the actual German defensive positions.

The British were also active and sent patrols out each night into no man's land. The 2/66 had a blinker apparatus in its sector that was used extensively at night to send messages to the rear. In the night of 12/13 September trench sentries observed what appeared to be a raiding party near Sectors C1 and C3. Their suspicions were confirmed when both sectors came under intense artillery and mine fire, all of this indicating a strong enemy attack was imminent. The blinker apparatus was used to alert the batteries in the rear and

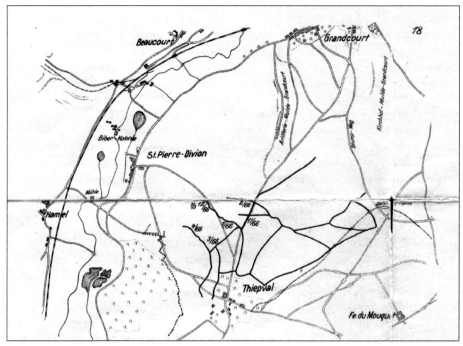

Positions of IR 66 by Thiepval.

in a few moments, the British front line was blanketed with artillery fire, the attack never materialized. Afterward, a patrol brought in a wounded Englishman, who appeared to be completely inebriated. At 12.35 a.m. the 10/66 reported that the enemy's first trench and saps were densely packed with men and gave the appearance of preparing to attack. Once more, the blinker apparatus was used to call up artillery support fire and apparently prevented any attack from forming.

The enemy's pattern of activity continued through the morning when at 7.30 a.m. preparation fire was placed upon the entire sector of the right battalion. The trenches were badly damaged, especially those held by the 10/66, where a mined dugout partially collapsed. With all the signs pointing to an enemy attack, the 10/66 requested barrage fire and the German defensive fire appeared to once again stifle any attack.

Similar events were taking place north of the Ancre in the sector held by RIR 55. A strong artillery fire raid, accompanied by the discharge of smoke clouds and infantry fire on the German front line all indicated that there was an impending attack, however; no such attack materialized Following these strange events, the enemy aerial activity noticeably increased from one day to the next.

Shortly after sunrise on 13 September, enemy pilots appeared over the sector held by RIR 77 observing traffic in the trenches, which, at this time, was especially active. The observation aircraft frequently used horns and flares as signals to the British artillery of German concentrations. What had started as artillery fire, mainly from field guns and light field howitzers, grew in size starting from 10 a.m. when the enemy employed heavy guns as well. The main targets were the dugouts and any positions where the men were observed to be working on the trenches. In addition to the heavy shells, the sector held by

RIR 77 received about 1,000 shrapnel and light shells on this day that completely leveled the trenches at many locations.

Something seemed to be occurring in the enemy lines. The recent events north and south of the Ancre seemed to have been feints, perhaps only used to determine what sort of German response an attack might receive. Perhaps it was being used to establish the locations of the German batteries, or, possibly to deceive the Germans by drawing attention away from the sector where an attack was being planned.

During the night of 13/14 September there was a powerful fire raid on Thiepval and the sector to the right neighboring regiment. As a result, the rear trenches in the sector of RIR 77 were held under constant shrapnel fire. In the early morning hours, at daybreak, dense fog covered the battlefield. The poor visibility resulting from the fog put a stop to all enemy aerial activity and there was relative calm in the sector for the entire day. The men of RIR 77 had already come to the conclusion that the British were only firing their artillery under aerial observation. The events of 14 September seemed to confirm this conclusion. 14 September brought much the same to the Thiepval Sector as the previous few days. A partial enemy attack south of Thiepval at 8 p.m. on the 14th also affected the positions of IR 66, even though the sector was not under direct attack.

The British advances from the south against Mouquet farm; the *Fabeck Graben* and Courcelette increasingly threatened the left flank of the Thiepval Sector. On 15 September strong British attacks had captured Courcelette, allowing the enemy to become firmly installed in the *Fabeck Graben* and captured the *Wundtwerk*. Additionally the *Hohenzollern Stellung* was also captured by the neighboring division.

Ever since the attacks of 3 September, the sector being held by IR 180 by Thiepval had not been bothered very much by British artillery fire, including the regimental battle headquarters in the upper *Stump Weg*. However, each day the enemy fire moved closer and fire-over events with gas shells forced the men to put on their gas masks numerous times.

Day by day the situation deteriorated, particularly when the *Wundtwerk* fell on the 14th and Courcelette on the 15 September. It was becoming all too clear that the projecting corner of Thiepval could not be held if faced by a large-scale enemy attack on its left flank. Despite the situation, the orders had remained the same: 'Hold out to the last man.'

During the same night that the II/180 was being relieved from Thiepval, the 4/66 repulsed an enemy patrol advancing against C3. Following a short hand grenade battle, a patrol from the 4th Company brought in a dead enemy soldier in order to obtain the unit identification.

Feste Schwaben also lay under heavy enemy fire during the British attacks of 15 September.

Up to the morning of 15 September we had generally made ourselves familiar with our position, which the Englishmen could now quietly come. We were on guard. And they came.

7.30 a.m. fire raged and iron rained down upon us. 'Alarm!' "Every man stood ready to fight with rifles and hand grenades. Our artillery was still silent. In the first trench hand grenades and rifle fire. The fire lying on us ends or goes away over us. We fired red flares, and therefore now awakened our artillery and produced barrage fire. Over there, to our left, where once Thiepval stood, we see the Englishmen in the first trench of the 180er; we open active rifle fire on them at approximately 500 meters. On the right beside us they come until in the shell holes of the 2nd Company, where they then through close combat, seized from all sides, become crushed. So that the Englishmen had a tough time of it on the 15th of September. *Vizefeldwebel* Collet, 4/66 [16]

Vizefeldwebel Collet may have opened fire on enemy soldiers in the vicinity of Thiepval but as of this date, no direct attacks had been made against IR 180.

The neighboring RIR 77 reported that the weather cleared on the 15th, and as soon as it was light enough, enemy airplanes were again very active over its position. At 10 a.m enemy artillery fire fell upon the entire sector with considerable strength and continued the rest of the day in undiminished intensity. Every man in the different companies was put to work repairing trenches that were being badly damaged in the artillery fire. The 26th Reserve Division sent orders to the regiment to specifically maintain the *Martins Pfad* in a usable condition. This trench had been utilized extensively as the main access trench to the village of Thiepval. The *Martins Pfad* lay under constant artillery fire and was leveled for the most part and accordingly offered little or no cover in many places.

The drain on experienced officers in the 26th Reserve Division continued to occur as seasoned officers became promoted; losses it could ill afford. On 16 September *Oberst* Josenhans, commander of RIR 121 since the start of the war, was promoted as the brigade commander of the 107th Reserve Infantry Brigade and transferred to the 54th Reserve Division.[18] *Major* Schmidt, from *Landwehr* IR 124, took command of RIR 121 in his place

The threat facing the Thiepval Sector continued to grow each day as more enemy pressure was being placed against the sector and more importantly, on the left flank of the sector. Adjustments to troop dispositions were needed in the Thiepval Sector to best meet the growing British threat. As the enemy encroached on the Thiepval Sector, more and more of the existing headquarters locations became vulnerable to enemy fire or of being captured in the event of a strong enemy attack.

In the night from 16/17 September orders were sent to IR 180. The regimental staff as well as the staff of Artillery Group Berta were to transfer to a command post at the eastern exit of Grandcourt. *Oberst* Vischer had already considered this as a possibility and had anticipated that such an order might be given and accordingly, , had previously ordered the construction of the fire proof dugout at location There would be no delay in moving both headquarters to Grandcourt as the dugout had been completed and ready for use.

On 16 September, an exciting fight played out on the right wing of the III/66 that rested on the Ancre. From their vantage point, the men of IR 66 could watch the British bombardment of the German trenches on the northern bank of the river. Most were very grateful that it was not falling on them.

From the numerous fights I especially recall an attack by the Englishmen on the Beaumont heights on the Ancre stream in the middle of September 1916. In advance of the attack went a fierce drum-fire of approximately 3 days and 3 nights. *Offizier Stellvertreter* Schmerling especially remains in my memory, who despite the severe bombardments in his 'Ernst August' calmness, smoking cigarettes with the beautiful snap fastener, further *Leutnant* Rödlingshöfer and *Leutnant* Angott. I do not want it to be left unsaid also, the three lads, the 'tall Heinrich' and the two others, of which I with certainty know that the youngest, the lad of Schmeling, had fallen. After this crazy drum-fire then the Englishmen attempted their attack. I led a platoon of the 6th Coy in the front line, i.e. one could hardly say line; because it only existed out of shell craters. The British became prevented from penetrating our trench through our hand grenades, machine gun and rifle fire into them, plenty of dead men lay in front of the barbed wire, until suddenly from the left side, probably from the Ancre stream, the Englishmen were successful in entering into the front trench. In the meantime the drum-fire became transferred on the second trench and on the support position. We then succeeded to block off the enemy and in close combat rolled them up and threw them out again of the neighboring trench on the left of us. The attack and the defense had lasted approximately 4 hours and we had once again a few hours rest up to the next drum-fire, and so this game repeated itself, the nightly preparation artillery drum-fire and the attacks following it almost all two up to three days. *Minenwerfer* were used during this attack by the Company Leader *Leutnant* Angott, who, I, in his beaming health, his blooming appearance, his whole character attributes and his personal employment could hardly forget. He was always with a rather confused comrade. *Leutnant* Helmich, 6/R55.[19]

From all indications, the British were preparing to attack the sector held by RIR 77. On 16 September the weather was clear and sunny, therefore the enemy artillery was once again very active. Their shellfire was very accurate as they took full advantage of their aerial observation, mainly with heavy caliber guns on different locations in the position. In total, the sector received 800 shrapnel shells and 150 heavy shells. During the afternoon extremely severe artillery fire was placed on the parts of the front located south of Thiepval, on the *Türken* and *Zollern Stellung*, which after some time, was followed up with strong rifle and machine gun fire.

Red light balls suddenly climbed into the sky at the same time as the heavy enemy fire reached its climax, the anticipated attack had begun. Even the rapid employment of barrage fire from the German artillery batteries could not stop the enemy advance. The British quickly penetrated into the *Türken* and *Hohenzollern Stellung*. A subsequent counterattack arranged by the neighboring IR 209 and IR 213 was unsuccessful. The sector *Thiepval-Nord* was not directly involved in this fighting; however, throughout the afternoon the enemy bombarded the second trench in C4 more severely than usual with shrapnel and high explosive shells.

Considering all of the events taking place so close to Thiepval, and the desperate need for more men, RIR 119 received orders on 16 September to be ready to march. By evening the III/R119 moved forward to Achiet le Grand. The time for rest was over; the time to rejoin the fight was at hand.

Shortly before sunrise on 17 September the headquarters staff of IR 180 left their old dugout by individual Groups. They moved down the valley, past the battery positions that were now abandoned but still gave the appearance of being occupied and consequently had drawn accurate fire by the British. During the journey to Grandcourt the men noted a strong odor of rotten fruit that continued the entire way to the new headquarters dugout. The troops concluded that the entire area must have been heavily gassed during the night. Fortunately, the headquarters staff was subjected to only a few random shrapnel shells that whistled above their heads. Soon after, they climbed down into the depths of the new battle headquarters.

The men in RIR 119 probably knew more about the overall situation facing the Germans than most of their comrades at the front. On the morning of 17 September the two remaining battalions of the regiment moved toward the front. The I/R119 was sent to Achiet le Petit, the regimental staff and II/R119 to Bihucourt. The following night the regiment was supposed to work on the *Staufen Riegel* between the *Stall Mulde* by Grandcourt and the *Below Riegel* by Pys. Nearby lay Courcelette, completely enveloped in flames as enemy light rockets constantly climbed high into the air, seemingly without end.

On the German side of the front, everything was dark and quiet. In front of RIR 119 were only a few weak Groups that were not capable of holding back an enemy attack. Once the work had been completed on the *Staufen Riegel*, the regiment would commence creating the *Miraumont Riegel*. This would be a position turning toward the south on the northern side of the Ancre. This position was necessary due to the increasing British threat from the south that had become increasingly stronger. The British had driven a deep, wide wedge into the German front and now threatened the Thiepval and Ancre positions from the flank and the rear.

The smell of rotten fruit that the men in IR 180 had encountered had indeed been the result of enemy gas shells. At 12.10 a.m., near the front lines by the Ancre, Company Pitschke/66 had observed the British working on their front trench opposite its position and in front of C3 there were further reports of a noticeable smell of gas.

At 12.30 a.m. on 17 September, a sentry in the 2nd trench of RIR 77 observed British soldiers at individual positions directly in front of the right wing of C4. He also noted that further to the right of them, the enemy had also left their trenches. The same observation was made by a sentry in C3. The sentry in C3 immediately fired off red light balls, the signal to the artillery for barrage fire. The resulting wall of fire that was accompanied by nearly every machine gun in the front and every *Minenwerfer* apparently destroyed any intended enemy attack. By 12.45 a.m. it became quiet again.

In addition to these events, sentry posts from IR 66 near the Ancre came under fire from a 15 man strong British patrol. The patrol was attempting to work closer to the Magdeburger's position using the artillery and gas fire on the northern bank of the Ancre as cover. It was later determined that the enemy patrol had already laid a plank across the shallow river in the vicinity of a double sentry post situated by the river bank.

Musketiers Kohlrausch, Einbrodt, Herbert Schmidt and Hasenkrug from the double sentry post, immediately alerted the trench garrison when they observed the British patrol. The darkness was lit up with the sudden flash of rifle fire coming from both sides and the crash of hand grenades. One Group was immediately sent out of a nearby tunnel as reinforcements for the four *Musketiers*. The fighting continued for a short time until suddenly, the British appeared to have withdrawn and the night grew relatively quiet once more.

The British had been forced to retreat after suffering a number of losses. At 2.30 a.m. the enemy returned to the scene of the fighting and attempted to retrieve their wounded comrades under the protection of a machine gun but they were prevented from completing their rescue by the sentries from IR 66. At dawn, *Musketier* Pitschinetz swam through the Ancre and dragged the bridge brought by the British back over the river. The bridge was approximately 8 meters long, 1/2 meter wide and had treads nailed on the lower side. A wounded First Lieutenant, who was already lying on a stretcher, one dead Captain and one dead Private were brought into the German lines. Only one man was lost from the double sentry post, *Musketier* Hasenkrug, 11/66, was killed during the fighting.

A similar event occurred during the following night by the 10/66 when an enemy patrol approached its position, again under the protection of artillery fire. The British were attempting a raid at the left sap of this company. They were driven back with hand grenades and rifle fire by the sentries inside the sap. One enemy officer and two soldiers were shot down and brought in.

One larger enemy attack on 17 September was directed toward Thiepval. At 7.45 p.m. a large British force was observed approaching the German lines below the village. The garrison located in C4 assisted their comrades in repulsing this attack by directing the fire of the machine guns in their position at the advancing enemy waves.

17 September brought a huge drama. About evening the Englishmen attacked out of their slightly higher lying position below Thiepval. Next to my dugout was an artillery officer as an observer. He had now brought his telephone wire in order again with his repair troops, which had already been unserviceable for days. He stood in his concrete blockhouse on the telephone and directed the barrage fire on the attackers. We received almost no fire and everyone stood in the trench. In a width of 200-300 meters the Englishmen poured in out of their trenches in broad swarms towards the somewhat deep lying Thiepval. Always new masses followed. From the English up to the Germans position was only a single line of men. We fired plenty of ammunition into them. One couldn't see any effect, because our artillery was employed. They closed off our position along the first trench through a powerful wall of fire. The Englishmen faltered, turned around and flooded backwards. Then there was a second fire wall on the English exit position and in the middle of the terrain by 15 and 21cm shells. Since there was no more support, the attackers ran in all directions, were thrown high into the air by the heavy shells; they were blocked off by the fire all around them. We had forgotten to fire in the rejoicing over this wonderful defense. A machine gun with a glowing red barrel still worked beside us, it has probably more worthwhile targets than it had in the entire war. The attacker was literally crushed. *Vizefeldwebel* Collet, 4/66 [19]

As a result of the constant British attacks further south of Thiepval, the 89th Reserve Infantry Brigade from the 207th Infantry Division had suffered extremely heavy losses as had the troops further to the left of it. On 18 September, the 207th Infantry Division was replaced by the 8th Infantry Division; the 7th Infantry Division (both from the German IV Corps) took over the front line further on the left.

This exchange of troops was accomplished with few losses because of the rainy weather that started on 18 September. With the steady rain, all fighting on both sides died down to an occasional rifle shot or machine gun burst. Only weak shrapnel fire lay on the sector. The persistent rain soon filled the trenches with mud and made any movement in them almost impossible. The men stood knee deep in the muck and tried everything to stay warm and dry, without much success. Many parts of the trenches collapsed, and repairs were only possible in a limited manner, mainly because the men lacked the necessary tools needed to scoop out the water and mud. Still, a silver lining to the terrible weather was, the much hated enemy pilots were rarely seen overhead; perhaps the rain was God sent after all.

The poor weather did not last long. By the afternoon of 19 September the skies cleared up, and the dreaded enemy pilots immediately appeared in large numbers over the position. Trench observers and sentries remained vigilant at their posts in order to prevent any sudden enemy surprise attack. At 4 p.m. an observer in RIR 77 in the *Auwärter Weg* saw a company of British infantry moving into the enemy trenches south of Thiepval. He immediately notified the artillery, which opened fire on the target.

New orders issued from IR 180 in the evening sent the 1/R77 to a position at the southern edge of Thiepval. This was being done as it had been decided that the forward line of the garrison of Thiepval required reinforcements. The 1/R77 was replaced in the *Bulgaren Weg* by the 11/180. Despite random enemy fire, the relief was carried out as expected, smoothly and without losses. The 1/R77 was no longer in the association of the I/R77 and had moved under the control of the Sector commander of *Thiepval-Süd, Major* Kerl of the II/180.

With this shift of troops, *Thiepval-Nord* under *Hauptmann* von Heugel contained the following units: In C4: 4/R77 (Company leader *Oberleutnant der Reserve* Sauerbrey) in the *Bulgaren Weg*: 11/180 (Company leader *Leutnant* Köhner), in the *Auwärter Weg*: 9/180 (Company leader *Leutnant* Wagner).

It was becoming evident to every regiment and company holding the Thiepval-Grandcourt positions that the situation facing them was reaching a critical point. Brigade orders from 19 September were ominous at best: 'The Regiments 66 and 180 are to clarify themselves about the situation through all means. Both regiments will take care of their own reserves independently' and 'regiments will necessarily hold their positions there where they are. The enemy has penetrated into Courcelette' gave sufficient weight to the seriousness of the situation. It was also expected that the regimental sectors C3 and C4 would be drawn into this attack, which were occupied by the 2nd and 4/66.

The I/180 that had been withdrawn to Marquion to be rested, already returned forward again on 20 September to replace the II/180 in the occupation of Thiepval. The II/180 would now go to Marquion during the night of 20/21 September. *Major* Weeber, who had arrived shortly before from LIR 125 to command the I Battalion, now became commander of Thiepval. When *Major* Weeber reported to the division headquarters on the 20th, he was dismissed by the division commander with the words: 'I entrust Thiepval to you.' He replied, 'and I will hold it up to the last man'. The Regimental staff of IR 180 had no battle headquarter positions beyond the eastern exit of Grandcourt. *Major* Weeber had full command and control over this critical sector and had no one else to rely upon in the event of a major attack.

Even though the situation at Thiepval was menacing, it was decided to send RIR 119 back to its rest quarters on 21 September as it was determined that the regiment could be spared. While in rest quarters a 3rd Machine Gun Company was formed in RIR 119, substantially adding to the overall firepower of the Württemberg regiment.

The decision to return RIR 119 to its rest quarters tuned out to be premature. New enemy attacks began on 22 September by Courcelette, Combles and Rancourt. Everything pointed to further attacks at other locations as well. RIR 119 was placed on alert once more and the men made all preparations to move if the situation called for additional reinforcements.

While not directly under attack, the sector being held by IR 66 came under lively artillery fire from all calibers against the entire front. It all seemed to indicate there would be new attacks against the Thiepval Sector in the near future. Numerous dugouts were smashed in under the heavy shells and many losses occurred in the regiment as a result. Observers also noted that the British were manufacturing another footbridge across the Ancre.

Because of the enemy attack against the left neighboring group, the German batteries fired gas shells into Hamel and Thiepval Wood upon suspected troop concentrations, saturating both locations. The threat of an enemy attack and the German gas attack meant that the intended relief of the III/66 by the II/66 could not be implemented yet. The men of the III/66 would have to wait just a bit longer before they could be sent to the rear for rest.

By the evening of 22 September the fire from the enemy heavy artillery had increased so significantly on the trenches held by RIR 77 that the men were forced to remain on high alert. This constant state of extreme tension, waiting each day for a major attack, was sapping the strength of the men. The troops holding the front line were becoming apathetic under the constant shelling and enemy patrol activity. Soon, the garrison of the entire front line would need to be relieved.

On 22 September, approximately 400 heavy shells fell on the rear areas of the sector held by RIR 77. At 9.30 p.m. the men could clearly hear lively infantry fire and observed red light balls ascend in the area of Courcelette and Mouquet farm. News came that an extremely violent enemy attack had taken place against the positions by Courcelette. Sector *Thiepval-Nord* still remained undisturbed throughout the noisy commotion taking place nearby. It was determined the next day that the enemy had captured ground northeast and east of Courcelette. The noose was tightening around Thiepval with each passing day.

There was little the Germans could do to prevent the British from approaching Thiepval. The German batteries were not strong enough to push the British back or substantially delay their advance. Still, everything possible was being done to hinder the enemy efforts. Starting at 12 midnight elevated gas readiness was ordered for all parts of the 26th Reserve Division in preparation of a gas attack. Commencing at 1 a.m. on 23 September, a pre-emptive gas attack that had been organized over the last four days: 3,000 *Grünkreuz* shells and 2,200 gas mines were fired against Hamel and Thiepval Wood. The gas attack proceeded systematically and without any enemy disturbance.

The gas shells and mines did little to deter enemy activity. During the night 23/24 September, a new enemy trench appeared from the junction of the upper *Mesnil Weg* in the *König Strasse* to the *Zwölfer Graben*. This trench brought the enemy troops that much closer to the southern edge of Thiepval, shortening the attack distance considerably.

The companies of RIR 77 worked on the mud filled trenches in the early morning hours so that they could become moderately passable. The sun and wind also helped to dry out the ground, making life in the trenches just slightly more tolerable. The sun and clear skies also brought enemy aircraft. During the good weather enemy pilots flew over the trenches with impunity and at incredibly low altitudes. The pilots and observers could clearly see every movement being made in the trenches. With aerial observation came heavy and accurate artillery fire as well, particularly on *Feste Schwaben* and the trenches in the rear.

It was quite conspicuous that Sector C4 received far less fire than the rearward connections. This led to the conclusion that something would be undertaken against the parts of the front lying further to the south. The British artillery pounded the *Martins Pfad* and *Zollern Graben* in the afternoon with their heaviest caliber shells, as well as the village of Thiepval. The shell fragments from the massive explosions of the heavy projectiles fell to earth as far back as *Feste Schwaben*.

The heavy bombardment of the rear terrain continued throughout the night. The British fire decreased slightly in the early morning hours of the 24th when suddenly, at 10 a.m. it was deployed again with an even greater ferocity . *Feste Staufen, Feste Zollern* and *Feste Schwaben* as well as all of the trenches leading from these strongpoints to the front were pounded by this renewed bombardment. Two dugout entrances were crushed in the *Bulgaren Weg* as well as the artillery observation post.

The heavy caliber shells continued to rain down on the German defenders throughout the afternoon; however, only on the rear terrain. Sector C4 was spared and received only a few shrapnel and light shells. 38cm shells shrieked through the air, the impacts creating immense geysers of earth and smoke as they smashed into Thiepval and the positions east of the village. The ground literally shook under these massive impacts like small earthquakes. At 6 p.m. the British fired gas shells on *Feste Schwaben* and Sector C4.

The first sign of gas being present was a sweetish smell that was suddenly noticeable in the battalion battle headquarters. The men immediately recognized it as gas, probably coming from gas shells that were mixed in together with the conventional high explosive shells. The gas alarm was sounded and anti-gas procedures activated. The gas was driven out of the dugouts using small fires or by swinging blankets to form a draft; the efforts were so successful that after only 20 minutes the men could remove their gas masks.

Everyone was expecting an attack by that evening or, at the latest, the next morning. By 8.30 p.m. red and green flares rose up into the air from the British lines to the east and southeast of Thiepval; however, nothing of any consequences followed the pyrotechnic display. The men came to the conclusion that the enemy was trying to deceive them. But surely, they reasoned, with such an immense expenditure of ammunition, an attack would have to take place soon.

On 24 September the entire sector of IR 66 lay under fire from heavy caliber shells. Despite the heavy fire, III/66 was able to relieve the II/66 the same night. The III Battalion had found that the II/66 had eagerly worked on the extension of the position in S1 and the *Hansa Stellung* during the time it had occupied them. In S1 the III/66 found 30 dugout entrances had already been started. Now, with fresh troops, all of the dugouts, including the smaller recesses were completed. The wire entanglements were reinforced with the installation of 700 coils of barbed wire. A new trench, the *Hansa Riegel* that was about 500 meters in length, was created and prepared for defense.

IR 180 reported that during the nights running over 24/25 and 25/26 September the British had created a new connection between the western end of the *Hafen Graben* and the old English position in Thiepval Wood. The telephone connection to the positions in Thiepval had already been interrupted for several days by this time. All of the attempts to restore the buried cables or create new connections through newly laid down high performance wires failed in the nonstop bombardment of Thiepval and the trenches lying to the rear. The connection with *Feste Schwaben* and *Feste Staufen* could only be restored for a few minutes before being cut once again. Any chance of maintaining the telephone lines required the use of numerous repair troops who had to go out into the heavy fire over and over again.

Soon, with losses among the repair troops increasing at an alarming rate and, with the lines being concurrently cut in dozens of places, all attempts at repairing the wires were called off, it was simply too much to overcome. Starting from 26 September a chain of runners was virtually the only method of transmitting orders and messages between the egiments and the battalions.

The British maintained pressure along the entire German front line by Thiepval. Artillery fire was even directed against Bapaume and enemy aerial activity increased to unbearable limits, no counter measures were enough to stop it. The area around Bapaume formed the focus of the fighting in the air. Bombing raids became a regular occurrence, especially against the railway unloading position in Irles. No part of the rear terrain, especially Corps Headquarters, was immune from the enemy activity.

Along the front line, 24 British observation balloons swayed in the breeze, one next to the other. The observers could see the entire German front from Martinpuich to Courcelette. Bapaume was developed into a fortress in the expectation of an enemy breakthrough. Rows of bridges across the Ancre became targets for enemy artillery fire and bombing raids by aircraft. Because of heavy fire, the battle headquarters of the 52nd Reserve Infantry Brigade, General von Auwärter, was transferred from Irles back to Vaulx. Even in Biefvillers the division staff made preparations to move further back, after the village received continuous heavy fire. The main dressing station was moved from the medical hollow by *Klein Miraumont* and transported back to Sapignies. It was evident that at least one long barreled gun appeared to have been allotted by the enemy to fire exclusively at the villages in the rear and assembly points in the areas that were apparently going to be attacked.

The night of the 24/25 September was relatively quiet, as were the early morning hours. It was damp and foggy and as a result no enemy aircraft were seen overhead. The weather did not clear up until about noon when it became bright and within a very short time the enemy pilots and artillery became active again. The entire rear area, especially *Feste Staufen*, lay under incessant fire that included guns of the heaviest calibers and that continued throughout the entire afternoon until the late evening. The front by Courcelette also came under heavy bombardment with heavy caliber guns, however once again, no attack materialized.

On 25 September a new attack had begun against the Combles-Flers line. Geuedecourt, Morval and Lesboeufs fell to the enemy on this day. Their fall would finally decide the fate of Thiepval. Later, the enemy bombardment increased to the highest possible strength and continued unceasingly throughout the night of 25/26 September in almost undiminished strength. Due to the weight of fire, the important Artillery Observation Post at *Feste Staufen* had to be evacuated. In addition to the artillery activity, the work being performed by the enemy infantry during the day in the *Hafen Graben*, upper *Mesnil Weg* and *Wundtwerk* also pointed to an imminent attack against Thiepval.

On the morning of 26 September the fighting continued to rage between Geuedecourt and Combles while in the sector of Group Stein it was comparatively quiet with the exception of the strong artillery fire falling along the front lines. After the capture of Geuedecourt and Combles had been accomplished early on 26 September, the British turned their attention toward Thiepval.

By the early morning of the 26th the enemy heavy artillery fire began again after a short pause during the previous night and continued throughout the morning. Suddenly, at 1.45 p.m. enormously powerful drum fire began to rain down upon Thiepval and the parts of the front line situated to the east of the village. At the same time the approach trenches, especially the *Lach Weg*, were taken under barrage fire of a strength never experienced before. Any existing telephone connections to the rear were destroyed after a few minutes. The only telephone wires still functioning remained near C4.

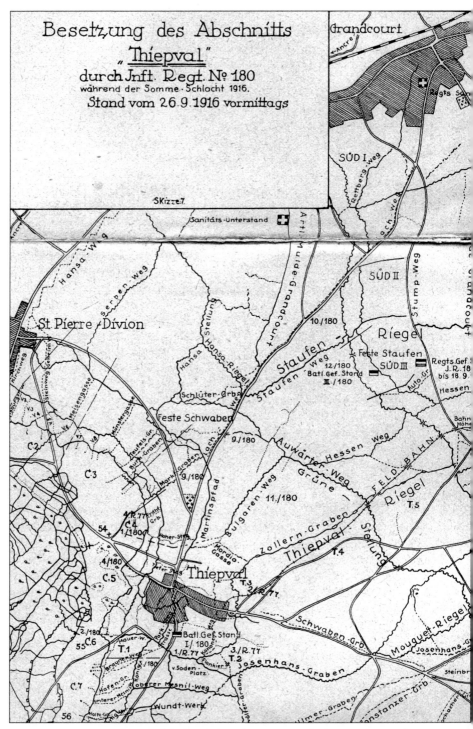

Position of IR 180 by Thiepval on the morning of 26 September 1916.

The company leader, *Oberleutnant* Sauerbrey, 4/R77, reported by telephone that Thiepval was being heavily bombarded. The drum fire lasted for hours in undiminished strength. An attempt was made to observe toward the front nearby the battalion battle headquarters from the edge of the trench; however, the entire area of Thiepval was shrouded in a dense smoke cloud that made any observation impossible.

In spite of all of the ominous news, the division staff always appeared to be in a confident mood. During the early afternoon of the 26th, immediately following the midday meal, *General-Adjutant* von Plessen appeared at headquarters to convey the personal thanks of His Majesty the Kaiser to the troops fighting at the Somme, especially the 26th Reserve Division. He was also going to distribute various awards to different officers and men. This visit suddenly became abruptly interrupted when a message was received at 2 o'clock 'The enemy has pressed into Thiepval. Further details unknown.'

The systematic bombardment of Thiepval had been going on day after day with great strength. Just like the preparations made for the attack on 3 September on C1 and C3, the enemy had now also systematically taken Thiepval, the left wing of C6 and C7, the *Brauner Weg, Mauer Weg*, T1, T2 and T3 and all dugouts under fire with heavy artillery and mines. Any attempt to work on the trenches and dugouts was impossible. As far back as 24 September there were only small remnants of wire obstacles remaining in front of the Sectors T2 and T3, and a few dugouts had already been destroyed.

In the afternoon, individual gas shells were directed against the position and between 6 and 7.30 p.m. gas mines fell in large numbers. All of this gas forced the men to wear their gas masks for hours at a time. The gas shells irritated their eyes, causing the men to cry, while the gas mines produced headaches. The fire on these days increased considerably until it reached its greatest strength on 26 September. On this day alone about 70 torpedo mines were fired into the sector with the span of one hour.

Following the extensive artillery preparation on Thiepval and the rearward connections, the main British attack finally began during the afternoon, at 2 PM, in the bright light of day. Apparently the British felt that an attack at this unaccustomed hour might not be expected by the German defenders. The assault came out of the line Courcelette-Authuille by the 11th and 18th British Divisions against the front *Zollern*, Mouquet farm, Thiepval and from the 1st and 2nd Canadian Divisions against succeeding trenches north of Courcelette (*Zollern Graben*). For support of the attack several of the new tanks had been brought forward.

The details of the actual events of the attacks against Thiepval were not fully known by the German Army until significantly later. The timeline and events of the final battle were pieced together from various news reports, enemy statements, a few accounts from survivors and in some instances, assumptions; of the defenders, there were few left to tell the story of what happened on 26 September.

In the first attempt, the British and Canadians succeeded in overrunning *Feste Zollern* and the outer works of Mouquet farm with their right wing in the sector of the German 8th Infantry Division, when, shortly after 2 p.m. the enemy became firmly established in the *Zollern Graben*. From this location, the British attempted to advance against the *Staufen Riegel* and the northern edge of Thiepval, *Feste Staufen,* or Stuff Redoubt as the British called it, and in the process capture *Feste Schwaben* and surround the village of Thiepval from the north.

This plan was apparently disrupted when the British came up against stubborn resistance at *Feste Staufen* by the III/180, Battalion Scupin. The enemy was also having difficulty overpowering the garrison in and under Mouquet farm where the 8th Infantry Division continued to fight in the cellars, tunnels and dugouts up until the evening.

Finally, there were the attacks on the left wing against the village and *Château* Thiepval that began at 2.15 p.m. This was the series of attack that were designed to encompass the village from three sides: the south, southeast and north. Three separate battle groups had been created for this purpose. The attack was conducted in three waves and when the southern column advanced out of the *Wundtwerk* the enemy ran into stubborn opposition by the I/180 and was not able to penetrate into the village.

The middle column advancing from the direction of Pozières along the Pozières-Thiepval-Hamel road broke through the positions of IR 153 from the 8th Division west of Mouquet farm and along the *Schwaben Graben* to break into the southeast corner of the village with direct support from batteries that had driven up to the battle front in the open. This column succeeded in overrunning three companies of RIR 77 holding the trenches there. The British then continued to advance into the village from the direction of the Thiepval chapel.

The initial British attack south of Thiepval was simply overpowering. The artillery and mine fire had shattered the defenses and forced the men, with the exception of trench sentries, to remain below ground inside the dugouts that had not been too badly damaged. The British followed directly behind the barrage fire and there was no time for the trench sentries to raise the alarm before the British were upon them. Given these circumstances, the German command accepted that the 1st, 2nd and 3/R77 and the men from the I/180, except for weak remnants, had either been killed or taken into captivity.

On the morning of 26 September, as usual, the artillery fire was on the position, until suddenly about 12.30 o'clock p.m. a furious shrapnel fire began. I went up out of my dugout however I had to linger for a moment in the entrance, because the overhang was blocked through machine gun fire from an aircraft. Furthermore while crawling out I immediately became greeted with a hand grenade from an Englishman standing in front of the dugout. Sacks with bread piled up in front of the cover protected me, and I fired at my attacker with my pistol. At this moment I became thrown down the stairway again together with some bread sacks from the force of further exploding hand grenades. I made it below still uninjured, but I was wounded on the left thigh and on the right heel from a hand grenade thrown after me. The sentry in front of my dugout was dead.

The British had broken through our line in our rear between Mouquet farm and the sector of the Regiment 153, the sentries were killed and the entrances of the dugouts were occupied. A frontal attack before our trench had not occurred, and the penetration by the enemy at different positions could not be observed by us because of the terrain. Now we had no other option remaining than to hold out as long as possible in our dugout, in the hope of becoming rescued through a counterattack. Meanwhile the enemy threw one hand grenade after the other into the dugout that exploded at the lowest treads, where approximately 700 hand grenades were stored. Fortunately however, they did not explode. The telephone connection was, like all days, torn. The telephone box as well as all maps and documents were destroyed. We were finally forced to leave the dugout by a sulphur cartridge with its suffocating smoke. I reached freedom with effort just before becoming unconscious.

No one was to be seen in front of the dugout, and I already had the hope, to escape yet; however at the next bend of the trench suddenly five Englishmen stood in front of me with rifles pointed at me, who took me prisoner. While four rifle barrels were pointed at my chest, a corporal plundered me. The most painful loss was the saddest for me. Under the care of my five guards I still remained approximately one hour in the trench and now endured the fire of our own artillery that in comparison to the customary English fire however was only moderate. Of the men of my company I saw no one more. They had apparently already been taken away. Then they brought me to the English lines. The trenches were full of assault troops, who moved upon Thiepval. They would have been a gratifying target for our artillery, but this presented only weak fire. As I would later realize, our artillery had withdrawn by the evening before the attack, because we had intended to give up Thiepval on the same night. *Leutnant der Landwehr* Onken, RIR 77.[21]

Parts of the enemy column encountered by *Leutnant* Onken then swung left into the rear of the German garrison at the western edge of Thiepval where a hand grenade battle occurred. The northern column reached the *Bulgaren Graben* and the *Martins Pfad* and moved forward against the *Château* from the north. It should be understood that the locations: Thiepval Chapel, the *Château*, Mouquet farm, etc. are being used to provide orientation to the reader and that, by September 1916, nothing above ground remained to even indicate they once existed other than possibly some fractured pieces of brick and red brick dust in the soil.

The few survivors from IR 180 provided a few pieces of the puzzle on what was taking place in and around Thiepval. The enemy attack was delivered in waves and moved with its left wing against C7 and the southern part of C6 at the intersection with the Thiepval - Authuille road.

The forward projecting triangle: *Mauerweg–C7–Braunerweg* that was occupied with one platoon from the 2/180 and sentries from the 2nd and 3/180 was quickly lost, as was anticipated should the position face a strong enemy attack. It was simply too exposed to hold out for any length of time.

The first real resistance was offered by the garrison in the *Mauer Weg*. The first wave of attackers was reported to be almost completely destroyed through infantry and machine gun fire before they had reached the remnants of the wire obstacles. The second, denser wave, flooded back with heavy losses as well. The third wave was accompanied by a tank and came up from Authuille Wood. Under the protection of the tank, with the third wave moving behind and alongside it, the retreating enemy soldiers of the second wave were stopped and in conjunction with the tank, worked closer to the German trenches until they were in front of the wire obstacles. However, this final wave also came to a halt due to the concentrated German defensive fire. Attackers and defenders now faced each other in a fierce fire fight.

This situation facing IR 180 became critical when the left wing and middle of the 3/180 were suddenly attacked from the rear with hand grenades. The British appeared to have penetrated the southeast and eastern front of Thiepval and were now rolling up the trenches from behind. More and more enemy troops were advancing to the south and southwest from the direction of the church and *Château* ruins.

The 3/180, attacked in the front and rear and threatened from the flank, was forced back from the left wing, the survivors withdrawing to C6. Despite repeated attacks, the enemy was not able to penetrate into C6 from the south through the *Mauer Weg*. Despite the tenacious defense of the barricade by the *Mauer Weg*, time was running out for the men of the 3/180. After repeated British attacks coming from the direction of Thiepval, the British began to make headway. Finally, the barricade at the junction of the *Mauer Weg* in C6 had to be transferred further to the rear. This move was necessary, otherwise the barricade and the defenders would have been circumvented by the enemy and surrounded.

The same situation that allowed the British to capture the western front of the village coming from the east, and, the southern front coming from the north, also allowed them to quickly occupy the northeastern and eastern parts of Thiepval. The British then succeeded in establishing a foothold in the *Martins Pfad* and part of the *Bulgaren Weg*. The weak forces that still remained in these positions were the only German troops left to prevent the enemy from advancing any deeper into the German defenses. The survivors of the initial British attack quickly erected barricades east of the intersection of the *Martins Pfad* with the second trench and in the *Bulgaren Weg* about 100 meters northeast of the junction with the *Mordio Gasse*.

Approximately 30-40 minutes after the start of the attack the British had already penetrated into the *Grünen Stellung* and in the *Zollern Graben*. From the *Grünen Stellung* and across the open ground from the *Zollern Graben* the enemy would be able to penetrate the *Hessen Graben* with strong forces. At this point in the fighting, approximately 30-40 British soldiers had already crossed over the *Hessen Weg* and were fighting at the *Lach Weg*. This small group was eventually driven back by the 9/180, who afterward erected a barricade southeast of the intersection of the *Grüne Stellung* and *Bulgaren Weg*.

At 4 p.m., a few members of the 9/180 came running out of the *Auwärter Graben* past the battalion battle headquarters of the I/R77. They reported that the British were advancing close behind them. The men were reorganized and ordered to occupy positions in the *Auwärter Weg*. As no other news had reached the battalion since the start of the attack the battalion commander, *Hauptmann* von Heugel, quickly ordered that a reconnaissance of the front lines must be made in order to clarify the overall situation.

The battalion adjutant, *Leutnant der Reserve* Eilers, proceeded toward the front lines with an orderly from the 9/180. The two men firmly established that the British had advanced almost up to the intersection of the *Bulgaren Weg* where it joined the *Auwärter Weg*. When the patrol reached this intersection they found that it was under extremely heavy fire. Fortunately, part of the 9/180 had erected a barricade there and held off any further advance by the enemy toward *Feste Schwaben*.

The *Auwärter Weg* was being held by the 11/180 and parts of the 1st and 2/R77. The 11/180 numbered only 35 men and the 1st and 2/R77 were comprised of approximately 20 men so that the entire garrison of the *Bulgaren Weg* consisted of approximately 50 men in total. The machine gun that had been positioned in the *Auwärter Weg* had been moved and placed near the barricade in the *Bulgaren Weg*. The *Zollern Graben* was already lost to the enemy, and the British had also successfully penetrated through the *Mordio Gasse* into the southern part of the *Bulgaren Weg* and the *Martins Pfad*.

The 1st and 2/R77 urgently asked for reinforcements or they could not be expected to hold their positions with such a small number of men. The only reserve for the I/R77 was a support platoon of 30 men in the *Markt Graben* that had been placed under the control of the 9/180. The Sector commander of the right neighboring regiment IR 66, *Hauptmann* Niemeyer, who was positioned not far from the I/R77 Battalion battle headquarters, was then asked if he could provide any support.

While the sectors held by IR 66 had not been attacked directly on the 26th, the regiment was still faced with a threat on its left flank. Apparently the intention of the enemy was to roll up the German front from the south. With the fall of Courcelette the enemy came into possession of the ridge that dominated the entire area and the next logical step would be for the enemy to take possession of *Feste Schwaben* by approaching it from the south.

The situation, as it was assessed by *Hauptmann* Niemeyer, showed the British succeeding in repressing the 4/180 back to the *Hoher Steg* which was still occupied and held by the 4/R77 and parts of the 1/180. They had penetrated into the *Martins Pfad* and *Bulgaren Weg*, so that *Leutnant* Armbrüster, 9/180 had to block off the intersection of the *Bulgaren Graben* with the *Auwärter Weg*. The enemy had also succeeded in penetrating further into the *Zollern Graben* and *Gassenweg*.

Hauptmann Niemeyer initially placed two groups of the 1/IR 66 to the possession of the 1st and 2/R77. In addition, all available Other Ranks with the battalion staff including runners and orderlies were sent into the *Auwärter Weg* as reinforcements. At that time, the Communication Trench Officer for RIR 77, *Leutnant der Reserve* Höltzenbein, who had been sent on reconnaissance, returned to the battalion battle headquarters through the barrage fire falling on C4 and reported the enemy break-in by Thiepval.

The British had attacked the position southwest of Thiepval with two tanks driving up on the road from Authuille to Thiepval. The tanks eventually became stuck in shell craters and at one point were attacked with hand grenades and naked steel by the men of IR 180 who swarmed over them in an attempt to destroy them.

The thrilling adventure of one of the new 'Land-armor' (tank) might be imagined here. On its own responsibility, it had the direction and it had smashed an enemy fire trench below the town. So it came upon a broad and deep opening on its solitary advance, in that seemingly soldiers hid. The tank wanted to place itself cozily over this trench, however it was suddenly stuck. At the same moment Germans hurled forth from their hiding places and swarmed around the wagon like bees. They showed an exceptional courage. Although the batteries kept hidden by the wagon showered them with a hail of projectiles, they attempted with desperate strength to storm the wandering tank-fort and kill its Other Ranks. In spite of the ceaseless machine gun fire they climbed on the roof, in that they lifted each other up to the top. They probably hoped to find to gaps or openings into the interior of the tank, but they could have just as well attacked a battleship with spades. It was an indescribable sight, this struggle of man against machine. The crew in the interior was filled with horror. In their wildest dreams our men had not considered it possible to become attacked. A blind enthusiasm goaded these Germans on and allowed in the madness them to lose their lives in the pounding work. They fought like the old infantry battalions at the beginning of the war. They came still like the first armies that swept along like the storm wind over Belgium and France. The deep cellar-vaults of Thiepval had preserved their clout in their entire undiminished strength, until the hour also came for them. [22]

The company leader in C4 asked about immediate reinforcements because of the strong enemy pressure, especially for clearing the *Martins Pfad* and establishing a connection with the 4/R77 through the *Hoher Steg*. Furthermore, *Leutnant der Reserve* Höltzenbein confirmed that no attack had taken place on the western front between C1 and C4. The company leader of the 11/180 then delivered orders to *Leutnant der Reserve* Höltzenbein to repel the enemy who had penetrated into the *Bulgaren Weg* and to establish a connection to the *Hoher Steg*.

The defenders were growing weaker with each enemy attack. The German defenses were in shambles and the British were advancing deeper into the Thiepval Sector. The situation had now become extremely dangerous for IR 66. Most of all for the 3rd and 4/66 lying in C3 and C4, and the 1st and 2/66 in *Feste Schwaben*. Any further advance by the enemy into the rear of the I/66 had to be avoided at all cost. The front facing south, being held by parts of IR 180 and RIR 77, desperately needed reinforcements. Now, an entire platoon from the 1/66 was sent to occupy the *Auwärter Graben* on the left of the *Lach Weg*. Two platoons of the company were sent to clear the *Martins Pfad*, in which a British nest had become firmly established. All three platoons were placed under the command of the I/R77. The *Schwaben Riegel* was occupied and held by the 2/66. However, in order to be able to hold *Feste Schwaben*, further reinforcements were urgently required; the lines were being stretched too thin.

Additional reinforcements were already on their way, moving into place as the fighting continued. Even without any specific information about the enemy attack and the status of the defenses, division and corps headquarters had made arrangements for every available man to be sent to the Thiepval Sector. Group Stein, and especially the 26th Reserve Division, had alerted all of the reserves in the rear at the start of the enemy attacks and ordered them to proceed toward the front with all dispatch. Once the reinforcements arrived, the local commanders would be able to deploy them where they were needed most. As the different units arrived at the front they were quickly placed at different blocking positions intended to prevent any possible enemy breakthrough.

During the course of the afternoon the 26th Reserve Division and the 52nd Reserve Infantry Brigade in Irles were provided with additional reserves: the Recruit Companies of RIR 121 and RIR 99. These companies were sent to occupy the *Miraumont Riegel*, *Landwehr Brigade Ersatz* Battalion 55 was sent to the *Grandcourt Riegel*, the IV/R99 was placed in the eastern half of the *Staufen Riegel*, a combined battalion from the 2nd Guard Reserve Division von Obernitz consisting of two companies each from RIR 15 and RIR 91, were placed in the western half of the *Staufen Riegel*. The *Below Stellung* and the *Gallwitz Riegel* were occupied by the regiments of the IV Army Corps.

50 *Musketen* arrived at the front and the massive firepower provided by these weapons was an invaluable asset to the defense of the sector. These weapons were deployed in the *Staufen Riegel* and in *Feste Schwaben*. Orders were also sent to IR 66 to provide additional reinforcements for all sectors of the 2nd position by IR 180.

RIR 119 was far to the rear enjoying a brief respite from the front lines. It too was targeted during the preliminary preparations for the British attack on the 26th. Enemy aircraft had dropped bombs during the night on the factory by Inchy, without hitting the buildings or the men of the 12/R119 who were billeted inside.

At 2 p.m. on 26 September alarm orders arrived at the regimental headquarters and *Radfahrer* were sent through the streets and alleys to assemble the companies. Every man hurried to his quarters and quickly packed up his equipment. By 3 p.m. the men were loaded into motorized columns that transported the unit to the front. The I/R119 was sent to Sapignies, the II/R119 to Bihucourt and the III/R119 to Behagnies. The II/R119 then marched toward Grandcourt where it arrived by the evening.

A small village in the Artois. Vivid red tile roofs lay in the luxuriant dark green of mighty trees. The September sun shined warmly in the wide village street. German soldiers stroll comfortably there. Villagers stand in the doors of the houses, after, they looked worried. White aircraft rock in the autumn blue of the ether and move to the front. The brazen throb of the drum fire rumbles hollowly from the distance. In Reserve!

Four cyclists pedal urgently out of a side alley. Where they come past, they shout a few words to those walking. A whirlwind appears to sweep behind them and carry away the soldiers. Everyone hurries, running toward their quarters. What is it? Alarm! Departure in ten minutes.

A long automobile column whirling dust around rattles into the village and stopped at the exit. Already a company comes up marching. The leader reports, divides his Other Ranks in groups and points them out to the vehicles. Climbing, lifting, pulling, shouting, yells, curses, swearing! The company is loaded and drives off. The other follow and it suddenly becomes quiet in the village. *Leutnant der Landwehr* Matthias Gerster, RIR 119.[23]

With the arrival of these reinforcements, everything possible was being done to prevent a larger breakthrough along the line Miraumont-Grandcourt. The numerous *Riegelstellungen* that had been constructed prior to this enemy attack also quickly demonstrated how important these preparations had been. The construction of the new positions had been reviled by the men performing the work night after night. Now, when the threat of an enemy breakthrough became a reality, this elaborate trench system was seen as critical components in preventing this potential disaster from becoming reality.

When the reinforcements arrived in their positions, rumors began to spread quickly through the ranks. 'Thiepval had fallen', 'Feste Schwaben stood like a rock in the frenzied sea.' The men soon learned that the British masses had stormed the *Hoher Steg* and the *Martins Pfad* that were defended by the remnants of the I/180. They also found out that enemy attacks had taken place along the entire line Thiepval-Courcelette, over the *Hessen Weg*, *Staufen Riegel* and *Grandcourt Riegel* toward Grandcourt and the enemy was attempting to take *Feste Schwaben* from the rear. If this occurred, it was as if the enemy wanted 'to take it out of the strong iron wreath of the German fortifications.' With this looming threat, the 26th Reserve Division ordered RIR 119 to occupy the *Grandcourt Riegel* with one battalion in the evening of 26 September.

Thiepval had fallen. The heroic Swabian regiment, IR 180, attacked in the flank and rear, was no longer able to hold the position. However, the defenders tenaciously held on to every trench piece, every shell crater they could while the British pressed relentlessly on the fortifications around Grandcourt: *Feste Schwaben*, *Feste Staufen* and the *Staufen Riegel*.

At 7.45 p.m. the 12/66 and one machine gun moved forward to *Feste Schwaben*. Upon orders from the brigade the 10/66 occupied the *Bulgaren Weg* during the night and the 11/66 occupied the *Auwärter Weg* and a part of the *Martins Pfad*. The 12/66 reinforced the 1/66 and together occupied part of the *Strassburger Steige* with the 2/66. For the companies of IR 66 that had been withdrawn from Sector S1, the 6/R15 and 5/R91 arrived to take their place.

This was the situation, when, at 10.30 p.m., *Leutnant* Köhler from the 10/66 arrived in the battalion battle headquarters and reported that two companies, the 10th and 11/66 were approaching as support. The 10/66 was immediately inserted in the *Bulgaren Weg* The 11/66 sent one platoon into the *Martins Pfad and* two platoons into the *Auwärter Weg* In the darkness, parts of both companies got lost in the confusing terrain; they did not rejoin their companies until much later. The men who had arrived attempted to clear the *Martins Pfad* up to the *Hoher Steg* of the enemy, in vain. By the evening of 26 September the front went to the south through the *Hoher Steg, Bulgaren Graben, Zollern Graben* and *Hessen Weg.*

The losses were heavy on both sides throughout the fighting. One attack against *Feste Staufen* came to halt after the British had achieved some initial success. The Germans bolstered their defenses by inserting two platoons of *Musketen* in *Feste Schwaben* and *Süd-I* By the evening of the 26th, the enemy had been able to occupy the *Hoher Steg* and *Hessen Weg. Feste Staufen* and the *Hessen Weg,* east of *Feste Staufen,* still held out until the morning; then the southern part of *Feste Staufen* was lost to the British by the late afternoon.

Division and brigade headquarters had only received sparse news about the swift course of the fighting. The headquarters staff felt helpless in the current situation. Hours filled with anxiousness had passed since that alarming message has arrived at 2 p.m. the previous day in the presence of General von Plessen. Up until evening no one was even capable of piecing together even a moderate picture of the situation, because the telephone connections had been destroyed and the orderly officers sent to the front to become familiar about the situation had not returned yet.

The first solid news to came out of Thiepval arrived by messenger pigeon that reached headquarters at 6.30 p.m. The small handwritten note stated '1 Unteroffizier, 17 men from the *Unterstab* I Battalion are still in the Battalion dugout, isolated from all companies and surrounded by Englishmen. Signed: Gossers, Patrol Leader. Belthle, Battalion *Tambour.*'[24] A second report received by messenger pigeon said that *Major* Weeber, who had previously disappeared and was thought to be dead had been seen at 9 p.m. at the well in front of the church of Thiepval. He was surrounded by the enemy and involved in a hand grenade battle.

Since then, no one has ever seen or heard anything again from *Major* Weeber, the last commander of Thiepval. He had given his promise to the division commander, 'To hold Thiepval to the last man,' and apparently he was living up to his word.

The III/180 now took over the protection of *Feste Staufen* and blocked it off to the south, while reinforcements arrived from different regiments in the second position and *Staufen Riegel* that would serve as support. In the course of the night it became known that the remnants of the I/180, about 100 men in total with parts of the I/R77, had assembled at 8 p.m. in the northern part of Thiepval under *Leutnant der Reserve* Kimmich, 2/180. In the confusion this small group broke through the British lines and reached the *Hoher Steg.* It was later learned that there was still fighting going on in the trenches at the northwest corner of the village of Thiepval until 8 a.m. the next morning.

On the evening of 26 September the new front lines were described based on the suggestion of the commander of the 52nd Reserve Infantry Brigade as the northern edge of Thiepval, *Bulgaren Graben, Feste Schwaben* and *Staufen Riegel.* The sector border towards the IV Army Corps was determined to be the *Köhler Pfad.*

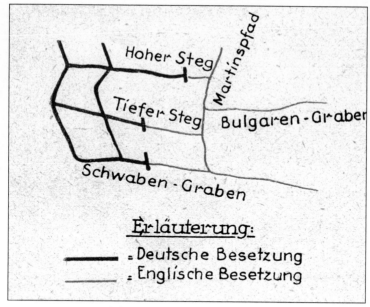

State of the fighting near Thiepval at 9 p.m.

The 8th Division had held the eastern part of the *Staufen Riegel*. Strong reserves of the IV Army Corps were in the *Below Stellung* and in the *Gallwitz Riegel*. Finally, after what seemed an eternity, the enemy artillery fire died down along the entire in the course of the evening. While the men enjoyed being out from under the constant bombardments, they were still under the watchful eyes of enemy observation aircraft and numerous observation balloons tracked every movement in the German trenches.

Some of the first real news of the events taking place by Thiepval came on the early morning of 27 September. The company commander of the 1/180 sent a report to headquarters outlining the situation of his men on the evening of the previous day.

1. The *Leutnant der Reserve* Mayer, Company Leader 1/180,
a) State of the fighting at 9 o'clock in the evening, see sketch.
b) So far as it was allowed to assess, the 2nd and 3rd Companies still each consisted out of one quarter of their former strength, the 1st and 4th Companies consisted out of only one third of their former strength.
Signed Mayer, *Leutnant der Reserve*, 1/180.
2. The officer patrol of *Leutnant der Reserve* Mutschler reported: 'Englishmen sit in the *Hoher Steg* on the Grandcourt-Thiepval road up to the *Bulgaren Weg*, 100 meters east of the junction of the *Mordio Gasse*. Counterattack by IR 66 commenced.' The food of the regiment came from iron rations on this day. Further food and close combat methods became brought up by carrying troops.
Reported losses on 26 September: *Leutnant der Reserve* Rieder dead, *Leutnant der Reserve* Armbruster wounded, *Leutnant der Reserve* Lindemann gas sick; 14 men dead, 54 wounded, 65 missing. [25]
A second message arrives from the 2/180 at 10.25 a.m.:

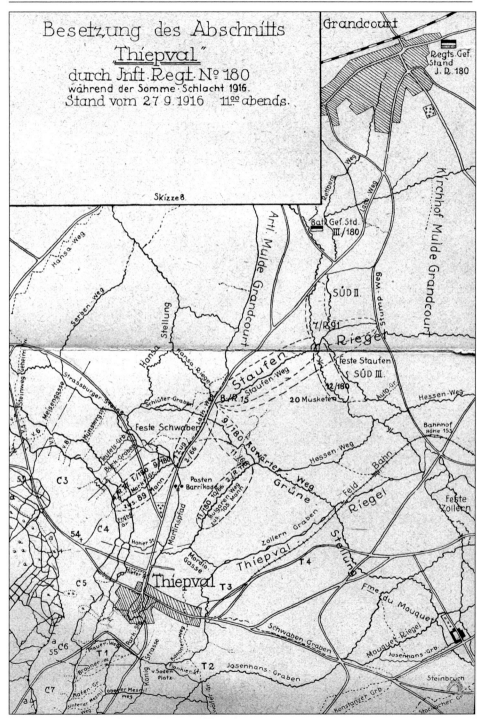

Position of IR 180 by Thiepval on the evening of 27 September 1916.

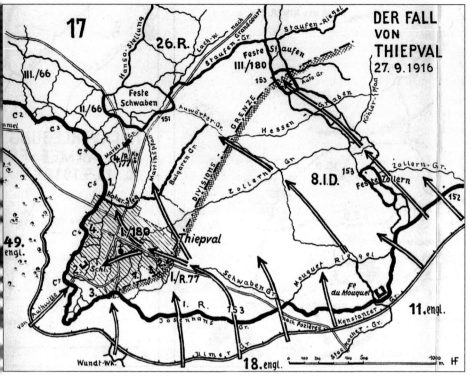

The fall of Thiepval, 27 September 1916.

Situation: I am with the remnants of the Battalion, approximately 100 men, in the *Hoher Steg* and in the 1st and 2nd trenches of C5. The enemy pressed into the *Hoher Steg* and fired from out of the *Martins Pfad* into the rear of the garrison. I will hold the *Hoher Steg* as long as possible. If support does not come, we will be pressed into C4, because close combat methods have become scarce. Signed. Kimmich, *Leutnant der Reserve* and Company leader 2/180. [26]

The reconnaissance undertaken in the night by officers from IR 180 made the following determinations on the morning of 27 September: The front was along the line: C4 – *Hoher Steg* – *Bulgaren Graben* and *Hessen Graben* on both sides of the second defensive position. This line was interrupted twice by British nests.

The first enemy nest stretched approximately 20 meters north of the junction of the *Martins Pfad* in the *Hoher Steg* up to the *Bulgaren Graben*, approximately 100 meters east of the junction of the *Mordio Gasse* in the *Bulgaren Graben*, the other from the junction of the *Bulgaren Graben* in the *Grüne Stellung* up to the *Hessen Graben*, approximately 100 meters east of the intersection of the *Hessen Graben – Grüne Stellung*.

In the afternoon the enemy intensified his artillery fire upon *Feste Staufen* to the greatest possible strength. Then, in the evening, when the report was received that the enemy had taken *Feste Staufen*, the II/R119 was placed under the command of IR 180. The 6th and 8/R119 advanced at night in a counterattack only to find the *Stumpf Weg* up to the *Auto Graben* strongly occupied by German troops and that there was still stubborn resistance in the second position by *Feste Staufen*. As such, the first trench north of the junction of the *Auto Graben* and the second trench in the middle between the *Auto Graben* and *Staufen Riegel* were sealed off.

The German command felt that it was sheer luck and, in their opinion, actually incomprehensible, that the enemy commander-in-chief did not decide to simultaneously attack the western front of Thiepval with the 49th Division on 27 September; from there to penetrate into *Feste Schwaben*. If this had been done, it would have been an unmitigated catastrophe for all German troops fighting south of the Ancre.

While both sides fought over the possession of Thiepval, the enemy also advanced on his right wing against *Feste Staufen* and *Feste Schwaben*. Fierce fighting developed around both of these strongpoints, with *Feste Staufen* defended by the III/180 and *Feste Schwaben* by IR 66. For the Germans, any thought of retaking the lost strongpoint of Thiepval appeared to be hopeless considering the overall situation in the southern sector.

The targeting of Thiepval by the British had always been anticipated at some point in the great battle. The village and surrounding terrain had formed a key point in the German lines on the Somme and had been viciously contested up to the very end. The enemy newspapers printed a number of stories about the capture of this important location, some comparing it with Sebastopol from the Crimean War. The defeat of IR 180 was honorable, and the captive comrades of IR 180 were judged by the Englishmen to be equal the elite 'Prussian Guards'. Thus did Thiepval, the 'hinge-point of the German western front,' fall in the hands of the enemy.

Many German histories written during and shortly after the war had to rely upon the enemy's own words in order to describe the 'heroic' fighting by the German defenders of Thiepval. It seemed only fitting that the enemy would have provided the epitaph for the German defenders.

> With what unprecedented bravery and sacrifice our I Battalion fought here in union with the I and III/IR 180, just for once we want to let the enemy tell. An English newspaper, the "Manchester Guardian," gives the following narrative on 29th September 1916: 'Yesterday afternoon Thiepval had been taken by our troops, but its conquest was costly, heavy fighting. Nowhere on the entire western front has the enemy afforded such furious opposition against our superior strength, nowhere has he caused us so many difficulties in his subterranean works. These battle proven troops that have defended Thiepval, only gave up after they were threatened with immediate annihilation. The prisoners attempted to organize themselves again and overpower their guards. The conquerors honestly recognized the stubborn fighting by which the Württemberger and the Guard Reserve conducted themselves. Although Thiepval was already lost by the enemy yesterday afternoon at 3 o'clock, the fighting still raged further the entire afternoon and the whole following night in the smashed trenches; and when this morning as I turned and looked for the last time at the shapeless ruined houses on the mountain ridge, the wild battle still raged under the earth in the dugouts defended to the utmost. The subterranean fighting now reached its highpoint in these hours. We know of the caves and tunnel of the Germans. Already examples of their catacomb construction required much admiration by of what they have produced under the hills and valleys of all of Northern France; a refined, important network of dry and electrically lit corridors that merged into a row of

Rieder
Leutnant d. R. im Inf.=Regt. 180
gefallen bei Thiepval
am 26. September 1916

(*Kriegstagebuch aus Schwaben*)

smaller chambers and further vaults, in which entire battalions could find protection. However, what was achieved here in Thiepval; must be considered as the masterpiece of German mole work. [27]

No man's land between the fires trenches had been deserted there the entire time. However when the English infantry attempted to advance, it was suddenly peppered by German weapons as if by magic. The building ruins which were at the orchard situated at the southern edge of the village hid gunners, and a large pile of earth and bricks, the former château at the western edge of the village, vomited flames and hand grenades. In the buried streets, under the ruins machine guns barked forth at the approaching figures in khaki. They lurked behind the charred tree stumps at the end of the route Pozières, behind the cemetery. Wherever one looked, machine guns sent forth death with frightening certainty. Finally three fourths of Thiepval was in our possession. Only the chateau held out. No human being could withstand the murderous fire of his gunners. A company leader held the fort and fired with his man, until they were face to face confronting the British. For a while it really seemed as if the defenders had the upper hand, when a land tank came to help that attacked the hill made out of earth and bricks like a storm boat. The château crumbled down, the gunners finally stopped firing. Yes, the spirit of Thiepval didn't become easily broken. [28]

Additional stories had appeared in newspapers such as the *Daily Mail* from 28 September 1916.

When 61 years earlier the fortress Sebastopol fell, there was a large outbreak of joy in England. With this opportunity the number of the fallen troops was insignificant, and the results were not much more than an episode in the war that was conducted in a comparatively modest scale.

It is evidence for the clearer understanding of the nature of the present war that two brilliant successes like the seizure of Thiepval and Combles have not been accompanied with a similar outbreak of joy. Everyone that was at these places, which concerned their opposition power, considered the fortress Sebastopol important. There were not even any modern European fortresses that were superior, even Metz or Verdun. Thiepval and Combles had been constructed according to the experiences of this war.

We could probably say that no army in the past has ever had to face a similar action, like the taking of the fortresses of Thiepval and Combles; especially if in consideration that the army standing opposite was a large well equipped field army, which was thoroughly equipped and was led by one of the best staffs.[29]

In the *Times* from 29 September a detailed report was mentioned in the section 'The storm troops were heavily bombarded.'

The British troops were severely bombarded the entire night through. They dug themselves in around the northern and northeastern part of the village of Thiepval; however, fierce hand grenade battles expelled them again. However, as soon as they had withdrawn, they dug themselves in once again. In the captured trenches the English soldiers advanced with hand grenades and naked steel on the endlessly steep steps into the subterranean areas, and here they arrived on the remnants of the garrison, who awaited them in the unavoidable close combat. Most of the Germans had died fighting. There were large dugouts, whose narrow doors were plugged up with barricades made from corpses. Other surrendered in the light of the electric lamps and then climbed out of the darkness into the open, where they ended up in danger from their own barrage fire. A large number of the prisoners must then still lose their lives while being transported back to the British lines. [30]

With the fall of Thiepval the British had still not completely fulfilled their goals. The Germans still held the key positions overlooking the Ancre with the strongpoints *Feste Schwaben* and *Feste Staufen* (Hills 151 and 153) in their hands. Before these strongpoints could be taken, major attacks would have to be once again undertaken.. The enemy continued to pound away on the German line *Staufen Riegel – Feste Staufen – Staufen Graben – Feste Schwaben* on 27 September and on the following days. Despite the participation of new divisions and an immense amount of material, no significant success was achieved..

Feste Staufen was being defended by the III/180 and neighboring troops, which stood immovable against all attacks. The II/R119 was moved here during the night of 26/27 September from Bihucourt, and put into the *Grandcourt Riegel*. The sheer weight of the enemy attacks eventually succeeded in gaining some ground on 27 September at *Feste Schwaben*

Parts of five German divisions had been involved in the fighting during the latest attacks. Most of the units were heavily intermixed as they were often placed in the front line by company or battalion in a piecemeal fashion; the 26th Reserve Division, 52nd Infantry Division, 2nd Guard Reserve Division, 7th and 8th Infantry Divisions. The defenders were drawn from nine regiments; IR 180, IR 66, RIR 119, RIR 15 RIR 77, RIR 91, RIR 99, IR 93, IR 153 and IR 165.

While it was generally quite difficult to oversee so many different units in a major battle, the energetic commander of the 52nd Reserve Infantry Brigade, *Generalleutnant* von Auwärter, masterfully directed the coordinated efforts of every unit from his battle headquarters at Irles and he refused to allow any news, good or bad, to distract him from conducting the fight

On 27 September the 26th Reserve Division headquarters was transferred from Biefvillers, where it was located since 15 March 1916, to Vaulx, some 10 kilometers further back. This occurred on the request of the commanding general, because Biefvillers was gradually becoming threatened by enemy artillery fire and bombing raids. Shortly before the departure of the division headquarters a direct hit struck the kitchen of the headquarters château, without causing injury.

There were no mined dugouts in Biefvillers save for a deep, but dangerous chalk cave, which offered any protection. The Artillery Staff had already transferred to Vaulx-Vraucourt from Biefvillers a few days earlier. The route to the front was far longer than before and as such personal visits to the front by the division commander were now more difficult and were limited.

At 3 a.m. on 27 September a runner was sent from the headquarters of the III/180 to deliver an express order meant for the 9/180. This order stated that the troops in sector *Thiepval-Nord* were to be placed under the command of *Major* Scupin, III/180, as was the staff of the I/R77. The order included the message that a British nest was located in the *Martins Pfad*. Two companies from IR 66 and the 11/180 were to be used for the counterattack to eliminate it. Furthermore, according to the orders of *Major* Scupin, the 10/180 was approaching as reinforcements. This company would occupy the *Markt Graben* with two platoons and the northern part of the *Auwärter Weg* with one platoon.

However this order, like many others from IR 180, did not make it to its destination. It was later determined that the order had indeed been sent by the battalion, but the messenger could not make it through the heavy enemy fire. Actually, as the I/R77 had no knowledge of the changeover of command to *Major* Scupin and in particular, of the approach of the 10/180 as further reinforcements, the I/R77 ordered the 10th and 11/66 to be inserted into the *Markt Graben* and the northern part of the *Auwärter Weg*.

Major Scupin, who was in *Feste Staufen*, immediately became notified of the movements of the 10th and 11/66 by runner who had managed to survive the difficult journey. To avoid confusion, the order that had been issued by the I/RIR 77 was not rescinded as it generally corresponded to the desired distribution of forces.

According to a message from *Leutnant* Köhler, 10/66, who was located at the headquarters of the I/R77 with three of his men, such heavy artillery fire lay on the *Martins Pfad*, where the rest of the platoon was inserted that it was impossible for troops to occupy it; neither friend nor foe could hold this trench. *Leutnant* Höltzenbein, who had been sent out to investigate the situation by the I/R77 confirmed that the *Martins Pfad* was full of dead. There were no German or British troops in the trench, which remained continuously under heavy enemy fire.

Later in the morning the telephone connection from RIR 77 to IR 180 was re-established for a brief time. It was confirmed that the staff of the I/RIR 77 was now subordinate to *Major* Scupin. The regiment ordered Scupin to act independently as circumstances dictated after he had had the opportunity to evaluate the situation. He was to act within the context of the commander's intent provided by RIR 77. The telephone lines were expected to be cut at any moment and he was expected to act in an autonomous manner in the execution of his orders.

Additional reinforcements continued to arrive at the front. In the early morning hours of 27 September the II/R119 marched from Bihucourt and moved into position, which in part was barely knee deep and besides a few recently started tunnel entrances, it possessed only a few complete dugouts.

Towards noon, *Oberleutnant der Reserve* Sauerbrey sent runners from Sector C4 to report he could no longer withstand the immense pressure by the British in the *Hoher Steg*. The British were pressing his men with far superior strength and had gradually forced him to evacuate the first and second trench in C4. Sauerbrey and his men first withdrew to the *Friedhof Graben*, then up to the *Markt Graben*.

Sauerbrey and his small force were able to hold the *Markt Graben* and blocked off the first and second trenches in C4. Reinforcements were urgently required, because the men of the 4/R77 and the 1/180 had been in a hand grenade battle for 22 hours and were completely exhausted; no longer capable of even the thought of throwing another hand grenade.

This message was sent through to *Feste Staufen* to *Major* Scupin by runners, because the I/R77 had no available reserves on hand to offer any assistance. There was simply no one nearby who could bring any help to the garrison of the *Markt Graben*. Further messages arrived from *Oberleutnant der Reserve* Sauerbrey, in which requests for reinforcements grew even more urgent until finally, Sauerbrey asked permission for his men to be relieved. All of these messages were forwarded to *Major* Scupin but he was unable to help in any way.

The strain on the men from the increasingly long wait for reinforcements or relief was appalling. Only small amounts of food and ammunition were able to be brought up to the 4/R77 by the few orderlies still left in the I/R77. The remaining companies of the battalion also received much needed supplies in equally small quantities. In one of the last messages sent by *Oberleutnant* Sauerbrey, he reported that the British had captured two dugouts in C4 through heavy hand grenade fighting. His tenuous grip on the critical position was almost gone.

Meanwhile, the battalion staff I/R77, on orders from IR 180, had to evacuate the dugouts in the *Lach Weg*. The I/R77 would have to move into the dugouts lying in the northern trench of *Feste Schwaben* where the sector commander of IR 66 was located. The abandoned dugouts in the *Lach Weg* were to be filled with one platoon from the 1/IR 66 so that the position would maintain at least a small garrison.

Later in the evening of 27 September, the II/180 arrived at the front, moving towards Miraumont from Marquion. The II/180 was placed under the direction of *Major* von Stöcklern, commander of IR 66 so that the remaining parts of IR 180 situated adjacent to his regiment could be withdrawn.

At 11.45 p.m. on 27 September IR 180 took stock of its losses in the heavy fighting on the previous day: *Leutnants der Reserve* Gussmann and Steinhilber dead; *Leutnants der Reserve* Knapp and Engel wounded; missing: *Major* Weeber, commander I/180, *Leutnant der Reserve* von Jan, Adjutant I/180, *Leutnants der Reserve* Schleich, Zeller, Göhner Schwaibold, *Leutnant* Merker, *Assistenzarzt* Dr. Spaich. 21 men dead, 90 wounded and 391 missing. Many weeks or months would pass before the fate of the missing became known.

While the Germans made do with the troops available to them, the British had the

Gußmann
Leutnant d. R. im Inf.-Regt. 180
gefallen bei Thiepval
am 26. September 1916

v. Jan
Leutnant d. R. im Inf.-Regt. 180
gefallen bei Thiepval
am 26. September 1916

Schleich
Leutnant d. R. im Inf.-Regt. 180
gefallen bei Thiepval
am 26. September 1916

(*Kriegstagebuch aus Schwaben*)

Leutn. d. R. Bleibler
gef. bei Grandcourt 26. 9. 1916

Hauptmann Burk
gef. bei Puisieux 27. 9. 1916

(Both photos from *Das Württembergisches Reserve-Feldartillerie-Regiment Nr. 26 im Weltkrieg 1914-1918*)

luxury of withdrawing their worn-out troops and replacing them with three fresh divisions. After severe drum fire, the attack began once again by *Feste Schwaben* and *Feste Staufen* at 11 a.m. An attack by the 2nd English Division against the *Stall Mulde* behind Grandcourt was repulsed after bloody close combat. Each attempt resulted in heavy casualties amongst the attacking troops.

However, it seemed as if the enemy wanted to take possession of the hill crest line, especially the *Hessen Graben* and *Feste Staufen* at any cost. The British attacked relentlessly and managed to penetrate into the *Hessen Graben* east of the *Köhler Pfad* and the southern part of *Feste Staufen* despite monstrous losses. Now, as *Feste Staufen* formed the key point of the entire defensive system that protected Grandcourt and the rear of Thiepval, it had to be retaken. The newly arrived 6th and 8/R119 received the seemingly impossible task of recapturing this vital position.

All of the counterattacks, restoration work on the defenses and need for support troops to prevent an enemy breakthrough required more men than were available. As a result, while the III/R119 worked on fortifying the villages of Behagnies and Sapignies the I/R119 was moved to Achiet-le-Petit in the night from 27 to 28 September in order to be closer to the front.

In the course of the night from 27/28 September, the sector commander of IR 66, *Hauptmann* Niemeyer, received a brigade order. According to this order, the entire sector of Brigade Auwärter would be divided into two parts. The right sector would be under IR 66. The southern boundary was the *Bulgaren Weg* and the *Markt Graben*. The parts of the front situated further east and southeast of the front belonged to the command area of IR 93; IR 180 was not been mentioned in the brigade order.

Separate orders had been sent to IR 180 and the I/RIR 77. Niemeyer assumed that IR 180, with its very heavy losses, must have been extracted or would become extracted from the front. No messages had been received from IR 180 for some time, because every connection, even runners, had broken down. It was later determined, the corresponding order sent to IR 180 had never reached the regiment. All of the runners were either wounded or killed attempting to deliver their messages. Finally, contact was made with the units from IR 180 and RIR 77, all of which were in desperate need of relief.

When, at about 3 a.m., the sector commander of IR 66 received orders from regimental headquarters to move his battle headquarters further back into the *Hansa Stellung*, the battalion staff of the I/RIR 77 decided to turn over the abandoned regimental battle headquarters to what was left of IR 180 and, if at all possible, to extract the meager remnants of the I/R77 from the front line.

Extremely powerful artillery fire had fallen on *Feste Schwaben* and the *Lach Weg* the entire night. At 7 a.m. the following morning the battalion staff of the I/R77 left the shelter of the sector commander of IR 66. The staff arrived at the regimental battle headquarters of IR 180 in Grandcourt around 8.30 a.m. and reported to the regimental commander, *Oberstleutnant* Fischer. Fischer was immediately advised that neither the remnants of IR 180 nor the I/RIR 77 could be pulled out from the front line despite the fact that the latter battalion amounted to only 42 men present for duty.

Early on the morning of 28 September, bombing parties from the 8/R119 advanced in the *Stumpf Weg* above *Feste Staufen* in an attempt to recapture the position. They advanced a considerable distance in the maze of trenches without bumping into the enemy. The 6/R119 sent Platoon Bohnert through the first trench of *Feste Staufen* and Platoon Welte through the second trench. Unlike the 8/R119, the two platoons from the 6/R119 quickly ran into nests of enemy troops and in the subsequent fighting, either expelled or destroyed them. Following their successful advance, the platoons were able to re-establish a connection through the *Auto Graben* and erected barricades to consolidate their gains.

At 10 a.m. the strongpoint *Feste Staufen* was in German hands again; the 6/R119 remained subordinate to *Hauptmann* Obernitz, who directed the defenses in the *Feste*. The British counterattacked twice, at 10 a.m. and at 12 noon; however they were repulsed both

Welte
Leutnant b. L. im Ref.=Regt. 119
gefallen bei Grandcourt
am 29. September 1916

(*Kriegstagebuch aus Schwaben*)

Leutn. b. R. Ackermann
gef. bei Thiepval 29. 9. 1916

(*Das Württembergisches Reserve-
Feldartillerie-Regiment Nr. 26
im Weltkrieg 1914-1918*)

times by the 6/R119 using hand grenades. At 6 p.m., the 8/R119 returned to the battalion in the *Grandcourt Riegel* on orders from the sector commander, where the men received shelter from the steep slope on the road to Miraumont. The 7/R119 was then inserted into the *Staufen Riegel* and at the *Köhler Pfad*.

When the I/R77 commander, *Hauptmann* von Heugel, found out that he could do nothing to replace his people in the front line, he was determined that every last wounded or injured man in his battalion would be extracted safely from the battlefield and issued orders accordingly. Towards evening, the British, who had already occupied the *Bulgaren Weg* and the *Auwärter Weg* during the afternoon, also attacked from the east and rolled up the *Markt Graben* where the remnants of the 4/R77 were located. Only a pitifully small number of men returned from the 4th Company following this attack. In the late afternoon, the staff of the I/R77 moved off from Grandcourt to Courcelles.

It had not been until the battalion leader personally spoke with the division commander, *His Excellenz Frhr.* von *Soden* of his well-founded concerns for his men, that his efforts rewarded. The I and III/180 as well as the I/R77 would be relieved by the II/180. This was originally scheduled to take place the same evening while the battalion staff from the I/R77 was relieved immediately. However, events taking place on the front would delay the relief von Heugel had worked so hard to achieve. After all, the needs of the army outweighed the needs of individual soldiers.

While *Hauptmann* von Heugel was making every effort to have his men withdrawn before his battalion was completely destroyed, further to the south and west, by *Feste Schwaben*, the British continued their efforts to capture this key point in the German defenses. There was stubborn hand grenade fighting at the *Martins Pfad* and in the *Bulgaren*

IR 180 following their relief from Thiepval. (*Die 26. Reserve Division 1914-1918*)

Graben all day long. The British suffered numerous losses assaulting the *Bulgaren Graben* and the *Auwärter Weg*, which failed in the face of tenacious opposition afforded by the 10th and 11/66 and the remnants of the 9th and 10/180. However, with each attack, the number of defenders grew smaller and smaller.

At approximately 9 a.m. another attack took place upon the entire front of IR 66. The initial assault struck the completely exhausted remnants of the 10th and 11/66 and 9th and 10/180, in total about 200 men, in the *Bulgaren Graben* and *Auwärter Weg* following a short, violent drum fire. After fierce close combat, during which all of the officers became wounded, the enemy finally succeeded in taking both trenches by 11 a.m..

Prior to this attack, the I/66 had been given orders by regimental headquarters to evacuate the command post in *Schwaben Riegel* and proceed to a new location in the northern part of the *Hansa Stellung*. With all battalion officers now further in the rear, *Stabsarzt* Dr. Sage, whose medical dugout was located in the *Artillerie Mulde*, was the senior office remaining onsite. He was personally instrumental in stopping the men from IR 66 and IR 180 who were streaming back in disorder as a result of the latest enemy attack. Dr. Sage collected every man he could as they ran past and reformed them in a nearby trench. It was becoming apparent that the men could no longer withstand the constant fighting; something desperately needed to be done before the entire line collapsed.

At approximately 12 noon new, strong drum fire, of all calibers, was placed against the entire regimental sector of IR 66 once more. At 1.30 p.m. a strong British attack followed the bombardment against C3 and C4 from the west and against the *Lach Weg* and *Schwaben Riegel* from the east. Despite the weight of fire, the frontal attacks against C3 and C4 were completely repulsed.

During this phase of the enemy attack the 2/66 under *Leutnant* Lorleberg and the 1/66 under *Leutnant* Henze succeeded in pushing the enemy out of the *Lach Weg* and the *Auwärter Weg* through a counterattack. The fighting at the barricades in the first and second trenches of Sector C4 was severe as both sides tried to gain the upper hand. *Leutnant der Reserve* Mau, who had already been severely wounded in the morning, was killed at the barricade in the first trench when he was struck by hand grenade fragments. *Leutnant der Reserve* Höger was wounded at the barricade in the second trench, as was *Unteroffizier* Heine. *Vizefeldwebel* Kremkan took over command and provided energetic opposition of the enemy attempts to capture the barricade.

While the 3/66 held out against a frontal and flank attack, the British broke through the *Markt Graben* that was lightly held by the exhausted survivors of the 4/R77. Even after numerous requests for support or relief, *Oberleutnant* Sauerbrey and his dwindling pool of men still held the *Markt Graben*. Now, it appears that Sauerbrey and his men had been finally overwhelmed. The British, once through the *Markt Graben,* attacked the 3/66 in the rear. Attacked on three sides, the 3/66 was forced to give up its position and suffered heavy losses.

On 24 September we relieved the 2/66 in C4. In the left portion of the first trench lay the platoon of *Leutnant* Elsmann, on the right *Leutnant der Reserve* Mau. In the second trench *Leutnant der Reserve* Höger lay on the left with his platoon. The 4/66 was in C3 and south of the 3/66 was the 4/R77, its left resting against Thiepval. On 26 September *Feste* Thiepval fell, after an extremely brave defense by IR 180, the hinge point of the German front of that time. When one group of IR 180, who evaded the enemy penetration, with a machine gun passed C4, they were held on to, because the company located there, weakened through very heavy losses in the last weeks – from the original 270 men they still had about 110 men left – they had to take advantage of any forces that were available to them. The 4/R77 which occupied the *Hoher Steg* had the enemy in the trench, and blocked off the first and second trench through barricades. However the enemy that was in the *Martins Pfad* advanced out over the *Hoher Steg*, so that the 4/R77 in the *Hoher Steg* received fire from behind and had numerous losses. Subsequently the company leader of the 4/R77, *Oberleutnant der Reserve* Sauerbrey, came to me and we united in the manner that the 4/R77 went back upon on the *Markt Graben*. On the other hand by the 3/66 the defensive trench between the first and second trench in the prolongation of the *Markt Graben* became occupied by Platoon Höger and simultaneously the first and second trench were blocked off with barricades. This was the situation on the evening of 27 September. For me, the following was clear on 27 September: the enemy will attempt to penetrate over the barricades into the first and second trench. The defensive position in the *Markt Graben* up to the first trench was without dugouts, so that the enemy's strong artillery bombardment could inflict heavy losses on the troops lying there. Furthermore the enemy delivered his attack against us in our rear from out from the hill. If the troops held *Feste Schwaben* behind us, then we were saved. I began 28 September with this belief. Then, *Leutnant* Elsmann reported sick: The young, dashing officer had been struck with a severe nervous breakdown. *Leutnant* Mau took on the position at Barricade I. Shortly following, it might have been about 5 o'clock in the morning *Leutnant der Reserve* Mau became severely wounded on the jaw from a shell splinter. The first trench was without any officers. I was thinking about taking over the position at barricade I. However, something completely unexpected occurred: *Leutnant* Mau appeared again with bandages drenched through with blood and placed himself in command again with the manly words: 'I intend to remain and be with my men.' At midday a terrible cannonade began. The fighting at the barricades was valiant. *Leutnant der Reserve* Höger must leave his platoon because of being shot in the arm, *Vizefeldwebel* Kremkau directed the defense. *Leutnant* Mau, standing high above on the edge of the trench, a sack of hand grenades alongside him, greeted the Englishmen, with his brave men at his side. They all died a hero's death with him. The barricades were held. Then the enemy appeared in the rear, coming from the hill. He had broken through the left wing of the 4/R77 in the *Markt Graben*, had pressed back the 11th and 12/66 in the *Martins Pfad* and dealt with the 1/66 through rear and frontal attacks. The weak force of the 3/66 that was still available for this attack – the main part fought at the barricades – could not keep the Englishmen back. With a few men, amongst them my three good subordinates, I attempted to face the enemy opposition. However direct hits by several hand grenades struck the largest part of the men to the ground. I received a hand grenade wound in the side. Then I wanted to help my severely wounded battle orderly – the poor Charles Mummeldey who had received 4 shots through the lungs. Both of us were prisoners of war, a confused mass of humanity rolled about us on the ground. *Leutnant der Reserve* Heine, 3/66 [30]

Despite the fiercest resistance by the 4/66 the British also penetrated into C3. Here, they were supported by low flying pilots, communicating with the infantry using horn signals. While the 1/66 stubbornly defended its trench further to the south, they too were engaged from the rear and finally dealt with by the enemy who had penetrated from the west. *Leutnant* Henze was severely wounded and captured. The fight of the 4th Company was described by *Vizefeldwebel* Collet.

About noon the heaviest drum fire fell like a blow, which died down about 1 o'clock. Individual wounded from the 3rd Company come toward us and reported the advance of the Englishmen, of which we, in the meantime, still saw nothing. Our company leader, *Leutnant der Reserve* Kühne, allowed the shell holes all around to be occupied, yet shells and shrapnel still continuously smashed by us, and then the rest of the 3rd Company came, which we absorbed. We see the first Englishmen appear half on the left behind us at *Feste Schwaben*. These we took under fire, the frontal attack against our first trench is refused outright. A pilot comes down quite close to us, we hear him from above the noise of the storm, he fired at us with machine guns. We take him under fire. He directs the fire of the artillery on us, which then slowly placed shot after shot in the middle of us. We have heavy losses. With it our company leader is also hit, I move into his position and await the Englishmen with pistol and hand grenades in my hands. It doesn't take long; the first of them comes through the end of the connection route. I shout: 'Halt, hands up!' and open fire on them, the first yields back. Now a sharp hand grenade fight starts, then the Englishmen attempt to hold us down with machine gun fire, in vain. The attack is finished. The pilot comes down to us again and works on us with machine gun and the storm roars continuously. We took him under fire and strike down the Englishmen that were attacking over and over again with hand grenades. We are in the fight for two hours, the gaps in our ranks become ever larger, hand grenades flew back and forth. I sent the wounded away, as far as they are still able to walk, they will see about reinforcements and ammunition. The hand grenades are running out quickly. I order that no more than one hand grenade is to be thrown, we must ration them. I take my tunic off, while two men observe, all others have gone into cover. Slowly and carefully I now throw one hand grenade after the other, anyplace over there where an enemy shows himself. The men in the cover work on the pilots. So one hour after the other passes in the hope that at any moment help must arrive. The hand grenades are almost exhausted, I have everyone search for what still could be found. Ten of them come back together. However, now the matter could become dangerous for us. I tell everyone: 'Whoever is wounded and could drag himself away, should set off.' Two first-aid men remained with the severely wounded. So I still stand alone behind the quickly piled up barricade with both observers slightly behind me by the next dugout. The hand grenades run out, five more, four more, I turn each one three times in my hand, before I throw them off. The first-aid men have placed their flag in front of the dugout; in the dugout are still only severely wounded men. I put my tunic on again and throw the third to last hand grenade at the enemy; then I go unobserved to the dugout, greet my severely wounded soldiers again and slowly go backward with my Schulze and the two observers. *Vizefeldwebel* Collet, 4/66 [31]

Further advance attempts by the enemy failed at the *Strassburger Steige* as a result of the courageous opposition of the 2nd and 12/66 under the command of *Leutnant* Lorleberg and the Machine Gun Company under *Leutnant* Caesar and *Vizefeldwebel* Kienader. At approximately 5 p.m. the British attempted a further advance in C2. The enemy attacked the first and second trench on the flank, while simultaneously a detachment attacked frontally following the signals of a pilot. The detachment attacking frontally became shot down immediately by the infantry in the first trench and the guns of the 1st Machine Gun Company under *Unteroffizier* Jütte located in the second trench. In the meantime, the leader of the left wing platoon in the first trench, *Leutnant* Krause, was killed. His replacement, *Vizefeldwebel* Voigt, was then severely wounded. As a result of the heavy losses, the enemy succeeded in pressing back the left platoon of the company in the first trench. However, the enemy did not advance any further. *Leutnant* Seyffert, with his platoon, took over command at a hastily erected barricade and stopped them.

In the second trench, *Vizefeldwebel* Fickenday, along with a few men, held the enemy at the junction of *Verbindungsgraben* 7 (V7) in a hand grenade fight. Therefore, the enemy attempts to penetrate into V7 from the first trench were in vain as a result of the actions of the company leader and six men. After a short hand grenade battle the enemy gave up all further attacks, and a barricade was formed at the junction of V7 where it joined first trench. Reinforcements arriving from the 8/66 under *Leutnant* Eifrig unsuccessfully attempted to take the opposite enemy barricade at 10 p.m. on the same evening. IR 66 had brought the attack waves coming from the south to a halt, and consequently had postponed the loss of St. Pierre-Divion and with it the southern Ancre shore for about 6 weeks.

Over the course of the afternoon, the 3rd and 4/R119 in the *Sanitäts Mulde* by Miraumont, and the 1st and 2/R119, moved into the *Miraumont Riegel* and at the steep slope by *Klein Miraumont*. The III/R119 moved to Achiet-le-Petit and from the heights that it moved across in the brightness of midday, could see the plateau of Thiepval covered with smokes from impacting projectiles. Pilots dropped bombs and pyrotechnics by Achiet le-Grand and the village edge was then shelled by British heavy artillery.

The battalion had barely moved into billets in Achiet-le-Petit on the evening of 28 September when it received orders to move to Grandcourt and into the position of the I/R119. In Irles the companies took hand grenades, and flare cartridges and hurried through the badly damaged village of Miraumont at the run, which was also being held under fire by the enemy artillery.

Upon arriving at their destination, the companies waited for new orders in their makeshift holes. The sun had shone the entire day. Now a fine rain started that transformed the badly torn up and pulverized ground into slippery mud. Man after man started to feel chilled and everyone tried fight back the cold feeling that crawled up their bodies from their feet. No one knew what was happening at the front.

Dispersed into platoons, the III Battalion of Reserve Regiment 119 marched to the front, behind the crest of a hill, in the cleft of a valley, behind a wooded village edge looking for cover. Like balled lumps, British tethered observation balloons stand by Albert in the red evening. British shells strike at the village edge. Pilots drop bombs on German columns on the neighboring street. The last village was reached. The darkness should guide us into the battle terrain.

10.00 p.m. The companies marched on. Columns rattle past at the trot, to the front, from the front. Hand grenades and light cartridges were grabbed at the *pionier* park. A German battery fired in the vicinity. The Englishmen answer angrily. The horizon was lit up with flashes everywhere. Pillars of fire climbed up out of Miraumont from the bursting shells. Through! Walk, at the double, walk, debris, nothing but debris on the left and right of the road! We lived here a long time ago, in this, in that home, now burnt, destroyed, collapsed! It smells like fire, like mustiness. No one lives here anymore.

Two companies assemble at the exit to Grandcourt, looking for protection against shrapnel on the hillside. The night is cold and the rain falls on the road. The Other Ranks attempt to sleep on their knapsacks. The ammunition wagon brings infantry ammunition. A Construction Company hurries past. A report of shells hitting the road. Running, screams, whimpers. A couple of wounded limp by here. Salvo after salvo hits into the village. The company leader sits freezing on the cartridge boxes. The sound of fighting subsided, swells to a terrible crescendo and subsides again.

Midnight goes past. The adjutant brings orders! *Feste Schwaben* is lost and should be stormed in the morning dawn. The III Battalion was moved forward to Grandcourt. "Make ready assault packs!" The Other Ranks got up out of their half slumber and made ready. Cartridges become distributed, the knapsacks put together. A few men remain behind as guards, until they are collected.

We arrive at Grandcourt without losses. There we find out that even the I Battalion is about to become inserted. Also here shrapnel and shells! And debris! An orderly arrives. Only the 9th Company is required for the storm. The other companies nest in holes in the embankment by the roadside. The rain becomes heavier. Ponds become established on the filthy street. The side of the road becomes like a swamp. Vehicles with food and ammunition, field kitchens, Medical ambulances rattle past. Slightly wounded men stream back. *Leutnant der Landwehr* Matthias Gerster, RIR 119 [32]

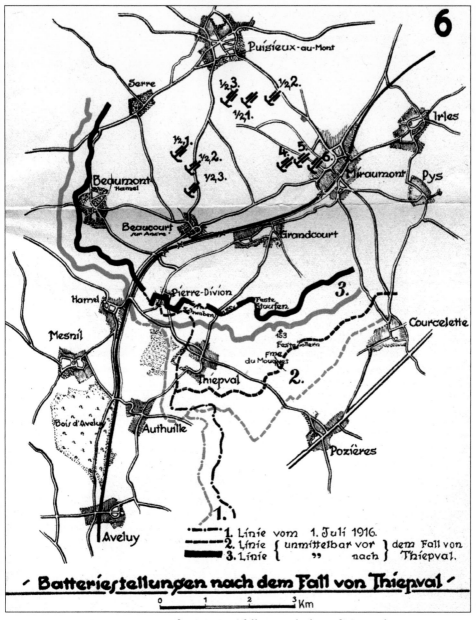

Battery positions for RFAR 26 following the loss of Thiepval.

The British had thrown all of their strength at *Feste Schwaben*; they circumvented the strongpoint, then attacked it from the north and forced the defenders into the northwestern corner, where they were then attacked from three sides. At same time the enemy had also attacked south of the village of St. Pierre-Divion, taken the first and second trenches and had pushed forward until they were into the *Strassburger Steige*.

This would not be the end of the fighting as the 26th Reserve Division issued new

Direct hit on a 7.7cm field gun from the 6/RFAR 26, September
1916. (*Die 26. Reserve Division 1914-1918*)

orders: '*Feste Schwaben* is to be cleared of the enemy. C3 and C4 are to be taken again.'
In order to accomplish these tasks, the division commander placed the II/180, I and III/
R119 at the disposal of IR 66. This difficult task would become even harder when the last
batteries still standing on the southern Ancre bank belonging to the 26th Reserve Division
had to be taken back to new positions. The batteries would be moved into prepared battery
positions on the northern bank in the area of Miraumont-Puisieux on the same day the
new attack orders were issued, according to orders sent out by Artillery Commander
Maur. While the movement of the guns was expected to take place smoothly, there was no
guarantee that all of the guns would be in place in time for the attack and the loss of even a
small portion of the artillery support could be disastrous.

Finally, the small remnants of the I and III/180 were extracted from the front in the
night from 28 to 29 September. On 29 September the battalions were marched in the
direction of Noreuil, where the regiment would be assembled. At 8 a.m. on 29 September
the regimental staff was relieved by the regimental staff of RIR 119. *Oberst Frhr* von
Ziegesar, the commander of RIR 119, took over the sector. *Oberleutnant* Guth, IR 180,
acting Regimental adjutant in the place of the regimental adjutant *Oberleutnant* Liebfried
who had been was sent home sick, remained in the regimental command post until the
following day for the orientation of RIR 119. The terrain was covered in thick fog and only
a few shrapnel shells were fired on the Grandcourt-Miraumont road making the exchange
far easier than expected.

The I and III /180 made their way along the road in small groups, *Major* Scupin with the officers of his staff attached to one group.

We followed a footpath in the Ancre valley on the side of the road and soon reached the catwalks, which our pioneers had built over the numerous water arms of the Ancre stream, to the railway embankment where we continued the march to Miraumont and continued beyond to the unloading place. Throughout the fog one could see the destructive work of the English shells upon Miraumont. The church steeple was shot off, there was a giant gap in the church roof, no house remained spared; one saw only ruins and wreckage. From the unloading place the road then rises via Achiet le Petit to Bihucourt, and from out of there to Noreuil, our first quarters and rendezvous for all parts of the regiment being withdrawn.[33]

Despite the heavy losses and difficult conditions the division had issued orders for a large set counterattack that was supposed to bring *Feste Schwaben* and the adjacent trenches into the possession of the Germans again, in order to prevent any follow-up thrust by the British into the *Artillerie Mulde* by all means.

In order to prevent any further advance by the enemy to the north, the 5/R91 was assigned to reinforce the companies fighting in *Feste Schwaben*. The 26th Reserve Division ordered IR 66 in St. Pierre-Divion to take over *Feste Schwaben* in the night from 28 to 29 September and placed two companies from the II and the entire III/R119 in its possession. While the I/R119 moved to the western exit of Grandcourt, the III/R119 pushed toward the eastern exit of this village.

Further Brigade orders that followed continued to press for the recapture of the lost terrain and assigned the II/180 and I/R119 to assist in the attack. At 3.50 a.m. on 29 September the following regimental order reached *Oberst* von Ziegesar: 'Hauptmann Niemeyer with the 8/180 would reinforce the *Strassburger Steige*. The overall *Feste Schwaben* would be taken back by the 5/180 and 7/180, also the 9/R119 with two machine guns that arrived in the *Hansa Stellung* at 5 a.m. Commencement of the attack will be 6 a.m. from the *Meisengasse*, respectively the *Schwaben Riegel*.'

In preparation for the counterattacks Thiepval Wood was targeted with effective fire the entire night by the heavy artillery. Furthermore, all entrances out of C3 and C4, Thiepval and the *Zollern Graben* that led toward *Feste Schwaben* would be closed off the entire night through artillery fire. The commander of IR 66 gave orders that the counterattack would begin at 6 a.m. on 29 September. It would be conducted in three groups under the leadership of *Hauptmann* Niemeyer, commander of the I/66 from the northwest, from the north by IR 180 and from the east by RIR 119.

All of the advance roads and nearby villages lay under enemy shell and shrapnel fire making it difficult to bring all of the troops into position; two direct hits in the 11/R119 placed an entire platoon out of action. The 1st, 2nd and 9/R119 with two platoons from the 3rd Machine Gun Company were more fortunate and managed to reach the *Hansa Stellung*, where the attack should begin at 6 a.m., with minimal losses; however, the trench the men found was completely leveled. The troops were forced to jump from shell crater to shell crater, while loaded down with hand grenades, ammunition and machine guns.

Despite these difficulties the attack was executed as ordered. The fighting was tough from the very start as the British afforded stubborn opposition and only retreated step by step. The three companies under *Hauptmann* Stapf, the 7/180, 5/180 and 9/R119, attacked from the north, while the two other Groups attacked from the northwest and southeast.

Even though the three groups started their attacks on time, disruptions and interruptions of every type prevented the scheduled attack from being developed in a coordinated manner. The 7/180 advanced at the head of the column and ran into an enemy nest in the *Schwaben Riegel* that slowed them down briefly until the threat was eliminated. The 9/R119 reached their goal by 10 a.m. aided by the dense fog but also suffering heavy losses from artillery fire despite the protection from the mist. Enemy artillery fire fell uninterrupted on the hill and its eastern slope, one heavy shell alone buried the bombing party at the head of the detachment and destroyed all of the close combat methods they carried.

It almost seemed too late to continue with the attack in the growing daylight. None of the different groups knew what was happening in the churned up terrain and at first the different companies were content to simply explore the nearby enemy trench and their own position. They dug in and eventually established a connection with the neighboring troops. About 10 a.m. two platoons from the 1/R119 were sent forward to reinforce the 5/180, while the third platoon was assigned to bring up supplies. The 10/R119 moved into its place in the *Hansa Stellung* with two platoons of machine guns that had still been positioned at the eastern exit of Grandcourt. Once the companies had been reinforced, the assault groups pressed forward into *Feste Schwaben*.

By midday, the assault groups had succeeded in recapturing parts of *Feste Schwaben* Hauptmann Stapf, the leader of the middle column particularly distinguished himself here, with the 5th and 7/180 as well as the 9/R119. The fighting about *Feste Schwaben* continued up until the evening with fluctuating success and further losses on both sides. The parts of IR 66 that were involved in the fighting had suffered very heavy losses. During this time, the command over *Sector Staufen* was assumed by *Oberst Frhr.* von Ziegesar, commanding RIR 119, from *Oberst* Vischer, the commander of IR 180. About midday IR 66 occupied the northern part of *Feste Schwaben and* the western part of the *Schwaben Riegel*.

There was good news for several units amidst the constant fighting. On the basis of a brigade order, all men who belonged to the I/R77 and I/180 would be extracted out of the position in the night of 29/30 September. The I/66 under *Hauptmann* Niemeyer also was relieved by the II/180.

The 10th Company was inserted. A misty rainy day begins. How is it in the front? Nobody knows. Wounded tell horror stories. The fire rages further continuously. Heavy British shells hit into the marshy floor of the valley. The day passes, the night passes. The new day brings new fighting. The British have penetrated into part of *Feste Staufen*.

> The bombing party of the 12th Company becomes sent for support and to throw out the adversaries again. However the garrison of the *Feste* has already thrown him back. The defenders of Thiepval become replaced and come back, dirty, tattered, wan, gaunt, drooping, the steel helmet pushed on the neck. The terrible fighting has cut its Runes in these faces with a brazen stylus, out of which rage and anger flashed. Silently, we watch the fighters of Thiepval pass by. *Swabian* heroes! *Leutnant der Landwehr* Matthias Gerster, RIR 119 [34]

In Sector Ziegesar the enemy undertook three large attacks at 1 p.m. after a short period of drum fire and bombardments with heavy mines. All three attempts were repulsed

Karl Schnek, KIA by shell splinter between 5.15 and 5.30 pm. (Author's collection)

by the IV/R99 under *Hauptmann* Leiling who was the commander of *Feste Staufen* at this time. A spirited counterattack by the 6/R119 following the British attempts even brought the previously lost *Auto Graben* back into German hands again.

The fighting by *Feste Staufen* continued up to the evening. For support, the brigade commander was required to move up further companies from RIR 119 to *Feste Staufen*, so that there were now six companies from RIR 119 in *Feste Staufen* and the remaining six companies from the regiment in and near *Feste Schwaben*. The exhausted men of IR 66 were very thankful when the reinforcements from RIR 119 arrived.

In the evening the third platoon of the 1/R119 moved into *Feste Schwaben*, so that the entire 1st and 9/R119 had been put in with the 5/180. When *Hauptmann* Stapf was fatally wounded in the evening, *Oberleutnant der Reserve* Zettler took over command of the redoubt. The troops spent the cold night without any protection in the destroyed trenches and in shell holes.

In the night to 30 September the entire garrison at *Feste Schwaben* was relieved by the I/170 and III/170 in accordance with orders from Group Stein. During the relief, the 1/170, which marched through the *Artillerie Mulde* and *Lach Weg*, ran into British opposition at the intersection of the *Lach Weg* with the *Schwaben Riegel*. In the meantime, the 9/R119 and 5/R91, which had not received the regimental order, were pressed back until they were in the *Schwaben Riegel*. The 1/170, badly cut up from its brief fight with the enemy, assembled in the *Artillerie Mulde* again while the II/66 remained in its position.

[O]n 29th September the order to march off to the south arrived. We all knew what that signified for us. Not at all far from us in the south, the battle already raged for weeks with unabated intensity. From the fire trench in a (mildly expressed) very restless position in nightly trench marches directly into the Hell of the Ancre valley, the I Battalion was content with this fate. It was only weak consolation, when one told us we were only coming into the second position, and tonight we went only a few kilometers to the south. We moved off by companies. tired and weary we came into the described sector towards morning, somewhat north of the Ancre valley, therefore directly by the battle border, where it was known to get a lot of artillery fire.

When I crawled out of my shelter about 10 a.m.; the Fall sun dazzled me [*Leutnant der Reserve* Grimm, leader of the 3/170] and presented me with a beautiful Fall morning with a splendid prospect in an unfamiliar and however so much mentioned area. Before us lay the ruins of the villages of Beaumont-Hamel and Beaucourt, on the left of the Ancre valley with the destroyed village Grandcourt and the steeply ascending heights of Thiepval, where everything was covered from the fumes and smoke of the bursting shells. Also this 'smoke-song' yonder there, that becomes our march-goal tonight and maybe our grave, I thought. If for a moment the area thinned out, one saw a snow white field, like an enchanted winter picture. The shells had thrown the chalk that was underneath the rocks up above and completely covered the brown earth. The day passed pleasantly, and towards evening we started at a goose step down the steep hillside into the valley of the Ancre brook, through the quite wide swamp terrain across to Grandcourt. In spite of the greatest difficulties our heroic food carriers, who had still previously been ordered, succeeded in bringing the field kitchens until to Puisieux and to give out the food still before the march off. I was quite aware that this meal would be the last warm meal for many of us. Further orders would be given out in Grandcourt.

At the exit situated facing the enemy of the former village was the regimental battle headquarters, where the regimental staff IR 170 had just relieved the staff of our division Regiment 66. The companies camped in the vicinity, while the company leaders became ordered into the battle headquarters to receive the orders. In the very spacious dugout it just swarmed with orderlies, telephonists, runners, etc. We received insights about the situation and our respective field-sectors with maps. The image that I as an old battle-soldier, who now was there already since the beginning of the war that in practice everything looks completely different than in theory. When already, it is theoretically clear, everything gray is gray, then outside in the trench, "practically taking" has first place.

The 3rd Coy received the sector *Strassburger Steige*, on the left a connection to the Feste Schwaben, to the right on the Württemberg IR 180. According to the map, my zone had a width of about 100 meters. An English attack had occurred there in the afternoon and had been refused. While we transcribed our orders, what had to be used later became distributed outside to the Other Ranks: hand grenades, K-Ammunition, seltzer water, preserved meat, everything iron that existed for the time of the approaching need. Naturally would the men hereby be more of more burdened and hindered in his mobility. However everyone knew that these things were as necessary, how possibly like bread. In the front it is nothing, however nothing other than death and corpses. With gas masks on the men must take these things; because the British had already started to gas the exit of the village the entire time.

Finally we were so far underneath and only had to set our watches. It was namely the historic night from 30 September to 1 October, where 'Summer time" was first introduced in the "winter time," that is normal time was changed. The night is when one in Germany at home agreeably attributed to that one sleeps one hour longer. Actually we should have set back the clocks at 1 o'clock at night to 12 o'clock, so was the rule. However for us it was really no matter, when we set the clocks back, for us this historic night did not bring one hour longer of sleep, probably however one hour longer of pain, altogether no sleep, for many however the eternal sleep.

Each company received a soldier from IR 66 as a guide. When I climbed up the stairs with my leader, I hear perchance, how a 66er soldier remarked saying: "Well, comrade, where must your company be taken?" "In the *Strassburger Steige*," was the reply. "There however the shroud still clings on, comrade; I hope that you come back safely again, because the *Strassburger Steige* is so close above the breeziest corner." Not without a mild scare had I listened to this low voiced amusement and for me I thought: It could become good there if the runners already talk like this among themselves.

However, there was no time now for such considerations; it must become acted. It was especially valid, to get away from the village exit held under continuous gassing. I therefore call to my men: "Everyone make ready!" discuss in all haste the most necessary with the platoon leaders; long explanations about the situation, position, etc. however were pointless. That must result in everyone being at his place and position. The guide informed us that we would come out of that gas waves once we reached the western exit of the village. Therefore then under coughing and gasping as soon as possible to get out of the gas so that one with very handicapped respiration through the heavy packs could at least grab fresh air again. We also happily reached the road out of the village that led to Thiepval. We had to travel on the road about 20 minutes. The guide now made me aware of it that the march upon the road would probably proceed without hardly any losses. Because the road lay under artillery fire, because the enemy probably knew through his pilots that here at night there had to be heavy traffic. The road however also looked it accordingly, so that soon each man saw why I in front with my guide at the head struck up a rather stalwart pace. However, one feels safer in the communication trench than on the open road.

A completely excruciating picture offered this so-called, or better to say, former highway. It had become completely dark, so had the shadows of the night made the dim pictures only more hideous to us. Many, many dead comrades in all possible positions, how the angel of death had reached them now, lay on and by the road. High poplars lay fallen, criss-crossed on the road, vehicles of all types remaining stuck or completely shot up, horse cadavers with bloated flesh and wide stretched out legs completed the picture of the fighting. What feelings probably had passed through the individual when he hurriedly strode past by these nocturnal spooky figures! We didn't have to hasten our steps to get away as fast as possible from this place of horror. And however there was no reason for us, to encourage the foot too greater speed. Because however we were already too very familiar with the frightfulness of modern warfare, to not say anything: when it was behind us here, therefore not at all in the actual battle-line, then how would it already look in the battle position at the front!

It almost seemed, as if the false claim of my guide was being punished that it would probably not go without losses. We had come up to the position without losses, where according to the supposition of the guide the communication trench from the hill opened up down in the road. The guide looked for this position in the dark and I allowed the company to stop, so as to not go past that approaching junction. Now the guide had found the position, I jumped along by the hillside, to convince myself from this elevated position that everyone would turn off into the trench – there a comes medium caliber shell and hits the ground on the road where a large part of the company still stands, because there is always stopping at such turn offs. The shell rushed away above my head that we now became as if the head became torn from the neck. And the consequences? 6 men dead and more than 10 wounded. The stretcher bearers take them immediately after they arrived, but we must still get away as quickly as possible from this dangerous corner, otherwise the losses will still become larger.

We ascend up the *Hansastellung* and according to my map through the *Serbengraben* to the *Strassburger Steige*, our goal. Soon it becomes clear then that my guide does not know this trench at all and states that he must lead us via *Feste Schwaben*. That this path was further and anyway is also full of more danger was immediately clear to me. It demonstrated that my presumption was right. Soon we were in real drum-fire, and no more trace of a trench. Jumping, always as long as the breath lasted, we ran through the fire, most coming out of the flank, from shell crater to shell crater. You allowed yourself to believe that thereby the company was often torn apart. In the meantime it had become 3.00 a.m., and according to my estimation we had to have been for a long time at the place and position. Many pieces of equipment lying around and more of more dead Englishmen show me that we had to be close to the battle line, maybe already very far over it. I declared to my guide, here under no further circumstances to go any further. I didn't want my entire company to walk into the hands of the Englishmen; because one didn't see any German soldier far and wide. My guide finally gave a small sound that he no longer knew and apparently led us on a wrong road. The guide was completely dependable to me, and given to be quite familiar with the terrain. I also made no reproach to the man; because in such murderous shell fire in the dark night across completely shot up trenches, to find one's way with certainty and stalwartly, because already hear now how this was also more strength than a man had.

Therefore, we crouched down into the shell craters as good as it could be and waited. There came part of the 2nd Company, which might probably be going as similar as we might be. That guide however knew information and showed us the path to the *Strassburger Steige*. It was already day now, when we arrived in our sector. [35]

The attack by *Feste Schwaben* proceeded on the morning of 30 September. The 1/R119 under *Leutnant der Reserve* Hahn cleared a section of trench 280 meters long in stubborn fighting and destroyed the enemy troops holding the trench; however, the Germans also suffered heavy losses. Shortly following the assault, enemy barrage fire began to fall over the entire position, which effectively ended any further advance.

Later, the 9/R119 pushed out from the *Lach Weg* into the *Auwärter Weg* and overpowered the enemy who was stubbornly defending that trench. However the assault groups from the two companies from RIR 119 ended up facing a British attack that was taking place at the same time as theirs. The enemy infantry pressed both companies back step by step. The ability of the men of the 1st and 9/R119 to resist the enemy advance was

Stapf

Hauptmann im Inf.=Regt. 180
gestorben am 1. Oktober 1916 an den
bei Thiepval erhaltenen Wunden

(Kriegstagebuch aus Schwaben)

severely curtailed when both groups ran out of hand grenades.

Finally the last two companies were put in, the 11th as reserve, the 12th in the *Staufenriegel*. Through a hollow they go past by the churchyard past, over shell plowed fields. Destroyed telegraph poles serve the battle orderlies who know the place as road signs. One becomes oriented during the glow of British light balls. The fire is silent. The light signals came closer. Where is our trench? The orderlies were uncertain. The company waits in shell craters, meanwhile the company leader looks for the *Staufenriegel* with them. Finally he has located it. Orders of the sector commander: The 12th Company shall relieve a different, weakened company. It went into that position in front over completely leveled trench parts, the *'Köhler Graben'*, an approximately 200 meter long communication trench that sticks out from the main position and of which approximately 50 meters was already in the possession of the enemy.

Here we meet part of the brave 7th Company that is glad to be united with their regiment again. At the barricade that closes off the trench against the British, stands the bombing party. The English barricade is in throwing distance. Hand grenades flew back and forth from time to time. Only one dugout is found in the trench. The largest part of the company is in the trench, lying in holes, defenseless. Suddenly the British artillery places its fire upon the trench. Have their movement inside been reported? The shells pound furiously. Man next to man pressed into the dugout, on the stairway, on the ground. Only the sentries stand. And sentries fell. Others took their place. One platoon found shelter in the *Staufen Riegel*. However the enemy doesn't attack and it

The grave of a friend, IR 170. (Author's collection)

becomes quieter again. *Leutnant der Landwehr* Matthias Gerster, RIR 119 [36]

At 10 a.m. the 10/R119 was moved forward as reinforcements for the hard pressed front line troops. However, this company also ended up engulfed in the severe enemy drum fire that was landing in preparation for a new British attack. The losses in the company quickly increased at an alarming rate with most of the leaders being killed or wounded. A strong British assault followed the bombardment shortly after 5 p.m. The 1/R119 was now being attacked simultaneously from the front and from the side; however the company was able to force the British troops, who had been able to make their way through the German defensive barrage fire, back with rifle and machine gun fire.

The day starts. In the dusk individual Groups of Englishmen attempted to advance out of an old German battery position. Rifle fire from out of the barricade drives them back. Soon following they waved with the Red Cross Flag. They want to save their wounded. The German is humane. Our fire is silent. Dead and objects of equipment still lay in the trench from the previous heavy, bloody day of fighting. The weapons become collected. The dead are buried in the night. The day passes under the usual artillery fire. And night and day exchange and death swings his scythe on the hills about Grandcourt. *Leutnant der Landwehr* Matthias Gerster, RIR 119 [37]

The 9/R119 had been able to procure a fresh supply of hand grenades and could then successfully defend their position against enemy frontal assaults. However, the British suddenly approached the 9/R119 from the flank where they had broken through the German defenses. The British also came from the rear, cutting off the rest of the men of the 9th Coy, many of whom had become hors de combat, and surrounded them. The machine guns of the 3rd Machine Gun Company that had been assigned to the 9/R119 were also placed out of action.

The few remaining men in the 9th Company still capable of offering any resistance stood by the side of the leader, *Leutnant der Reserve* Buck, and took part in the close combat. *Leutnant* Buck became wounded and then *Leutnant der Reserve* Osswald, as the last officer in the company still uninjured, was killed; while most of the Other Ranks were killed or captured. Only a few men along with a single machine gun they had managed to save succeeded in making their way back into the *Hansa Stellung*, where the 2/R119 was positioned. The fighting in *Feste Schwaben* went back and forth the entire evening. At 10 p.m. the northern part of the redoubt was in German hands, the British held the remainder.

The enemy had still not achieved their desired goal, the final capture of the German strongpoints of *Feste Schwaben* and *Feste Staufen*. An attack undertaken against both strongpoints at 5.30 p.m. had was repulsed by parts of RIR 119, during which the 1/R119 suffered heavy losses. When the attack was over a large part of *Feste Schwaben* was still in German hands.

There was also heavy fighting in Sector C3 on this day. A *Sturm Abteilung* had arrived from the XIV Reserve Corps to assist in the execution of a proposed attack. The men in the *Sturm Abteilung* were assigned to an assault column, which would be joined by one officer and 100 men from the II/66. The German batteries in support of the assault had been ordered to place blocking fire around the enemy target trenches to prevent any potential enemy reinforcements from interfering.

In order to hold the trenches that were expected to be captured during the attack, infantry companies with machine guns, each with 6,000 belted cartridges would follow. The assault column formed from the II/66 had the task to clear the second trench from C3 up to the junction of the *Münstergasse*. Simultaneously the 3/170 would advance into the *Münstergasse* from the *Strassburger Steige* and establish a connection with the II/66. An *Infanterie Geschützbatterie* would make the second trench from C3 to the *Münstergasse* ripe for the attack.

For the execution of this task a detachment of 50 men each were assembled from the 5/66 and 8/66 with the allotment of one machine gun under the command of *Leutnant* Kühne. The counterattacks would take place simultaneously at 6 a.m. However, problems occurred at the very onset of the attack. The artillery preparation fire that was expected to block off the enemy trenches did not take place. Despite the lack of preparation fire, the infantry attack started as planned. Soon after leaping over the first enemy barricade, *Leutnant* Kühne and a number of his men became severely wounded. *Vizefeldwebel* Schütte, 5/66, quickly took over command.

Without blocking artillery fire, the enemy was able to quickly move up reinforcements and a hand grenade battle developed at the barricade. Men began to fall, killed or wounded by the constant rain of British hand grenades dropping all about them. *Leutnant* Seyffert was one of the many officers killed while attempting to take the enemy barricade.

A patrol was sent out from the 5/66 to make contact with the 6/170, of which only a few men had actually advanced into the *Münstergasse*. Meanwhile, *Vizefeldwebel* Fickenday 7/66, attacked with two Groups. He captured the first barricade with the initial advance; then overran two further enemy barricades and finally erected a new barricade close in front of the junction of V7 with the second trench. Once the attacks had stopped, the men from IR 66 and IR 170 reinforced their individual barricades and prepared for the inevitable enemy counterattack.

For a time following the German attack, the British behaved quietly. Then, at 5 p.m the British began a counterattack against the new barricade after a brief but destructive period of mine fire, in order to retake the lost section of trench. *Leutnant* Peyer, who was in command at one barricade, held it against repeated enemy attacks. Hand grenades were freely used on both sides and losses began to increase with each passing moment, neither side making any progress.

While the fighting continued into the night, at 9.30 p.m. the II/66 was relieved by the II/170 and moved to rest quarters in Bois de Logeast, where the regimental Recruit Companies be replenished the large gaps in the ranks of the battalion. In the afternoon of the following day, the division commander visited the II/66 and spoke to the troops of his admiration of their deeds. In the parting order from the 26th Reserve Division it was said: 'I have followed the actions of the regiment with admiration and I am proud, to have such iron and heroic troops under my command.'

The fighting on the Somme at the end of September had been intense. The enemy attacks had all been supported by increasingly active aerial support. At times, up to 18 enemy airplanes could be seen overhead simultaneously. Despite the force being applied in the capture of the German defenses south of the Ancre, the Germans still held out and prevented any disastrous breakthrough.

The survivors of the I/R77 were finally replaced and withdrawn from the front. The heavy losses of the battalion were more than enough evidence of the bitter fighting of the last few days. The 1/R77 and battalion staff had marched out with 6 officers and 167 men. It returned with 4 officers and 62 men. The 2/R77 had marched out with 3 officers and 178 men. It returned with 53 men. The 3/R77 marched out with 3 officers and 158 men. It returned with 21 men. The 4/R77 marched out with 3 officers and 155 men. It returned with 26 men. The losses in the I/R77 amounted to 75% of the officers and 75% of the men who had been sent into the fighting. The regimental account left the impression that the I/RIR 77 had been sacrificed with the exception of a very small group. While some men were known to be dead or wounded there was no news about the fate of the many individuals who were simply listed as missing.

Among the officers reported missing were: 1/R77: *Leutnant der Landwehr* Onken, *Leutnant der Reserve* Oelze. 2/R77: *Hauptmann der Reserve* Borchers; *Leutnant der Reserve* Haessler; *Offizier Stellvertreter* Quart. 3/R77: *Leutnants der Reserve* Lohmann, Jacobs and Hoops. 4/R77: *Oberleutnant der Reserve* Sauerbrey; *Leutnant der Reserve* Schütt.

One of the problems facing the Germans defending the Thiepval-Grandcourt Sector was exhaustion. The troops had been involved in heavy fighting for weeks without being

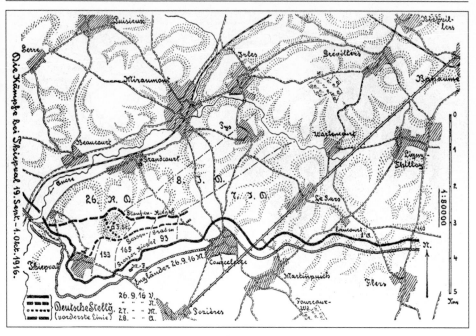

German positions south of the Ancre up to 28 September.

relieved. The weather had turned colder and rainy, increasing the number of troops reporting sick and making the lives of the men who remained at the front even more miserable. Most of the units that had been involved in the fighting had been scheduled for replacement and were barely maintaining effectiveness.

The recent enemy attack had succeeded in taking a portion of *Feste Schwaben* and, subsequently, the trenches on the right and on the left of it. The orders from the brigade commander for immediate counterattacks and the recapturing of these positions had not been completely successful. A particularly tenacious nest of British troops had become firmly established at the eastern edge of *Feste Schwaben*, in the *Lach Weg* on the Thiepval-Grandcourt road, where the *Grandcourt Mulde* approached.

This enemy nest had proven to be impossible to eliminate and it was decided that clearing this troublesome opposition should be left up to special assault troops. The division requested the new *Sturm Trupp* from Army Group Stein to retake the critical position, which was scheduled to take place in October.

The 5th and 7/180 were withdrawn to the *Grandcourt Riegel* after the fatal wounding of *Hauptmann* Stapf. The I and III/66 became replaced in the night from 30 September to 1 October through two battalions from IR 170 (52nd Infantry Division). In the meantime, the command over the sector west of Grandcourt was temporarily retained by the commander of IR 66, *Major* von Stöcklern *bei* Grünholzeck. General von Wundt, who had left the front lines on 7 September in order to rest, returned and relieved the staff of the 26th Reserve Infantry Brigade under *Oberst* Lessing, on 30 September. Wundt's battle headquarters was located south of Puisieux.

The officers and men of IR 66 were proud of what they had achieved in the fighting between St. Pierre-Division and Thiepval. However, the cost paid for such results had been

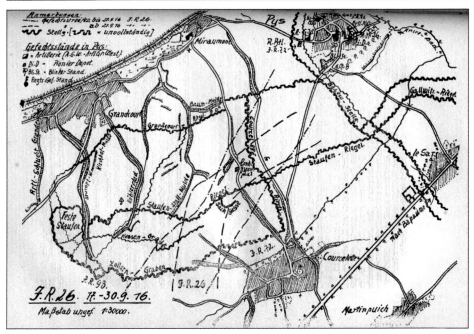

German positions on the left flank of the 26th Reserve Division, 30 September 1916.

heavy for the Magdeburgers. By the time the regiment was relieved it had lost a total of 35 officers and 1,716 men. The battle strength of the I Battalion now amounted to 349 men, the II Battalion 666 men, the III Battalion 335 men. All officers from the Recruit Depot had to be transferred to the regiment in order to fill up the Company leader positions with officers again.

During all of the enemy attacks taking place south of the Ancre, the troops of the 51st Reserve Infantry Brigade located on the northern side of the Ancre had not been ignored. Instead of facing any direct attacks, the enemy continuously bombarded the trenches being held by RIR 55 and RIR 121. New mine explosions occurred, while the British continued sapping forward toward the German front lines, all of which were designed to keep the garrisons of RIR 121 and RIR 55 in a constant state of alarm. All of this enemy activity prevented the men from getting any rest as the men holding the front lines never knew if and when an enemy attack might take place against their positions.

While their comrades on the southern bank of the river were fighting with rifles, machine guns and hand grenades, the men on the northern shore fought with the pick and spade. Day after day the entire position became shot up by enemy artillery fire raids. Each night they must be repaired again and the badly damaged or destroyed wire obstacles replaced. The connections to the rear lay under fire day and night. Beaumont could no longer be safely reached anymore by wagon or motor vehicles. The field-railways were so badly damaged that they could barely be repaired anymore. The traffic to and from the positions had to take considerable detours via Puisieux. The wounded and sick must often wait for days before they could become transported to the rear.

After fighting on the Somme for the past two years, many men in the 26th Reserve Division urgently wished for relief and a change in the theater of war. This wish would eventually be fulfilled for the division, but not yet it seems. As October approached, rumors began to circulate that old friends of the 26th Reserve Division might be returning to the Somme, the men of the 28th Reserve Division that had been gone since the first days of July. It was more than three months since the two divisions had been in close proximity and a great deal had happened to the men from both divisions during this time.

Notes

1. Vischer, op. cit., p. 49.
2. *Priester Granatenwerfer* was also designated as the *Granatenwerfer* 16, a spigot mortar that had an effective range of 300 meters. It received the name *Priester* because it had been originally developed by a Hungarian priest.
3. Gerster, Matthäus, *Die Schwaben an der Ancre*, p. 144.
4. *Feldpost* letter, *Leutnant* Albert Reihling, RIR 119.
5. Korfes, *Hauptmann* a.D. Dr. Otto, *Das 3. Magdeburgische Infanterie-Regiment Nr. 66 im Weltkriege*, p. 211.
6. The designation 'Pope's Nose' was reportedly given to this part of the German lines by the men of the 36th (Ulster) Division, formed by Irish Protestants, as meaning something to hit hard. One other account indicated that it was a derogatory name, as it supposedly referenced the shape of the Pope's nose? Whether these or any other explanations are correct is not known to the author.
7. Gerster, op. cit. pp. 142-146.
8. Edmonds, Brigadier-General Sir James E., *History of the Great War. Military Operations France and Belgium 1916. Battle of the Somme*, London, 1932, p. 280. To the author it almost seems as if these men, in particular the platoon leaders, were simply thrown away.
9. Korfes, op. cit., p. 213.
10. Korfes, op. cit., pp. 213-214.
11. Korfes, op. cit., p. 214.
12. Korfes, op. cit., pp. 214-215.
13. On 23 October 1916 General Ludendorff issued orders that each army on the western front should contain a *Sturmbataillon*.
14. *Grünkreuz* (Green Cross) gas shells had three different fillings. First, Diphosgene, a lethal gas. Second, Diphosgene with 30-66% Chloropicrin, a lethal gas. Third, 60% Phosgene, 25-30% Diphosgene, 10-15% Diphenylchlorarsine, resulting in a combination of a sneezing agent and lethal gas.
15. Gerster, Matthäus, *Das Württembergische Reserve-Infanterie-Regiment Nr. 119 im Weltkrieg*, p. 59.
16. *Oberstleutnant* Bornemann, was made the Director of the Württemberg Officer's Association after the war, he died on 7 October 1935 after a long, severe illness that he had suffered from since the war.
17. Korfes, op. cit., p. 216.
18. *Oberst* Josenhanss was not in good health when he was transferred to the 54th Reserve Division in September 1916. He died soon after the end of the war on 31 July 1919.
19. *Oberst* von Wissmann, *Das Reserve Infanterie Regiment Nr. 55 im Weltkrieg*, pp. 124-125.
20. Korfes, op. cit., pp. 217-218.
21. Wohlenberg, *Oberleutnant d.R. a.D. Rektor Alfred, Das Reserve-Infanterie-Regiment Nr. 77 im Weltkriege 1914-18*, pp. 226-227.
22. Wohlenberg, op. cit., pp. 231-232.
23. Anon, *Kriegstagebuch aus Schwaben*, p. 1,485.
24. Vischer, op. cit., p. 53. According to later sources, *Major* Weeber had already been killed in the afternoon at the well in front of the church. At 9 p.m. the Battalion Under Staff fought under the command of the Battalion *Tambour* Belthle.

25. Vischer, op. cit., p. 53.

26. Vischer, op. cit., p. 54.

27. Wohlenberg, op. cit., pp. 230-231.

28. Wohlenberg, op. cit., p. 232.

29. Wohlenberg, op. cit., pp. 232-233.

30. Korfes, op. cit., pp. 221-222.

31. Korfes, op. cit., pp. 222-223.

32. Anon, *Kriegstagebuch aus Schwaben*, p. 1,485.

33. Vischer, op. cit., p. 54.

34. Anon, *Kriegstagebuch aus Schwaben*, p. 1,485.

35. Müller-Loebnitz, Oberstleutnant Wilhelm, *Die Badener im Weltkrieg*, pp. 221-224.

36. Anon, *Kriegstagebuch aus Schwaben*, p. 1,485.

37. IBID, p. 1,486.

3

In the Champagne with the 28th Reserve Division

Before looking at the events that were to take place in October on the Somme, we need to look back to the period of time just after the 28th Reserve Division was relieved from the Somme following the heavy losses the division had suffered in the first days of the battle.

Following the heavy fighting on 1st, 2nd and 3 July 1916 the 28th Reserve Division was almost destroyed as a fighting unit. Not every regiment in the division suffered the same heavy losses as RIR 109; 2,148 officers and men killed, wounded or missing of which 556 had been killed on 1 July alone. However, the total numbers of men killed, wounded and missing in all three regiments of the 28th Reserve Division made it imperative that it be withdrawn from the Somme and allowed to refit and receive reinforcements on a quieter sector of the front.

The available reserves of the German Army were strained at this time of the war with the start of the Somme Offensive taking place simultaneously with the continuation of the heavy fighting at Verdun that was still raging further south and major fighting on the Eastern Front. As a result of these events, it was not possible for troops withdrawn from a battle front to be allowed to rest for any great length of time. The newly relieved troops would have to replace other divisions in quiet sectors so that the fresh troops could be utilized at the front where they were needed most. As such, the 28th Reserve Division was designated to relieve the active 28th Infantry Division in the Champagne sector.

As each regiment was taken out of the front line, a replacement unit or a composite group took over their sectors. The regimental position of RIR 109 was formally taken over by the 16th Bavarian Infantry Regiment from the 10th Bavarian Division. The remnants of *Landwehr Brigade Ersatz Battalion* 55 then moved into the 2nd position in the line Contalmaison-Bazentin-Longueval. The front line was now considered stable with the insertion of fresh troops.

RIR 109, or what was left of the regiment, was then assembled in Le Transloy and transported into the area southeast of Havrincourt. While in Le Transloy, the construction company, Company Ganter was disbanded and the men moved back to their former infantry companies. The men from Company Ganter were newly equipped to act as combat infantry, not construction troops. For many, this was a shock as it had been months or years since they had to take part in the fighting on the front lines. Most had not fired a rifle for many months or ever thrown a hand grenade. Just how effective some of these men might be in a fight was questionable.

Due to the heavy losses among officers and senior non-commissioned officers in RIR 109, numerous replacements and promotions were required in order to keep the regiment functioning. While plans were under way to transport the regiment to the rear, it was hoped that there were still Other Ranks who had become separated from the regiment

215

The old look. Infantryman of IR 111. (Author's collection)

during the fighting and would still find their way back to their commands. The I/R109 made arrangements for a collection squad and positioned it on the road to Flers under the command of *Vizefeldwebel* Weickel. Weickel and his men would assemble any stragglers from the regiment and after a specified time, march the men back to RIR 109. Similar actions were also being taken in RIR 110 and RIR 111.

At 2 p.m. on 2 July the I/R109 marched to Ribécourt by Marcoing and received billets for the night. The 1st and 2nd Machine Gun Companies also followed there. After a few days of rest and following the return of stragglers who had become separated from the regiment, RIR 109 was to be transferred into the area southeast of Havrincourt on 4 July. The regiment reached its destination, following a night march. The regimental staff and the II/R109 with the First Line Transport took quarters in Trescault, the III/R109 in Villers-Plouich. The Baggage Section of the Train and the First Line Transport of the III/R109 then rejoined the regiment and was quartered in Barastre. The I/R109 remained in Ribécourt.

The regiment that had defended La Boisselle, RIR 110, was relieved by IR 190 after three days of fighting. The remnants of the regiment, marched to Eaucourt-L'Abbaye through British barrage fire. Once in Eaucourt-L'Abbaye, the men were assembled and they received some of the first hot food they had seen in over a week. Once rested, the men of RIR 110 marched to Beaulencourt via Geuedecourt. The survivors of RIR 111 were thankful to be taken out of the battle on 3 and 4 July, especially after the intense fighting the regiment had experienced at Fricourt. There were many missing faces and the true level of the losses suffered by the regiments could be seen in the thin ranks when the full division was assembled for review, it was only a shadow of what it had been a week earlier.

The reports of the heavy losses suffered by the regiments of the 28th Reserve Division had not reached home in the days following the relief and the news, either by official notification or through the published *Verlustlisten* would take time to reach each individual family. Still, anyone who read the local newspaper knew full well that a major battle had started on the Somme and that the 28th Reserve Division would have been caught up in the fighting. Waiting for news of their husbands, fathers, brothers and nephews must have been agonizing for the families who did not know if their loved ones were dead or alive. Even when the notifications were sent out and the *Verlustlisten* published,[1] the men listed as *Vermisst* (missing) would have to wait even longer before their fate could be determined.

In the weeks and months following 1 July inquiries about the fate of individual soldiers were being received by each regiment in the hopes that additional news might be available. These often came in the form of private letters sent to the friends of a particular soldier or to the regimental staff. Other inquiries came from associations such as *Frauendienst*.[2] Some details about the fate of individual soldiers became known through correspondence or affidavits received from fellow prisoners of war where details concerning the disposition of their comrades was provided to the authorities. As the months passed more and more information became known of the missing men and the casualty returns were corrected accordingly. Still, for a small percentage of families, the details of what happened to their loved ones would never be fully determined until after the war had ended.

For some families, a reassuring letter from a son, father or brother who had survived the terrible fighting at the beginning of July allowed the family to be spared the worry about their fate.

Oberleutnant & Company Leader Boy, 2nd MGK RIR 111
In the Field, 18 July 1916
Dear Mother!
.... . Your lines speak of a certain concern for me, which it totally unfounded. We look here at our existence and are happy not to have been withdrawn to rest too far behind the front, because then we would be a 'rested' unit in a short time and still be returned to the biggest mess. We are already here now 3 days in a new position and have not had a single man killed ... . You are all sincerely greeted, Erwin [3]

Now, as the division was so understrength, immediate action had to be taken even before the regiments were removed from the Somme region. Replacements were urgently required to fill out the regiments, even if they could not be brought up to full strength immediately. These needs had already been anticipated, though not in the number that was required. As early as 1 July, any man who was rated *Kriegsverwendungsfähig* [Fit for active service] or as was the normal abbreviation, K.V. in the *Ersatz* Battalion was made ready to march and on 2 July was transported to Barastre, where more than 1,000 Replacement Other Ranks quickly became assembled. However, these were partially untrained men, and even when they were eventually placed in one of the regiments they were unfamiliar faces

The old look. Infantryman of RIR 109. (Author's collection)

to the veterans of these regiments, and it would be some time before these units could be considered a cohesive fighting force once more.

Initially, the situation faced by the new replacements was bearable. Despite the non-stop rumbling of the artillery in the distance, the men were not faced with becoming involved in direct combat with the enemy. Still, being behind the front was not the safest place to be as long range enemy artillery dropped shells at different locations and enemy aircraft strafed and bombed targets of opportunity they had identified.

The first task of the replacement troops was to march back and forth behind the front in order to imitate troop shifts and new reinforcements for the battle. Afterward, once the men had been marched around for some time, they were loaded aboard rail cars that were meant to imitate troop transports and they became shifted behind the front once again. The deception proved to work to one degree or another. Very soon, enemy aircraft spotted the columns and then the trains and the replacement troops came under regular air attack with machine guns and bombs.

Due to the frequent attacks by enemy pilots the mood of the men was not always good. For most, this was their first taste of being under fire and it made many of the new recruits very uncomfortable. Following an air attack, neither the marching columns nor trains would move very far from their current position for several hours until the threat of a new bombing attack from the air was considered past.

The men involved in the deceptive troop movements soon took on a confident fighting mood. Many began to have the desire to come to grips with the enemy instead being killed as a defenseless victim to 'stupid aircraft bombs'. For most it was a relief when 500 of the new replacements were allotted to RIR 109 and were officially assigned to the 28th Reserve Division in Honnecourt on 8 July. The decision of which men to send to the regiment had been decided by the officers in the Field Recruit Depot. Each soldier had been strictly inspected for a second time, and those chosen were provided with two sets of clothing and a second pair of boots when he was sent to the regiment.

Along with the soldier's normal equipment; rifle, ammunition, entrenching tool, etc. this unusually heavy load was made very noticeable in a most disagreeable manner while on the march. Many of the new replacements had had never sweated so much in their lives, as they did marching in the blistering July sun. Once the new replacements arrived in the regiment they did not have to worry about any ridicule from the veteran soldiers about their clean appearance, at least not on this occasion.

On 5 July the men of RIR 110 were marched from Beaulencourt to Banteux and Bantouzelle and provided with quarters in both villages; the regimental staff in the château by Banteux. The regimental commander, *Oberst* von Vietinghoff, was granted time off for a furlough home following the intense fighting. He would never return to the regiment as he was transferred to army headquarters upon completing his furlough. RIR 110 was slowly filled up again and in the period of time from 6 to 9 July, RIR 110 received new replacements consisting of 16 officers and 400 men from the Field Recruit Depot and an additional 180 men directly from Germany.

On 9 July, a Field Church service was held for the men of RIR 109 in the park of Trescault in a modest manner for the celebration of the birthday of His Royal Highness the Grand Duke of Baden. During the service the following order was read to the men of all three regiments of the division.

> Division order of the 28th Reserve Division from 9th July 1916:
> Tonight the last part of the division came back out of the battle that in total was in the fighting since 21st June. The enemy has won ground because of the use of excessive artillery and additionally enormous masses of infantry; however, his break through attempt failed by the stubborn bravery of our troops. Your performances, officers and soldiers of the 28th Reserve Division will become praised later in history. Today I speak to you of my thanks and my appreciation. Signed: Von Hahn. [4]

As well as the following order from the XIV Reserve Corps.

> Order of Army Group von Stein, Abt. IIa Nr. 20 154 from 9th July 1916.
> In a momentous time the 28th Reserve Division separates out of the ranks of my army after severe, but honorable fighting. Faithfully connected with the XIV Reserve Corps since the beginning of the war, the division fought gloriously with it in the Vosges, as well as in the battles and skirmishes in northern France.
> I remember here of the days of battle at the Donon, at La Boisselle, Fricourt and Mametz that will forever form a glorious page in the history of the 28th Reserve Division With its separation I speak to the division of my thanks and my full appreciation, in the firm conviction that the same will also faithfully perform

their full duty in their new association in battle and victory, up to an honorable peace. Signed: von Stein [5]

The survivors of RIR 109 were also reminded of what they had endured in these days of heavy fighting and how they had afforded 'superhuman effort'. By their persistence up to the last moment, up to death, up to being captured or up to the happy escape out of this Hell they also contributed to break the first momentum of the enemy's mass attack.

In the course of 10 July the battalions of RIR 111, whose ranks had been filled again with men from the Field Recruit Depot and by replacements from Germany, became embarked on troop transport trains in Marcoing. Following a journey of approximately 14 hours through Valenciennes – Maubege – Hirson – Vouziers the transports finally reached Savigny in the Aisne Valley on 11 July.

In the night from 11/12 July RIR 110 was transported to Cambrai-Annere and the regiment was unloaded in Brizy, Bandy Candreuve, and in Savigny. The battalions marched to their respective quarters by foot: the regimental staff, I Battalion and Machine Gun Coy in Falaise, II and III Battalions, 2nd Machine Gun Coy and Machine Gun Marksman Detachment in the artillery camp Brieres.

The regimental staff of RIR 111, I Battalion and the 1st Machine Gun Coy were accommodated in houses and barracks in Savigny. The II/R111 marched to Monthois, located approximately 3 kilometers south of Savigny and the III/R111 received accommodations in camps constructed not far from Monthois, named *Fliegerhang Nord* and *Jonas Lager*. The 2nd Machine Gun Coy and the Construction Company received billets in the Marvaux *Lager*. The division was now in the Champagne, in the sector of the 3rd Army under *Generalobersten* von Einem.

All three regiments had continued to receive a regular influx of replacements in the time they had left the Somme to the time they reached the Champagne. With the arrival of the latest group of replacements, the three battalions of RIR 111 could now report an average battle-strength of 1,000 rifles each. On 10 July RIR 109 was transported by train from Hermies. Shortly before leaving this village an additional 587 *Unteroffiziere* and Other Ranks arrived as replacements. The much larger regiment then travelled via Lille, Mons, Hirson to Pont Faverger northeast of Reims.

With the first requirement well under way, the replenishment of the regiments, it was time to reflect upon the lessons learned during the recent battle. One of the very first the regiments had learned was that in trench warfare the front width of a platoon at war strength had been stretched too far. As a result, the companies became divided into four instead of the normal three platoons each so that more men could hold the front line company sector and still have a substantial reserve located nearby.

The unusually high number of losses among the officers in the regiments also needed to be addressed as quickly as possible. Part of the needs of RIR 111 came from officers who were transferred from the active XIV Army Corps into the regiment. Fortunately, these officers knew the Champagne and all of its idiosyncrasies, which would prove particularly helpful to RIR 111 as the regiment took over a sector that was quite different than the one the men were familiar with.

When the men of RIR 111 discovered they were being transferred to the Champagne region, many had expected it to look similar to the hillsides of the Black forest. Most had expected to see numerous vineyards and rolling hills and forests as they would at

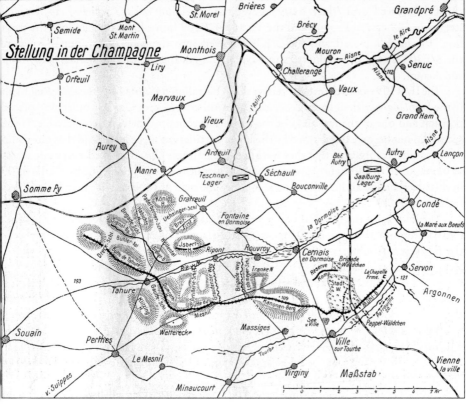

Overview of the Champagne Sector.

home. These views were nowhere to be found. The countryside facing the men gave off a monotonous impression; small valleys with streams and abrupt, steep slopes that were occasionally interrupted by small wooded parcels. The ground looked even gloomier because of the grey-white coloring from the infamous Champagne chalk that made up most of the terrain.

In the dry weather the dense dust produced by the chalk could reach depths of one foot or more and was extremely disagreeable when walking or marching through it. When it rained, the dust was transformed into an impervious glue like substance that stuck to uniforms and boots, clogged rifles and made it extremely difficult to move about the trenches. It had become so bad at times that paths and roads could only be used in the wet weather if they were covered with wooden slats or planks. Even the mud of the Somme was preferable to this morass.

There were very few villages or towns behind the front lines. Apart from Ripont, Rouvroy, Fontaine, Gratreuil and Ardeuil there were only small hamlets scattered about the countryside. Of these villages or hamlets, the houses that had been constructed using Champagne chalk had become ruined by the enemy shells and had simply melted away with time and weather.

On the evening of the arrival of RIR 109 on 11 July, the I and II/R109 went into position by Prosnes and Aubérive and in part were made subordinate to Division Fortmüller, from the XII Reserve Corps. The I/R109 relieved the I Battalion of the *Badische Leibgrenadier* Regiment 109 east of Prosnes and the 1st and 4/R109 immediately moved into the front line. The battalion staff and the 2/R109 moved into the support position *Bärenburg*, the 3/R109 was provided quarters in *Kipsdorf Lager*. The Sector commander was *Major* von Arnim.

The II/R109 would eventually relieve the II Battalion *Badische Leibgrenadier* Regiment in the *Sachiengrund* designated as Sector C1, at Aubérive. Sector C1 was a quiet, well placed position and one of the few areas of the front that contained pleasant countryside. If the sector did not become bombarded by the French artillery at night it was said that one could have completely forgotten that they were in the war. It was also considered a very safe sector to be stationed in. In slightly over four weeks of continuous position time by the II/R109 in this area, the battalion suffered losses of only one man missing and one man killed, both from the 7/R109.

The journey of the III/R109 to its new destination didn't go as smoothly as the other two battalions of the regiment. There were delays obtaining sufficient rail cars to transport the far larger battalion and its equipment the battalion now contained. Finally, after a second train had been located there was a delay of several hours until only one of the trains began to move. This was eventually followed by the second train some hours later and even then the trains moved at a snail's pace; many in the battalion felt they would never reach their destination at this rate. The delays were most likely caused by the unexpected arrival of reinforcements for the fighting on the Somme that had taken up most of the available rail lines. Once all of the delays were overcome, the battalion travelled quickly via Lille, Douai, St. Ghislain, Mons, Aulnoye and Hirson and at 3.30 a.m. on 12 July the journey ended in St. Morel at Vouziers.

After marching for 30 minutes the III/R109 reached Vieux. The battalion would now be attached to the *Badische Leibgrenadier* Regiment 109 as the IV Battalion of this regiment. It now belonged to the 28th Infantry Division in the XIV Army Corps where the *Leibgrenadier* Regiment formed the left wing of the 3rd Army.

Over the next days and weeks further replacements continued to arrive at the regiments of the 28th Reserve Division. As in RIR 111, some of the officers who assumed positions in RIR 109 and RIR 110 had been transferred from the active 28th Infantry Division. On 13 July *Hauptmann* von Wolff from *Jäger* Battalion 5 took over the leadership of the III/R109. On the same evening this battalion was reinforced through 8 officers, 3 *Offizier Stellvertreter* and 140 men that had just arrived from Germany as replacements. On 14 July *Leutnants* Hell and Riemann, formerly in the *Badische Leibgrenadier* Regiment 109 also joined the battalion.

On 12 July 18 officers and 400 men arrived at RIR 110 who had come directly from Mannheim, so that the regiment was now almost back to full strength. A few days later, 14 July, the men of RIR 110 were ordered to replace the troops of Infantry Regiment *Markgraf* Ludwig Nr. 111. The relief held in the night from 14 to 15 July was conducted without any French interference. On the right wing lay the *Pionierberg*, on the left the *Kanonenberg*. Both of these interrelated hills, approximately 200 meters apart, stretched south of the Dormoise valley. An advantageous defensive sector ran through the Dormoise valley, some 5 kilometers to the north, approximately in the line from the hills north of La Fontaine en Dormoise to Bouconville.

The sector that RIR 111 was to take over lay about one kilometer south of Ripont,

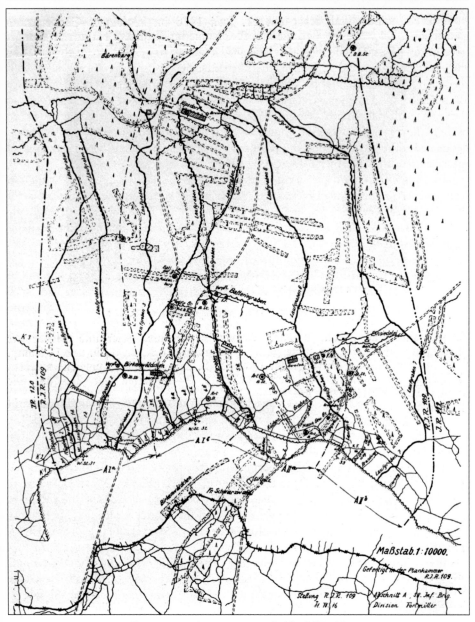

Prosnes trench system occupied by RIR 109.

where from 14 to 17 July the regiment relieved *Füsilier* Regiment 40. This sector was nestled in the deep notched Dormoise valley. The trenches located on both sides of the line were on the slopes rising up from the valley to the high road by the Champagne farm position. The distance between the opposing sides averaged between 100 up to 200 meters. However, in some locations the lines approached to within 20 meters, in a few instances even closer. The *Liebert Schlucht* ran directly through the battle sector, running in a north-south direction from the Dormoise. The III/R111 took over the trenches to the west of this ravine with a connection to IR 113 in the right sector, while on the left was the I/R110.

The machine gun companies that contained a total of ten guns were distributed along the front. The regimental staff moved to its battle headquarters in the Dormoise *Lager* on the road to Tahure. The rest battalion, the II/R111, came to Savigny as the army reserve. The billets for this battalion were in barracks that were on the Aisne River. Being so close to the water resulted in the men being exposed to clouds of annoying gnats during the day and by night the area was crawling with numerous rats that disturbed the men's rest. Even when designated as the 'rest' battalion, one company was brought forward to Vieux and assigned special entrenching duty by the division.

By 18 July the once depleted ranks of RIR 109 were almost completely filled. Fresh replacements and occasionally a seasoned officer helped to restore the regiment. One of the last replacement officers to arrive was *Hauptmann der Landwehr* Hanze, originally from *Jäger* Battalion Nr. 8. He arrived on the 18th and assumed command of the 12/R109. With the new replacements the III/R109 could be placed in the front lines once again. On 20 July the newly formed battalion moved into the *Kanonenberg Stellung*. The 9th and 10/R109 took over the front line of the *Kanonenberg Stellung*, Sector J3 and J4 south of Rouvroy. The 11th and 12/R019 occupied the support trench east of the sunken road. With the insertion of the III/R109 the III/*Badische Leibgrenadier* Regiment could finally be withdrawn.

By the end of the month of July, RIR 109 had received no fewer than 1,872 replacements. With the arrival of so many men, all companies could be brought up to the prescribed battle-strength once more. The new men, mostly untrained recruits sprinkled with a few of the surviving veterans, found the network of trenches assigned to them was in very bad shape. Much of it was destroyed and damaged as a result of the lively activity of close combat methods, of which the large French winged mines were especially feared. The dugouts the men found were not bombproof, as well as being far too few to house all of the men in the companies.

The difficult task of repairing and maintaining the position never finished during the stay of the 28th Reserve Division in the Champagne. Everywhere the men looked there were shortcomings and major changes that needed to be completed. Considering the efforts the division had made in creating their trenches on the Somme it must have been quite frustrating to the veterans in the regiments to see the sorry state of affairs left behind by an active Baden infantry division.

It was incomprehensible to everyone that the telephone wires they found were still affixed in the open, on the walls of the trenches. As such, they were extremely vulnerable to enemy fire as well as from the possibility of the soldiers damaging or cutting the wire by accident. Steps were taken immediately to bury the telephone cables in the ground as deep as possible.

At first, the companies inserted into the front line only remained a few days at a time, mainly because of the continuous bombardment of the trenches by French mines ate away at the nerves of the new men. Therefore, the companies were quickly relieved from the front lines and sent to the rear in reserve or to rest. The constant rotation helped the men to become familiar with the dangers of trench warfare in a measured manner.

Despite the exposure to French mines and the inexperience of many of the men the losses were moderately low. The III/R109 reported a total of 7 killed, 14 severely wounded

Getting ready to lay telephone wire, RIR 111. (Author's collection)

and 22 slightly wounded in the period from the 20th until the 31st of July. The battalion suffered far more losses as a result of illness than enemy fire. 60 men reported ill in the same time period, mostly complaining of intestinal illness, a direct result of drinking bad water.

Drinking water was apparently always a concern in the Champagne. The water used for the entire sector was supplied by two wells and a third source inside a dugout called *Tränke Nord*. It was also quickly realized that the water could only be used for drinking if it was first boiled. No one was immune from the problems associated with the drinking water, even *Hauptmann* Henze, 12/R109 reported sick after experiencing severe intestinal cramps. *Leutnant* Martin took over the leadership of the 12th Company in place of Henze.

When RIR 110 took over the *Pionierberg-Kanonenberg* position, it only had a depth of 200 meters from the front line to the rear positions. This forced the sector reserve to stay too far behind the front lines in order to be protected from enemy fire; otherwise the losses would be unacceptable in the exposed positions. The solution to this problem was in the completion of a tunnel that had already been started by the previous regiment. The tunnel, when finished, would allow the reserve to reach the front line safely and in the fastest possible time from the distant support areas. Progress on the tunnel was slow as the men worked their way through the hard rock.

The Dormoise valley was held under constant enemy fire the entire day. Only ruins

Trench armor worn in exposed positions. (*Das Reserve-Infanterie-Regiment Nr. 109 im Weltkrieg 1914 bis 1918*)

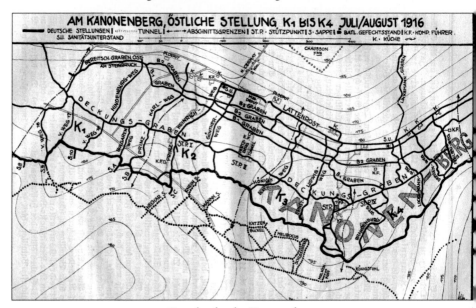

Trenches by the Kanonenberg.

Extension
of previous
map showing
trenches by the
Kanonenberg.

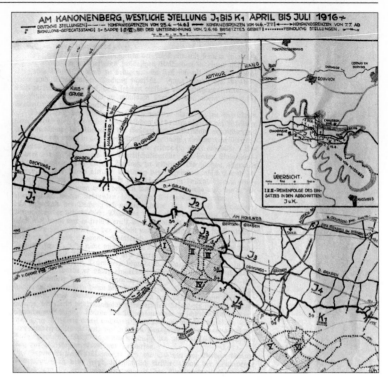

remained of the villages of Cernais en Dormoise and Rouvroy, likewise the hollow between the *Pionierberg* and *Kanonenberg*. As a result of this fire, traffic between both parts of the position was very difficult, likewise the traffic to and from the position. Most of the movement of men, supplies, food, etc. had to be made at night under the cover of darkness. Fortunately the light gage (60cm.) railway from Vouziers to Challerange and beyond could be utilized to transport Other Ranks and materials toward the front lines. Another light gage railway was also positioned along the road to Tahure which was also used for the quick transportation of men and equipment to and from the front line.

Once the trains had been unloaded there was still a short distance to travel that was often under enemy fire during the night. Teams of oxen and donkeys were used to haul the heavy loads up to the trenches where carrying parties could finish the journey. All of these activities placed a heavy strain on the men and animals as they worked around the clock to maintain the position.

The men in RIR 110 also found the newly assigned position to be far less developed than in comparison to their previous positions at La Boisselle and the *Lehmgrubenhöhe*. On the left wing of the sector there was only one battle trench in several areas. Shell proof dugouts did exist at the front but not in sufficient numbers to house the entire trench garrison.

The reserve position in the *Lohmeyer Schlucht* where the reserve companies were housed was completely exposed to enemy fire. Even the huts used by the men could be reached by light artillery, and only a single inadequate mined tunnel was available for protection in the event of a bombardment. The existing dugouts were very damp and so narrow that the

RIR 109 on the Kanonenberg. (*Das Reserve-Infanterie-Regiment Nr. 109 im Weltkrieg 1914 bis 1918*)

men's knapsacks could barely fit. The communication trenches were also very narrow and would have to be widened so that two men could pass one another at the same time.

The distance between the opposing trenches alternated between 80 meters on the right of this sector up to 350 meters on the left wing. The enemy trenches could not be seen from the German front line, so that concrete observation posts had to be created higher up, further in the rear, from where the French trenches were visible. At least the wire obstacles in front of the position were considered to be adequate.

After the stress of being under the constant threat of enemy mine warfare while on the Somme, the absence of this method of fighting was considered to be quite beneficial by the older Other Ranks who had survived mine warfare by La Boisselle. Many of them considered that the sector almost had the characteristics of a rest area, if it were not for the enormous requests for labor placed on the troops.

Once the new men had become accustomed to the sights and sounds of trench warfare, the rotation of the troops became the same as what had been used on the Somme. 20 days of position duty, then 10 days rest in Falaise. Each sector battalion had two companies in the front line, one in support. One company each from the battalion together with two thirds of the Construction Company formed the regimental reserve. The machine guns were all placed in accordance with the experiences learned in La Boisselle; in the 2nd and 3rd trenches and even further to the rear. The *pioniers* who were particularly necessary for the construction of the tunnels lay close by in dugouts named *Tränke Nord* and *Pionierberg*.

Usually, the position battalion worked on their trenches, especially in the construction of sufficient bombproof housing of the Other Ranks. The regimental reserve companies first of all improved their own dugouts in the rear and in the remaining time provided temporary workers along with the *pioniers* for tunnel construction.

Life in the front line trenches was also generally the same as the men had experienced on the Somme. The numerous replacement Other Ranks in the companies had to quickly become accustomed to the harsh reality of war and become trained in trench warfare. The first noticeable difference between the older veterans and new replacements could be seen when the men were entrenching. The results of entrenching by the new replacements could not match the performances of the old, experienced troops. It quickly became evident that many of the new replacements had never had to perform the heavy labor required to dig out large sections of a trench in the shortest possible time.

The older veterans simply went to work and kept up a steady pace that soon produced a reasonably deep trench while the newer replacements had difficulty trying to dig in the confinement of a narrow trench, had to rest far more often and their results were mediocre at best. Fortunately for the new men, digging in the soil of the Champagne was easier than it had been in the flinty chalk soil of the Somme.

The new replacement troops would soon have the opportunity to master the hard work required to create and maintain the trench system. Wide, deep trenches, splinter proof sentry posts and the necessary numbers of shell-proof dugouts were missing. In addition, the connecting communication trenches to the rear were non-existent in places. The new men had plenty of work ahead of them.

The men quickly realized that they were occupying what could be called a 'quiet position'. It was suspected that both the German and French troops occupying the trenches had been sent to the Champagne from active parts of the front in order to rest and refit. While it was considered a quiet sector there was still the daily brushes with the enemy in the form of rifle and machine gun fire, hand grenades, mine throwers and occasional artillery fire. The air was often filled with aircraft from both sides that would attack the opposing trench garrisons and cause losses now and then.

As on the Somme, losses occurred simply when the men were at the wrong place at the wrong time when a mine or artillery shell fell. One of the first men lost was regimental Adjutant, *Oberleutnant* Edinger-Hodapp, who was struck by a shell splinter in the thigh on 20 July while he was at the battle headquarters. On 21 July *Leutnant* Krämer, the leader of the 2/R111 became fatally wounded.

If there was one constant other than the tedious work of entrenching, it was gathering intelligence. The need for intelligence information had not changed at all from the days on the Somme. Orders soon came down to the division to send out patrols and raiding parties in order to positively identify the enemy units opposite each regiment. Patrols were sent out into no man's land on a nightly basis and a number of raids were planned and executed in order to take prisoners.

In the case of RIR 111 it appeared that the regiment was very unlucky when it came to taking prisoners. In each instance, the raids held by this regiment failed in their goal and at the same time the regiment suffered a number of losses during each attempt. During one raid held on 22 July, *Leutnant* Eckert, 11/R111, who was directly in front of the French wire entanglements was severely wounded by a close range rifle shot. Despite heavy French fire his men were able to rescue their wounded leader and carry him back to the German lines. His wound proved to be too severe and *Leutnant* Eckert died a short time later.

At the end of July the III/R109 was relieved from the front lines and sent back to the infantry camp at Brieres for a rest period. The next 10 days were used productively to continue the training the new replacement men desperately needed. Physical exercise

Trenches in the Champagne. (*Das Reserve-Infanterie-Regiment Nr. 109 im Weltkrieg 1914 bis 1918*)

was performed on a daily basis. The men were shown how to maintain their uniforms equipment and in particular their weapons. Special courses in the art of throwing hand grenades were held to allow them to become comfortable in the use of this close range weapon and to utilize them accurately. Hand grenades had taken on such an important role in trench warfare that the training was made as realistic as possible. For the first time in the war, men from RIR 109 were injured during the practice with live hand grenades. Squads were also provided with training on the technical aspects of the *Priesterwerfer*, *Minenwerfer*, machine guns, and other close range weapons.

At this time the I and II/R109 were still in position in the quiet sectors by Aubérive and Prosnes. Each battalion had the luxury of positioning two companies in the front line, one company in reserve and one company in rest. As such, the companies were relieved and exchanged places on a rotating basis every six days. The regimental staff had also received new quarters in the *Kipsdorf Lager*.

Unlike many of the sectors in the Champagne, the position in front of Prosnes had been well developed. There were deep trenches and dugouts and the entire sector was protected by strong wire obstacles. The distance between the opposing lines was slightly wider at this location as well, on average amounting to 400 to 600 meters.

While at the Prosnes sector the men of RIR 109 were kept busy on a daily basis in constructing new trenches, reinforcing the existing defenses and generally keeping the entire defensive system in good repair. This work did not go unnoticed by the French and at the beginning of August both the enemy infantry and artillery fire focused somewhat on the Badener during the night and early morning hours in order to disrupt the Germans

Well-kept graves of IR 111.
(Author's collection)

Granatwerfer training. (*Das
Reserve-Infanterie-Regiment Nr. 109
im Weltkrieg 1914 bis 1918*)

from entrenching at a location named the Pilz.

The two main areas of concern for the French were the *Schwarzwald Graben*, an access route to the Pilz, and the new trench being constructed in the Pilz. Both areas became particular targets for the French guns over and over again. In spite of the heavy artillery bombardments the work performed by the men of RIR 109 had paid off and the losses to the regiment by Prosnes were very small. The I/R109 only had one casualty when one man was slightly injured in the time period from 11 July to 13 August.

On 9 August, the second anniversary of the day, on which the regiment had first moved into the field, *Oberstleutnant* von Baumbach reminded the men in the regimental orders of their comrades who had found the heroes death in the Vosges and in Northern France. He particularly pointed out the many Badeners who had been killed as well as men from Hohenzollern, East Prussia, Thuringia, Uckermärk, Schleswig-Holstein, Braunschweig and Westphalia, who also had followed the flags of the regiment.

In the night of 10/11 August the I and II/R109 were relieved by Grenadier Regiment 8. The crews of the revolver cannons and *Granatwerfer* had to remain in their position until the evening of 12 August, until the squads being trained in Moronvillers and Bärenburg could replace them. The II/R109 was loaded onto trains on 12 August in Pont Faverger and transported via Rethel to St. Morel, where the men received billets in the infantry *Lager* Brieres. The regimental staff, the I Battalion and the 2nd Machine Gun Company followed there on the next day.

During this time the men of RIR 110 were positioned on and near the *Pionierberg*, where, in the eyes of the men from the regiment, the state of the defenses was inadequate. A great deal of work would be needed in order to improve the position to a point where the men of the regiment considered it to be satisfactory. One of the first tasks taken on was to provide safe and easy access to the front lines from the support areas.

Potable water was still also a great concern. Detachments from the Construction Company drilled a number of new wells inside the tunnels. They were also kept very busy making repairs to the regimental command post and constructed light signal stations on the *Pionierberg*. The latter was very important in the event the telephone connections were disrupted so that contact with the command positions in the rear could be maintained at all times.

As the battalions from each regiment were moved into different parts of the front line they quickly learned which sectors were the safest and which ones were the deadliest. When the I and II/R109 found out that they would be taking over the sector that formed left wing of the 3rd Army they suspected it would not be as comfortable as the sectors they had previously occupied. When the men of the I and II/R109 also learned how many more losses the III/R109 had suffered in the same sector than what they had at Prosnes and Aubérive, their fears were confirmed.

The I and II/R109 moved into their new sectors from 14 to 17 August; the men being equipped with assault packs, and, for the first time with steel helmets. The first day in the new position was very restless. The German artillery and *Minenwerfer* fired on the enemy trenches. The French replied in kind and trenches and dugout entrances had to be repaired over and over. The III/R109 had made good use of its time in the position and the improvements made by the battalion prevented many casualties. The I and II Battalions only had one man killed and one man severely wounded in the first days in the position, almost miraculous considering the weight of shells and mines that had fallen on their

Men from RIR 109 in Champagne barracks, August 1916. (Author's collection)

trenches. Shortly afterward an eerie silence fell over the sector. The men soon concluded that the French had moved fresh troops into the trenches opposite RIR 109 and it would be a few days before the enemy would become active once more.

Once the men of RIR 109 became familiar with their new sector they were able to take stock at what they had inherited. The battle fighting position moved along the hill, also on the side of the *Kanonenberg*. It consisted of the battle trench and the cover and support trenches. A number of communication trenches ran from the valley up on to the hill. The trench walls suffered badly from French mine bombardments; the earth filled wicker baskets used to support the trench walls had to be constantly replaced.

The gaps in the wire entanglements were very difficult to repair because of the close proximity to the French. One method to solve this problem came from the support companies, which created Spanish riders and wire hedgehogs during the day at the *pionier* depot in the Hertzberg tunnel. With these, the gaps in the wire entanglements created from shells and mines during the night could be quickly and safely filled in during the day.

Secure dugouts were lacking for the sentries. With hard work, well positioned galleries were created, like the *Prinz Heinrich Stollen, Pionier Stollen* and *Hertzberg Stollen*, all provided secure connections with the front line for the support companies. Each battalion provided 80 men for duty in the newly formed Construction Company that was commanded once again by *Leutnant* Ganter, who was quite familiar with the construction needs of the regiment and within a short time most of the deficiencies in the defenses had been corrected.

The *pionier* park in front of the western entrance position of the *Hertzberg Stollen* was a frequent target of enemy mines up to the heaviest calibers. In order to be prepared against surprise attacks, alarm sentry positions were placed higher up on the mountain that could hear the firing of enemy mines and gave warning to the men below using klaxon horns. They did the same when they observed enemy pilots overhead. Despite these precautions,

The new look: Trench sentry from RIR 109. (*Das Reserve-Infanterie-Regiment Nr. 109 im Weltkrieg 1914 bis 1918*)

many men, who were preoccupied in conversation or work, did not pay attention to the klaxon horn signal. These men paid a heavy price for their inattention.

Frequent fire raids were held, especially on the Dormoise valley that was almost constantly under fire. A connection between the *Pionierberg* and *Kanonenberg* could not be created to a depth necessary to protect the men crossing from one position to the other because of the swampy ground of the Dormoise valley. As such, most of the losses suffered by the regiment occurred in this area. On 2 September *Hauptmann* Steiner from RIR 110 fell victim to French fire while crossing this dangerous spot. He was so severely wounded by mine splinters that he would never rejoin the regiment.

Despite all of the hard work, most of the existing listening saps were not deep enough to provide any cover for the men on listening duty and had inadequate wire entanglements needed to protect the exposed positions. Still, saps extending from both sides of the wire were a common site. Often the saps were the closest points between the French and German trenches and it was not uncommon for the men occupying the saps to become involved in hand grenade battles with one another. One sap in particular, the *Anna Sap* in the right sector and the French sap lying opposite was often the scene of intense hand grenade fighting. As a result this sap became closed off with wire obstacles, and only the entrance of the sap head remained occupied by sentries.

Toward the end of August, all French patrols that attempted to approach the German position by the *Anna Sap* were expelled with hand grenades thrown from trench sentries. These prompt responses to the enemy activity apparently prevented any further attempts

Entrance to the Hertzberg Stollen. (*Das Reserve-Infanterie-Regiment Nr. 109 im Weltkrieg 1914 bis 1918*)

by the French to approach the German trenches in the weeks that followed. In the time following this period, the French did not even venture out of their trenches very often and the patrols from RIR 110 who went in search of prisoners in no man's land came back empty handed each night. Not even pieces of enemy equipment could be found lying about. Still, the need for prisoners was still considered urgent, so plans were prepared for a larger raid against the French lines.

One of these raids was carried out a few days later, in the night of 2/3 September, by IR 112, and RIR 109, on the left flank and the right flank of RIR 110 respectively. Since RIR 110 was directly in the middle of the two raids, it was decided that I/R110 would create a simulated raid using straw filled puppets dressed in German uniforms.

The III/R109 was the battalion assigned to hold the raid against the French lines on the night of 2/3 September. The III Battalion occupied the trenches in sectors K1 and K2 and the I/R109 occupied the trenches in sectors K3 and K4. The planners of the raid had coordinated the infantry attack with the artillery, *Minenwerfer* and *Granatwerfer* against the enemy sector designated *Blaupunkt* 35 and *Blaupunkt* 37, which lay in front of sectors K2 and K3. The raid was given the code name '*Kölnische Zeitung*'. In total, three separate patrols would be sent out in a coordinated attack. The patrols were commanded by *Leutnants* Albrecht and Lindenberg and *Vizefeldwebel* Hainmüller.

The Other Ranks who would form the raiding parties were selected with great care in order to ensure success of the undertaking. For several days before the raid the attack was rehearsed at an exact copy of the enemy trenches that had been reproduced behind the front. At the same time the infantry were being trained, the *Minenwerfer* and artillery fired on the specified targets, in part as registering their fire and in part to soften up the position.

Battle trench in Sector K3. (*Das Reserve-Infanterie-Regiment Nr. 109 im Weltkrieg 1914 bis 1918*)

Unfortunately, it appears that this increase of fire against the French trenches served simply to warn the enemy that something was going to happen in the near future. Following the artillery and *Minenwerfer* fire the opposing French infantry became increasingly restless. The French were quick to react to the heavy German fire and on the day before the raid, 2 September, the French placed extremely heavy mine fire on the entire sector of RIR 109.

Despite the French fire, the raid was going to take place as scheduled. Punctually, at 1 a.m., all of the batteries, *Minenwerfer* and *Granatwerfer* that were available to the regiment opened fire. Within moments the French artillery and mine throwers also opened fire, with a heavy bombardment of the German front line trenches. For the men of RIR 109 who were not directly involved in the raid the flashes and explosions of the French projectiles, the fiery tail of the hated winged mines, the different colored, almost numberless light balls offered an extremely terrifying but also beautiful spectacle.

The German trench garrison continued to suffer under the weight of French fire that fell on them without interruption. The German positions became considerably damaged in numerous locations under the massive shell impacts. No fewer than 19 *Granatwerfer* became placed out of action as a result of the concentrated French fire. This proved to be a problem as the fire effect that was expected from these weapons at the point where the enemy line was to be entered by the raiding parties was essentially ruined. As a result, overwhelming the French close combat weapons was not achieved.

The immediate French response to the German bombardment, the destruction of so many of the *Granatwerfer* had a combined effect on the planned raid and the undertaking did not have the success that had been expected. In fact, only two of the patrols succeeded in even exiting the German trenches, however, these men found it impossible to enter the French trenches because the wire entanglement were not damaged sufficiently and the French had strongly occupied their front line.

Once it had been realized that there was no hope of entering the enemy trench, the two raiding parties made their way back to the German lines and reported their failure. The only real success occurred by RIR 110. Apparently the regiment was quite successful in fooling the French in thinking that a raid was also being held on their part of the front line because the enemy employed massive artillery and mine fire against the puppets. Other than damaged uniforms, the men of RIR 110 did not suffer any losses.

The other regiments were not as fortunate. The losses from the raid for RIR 109 were: three Other Ranks from the raiding parties wounded. One man was injured from the crews of the *Granatwerfer* and five men wounded and one killed from the trench garrison. The *Granatwerfer* crews suffered very small losses despite losing so many of their weapons. This was probably due to the practice of operating the weapons using a long lanyard on order to fire them. This was done in order to prevent losses in the event the *Granatwerfer* shell exploded prematurely when being fire. As such, the crews were under cover for most of the time the French bombarded the German trenches.

The I/R111 held the next major raid in a bid to finally take an enemy prisoner using stealth and surprise. The target was two enemy sentries located in a nearby listening post. In the night from 6/7 September a raiding party under the command of *Hauptmann* Short was divided into two groups and placed on both sides of the *Liebert Schlucht*. At the appointed time, the two raiding parties worked forward along the hillsides of the ravine.

On the eastern side of the ravine was *Leutnant* Heberle, 2/R111, accompanied by one *Unteroffizier* and four men. They had crept up to the enemy sentry post in order to observe the French lines during the relief of the sentries. When the opportunity was right, Heberle crawled through the wire entanglements with two of his men and fell upon the Frenchman. However, the sentry had time to give the alarm by his screams for help, and in the subsequent close combat *Leutnant* Heberle was fatally wounded. Of the two men who had accompanied Heberle into the French trench only one, also wounded, succeeded in exiting out of the trench.

The *Unteroffizier* assigned to the patrol quickly hurried to help the wounded man however he also became shot almost immediately. The *Unteroffizier* was then helped back to the German trenches by the last man of the patrol who was still unwounded. On the western side of the ravine *Vizefeldwebel* Krämer's patrol came upon thick wire obstacles. While Krämer and his men made their way closer to the French listening post he could observe a strong enemy garrison in the trench lying behind it. As his men were hopelessly outnumbered Krämer gave up the idea of attacking the enemy sentries.

The I/R111 tried one more raid in the night from 24/25 September when four patrols of the battalion, in conjunction with raids that were simultaneous being held by IR 113 and RIR 109, attempted to penetrate into French saps east of the *Liebert Schlucht*. The target of the raid had been bombarded by the division artillery on the previous day along with numerous medium and heavy *Minenwerfer* shells.

Under cover of darkness, the raiding party slowly crawled through no man's land toward the French trenches, taking almost an hour to reach them. It was later suspected that an alert French sentry had observed the raiding party approaching his position because the patrol found the enemy battle trench strongly occupied. Within a few seconds of their discovery, the men became greeted with a barrage of hand grenades, which quickly resulted in losses.

The surprise raid instantly turned into fierce close combat, in which the French quickly employed artillery fire and rifle grenades. With such heavy fire, any penetration into the enemy trench was impossible. The raiding party withdrew in the face of such stiff opposition leaving behind five dead. Five wounded Other Ranks were able to be rescued by the support troops. Success still eluded the men of RIR 111 and this latest attempt failed to have any tangible success. Most often, the failure of each attempt was primarily due to the alertness of the French garrison.

Part of the problems faced by the men of the 28th Reserve Division in sending out patrols and attempting raids on the French lines was due to that much of the enemy trench system could not be observed from the German front lines due to the nature of the terrain. This lack of observation made it almost impossible for some portions of the line to even be considered for a raid and therefore narrowed down the potential sites that could be utilized. It is probable that the French were also aware of this shortcoming and were able to concentrate their defensive efforts in the areas most vulnerable to a surprise attack.

The need to be able to observe all of the French lines took on greater importance over time and led to the creation of a special observation service named 'Lux' was formed in each regiment of the division. In each sector a capable Unteroffizier was appointed as the Battalion Lux, for each company one was specified as the Company Lux. The battalions and companies maintained Lux books and reported to the Lux officer of the regiment, Leutnant der Reserve Berthold, who as director was responsible for the overall observation service. The Lux position at the Kanonenberg located by RIR 109 had the task to observe every change by the enemy exactly, determine the enemy sentry lineup and to find their machine guns.

All of the hard work performed on maintaining the defensive system and extending the position was making good progress in the last few months. Large numbers of new dugouts were completed or close to being finished. The work on the deep dugouts required a great deal of time and effort because the Champagne chalk took on a rock like character as the men went deeper into the ground, and all necessary mechanical aids were lacking. The manpower of the regiments was limited despite the influx of thousands of replacement troops.

The lack of manpower was still mainly due to the high numbers of men who reported sick in each regiment. They were all affected by the Champagne illness, an intestinal disorder everyone was probably infested with. According to popular belief, it was most likely brought on by water trapped in the lime. Illnesses among the men proved far more draining to the manpower issue than enemy fire. In August the III/R109 reported a loss of 6 men killed and 72 men out sick from intestinal illness. The large number of sick in the division was frustrating despite the precautions of only using boiled water for drinking by the men. The idea of adding Schnapps was thought to help counteract the pestilence. The only problem with this last theory was that anyone who did not have a fever was not considered to be sick! And therefore no Schnapps!

The overall health of the men was improved by planting large gardens in the rest camps where fresh vegetables could be grown. One company from the rest battalion was sent out to the rear on a daily basis to help bring in the local harvest. This was done in order to assist in providing a supplement the normal army diet with a supply of fresh food. This food was a welcome improvement to army rations and essentially sustained the good health condition of the troops. Because Marmalade was gradually beginning to play an important role in the nutrition of the troops, practical jokers among the men had apparently decided to create

The *Kanonenberg Stellung*. (*Das Reserve-Infanterie-Regiment Nr. 109 im Weltkrieg 1914 bis 1918*)

a mountainous pile of chalk on the *Kanonenberg* with the use of a large number of empty Marmalade cans in a pile, the so called Marmalade monument.

At least one officer in RIR 111 regretted having left behind so many delicacies on the Somme when the regiment was transferred to the Champagne:

> The speech of an English officer was in a letter written from my lovely landscaped garden in Bazentin, which was printed in a Cologne newspaper. Too bad we cannot eat even now certainly ripe tomatoes and cucumbers, not to mention the 2,000 radishes.[6]

The battle strength of the companies, already reduced by illness, was decreased even further when troops were reassigned to perform labor duties and any number of different details required for the numerous facilities behind the front, in part agricultural and in part industrial in nature. These requirements took numerous men to operate properly and the only source of men came from the battle strength of the army. The loss of so many men, most of whom were still barely trained, was agonizing for the troop leaders. In the time from 6 to 15 August the 10/R111 was removed from the regimental sector entirely; the company had become transported by motor lorries to the Saxon Division Fortmüller, further west by St. Maria à Pys, where they were assigned to construct dugouts there.

Something new was now added to the training schedule of the officers and men of the 28th Reserve Division, an assault school, a *Sturmschule*. At first, officers from the regiments were sent to Falaise where they attended lectures and field training in the XIV Army Corps *Sturmschule*. Once the officers had been introduced to the school, selected Other Ranks were sent to attend the course. Senior non-commissioned officers would also be expected to assist with Storm training once they returned to their respective regiments.

Close quarters: Mealtime in a dugout. (*Das Reserve-Infanterie-Regiment Nr. 109 im Weltkrieg 1914 bis 1918*)

The issue of replacements, both in the numbers that were required by the different regiments, but more importantly, in the quality of the men they were receiving indicated that the German army was already facing a shortage of trained men to replace the numerous casualties suffered each month. This was a problem that would only grow worse over time.

The three regiments of the 28th Reserve Division had received thousands of replacement troops in order to restore the division at full strength. The new men who had come from the Recruit Depots or training camps in Germany would all be eventually trained and experienced soldiers if they could only survive life in the trenches.

RIR 109 was still short of men, even with the influx of so many replacements in July and early August. This problem was eventually solved by the end of August when two drafts of new replacements arrived at the regiment. First 115 men, then 175 men; most were *Landsturmmann*, Train soldiers and drivers, who only possessed the very basics of infantry training. It was quickly discovered that many of these men had not ever fired live ammunition before. Before these men could even be considered for front line duty it was necessary to assemble them into a training company under the command of *Leutnant* Riemann.

In Champagne: Men from RIR 109, . (Author's collection)

Also, in order to free up trained troops for use in other divisions on the front where the need was the greatest, Other Ranks who had been designated suitable for garrison employment, Gv. or *Garnisonsverwendungsfähig*, were transferred to regiments such as RIR 111 in September. The corresponding number men who were fit for active duty, K.V. or *Kriegsverwendungsfähig*, had to be turned over to be delivered to other formations. Both the arrival of poorly trained men and the exchange of men fit for front line duty with those better suited to garrison duties had a material effect on the actual combat strength of the 28th Reserve Division. It was always expected that once the division had been rested and brought up to full strength it would become deployed on an active front once more. Just how would the division perform with so many men who were not fit to man the front lines in battle?

Still, not everything was hard work and danger for the men of the 28th Reserve Division while in the Champagne. With the arrival of so many new men in RIR 109 it was not long before the regimental band could be restored. Many of the original members had become casualties during the fighting on the Somme on 1 July, now, brought back to full strength, the band played music almost nightly in the *Brierlager* and helped the men to relax and forget about the war, even if only for a short while.

Even parts of the front line could be utilized by the men for relaxation on the *Kanonenberg*. Despite French mines, shells and other dangers, quiet, safe locations could be found there. In these locations the men were able to expose their weakened limbs to the August sun and add some color to their pasty white skin.

In the middle of September the regiments of the 28th Reserve Division received an important visitor from home, His Royal Highness *Grossherzog* Friedrich II von Baden. Friedrich II visited the rest battalions of each regiment and spoke to the assembled men of his acknowledgment and his thanks for its performance in the field until now. He also passed out a number of Baden awards to men who were being recognized for bravery in the field, something that always raised the morale of the troops. Friedrich II was well liked by the men of the division and he mingled with the troops in his normal genial and

Sunbathing in a protected position. (*Das Reserve-Infanterie-Regiment Nr. 109 im Weltkrieg 1914 bis 1918*)

attentive manner.

In the same time period as the royal visit, the War Ministry had decreed that each regiment was to be provided with an additional machine gun company. Now, there would be three machine gun companies, one attached to each battalion in the regiment. The lessons learned in the fighting on the Somme and at Verdun had clearly demonstrated the importance of these weapons and the need to expand their use. Perhaps the increase in fire power could offset the loss of so many trained men in the division as well.

On 11 September RIR 111 received its 3rd Machine Gun Company, which was to be designated as the 1st Machine Gun Company, with *Oberleutnant* Born as the commander. This company would become subordinate to the I/R111. The Machine Gun Company that had been with the regiment since the beginning of the war became designated as the 3rd Machine Gun Company and attached to the III/R111.

The three machine gun companies attached to RIR 109 were under the command of *Leutnants* Affolter, Degener and Sattler. *Hauptmann* Block became appointed as the Machine Gun Officer attached to the regimental staff. Block became responsible for the handling and needs of all three machine gun companies so that they could be used to the greatest advantage in the future.

In RIR110 a third Machine Gun Company was formed on 15 September out of the two already existing. The 1MG/R110 had 6 guns, the 2MG/R110 and 3MG/R110 would

Enjoying the warm sun. (*Das Reserve-Infanterie-Regiment Nr. 109 im Weltkrieg 1914 bis 1918*)

have four guns each. A fifth gun was later moved to the latter. The company leader of the 1MG/R110 was *Leutnant der Reserve* Lusch, for the 2MG/R110 *Leutnant der Reserve* Gerstner and for the 3MG/R110 *Leutnant der Reserve* Fleck.

By late September the question of which unit was opposite the division had still not been determined. No prisoners had been taken in any of the numerous raids and patrols sent out by the three regiments of the division. It was decided to try once more to finally capture a French soldier. The raid was to be carried out by the men of RIR 109 in the night from 24/25 September under the password '*Kuhstrich*'. It would be directed against *Blaupunkt* 49. *Leutnant* Albrecht from the 4/R109 was given command of the raid once again.

Preparations for the undertaking were to be completed in the time period from 18 until 24 September. The network of French trenches where the raiding party was to break-in at *Blaupunkt* 49 was re-created at Briere farm, where the Other Ranks of the raiding party rehearsed their attack each day. It was considered imperative that the men know their duties exactly and also to become as familiar with the enemy trench system as possible.

At 9.55 on the evening of 25 September the raiding party left the German trench from sector K4. The men followed an old, collapsing trench from which they could come up to within 12 meters of *Blaupunkt* 49 without being observed. At 11.55 p.m. an underground mine that had been placed near *Blaupunkt* 49 was detonated as planned. The explosion removed the wire obstacles up to the sandbag barricade and also part of the barricade, opening a route into the French trenches.

The patrol made its way through the gap and past the sandbag barricade only to advance upon a further wire obstacle located several meters behind the barricade. The raiding party also discovered the actual French trench was also closed off with sandbags behind which, was a sentry post. The obstacles were so strong that the raiders could not overcome them.

In this situation, the raid was in danger of failing like the previous ones. *Unteroffizier* Holler, 10/R109, who was at the head of the patrol, looked for a route outside the trench. He discovered a location where the wire obstacles were weaker and he was able to reach the enemy trench, he was quickly followed by the men of the patrol who split into two groups in order to explore the French front line trench.

Unteroffizier Holler's group could see how few Frenchmen had been left behind in the front line trench. Holler entered the French trench as ordered and found two empty dugouts there. Next he and his men advanced along the trench until they reached a location where four trenches intersected. Just as the raiding party reached the trench intersection A Frenchman came towards them, walking along one of the trenches. When Holler called out to the French soldier he instantly turned around and tried to flee back up the trench he had been walking through. Holler quickly used his bayonet and killed the Frenchman with a thrust. While Holler removed his bayonet from the dead enemy soldier lying on front of him he could see no other French soldiers in his vicinity.

The second part of the patrol, under *Unteroffizier* Geiger, 4/R019, was luckier in finding a captive and they quickly wanted to take their prisoner back across no man's land to the German lines. Their luck ran out, however, when their prisoner was shot in the back of the head by a French bullet while he was climbing over the sandbag barricade and was killed instantly. Geiger quickly removed the regimental number off of the tunic collar from the fallen man and left the body behind.

The third part of the patrol had received orders from *Leutnant* Albrecht, not to penetrate into the French trench, but instead to remove any obstacles and open the route for the withdrawal of the other two parties. When *Leutnant* Albrecht was informed that a prisoner had been taken by *Unteroffizier* Geiger's patrol and that the task of the raid had been fulfilled, he gave the command for the men to withdraw, at which point the patrols moved back. The three patrol groups had a total of four slightly injured men.

While the only prisoner had been killed, the undertaking was considered a success with the identification of French Regiment 124 being opposite RIR 109. This apparently was particularly important for General Headquarters for the determination of the distribution of the enemy strength. Ever since *Generalfeldmarschall* von Hindenburg had been appointed as Chief of the General Staff of the army on 29 August, requests constantly arrived at division headquarters for up to date battle information on enemy troop strength and the location of enemy units.

This need for accurate intelligence information apparently went hand in hand with a recent crackdown on the lax German practice of allowing the men to provide possibly damaging information in their letters home. Until 1916 there had been no one rule regarding what the men placed inside their letters or any concerted effort at censorship. By this point in the war it had become obvious that this failure to regulate the flow of information, from the published *Verlustlisten* down to the *Feldpost* that could provide valuable intelligence information to the enemy. New measures would soon be taken in regard to the *Verlustlisten* but for now, greater censorship was implemented when it came to the *Feldpost*.

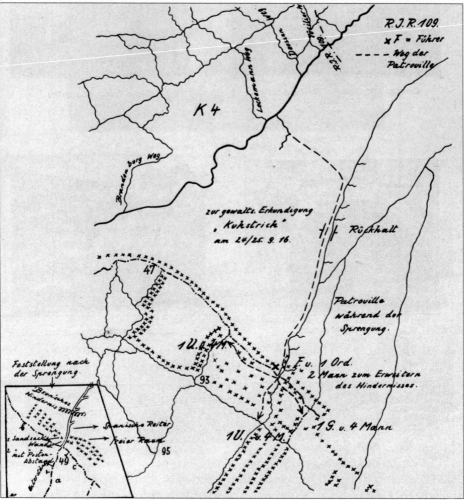

Patrol Undertaking, RIR 109.

In the field, August 23, 1916

My Dear Mother!

I have just received your dear long letter from 20. 8. And I want to thank you for the same. However, I wrote to you on 13 August. From time to time the entire mail of a division are retained to be examined whether the treat about military affairs. Probably my letter has fallen victim to such censorship and will still yet arrive, etc ... .. [7]

The time spent by the 28th Reserve Division in the Champagne was quickly coming to an end. Occurrences in the war always led to rumors that in some cases, more or less, were true. One such rumor that started in the middle of September said that the 28th Reserve Division was to be employed on the Somme again, where the French and English attacks had occurred almost continuously since July.

A number of events occurred in the following weeks that provided pieces of the puzzle

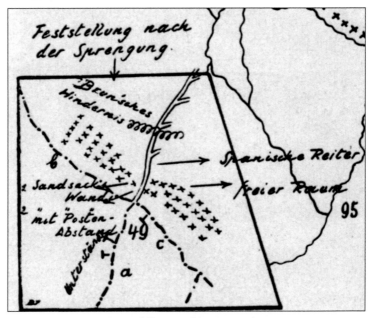

Situation following the mine explosion.

about the next deployment of the division. Towards the end of the month, 26 September the II/R110 that had been in rest, was moved into the sector of the 29th Infantry Division by Tahure and relieved the III/112 from the front line on 28 September. In the days from 30 September to 3 October the remaining battalions of RIR 110 were relieved by LIR 71 and made available for other uses. While in the Champagne RIR 110 had suffered losses amounting to 11 men killed, 2 officers, 49 men wounded. The battle strength of the regiment was now 61 officers and 2,500 men.

The extraction of RIR 111 from the Champagne position began in the night from 25/26 September with the I Battalion that was relieved by the III/R111. In the following night the I/R111 was then used to free up troops from the 29th Infantry Division; parts of IR 112 and IR 142, in the sector between Ripont mill and Tahure.

An undertaking that had been planned by the *Sturmschule* for 1 October, in which the III/R109 was scheduled to take part was suddenly cancelled. Also, in the night to 1 October orders were suddenly received that the III/R109 was to be relieved by the I/LIR 71 and would then receive quarters in Primat. The men were assembled with full equipment on 1 October where they received four days of iron rations. The sudden relief, the parade with full equipment and now iron rations gave rise to any number of rumors about an imminent movement of the division. This suspicion was quickly confirmed when at 11 p.m. the battalion was marched off to the railway station at Savigny-West, where *Oberstleutnant* von Baumbach said farewell to the battalion. Before the III/R109 departed von Baumbach awarded a number of Other Ranks with the Iron Cross II Class.

The relief of the I/R109 took place on the following day with the same preparations and equipment as the III Battalion. The II Battalion, as the last in the position on the *Kanonenberg*, was relieved in the night to the 4 October by RIR 234. The II/R109 traveled from Ardeuil to Vouziers, where it was given housing in the *Kürassier Kaserne*. The men were allowed to thoroughly clean themselves and their uniforms in order to be ready to be transported away.

IR 111 took over the position of the I/R111 on the evening of 2 October and the I/R111 became billeted in the *Kürassier Kaserne* in Vouziers. On the early morning of 4 October the battalion departed to Sancourt north of Cambrai, from where the battalion marched to its quarters in Marquion. In the night 30 September/1 October the III/R111 had also moved out of the position; The regimental sector was occupied in part by the I/LIR 71.

The III/R111 was transported on the evening of 1 October from Savigny to Rumilly south of Cambrai. It arrived there in the morning of 2 October and reached Sains les Marquion via Cambrai that was situated 15 kilometers west of the city after an exhausting foot march. In the meantime RIR 235 had arrived in the Champagne, and in the night from 3/4 October relieved the II/R111 from the front line. On 5 October the battalion was transported from Vouziers to Sancourt and billeted in Sauchy-Lestrée. On the same day the regimental staff reached Marquion.

While in Vouziers, the Other Ranks of the II/R109 and RIR 111 were given time to visit the local cinema and the opportunity to drink a good glass of beer, something the men had done without for quite some time. On 5 October the II/R109 departed from the Champagne.

The time spent in the Champagne had been used to make the regiments capable of fighting once again after the heavy losses they suffered on the Somme. Most of the replacements that arrived from Germany came from the Class of 1896. However, despite the time spent in the Champagne and with the loss of men rated as K.V. being replaced by men rated as Gv. there were only a few men in each company with any real combat experience.

While the new Other Ranks were learning how to survive trench warfare there were inevitable losses, many as a result of the lack of experience of the newer men. Large parts of the *Unteroffiziere* were still inexperienced in position warfare and this was considered to be a serious problem when the regiment went into action once again. Also, only a fraction of the heavy losses of officers lost on the Somme could be made up. Many of the newer officers would also have to learn their duties the hard way, by being thrown into action and learn on the job.

With the recent troop movements, the 28th Reserve Division had returned to its old sector on the Somme. The densely occupied villages, the industrious activity by the staffs, the numerous columns and military hospitals indicated that the men were behind a front that was involved in serious fighting.

The noise of the artillery thunder resounded across from a westerly direction and clearly indicated the battle was still raging. The replacements which had been educated in trench warfare in the Champagne were being thrown into the raging battle on the Somme for the first time. The trusted fighting spirit and the sense of honour of the few old Somme fighters still in the ranks were going to experience the horrors of the Somme for a second time. Under these circumstances, the leaders and troops walked forward with hope and trust onto the soil of the Somme.

Notes

1. *Verlustlisten* for the 28th Reserve Division were published on 26 July, 28 July and 23 August 1916.
2. The *Frauendienst* or Women's Service was formed during the war to aid in the war effort.

3.   *Feldpost* letter *Oberleutnant* Erwin Boy, 2MG/R111. Courtesy of Felix Fregin.

4.   Frisch, Georg, *Das Reserve-Infanterie-Regiment Nr. 109 im Weltkrieg 1914 bis 1918*, P.131.

5.   IBID.

6.   *Feldpost* letter *Oberleutnant* Erwin Boy, 2MG/R111. Courtesy of Felix Fregin.

7.   *Feldpost* letter *Oberleutnant* Erwin Boy, 2MG/R111. Courtesy of Felix Fregin.

Chapter 4

28th Reserve Division

2nd tour of duty on the Somme: October 1916, Grandcourt

The 28th Reserve Division was destined to return to the Battle of the Somme for the second time. The division was being sent back to the Somme to occupy a sector that had recently become severely threatened by determined British attacks; Grandcourt and Thiepval. The actual destination of the division was kept secret from the men but once the division had reached the vicinity of the Somme it did not take long for the troops to guess that this was their journey's end. For weeks, the newspapers had followed on a daily basis the heavy fighting along the Ancre and the fighting surging back and forth at this key location. While the 28th Reserve Division had originally fought further south of Thiepval, the area by the Ancre was not unknown to some of the men who had fought there in 1914.

The new sector assigned to the division was in front of Grandcourt and in the Ancre valley. The positions had been well constructed and had withstood the initial attacks by the British on 1 July and the weeks following. However, after months of tenacious resistance against the constant pressure exerted by the enemy on this sector, the front line had gradually been pressed back until it now consisted of what had once been the second line on 1 July.

The Grandcourt Sector was tactically very important, but also proving very difficult to defend when the 28th Reserve Division arrived at the beginning of October. The position contained the critically important Hill 151, which projected from the German line in front of Grandcourt. On the right of it was the swampy Ancre valley that was almost impassable, however its entire length was exposed to direct fire by the British up to the rear exit of Grandcourt. The connection to the left was curved back toward Courcelette. If the British succeeded in advancing further on the left or on the right of Grandcourt, the line of retreat for the garrison holding this position could be cut off and the men would be trapped.

The formerly well-constructed positions of the 26th Reserve Division no longer existed. Only a few dugouts were still intact in the communication trenches leading to the line *Feste Schwaben-Feste Staufen*. The fire trenches had been virtually leveled and the front line mainly consisted of one crater next to another where the men had been able to connect them with crude passageways. The route into the front line was only recognized with great difficulty by the footpaths left by the men as they travelled across the front. The line, as it existed, was easy to miss and in many instances, this resulted in men walking into the hands of the British.

The British it seems had been pursuing a successful tactic of late. When they discovered that a unit was being relieved from the German front line, the British attacked and, in the confusion inside the German lines, they usually had some success, mainly because the new troops had not had the opportunity to become oriented in the difficult terrain. To effectively prevent this type of attack, the insertion of the 28th Reserve Division took place piecemeal, battalion by battalion, one after the other.

What the men also quickly discovered was that both sides held to an unspoken humane agreement. The wounded men lying in no man's land in the early morning hours were recovered both by the British and the Germans under the protection of Red Cross flags. During this time both sides stopped all fire activity. The picture of stretcher bearers carrying a large Red Cross flag on a long pole would remain indelibly linked for many post war veterans with the memory of Grandcourt from October 1916.

While plans were being drawn up for the deployment of the 28th Reserve Division, the intensity of the fighting by *Feste Staufen* had not diminished. As the battle surged back and forth, men fought and died for small parcels of ground from defensive positions that could barely be recognized as such any longer.

So comes the 1st of October here. A day of great fighting! It throbs since dawn on the entire line. On the left, hardly 600 meters distant, already rages hand grenade fighting. One clearly sees the British, clearly sees the German stick hand grenades with their projectiles. The wire obstacles fly up in shreds. Direct hits destroyed the trench, explosions roar, rending the eardrum. Splinters whistled and whizzed.

The *Sanitäts Unteroffizier* quietly and undaunted performs his duty and brings the wounded into the mined dugout. Already the English trenches are filled. Bayonets flash above the breastworks. Steel helmet presses against steel helmet. The Other Ranks rush out of the mined dugout in the battle excitement, to repel the storm. It is still too early. The leader must push them back with crude words, to avoid unnecessary losses. Light balls demand barrage fire from the German artillery, as far as one can see!

Now the adversary breaks forth. Out! The trench is occupied in a moment. A machine gun was brought into position. And out of 100 firing mouths flies death by naked projectiles towards the Englishmen. See, how he falters, puzzled, hesitates, throw themselves down and look for protection. Slow fire! Measured target shooting replaces the initial emotional rapid fire. Where an English head shows itself, German bullets fly about his ears. There we attempt to come from the right into the rear of the enemy. The position is bad. We could not shoot to the right. A few groups jump out of the German trench, taking front to the new attacker and make him ready for the fate of his brothers. The German artillery is employed. However a battery shoots too short. Light signals indicate it to them.

Hand grenades crash at the barricade. A brave *Vizefeldwebel* with his stout flock fights off all attacks. How long already? No one knows. The time flew by. Already it is the evening. Furious about the failed attack the British artillery pounds down anew. The enemy attempted a new thrust also. His bombing parties advance in the communication trench. And our hand grenades are running out. Fire on the advancing British! In vain! Bending down, they find protection in the half destroyed trench. A bullet struck the company leader and shattered his arm. The platoon leader is wounded. The only officer took over the company. With the last remains of the hand grenades the brave men standing at the barricade held. One after the other falls. The last hand grenade! Defenseless in the unequal fighting, the defenders moved back. The British pressed on until they were by the dugout, in where the wounded lay. They look to drive out the garrison with hand grenades and smoke bombs. However, no one surrenders. They know that there are no comrades left.

The situation is serious. Individual groups look to take the lost trench, in vain.

Weber

Leutnant d. R. im Juf.-Regt. 180
gefallen bei St. Pierre-Divion
am 2. Oktober 1916

(*Kriegstagebuch aus Schwaben*)

The lack of hand grenades makes all attempts futile. The British bring a machine gun into position. Two brave men attempt to silence it with hand grenades. In vain! They were wounded. Finally the carrying troops bring new ammunition. Now it must continue. Parts of the 7th, 8th and 12th Companies fall on the invading enemy in a fresh assault with spades and hand grenades. Furious close fighting; explosions, bloody spades, screams and shouts.

At 8 p.m. the entire blood-drenched trench is German again. Again a bombing party stands alert at the barricade and the night makes ready its compassionate its dark veil over the suffering and miseries of the day. *Leutnant der Landwehr* Matthias Gerster RIR 119 [1]

The men of the 28th Reserve Division had come at the right time in order to relieve the exhausted men who had been defending the front line and who had reached the end of their strength. The sector assigned to RIR 111 was *Sector Staufen,* located south of Grandcourt. The position lay about 4 kilometers north of Ovillers, a village well-known to the men of RIR 111. This village and the subsequent terrain east of it as well as south encompassing the ruins of Martinpuich, Le Sars, Bazentin le Petit, had already been captured by the British while the regiment was in the Champagne.

The German line north of the Ancre was still as intact as it had been on 1 July when all enemy attacks were repulsed. The positions north of the river were experiencing regular artillery and mine fire as well as the occasional raid or patrol fight since the last enemy attack in early September. The sector south of the Ancre that would be occupied by the regiments of the 28th Reserve Division included St. Pierre-Divion and battle trenches that had formerly been the communication trenches of the 26th Reserve Division. The new line faced west at some points close to the Ancre, and south at other locations.

In the days from 6 to 8 October the battalions of RIR 111 were transported to Noreuil. From here the men would be taken up to the battle front at Grandcourt. This would mean a foot march of 22 kilometers or more, an onerous undertaking at the best of times. To ensure that the men were in a condition that would allow them to man the front lines the Other Ranks and packs were carried on food wagons as far as Sapignies. The rations were distributed in this village and a religious field service was held in the local church.

When RIR 111 finally occupied its new sector, the first task was to rebuild the defensive positions. Just recently, at the end of September, Thiepval, and other key positions located nearby had been captured by the enemy and the fighting continued to take place daily. The battle battalions were not ready for what they found, a series of shell holes that had been connected together to form a crude defensive line.

There was almost no shell proof housing for the supports. The garrison in the front line had become crowded together in the few remaining dugouts, a few tunnel entrances that had recently been started and some scattered concrete shelters. The largest part of the men only found some protection from the British shell fire in quickly created shelters, usually small recesses cut into the front of the trench wall or side of a large crater, known as

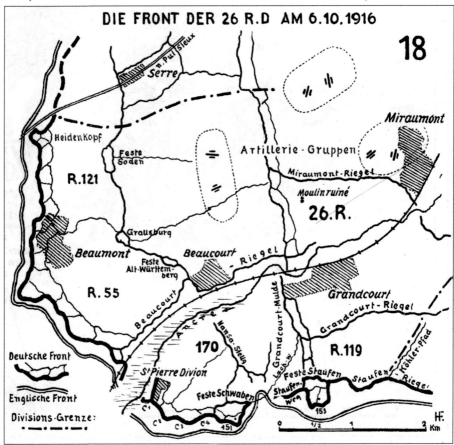

The front of the 26th Reserve Division on 6 October 1916.

Karnickellöcher, or rabbit holes.

Almost every wire obstacle had been swept away in the constant enemy artillery fire. Any attempt to set up new entanglements only led to increased casualties amongst the men. Because of the direction of the front line, the British had the advantage that his batteries north of the Ancre could place shell on the German line from the right flank and from the rear. This often led to the suspicion by the men that the German batteries were firing too short.

Despite all of the drawbacks of the position, it was extremely important that it be held. If the British succeeded in breaking through and crossing the Ancre, then the positions north of the river would be threatened from the rear. The men in RIR 111 were fully aware of the importance of the position and how serious their task would be.

As soon as the battalions were inserted into the front line, the men immediately took all measures to remedy the shortcomings of the sector. While some progress was made, the daily requirements needed to defend the position used up almost all of the available strength of the battalions and very little effort could be dedicated to improving the position. In addition, much of the work performed each night was destroyed by the enemy artillery on the following morning.

RIR110 was also being sent up to the front lines at this time. At 2 p.m. and 7 p.m. on 6 October the I/R110 travelled toward Grandcourt in half battalions. According to the arrangements made by the commander of IR 170 under whose command the battalion was placed, the battalion would occupy *Feste Schwaben* in the Grandcourt position. The battalion staff arrived at the battle headquarters in the *Hansa Stellung* at 10 p.m. in which the 9th, 10th and 12/170 would later become the sector reserve.

7 October

When the men from the I/R110 arrived at the front they would relieve the badly frayed companies, the 1st, 2nd, 4th, 6th and 11/170, which were lying in *Feste Schwaben*. The first two companies from the I/R110 arrived at 1 a.m., the remaining two companies at 3 a.m. The 1st and 4/R99 that until now had been subordinate to IR 170, were now subordinate to the commander of the I/R110.

The position that was to be taken over from IR 170 ran from the Ancre ground via point 151 – *Feste Schwaben* in the direction of Point 153 west of Courcelette – *Feste Staufen*. At the beginning of the Somme battle the line St. Pierre-Divion-Thiepval-Ovillers had been occupied by the 26th Reserve Division and was successfully defended. After Thiepval fell and the German line was pressed back, the new front line position carried designation names reminiscent of the *Württembergers*, respectively the old garrison of IR 126.

Four fairly intact strongpoints still existed in the sector: St. Pierre-Divion, *Feste Schwaben*, the *Hansa Stellung* and *Feste Staufen*. In the latter there were a few still existing dugouts. As these dugouts had originally been built as accommodations for the reserves supporting a battle position, many were too large, in that they could hold an average of 50 men. Some were even larger, where there was room for up to 100 men. These large dugouts took on an ominous reputation in the regiment during the course of the time it was in the position.

There had always been the possibility that dugout occupants could not man the battle trench quickly enough to repel an attack, a fundamental requirement for a successful defense of the position. These larger dugouts had few exits and in case of an emergency, they could not be exited quickly enough by the large number of men inside them. With the close proximity to the British position these shortcomings could only help the enemy in any surprise attack. However, for better or worse, these dugouts were utilized as some of the only safe locations at the front.

> One wrote on 7 October 1916, when we occupied the position by Grandcourt. You were under all of the guns: no more wire entanglements, no dugouts; the trench was fully of dirt and mud. The terrain was completely plowed up through the numerous shells. In front of us was a dugout destroyed by a direct hit with a cross affixed, upon it was written that here seven comrades lay buried. This cross spoke a solemn language to us. With effort, the company came down into a half destroyed artillery dugout. Otto Hengel, 9/R111[2]

There were few, if any, wire obstacles before the front line, and likewise there were few continuous access routes leading from the rear to the battle trench. One such trench the *Meisengasse*, a communication route running between the old first and second trench lines, had been captured by the enemy in an earlier period of fighting. Therefore, the left wings of the first and second trenches were blocked off with barricades, one side occupied by German troops, the other side by the enemy.

Corresponding to the desolate condition of the communication trenches was the telephone connections between the command posts. Working telephone lines could only be maintained with the greatest exertion by the telephone troops. Even if a connection to the rear was established, at best, it only lasted for a few hours. The wires would then become destroyed once again. Since secure communications through the telephone was not guaranteed, it had to be accomplished through runners. This method of transmitting orders and messages was also of dubious reliability due the severity of the deadly enemy barrage fire.

It did not take long before the men of RIR 110 were in the thick of things once again. For most of the day on 7 October there was strong artillery and mine fire upon the regimental position accompanied by numerous enemy observation aircraft flying over the German front line, obviously directing the artillery fire. At 7 p.m. enemy raiding parties approached the *Strassburger Steig, Münstergasse* and the *Schwaben Riegel*. They were all repulsed following intense hand grenade battles. Once the raiding parties had been driven off and the artillery fire had died down somewhat, an accounting could be taken of the losses suffered by the regiment. It was discovered that 7 men had been killed and 28 men had been wounded during the day.

8 October

On the following day, 8 October, it was the turn of the German infantry to take offensive action. At 6 a.m., IR 170 undertook an attack, with two *Sturm Trupp* and a *Flammenwerfer* detachment followed by two further infantry groups, on a position called the *Kreuzungpunkt* located near *Feste Schwaben*. The 3/R110 was also participating in the attack and was being held in support, ready to occupy and develop the captured trench.

The 1st and 4/R110 were also active at this time, with the companies being involved in trying to expand their position by pressing back the enemy located on both wings of the regimental sector. Bombing parties, along with infantry support, advanced through the makeshift trench line, forcing the British back from crater to crater.

The attacks by IR 170 and the two companies of RIR 110 succeeded in overwhelming the enemy defenders with the help of supporting artillery, machine gun and *Minenwerfer* fire. However, the enemy trench captured by IR 170 proved to be too difficult to hold. By 6.30 p.m., the men of IR 170 and the 3/R110 occupying the captured position suffered numerous losses under very strong retaliatory mine, machine gun and shell fire from the British. In light of the increasingly heavy casualties, it was decided that the captured position had to be abandoned and the men were ordered to evacuate the hard won ground and withdraw to the old German line. Among the fatal losses suffered during this fighting was *Leutnant* Thietje, 3/R110 and five men from his company. Many more sustained wounds and were sent to the rear for medical treatment.

In the neighboring RIR 111, the III/R111, under the command of *Major* Oloff, relieved a battalion from RIR 119 from the positions at the left wing of the division sector in the early morning hours. The III/R111 now occupied the *Staufen Riegel*. The 9/R111 was on the right of the new position; the 11th and 12/R111 followed, occupying the *Staufen Riegel* up to the *Köhlersappe*.

A large dugout was located at the left wing of the III/R111, the *Leyling Stollen*. At first, the dugout was utilized as the battalion headquarters and accommodated the entire staff. It was soon discovered; however, that the battalion headquarters was perilously close to the front line. It was decided that it was far too dangerous to have the battle leadership of the sector where it could be quickly overwhelmed during an enemy attack. As a result, the battalion headquarters was transferred further to the rear in the *Kirchhof Mulde* Grandcourt.

After taking stock of their situation, the III/R111 discovered that there was no connection with the neighboring Marine Infantry Regiment 2; all contact and communication had to be established using patrols. The 10/R111 was the battalion reserve, located behind the right wing of the battalion. The 10th Company was accommodated in the *Stump Weg* that led toward Grandcourt. Later that night, the I/R111 under *Hauptmann* Steffan took up position on the right of the III/R111 after relieving parts of RIR 99 and RIR 119.

The 3/R111 occupied *Feste Staufen*, a part of the position located on a rise that projected toward the enemy, with the 9/R111 connecting on the left. *Feste Staufen* was a strongpoint that had been previously located in the second line of the German defenses on 1 July 1916. Now, all that remained of the powerful position were a few paltry, destroyed trenches. The narrow, projecting position of *Feste Staufen* approached very close to the British line. Due to the relentless enemy advances, the flank of this strongpoint was seriously threatened as enemy fire could be concentrated on the position from almost every direction. It was considered to be the most exposed part of the German line in this sector because of this.

Despite the vulnerability of the position, it could not be abandoned in order to straighten the German line. If the British were to take *Feste Staufen* they would have an unrestricted view into the Ancre valley by Grandcourt. The men of the 28th Reserve Division felt that there was another reason for the obsession with holding this point of the German line, the importance apparently placed on it by the enemy.

The British name for *Feste Staufen* was Stuff Redoubt and was frequently mentioned in British reports. *Oberst* Ley had a different opinion of the position he was given. In his diary he wrote that instead of calling the strongpoint *Feste Staufen*, it should really have been called fortress 'Mausefalle' [Mousetrap] Staufen.

Just to the right of the 3/R111 was the 2/R111, which was positioned in the Staufen Graben. The connection to RIR 110 in Feste Schwaben was not secure and a gap had opened in the German lines. The 1/R111 lay behind the middle of the sector in a communication trench that ran from Feste Staufen to Grandcourt. The battalion command post was located at the intersection of that communication trench with the Lach Weg. The 4/R111 was supporting the regiment and was located in the vicinity of the regimental command post at the exit of the village of Grandcourt, where the men had dug out Karnickellöcher into a nearby hillside.

The machine guns of the 2nd Machine Gun Company were located with the I/R111. Those of the 3rd Machine Gun Company were with the III Battalion, all of which were distributed in the front line. The men of RIR 111 were being supported by an extremely exhausted battalion from RIR 99, located in the second line in the Grandcourt Riegel. During the night from the 9/10 October the 6th and 8/R111 were moved into the right wing of the Grandcourt Riegel, while the 5th and 7/R111 were kept further back on the Miraumont-Grandcourt road as reserve. The staff of the II/R111 under Hauptmann Bumiller was placed in a dugout in the Kirchhof Mulde, located behind the Grandcourt Riegel. The 1st Machine Gun Company was subordinate to this battalion.

For the men who were returning to the Somme for the second time, the movement through the sector had dredged up memories of the days by Fricourt. All of the routes and communication trenches were covered with shrapnel; crossing-points, command posts, kitchens and hollows were blanketed with high explosive shells. The front lines were no better; they were covered with shells and mines of every caliber, which rained down on the

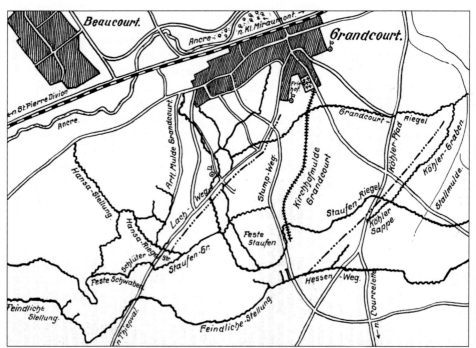

Positions defended by the 28th Reserve Division in October 1916.

positions. Under these circumstances, losses were inevitable.

While RIR 111 had brought up all three battalions into the front line, more men were needed. On 8 October, the II/R110 marched from Vaux through Sapigny and Achiet le Petit in the defensive positions by Miraumont. The battalion finally arrived at its destination at 12 midnight and was allowed to rest with the men being accommodated in dugouts.

9 October

The night from 8/9 October had been relatively quiet for the men of RIR 110. While the shelling had never completely stopped, the volume of fire had decreased to such an extent that it allowed some of the men to rest and others to make a few improvements to the position. The peacefulness did not last very long as, in the early morning darkness; British patrols began to probe the German positions at numerous locations. In each case the alert sentries inside the German trenches were able to alarm the garrison and the enemy patrols were expelled, primarily with hand grenades.

Then, at 5.30 a.m., the enemy infantry attacked the entire German line, advancing in five waves. On the left wing of the I/R110 the advancing enemy waves were only able to approach the German trenches, but were unable to penetrate due to the volume of defensive fire, assisted by artillery, *Minenwerfer* and *Granatwerfer* fire.

The British had better success on the right wing of the I/R1110 and a small group of enemy soldiers had managed to penetrate the German lines at the *Schwaben Riegel*. A counterattack was quickly formed by the men of the I/R110 and they immediately recaptured the lost section of trench after heavy hand grenade fighting. The British had suffered numerous losses crossing no man's land and the small group inside the *Schwaben Riegel*, was completely overwhelmed. Once the portion of the line had been restored, a British corporal and two other men were taken prisoner and sent to the rear.

All of the fighting that had surged back and forth in the morning had also caused heavy losses among the companies of the I/R110. It was decided to send reinforcements so that the position could be held. The 9/170 was alarmed and positioned in the *Hansa Stellung*, directly behind the *Schwaben Riegel*, where the company could provide timely support at any critical location.

At 1.30 p.m. observers noted that the British were filling up their trenches with infantry once more and a new attack was expected at any moment. Messages were sent back to the rear to the artillery positions which opened fire. The accurate German *Vernichtungsfeuer* [annihilation fire] came down on the British assembly trenches and apparently caused enough losses that the British did not attack that afternoon.

As darkness fell over the battlefield once more, *Unteroffizier* Blohm, 1/R110, who had been missing the entire day, suddenly returned to the German trenches accompanied by a British prisoner. Apparently Blohm had been caught out in no man's land during the British attack and had managed to capture the enemy soldier. Due to the heavy fire and probability that neither man would survive being exposed in daylight, he had detained his prisoner the entire day in a shell crater about 80 meters in front of the German lines. Once it was safe, he returned with his prize. With the return of Blohm, the casualty list for the I/R110 dropped by one man. The total losses for this day of fighting were 30 men killed, 120 men wounded and 1 man missing.

While the I/R110 was involved in heavy fighting for much of the day, the sister battalion, the II/R110 spent the day constructing dugouts in the *Miraumont Riegel*. At one point in the morning, the 5/R110 was sent forward to reinforce the I/R110. The 5th Company arrived at the front in the afternoon, at a time when especially heavy artillery fire was being focussed upon the *Hansa Stellung*. Fortunately, no enemy infantry attack followed.

While heavy fighting was taking place in the sector held by RIR 110, the neighboring RIR 111 was only experiencing strong artillery fire. Among the men who were killed or wounded during the bombardment was *Major* Oloff, commander of the III/R111 who was placed out of action early in the morning due to shell splinters. As there was a shortage of officers, *Oberleutnant* Born assumed command of the battalion in his place.

Overseeing the bombardment were numerous enemy aircraft that flew back and forth above the position. Further in the enemy rear, numerous tethered observation balloons appeared across the horizon.. The scene reminded many of the veterans in the regiment of the start of the Somme battle in July. Now, instead of attacking across a wide expanse, the enemy was attacking much smaller fronts with concentrated forces. It was only a matter of time until the British turned their attention to the men of RIR 111. In the early afternoon of 9 October the enemy artillery fire increased to a level consistent with severe drum fire on the 2 kilometer wide sector of RIR 111.

Messages were sent to the rear requesting the German batteries to provide artillery support for the expected British attack. The German guns did open fire but could not match the numbers and calibers of the British guns owing to fewer guns being available. The attack commenced at 4 p.m., along the entire front of the regiment. The enemy assault waves on the right and left wings of the regimental sector quickly ran into trouble when they were met with heavy infantry, mine and artillery fire. The British troops in these locations were forced to take cover in shell craters in front of the German line and were unable to advance any further.

A small contingent of British troops, estimated to be about the size of two companies, managed to penetrate into the southern trench of *Feste Staufen*, into the *Auto Graben*. The machine gun from the 3rd Machine Gun Company that had been positioned in the *Auto Graben* had been destroyed by a direct hit. Without the additional firepower of this weapon, the enemy infantry had been able to enter the badly damaged trench and quickly engaged in bitter close combat with parts of the 3rd and 9/R111. Segments of the 9/R111 were immediately pressed back into the southern corner of the *Stump Weg* and further back into *Feste Staufen*. The British forces continued to advance deeper into the German defenses, driving their way further into the *Stump Weg*. It was here where most Groups of the 9/R111 along with two machine guns were accommodated in a large dugout, a former command post. The entrance to the dugout had been blown in during the bombardment and before the garrison could clear the entrance, the enemy was in control of the exit into the trench.

Reports came in that the British were employing flamethrowers to clear out the dugouts and pockets of German resistance. The fumes from these terrifying weapons were enough to incapacitate any man and, when combined with the close confines of a deep dugout, they could also quickly suffocate anyone trapped below. What happened to the men inside the dugout was only guessed at by the regiment. It was suspected that they had defended their position as best they could before being overwhelmed.

What did eventually become known was that *Leutnant* Räuchle had been killed here. However, a large part of the 9th Company along with the company leader, *Leutnant* Biermann, and *Feldwebel* Reitze had ended up in captivity. The garrison of *Feste Staufen* could do little to help their comrades trapped inside the *Stump Weg* and watched as smoke from the burning dugout rose high into the air as it slowly burned out over the course of the day.

The enemy now had an open path into the German rear through the *Stump Weg* which they attempted to exploit before being brought to a stop by a counterattack led by the 10/R111 moving up the *Stump Weg* from the direction of Grandcourt. The British then quickly constructed a barricade inside the *Stump Weg*, trying to secure their gains. The men of the 10/R111 drove over the makeshift barricade using hand grenade attack, forcing the British defenders back up the trench toward the old British lines.

As the men of the 10/R111 advanced through the trench they were able to free a number of men from the 9/R111 trapped inside partially collapsed dugouts. Finally, the enemy was thrown back out of the eastern part of *Feste Staufen,* all the way back until they were almost at the junction where the *Staufen Riegel* intersected the *Stump Weg.* The fighting continued to surge back and forth as the British attempted to advance back down the *Stump Weg* once more, only to be stopped in their tracks by the men of the 10/R111 who maintained their positions despite suffering heavy losses. During the fighting the company leader, *Leutnant* Rupp, and *Leutnant* Hugo Mayer were both wounded, further reducing the number of trained officers left in the regiment.

After two days it was already so precarious that we could hardly leave the dugout. We were continuously bothered by English flyers, and the English artillery made our lives miserable in every possible manner. We should certainly establish the destroyed telephone wire to the battalion, but it was almost impossible in the strong fire. It came, as we had expected; strong drum fire started in the afternoon, and they came closely behind it, before we could see them, the Tommys attacked and threw hand grenades into our dugouts as they ran past, fortunately without causing any losses. Now the situation was difficult. In front of us the English, behind us the English, in the middle the raging fire – what should we do? Everyone thought we were lost! Finally nothing remained for us other than to unfasten our equipment and yield to the superior strength. However with it the pressure was still not over. Our biggest danger we still had to survive, when we had to run the gauntlet between the fixed bayonets of the Tommys. At the same time the German fire started with such intensity that it became hell for the British. Therefore many still became wounded or killed by our own comrades. Finally the biggest number of us came under the leadership of a slightly wounded Englishman, who was armed only with a German light pistol, came to the English dressing station. Here we received water to drink, and were gaped at by a number of English soldiers. Fortunately we were not robbed by them. This was attributed to the circumstances that we were not merely a couple of prisoners, but about 50-60 men. So nothing was made of any 'souvenirs' by us and the Englishmen must leave with empty hands. I only got it generally out of the escorts, with whom I later talked to in my broken English, so that I gave him a piece of German money, wherefore he thanked me quite politely. After an approximately two hours march, during that we passed our old positions by Thiepval and therefore crossed over the Ancre on the right of Albert, were we temporarily at our destination. Otto Hengel, 9/R111[3]

While the fighting was taking place inside the *Stump Weg*, there was also close combat taking place against the British located in parts of *Feste Staufen. Leutnant* Weissensee, the

Zur frommen Erinnerung im Gebete
an

Joseph Hipp

Grenadier im Res..Inf.-Regt 119, 3. Komp.
Inhaber des Eisernen Kreuzes II. Kl.
geboren am 5. November 1894 in Nendingen
gefallen am 9. Oktober 1916 bei Thiepval
an der Somme.
✠

Er kämpft fürs teure Vaterland
Als Grenadier mit Herz und Hand
Und gab sein junges Blut so rot
Für uns getreu bis in den Tod.
Wir wollen sein in Lieb' gedenken
Und ihm mit Dank die Bitte schenken:
Herr Jesus, nimm ihn auf in's Licht;
Zeig ihm Dein göttlich Angesicht
Und laß ihn ruh'n in Deinem Frieden;
Er focht den guten Kampf hienieden!

Gebet.

O Vater der Barmherzigkeit und Gott alles Trostes! Wir empfehlen Dir die Seele unseres Mitbruders *Joseph*, welchen Du nach Deinem unerforschlichen Ratschlusse aus dieser Zeitlichkeit abgerufen hast. Laß die Mühen und Schmerzen, die er während des Krieges auf sich genommen und das Opfer des Lebens, das er in Verteidigung seines Vaterlandes gebracht hat, ihm gnädig zur Sühne gereichen für alle Sünden, die die er auf seiner irdischen Pilgerschaft aus menschlicher Schwachheit begangen, und verleihe ihm für den Heldenmut, mit dem er für das Vaterland gekämpft, und für alles Gute, das er je hienieden getan, zum Lohne gnädig die Siegeskrone des ewigen Lebens. Amen.

Vater unser . . . Gegrüßet . . .

Barmherziger Jesus, gib ihm die ewige Ruhe! (7 Jahre u. 7 Quadr. Ablaß.)

Süßes Herz Mariä, sei meine Rettung! (300 Tage Ablaß jedesmal.)

(Author's collection)

leader of the 3/R111 sent a bombing party from his company against the British in the western trench sections of *Feste Staufen*. By late afternoon, the bombing party had recaptured most of the trenches that had been lost earlier. During the counterattack, Groups from the 2/R111 under *Leutnant* Holzhauser provided effective fire support, engaging the enemy from the right, out of the *Staufen Graben*.

The 1/R111 under *Leutnant* Koch served as rear-support in the northern *Quergraben* of *Feste Staufen*. The fighting was desperate, *Leutnant* Göbel, 2/R111, was killed along with many brave *Unteroffiziere* and men from his company. *Leutnant* Straub, 3/R111, was among the numerous wounded.

The British troops still inside the German trenches defended their hard won positions with the utmost stubbornness and as a result, the men of RIR 111 were unable to completely eject the British from the *Auto Graben*. When there was a lull in the fighting, as much resulting from the onset of darkness as from the exhaustion of the men on both sides, the recaptured trench pieces was blocked off with barricades. *Feste Staufen* now existed as three barricaded sap heads.

Still, the fighting was not finished. Further German attacks recommenced at 5 p.m. as the regiment had ordered that every attempt should be made to throw the enemy completely out of *Feste Staufen*. In order to accomplish this, one platoon each from the 4/R111 was placed under the command of the I and III/R111 that were then attached to the 3rd and 10/R111. In addition to providing men for the assault parties, the two platoons would also provide critical transportation of ammunition and food needed for the assault.

However the counterattack did not develop very effectively due to strong enemy artillery fire. The enemy was not having any better luck, all of their attempts to advance deeper into the German trenches also failed as a result of strong defensive fire. The continuous fighting around the barricades used up all of the available strength on both sides, fresh troops were desperately needed. Arrangements were made during the night of 9/10 October for the 5/R111 under *Leutnant* Meichelt to move forward from Grandcourt. One platoon would reinforce the garrison of *Feste Staufen*, two platoons were held back at the *Lach Weg* as a reserve for the I/R111.

10 October

10 October was a relatively quiet day for the men in RIR 110. Once the sun had risen, enemy aircraft appeared as per normal overhead in large numbers as the pilots and observers continued to monitor every movement made in the German lines. In addition, numerous tethered observation balloons climbed high into the sky across the horizon once again. The men of RIR 110 felt as if they were under the microscope and all unnecessary movement was avoided; to many it felt as if the enemy had someone watching every single man inside the trenches.

The fighting to recapture the lost positions adjacent to *Feste Staufen* had gone on all during the night, which only briefly subsided in the early morning hours. Then, in the pre-dawn hours, German batteries and *Minenwerfer* covered the enemy occupied *Auto Graben* with heavy fire, the explosions lighting up the darkness as if it were daytime. Once the position had been considered sufficiently prepared, several assault groups from *Feste Staufen* attacked the *Auto Graben*. At 7 a.m. Groups from the 3rd, 4th and 5/R111 advanced from the right, while simultaneously parts of the 9th and 10/R111 advanced from the left of the strongpoint. Both detachments were supported by a *Sturm Trupp* from the II/R111.

The assault parties moved quickly over the open ground and through the damaged trenches and craters, attacking the British defenders of the *Auto Graben* with hand grenades. The British response was swift and deadly. During the night, the enemy had brought up a number of machine guns and had positioned them so that they could spread their fire along the length of the *Stump Weg*. When the first German assault troops made their appearance, the enemy called up defensive artillery and mine fire, within moments, the attackers were smothered under heavy barrage and annihilation fire. Not to be left out, enemy aircraft overhead would suddenly turn and dive down on the attacking Germans, raking the men of RIR 111 with machine gun fire. .

Despite the intense enemy opposition, the assault detachments from RIR 111 continued their attacks. As each advance was disrupted, the men were reformed and tried once more. This was repeated a number of times until finally, some success had been achieved. *Leutnant* Müller, 7/R111, was able to occupy the barricade located at the *Stump Weg* with a portion of his men. However, it proved impossible to exploit their success in the hurricane of fire directed against them. The fighting around the barricade involved the plentiful use of hand grenades on both sides as well as close fighting throughout the remainder of the day and well into the night without any noticeable change in the situation.

The relative calm being enjoyed by the men of the neighboring RIR 110 came to an end in the afternoon when the British focussedstrong artillery fire upon the rear positions of the sector. Everything pointed to the possibility of an attack taking place at any time. While the men remained on high alert, constantly scanning the foreground for signs of an attack, none appeared.

During all of this, the III/R110 reached Vaulx, marching from Saudemont. The battalion was ordered to relieve the II/170 from the front line where it was positioned with the II/R110. The III/R110 marched via Sapigny-Miraumont to St. Pierre-Divion where the companies would pick up guides who would direct the companies into their new positions Starting from 10 p.m., the parts of IR 170 which were still remaining in the position with the II/R110 were relieved. When the exchange was completed, the III/R110 occupied the right sub-sector whose right wing was on the river Ancre. The battalion battle headquarters was located at the northwest exit of the village of Grandcourt.

11 October

On the morning of 11 October, all of the companies of the III/R110 were in position. The 11/R110 was positioned in the first trench on the right wing of the sector, connecting to 12/R110 on the left. Parts of the 12/R110 were also on the right wing in the second trench up to the *Strassburger Steig*. The 9/R110, save for one platoon, was positioned in the *Strassburger Steig* up to the *Münstergasse*. The battalion staff with one platoon from the 9/R110 acting as the sector reserve, were in the *Biber Kolonie* on the left bank of the Ancre. The right bank of the Ancre was occupied by the III/R55.

Following the relief, the companies from the II/R110 were repositioned so that the battalion would be able to relieve the I/R110 from the front line. In the short time the I/R110 had been in the thick of the fighting, the battalion had lost 1 officer, 39 men killed; 19 men wounded and 18 men missing. In order to provide the maximum protection for the sector, the 7/R110 was placed into *Feste Schwaben* and in the southern part of the *Hansa Stellung*, where the company could support the I/R110. The 6/R110 was positioned in the *Artillerie Mulde*, where a detachment was sent out on picket duty and positioned in the southern portion of the *Artillerie Mulde*. The 8/R110 was placed in reserve and positioned directly south of Grandcourt, near the regimental battle headquarters, and the 5/R110 occupied *Hansa Stellung Nord*. The battalion headquarters moved into the dugouts at the battle headquarters at the southern exit of Grandcourt. The 2/R110 was attached to the battalion as reinforcements and assumed resonsibility forthe field sentry position on the heights of the *Lach Weg*.

When the sun rose on the morning of 11 October, the garrison of *Feste Staufen* was exhausted following the relentless combat the men had been involved in. All three defending battalions were so intermingled that it was impossible to separate them into the original companies. However, despite the confusion and disorder, the garrison, under the command of *Leutnant* Weissensee, had not lost a single foot of ground despite numerous attempts by the enemy to expand his earlier gains. All of the barricade positions were still firmly in German hands.

At the same time however, the British still sat in the *Auto Graben*. While the British had also suffered heavy losses in the close combat and hand grenade battles, new troops always seemed to appear in the position. During the fighting overnight, the men of RIR 111 had captured one prisoner and the enemy had also been forced to abandon one machine gun and other pieces of equipment.

Violent attacks had also taken place on the right towards the *Staufen Graben*. The distance between the opposing lines was quite far at this part of the line and the defensive fire of the garrison and the artillery support had been able to stop the enemy advance before it could reach the German position. Afterward, three British soldiers who became trapped in shell holes in no man's land as a result of the German barrage fire were brought in as prisoners by patrols from the 2/R111.

Panzerstand im Staufengraben

Reinforced concrete shelter in the Staufen Graben. (Author's collection)

Following this latest attack, the fighting began to subside as both sides recuperated and rested. For the exhausted Germans however, there was littlerespite. It was only a matter of time before the next wave of attacks would descend upon the defenders and every second was needed to ensure that the position could be held.

The men from RIR 111 quickly transitioned from the use of hand grenades and rifles and replaced them with picks and shovels. Ever since *Feste Staufen* had been transformed into three unconnected saps, it was deemed to be imperative that the individual barricades should become connected to each other. Equally important was the construction of a new communication trench leading to the *Hansa Riegel* where RIR 110 was positioned.

With the almost constant stream of losses at the front, it was vital that the support troops that were positioned in a trench line between the *Grandcourt Riegel* and the front line be protected from enemy artillery and mine fire. Unfortunately, the support trench lacked in almost any protection against this type of fire. This was painfully obvious as the support troops continued to suffer unnecessarily high losses from shell splinters, shrapnel and being buried under collapsing trench walls when high explosive shells impacted nearby.

The only sure method to provide the necessary protection was in the creation of new dugouts. Without these, the support troops could no longer remain in their position without becoming combat ineffective. The men were quickly set to work creating dugouts at intervals along the front wall of the support trench. Not only would the dugouts provide secure housing for the men, it would allow the support line to be fully manned in the event of further enemy attacks.

Dugouts were also started in the battle trenchs that were also very suseptable to British fire and that offered almost no protection to the garrison. The work on the dugouts was immediately started in the *Köhlerpfad* and the *Stump Weg*. Most importantly, secure dugouts and associated emplacements needed to be created for the machine guns in the

Men from RIR 111 in the Hansa Riegel. (*Das Reserve-Infanterie-Regiment Nr. 111 im Weltkrieg 1914 bis 1918*)

second trench and the support trench. One of the lessons already learned during the Battle of the Somme was that machine guns located inside the battle trench were not always ready to fire in the event of an enemy attack, especially if the distance between the opposing lines was quite close. The enemy infantry had shown themselves capable of easily overrunning the front line before the machine guns could be brought into position and open fire.

It was also found that the heavy shelling, combined with the mud and filth, could foul the machine gun mechanism or prevent the ammunition from being fed into the *Zuführer* [feeder] if the canvas belts or the cartridges were dirty. In either case, the machine gun could not be operated in a time of need. The new machine gun emplacements and secure dugouts for the gun and gun crews in the rear trenches would ensure the best use of the massive firepower of these weapons.

Most of the men in the 7/R111 were being used to construct the new emplacements. The materials needed to create the dugouts would come from the Construction Company depot located near Grandcourt, which was under the command of *Leutnant* Lantelme. Carrying parties were quickly assembled from men found in the regimental billets and First Line Transport in Miraumont, Irles and Sapignies. These carrying parties were given the duty of transporting all of the required materials to the front line by hand under the direction of the Supply Officers who also had the task of bringing food and water to the front line troops.

Food and water were recognizedas critical supplies in the heavy fighting taking place near Grandcourt. While there were still ample quantities of food to provide to the troops, it was proving impossible to bring warm food into the trenches. It was also considered impractical to have the front line troops send men back to Grandcourt to obtain the food

'Somme 1916'. Survivors of the fighting. (Author's collection)

and then carry it back to their comrades. This could seriously weaken the strength of the trench garrison at a critical moment.

At this time of the fighting, the field kitchens were still able to travel up to Grandcourt under cover of darkness. The hot food was then transferred to containers and carrying parties transported the food through the devastated terrain and, if luck was with them, deliver the food to the correct locations.

Warm food was seen as being fundamental to maintaining the morale of the men at the front. Generally, the journey to the front took so long that the food was almost always cold when it arrived. In order to allow the front line troops to heat up the food after the carrying parties had dropped it off, solidified alcohol was also brought to the front line. This method of re-heating the food would give off the least amount of smoke which was considered necessary to prevent the enemy from observing their location.

The men who made up the carrying parties received very little recognition for their difficult task. Not only did they have to carry heavy loads across a shell cratered terrain, they had to make the return journey across the same shattered ground. It was not uncommon for the men to become lost in the featureless terrain and in some cases carrying troops simply walked into the enemy lines by mistake. This problem was not confined to the Germans as British troops also ended up in the wrong trench on occasion.

The treatment of the wounded had also been of great concern since the 28th Reserve Division returned to the Somme. There were a limited number of usable dugouts for the number of men inside the trenches. Some of these had to be used as dressing stations where severely wounded men could receive immediate treatment from the regimental surgeons or where slightly wounded men could find shelter on their journey to the rear.

The stretcher bearers were constantly active as they roamed the battlefield in search of wounded men, especially those who were immobile as a result of their wounds. The unspoken agreement utilized by both sides to respect the Red Cross flag was instrumental in saving dozens of men from a lingering death from loss of blood, exposure or random shell fire. Without this agreement, it would have been impossible to recover the wounded in order to receive medical help during daylight hours.

The hard work required to improve the overall position quickly paid off when the British renewed their attacks against *Feste Staufen* in the afternoon of 11 October. All of the attacks were smashed by the defensive fire from the German infantry and supporting artillery barrage fire. Recapturing the lost trench pieces was considered of great importance to the honor of the Baden regiment, RIR 111. Perhaps more importantly, by regaining the lost trench sections, the position would be inherently stronger and easier to hold against future attacks. The wedge driven into the division sector needed to be eliminated; bringing the entire position back into German hands needed to be accomplished at all costs..

During the night, the 7/R110, positioned in *Feste Schwaben* covering off the left sector was reinforced by a platoon from the 6/R110. The 7/R110 losses had reduced its strength to the point where it did not have enough men available to cover the entire strongpoint unilaterally.

12 October

On the morning of 12 October, the *Sturm Trupp* of the I/R111 attempted a surprise attack against the *Auto Graben* without any artillery or *Minenwerfer* preparation fire. However the British were on the alert for just such a move and quickly employed barrage fire from mine throwers and flanking machine gun fire. The attack quickly fell apart in the face of such heavy opposition and the survivors made their way back to the German trenches.

Another effort to attack the *Auto Graben* was attempted in the evening; this time after the German batteries had violently bombarded the enemy occupied position and then placed a fire barrier around the *Auto Graben* that should effectively block any reinforcements from reaching the defenders. The British once again responded to this threat quickly and effectively, with artillery, mine and machine gun fire.

One of the numerous enemy shells struck the entrance to the dugout of *Leutnant* Weissensee, who was tirelessly directing the defense of *Feste Staufen* and the counterattack against the *Auto Graben*. It took some time before the entrance shaft could be cleared of dirt and crushed wood beams in order to free the occupants. The sandbag barricade at the *Stump Weg*, which had already been destroyed several times in the enemy fire, also had to be reconstructed over and over again during fierce hand grenade fighting, in order to have a secure exit for the next assault on the *Auto Graben*.

Throughout most of the day thrust pushed up against counter-thrust as both sides tried to gain the upper hand at the barricades. By the fall of darkness the British occupied the barrier by the *Stump Weg*. Then, just as quickly as it had been lost, *Vizefeldwebel* Schuler, 11/R111, snatched the barricade from the enemy once again, and *Leutnant* Beck with a *Sturm Abteilung* stormed forward up to the *Auto Graben*. However, Beck and his men ended up in such severe enemy machine gun fire that they could not remain in their position in front of the barricade.

At the western barricade the struggle of the *Sturm Abteilung* of *Leutnant* Helbig, *Leutnant* Kohler and *Offizier Stellvertreter* Wurth shot down the British troops defending their barricades and almost managed to recapture the entire *Auto Graben*. Both *Leutnants* Helbig and Kohler were wounded in this fighting along with numerous losses among the Other Ranks.

Once the initial momentum was lost in the face of stiff enemy opposition, a new barricade was quickly constructed in order to retain possession of the captured ground. While the men worked on the barricade, *Offizier Stellvertreter* Wurth stood in the front ranks throwing one hand grenade after the other into the British lines. Suddenly Wurth collapsed to the ground, severely wounded by enemy fire. He was just one of many men who became casualties in the close fighting; the number of troops from the *Sturm Abteilung* still on their feet diminished with each passing minute.

No further reinforcements could reach the men from RIR 111 because the British had also placed a wall of artillery fire around the German positions. While the German guns attempted to block off the British trenches in the same manner, the fire was not as strong or as effective as their opponents. Because of this, the British could send reinforcements to the threatened sector and tip the balance in their favor. In the subsequent unequal fighting, part of what had been recaptured by RIR 111 was lost once again.

When the fighting eventually died down, it was time to take stock of the situation. RIR 111 and the opposing British troops had both suffered numerous casualties in the fight for the *Auto Graben*. In the end, the Germans were in possession of approximately 50 meters of this trench, or, more accurately, 50 meters of what had once been a trench. The position had been utterly destroyed in the artillery and mine fire and was barely recognizable as a former trench. It now consisted of a row of shell craters that were roughly joined together.

The rest of the surrounding positions looked no better. The *Staufen Stellung* and the subsequent sector were all heavily damaged. All of the painstakingly created defensive facilities were virtually leveled once again. Many of the trenches that still existed were barely waist deep. Worst of all, the trench garrison was completely mixed together and the men were extremely exhausted. Despite the fatigue, many of the men who had survived managed to inform their families that they were still alive and unharmed.

In the field, October 13, 1916
My Dear Emil!
Only brief greetings with the message that I am still well. This will mean much. Yesterday we rejected three violent attacks by the English. This night we captured a trench piece, but had to give it up again because of the heavy artillery fire. The very first day we lost about 300 men. Despite all of this, I feel honored. I think of you, your Erwin. [4]

The neighboring III/R110 used all of the available men in the battalion to improve its position on 12 October. Dugout corridors were cleared of earth and debris, opening them up for use by the men if the interiors were still intact. The depth of the trenches and connected crater positions was increased as much as possible and a connection route to the second trench and the *Serben Weg* up to the *Strassburger Steig* was dug out again. The hard work was constantly being disrupted by British artillery fire that was being directed upon the work parties by the seemingly endless enemy observation aircraft that flew overhead from dawn until dark.

Throughout 12 October *Feste Schwaben* was continuously bombarded with shrapnel, while the *Hansa Stellung* was covered in heavy caliber shells. Under cover of darkness, in the night to the 13th the 6/R110 created a new trench that ran from the *Hansa Stellung* to the *Artillerie Mulde*, which would be utilized to house support troops for *Feste Schwaben*.

One further platoon of this company was inserted between the 5th and 7/R110 at *Feste Schwaben* because the casualties suffered by the 5/R110 had increased substantially.

The attempt by one platoon of the 8/R110 to develop a connection trench between the *Schlüter Graben* with RIR 111 to the left of the regiment failed as a result of the heavy artillery fire that was placed on *Feste Schwaben* and on *Feste Staufen* throughout the entire night. Three platoons of the 8/R110 simultaneously worked on a new communication trench running from the *Hansa Stellung* to *Feste Schwaben*. By the end of the night, a shallow trench approximately 200 meters long had been created.

13 October

13 October was a quiet day by Somme standards. While there were no enemy infantry attacks, the men in RIR 110 were unable to perform any work on the defenses because of the extremely active enemy observation aircraft, tethered observation balloons and the heavy bombardment of the *Hansa Stellung* and *Feste Schwaben*. All of the approach routes leading into the regimental sector were also under very strong artillery fire.

Darkness afforded some protection against enemy observers who were directing the intense bombardment of the German positions and the artillery fire had lessened somewhat. The men crawled out of their shelters and set off to work once more. During the night to 14 October, 150 meters of the *Schlüter Graben* was dug out by one platoon from the 8/R110. Two platoons of the 6/R110 worked on the new trench running from the *Hansa Stellung*

Filling in a massive crater behind a 7.7cm field gun position, 6/RFAR 26, October 1916. (*Die 26.(Württembergische) Reserve-Division im Weltkrieg 1914-1918*)

to the *Artillerie Mulde* that had been destroyed the day before, while the rest of the 8/R110 started work on a communication trench to *Feste Schwaben*. However, by the following morning, the garrison in the *Schlüter Graben* had to be withdrawn again because the men did not have any protection against the heavy British artillery fire that recommenced once it had become light.

The heavy fighting for the *Auto Graben* on the previous day had apparently exhausted both sides and no new attacks were undertaken by the British or the Germans. There was the normal sniping, machine gun fire and occasional hand grenade but nothing more. The I/R111 remained in the front line throughout the day. Later in the afternoon, good news spread through the trenches, the battalion would be relieved during the night. Now there was some hope for the survivors that they might actually live to see another day. As anticipated, the I/R111 was relieved by the II/R111 in the hours of darkness and the few surviving men of the I Battalion slowly made their way to the rear through the shattered terrain in expectation of warm food and a comfortable and safe place to rest.

14 October

The relief of RIR 111 was successfully accomplished in small squads despite fierce enemy bombardments. On the morning of 14 October the 8/R111 under *Leutnant* Bier was in the *Staufen Graben* in place of the 2/R111 and the 6/R111 under *Leutnant* Wittwer was in *Feste Staufen*. The border of the sector connecting to the III/R111 wasextended on the left until it was 50 meters east of the *Stump Weg* in order to provide assistance with the defense of *Feste Staufen*. The 5/R111, that had already been heavily involved in the fighting, was assembled in the northern part of *Feste Staufen* in place of the 1/R111, and the 7/R111 was located in the *Lach Weg* as support. However, instead of moving to warm, clean billets further in the rear, the companies of the I/R111 occupied the *Grandcourt Riegel* on both sides of the *Kirchhof Mulde*. *Hauptmann* Steffan remained in his sector and retained leadership over the companies of the II Battalion. The I/R111 was taken on by *Hauptmann* von Stockhausen who had returned to the regiment following a furlough home.

On the early morning of 14 October strong British artillery fire, including gas shells, fell across the regimental sector, especially on the left wing of the regiment, where the densely occupied *Leiling Stollen* was located. The fire become so intense by the *Leiling Stollen* that one half of a platoon of the 12/R111 was moved further back into the barely started tunnels of the new intermediate position.

Reports from observers stated that the enemy was filling up his trenches. The German support batteries were notified of this and they opened annihilation fire against the enemy positions. During the bombardment, a British ammunition depot in a sap located in front of the 12/R111 was set on fire and burned fiercely. At 4 p.m. strong enemy attack waves advanced against *Feste Schwaben* and against the front of RIR 111 despite the German defensive artillery fire. The result was the same as 9 October: the attack broke down completely along the entire frontage of the regiment. The only place where the enemy made any headway was at the projecting corner of *Feste Staufen* where the opposing sides became involved in a bitter hand grenade fight.

The fighting surged back and forth as it consumed more and more men on both sides. The men from RIR 111 soon gained the upper hand, repulsed the enemy back and managed to penetrate into the *Auto Graben*. Then, the fortunes of war changed once more and the British, who were apparently receiving a constant flow of fresh troops, regained the upper hand and retook some of the ground they had lost. Finally, the British succeeded in penetrating into the sap head of *Feste Staufen* on both flanks and cut off the defenders located there.

Immediate counterattacks by the remnants of the 6/R111 with *Unteroffiziers* Hermannsa and Haus, a few Groups from the 5/R111 under *Leutnant* Meichelt and Sergeant Schwöbel, supported from parts of the 8/R111 under *Feldwebel* Hirschauer from their position in the *Staufen Graben*, formed a barrier against any further enemy penetration into the German defenses and even forced the British back in places. Despite all of this effort, they did not succeed in making it through to the platoons of the 6/R111 that were trapped inside the sap head. As a result, a large part of the 6/R111 along with the company leader, *Leutnant* Wittwer, and *Leutnant* Strässle, ended up as prisoners. By the evening of the 14th the final result of the fighting was that the British had managed to push their barricades forward about 50 meters.

The largest part of *Feste Staufen* was successfully defended by the last Groups of the 5th and 6/R111, which received reinforcements from platoons of the 4th and 7/R111 While the enemy attack against the front of RIR 111 was generally unsuccessful, the enemy was able to firmly established themselves on the right in *Feste Schwaben* and, from this position, threaten the right flank of the regiment. RIR 111 now had no connection with the neighboring troops on the right or the left flank. The new front ran in a northwestern direction, approximately along the route of the *Hansa Riegel*.

Later in the evening, the 8/R111, with *Leutnant* Bier, though already wounded succeeded in establishing contact with the *Staufen Graben* once again. In order to support this company in its dangerous situation, parts of the 2/R111 were moved to the right into the *Lach Weg*, and one platoon of the *Bau* Company brought fresh supplies of hand grenades up to the front. The command in the right sector now passed to *Hauptmann* Bumiller while *Hauptmann* Steffan assumed the leadership over the III/R111 in the left sector.

For one week, all parts of RIR 111 were exposed to extremely difficult conditions during the fighting. The leaders, like the men who were inside shell holes or in makeshift shelters day and night, were continuously exposed to enemy projectiles and were constantly under the highest levels of tension from the threat of an attack. In order for there to be any possibility of preserving the fighting strength of the garrison, dugout construction was undertaken with with frantic eagerness, but progress was still slow. Enemy shells during the day often destroyed the hard work of the previous night. The men shouted at the carrying parties 'bring wooden frames, only wooden frames!'

The exhausted carrying parties did all that was humanly possible to supply their comrades at the front. As the enemy fire continued, it also became even more difficult to bring construction materials and food to the front line. The field kitchens could barely make it through the fire barrier and one that served the 11/R111 had already been destroyed from a direct hit. With the reduction in food supplies, many of the men had to resort to eating their iron rations.

In the course of the morning the enemy was showing signs of increased activity according to reports made by observers in RIR 110. At times four to six aircraft flew above the position; four tethered observation balloons appeared above the enemy lines. The British artillery fire, an ever present scourge, appeared to die down during the midday hours. Then, when observers in RIR 110 noticed that British troops were filling up the trenches opposite RIR 111, a call was made to the rear on one of the few working telephone lines, requesting artillery barrage fire on the enemy trench. At 3.45 p.m. the observation officer from RIR 110 reported an enemy gas attack upon the neighboring sector, west of the village of Beaucourt, north of the Ancre where RIR 55 was located. Five minutes later, at 3.50 p.m. drum fire began to fall upon *Feste Schwaben* and *Feste Staufen*, and within minutes, an enemy infantry attack commenced against *Feste Schwaben*.

At 4 p.m. red light signals climbed up into the sky from *Feste Schwaben*, following which, German artillery barrage fire fell from the *Meisengasse* up to *Feste Staufen*. All communications with *Feste Staufen*, including the telephone lines, had been cut off. The enemy barrage fire came from the direction of Beaumont, essentially from the rear of the strongpoint, making it even more destructive than usual. Reports from artillery observers stated that British troops could be seen pressing into *Feste Staufen* while red and white light signals could be seen repeatedly ascending into the sky from the *Feste*.

Between 4 and 5 p.m. the British fire on *Feste Staufen* gradually decreased and then shifted suddenly until the full fury of the enemy artillery fire now fell upon *Feste Schwaben* and the entire regimental sector up to the north of the Ancre. The situation existing in *Feste Staufen* and *Feste Schwaben* was completely unknown to the commanders in the rear; the damaged telephone wires could not be repaired, the runner service had broken down in the heavy shell fire and the smoke and debris thrown into the air prevented any blinker signals from being seen.

At the same time that both German strongpoints were being attacked, the British also attacked the German lines further west following a severe artillery fire raid. The left wing of the enemy assault troops successfully advanced across the *Münstergasse* that was occupied by the 5/R110.

All of a sudden, enemy troops penetrated into the eastern part of the *Strassburger Steige* where the 9/R110 was positioned. The British troops had apparently made good use of the cover provided by the numerous deep shell craters to approach the German position unseen, finally arriving at a point immediately in front of the German trench. *Leutnant der Reserve* Weiss spotted the advancing enemy troops directly in front of his position at the last moment and immediately alerted his platoon. However, it was already too late to prevent the British from penetrating into the trench.

Leutnant der Reserve Weiss and his Half Platoon leader *Vizefeldwebel* Albrecht were both wounded early in the attack rendering the platoon leaderless. Despite this, the platoon poured out of their dugouts and shelters and prevented any further advance by the enemy to the west. About 90 meters of trench west of the *Münstergasse* was lost to the enemy. The remaining part of the *Strassburger Steige* lay under strong fire until 6.30 p.m., which prevented any connection to the other platoons of the 9/R110.

It was the 14th of October 1916 ... ... For three days we now lay opposite the Englishmen in *Feste Schwaben* near Thiepval – St. Pierre-Divion and waited at an especially dangerous corner, at the commencement of new fighting for life and death.

However, besides the usual shell bombardment, until now we could determine 'nothing new from the enemy', a fact that we gladly exploited to restore the badly shot up position again as best we could. In the afternoon about 4 o'clock I sat in my so-called dugout, a few meters under the ground, at the left wing of my company with connection to the neighboring 5th Company, when suddenly my sentry in front of the dugout yelled down in a loud voice: '*Herr Leutnant* come up quickly, a gas attack!'

Killed by an artillery shell. (Author's collection)

With a jump I landed by the sentry with the gas mask in my hand and came directly to the right place and there was one of the greatest gas attacks I had ever seen before. Beyond the Ancre stream the terrain climbed gently and from out of our position we Germans, had a wonderful view of the enemy lines. My sentry was right. The English had employed a huge gas cloud attack. Heavy white, yellow clouds streamed out gas cylinders from a further line in an immense smoke screen and moved sluggishly, however unstoppable, over the German front in the rear terrain, between bursting gas shells and shrapnel and soon the gas alarm siren in the neighboring regiment sounded across to us. The German artillery hesitantly placed fire on it and we waited full of tension for the further development. With us, everything remained quiet, so eerily quiet that it was quite uncanny to me and I sent several orderlies through the trench to place it on alert. We knew the tactics of the English and we were able to make sure that we would not get greased. It also did not last long, because the English artillery showered us with drum fire that we heard and saw. Quickly, we dispersed into our dugout again and with the watch in hand, we now waited from minute to minute for the alarm cry of our sentries, however; nothing came of it. The whirlwind of fire continued to increase. Our sentry soon came crawling down to us and reported that above it only hailed like this from shells and shrapnel balls. However I must observe and so then I jumped up into the trench in an instant, stretched my nose above the cover towards the enemy, saw nothing and vanished again in full cover. Suddenly, I recognized in our own trench khaki-brown figures bent down behind a traverse with English steel helmets coming toward us, heavy sack of hand grenades over their shoulders, the rifles with fixed bayonet in their hands. Only the traverse and the rather shot up trench piece lying in front of us separated us from each other.

The terrible situation was recognized as fast as lightning – a shouting cry into the dugout- a jump to the traverse – one, two shots from the revolvers in the middle of the advancing Englishmen – bursting forth of a hand grenade – all without thought, purely mechanical however logically executed that in the fraction of a minute caused hesitation among the Englishmen and was sufficient, to withdraw again behind the protection of the traverse, meanwhile my men come up from out of the dugout with a few words of explanation and to cause a murderous hand grenade fire on the bewildered Englishman. Our hand grenades rained blow upon blow into the crowd of Englishmen who were stunned and who quickly withdrew and in no time our trench piece was free again, especially as my infuriated men pressed forward and went bodily against the Englishmen so that it was such a delight.

However they had also soon assembled themselves again and recovered from the first shock. Already the first English egg hand grenades came flying, already they crashed on the embankment and in the trench piece in front of us. Soon a regular large hand grenade fight was taking place and suddenly one comes flying directly at me, already it fell on the embankment, rolls down, directly at me, I throw myself backward, sliding back. A crash and already I sensed a piercing pain in the left shoulder. Up again and under the circumstances, the fellows should get to know us. I feel nothing more, we throw ourselves into the shell holes on the right and on the left, blocked off from the trench and rush forward into the next shell crater, always on, always frantic, as if intoxicated. However, gradually the pain became noticeable, not only in the shoulder, also on the chin, the left upper and lower leg. The left hand with the revolver sinks down powerless, blue rings form, circling before my eyes, weakness grabs me and when I see my faithful *Vizefeldwebel* Albrecht at this critical moment beside me, I hand over the command to him and attempted to walk back slowly to the dressing station dugout of the battalion, in the knowledge that the Englishmen who were attempting to roll up our trench had been prevented and the lost trench piece was already recaptured by our own company again and quite a bit of the neighboring company, and, had been cleared from the enemy. The fighting had lasted over an hour, no wonder that the blood loss and nerve weakness made itself so noticeable now. However it still went entirely well and even worse for wear, the approaching reserves kindled my courage again. When I informed the leader about which direction he should proceed, a heavy English shell crashes in close proximity and tears up my entire right hand. Looking at me ashen, my comrade wanted to support me before I fell over, however he must continue forward, to help the others until the last Englishman is outside again. Supported by a Medical soldier he takes me to the bank of a trench, takes a belt from the bag, allows my artery to be bound up and from the gigantic red cloth bag of the Medical soldier (who I never forgot) applies an emergency pressure bandage; our bandage packets this time were on hand and had remained in the dugout. And now – I must still reach the Battalion. I staggered back and forth like a mad man through the crater terrain, instinctively I still knew the approximate direction and finally landed in front of the Battalion dugout, in front of the commander and waved and shouted as if I was possessed, I navigated over to him and after sufficient attempts, reported in a fairly military posture, unconscious, he caught me in his arms. *Leutnant der Reserve* Weiss [5]

Reinforced concrete shelter in the Staufen Graben. (Author's collection)

At 5.30 in the afternoon the I Battalion reported that Battalion Stephan (connection Battalion RIR 111) had asked for support because the enemy had penetrated into the western part of *Feste Staufen*. While all of these events were taking place in *Feste Schwaben*, the British had also advanced out of the southern end of the *Meisengasse* and attacked both German barricades at the end of the first and second trenches, therefore against the flank of the 10th and 11/R110. Platoon Hopf, which was holding the barricade in the first trench, had been quickly alerted to the enemy advance. While the enemy detachment, about 60 men strong, was forced to give way 50 meters from the first trench by the rapid rifle fire of Platoon Hopf, the enemy succeeded in temporarily penetrating into the eastern part of the second trench.

Because of the heavy fighting raging in *Feste Staufen* and in the *Staufen Graben*, and following repeated urgent pleas from RIR 111, two platoons from the 4/R110 were inserted by the 6/R111 as reinforcements at 6 p.m. Once in position, the men of RIR 110 immediately became involved in fierce hand grenade fighting against the enemy. At 6 p.m. a message from the 51st Infantry Brigade arrived at the regimental headquarters of RIR 110 indicating that apparently part of the *Strassburger Steige*, *Feste Schwaben*, and positions south of the *Hansa Stellung* and *Schlüter Graben* were in British hands. Despite this message, no additional supports were sent forward. An officer from the regimental staff who had been sent to meet with the commander of the II/R110 for orientation about the situation, returned at 7 p.m. with the report that it was not possible to make it through to the battalion headquarters because of the heavy barrage fire.

It was proving to be extremely difficult to transmit orders and messages in the confusing situation with all of the telephone lines cut in the shell fire and the long periods of time needed for runners to make their way through the badly damaged landscape and heavy fire, if they made it through alive at all. The first report from the II/R110 about the overall situation did not arrive at the Regimental headquarters until 7.25 p.m. Shortly afterwards, the telephone repair troops managed to restore the telephone connection with the neighboring battalion from RIR 55, located on the north shore of the Ancre. RIR 55 was then asked to send a runner to the headquarters of the III/R110 so that they could transmit an order that had been given to it through the telephone. Such lengthy and complicated detours were becoming the norm. The delays inherent in such methods of sending orders and messages proved to be very damaging as many of the orders and messages being sent were no longer applicable once they arrived at their final destination as the situation had already changed.

Under these difficult circumstances, the training and doctrine of the junior officers served the Germans well as took decisive action on their own initiative. *Feldwebel Leutnant* Aullen with the *Sturm Trupp* of the 8/R110, followed by the rest of the company, advanced in a counterattack against *Feste Schwaben*. However, because of the wall of barrage fire placed in front of the strongpoint, Aullen and his men could not reach their goal and he was forced to withdraw under heavy losses for the 8/R110. *Feldwebel Leutnant* Aullen was also among the men wounded during this attempt.

The attack by the 8/R110 clearly proved that a frontal attack against *Feste Schwaben* was hopeless under the current circumstances. Next, there was a proposal from the II/R110, to advance against *Feste Schwaben* from the *Artillerie Mulde* and the *Strassburger Steige* with the eventual goal of surrounding it. This proposal was the same as one put forth by *Leutnant der Reserve* Gutleben and attack orders were duly issued for all available units to participate in the attempt. The attack would include the 1st, 2nd and 9/R110 along with one platoon from Machine Gun Marksman Detachment 152 under the command of *Hauptmann* Humricht that was seconded for the attack to the II/R110.

The counterattack was planned as follows: The 1st and 2/R110 and Machine Gun Marksman Detachment 152 would advance from the *Artillerie Mulde* against the left corner of *Feste Schwaben*. The 8/R110 would advance against the front of *Feste Schwaben* and the 9/R110 would advance against the right corner. The signal for the attack would be the firing of one red and one green light ball, three times in a row. In consideration of the extreme difficulty in transmitting messages and orders, *Major* Schröder should have taken the opportunity of making his preparations and setting a specific time for the attack so that each group could receive the orders and get into their places concurrently in order to be ready.

Unfortunately, this was not the case. The time set for the attack came from the senior command and was scheduled for 12.15 a.m. This methodology, as with many previous late night attacks, had often proved to be disastrous. The orders for the attack did not reach the III/R110 until 11.30 p.m. and it would be impossible to have the 9/R110 in position, ready to start 45 minutes later. In anticipation of the attack, the 9/R110 was reinforced by one platoon from the 12/R110 under *Leutnant der Reserve* Götz and later by an additional platoon from the 11/R110 under *Vizefeldwebel* Müller.

The leader of the III/R110, *Hauptmann* von Borell, requested a one hour postponement of the attack to get his men into position. While this was considered a very reasonable request, it was contrary to the express orders by the division and the regimental commander refused the request as, in his opinion, the original order had to be obeyed.

The attack signal was given promptly at 12.15 a.m. but for one reason or another, it was not seen by part of the troops scheduled to attack, especially not by Company Hänlein.

Also, different detachments had still not reached their jumping off places by this time, and as such, the three pronged attack did not take place simultaneously as anticipate. The results were tragic and predictable. Without any coordination between the three assault groups, the enemy was able to concentrate all of his defensive fire against each individual part, therefore easily driving them all back, one by one, with heavy losses. With the increasing number of men being lost, preparations were made to throw the last reserves of the 28th Reserve Division into the battle.

Until now, the two regiments, RIR 110 and RIR 111 had shouldered the brunt of the fighting, while RIR 109 remained in the rear. Now, it was the turn of the former defenders of Montauban to take over the front line on the Somme once more.

At 6.30 p.m. on 14 October, the II/R109 in Sapignies was alarmed and received orders to march to Irles, where they would be under the 56th Reserve Infantry Brigade. After reaching Irles the 6th and 8/R109 received orders to move forward into the *Hansa Stellung* where they were placed under the command of the II/R110 while the battalion staff, 5th and 7/R109 moved to *Süd-I* by Grandcourt where they also came under the command of RIR 110. All of the companies were fully equipped with entrenching tools and the new steel helmets.

Finally the march begins. I walked there as the last one from the battalion. The fighting raged in the west and northwest. The drum fire raged. It sounded as if a loaded wagon drawn by 100 heavy horses traveled over a long, wooden bridge; the fighting and crashing all around becomes more like the rolling, surging sound of thunder. Now and then the individual, powerful shriek of a giant gun that sang differently sounded across; after that again the revolving, surging, crashing about, raged on. In the heavens, in the gray and black drifting clouds that rolled there like drift ice in the great west wind, is a constant glimmer and glitter from distant and nearby firing and impacts, continuous and restless like the shimmer of ghostly tubes in the changing current. And close on the horizon the light balls play. If you have already once watched a proficient downfall, as with the explosive downpour everyone dropped down, they now spring up again from the ground, jump up in a steep arc and again fall down! So climbed the light balls, glowing white, red, green, by the dozens, by the hundreds and falling down again in a full arc, and each sinking also excites new ones again that suddenly shoot up. The clouds divide, and from the wan moonlight cast from above lies Irles in front of us. An expression of untold nakedness lies on these ruins that are split apart. The houses are knocked open as with giant fists, they are missing the walls, the roof hangs at the nape like a smashed hat; here, along our path, lies the stones of the church, burst wide open.

In long spacing, man behind man, we hurry to that place. All is mute and gray in the moonlight like ghosts, Miraumont is destroyed. Here and there lay a dead nag and the odor of corpses wave over us there like an evil reminder of the lurking death.

At the end of the village an embankment runs crosswise to the road, high and wide. We follow in the protection of the embankment, while on the left of it the Ancre was connected with our path. A quaint brook between moonlit meadows, elms and shrubs in graceful groups. However there were huge water filled shell craters. Crater upon crater, and many thick elm trunks were sheered and torn apart. A route goes above it on the embankment; the shells move howling over us. There everyone probably thanks his good fortune that none impact and he is not conveyed into the Ancre swamp by the atmospheric pressure; because round craters gape, and the rails hang there like intestine out of a hacked corpse.

On a narrow beam bridge we go over the swamp, shining in the moonlight. On the road, past by destroyed wagons, horse cadavers, torn apart limbers, away past lost materials, wooden frames, ammunition boxes, then – finally having reached Grandcourt. *Feldunterarzt* Ganter, II/R109 [6]

15 October

Relief for the exhausted men of RIR 110 and RIR 111 was at hand. The III/R109 under the leadership of *Hauptmann* von Wolff, started to march out of Mory at 4.30 p.m. on the afternoon of 15 October, with assault packs and rations for six days. The battalion had orders to take back *Feste Schwaben* in the night from the 15th to the 16th. The command over the assault was given to *Hauptmann* Block, to which the III/R109, as well as five *Sturm Trupp* and eight *Flammenwerfer* were subordinate.

Because of numerous delays, from the receipt of ammunition to provisions, the companies did not arrive in *Grandcourt Ost* until 10.45 p.m. Once in *Grandcourt Ost*, the company leaders received the attack orders from *Hauptmann* von Wolff; however, due to the late hour and darkness, there was no possibility of becoming oriented to the terrain. The different companies would have to rely upon existing maps of the sector, most of which were completely outdated.

The companies moved forward at the quick march, in order to reach the different starting points called for in the orders and to be ready for the attack scheduled at 12 midnight. The *Flammenwerfer* that had been assigned to each detachment however, had not arrived yet. Three storm columns were prepared for the attack. The 10/R109 under the leadership of *Leutnant* Rösiger with one *Sturm Trupp* and two *Flammenwerfer* would attack the *Meisengasse-Münster Graben-Strassburger Steige-Feste Schwaben* line; the 12/R109 under the leadership of *Leutnant* Armbruster with two *Sturm Trupp* and three *flame Flammenwerfer* would proceed against the *Schwaben Riegel*; the 11/R109 under the leadership of *Leutnant* Ruf with one *Sturm Trupp* and two *Flammenwerfer* would be positioned at the *Lach Weg* and proceed from there against the triangle formed by the *Schlüter Graben-Hill 151-Schwaben Riegel*. The 9/R109 under the leadership of *Oberleutnant* Bürger with one *Sturm Trupp* and one *Flammenwerfer* were placed in the *Artillerie Mulde* as support for the attack and came under the control of *Hauptmann* von Wolff.

The password given for the attack was *Sonntag*. Since many of the *Flammenwerfer* had still not arrived at midnight, some of the detachments advanced without them. Additionally, not all of the detachments advanced as scheduled. With the lack of any telephone connections, the quick transmission of orders and reports was not possible. Some of the formations were not able to move quickly enough through the unfamiliar terrain because of the strong enemy artillery fire. With the failure of the three assault detachments proceeding at the same time, the momentum of the attack was destroyed. Instead of facing attacks from three directions simultaneously, the enemy was faced with only one detachment at a time and therefore the smaller threats could easily be parried by the British once again.

The 10/R109 was in St. Pierre-Divion with two *Flammenwerfer* in its possession;

however, only one of them was working. The 10th Company succeeded in advancing a great distance toward the British lines, in part across the open terrain. About 2.30 a.m. *Leutnant* Vorbach, as well as *Unteroffizier* Sauer, were placed out of action by enemy fire. As losses among the assault party increased during the advance, *Leutnant* Rösiger halted the men and took shelter in a badly damaged empty trench and evaluated his situation. After long consideration, he gave orders to retreat back into the protection of the tunnel at St. Pierre-Divion in order to avoid further unnecessary casualties. The primary reason given for the retreat was because the trench the men were sheltering in was under heavy enemy fire. If the opposing British troops added the fire from machine guns, this would only have caused comparatively higher losses. While this was the basis for the decision, the actual losses suffered by the 10/R109 were quite low, two men killed, one man missing, one officer and two men wounded. The attached *Sturm Trupp* had lost one man killed and four men wounded.

The losses in the 12/R109 after reaching the *Hansa Stellung* following the initial advance, were equally small; one man killed and one man slightly wounded. The men of the 12/R109 were unable to advance any further as a result of heavy enemy barrage fire falling in front of and behind their trench. As a result, the men were told to dig in at the upper part of the *Hansa Stellung*. When it became somewhat quieter, *Leutnant* Armbruster positioned at the head of his company, pushed forward up to the fork of the *Hansa Stellung* shortly before it joined with *Feste Schwaben*.

Now the company ran into unexpected obstacles, ones caused by German artillery fire. There were numerous shell craters opposite the men of the 12/R109 and they were as deep as a man and quite wide; all resulting from the German 21cm shells, known to the enemy as 'Jack Johnsons' because of the thick black smoke produced by the exploding shells. These deep, wide craters formed huge obstacles to any orderly advance. Man after man had to jump from one hole to another, an especially difficult task for the men carrying any heavy equipment.

Progress through the craters was slow and cumbersome and, with so few men in the assault detachment and the lack of any *Flammenwerfer,* the attack leaders doubted their ability to accomplish their tasks. The terrain was so badly shot up that no one could make out the former positions that had once existed there and the route to *Feste Schwaben* was completely obliterated. While the assault force made its way slowly through the cratered field, two enemy machine guns opened up and took the company under effective flanking fire. Now, any thought of continuing the advance in such heavy fire was considered pointless and the men were ordered to dig in where they were.

Finally, at 5 a.m., the two *Flammenwerfer* that had been missing when the attack had started showed up. With the arrival of these weapons, the 12/R109 decided to attempt the attack once again, however without any success. The odds were simply too heavily stacked in the favor of the British who could direct a great deal of fire against the small assaulting force. Once the latest German attack had been repulsed, it was the turn of the British to counterattack.

The enemy had no better luck than the men of the 12/R109 in the difficult terrain. The British troops were forced to withdraw under a constant hail of hand grenades and both sides settled down in their positions to evaluate the situation. The men of the 12/R109 were instructed to quickly connect their individual shell craters and create a makeshift defensive trench. Further attacks by the British were held down through artillery barrage fire from the German batteries supporting the attack. Later in the evening the company returned to the picket position it had started from. The losses for the day: three men killed, and *Vizefeldwebel* Freiburger severely wounded from being shot in the chest.

The 11/R109 pressed forward from *Grandcourt Süd* in the *Artillerie Mulde* under heavy artillery fire. The men were unable to participate in the attack scheduled for 12 midnight, because they did not first reach the starting point for the undertaking until 12.45 a.m. Hours passed before it was finally decided to attempt a second attack at 4 a.m. However, even this second planned attack did not take place by the 11/R109. The commander of the attached *Sturm Trupp* had orders, not to begin an attack until the *Flammenwerfer* with the neighboring assault company, 12/R109, had been observed being used. Since nothing could be seen of any *Flammenwerfer* activity by the 12th Company, the commander of the *Sturm Trupp* believed that the attack had been postponed and he decided to wait until they were deployed. Finally, at 6 a.m. the company leader, *Leutnant* Ruf, gave the order to dig in. An hour later the 11/R109 and attached *Sturm Trupp* were withdrawn to *Grandcourt Süd I*.

With all of the events taking place on the morning of 15 October, the participation of the 9/R109, was no longer required. The 8/R110 was then moved forward up to the mouth of the *Hansa Riegel* and awaited further orders there. The situation by RIR 110 was basically the same as experienced by RIR 109. The 6/R109 had received orders to support an attack by RIR 110 upon *Feste Schwaben*. Two platoons, Hainmüller and Willmann, were assigned to assist RIR 110 in the undertaking; however the two platoons were unable to establish any contact with RIR 110. It was doubtful that even with the addition of two platoons, the attack by RIR 110 would have had any success. The early morning assault was stopped cold by heavy British fire and no headway could be made against the entrenched enemy.

Despite the utter failure of every attack made on 15 October, division headquarters was considering another series of attacks at 5.30 a.m. on 16 October on *Feste Schwaben*. For this second attempt, RIR 111 would also participate in the advance. Several assault groups were prepared for the new attack. Group Humricht, consisting of the 1st, 2/R110 and parts of the III/R110 was in the *Artillerie Mulde* with a connection to the *Lach Weg*. Group Schröder consisting of the 6th and 8/R110 and 6th and 8/R109 would be on the right of Group Humricht, with the 9/R110 located in the *Strassburger Steige*.

When the failed attacks of 15 October were evaluated, it was determined that the assault units had been given insufficient time to become orientated for the attack. The officers and men lacked any familiarity with the terrain and the attacking troops were greatly fatigued from the long advance and from carrying the heavy assault kit. There was no communications between the different units because of the extremely difficult terrain that was literally inundated with numerous shell craters and the absence of sufficient artillery support before the attack. All of these reasons had prevented a coordinated advance thereby minimizing any possibility of success.

However, there was at least one place where the Germans had been successful. In connection with the latest attack by RIR 109 in the night to 16 October, *Leutnant* Beck and *Vizefeldwebel* Hirschauer with a *Sturm Trupp* from the 7/R109 pressed forward against a lost trench piece and were able to recapture 20-30 meters of the crater terrain from the enemy. While only a small gain, it was seen as a notable success.

Allzufrüh, Du tapferer Streiter
Fällst Du von des Todes Hand,
Auf dem Feld des Ruhms, der Ehre
Ferne in dem Feindesland
Ausgelitten, ausgerungen,
Hat Dein gutes, edles Herz
Dein gedenkend steh'n wir weinend
Und gebeugt vom tiefen Schmerz
Schlaf in Ruhe, schlaf in Frieden
Fern auf fremder weiter Au,
Bis der Herr Dich einstens wieder
Ruft zur großen Heeresschau.

M. LIEHNER'S HOFBUCHDRUCKEREI u. m. H. H. SIGMA (INGEN

Zur frommen Erinnerung
im Gebete an
Eugen Schlegel
Musketier im Res.-Inf.-Reg. Nr. 111
geb. am 26. August 1896
gefallen am 16. Okt. 1916 durch einen
Granatschuß bei Grandcourt (Nordfr.)

Gebet.

Vater der Barmherzigkeit und Gott alles
Trostes, erbarme Dich De nes Dieners **Eugen,**
der für sein Vaterland gefallen ist. Fern von
der Heimat liegt er begraben, doch Du, o Vater,
sei ihm nahe durch Deine Liebe. Vergib ihm die
Vergehung n. laß ihm alle zeitlichen Sünden-
strafen nach, lohne seinen Tod, den er für das
Vaterland erduldet hat, mit dem ewigen Leben,
schmücke ihn mit dem Siegeskranz des treuen
Soldaten und gib uns allen die Freude des
Wiedersehens im Himmel. Durch Christus, unsern Herrn. Amen. Vater unser.
Mein Jesus Barmherzigkeit!   (300 Tg. Abl.)
Barmherziger Jesus, gib ihm die ewige Ruhe.
(7 Jahre, 7 Quadr.)
Süßes Herz Mariä sei meine Rettung!
(300 Tg. Abl.)

Killed by an artillery shell. (Author's collection)

16 October

The time on the Somme for the men of RIR 110 was almost at an end. Plans were in place for 17 October to have the II and III/R109 take over the positions held by RIR 110 and to allow the exhausted regiment to be relieved. Until then, there was still one more attack to take place and, as a result, for many in RIR 110, the relief was one day too late.

At 5.30 a.m. the attack began in accordance with orders. On the left wing *Leutnant der Reserve* Hofheinz with parts of the I Battalion advanced and succeeded in penetrating into the *Schwaben Riegel* moving through the position up to the old battalion dugout. Individual detachments from Group Schröder made spirited attacks over and over, however they were thrown back due to enemy machine gun and infantry fire. Additionally, the volume of enemy fire, resulted in a large part of the troops from the 6/R109 and 8/R110 being unable to withdraw into the *Hansa Stellung*; they remained scattered across the battlefield in shell holes for the rest of the day and, on the slope in front of the enemy position.

Because Group Schröder had failed to make any headway, the success achieved by *Leutnant der Reserve* Hofheinz and his men had to be abandoned. Hofheinz had been counting on support from the 6/R109 and when this did not take place, Hofheinz called for his men to withdraw from their position and return to the starting place; *Feste Schwaben* remained in enemy hands.

Following this failed attempt to recapture *Feste Schwaben*, the troops assumed the following positions: the picket positions on the left wing were occupied by men from the 1st and 3/R110, similarly the connection between them and the dugouts in the *Artillerie Mulde*. Parts of the 2nd and 3/R110 were in the *Hansa Stellung*, the 8th and 6/R109 were in the newly dug out trench running from the *Artillerie Mulde* to the *Hansa Stellung*; the 6/R110 and parts of the 8/R110 held the *Serben Weg*.

After the unsuccessful attacks in the morning, the British displayed undertook active aerial observation and in the afternoon, strong artillery fire fell upon the German positions, without the enemy making any attempt to attack. The Germans suspected that their repeated attacks during the night and the morning hours had somehow prevented the enemy from coming out of his newly captured positions. More likely, the British infantry were busy consolidating their gains while their artillery fire helped prevent the Germans from attacking again.

In the course of the night the remnants of the I and II/R110 were finally relieved by the II/R109 under *Major* Dunklenberg. The two battalions moved toward the rear and were then placed in the *Beaucourt Riegel* west of Grandcourt. Here they found the Other Ranks of the 8/R110 that had spent the day in shell craters in front of the enemy position. The regimental commander of RIR 109 now arrived and took over the Grandcourt Sector with two of his battalions. The III/R110 located in St. Pierre-Divion remained subordinate to him.

On 16 October the regimental staff, I and II/R110 moved to the rear to Behagnies and Sapigny and received billets in these villages. The weak remnants of the battalions would have little time to rest after their long ordeal. The men were scheduled to dig new trenches in Sapigny on the following day.

The idea of recapturing *Feste Schwaben* had not been abandoned despite the recent setbacks. A new attack was attempted by portions of RIR 109 on 16 October to recover *Feste Schwaben*, it too failed. Following this latest attack, the *Strassburger Steige* up to the *Serben Weg* had to be evacuated. The southern part of the *Strassburger Steige* was still occupied by the 9/R110, reinforced by one platoon from the 11/R110. The 10/R110 and two thirds of the 11/R110 had previously held the position until being relieved. Part of the 12/R110 lay in the second trench, part of this company was in the *Biber Kolonie*.

17 October

17 October was a very quiet day in comparison to the previous week. Despite continued artillery fire, the men tried to rest when not working on the position. One of the only notable events occurred when *Oberstleutnant* von Baumbach assumed the command over the Grandcourt sector.

18 October

Work on improving the position continued through the night of 17/18 October. RIR 109 worked feverishly on the creation of a new *Schwaben Riegel*. While working on the new positions, the trench garrison could only find refuge in *Karnickellöcher* that had been dug into the trench wall. As these were simply earth holes without any type of support, men were often buried as a result of nearby exploding shells.

On the evening of 18 October the I/R109 moved into the position under *Hauptmann* Dahlke. The 1st and 2/R109 were placed in the *Beaucourt Riegel*, the 3/R109 in the *Artillerie Mulde* and the 4/R109 in the tunnel of St. Pierre-Divion, where the battle headquarters of the battalion was also located.

At the same time that the men were hard at work creating new positions or simply trying to restore the older ones, small scale fighting continued. In the early morning hours of 18 October, RIR 111 sent out bombing parties under *Vizefeldwebel* Volk and men assembled from the II/R111. These bombing parties attacked both enemy barricades in the western *Sappen Gräben* under the cover of fog and darkness. They managed to force the British back approximately 30 meters at both barricades following intense hand grenade battles. Later in the night, further small scale attacks were conducted in a similar manner and they managed to capture a few more meters of the badly damaged trench. However the meager portion of the trench recovered in these actions also sapped the strength of the regiment as each attack resulted in irreplaceable losses.

It soon became very evident to the men in RIR 111 that their small, local attacks were insignificant in comparison to what the enemy had been throwing against them in the last few days. The bombing raids, while capturing small sections of trench, would do little to deter the British from continuing their attacks. From all indications, the British appeared to be planning major new assaults in the near future in order to capture this vital portion of the German line.

The British also appeared to have an unlimited supply of ammunition, judging by the constant heavy artillery fire that fell across the German positions day and night. New enemy batteries were identified by the observers as having joined in the fighting. Enemy aircraft that were flying over the German positions at low altitudes continued to increase in numbers, so many more that the German squadrons had no chance of disrupting their operations.. The garrison of the German front line sent back numerous reports of encounters with large British patrols who were clearly attempting to locate weak points by probing the German defenses across the entire line.

19 October

All of the next day and night, 19 October, the men in RIR 109 worked almost exclusively on restoring the badly damaged position. The shelters used by the men had advanced slightly from the *Karnickellöcher*. Now there were a few dugout entrances covered with thin sheet metal. Unfortunately, these shelters were actually not much of an improvement over the *Karnickellöcher*. They were not deep enough to adequately protect the men from enemy artillery fire and the entrances were constantly being crushed by direct hits from high explosive shells, killing or wounding everyone inside. Heavy enemy artillery fire fell almost constantly on the men the entire time that they were working.

Indications of an impending enemy attack continued to grow as the days passed. On 19 October, observers in the III/R111 reported seeing the enemy entrenching far in front of their position as well as in front of the neighboring sector that was being held by *Landwehr* IR 74. *Landwehr* IR 74 had only recently taken over the trenches in place of the neighboring Marine Infantry Regiment 2. In order to determine exactly what the enemy was up to, a patrol under *Vizefeldwebel* Hilpert with one *Unteroffizier* and 10 men from the 9/R111 crept out into no man's land to get a better look at the enemy's activity.

The patrol quickly realized that the British were working closer to both German sectors in order to reduce the distance needed for the attack waves to cross no man's land. Very soon afterward, the patrol also determined that machine guns had been positioned inside the newly created enemy trenches. All of this information indicated that the enemy was expanding his front to the east and it was only a matter of time before a new attack began.

Armed with this new intelligence, it was all the more urgent that the Intermediate position behind the left sector, between the *Stump Weg* and *Köhlerpfad,* be made defensible. The I/R111, which during the entire day lay at the eastern slope of Grandcourt and in the *Stall Mulde* as the regimental reserve, now worked on the *Staufen Riegel* throughout the

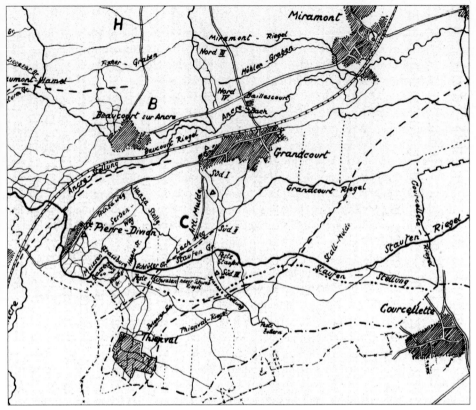

Thiepval-Grandcourt Sector

night. The companies were replaced in the *Grandcourt Riegel* by Reserve *Jäger* Battalion 13. The III/R111 also created a new barricade protected by thick wire entanglements in the *Köhlerpfad*, while the 5th and 7/R111 attempted to establish a connection between the sap by *Feste Staufen* and the *Stump Weg*.

The batteries on both sides continued to fire continuously throughout this period. The German guns attempted to protect all of the work being performed by the infantry, and made every attempt to silence the constantly increasing British fire but without much success. They had too few guns and were spread very thin across a wide sector. The numerous British guns continued to systematically destroy all of the positions created by RIR 111 and the other units.

British pilots could easily observe the lively activity inside the German trenches and directed the fire of more and more batteries against them. The constant enemy shell fire made the work very difficult and each passing hour brought more losses to RIR 111. As if the situation could not get worse, it started to rain. The numerous shell holes quickly became filled with mud and water and foot traffic inside the trenches was almost impossible as the men sank deeper and deeper into the slimy mud. Still, this could be also be an advantage as the enemy would have to cross open ground in any attack and the enemy infantry would be vulnerable as the men also became bogged down in the thick morass.

20 October

On 20 October, the southern part of the *Meisengasse* was ordered to be cleared of the enemy by a surprise attack. Four *Sturm Abteilung* from RIR 110, each containing one leader and ten men had been carefully chosen for the task. They would creep forward, out of the German position and from the barricade near the *Meisengasse* under the cover of darkness. Once in position, the medium *Minenwerfer* would fire several shots into the enemy trenches, at which time the *Sturm Abteilung* would enter the British position. Reserve troops would follow the attack; carrying materials to create a new barricade as well as bringing up ammunition, hand grenades and other supplies the men needed. After delivering their loads, they would join the assault groups inside the enemy trench.

This well-prepared plan failed at the start because of one man's refusal to obey orders. The men in the *Sturm Abteilung* had been given strict orders to advance toward the enemy position only by crawling along the ground so the enemy sentries would not see them in the darkness. One man, who apparently had a great dislike of wet, muddy ground, advanced by bending over at the waist and by moving in leaps and jumps.

The British sentries quickly spotted his silhouette in the dark sky and alerted the trench garrison. As the raiding parties came closer to the British position they were suddenly met by a hail of machine gun fire and hand grenades. It quickly became evident that the attack could not proceed in the face of such fierce opposition and the signal to withdraw was given. The *Sturm Abteilung* managed to withdraw from the firefight and return to the German lines with two men killed and ten men wounded. It is not known if the troublesome soldier who gave away the attack was among the casualties.

Meanwhile, the men in RIR 111 continued to work on their defenses and constantly wondered just when the British would attack next. The men in the regiment suddenly received very good news and could breathe a sigh of relief when orders arrived at headquarters in the morning of 20 October that the regiment was being replaced. The long awaited relief would begin later in the night when one battalion from IR 94 would relieve the I/R111. The remaining battalions would be relieved shortly afterward, each by a corresponding battalion from IR 94.

21 October

While the men in RIR 111 were enjoying the feeling that comes with the expectation of being relieved from a dangerous position, the men in RIR 109 would remain in the thick of it for some time to come. On 21 October a new attack was ordered to recapture *Feste Schwaben*. The I/R109 was assigned to execute this attack and had been allowed two days and nights to prepare for it. The 3rd and 4/R109 were designated as the assault companies. During the preparation time, the British position was explored by patrols, relay posts were created, ammunition and medical supplies were stockpiled at convenient locations and the timetable for the attack was finalized. Everything possible was being done in this short period of time to ensure success.

At 5.45 a.m. the 3/R109 began its attack against *Feste Schwaben* after being reinforced by *Flammenwerfer* and specialized *Stosstrupps*. The attack was proceeding as planned and the 3/R109 succeeded in occupying the *Schlüter Graben*, as well as a small part of the *Schwaben Riegel*. Then problems began, when the 3/R109 could not establish any connection with the 4/R109 that had concurrently advanced from the *Strassburger Steige*. This assault included some men from the newly formed and recently trained

Sturmabteilung assigned to the 28th Reserve Division. The men in the *Sturmabteilung* had received their *sturm* training near Cambrai and were excited about the prospect of putting their knowledge to use. By utilizing these specialty troops, it was hoped that the plan to recapture *Feste Schwaben* would be successful despite the anticipated strong enemy resistance.

On 21 October from 1.00 a.m. to 5 a.m. we left our location that lay about 40 kilometers behind the front, we reached the ordered position in the front in the Sector of RIR 109 and were still able to get a few hours of rest in one of the few dugouts that had survived the drum fire, although it was very cramped. At exactly 5 p.m., after our artillery fire on the trench taken by the British had been reinforced, we moved – 16 assault troops, behind a company of RIR 109 – and we worked our way forward until we were close up by the sentry post in the sap without becoming noticed by the enemy. The latter, two bearded Canadians, were dealt with by us after brave resistance, and now we went further, first the *Flammenwerfer* of the *Guard Pioniers*, against which the Tommy paid heed to. Our well-aimed hand grenades we threw made them go back further, so that already, after scarcely half an hour, we had reached our attack goal, '*Feste Schwaben*'.

Unfortunately, for our own security, we blew up all of the dugouts here by means of explosive charges, because the garrison did not come up after our invitation to give themselves up, not the consequences we wanted to achieve. During this time we received machine gun fire from the left flank that straightaway a few of my man fell victim to. We dammed off the barely chest deep trench toward the left, smoked the machine gun nest with well-aimed stick grenades and began to make ourselves at home. It worked out now that the enemy was not content and pelted us proficiently with Disk grenades, but most of these also went too short or too far. Anyway, I had not observed any losses within my sector from these hand grenades. However, both *Flammenwerfer* were presumably knocked out by our artillery firing short now and then, and also our musician with the Light pistol was missing, so that we lacked the possibility of communicating with our artillery. After some time the noise of fighting to the right of us had died down more and more attracted my attention and finally, from the neighboring troops, *Flammenwerfer*, etc. altogether there was nothing further was observed. In the assumption that the latter rolled up the trench to the right in accordance with the mission, I ran with two men of my squad around the next traverse. To our astonishment we saw ourselves opposite an English double sentry post after a few steps. The Tommys were not a little dumfounded and stared at us several seconds, without being able to bring themselves to a decision. In want of other weapons – we had completely used up our ammunition – I gathered a handful of earth up and threw it at the English sentry, who meanwhile – visibly nervous – fell to his knees in front of us.

We used this unexpected pause by the enemy- we assault troops were definitely not made like this apparently still inexperienced chap – to quickly warn those around us, that is to say, to walk back around the traverse. The sight, which now offered itself to us, was frightening. Meanwhile, the Englishmen were in the trench piece that had been occupied by us, after they had shot down the garrison, and at the same time killed everyone who still lived, yet our poor comrades, by waving cloths and other gestures that are recognized as indicating surrender, made it known that they wanted to yield. Under this impression the three of us quickly jumped out of the trench with determination, to reach our exit-position again, however we were immediately taken under fire. I received a dull blow against the right thigh that threw me headlong into a deep shell crater. The leg was shattered. A second hit struck me squarely in the left upper arm, also coming from a rifle or machine gun bullet. Well wasn't that cheerful; lying helpless in a deep hole half filled with muddy water a few meters in front of the enemy, without the prospect of being found by our side and being able to become saved – therefore either I would allow myself be dealt with by the increasingly wild Tommys or to slowly die of thirst and to starve!

First of all, I put on both of my field dressing bandage packets as best I could and lit myself a cigarette. I had completely drunk all of the water out of my canteen before. I had no food. Suddenly I heard noises behind me. I looked up and saw two of our men, who quickly took cover in my shell hole against machine gun fire, which swept over us. They recognized me immediately and promised to carry me carefully and that I would be fetched after the onset of darkness. After that, they crawled out, one after the other and ran further. I look at my watch and firmly determine that it was eight thirty in the morning; therefore I could still have all sorts of experiences up to the onset of darkness. However not many came to pass, apart from a number of our heavy shells and shrapnel, which smashed in my proximity. Once a lead ball flew towards me and hit my right foot however without penetrating it. The Tommys in front of me worked in his trench, and I heard quite clearly, how the men talked. The smoke of their tobacco pipes penetrated up to me also, and still after months I suppose the smell of scented tobacco genuinely increased my memories about my situation at that time.

The day passed faster than I expected; I might have also slept many hours. The suffering from thirst was indescribable. However now, because it was dark, I hoped to become collected soon. What all went through my head in these hours I no longer know today. *Unteroffizier* W. Liebrich, 1/R111, *Sturmabteilung* 28th Reserve Division [7]

The attack by the neighboring 4/R109 had not gone smoothly. The men in the 4/R109 advanced at the scheduled time and unexpectedly ran into a trench that was filled with British troops. The enemy trench garrison immediately opened lively rifle fire and threw hand grenades into the ranks of the attacking Germans. When it became known in the rear that the 4/R109 had run into stiff opposition, parts of the 2/R109 were sent forward as reinforcements. Even with the extra men, it quickly proved to be impossible to continue the attack and the men were ordered to return to their exit positions. Shortly after the 4/R109 had withdrawn, several strong British patrols followed after them, which were quickly repulsed at the barricade. Immediately following the patrols, a British bayonet attack took place by a larger force; this too was repulsed.

While the attack by the 4/R109 had stalled, the 3/R109 was able to continue its attack and left the shelter of the *Schwaben Riegel* and moved in the direction of Thiepval. The 3/R109 quickly ran into strong opposition from British reinforcements that had moved up to the front line from the enemy rear. The British counterattacked and forced the 3/R109 back into the *Schwaben Riegel*. The losses of the 3/R109 were very high as a result of this fighting. The remnants of the company, approximately one platoon in strength

(Author's collection)

occupied the *Schwaben Riegel* once again and from there, fended off several more British counterattacks.

Then, disaster struck the survivors of the 3/R109. The British were able to set up a machine gun that flanked their position in the *Schwaben Riegel*. The heavy machine gun fire decimated the defenders so much so that the few men still capable of fighting could no longer resist the British counterattacks approaching them from three sides. The 3/R109 was overrun by the British masses, and whoever had not been killed, ended up as a prisoner.

For one soldier in RIR 109 who had survived the fighting on the Somme on 1 July and the months of trench duty in the Champagne, his war had come to an end.

> All of a sudden our artillery stopped and everything was quiet. I jumped into a big shell hole and 2 young fellows from a Saxon regiment jumped in, too. They said, 'we're going to go back,' and I said, 'you don't go back, they're going to kill you. We'll stay 'til dark and then we'll go back.' No. they wouldn't stay. Both were killed. One fell in the hole and the other one fell outside. When I looked up, 3 or 4 Englishmen were standing there and told me to put the rifle down. I did and that was the end of the fighting for me. Emil Goebelbecker, RIR 109 [8]

The large-scale enemy attack that had been anticipated for so long finally occurred. On the afternoon of 21 October the sectors of RIR 109 and RIR 111 came under strong artillery fire once again. Soon afterward, the British attacked in dense waves from the *Staufen Graben*, one following after another. RIR 111 was forced to relinquish part of its sector in this attack and the connection between RIR 111 and RIR 109 was broken. It appeared as if the enemy might actually find a way through the German defenses when the concentrated fire of numerous German machine guns forced the enemy to withdraw back

Zur frommen Erinnerung
im Gebete an

Johann Jörg

Unteroff. bei der Minenwerfer=Komp. 226
Inh. des Eisernen Kreuzes und der
Silbernen Verdienst-Medaille
geb. am 11. Juni 1887 in Laupheim
gef. am 21. Oft. in Grandfourt.

Dein Grab im fernen Feindeslande,
Ift uns wohl eine schwere Pein,
Doch nimm dies Wort zum Unterpfande:
Dein Gras soll nicht verlassen sein.
Allabends, wenn die Glocken summen,
Zieht lieben unser Geist dorthin,
Und streut dir betend Andachtsblumen
Auf's Heldengrab mit frohen Sinn.

„Ich habe den guten Kampf gekämpft
den Lauf vollendet, den Glauben bewahrt.„
(2. Tim. 4. 7.)

„Ihr habt jetzt zwar Trauer; aber ich werde
euch wiedersehen und euer Herz wird sich
freuen und eure Freude wird niemand von
euch nehmen.„   (Joh. 16. 22.)

Gebete.

Wir empfehlen Dir, o Gott, die Seele
Deines Dieners **Johann**, welcher in
der Hoffnung auf Dein Erbarmen den Hel-
dentod für das Vaterland gestorben ist.
Nimm ihn gnädig auf unter die Zahl der
Auserwählten, damit er selig in Deiner
Anschauung auch für uns bitte, die wir
hienieden seiner liebend gedenken. Durch
Jesum Christum, unsern Herrn. Amen.
„Barmherziger Jesus, gib ihm die ewige
Ruhe.„

Süßes Herz Mariä, sei meine Rettung !

(Felix Fregin)

into the *Staufen Graben* once again.

The British had also launched attacks against RIR 110 by the *Meisengasse*. Between 1 and 3 p.m. on 21 October the enemy attempted three separate times to penetrate into the second trench that was occupied by the 12/R110. The British advanced out of the *Meisengasse* following a short period of drum fire before each attack. All three attacks were repulsed by infantry fire from the 12/R110 manning a barricade and the effective fire of the supporting *Minenwerfer.*

The cost of these victories had been high, all but five men from the 12/R110 had become placed out of action; killed or wounded. The 12th Company had lost 14 killed and 41 wounded in the heavy fighting. During the repeated enemy attacks the *Sanitätsmannschaften* were constantly going out in the open, under the heaviest artillery fire, in order to rescue their stricken comrades and, as a result, were also losing men at a rapid rate.

The British were successful in their attack against the first trench of the nearby 10/R110 that occurred at the same time as the first attack against the 12/R110. Four medium mine throwers had been brought forward and opened fire on the barricade occupied by the 10/R110, firing from the *Meisengasse.*

Following this latest attack, when the *Meisengasse* filled up with enemy troops, the trench garrison of R110 was alarmed and the men quickly manned their positions. The British deployed concentrated mine fire once more to a width of 150 meters with the shells falling in a row in front of the first trench, then moving slowly over the German lines toward the rear. The British troops followed closely behind the rolling mine fire barrage, using it as cover, and successfully entered the German trench. The British troops continued o advance about 100 meters where they stopped and erected a new sandbag barricade. Attempts were made by the 10/R110 to retake the lost trench from the north, but all attacks failed in the face of enemy fire coming from the new barricade. Finally, the 10/R110 gave up the idea of recapturing the trench and erected a new barricade opposite the British one.

The III/R110 had no reserves available to offer any assistance to either company. The emnants of the 2nd and 4/R109 located in mined dugouts nearby consisted of five leaderless Groups; they were quickly assigned to the 10/R110. The men were ordered to assemble in tunnels where other parts of both companies were found. The battalion commander also placed the rest of the 4/R109 under the command of the company leader of the 12/R110. Two thirds of the 2/R109 remained in the mined dugouts as reserve for entrenching and carrying parties during the night. One of their highest priorities was to obtain new supplies of mines as the *Minenwerfer* had fired off all available ammunition in the earlier fighting.

However, most of all, they were to bring up as many hand grenades as the men could carry. This was proving to be the weapon of choice in the close confines of trench warfare. In order to recapture the first trench, the III/R110 demanded three additional medium *Minenwerfer*, because the *Minenwerfer* in its possession had become worn out and was no longer capable of precision shooting. No new weapons arrived, there were simply not enough available reserves to make up for the *Minenwerfer* that were damaged or destroyed and it would have been impossible to bring the 950 pound *Minenwerfer* through the mud and shell cratered terrain; let alone the shells that weighed 109.1 pounds apiece.

While their comrades were involved in the heavy fighting, the men of RIR 111 were still eagerly awaiting their anticipated relief. The 2nd, 3rd and 4/R111 finished digging in the intermediate position during the early morning hours of 21 October, when the men were assembled and marched out of the trenches to Sapignies, where they could rest and receive warm food. The few remaining defenders of the *Staufen Stellung* marched to Vaulx-Vraucourt accompanied by the regimental band where they arrived the same afternoon. Parts of all three battalion remained in the front as assault troops and for the orientation of the III/94 taking over the position. The men who were being sent to the rear were ecstatic about leaving the position, which was physically collapsing under the shell fire and rainy weather.

At 8 a.m. on 21 October *Hauptmann* Edinger-Hodapp who was reconnoitering at the barricade at the *Stump Weg*, observed enemy columns making preparations in the positions adjacent to this trench. Edinger-Hodapp immediately called for artillery fire against this target using flares. The heavy guns in the rear soon opened fire; however, the field artillery apparently did not see the signal flare until considerable time had passed. Fortunately, as a result of the defensive artillery fire or possibly for other reasons, no attack occurred at this time. Then, later in the morning, the enemy artillery grew in intensity once more until it reached the level of drum fire by midday against the entire sector south of the Ancre.

Just after 10 p.m., British infantry advanced in dense masses against the German lines. Men from RIR 111 fired off signal flares across the sector, calling for artillery barrage fire, but, there was no response. Apparently the fog, dust and the haze prevented the artillery from seeing the signals. All telephone connections had long since been cut by the heavy British fire. The men of RIR 111 grew anxious as the minutes passed without any defensive barrage, when, suddenly, the German batteries began to fire, but by this time it was almost too late.

The waves of enemy infantry had already approached the position of the 8/R111 in the

Staufen Graben and the 9th, 11th and 12/R111 in the *Staufen Riegel*. Every man in these companies had opened fire into the oncoming enemy waves and the German machine guns were as effective as ever, cutting down men in rows as the guns traversed the Khaki lines. Still, the intense defensive infantry fire could not prevent the British from overrunning the barricades of *Feste Staufen*.

The vast number of enemy troops simply overwhelmed the thin ranks of the defenders at the barricades. The fighting was vicious as the opposing sides fought at close quarters, with the British attempting to expand their gains while the remaining defenders trying desperately to hold them back. Losses mounted on both sides as rifles and hand grenades were used at close range, causing horrible wounds and killing men indiscriminately.

Losses among the defenders were reaching a critical point; if reinforcements did not arrive, the entire position would be lost. The 5th and 8/R111 suffered the most in the fighting. Among those killed were two well respected and capable officers, *Leutnants* Schulz and Fertig. Platoon Buntru, 5/R111, was completely cut down and whoever had not been killed, was taken prisoner.

British assault troops were attempting to roll up the *Staufen Graben* and the *Staufen Riegel* to the right and to the left of the point where they had penetrated the German lines and then, attack those positions from the rear. German opposition was fierce and the British were slowly driven back in bitter close combat as shell hole after shell hole was cleared of the enemy. Platoons from the 11th and 12/R111 advanced out of the new switch line against the enemy. They were supported by machine guns located in the *Kirchhof Mulde Grandcourt* from Platoon Kohber, 2MG/R111.

The left wing of the *Staufen Riegel* occupied by the 12/R111 succeeded in holding out against the enemy assaults. The sectors of the 9th and 11/R111 where the enemy had penetrated with the assistance of flamethrowers, finally succumbed to the repeated British attacks. The German resistance had been tenacious, but the enemy numbers soon won out. Only a few men from the 9th and 11/R111 managed to come to the rear out of this trench unwounded. The officers had all been killed or wounded including *Leutnants* Günther and Arnold who were killed and *Leutnants* Manger and Höfler who were wounded.

The 12/R111 blocked off the trench to its right with a barricade that was successfully defended by a detachment under the command of *Leutnant* Welcher. *Vizefeldwebel* Birzel and his Group fought in the *Köhler Sap*, where the British had penetrated earlier with heavy losses and which had been recaptured by RIR 111 once again. The company leader *Leutnant* Sardemann, with the rest of the company, took over the defenses on the left flank where the enemy could also be seen advancing east of the *Köhlerpfad*. The neighboring *Landwehr* IR 74 had apparently been overpowered in this attack, and the 12/R111 was forced to defend its crater field from three different sides.

Unteroffizier Kaim was sent back to battalion headquarters with a report about the situation and with the urgent plea for support. Two platoons from the III/94, which attempted to help, were unable to make it through the barrier created by the enemy artillery fire. The batteries supporting RIR 111 directed their fire in front of and on the *Köhler Sap* but even this was not enough to avert the fate of the garrison. The survivors of the 12/R111 bravely stood at their post until the very last. Everyone who had been involved in the fighting had either been killed or captured, including the company leader, *Leutnant* Sardemann, and *Leutnant* Welcker.

At the same time the 12/R111 was being annihilated, there was also fighting at the

Staufen Graben on the right wing of the regimental sector, which lasted until late afternoon. All attempts by the British to break through toward Grandcourt by the *Lach Weg* failed. This was due to the strong resistance by the front line garrison and supporting units that had been sent forward to hold the enemy back. At times, the defenders had even succeeded in throwing the British out of parts of the *Staufen Graben* once again.

Three companies of the III/94 under *Leutnant* Meichelt and Sergeant Woll from the 5/94 were supporting the II/R111 as well as parts of the III/R111. These companies were able to partially restore the situation through a successful counterattack. The men of both regiments then worked forward through heavy artillery fire; with men falling almost every meter they advanced toward the *Staufen Graben*. In order to maintain the connection between the two assault detachments from both regiments, the 1/R111, under *Leutnant* Thielenhaus, accompanied the attack by the left wing.

However, before the reinforcements were able to reach the *Staufen Graben*, the trench had already been lost. The defenders had been encircled from the right, the enemy coming from the direction of *Feste Schwaben*. The last British assault upon the *Staufen Graben* was thought to have either killed or captured the entire company; no one had come back from the 1/R111.

The loss of *Feste Schwaben* and the *Staufen Stellung* seriously weakened the overall German defenses on the Somme. The British, in the *Staufen Stellung*, now had an almost unrestricted view into the German rear toward Grandcourt and had taken steps to ensure that they would keep the hard won positions. The British quickly brought up machine guns, trench mortars and reportedly even trench guns and installed them in the newly captured positions. It would take considerable effort on the part of the Germans if they were to recapture these key points.

Still, the German High Command had not given up the idea of retaking the lost terrain from the enemy. In the late afternoon, the German batteries concentrated their fire upon *Feste Schwaben* and the *Staufen Stellung* in preparation of an assault later in the day. At 6 p.m. attack groups from the II and III/R111, the III/94 and Reserve *Jäger 13* advanced across the pockmarked terrain toward the British lines. The men could only advance slowly due to the poor condition of the ground and from the quickly deployed British barrage fire that the enemy had called down.

Finally, only very thin ranks still remained of the original assault groups. There were no reserves left to throw into the fight. Makeshift detachments were quickly assembled together consisting of men from the *Bau* Companies, runners and battle orderlies, to help close the gaps in the front line. This had proven to be harder than first expected; no one really knew where the front line was. Finally, a patrol under *Leutnant* Geissinger was sent forward to establish where the troops were located. Geissinger returned and reported that as at 8 pm there was still fighting going on across the sector.

He had brought good news when his report indicated that everywhere where the enemy had crossed the former German front line trenches, he had become thrown back. The remnants of the assault groups, which were extremely exhausted and completely intermingled, were along the *Lach Weg* and then on both sides of the *Stump Weg* at the beginning of the switch line until at the *Köhlerpfad*. No connection with any other troops existed on either wing.

22-28 October

After a hectic day of fighting, a feeling of calm came over the front by Thiepval in the late evening hours. It was gratefully appreciated by the men on both sides. At approximately 1 a.m. on 22 October a modest silence descended over the front line. The forces on both sides were simply exhausted from the heavy fighting of the previous days. Still, the entire terrain continued to be targeted by steady British artillery fire all day on the 22nd, but no infantry attack followed.

It was time to reorganize the German positions and try to make sense of where all of the different units were located. On the morning of 22 October the I/R109 was assigned to Sector *Grandcourt Süd I*. When the battalion arrived at the *Süd I* trench they found the 1/R109 and the remnants of the 3rd, 6th, 9th and 12/R109. Furthermore, the 1MG/R110 and Machine Gun Marksman Detachment 152 and two *Musketen* platoons. The I/R109 established a connection at the left wing with the I/94, which had already relieved part of RIR 111.

Towards the morning of 22 October, the remnants of RIR111 succeeded in making contact on the right with a picket from RIR 109 in the *Artillerie Mulde*. A hole still remained in the front line on the left, because *Landwehr* IR 74 had been forced to yield up to the *Grandcourt Riegel* by the attacks of 21 October. The switch line behind the front of the old RIR 111 sector now became occupied by Reserve *Jäger* Battalion 13.

While it was relatively quiet along the front, the rest of RIR 111 could finally be extracted out of the battle position. *Leutnant* Schwarz, Adjutant of the III/R111, guided the relieving troops from the II/94 forward in the early morning hours of 22 October. What still remained of RIR 111 became collected in Sapignies up until midday.

While the men of RIR 111 were being relieved, others like *Unteroffizier* W. Liebrich, 1/ R111, from the *Sturmabteilung* 28th Reserve Division was still lying wounded in no man's land, and wondering what was to become of him.

> Only one particularly remains in my memory, when the night also passed, the new day dawned [22 October], and I still lay in my shell hole, my life gradually ending and I wished that a beneficent shell would kill me. The feeling of thirst increased to an insufferable level, and my injured leg ached with the smallest movement I made. I fantasized in my sleep of fountains, full canteens, comrades, who brought me water, coffee and similar items and with it awakened with even ghastlier thirst.
>
> Also this day, a Sunday, passed without any new occurrence and the same on Monday. Now I wanted very much to make the attempt which until now my core resisted against, of falling into their hands. After all, the Englishmen noticeably drew attention to themselves. I heard them speaking as before, smelled their tobacco; I whistled on my trill-whistle once, twice, three times, waited some time, whistled again and repeated this often during several hours, but nothing took place following it. Now the thought came to me as fast as lightning to attempt, to crawl back alone with my own strength during the coming night. Believe, and do!
>
> Darkness had barely fallen when I made my preparations. I tore the straps off my haversack and gas mask, bound them together and fastened them so that my destroyed leg was good. After a few failed attempts I could roll on to my belly and by pulling myself up, with help from the tip of my foot of the good leg, crawled out of the shell crater. The main work was accomplished. The wound ached very much to be sure,

but I clenched my teeth together. My deliverance was meant to be, a new resolve to live had come over me. First of all, somewhat closer to the area I looked above and, after I had approximately determined the direction of our line according to the light balls and the muzzle fire of our guns, I crawled on. *Unteroffizier* W. Liebrich, 1/R111, *Sturmabteilung* 28th Reserve Division [8]

While Liebrich was desperately trying to stay alive, from 22 to 25 October, the men from RIR 110 continued the backbreaking work on extending its position and the new *Schwaben Riegel* from the first trench across via the second trench and the *Meisengasse* to the *Strassburger Steige*.

In the afternoon of 22 October, the III/R111 marched to the vicinity of Vaulx-Vraucourt; the II/R111 followed there on the morning of 23 October. The battalion staff, Machine Gun Company and the *Bau* Company were replaced by the early morning hours of 24 October. The regimental staff moved into quarters in Epinoy northwest of Cambrai, on the same day along with the II and III Battalion, while the I Battalion had been transferred back and moved to Raillencourt west of Cambrai.

When the regiment was fully assembled in the vicinity of Cambrai, it consisted of a small, exhausted group of men in comparison to the number that had gone into the second tour of the Somme battle at the beginning of October. In the time the regiment was deployed by Grandcourt, it had suffered losses of: 8 officers, 110 men killed. 14 officers, 459 men wounded. 8 officers, 535 men taken prisoner and 355 men missing, a total of 30 officers, 1,459 men.

From the 45 officers who were involved in the fighting, only 15 had come back. From the battle strength of approximately 2,750 men, over half of them had become a casualty. It was time to rebuild the regiment for a second time in only four months. Now, there were very few men who could state that they had been in the regiment since the start of the war. The old RIR 111 had virtually ceased to exist.

One of the men listed as missing was fortunate. He was destined to be saved though his future military career was in doubt.

It went damned slowly and more than once I slept from exhaustion. Finally I landed at an old entanglement; meanwhile it had become light, but everywhere was an almost opaque fog. The torment of thirst induced me to capture the dew drops on the wires. It was not much, only more of a moistening of the lips; however I now had hope; to soon be at our side. So on the other hand I crawled on a bit further, I suddenly saw in a distance, approximately 50 steps our forward line, recognizable by the steel helmets through the thinning fog. By waving I made myself noticeable, a sentry also saw me, called the Duty Officer, who gave a few men the mission, to get me. Three stout comrades did not hesitate despite the increasing daylight, jumping from shell crater to shell crater, running out, and one at the same time carried me on his back into the position. Thank God, saved! Still I could hardly believe it. Also today it is hardly imaginable to me. I came back for the biggest part of this journey in a type of semi-conscious state, created through the traumatic fever and feebleness. Since then however, I know what a person is capable of, when it gets toward the end. The skilled German doctor finally succeeded in not only saving my leg after thirteen-months of treatment in a military hospital, but also made it so movable again that externally little is noticeable of the injury. *Unteroffizier* W. Liebrich, 1/R111, *Sturmabteilung* 28th Reserve Division [10]

While *Unteroffizier* Liebrich, 1/R111 had managed to make it to safety, for hundreds of other men who had been captured, the future was uncertain. Prisoner of War Otto Hengel, 9/R111 and his companions captured earlier in the fighting were on the start of a long journey. When his large group arrived at their first destination they were met by fellow prisoners who had been captured on the same day.

In a farmyard we met further comrades who were prisoners, who had already arrived and that had been taken captive on the same day. We now became picked out and interrogated by a few German speaking English officers. The result was that except for a knife and notebook everything was undisturbed, even my watch. Through their questions the English officers did not extract the least information about the German positions and similar things.

Under open skies, within barbed wire, we spent the first night in the prisoner of war camp. Tired, cold and hungry we awaited the next morning, of sleep there was no discussion – it was already too cold – October! Moreover I did not even have an overcoat there. We lay closely pressed together under an apple tree, standing up if it became too cold for us, and through running to bring a little life back into the frozen limbs again. Instead of the hoped for hot tea there is only water on this morning and in place of bread we received hard biscuits and the well-known American Bully Beef, three men to a tin. Then in the course of the morning went further under the accompaniment of mounted Englishmen until at Acheux, where a camp for prisoners had been set up. Here we were separated from our *Feldwebel* and *Leutnants*, without previously being able to say goodbye to them. The latter went to England, we remained in France. After 4-5 days we were placed together with a large number of comrades from other regiments to be transported and loaded on the nearby railway. We traveled forty hours across and through France. Two nights and a day we did not where we would end up. 40 men were presently in a cattle car. We had meager straw for a bed, barely any blankets or similar items for a covering. Happy was he that could call an overcoat his own. The sanitary conditions were extremely insufficient, fresh air only came through a small opening into the wagon. Food was all that we got. The thirst was always the most severe! After we now had traveled further back up to Boulogne, we came into the vicinity of a small village Hersin-Coupigny, where a bleak farm-field, only enclosed with a wire entanglement, should become our first prisoner of war camp. Otto Hengel, 9/R111 [11]

RIR 110 was also being taken out of the front line as new troops arrived to take over the position. In the night of 26 October the regiment was relieved by troops from IR 95. The companies assembled in Achiet le Petit after being relieved and marched via Behagnies to Noreuil into alarm quarters. The losses of this regiment in the second participation in the Battle of the Somme had also been very high. The casualties in RIR 110 consisted of: 7 officers, 183 men killed. 7 officers, 491 men wounded, 484 men missing, a total of 14 officers and 1,158 men.

The XIV Reserve Corps orders issued on 24 October did not fail to acknowledge its appreciation to all of the troops.

The 28th Reserve Division leaves the XIV Reserve Corps for the second time after taking part in heavy fighting. The main force of the enemy attack in the great July battle struck the division. They had suffered heavy losses that however had not been in vain. The enemy could not enforce his intended breakthrough, because the rest of the divisions have afforded brave resistance to the last. In order to replace the losses, many young soldiers must be put in. In the Champagne they had the opportunity for further education and knowledge of trench warfare. Returning to the reserve corps, the division took over one of the most difficult sectors of the front south of the Ancre. Here, with few exceptions there were no carefully developed positions. Lack of trenches, which under continuous enemy fire were arduously created and became destroyed over and over again, and the position was created from shell craters. The division had also endured bravely here. It was also not successful, to hand over all parts of the position undertaken to the replacing troops, however the adversaries were removed multiple times from the lost trench pieces through counterattacks. I speak of my thanks to the determined leadership and brave troops for their devotion and

Men of RIR 109 following the fighting in October. (Author's collection)

fidelity to duty. I wish the division now finds the opportunity to recover in a quiet position. *Von* Stein [12]

Now, RIR109 was the only regiment of the 28th Reserve Division still involved in the fighting at the end of October. On the morning of 26 October a composite company was formed from men from RIR 109 under the leadership of *Leutnant* Armbruster. This company took part in an attack being undertaken by RIR 94 to recapture *Feste Staufen*. The attack failed before it began; it was simply not possible for the men to advance through the heavy British artillery and machine gun fire. The losses in the unsuccessful assault were unfortunately very high. The composite company from RIR 109 alone lost 40 men. This final act was soon followed by the relief of the regiment from the front.

Once the men from RIR 109 had been relieved, the troops assembled behind the front in Behagnies and Sapignies. From there they moved to Noreuil. The regimental staff moved into quarters in Vaulx after surrendering control of the regimental sector to IR 95. The German positions were still holding out despite constant enemy pressure along the entire front by Grandcourt. The cost to accomplish this had been high. From 14 to 28 October RIR 109 lost one officer and 73 men killed, 11 officers and 420 men wounded and 4 officers and 226 men missing for a total of 16 officers and 719 Other Ranks.

One reason why the regiments of the 28th Reserve Division had been able to withstand the constant British attacks with so few resources in men and artillery during the month of October is in part due to the extraordinary work performed by the supply service. When the 28th Reserve Division was heading to the Somme for the second time, it was made very clear that bringing supplies to the front line was a very difficult task, especially after the narrow gauge railway running through the Ancre valley had been destroyed. Once the British had advanced against Hill 151, it allowed the enemy to directly observe the entire railway-route. This vital supply line was then systematically destroyed using the heaviest caliber shells.

When the 28th Reserve Division was assigned to the Grandcourt Sector, a railway construction and supply detachment was created and placed under the command of *Leutnant* Ganter, former head of the construction unit called the *Ganterwerk* from the first deployment on the Somme. The new construction detachment was sent ahead of the division in order to guarantee that everything possible was being done to provide for the combat troops. Ganter received strict orders that the railway formerly line used to supply the position was to be in working order in the shortest possible time.

The *Swabians* in the 26th Reserve Division had already declared this to be impossible. *Leutnant* Ganter however, was aware that the very lives of his fellow soldiers in his regiment and division might rely upon the supplies being carried on this railway. He was determined to do whatever was possible to accomplish his orders.

For three straight nights the men in Ganter's construction unit worked on the railway embankment under a constant hail of shells. Gigantic craters torn into the embankment by 38cm shells were bridged one after the other. When dawn arrived, the men could no longer work on the exposed railway embankment without the possibility of being killed or wounded from artillery fire directed by observers on the ground and aircraft in the sky.

The men returned to their quarters and 'fell on their beds as if dead' according to *Leutnant* Ganter. When darkness fell once more, the men swarmed out again onto the embankment and continued their Herculean task. After three nights of such labor, *Leutnant*

Damaged rail line along the Ancre. (*Die 26.(Württembergische)*
Reserve-Division im Weltkrieg 1914-1918)

Ganter announced with great pride that the railway line was repaired and could be used to supply the front line immediately. Much of the credit can be given to *Offizier Stellvertreter* Müller, RIR 109, who directed the repairs each night, 'with tireless energy and boldness'. When the 28th Reserve Division first took over the position in early October, the first train also arrived in Grandcourt and brought all of the food, ammunition and construction materials that the fighting troops needed.

As long as the 28th Reserve Division was in the position, the trains travelled to and from the front line each night. Even though the railway line was in operation, it would not have remained intact if not for the nightly work performed by Ganter and his men. The British quickly determined that the railway had been repaired and redoubled their efforts to destroy it once more. Increased artillery fire was being directed at this target and the weight of shells was having an effect by causing serious damage to the embankment as well as the tracks.

Still, each night Ganter's men worked on repairing all of the damage caused during the day and each night the trains brought up fresh supplies. The division horses also benefited from this work. Now it was not necessary for transport horse and wagons to bring up supplies to Grandcourt, this was exclusively carried out by the light railway. The transport horses were only required to pull the Company field kitchens as close to the front as possible each night.

The men of the 28th Reserve Division had relinquished part of the front line that had been turned over to them at the start of the month. They had not been able to recapture the vital Hill 151 from the enemy. Still, when the fighting was over for the division, the men could look back with pride that they had still retained a section of Hill 151 and had not allowed the enemy to force them back completely and, above all, they had prevented an enemy breakthrough by Grandcourt.

When His Majesty, Kaiser Wilhelm visited the Western Front, parts of the 28th Reserve Division, amongst them a group from RIR 109 consisting of *Leutnant* Affolter and 24 men, appeared in the Château Park of St. Leger, where ten men were awarded the Iron Cross II Class and *Offizier Stellvertreter* Metzner was awarded the Iron Cross I Class.

Notes

1.   Anon, *Kriegstagebuch aus Schwaben*, pp. 1,486.

2.   Bachelin, *Major* Eduard, *Das Reserve-Infanterie-Regiment Nr. 111 im Weltkrieg 1914 bis 1918*, p. 310.

3.   IBID.

4.   *Feldpost* letter *Oberleutnant* Erwin Boy, 2MG/R111. Courtesy of Felix Fregin.

5.   Greiner & Vulpius, *Reserve-Infanterie-Regiment Nr. 110 im Weltkrieg 1914-1918*, pp. 149-150.

6.   Frisch, Georg, *Das Reserve-Infanterie-Regiment Nr. 109 im Weltkrieg 1914 bis 1918*, pp. 149-150.

7.   Bachelin, op. cit., pp. 307-309.

8.   Baumgartner, Richard (Ed.), 'The Somme 1 July 1916', *Der Angriff, A Journal of World War 1 History* No. 3, p. 6.

9.   Bachelin, op. cit., p. 309.

10.   Bachelin op. cit., pp. 309-310.

11.   Bachelin, op. cit., p. 311.

12.   Greiner & Vulpius, op. cit., pp. 153-154.

Chapter 5

26th Reserve Division

To the bitter end: The Battle of the Somme, November 1916

By 1 November 1916 the fighting on the Somme had already been raging four months. Now, as November started, the fighting continued into the fifth month with almost unabated strength. While the majority of the fighting so far had taken place south of the Ancre, now, following the heavy fighting in October by Grandcourt, it was the turn of the sector north of the Ancre. The sectors located north of the Ancre had held firm on 1 July and had resisted every subsequent enemy attempt to capture them. The recent increase in enemy activity north of the small river clearly indicated that this was to be the next focus of the Allied offensive. Coincidentally, many of the regiments that had fought so tenaciously against the enemy onslaught on 1 July 1916 would now be involved in the fighting at the very end of the battle. As a note to the reader, in an attempt to present the often confusing information regarding the fighting north of the Ancre I am presenting the material starting from the German left wing, RIR 55 by the Ancre, and then the subsequent regimental accounts further to the north.

At the beginning of November, the German positions directly north of the Ancre were being occupied by a number of regiments: RIR 55 from the 2nd Guard Reserve Division defended the line between the Ancre and Beaumont. RIR 121 from the 26th Reserve Division still defended the Beaumont sector including the *Heidenkopf*, a position it had held on 1 July on the opening day of the great battle. Further north, IR 23, from the 12th Infantry Division, would defend the line north of Beaumont. On 1 July this regiment had fought near Montauban and the area near Curlu. Within several days, IR 62, also from the 12th Infantry Division, would take over a portion of the front line as well. The area further to the north was occupied by the men of the 52nd Infantry Division, just as it had been on 1 July, 1916.

RIR 55 had been holding the front line position without relief since the beginning of September, eight long weeks. Throughout October, artillery and mine thrower fire fell on the regimental sector with increasing intensity. In addition to the constant enemy fire, there was another difficulty facing the men. As the weather grew colder with each passing week, it became even more important to provide warm food to the men in the front line positions. This was proving to be increasingly difficult due to the enemy fire but more so from the wet weather that turned the trenches into a quagmire.

Now, in November, the enemy began each day with drum fire from 6.30 until 7.30 a.m. After this intense period of fire, the shelling died down to a slow and steady rain of shells and mines with occasional pauses in the fire. All fire pauses had to be taken advantage of by the men of RIR 55 for repairs and restoration of the badly damaged positions. Like warm food, bringing up the critical trench materials only occurred with considerable difficulties as a result of enemy fire and the poor road conditions. In the eight weeks RIR 55 had been in the position it had lost 50 horses and numerous wagons, particularly on the Miraumont-

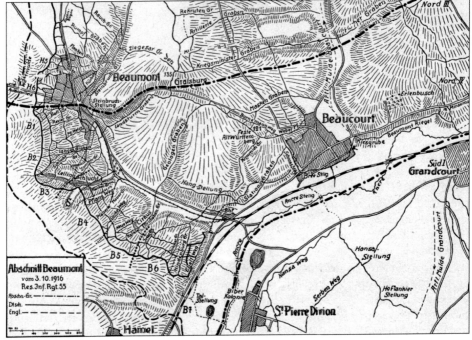

German positions along the Ancre.

Grandcourt-Beaucourt-Beaumont (Station Beaucourt) road. Heavy rain turned the roads into bogs making it almost impossible for the horses to pull the heavily loaded wagons through them. The rain also constantly filled the position with thick mud and while the men were working around the clock to keep them open, it was a losing battle.

Even when the trench garrison, the II/R55, received assistance from the I/R55 in the form of additional carrying parties, the forward most trenches barely remained passable, and only with the utmost effort on the part of the trench garrison. The accurate fire from the enemy mine throwers were the most feared weapons. The impact of the mines proved to have a devastating effect on the fragile defenses. Under these conditions, the men quickly became fatigued from the difficult work and the numbers of men reporting sick climbed higher each day. The constant enemy fire destroyed telephone lines over and over again. The Telephone repair troops continued to risk their lives as they worked trying to mend the damaged wires and many of them were killed or wounded when they were caught in the open by enemy shell fire.

Guns and mine throwers of the heaviest calibers destroyed wire obstacles and trenches in the shortest time. The shattered defences could no longer be repaired using conventional methods; they had to be replaced with the less effective Spanish riders. The enemy fire was being directed by low flying aircraft in numbers that had never been seen before, even during the heaviest fighting on the Somme during the summer months. Any man who moved inside the trenches during the day came under attack by them with machine gun fire. The German infantry longed for air support in order to keep the annoying enemy pilots away. Unfortunately, in the autumn of 1916, there were fewer German pilots in the air over the Somme. The men also felt that the German air force was technically inferior to the

Dismal conditions north of the Ancre. The wired trench would be difficult
for any attacker to see or destroy before an attack. (Author's collection)

enemy as they rarely saw a German aircraft flying over their positions, let alone flying across
to the enemy positions.

In spite of these dangers, German observers remained at their posts in the poor weather
and enemy fire and constantly watched the enemy position for any signs of an attack. It
appeared they did not have long to wait, when, at 7.45 a.m. on 2 November, continuous
drum fire fell on all of the trenches in IR 62 by Beaumont with only a short pauses at
midday and later around 6 p.m.

At 8 p.m. the enemy artillery started once again and for a short period of time had
reached a level that indicated an attack might follow. When no infantry attack occurred
and when the artillery fire eventually died down, a patrol was sent forward from Sector B1
from the 11/62. The patrol discovered a British corpse in the intermediate terrain, from
which the insignia was removed for identification. Shortly after this discovery the patrol
was spotted by enemy sentries and was prevented from any further advance through hand
grenades and machine gun fire.

On the afternoon of 3 November, orders were issued to IR 23 that the regiment would
relieve RIR 121 from the position north of Beaucourt. Advance parties were immediately
sent out following receipt of the order. The II/23 marched in the night of the 3/4 November
to Achiet le Grand, where it arrived at 6 a.m. and remained there for the next twelve hours.
At 7 p.m. the II/23 arrived in Achiet le Petit and relieved the II/R121 from the *Zwischen
Stellung*. The I/23 marched via Croisilles – St. Léger to Achiet le Grand, where it received
billets for the night from 4/5 November.

By the end of October, RIR 121 was at the end of its strength. The men from the
regiment had been in the front lines since 10 April without being relieved from the position
for any length of time since June 1916. For weeks and months following the heavy fighting

on 1 July, the regiment was not directly attacked but had been subjected to daily harassment fire that slowly ate away at the men's nerves. For a period of several weeks, at the end of October, there had been several hours of concentrated drum fire on the position day after day. Everyone was forced to work repairing the trenches, dugouts and wire entanglements in the time when the enemy fire had died down. This extra strain on men already close to exhaustion was simply too much and it could not continue to go on like this much longer.

Finally, in the night from 4/5 November the relief so desperately longed for by the men of RIR 121 holding the front line was going to take place. The men from IR 23 had arrived and by the night of 7 November the relief was finished. RIR 121 now became the Army Group reserve and was located in the following villages: Regimental staff: Sains les Marquion, I Battalion: Baralle, II Battalion Staff, 5th and 6th Companies Inchy-en Artois, 7th and 8th Companies Sains le Marquion: III Battalion: Pronville.

At 7 a.m. on 7 November *Major* Lemcke, IR 23, took command over the new sector of the regiment that ran from just south of Serre to Beaumont. The regiment was positioned as follows: H1 – 9/23, H2 – 12/23, H3 – 10/23, H4 – 2/23, 2nd trench behind H1, H2 and H4 one platoon each from the 7/23, *Röhrelegraben* – 6/23, *Brettauerweg* – 11/23, *Nagelgraben* – 8/23, *Zwischen Stellung* behind H3 and H4 – 4th and 3/23, *Feste Soden* – 5/23, *Nord I* – 1/23, Staff I Battalion in the *Sodenbogen*, staff of the II Battalion in *Feste Soden*, staff of the III Battalion in the *Röhrlegraben*. Regimental battle headquarters – *Zwischen Stellung*.

IR 23 received additional fire support when several groups of *Musketen* were assigned to the regimental sector. These weapons had been proven to be very effective in earlier fighting with the increase in firepower and often played a critical role in stopping enemy advances.

The men of IR 23 found that almost every trench was completely impassable because of the thick mud. In many locations the men sank up to their knees, in some areas even up to their hips and it often took several men to pull a single comrade from the relentless grip of the muck. It took considerable effort before trapped men were finally released from the morass; to be wounded in these conditions was terrifying in the extreme.

All telephone lines in the sector had been cut in numerous places by the British artillery fire and the misty, rainy weather made light signals useless. With the loss of most means of communications, especially telephones, the majority of reports and messages were carried by runners. Conditions made their task almost beyond the abilities of an average man as they worked through enemy fire and mud that threatened to suck them under at almost every step. It was not without reason that this period was often called 'Hell of the Somme'.

Even at times when the men tried to move through the trenches during the daylight hours, the efforts were almost useless because of the considerable enemy aerial activity and air attacks upon individual soldiers. All movement had to take place at night, under the cover of darkness. Then, because of the terrible conditions, movement was only possible on top, outside of the trenches, where the troops were exposed to enemy searching artillery and machine gun fire.

From the very first day the regiment took over the position, considerable artillery fire blanketed the sector. The constant shell fire made the horrible condition of the trenches even worse. The wire obstacles positioned in front of the trenches became damaged so badly that in most places they no longer constituted a barrier against an enemy advance and not even pre-fabricated obstacles could be set in place; the trenches in these locations were completely exposed.

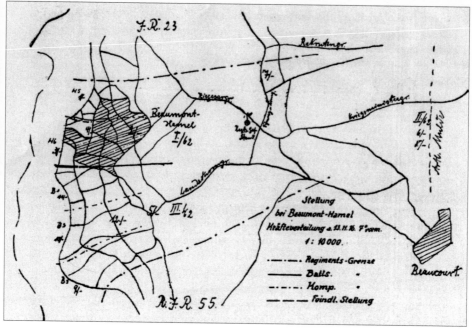

Beaumont-Hamel.

The once invaluable field railway by Achiet le Petit had been destroyed, so every roll of wire, every obstacle post, every item needed by the men at the front had to be carried up by hand. The small quantities of construction materials that made it to the front under these difficult circumstances, was simply not enough to restore the mud filled and badly damaged trenches to any state where they could be considered defensible again.

The situation facing the newly arrived men from IR 23 was not any better at the neighboring IR 62. On 6 November the enemy artillery and mine fire grew to a level rarely experienced before this time by the men of the regiment. The few wire obstacles remaining and still intact dugouts particularly suffered in the heavy fire. On the morning of 7 November the enemy artillery fire increased to drum fire that lasted for one hour. The sky was multiple shades of grey as far as the eye could see. Heavy downpours completely saturated the churned up earth and small pools of water began to join together and form small ponds. Breastworks and traverses collapsed into the trenches, as far as they had not already been destroyed by the shell fire. Communication trenches could no longer be distinguished from shell craters and the rain just continued to fall day after day.

Herewith I will indicate the enemy fire distribution. 7.5cm shells always came directly from the front. Shrapnel from the front and half left. I could not remember, if I had noticed if our company had also once become fired at from half right. In front of us stood heavy guns, firing away over us, with exception of 12 November 1916. The right wing of the company had suffered very much under shell fire, which according to the distribution of the craters had to have come from half on the left until directly on the left. The middle platoon suffered terribly under this mine fire. We received day by day, four hours alone of heavy ball mines. Lightweight mines (bottle mines) often at night, when working. The sentries must use all of their effort then to pay attention to the firing of the mines. This was especially difficult with the light mines. However they acquired it after all! The left wing remained peculiarly spared. This curious distribution that didn't change in the entire time was somehow connected with the organization of the English artillery, as far as they were unquestionably making ready for the attack. In the trench we often wracked our brains and we thought about what kind of attack was being prepared with this fire distribution. The fact that mining tunnels were being driven under the trench by the III/62 was well-known by us.

Our fields of fire at the left wing until in the hollow were good. It was somewhat unfavorable on the rise in the middle of the company. A stretch of foreground could not be covered with the rifle. The machine gun in the hollow was able to help out here. The right wing also had a fairly good field of fire.

Transmission of orders: *Leutnant* Scheer was connected with the company leader in the second line by telephone. *Feldwebel* Jacob and I had a runner. We both lived in the large dugout together with the Other Ranks. Also on the first days we were in possession of a telephone, unfortunately however the apparatus became removed. During a powerful bombardment a runner's report on what our situation was did not make it through.

Our pilots could not seriously oppose the lighter and graceful English planes with their older aircraft, despite the immense courage that their pilots demonstrated. They therefore did not appear by Beaumont altogether. I turn to a description of our stay in the trench: The first night in the trench proceeded well despite the continuous uttermost alarm readiness, which is to say, everyone had to sleep with their equipment buckled on. Nevertheless the troops were in the best mood, there were songs and jokes, one hoped for a proper attack, in order to wipe out the damn Tommys for their mine fire. *Unteroffizier* Olbrich, who was eternally hopeful, was happy about the rifle grenades. Together with *Unteroffizier* Hampel, whose accuracy and conscientiousness instantly allowed you to think of a bank official, he transmitted a Sunday morning greeting across to the Englishmen in the greatest delight, not realizing that they would take this terribly bad, because they could not afford something like this. I met him one day, as he viewed his 'Shooter' with pride. Because I dared to make a couple of bad jokes, he directed me to that device immediately in front to silence me. He wanted to save the rest of the shells for more serious times.

The men did everything they could to bring the trench in order. Initially each platoon still had its work group. *Unteroffizier* Belkner led the one from my platoon. They were tireless in the manufacturing of parapets and repairing damage. The Other Ranks vied with each other in zeal and ingenuity. However, soon they could no longer keep it up. A nasty rain sets in that shattered all work. The mud absolutely wanted to flow into the dugouts. *Fähnrich* Pukall, 3/62 [1]

The fire had grown to such an extent that from 7 November almost nothing in the position could be recognized any longer. Every command post, the *Zwischen Stellung* and the *Artillerie Mulde* were held under heavy fire. The sheer number of shells and mines falling on the trenches had already led to considerable losses in the regiment.

Regardless of the great hardships, the men still performed their assigned tasks as best they could. Runners defied serious injury or death as they continued working their way

:hrough the damaged battle trenches and destroyed communication trenches in order to :ransmit key orders and reports. Every attempt was made to repair the telephone lines. Telephone troops searched the churned up terrain looking for the breaks in the telephone .vires and quickly made repairs. Their efforts were not always in vain, at least the telephones .vorked at times, even if only for a short while before they required repairs once again. Still, .t was not hard to imagine that anyone who experienced these conditions had hoped to be :elieved, no matter how long they had manned the front lines.

Now it became uncomfortable and we hoped for relief that should occur on the 7th of November. The sentry groups had to help. The hollow could barely be walked through up to the 7th. The Englishmen constructed a new mine thrower for undoing everything. While they initially only fired occasionally, there is now two hours of fire daily, in the morning punctually at 8.30 o'clock, after a pause it goes on again for two hours. The stay in such constantly bombarded dugout is not among the most beautiful resting places that you could imagine. One hears the hollow noise of the explosions; atmospheric pressure penetrates into the shelter so that every light goes out. To sleep is out of the question and so one broods in darkness there and hears only the hail of stones banging down the stairway and sand trickling down between the wooden frameworks. An invisible pressure weighs on the skull. One wants to avenge himself, but how? The daily duty of the Englishmen seemed to be the same; it never seems to become disturbed. In the morning and in the evening our trench became taken under drum fire, always at the same time. Evening after evening the rearward connections became taken under fire. The sight was wonderful if when the entire horizon flamed up from the unnumbered guns firing. Above us it sang and then whistled and to sing on and then one heard the hollow explosion of the projectile far behind us. Two guns we noticed especially by their red muzzle flash. They stood close behind Auchonvillers.

The duty in the trench was soon no longer maintained in its original form. Also the food became worse daily, there are only 'entanglements.' Our strength rapidly declined with the exhausting duty. Many lived only on dry bread, which also only sparingly came up to us and coffee, because they claimed that dried meat and vegetables made their bowels sick. I wanted to compel them to eat that stuff, only so that they were able to work. Nevertheless I often caught someone who was pouring out his food. Candles rarely came to the front; the men took care of this by making 'Hindenburg lamps' out of margarine and good suet, so they did not have to sit eternally in darkness. Unfortunately I had to prohibit that in their best interest. The sentry duty had to be newly regulated, the work groups vanished. Everyone had to work, every sentry had to stand. The uniforms were wet, the seams of the boot rotted. In my platoon there were no complete boots any more. The men, without exception, were catching colds; some could hardly speak any more. Nevertheless no one had reported sick. There is still hardly any sleep and if so, then only for a few minutes. On the suggestion of Schrott, who was lost to a *Feldwebel*, Jacob and I threw our platoons together for work and sentry duty and so achieved that each man was only required to be taken only once every two days to work at night, while the sentry duty had to be executed day and night. The events sped up now. The Tommys had placed their destructive fire down even further forward and was now working on making the first position ripe for the storm. A regular sentry duty was now hardly possible anymore. Also, the company duty was not allowed to be executed any longer, because the trench was impassable during the fire. The platoon leader and *Unteroffizier* Hampel, who also rendered company duty, came over, and agreed that everyone had to pay attention to everything anytime he was in his sector. I often had duty mornings and evenings during the drum fire. At this time I stayed at the left wing, where there were few hits or, up in the sap. From both points one could safely overlook the company sector. The right wing also stood under fire very often, it also offered no cover and didn't allow any overview. It was something splendid to view the courage and the sense of duty of the sentries, of which many could barely stand straight because of the cold. Everyone knew that his comrades essentially relied upon on him and this feeling of responsibility allowed them to forget everything else. Often I said to my sentries: 'You come and go in, I will remain here' and always received the reply: 'No! They would also remain outside!'

The artillery fire increased in intensity. A spot half right behind us became remarkably completely inundated: Do they suspect that the Battalion dugout was there? Often I also viewed the bombardment of our communication trenches by 7.5cm shells with quiet admiration. It was astonishing, how precise the guns were arranged. Each shot crashed 10 meters in front of the previous one and all took hold exactly about the trench. Our connection routes to the rear were only passable at night or also at certain times. I can explain the impeccable shooting only with the superior pilots and tethered balloon observation that in no manner could be impaired by us. Runner and food carriers also had to run through the 1st Company at indeterminate times, because we constantly had wounded or dead. Also, a walk through the *Talweg Graben* at the left wing could not be managed without loss by day, because the slope to the hollow didn't offer any cover and was constantly threatened through mines and machine guns. The machine gun threatening us here was in a blockhouse in an English sap, as I discovered from the III/62. From there I also noted the Observation officer for all light and heavy Mine throwers that kept us constantly busy. Some of them were built into the embankment of a road. A field railway that we heard driving every night carried the mines until in front by the throwers. Upon or request a battery of 15cm guns was allotted to us. However our faithful comrades often could not shoot. Soon one heard only one gun; then this also seemed to be broken down. The English pilots were like a plague. They flew over us the entire day in great numbers, each fired at anyone who moved in the trench. Often the men grasping their rifles lay in wait, on the lookout to elude an overly impudent pilot. However, unfortunately without success! They seemed to especially observe the hollow. A pilot swooped down one morning like a bird, took a photograph of the sentry standing there and shot steeply into the air. This was the only time that I saw a pilot so close above the ground at the front. Later it became fashionable by the pilots; then it still seemed unbelievable. Our pilots were never seen, however on one morning a German pilot, came over the English lines, accompanied by our best wishes. Fortunately he also came back again, because the Englishmen had delivered only very puny defensive fire. Maybe he had also chosen a favorable time, because towards morning the Englishmen fired almost nothing at all, maybe they had breakfast. Or it was a type of Medical pause. One day a sentry yelled excitedly, a large number (27) German pilots came. We remarked, it was the registration pilots who would determine what was still held and we made the white cloths ready. However again they did not come far. It came to light during fighting with English pilots that one German plane swooped down, darting behind the Englishman like a bird of prey. Still for once the German pilot caught his machine; however the enemy gave him no rest.

We hoped for relief, while the Englishmen started to throw gas bombs. The enemy appeared to know our 'gas alarm' and had posted countless pilots above us, most likely to determine our trench strength. We were not fooled. After the bombardment I went into the sap in the hollow, where a severe gas smell was very noticeable. A bomb had fallen a few meters away next to the sap head. Nevertheless the sentry had continued to perform his duty for more than one hour, finally without a mask, because neither trench sentries nor the platoon service had come to him. He didn't want to leave his post without orders. I believe it was Knauer. I worried about his relief, because he was half broken down. The sap was given up. *Fähnrich* Pukall, 3/62 [2]

Despite the overwhelming enemy fire, the German *Minenwerfer* and guns did not sit silently under the increasingly heavy enemy bombardments. Even with far lower numbers of guns and *Minenwerfer* they had visible success in trying to combat the enemy mine throwers that were installed opposite Beaumont. Even with the occasional successes however, it was short lived. Within hours, new finned and ball mines fell upon the trenches and dugouts with massive explosions. The garrison sat inside the few intact dugouts, often closely packed together, crouching in every corner of the shelter and even on the stairways leading toward the surface. While the men usually sat in complete darkness, by the first week of November they were also being held in the highest state of alarm readiness. The men were always waiting for that moment, when they would be ordered to man their posts in order to repel an enemy attack.

The higher state of readiness would come in handy over the next few days. In addition to being subjected by daily artillery bombardments, the trenches of IR 62 were also being probed by strong enemy patrols on a daily basis. One such British patrol on 6 November against Sector H6 that was occupied by the 3/62, ran into the patrol of *Vizefeldwebel* Kille while still in no man's land. The British patrol was immediately attacked and, as a result of this sudden and unexpected assault, the enemy were scattered and hurried back into their position, all the while coming under machine gun fire from the guns positioned in H6. Additional patrols followed against Sectors H6 and B1 and, in each instance, managed to reach the German trenches. The patrols were spotted and came under heavy fire, in particular salvos of hand grenades, forcing them to withdraw. Following these aborted attacks, patrols from IR 62 found one wounded and one dead British soldier lying in front of the remnants of the German wire and carried them back into the German lines. The two enemy soldiers were identified as belonging to the 9th Royal Edinburgh Regiment (1/9th Royal Scots).

On the next morning I observed an English patrol of three men during the drum fire from the left wing of the company who approached the abandoned sap during the descent of a light ball. Although I immediately proceeded with a few men, I could not catch any. However, they do not seem to have reached our sap head. Anyway the greatest attention was required. At this time the attempt by *Vizefeldwebel* Kille, with the regimental patrol to make a forcible undertaking also failed and an alarm came from the subterranean sap. The trench was occupied in a moment; however, the

Englishmen seen by the sentries did not come. Maybe it was only an ordinary patrol.

Furthermore heard at this time was the attempt by the Englishmen to penetrate into the trench of *Leutnant* Scheer. The patrol now ran into the machine gun. I believe an Englishman became wounded then and brought in. Now followed a more serious gas attack that our sentries on the right of the hollow immediately observed. In the hollow a sentry had failed. He and his comrades had to pay for it. *Leutnant* Scheer was also gas sick and later died; two men to my knowledge were dead. As company duty I could restore order there, because in the excitement, the leaderless platoon had ended up somewhat disordered, which increased when men were sent forward out of the second line. *Unteroffizier* Hampel took over the command, which later *Leutnant* Walter led. I pained me to my soul, when I saw our resplendent Mittelstrass under the men who were gas sick, he had suffered severely. To my knowledge he was already over 45 years old and a father of 6 children. Nevertheless he was one of the most intrepid and most conscientious patrol participants. He no longer believed in his salvation. His hope was that his wife and children be looked after. *Fähnrich* Pukall, 3/62 [3]

IR 23 had also been under strong enemy fire raids during the night of 9/10 November. Strong drum fire fell on all the trenches in the regimental sector on 10 November between 6.30 and 7.30 a.m. however, in spite of the active fire the overall losses remained very small. IR 23 experienced a change in command at this time when on 10 November *Major* von Wedelstaedt took over the leadership of IR 23, *Major* Lemcke stepped down and became the commander of the III/23.

The British did not have a monopoly on all patrol and raiding activities at this time. In order to be able to determine the enemy intentions the I/62 received the task to conduct a raid with the intent of taking prisoners. The raiding party patrol advanced in the night from 9/10 November and despite all precautions, was observed by enemy sentries. The raiding party managed to penetrate into the enemy position despite lively defensive fire and shot down a double sentry post. The raiders then spread out into the trenches threw hand grenades into several nearby dugouts before withdrawing.

Numerous British soldiers lay dead inside the trench; primarily as a result of the intense artillery preparation fire. Within a short time a British detachment began a counterattack, and it quickly turned into a lively hand grenade fight between the opposing groups. The raiding party from IR 62 lost three men in the hand grenade battle and was forced to withdraw. Unfortunately, the patrol was unable to capture any prisoners and because of the intense enemy fire they could not bring back any enemy bodies with them.

The men in IR 62 had found the position by Beaumont to be especially disagreeable. The British flanked the German trenches from the southwest shore of the Ancre, at many positions the British were almost able to fire into the German trenches from the rear. The southern sector of the front was a particularly dangerous place to be stationed. This sector was being held by the III/62, which suffered greatly from the flanking fire and long range artillery fire coming from the rear from batteries located south of the Ancre where the new front lines had been pushed far to the east by Courcelette and Martinpuich. This was a situation that the men of RIR 121 did not have to contend with when holding the village of Beaumont during the previous months.

While there were only a few casualties being suffered in the increased enemy artillery and patrol activity north of the Ancre, even these minor losses reduced the effectiveness of

Medical dugout along the Ancre, 28 October–20 November, 1916. (Author's collection)

the companies holding the front line. Losses suffered by the regiment by Beaumont from late October up to 10 November, were: 38 men killed, 134 men wounded, 3 men missing. Since the companies had moved into the trenches with an average strength of 80-90 men each, these losses were very perceptible.

The 9/62, the left wing company, had suffered the most. However, under the present circumstances there could be no consideration of relieving the men. It was felt that only troops that were very familiar with the position, could successfully repulse the attacks that were expected almost daily. This was completely opposite the situation that had faced the regiment just before 1 July when it had been replaced by Bavarian RIR 6 on the eve of the great offensive.

The II/62, which was the reserve battalion, was also looking forward to a change of position. The losses of men being suffered by the battalion while undertaking carrying parties and entrenching duties near the front line had been no less that that suffered by the position battalions. At least, if you were in the front lines, you had a chance to come to grips with the enemy and not simply face the horrors of artillery fire where high explosive shells fell without much warning.

The regiment would have to remain in the position that was constantly being shot up and filled with mud as the rains fell. Almost every Other Rank in the regiment had a cold, many men were so sick as to barely be able to speak. Their clothing was completely soaked through to the skin; the boots were falling apart at the seams because of the constant exposure to water. Fortunately, by 10 November the enemy fire at night had died down somewhat.. This gift of time was being used to the best advantage by bringing up large quantities of food and ammunition into the front lines.

Because of the increasingly high number of losses from enemy shell fire and from illnesses, IR 23 had decided to make changes in the occupation of the different sectors.

In the night from 11/12 November some units were relieved and replaced within the regimental sector. On the morning of 12 November the sectors were occupied as follows H1 – two platoons of the 9/23. H2 – two platoons of the 12/23. H3 – the 4/23. H4 – the 2/23. Second trench behind H1-H4 one platoon from the 9th and 11/23. *Röhrlegraben* – the 10/23. *Brettauerweg* – one platoon of the 12/23. *Nagelgraben* – the 1/23. *Sodenbogen* and *Geschwindgraben* – the 3/23. *Zwischen Stellung* behind H3 and H4 – the 5/23. *Feste Soden* – the 7/23. *Nord I* – the 6th and 8/23.

The relief had proceeded with few casualties, despite a constant increase in the strength of the artillery fire day after day. On the morning of 11 November the entire sector north of the Ancre was taken under heavy fire. Because of the strong bombardment the food wagons were unable to reach even the position kitchens. On 12 November the sector was under constant shelling that increased to the level of drum fire in the morning between 6 and 8 a.m.

Entire trenches were leveled and most of the existing dugouts were pressed in. The wire obstacles in front of the 1st and 2nd trenches were completely destroyed. The wire in front of the *Zwischen Stellung* was badly damaged. The enemy batteries continued to rain down shells and shrapnel on the German positions. Because of the level of artillery and mine fire an enemy attack was continuously expected and the overall regimental sector was kept at the highest state of alarm readiness.

The heavy enemy fire falling along the German front left an indelible imprint on the memory of many men.

> On the next day [12th] there was a terrible drum fire of all calibers. Heavy shells exploded in our position, one could clearly see them before they impacted, Schrott had made me attentive to them. Particularly the right wing, where Olbrich resided with his men and was entirely isolated, received the biggest shells. An entrance of their dugout had already been pressed in previously, by which death had come to the friendly, always accommodating Lehmkull, who was paying attention on the steps as the gas sentry. Everyone that knew him will remember him with pleasure. We feared the worst for the dugout, however we later found its occupants glad and cheerful as always before. The dugout had held up well. We had also become bombarded with heavy shells and mines, so that we left the dugout, because we could no longer quite trust it. The trench looked completely devastated. The III Battalion and left wing had received fewer; the middle platoon had suffered badly. Two entrances of the big dugout had collapsed. The big traverse that protected the flank and that we arduously assembled again after every bombardment existed only out of an allusion. An unconscious rage grabbed us! All work destroyed again!
>
> The worst was seen at the right wing. Here was crater by crater of gigantic dimensions. I lost the direction of the trench during the patrol and I was soon in the intermediate terrain. A sentry, who according to his statement had already come to expect me, called me back. He had crouched in a small concrete sentry house for the entire bombardment. When I forbade him to do this in the future, because such courage was pointless, his answer almost offended me: 'If you have duty, you do not also go into any dugout!' Unfortunately the brave Batack, as he was called, was killed on the next day. A huge crater sat at the company border. *Fähnrich* Pukall, 3/62 [4]

During the time the British fire fell on the German trenches in unprecedented strength, not all activities were affected. The men in RIR 55 had been in their positions near the Ancre for the last 10 weeks without interruption and the spirit of the men was described as being excellent. On 11 November a patrol from the 12/R55 made its way across to the enemy trenches under the cover of darkness and managed to capture a particularly annoying British mine thrower in the enemy storm trench in front of Sector B7. The patrol also brought back 12 mines with them, the rest they had thrown into the Ancre, where presumably they still sit today. On the same day, *Infanterist* Pecko, an exceedingly good marksman, forced down a British aircraft by firing a bullet through the aircraft, which destroyed the motor. At least there was one less of the extremely annoying enemy aircraft that always seemed to be flying over the German lines at will.

By IR 62, there was no change in the enemy behavior on 11 and 12 November, the pattern of bombardments continued as in the previous days. The regimental headquarters had received numerous reminders from the brigade and also from the division that an enemy attack was pending. Every command post, as well as the trench garrison was in the highest alarm readiness. On 12 November an extremely dense fog covered the terrain, especially in the morning hours, which prevented any observation of the enemy lines. In order to counter this predicament extra precautions were taken and the number of Light ball posts was increased. In the event the telephone lines failed or runners were unable to get through the enemy fire, several Other Ranks from *Ulan* Regiment 2 along with messenger pigeons were positioned in the regimental battle headquarters.

On the right wing of *B-Mitte* was the 1/R55 under *Leutnant* Romberg in the B-Ravine. On the right flank of this company stood the 9/62, where already on the afternoon of 12 November an entire platoon had been placed out of action through gas shells. Observers in the I/R55 sector also sent back reports that the enemy storm trench was being filled up with men. The observers had quickly sent back reports to the support batteries that opened a moderately powerful barrage fire on the British trenches and as no attack followed, it was assumed that the barrage fire had been successful.. Otherwise, the night had passed quietly.

On 12 November the normal fire raids on the other sectors of RIR 55 were earlier than usual, especially on the rear positions and *Feste Alt Württemberg*, the regimental headquarters. The latter were also bombarded with heavy shells for several hours in the afternoon. By the evening of the 12th there were numerous reports from the front line observers that the British front line trenches were again being strongly occupied by troops, everything pointed to an attack taking place on the 13th. In light of these reports the trench garrisons north of the Ancre were all placed on alert and were advised to prepare for an attack to take place the following day.

The German front line was being held by elements from four German regiments. IR 95 held the ground along the northern bank of the Ancre west of Beaucourt. The front line west of Beaucourt and sectors B4, B5, B6 and B7 were occupied by the I and III/R55. The II/R55 occupied the second line in support of the front line. The I and III/62 occupied the sectors B1 to B4 as well as H5 and H6 in front of Beaumont, while IR 23 occupied the sectors north of Beaumont up until Serre.

The II/R55 occupied *Feste Alt Württemberg* at the *Beaucourt Riegel* of Sector N (*Zwischen Stellung*). The 5th Company, (*Leutnant* Lenze), lay in the *Beaucourt Riegel*, the 6th Company (*Leutnant* Tietse) in N III, the 7th Company (*Leutnant* Rödlingshöfer]) in N IV, the 8th Company (*Leutnant* Bollkämper) in *Feste Alt Württemberg* with the regimental staff. All of the positions were badly damaged due to the continuous artillery fire.

The four companies of the III/R55 could only muster a fighting strength of between 130 – 140 men apiece as a result of losses through illness, death and wounds. The high demands placed on the men during the seven week enemy bombardment from guns of all calibers and from heavy mines and the constant alert readiness had greatly weakened them. The positions were destroyed and, for the most part, were no longer 'defensible'. B7 consisted mainly of individual craters that were crudely interconnected and no wire entanglements existed in the front. Many of the mined dugout tunnel entrances had been badly damaged in the shell fire and required constant repairs in order to keep them moderately functional..

On the left of RIR 55, in a southeast direction, stood IR 95 but there was no actual connection between the two regiments. In September and October secure connection to the left Ancre shore had been maintained through nightly patrols. When the swampy riverbed became impassable because of the heavy rain, the connection between both sides of the river was broken. Attempts were still made to establish some sort of direct communication despite the dangerous conditions, without much success. On several occasions, men almost lost their lives trying to make it from one side of the river to the other. *Unteroffizier* Neuschäfer, 12/R55, almost drowned during such a patrol undertaking.

There were no longer any real defensive positions along the edge of the Ancre Valley since the rains had started. By the end of September the dugout that was mined into the steep slope descending to the embankment, whose occupation should effectively block off the embankment from the enemy, was almost uninhabitable. The ground water was so high that both Groups accommodated inside the dugout could only sit with their backs up against the dripping walls of the tunnel. The exits of this dugout had to be frequently reopened, because they were constantly being filled with debris from shell fire. The left wing platoon, 12/R55, and with it the immediate connection to the railway embankment was

The Ancre, November 1916. (Author's collection)

under the command of *Leutnant* Gerhard Weyland.

The night of 12/13 November was unusually quiet. The rain had stopped and the nearly full moon shone so brightly on the shattered terrain that the men could observe any movement at great distance, an ideal situation if the enemy was to attack as expected. The men sitting in the German trenches and shell craters, while pleased about the lack of rain and good visibility, wondered what this conspicuous and unaccustomed silence indicated. The men immediately began to experience an eerie sensation that something was just not right. They also worried about what the enemy was up to in the stillness and what activities it might be concealing.

Towards dawn, an increasingly dense fog covered the terrain and rendered any observation impossible. The German alarm sentries anxiously strained to listen for any sounds coming from the enemy lines in order to prevent their comrades from being surprised. By 6 a.m. still no sounds, still no enemy activity and no infantry or artillery fire fell in their vicinity. The eeriness only increased in intensity.

The night from 12/13 November was wonderful. A clear starry heaven was above us, the moon our staunch ally, shone with full strength and made an attack unlikely. Dead silence prevailed. No shot disturbed this silence; no light balls brought attention to themselves. Finally I could sleep a few hours at a time, after I had again inspected every sentry post through the terrain. However towards mornings I was in the trench again, because each night the Englishmen had worked in front of their trench around dawn and made a racket, possibly trying to make our sentries unwary. Nevertheless each morning we had occupied the entrances to our dugouts, ready for an attack. This constant highest alarm readiness had an exhausting effect.

Also today I listened across to the English position, once the moon sank and a light fog formed between the lines. On the right a sound could be heard! There our magnificent Huismann came running up, who I also learned was irreplaceable in this position, and he asked for permission to be allowed to fetch the mail. Three large sacks were lugged up here. I allowed each sentry to be relieved at his post so he could receive his mail. The first mail for three weeks, what joy! And for many it was the last! I only opened my letters, because the silence outdoors demanded our highest attention. Meanwhile the fog had become very dense, it was conspicuously quiet. I went to the hollow, where the double sentry reported: '*Damn* fog, otherwise everything quiet!' Then I went back to the left wing. There Geisemeyer called me, whose good eyes rendered special delight to me that I should come listen, it was so different today outdoors. I strained to listen; the frequent repetition of dull sounds could be heard. That could not be entrenching or cutting of obstacles. The Tommys undoubtedly marched on! I allowed my platoon to make ready and occupy the stairways and ran to the right wing. There the same sound could be heard. 'Make ready, highest alarm readiness!' I also ordered here. Then I ran to the hollow. At the right slope was also a reliable sentry, who had heard the sound in front of him and to the right. The hollow was free from sound. Therefore, consistent with the artillery preparation. *Fähnrich* Pukall, 3/62 [5]

While the men from IR 62 were experiencing an unusually quiet evening, it was not as peaceful just a short distance to the north and the south. At 3 a.m. gas shells began to fall near the III/R55 by the Ancre. This fire continued for several hours when, at 5 a.m., trench sentries sent back a report that the British assault trenches were filled with men.

Due to the extremely dense fog, all of the regiments along the front line had sent out extra patrols into no man's land in order to keep an eye on any enemy activity. One of the last reports sent back to the III/R55 and the 9/R55 at 6.10 a.m. mentioned that *Gefreiter* Preuss and *Musketier* Landauer, 11/R55, had been severely wounded while out on one of these patrols.

IR 23 reported that British artillery fire continued to fall on the regimental position north of Beaumont during the night of 12/13 November, especially on the communication trenches leading toward the rear. Clearly the enemy was up to something, but what?

The daily enemy drum fire started across all of the sectors promptly at 6 a.m. as usual. The German front line observers were almost blind as a result of extremely dense early morning fog that blanketed the terrain. It seemed that the British were also firing smoke bombs into the fog that only made the opaque wall even thicker; visibility was down to a few feet in some places.

The increased level of enemy fire drew the attention of regimental headquarters, who contacted the III/23 headquarters (Battalion Lemcke) in the right hand sector of the regiment by telephone. They simply asked: 'What is the situation?' The reply was: 'Besides the strongest artillery fire there was nothing unusual.' The telephone connections leading to the I/23 (Battalion Eichholz) in the left sector of the regiment had already been destroyed in the British artillery fire and all communications would have to rely upon runners as lamps signals were useless in the fog and smoke.

The II/R55 reported that since 6.30 a.m. strong drum fire lay upon the battalion and the rear terrain. *Leutnant* Dobberke from the Machine Gun Company was the AVO [Artillery Observation Officer] of the regiment in *Feste Alt Württemberg* with *Leutnant* Kracht, 6/R55, a Bavarian artillery observer, 4 *Unteroffizier*, 5 Telephonists, 6 runners and 2 officer's servants. Early on the 13th, at 6 a.m., a telephone report was received from the III/R55: 'The English storm trenches are occupied.' There would be a delay in transmitting this report to brigade headquarters and the supporting artillery as all telephone connections to the rear had been destroyed in the heavy fire.

When the enemy drum fire began, *Feste Alt Württemberg* was also strongly bombarded. The numerous light balls fired off at the front simply could not be seen, even by observers as close as *Feste Alt Württemberg*, because of the dense fog. *Leutnant* Dobberke reported to the regiment that observation was impossible. At 6.45 a.m. machine gun fire was audible and bullets were striking the ground around the position. Still, there was nothing that could be seen.

The enemy drum fire reached a crescendo, a previously unheard of intensity, at 6.45 a.m. Almost simultaneously a huge mine explosion occurred in Sectors B1 and B2 destroying wide stretches of these company sectors. One complete platoon from the 11/62 was destroyed or buried in the massive explosion.[6] The enemy infantry attacked simultaneously with the drum fire and the mine explosion; the long anticipated attack had begun.

> He had heavy losses everywhere in our infantry and machine gun fire. There, where the mine explosion had destroyed the garrison of our position, he could penetrate into the first trench. While the companies still were involved with the defense of the attack the enemy had employed on the front, strong enemy detachments penetrated into our

position from the rear, coming from Beaucourt, through the *Mittleren, Revier, Grenz* and *Karren Graben* and now also attacked the companies here further from the rear. After heavy losses the companies of the Sectors B1 and B2 yielded at 9.30 o'clock in the morning. Battalion commander, *Rittmeister* von Dresth, III/62 [7]

RIR 55 reported that the powerful drum fire was transferred to the rear positions at 6.45 a.m. and seemingly within minutes the enemy was already inside the German position. The 2/R55 under *Leutnant* Steffen, who commanded the middle platoon in Sector B4, had a total force of 4 *Unteroffiziere* and 31 Other Ranks. The wire obstacles in front of his sector had been totally destroyed and enemy troops were quite close, in some parts only 80 meter distant. *Leutnant* Steffen's men were at an even greater disadvantage; the enemy trench could not be seen from his position due to the lay of the ground. Considering this fact, the trench sentries remained on high alert in the dense fog during the bombardment. However, in a short time the trench was entirely leveled and all of the sentries were dead or wounded.

The 9/R55 under *Leutnant* Diekmann was in the first trench of B6 with three platoons. On the right was the 1st Platoon under *Leutnant* Meyenberg, alongside them the 2nd Platoon under *Leutnant* Ostrop, then the 3rd Platoon under *Unteroffizier* Schürmann. The company commander was in the second trench with 20 men and two platoons from the 10/R55 under *Leutnants* Knappmann and Besecke. The 3rd Platoon of the 10/R55 under *Leutnant* Keiser was in the third trench. The commander of the 10/R55, *Leutnant* Neise, was in the *Bismarck Stollen* with 20 men as well as the telephone switchboard that connected the sector to the battalion, however, quite a few of the lines had been destroyed in the enemy artillery fire. Gas shells also forced the men to wear their gas masks which placed an additional physical strain on the troops and reduced visibility even more.

The 11/R55 opened fire on the British trenches with *Minenwerfer, Priesterwerfer* and the *Erdmörser* in expectation of the probable enemy attack. Light balls fired into the air calling for defensive barrage fire went unanswered, due to the dense fog that covered the Ancre valley. As the events unfolded across the front lines, most of the regimental battle headquarters located further to the rear were in the dark about the situation at the front.

The attack had been detected in a timely fashion at the front line and every man was in their position on high alert. It was later determined that RIR 55 was being attacked in the front by the Royal Naval Division and a Canadian brigade. While the drum fire was still falling on the sector, enemy columns, which had successfully attacked south of the Ancre, crossed over the river. Now these troops used the cover of the dense fog to spring a surprise attack on the *Biber Kolonie* and the rear of the regimental position.

At 7.20 a.m. 60 British troops appeared at the *Bismarck Stollen*, approaching from the *Pionier Dorf* and dug in there. They were then forced to withdraw to the *Biber Kolonie* by the fire from a *Priesterwerfer*. At 7.45 a.m. the connection between the *Bismarck Stollen* and the battalion had ceased to exist. The *Albrecht Mörser* located in the middle of the third trench fired very effectively on the *Irles Graben*. It was not until early on 14 November when it was rendered unserviceable, similarly the *Priesterwerfer*. Both weapons were captured by the enemy at noon on 14 November.

At 7.50 a.m., strong enemy columns, which had probably crossed the bridge over the Ancre near the mill, advanced up the *Hang Stellung* and simultaneously dense skirmish lines approached, coming down from Beaucourt. Part then went to the north in the direction of *Feste Alt Württemberg*. Facing this unexpected threat, the garrison of the *Hang Stellung* was reinforced as fresh reserves arrived.

Within minutes of the initial enemy attack a *pionier* runner arrived at the regimental headquarters of RIR 55 from the *Pionier Dorf* carrying a message that the British were attacking and that numerous dugouts had been damaged and the exits blocked from the heavy fire. The adjutant of the III/R55, *Leutnant* Genest, also received a report over one of the few intact telephone lines that there was hand grenade fighting in Sector B5.

Hauptmann von Obernitz immediately sent battle orderlies to the *Pionier Dorf* and to the front. They did not get very far as the dugout entrances at the headquarters dugout were already occupied by British troops. Suddenly, explosions took place as hand grenades were thrown down into the dugout entrances and the staff of the III/R55 found they could no longer exit their shelter. The entire *Kolonie* was apparently occupied by the enemy and many of the dugouts located there were burning with thick columns of smoke and flames rising into the air.

Following the telephone message received by *Leutnant* Genest, all telephone lines were cut and regimental headquarters could not be advised of the critical situation taking place by the III/R55. All maps, documents and papers in the headquarters dugout were immediately burned in order to prevent anything of value from falling into enemy hands.

Hauptmann von Obernitz and *Leutnant* Thofern, leader of the 3rd Machine Gun Company, and two officer's servants were soon taken prisoner by British bombing parties and taken away through the position of the III/R55 Battalion toward the Ancre. Attacked from the front and the rear, the men in the front lines did not stand a chance under these circumstances.

The German batteries in the rear had still not opened a defensive barrage fire as expected in such moments. Apparently they could not see the flares being fired into the air because of the dense and fog which was only made worse by the explosions of the artillery shells and the burning dugouts. The dense fog was also affecting the sounds coming from the front, which were being muffled; as such the gunners were unaware of the magnitude of the enemy attack. With all other means of communication ineffective, runners would have to carry all messages to and from the front lines from now on.

The situation facing the III/R55 was growing worse minute by minute. The first trench on the left of the *Junker Graben* was overrun; the enemy was on the right wing of the second trench of B7. Some local successes were achieved such as when Machine Gun No. 4 and Group van Egern, 10/R55, forced the British back temporarily.

Leutnant Rittenbruch, 1MG/R55 and three men were wounded early in the fighting. Afterward, *Leutnant* Rittenbruch still fought very bravely with the 8/R55 where he was then shot through the body. The enemy attack was finally repulsed as a result of the work by Machine Gun No. 3. The platoon of *Leutnant* Ostrop then pursued the fleeing enemy and also threw them out of the shell holes in the foreground. A British flamethrower was reported being destroyed at the right wing and two British officers and 40 Other Ranks, half of them unwounded, were taken prisoner. The enemy prisoners were brought into the *Bismarck Stollen* where they would be protected from artillery fire. The German infantry were defending the position alone; the German batteries still did not fire.

Platoon Besecke blocked off the second trench of B6 by dugouts 39/40 and occupied the *Junker Graben* between the first and second trenches. Besecke then advanced in a counterattack with men from the 9th and 10/R55, by which *Unteroffizier* van Egern, *Gefreiter* Dabbel, *Musketier* Rars, 10/R55, and *Unteroffizier* Schürmann, 9/R55, behaved n a conspicuous manner. While the British troops had succeeded in taking possession of the largest part of the 1st and 2nd trenches of B7 after several hours of bitter fighting the British troops that had penetrated in B6 were thrown out again through the powerful counterattacks by the 9th and 10/R55 at 8.15 a.m.

Barricades were erected on the wings of the first trench of B6. Following orders from the battalion, *Leutnant* Keiser, 10/R55, launched a counterattack with the few available reserves out of the *Bismarck Stollen* through the third trench of B6. However, it soon became bogged down at B7 through the fiercest opposition and, as a result, Keiser was forced to block off B6. *Leutnant* Keiser was killed during the attack and his death was considered a great loss. Platoon Knappmann, 10/R55, with Platoon Schellewald, 3/R55, turned to the defense out of necessity. *Leutnant* Nolting, 3/R55, joined Machine Gun No. 6 in the front.

Little was known of the overall situation in the sector of the III/R55. In many cases the companies could only make sense of what was happening in their immediate vicinity and there was little coordination between units. The enemy drum fire lasted until 7.05 a.m. when much of the fire was transferred further to the rear. *Leutnant* Weyland was in the *Storchennest* trying to observe the enemy movements in the smoke and fog. *Unteroffizier* Nell and three men were sent out to reinforce the patrols that were still located somewhere in the front of the position. The machine guns opened fired upon the railway embankment in the hopes of slowing down the enemy advance. Several small fires inside the trenches caused by incendiary bombs were extinguished.

Early on the 13th, *Leutnant* Harald Haase, 12/R55 had his platoon standing ready in the dugout entrances while he crouched in the trench with his servant Wilczura, *Unteroffizier* Fiebig and a double sentry. 15 minutes after the beginning of the drum fire the first British soldier appeared out of the fog. Everyone was outside in a moment and greeted the enemy with a hail of hand grenades. Then the effort was made to have the men also use their rifles and not have everyone 'blow off powder' by using just hand grenades.

The British broke inton at 7.15 a.m. and the second platoon of the 12/R55 under *Vizefeldwebel* Cybulka hurried to help. The third platoon of *Leutnant* Harald Haase, who, immediately at the start of the attack were all in shell holes, was completely surrounded by 8 a.m. The fighting was vicious, with small groups of men from both sides engaged in close combat using whatever weapon they had at hand.

The machine gun allocated to the company suddenly stopped firing. It was carried down into a nearby dugout where it was determined that the feed mechanism had broken. Therefore the platoon could only defend the position using rifles and hand grenades. *Unteroffizier* Fiebig fired all of the flares into the sky in vain, because the fog was impenetrable. It was discovered that the enemy had broken through on the right and on the left of the platoon. At 8.15 a.m. *Leutnant* Haase was severely wounded twice.

Suddenly, the flat steel helmets of the Englishmen appeared on all sides, so that it was impossible, to establish a connection on the right to the 10th Company and on the left to the second platoon. The only thing remaining was to defend ourselves like a hedgehog and hope for the counterattack by the garrison of the second and third trenches or the 11th Company. As soon as the men of the third platoon (Haase) had some space, they shouted Hurrah, pointing out the way to the men lying behind them. They didn't suspect that the 11th Company had probably already been taken captive.

Through rifle fire and hand grenades the Englishmen shrank the platoon together. When out of the fog 1 officer and 2 men (Englishmen) appeared close behind *Leutnant* Haase, were they 'surrounded'? When an English squad with a machine gun approached from half right, *Leutnant* Haase succeeded in forcing them to turn back with losses with his pistol. Now *Leutnant* Haase a received a shot in the back of his head and fell there. His brain was injured. He went into the dugout to allow himself to be bandaged, where later, he was overpowered by superior strength, and was taken prisoner with a few men. He had later received the Iron Cross I Class upon the application of *Hauptmann* Winkelmann.[8]

Unteroffizier Fiebig took over the third platoon following the loss of the platoon leader Nearly everyone in the 12/R55 was dead or wounded. The last four men in the shell craters were finally taken prisoner. *Gefreiter* Glas with six men went into dugout No. 1 and remained hidden inside for a long time. Finally, at 11 a.m. on 15 November, Glas and one other man were taken prisoner. *Unteroffizier* Nell was among the men taken prisoner that day.

Losses continued to rise; two men suffocated in the *T-Stollen* after it had been set on fire. *Leutnant* Weyland, who had been forced from his observation post, attempted to retake the *Storchennest*, however he was taken prisoner as a result of his attempt. The *Schleusinger Haus*, occupied by *Unteroffizier* Gorsky and nine men, was close to the embankment and the *Ebeltweg*. It was attacked from the rear, and as a counterattack was not possible, it was also taken by the enemy. *Leutnant* Dreyer was killed at some point in the fighting. The railway embankment and the Ancre valley were now occupied by the British.

In the days following the intense fighting, *Leutnants* Weyland and Harald Haase *Unteroffiziers* Fiebig and Engelmann became nominated by *Major* Tauscher for the Iron Cross 1st Class. *Gefreiter* Bosenius, *Musketiers* Wilczura, Thomas, *Landsturmmann* Meyer *Musketier* Nowatzki, *Landsturmmann* Wiegel, *Fernsprecher* Bracht were nominated for the Iron Cross II Class. The total losses of the 12/R55 were 36 men killed, 67 men wounded and 30 men taken prisoner.

During this time, events at the right wing of RIR 55 were unfolding in much the same manner as on the left sector of the regiment. In the right hand sector the 3rd Platoon of the 1/R55, under *Leutnant* Finkeldey, and the machine gun in the sector were in the trench ready for action, as were the other platoons. The 3rd Platoon and the machine gun drove off the initial enemy attack with accurate defensive fire and hand grenades. On the left wing of the 1st Platoon a few British troops managed to penetrate the front line trench, but they were quickly thrown out with large losses.

However, the position of the 1/R55 was not secure; the enemy still remained in a flanking position on the slope of the ravine. The British had apparently taken the position of the neighboring IR 62. Dense enemy columns were observed moving through the *Sommer Graben* to the rear of the position. *Leutnant* Finkeldey continued to fire red flares into the air, in vain. These signals were never seen by the artillery in the rear and still no defensive barrage fire followed.

The 4/R55 under *Oberleutnant Graf* Matuschka was in B4. Every man in the company had also been on alert for signs of the enemy attack. The first British waves were met by a hail of infantry and machine gun fire and effectively prevented from penetrating the German line. Only the left wing of the company was overrun and then pressed back by the increasing numbers of British troops. The 4/R55 reported that some German batteries did respond to the light signals in its sector, however, in the dense fog, many of these shells fell on the men of the 4/R55, causing a number of losses.

Graf Matuschka had wanted to recapture the piece of the first trench that had been lost with a counterattack out of the second trench. Two dugouts with their garrisons had already become overrun, reducing the overall strength of the company considerably. *Leutnant* Krautscheid wanted to begin his attack at 7.15 a.m., when large numbers of the enemy suddenly came through the fog and engaged his forces.

The reserve company of the I/R55, the 3/R55 was commanded by *Leutnant* Nolting. One platoon from it under *Leutnant* Schellewald was extremely overextended in the second trench of B4 and B5 and it was tactically subordinate to Sector B5. Almost every man in the 3/R55 had been employed in the defense of the position. The other platoons of the 3/R55 were in the third trench of B5 with individual Groups in the trenches of B4. At 7 a.m. *Leutnant* Schellewald was attacked from the front and the right. His company was able to force the British back, took one prisoner and then became involved in a protracted hand grenade battle at the right wing of the company sector.

The 3rd Platoon of the 1/R55 was forced to defend its position from the front as well as the rear. At 7.45 a.m. an attack followed from the rear from out of the *Sommer Graben*. *Leutnant* Finkeldey was able to throw them back in a counterattack. The British also advanced through the *Leiling Schlucht* in the direction of the *Luna Weg* where *Leutnant* Romberg was fatally wounded at the exit of his dugout.[9]

The enemy was prevented from advancing through the *Luna Weg* by the 3rd Platoon using a considerable number of hand grenades. In the meantime, the garrison of the second and third trench under *Leutnant* Neuschäfer moved forward and defended the *Leiling Schlucht* against the enemy who continued to press deeper into the ravine. By 8 a.m. the connection by the 3rd Platoon with the 1/R55 had been re-established.. *Leutnant* Finkeldey had taken over the 1/R55 from *Leutnant* Romberg; however he remained with the 3rd Platoon.

One of the first orders he gave was that *Leutnant* Neuschäfer should defend the *Leiling Schlucht* on both sides, because he already knew that the British had penetrated into the *Kolonie* at 7 a.m. *Leutnant* Finkeldey also wanted to protect the position from the direction of IR 62 and ordered *Feldwebel Leutnant* Spieker, to defend the rear of the position and to preserve the connection with the 4/R55. Spieker was also ordered to direct the defense of the ravine where the British attempted to advance.

Further enemy attacks in the front wererepulsed by the 3rd Platoon using hand grenades and with support from the machine gun there. Finkeldey had correctly assessed the danger on his right flank when the British attempted to roll up the position of the I/R55 from the right on several occasions. A hand grenade attack by the 1/R55 finally cleared the position of IR 62 up to the vicinity of *Sommer Graben*.

The fighting around the *Leiling Schlucht* was like a scene from Dante's Inferno. All of dugouts were burning, flames and smoke pouring into the already dense fog. Dead and wounded men from both sides lay scattered throughout the landscape and every portion of the original defenses had been smashed into rubble. Finally, the bombing parties had to withdraw from their advanced position toward the right wing so they would not become cut off by British troops advancing from out of the *Sommer Graben*. The close fighting had caused heavy losses to the 1/R55. At 10 a.m. a message was sent to the battalion with the plea for reinforcements and ammunition; especially hand grenades.

Two mine explosions were reported in front of the company sector by the 2/R55 at 7 a.m. A massive enemy attack took place covered by British artillery fire, giving the defenders no time to occupy the positions before the attack. Fierce hand grenade fights broke out across the company sector and in a short time the connections to the rear and to both sides were broken. The surviving members of the garrison soon became crowded into the few remaining dugouts and were taken prisoner when the British began employing incendiary bombs; to remain inside the dugout meant certain death by smoke inhalation or by fire so the men wisely chose to surrender.

At 7.15 a.m. the trench sentries in the third trench reported: 'Individual Englishmen on the right.' Despite the report, it was still uncertain if the enemy was on the right or if it was actually other German troops as visibility was still poor. A patrol was sent to Sector B4 to make certain if the troops were friend or foe. The patrol firmly established that they were the enemy when they came under heavy infantry fire as they approached the group of men.

A runner was also sent to the battalion at 7.30 a.m. by the 4/R55, looking for reinforcements and ammunition, but there was none to spare. Dugout No 11 in the second trench was captured, the connection with the other companies was broken and at 8 a.m. *Vizefeldwebel* Paschenke was killed; the rest of the dugouts were soon besieged by the British as well.

At 7.45 a.m. the 2/R55 sent requests for help. The British were in front in B5, the connection with *Leutnant* Angott and the half platoon further on the right was broken. The communication route to the first trench and the second trench were already in part occupied by the British. There was still no connection to the 10/R55 on the left.

At 8 a.m. 30 British soldiers attacked the third trench from the right. They were repulsed and a wounded First Lieutenant was taken prisoner, along with a machine gun, two Plate guns [Lewis Guns] with ammunition. *Leutnant* Schäfer, who had been wounded in the head, fought on until his death. The connection with three Groups that were on the right of the *Zirkus Graben* [also known as the *Cirkus Graben* on some maps] was gone. At 8 a.m., an *Unteroffizier* with two men from the Machine Gun Company, who had come out of the *Kolonie*, also reported that this position had been taken by the British. *Leutnant* Nolting now also had to provide protection from the enemy threat in his rear. A runner from the battalion had come back; apparently he did not have any III Battalion Headquarters to report to. The dugouts burned everywhere, adding to the hellish scene facing the men *Leutnant* Nolting, 10/R55, brought down a machine gun from a position where it could not bring fire to bear on the enemy advance to a new position which would have a much better effect on the current fighting. It was positioned in the third trench and was used with good success, firing in the direction of B4. Confusion seemed to be prevalent on both sides as no one really knew who occupied a particular trench from minute to minute.

A British runner, who was coming from the recently captured *Kolonie*, ran into the hands of the 10/R55 and was taken prisoner. The British were definitely in the possession of the hillside position between Beaumont and Beaucourt, threatening the left flank and rear of the I and III/R55. *Leutnant* Nolting went to the leader the 10/R55, *Leutnant* Neise, in the *Bismarck Stollen* to discuss the overall situation. Both officers were determined to maintain their hold on the position.

By now, all telephone connections to battalion headquarters had been destroyed. *Leutnant* Nolting sent runners to the battalion and to *Leutnant* Schellewald to advise them of the situation. At 7.45 a.m. Nolting received a message, 'The Second trench running from B5 until the first communication route was held, *Leutnant* Schellewald asks about support.' In response to this request, *Leutnant* Neise, 10/R55, was only able to send a few men over to them.

The II/R55, located in the rear in support, knew little of what was taking place at the front. The sounds of fighting were coming from every direction and the visibility was still bad. Observers strained to see if they could make out anything that could provide some insight into the events at the front, without success. It was not until 8.30 a.m. when *Unteroffizier* Stratmann, 3/R55 who was wounded, approached the left wing of *Feste Alt Württemberg* with the report: 'The Englishmen have taken the forward position.'

Leutnant Buchholz, 6/R55, reported this to the regimental headquarters after which *Oberstleutnant* von Laue issued orders: 'The 8th Company should make a counterattack, *Leutnant* Buchholz with the platoon of the 6th Company should perform reconnaissance at the left wing of *Feste Alt Württemberg*.' Additional orders were sent to the II/R55: The adversary has broken through in B5. If the situation at the Ancre permits it, become inserted in the front. Report to the *Kolonie*.' This order did not arrive at its destination until very late. *Leutnant* Buchholz quickly determined that the British were already in the hollow of the *Kimmich Graben*, west of the *Schloss Stellung*.

At 10 a.m. two telephone men, Metting and Wagner went out from the headquarters of the II/R55 to mend the wires. At 10.30 a.m. the two men had managed to repair the wire and a telephone connection now existed to the regiment. The first message sent was: According to oral message by runners the Englishmen broke in at B5. The fighting was still taking place. Barrage fire signals were urgently required. The tower sentry reported: 'The Englishmen are already here. The dugout entrance is already occupied.'

When *Leutnant* Dobberke reported this to the regimental headquarters, *Leutnant* Giesecke shouted back: 'The Englishmen are already at our dugout!' This was the last news from the regimental staff, it was 10.30 a.m. At 11 a.m. the British continued to advance into their own artillery fire. There was still no sign of any defensive fire from the German batteries in the rear.

Leutnant Bollkämper had observed British troops in front of the *Zwischen Stellung*. However, he was unable to make a counterattack out of his extended position or the *Zwischen Stellung* or *Schloss Stellung* during the heavy drum fire. In a short time the British had also apparently attacking the regimental battle headquarters at *Feste Alt Württemberg*. *Oberstleutnant* von Laue and *Leutnant* Giesecke were able to ward off the initial attack with great effort. They knew that the position would be lost if additional enemy troops arrived.

Oberstleutnant von Laue and *Leutnant* Giesecke had decided that it would be safer at the II Battalion headquarters dugout in the *Artillerie Mulde*. At approximately 11 a.m. von Laue and Giesecke left the headquarters dugout with several men and proceeded toward the position of *Hauptmann* Minck. During the attempt, *Oberstleutnant* von Laue was killed by artillery fire and *Leutnant* Giesecke was reported missing. Two other men were with them, a cook who was apparently also killed and Telephonist August Metting.

Metting later stated that while hurrying toward the II/R55 headquarters dugout, the four men advanced by jumps from one shell crater to the next in some of the heaviest drum fire they had ever experienced. After the second jump, Telephonist Metting stated he lost consciousness and, when he awakened later, he could not locate any of his three companions. He then assumed that all three had been killed in the shell fire.

Metting continued to make his way toward Beaucourt and the only men he saw on his journey were either dead or seriously wounded. On 14 November, Metting was captured by the British and became a prisoner-of-war. *Oberstleutnant* von Laue and *Leutnant* Giesecke were later found and their death by artillery fire was confirmed.

As a result of the severe and ongoing artillery fire over the last days, the trenches of the *Beaucourt Riegel* that *Leutnant* Lenze had occupied with the 5/R55, was entirely leveled by 13 November. Also the *Feldwach Stellung*, the *Kiesgrube*, had become covered by artillery fire. As the companies of the II/R55 located in the forward line were now completely cut off from battalion headquarters. *Leutnant* Lenze, 5/R55, took on the leadership of the battle line. *Hauptmann* Minck did not receive the message about these events until later in the afternoon.

By the neighboring IR 62, the enemy drum fire reached its highest intensity at 6.45 a.m. Almost simultaneously, a huge mine explosion followed in Sectors B1 and B2, destroying wide stretches of two company sectors. Immediately following the massive explosion the enemy infantry began their attack. Before the first wave could reach the first trench, the Other Ranks, who were already sitting and standing on the stairways of the dugouts plunged out into the badly damaged trenches and shell craters and received the enemy attack with rifle and machine gun fire and hand grenades.

The British were only able to penetrate the front line of IR 62 where the garrison had already been destroyed or incapacitated by being buried by the mine explosion. Strong fire coming from the second and third trench stopped them from advancing any further. The second and third trenches were completely occupied and held out against the enemy onrush. Dead and wounded lay in large numbers before the front, individual British troops who had managed to penetrate the first German trench were taken prisoner. New attack waves did not follow and so the situation appeared under control in the regimental sector.

A joyous, celebratory mood came over the men from IR 62 holding the first trench. They were proud of their success. All discomforts of the last week were apparently forgotten in the moment.

> Now what was needed was to anticipate the Tommy. Now the tunnel exploded! Now the machine guns sparkled! Why did the machine gun in the hollow still not fire? I ran to the hollow, but I moved back after a few steps, horrified. What was that? A gigantic column of fire rustled to the heavens. The fog increased in ghostly volume and doesn't allow us to see where it went up and what range to maintain. It could be equally the same by *Leutnant* Scheer, as with the III Battalion. Simultaneously, machine gun fire never heard before raged along on the entire front and a hail of mines pattered down upon us here mixed with furious shrapnel fire. I ran back to my platoon, the sentry jumped into cover, attack!
>
> In the shortest time hand grenades were distributed, as much ammunition as they could carry was given out to everyone and the stairways were occupied again. I quickly looked around the bunks, if perhaps anyone had forgotten his duty, although I had nothing to fear. At each tunnel entrance a selected *Unteroffizier* stood with a light pistol and hand grenades that was to give the signal to occupy the trench as soon as the drum fire was transferred. At our exit stood the untiring, irreplaceable Schrott, a forester in his 40's. There also shouted the sap sentries already: "They come!" Immediately following a hand grenade crashed in the dugout that formed the exit into the sap. Following it flew a series of hand grenades in the old trench that connected the

sap with the new trench. 'Get out,' only two were allowed to remain behind, who were to have protected the subterranean sap and with it our dugout. The garrison of the trench, which was so immaculately equipped by us that I could never have dreamed of, now took place first on the right and on the left of the dugout by us in the manner that each man threw a hand grenade, whereupon the rifleman posted there went on the attack. Everyone had to run this way, also covering his path through the tossing of a hand grenade over the cover, jumped into his position and opened fire. This proved itself to be excellent in front of Beaumont, because the Englishmen advanced in their own drum fire. Also they did not come in a skirmish line, but in masses.

Individuals had come earlier, many later, many came alone. One Tommy was already in our trench, when we occupied it. A *Gefreiter* ran at him. Geisemeyer firmly believed that one Tommy with a lit cigarette and sloped rifle before the actual attack was in front of him and had to be shot. I saw red and white light balls go high in the hollow, which however in the dense fog only appeared as puny points of light. Therefore I immediately gave up launching red light balls, because I remarked, whoever has not seen the mine explosion from behind, whoever was not toppled out of their bunk because of the earth movement from the mine explosion and whoever did not hear the shooting, will also not notice such. Furthermore *Leutnant* Walter had a telephone that was possibly still in order. I therefore fired all light balls from our platoon at the ground, so that everyone who came past would become visible as shadow images in the fog. Others did not glow. We soon had calm, that is to say today I am still lacking any concept of time for the duration of the individual fighting. There, as we stood continuously in close combat, I abstained from making any time recordings in my report book. After daybreak we had to endure one more fierce close combat with hand grenades that I later saw as a large war picture in an English magazine. The most economical ammunition consumption was ordered, and was also executed impeccably. I have not seen anyone, who had become nervous. At this time I was very far to the left and came into an embarrassing situation, when a Lewis Gun appeared in front of me. I received hand grenades from half-right. *Unteroffizier* Belkner came to me in no time at all with hand grenades to help, without hesitating he jumped out of the cover and nearly hit two Tommys lying close in front of us with a hand grenade. He did not hear my shout to stop because of the battle noise. Before his hand grenade exploded, a rifle pattered again and Belkner was hit, he fell over backwards into the trench. I came safely away. I came back again into the same position with urgency, this time an Oldenburger helped me. The Tommy fell into our trench severely hit. After that we had to wait alone a long time. Out of all eyes shone the uplifting feeling, we have stood at our forlorn position! Those at home could look at these fighters with pride, who still yesterday had accomplished what was thought to be insane, in that they had held this hopeless position. The tight discipline, combined with self-control, tough energy and devotion by every individual, had accomplished that miracle. Forgotten was all of the lack of courage of the last days. An almost high spirited mood prevailed. I can still see the mischievous Ulka today pointing out to the dead and wounded lying in front of us with the words: "*Fähnrich*, I wonder if they have any cocoa and *schnapps*? Fähnrich Pukall, 3/62 [10]

The men enjoyed their initial success, when suddenly loud battle noises came from the rear of the front line. Infantry, machine gun fire and English cries of 'Hurra' could clearly be heard and it was soon observed in the thinning fog that the enemy was still developing his advance to the east and southeast. The British had mainly broken through to the south by RIR 55 and then turned in a northerly direction. So it came that the I and III/62 Battalion staff lying at the eastern edge of Beaumont were suddenly facing strong enemy forces. After the fighting had surged back and forth, during which the two battalion staff were repeatedly captured and then liberated as new reserves appeared that exchanged places with the company lying in the third trench, they ultimately ended up as prisoners of war.

Leutnant der Reserve and Battalion Adjutant Hofmann, I/62, drew particular attention to himself here. When he was being taken away as a prisoner, he struck down his escort and grabbed his rifle from him. He succeeded in making it through to the regimental staff even while severely wounded, being shot in the chest. Unfortunately this brave officer later died from his injuries. In the same manner, *Leutnant der Reserve* Römer and six men were also able to strike through to the rear and safety.

The intense drum fire followed by the mine explosion had been observed by the regimental staff. With all telephone lines cut by the artillery fire, attempts were made to contact the I and III/62 using battle runners and hopefully to obtain some information about the situation at the front. At 7.15 a.m. the battle runners bumped into a strong enemy infantry detachment about 300 meters west of the regimental battle headquarters. The British opened fire on the runners, forcing them to return to the regimental battle headquarters. Upon hearing the news from the runners, *Oberstleutnant* von Poser, guided by some orderlies, hurried through the heaviest enemy artillery fire to the *Zwischen Stellung* and alarmed the *Schanz* Company lying there and the 7/62 that had been moved there a few days before. It was not possible for the rest of the regimental staff to escape the headquarters dugout and withdraw to the *Zwischen Stellung*, because the exits of the dugout had become occupied by the enemy. Later they succeeded, escaping through a half collapsed exit, aided by the heavy smoke and fog.

While the defence was still being organized in the *Zwischen Stellung*, the first enemy patrols had already advanced against this position. An attempt to establish a connection with the battle battalion using one platoon from the 7/62 and a patrol from the *Bau* Company failed because of aggresively advancing British troops.

Fähnrich Pukall, after surviving the initial enemy attack at the front by Beaumont, was faced with a dilemma. While enjoying the success of repulsing the expected British attack from the front, it had become evident that the enemy was also in his rear. Pukall and his men had orders, to hold their positions and not give up any ground voluntarily. It was something they were determined to do at all cost.

> I was wondering if we could go not go back again into the dugouts, because the Tommys were repulsed after all, and because the cabbage vapor was getting stronger. This was unfortunately impossible, because I had noticed something incomprehensible. Still, throughout the fog, I had heard nonstop cheering from many voices in the area behind Beaumont. All clear voices! What on earth were our reserves doing back there? We needed them desperately! Since we were very busy, I could sometimes barely hold my rifle, the barrel was glowing hot and my arms were tired, so I did not listen any more. Now, where the fog lifted, I saw something different: Long groups in Field Grey came toward us. Thank God, the reserves! I thought and I stood up in full height with an

old *Gefreiter* upon the berm and waved. Thereupon the first group curved, coming directly toward us, off to the 1st Company also. Now I saw in front and behind two Englishmen: Now it was clear to me that I already saw ghosts. However there the *Gefreiter* already shouted: "They are so like Englishmen!" I would have gladly run over with some men to rescue them, had our ranks not already become so very thin and the reserves out of the second trench were still not there. We did not let the others know anything of our observation. There came *Unteroffizier* Schrott running: '*Fähnrich*, you can just see the Tommys sometimes at the right wing by the 1st Company.' I hung a new cartridge belt around me and hurried to Schrott's place. I did not trust my eyes, row upon row of Tommys walked, without lying down or ducking a single time, advancing toward the 1st Company. The 1st Company had no favorable field of fire, as we had said. However, had we had one or two machine guns here we could have delivered a devastating flanking fire. So we fired without any cover, kneeling to the half-right until the right. Individual Englishmen with sloped rifles still came toward us, then one of us commanded: "Ready, fire! Hold your finger, slowly squeeze!" Schrott, an old forester, probably had no bullet that was not a hit.

With this I did not want to forget an old *Gefreiter*, who always appeared to me as the type of a model soldier and front fighter. His bony face smiled at each hit, his dark hair appeared out of the always formally perched, neat cap and his black eyes looked for a new enemy. He rarely spoke a word. I could not remember his name, although we later became good friends in the prisoner of war camp.

For a moment I ran to the left wing of my platoon, where there was a new surprise. When I wanted to take my old place beside the dead Tommy, suddenly machine gun bullets whistled around my ears. In B5 an English machine gun arrived in the front instead of our support. I had to go back; simultaneously I asked an Oldenburger, if I might direct him to a new place, he constantly received machine gun fire from the other side of the hollow from the rear. I hoped it must possibly be the reserves, with any of the Englishmen who had already slid through the first line; therefore I cared little about what was going on behind us. Nevertheless I would gladly have the machine gun in B5. With our last 5 hand grenades and a *Gefreiter* I had to try. I threw and immediately when he noticed the English stopped firing he was to shoot the first Tommy who raised his head over the heap. Luck was however not with both of us. We were both hit! The further attempt, to achieve our goal with two rifles, we also had to forsake as completely hopeless. At the same time the *Gefreiter* received a number of shots in his tunic collar that fell to the ground in fragments, he remained miraculously intact. Since in the meantime the machine gun had zeroed in on the other side of the hollow, we had to abandon any further attempts and focus on the right. There one called to me to: Schrott is dead! A casualty, who lay in front of us, had to have underhandedly shot at him. A shot had penetrated in his temple. He lay in front of me in the trench, everyone's friend, he had untiringly worked for us; his experience was indispensable, indispensable also here in the battle. Now, all at once he would be no longer? I didn't want to believe it. However there was no time for mourning, it needed to be thoughts of what to do, we hung in the air. We had Englishmen on all sides. On the right they came through in masses and curved toward us on the extended Auchonvillers-Beaumont road. They also probably came through the mine crater, because where did the machine gun fire come from? Therefore a counter thrust probably had to be expected by the II Battalion. As a result, we waited further. Had they come, we could have taken the Tommys between two fires. However, our ammunition was almost gone. Everyone still had a few shots for receding troops; perhaps it would have been sufficient. We waited, waited further! Only now did I realize that there were so few men in the trench.

I asked the individuals. The answer I received was that they were shattered. Only Huismann, the merriest of all, indefatigable who with everything there, where it was needed to demonstrate perseverance and courage, was still laughing when the others could barely stand from exhaustion. A comrade, how one rarely finds them, always ready to give his life for the others, who went on patrols with enthusiasm, he also no longer stood at his place. When he was first outside during the attack he became slightly wounded. He and his friends had firmly promised not to leave each other during the attack. He had also not considered himself to be wounded, until a second shot hit his shoulder and he dropped his rifle. Only now would he be separated from his friends, to be allowed to be bandaged. I met him again as prisoners together. He walked alongside me, somewhat weak from his loss of blood we still spoke together; when he remained behind in a Medical station. In the separation he waved at us again to, I didn't suspect that it was our last greeting.

There suddenly appeared a shape in the background. A runner? Officer? He wore a steel helmet. We called him here, so that he did not run into the Tommys. We waited anxiously! He was a prisoner and was making ready for dispatch in "Direction France". He was an *Offizier Stellvertreter* and *Offizier Aspirant* from the *Minenwerfer*, in civilian life an architect. We did not trust our ears, when he reported to us, prepared, to answer each time: 2nd and 3rd lines were occupied man by man by Englishmen, as he has seen. The enemy pushed further forward to Miraumont, seemingly without becoming stopped. He was taken prisoner behind the 3rd line.

There was no question of going back now with our scarce ammunition. We discussed it for a long time; again I attempted to determine if Olbrich was still there and ran along the trench holding up my rifle. It was empty! There was no one to see from our right wing platoon. Suddenly I was in front of four Englishmen, which were contained in the trench. They immediately raised their hands high. I went over and called for Olbrich and the other. No answer, no shots. There I also noticed that the Tommys were going on, because they were not at all wounded, as I believed. However I fortunately came back. From the hill by the hollow I therefore heard nothing more. We could not go down because of the machine guns. Now I put it to Jacob and the *Offizier Stellvertreter*, who considered it foolish to allow the enemy to advance over our nine corpses under these circumstances. Then it came to me like a beaten dog. I had to toss away all of my ideals. Today, I find this terrible decision justified that these nine men, who were still with me, could be of more use to Germany than our bleached bones in France. What could we still do to harm the enemy that were in possession of masses of men, and where the route into our hinterland stood open for him? As the superior enemy approached us, we had to let the weapons drop.

The Englishmen, as drunk as they were, were happy that they had still not yet received a couple in the ribs from us, and I was still very anxious that they did not drive us in front of them as bullet traps. It was simply magnificent, when we came through the 2nd and 3rd lines. I wanted the others to clearly realize they had to pay attention to me, however I was immediately prevented. Unfortunately the English Officer who was with this drunken horde, pushed through and we were brought back. Any thoughts of escape that promised success, were now gone. I have really paid attention to every opportunity. Between both lines we received fire again, one man was wounded. Somewhere near us must still have held a sentry nest, unfortunately I could not discover it. *Leutnant* Walter with the left wing of the company was also taken prisoner after us. In view of the clear facts that the *Minenwerfer* told us, any hope and every breakthrough design, how I have also thought of later by the hundreds, to put into practice, was foolish. There was at this time nothing other than yes or no. Either bite the dust, which would not serve anything, or to live!

In the end I must still say, that the stand by our men was simply flawless. Also as prisoners they were proud of what they had accomplished and despised the souvenir voracious Tommys. I don't have any need to admonish a single one!

One more small recollection: English Officers went past by the long rows of prisoners. They remained standing by us and saw our shoulder straps, because one said: "O, see, here are 62er that is a very good regiment! *Fähnrich* Pukall, 3/62 [11]

Finally, it was evident that the reserve battalion would not be able to help their comrades at the front. The regiment declined to send any further men from the reserve battalion to Beaumont with a heavy heart. It was necessary to prevent any further enemy advances in the *Zwischen Stellung*. As a result of this decision, orders were issued at 10.30 a.m. that the 6th and 8/62 would move forward out of the *Artillerie Mulde* into the *Zwischen Stellung*; the regiment no longer had any available reserves.

The enemy artillery continued to fire on the *Zwischen Stellung* and on the terrain up to the *Artillerie Mulde*. As a result, both the 6th and 8/62 suffered considerable losses during their advance into the *Zwischen Stellung*. When the 6/62 arrived in the position the company received orders to press forward into the *Ziegesar Graben* and to establish a connection with the I and III/62. The 6/62 reached the former regimental battle headquarters without coming across any opposition. Then, 50 meters further west, the company came under active enemy infantry and machine gun fire, and within a short time, artillery fire also.,. The 6/62 did not succeed in advancing any further in the direction of Beaumont.

Until now only IR 23 was in the *Zwischen Stellung*, and maintaining a connection to the right. In order to re-establish a connection to RIR 55 on the left, patrols were sent out. The patrols returned with bad news. First of all it had been determined that *Feste Alt Württemberg* was no longer occupied by RIR 55. Additionally, the regimental staff was missing and it was later determined that the staff had already been taken prisoner at approximately 8.30 a.m. or shot down. It was not until late afternoon that IR 23 finally succeeded in establishing a connection with RIR 55.

There was fighting in the positions isolated by the enemy the entire morning. Individual groups combined to form defensive nests from which they desperately tried to fight off the enemy approaching from all sides. Parts of the regiment had bravely defended their positions until 4 p.m. and did not surrender until they had accepted that any hope for salvation through a counterattack had to be abandoned. The battalion commander of the III/62 provided one of the few accounts to survive of the fighting from this time. He made his report while sitting in a British prisoner-of-war camp.

In Sector B3 the 12/62 held a counterattack after defending against the first enemy attack, under the leadership of *Oberleutnant der Reserve* Holle. With this, 36 prisoners, 1 machine gun and 1 mine thrower were brought in. *Oberleutnant* Holle was killed. With him, the regiment lost an outstandingly brave and energetic officer. When the 12/62 was attacked from the rear, the company defended itself, fighting on all sides until about 4 o'clock in the afternoon. Not until then did the remnants surrender in the strength of three groups.

Also the 5/62 lying in the third trench defended itself bravely under the leadership of *Leutnant* Hopf until 2 p.m. The battalion staff was alarmed, as soon as the enemy attack was recognized; all of the existing reserves were in their possession. When at 7.00 a.m. the first Englishmen appeared in front of the battle dugout they were expelled through infantry fire. First of all the Englishmen occupied the dugout, in which the battalion doctor Dr. Schuhmacher was found with 20 wounded. *Vizefeldwebel* Christoph and *Fähnrich* Dinter attacked these enemies with hand grenades and prevented them from pressing forward any further. Both were wounded during this fighting. Later a *pionier* officer also succeeded in expelling the Englishmen here again.

Attempts, to establish a connection and reach the inserted companies through runners failed. None of the runners sent out returned back to the Battalion staff. On the other hand *Unteroffizier* Drzenga, 11/62 with 2 men from the regimental battle headquarters succeeded in reaching the battalion with a report. When at 9.30 a.m. enemy detachments from Beaucourt were observed advancing against our position here, the machine gun found with the battalion staff was brought into position. *Unteroffizier* Nietsch, who operated the machine gun, fired at this adversary until 11.45 o'clock with good effect.

Meanwhile, the enemy had brought up new troops here and began to entrench east of Beaumont and bring machine guns into position. Therefore the battalion battle headquarters here became bombarded with infantry fire from the north. Surrounded on all sides, the staff had to yield at 12.45 p.m. when 200 Englishmen, under the leadership of an Irish Captain advanced against the battle headquarters. *Rittmeister* von Dresth, III/62 [12]

Further north, by IR 23, the III/23 reported at 7 a.m. that there had been a huge mine explosion on the left, south of the battalion and that rifle fire could also be heard coming from that direction. The III/23 also reported being bombarded with gas shells mixed in with the shrapnel and high explosive shells. What the men from the III/23 did not realize was that while the enemy fire was falling on their front line trench, the first British attack waves had formed in no man's land under cover of the unusually dark morning and thick fog. The enemy infantry waves advanced under the protection of their new creeping barrage while also being shielded by the opaque fog. When the bombardment lifted from the German front line the enemy assault waves were almost on top of the *Winterfeldter* before they knew they were in danger. Using such tactics, a number of British troops had succeeded in penetrating the front line trenches held by Battalion Lemcke.

The enemy penetration into parts of the front line trenches was immediately reported to battalion headquarters. Once battalion headquarters heard of this threatening situation orders were issued to the 10th and 11/23 to counterattack and restore the situation. The two companies were quickly formed and advanced toward the threatened sector. When they arrived the companies became involved in close combat with the British troops and drove them back, completely out of the German trench. During the counterattack approximately 500 enemy prisoners and one machine gun were reported being captured. By 12 noon the forward trench of the III/23 was once more entirely in German hands.

The 9th and 12/23, which occupied the front line battle trenches during the early morning attack, had already suffered considerable losses on the previous days and barely had enough men to hold their sectors. Following the counterattack, the 10th and 11/23 were then ordered to remain in the forward and 2nd trench of the sector to reinforce the garrison.

The situation in the left sector of the regiment was completely unclear for a long time due to a lack of communication with the battalion or company headquarters. It was later determined that following the mine explosion in the neighboring sector the battalion leader, *Hauptmann* Eichholz, with his staff who were under the leadership of the battalion adjutant, *Leutnant* Apfeld, ordered the three exits of the dugout of the headquarters to be occupied and defended. Eichholz then personally went over to the nearby telephone dugout in order to obtain any information he could about the situation facing his battalion.

The leader of the 4/23, *Leutnant* May, who miraculously still had a functioning telephone connection to the battalion, reported shortly before the attack that the forward position of his sector in H3 was occupied and everyone was ready to defend it against an enemy attack. The telephone line to Sector H4, the 2/23, had already been destroyed and no connection could be established. A few minutes after *Leutnant* May had reported about Sector H3, another telephone call was received from the telephone operator of H3 who stated: 'Enemy infantry attack upon H3. *Leutnant* May was just severely wounded and become carried into the dugout. Immediately following, the enemy had broken through at the right wing of H3, they were already in the second trench.'

No other details were available and battalion headquarters and the telephone lines went dead after the last message. Eichholz was still in the dark about the overall situation facing the battalion sector. He came to the conclusion that the enemy had probably broken in to the German lines following the huge mine explosion, under the protection of the fog. Eichholz felt that strong British attack waves had surely flooded over the neighboring trench garrison in IR 62 that had been blown apart in the explosion and by all accounts, it appeared that the British had successfully swung to the north and had come up in the rear of the companies of the I/23. This being before the men affected by the explosion and artillery fire had completely regained consciousness or managed to exit their dugouts.

Following this assessment of the situation, *Hauptmann* Eichholz ordered, the fire steps on the right and on the left of the headquarters dugout to be occupied. The AVO, *Leutnant* Heinke from FAR 78, received orders to burn all maps and documents as a precaution. The now useless telephone communication equipment was dismantled. When the trench garrison reported seeing an enemy skirmish line approaching their position, the battalion leader returned to the men of his staff. They could clearly hear individual rifle shots coming from the front line as well as lively machine gun fire, especially from H3, and hand grenade fighting.

Fog and smoke still covered the terrain and only faint shadowy figures could be recognized in the dense mist. Red light balls were observed rising into the air all along the sectors H3 to H4 but they were quite dim and difficult to make out in the haze. At approximately 7.30 a.m. a few British troops were observed moving from the right into the *Soden Graben* and toward the left into the second trench, accompanied by the sounds of fighting.

After the men in the staff of the I/23 received increasing infantry fire from the rear they occupied the rear trench wall. After about 10 minutes a wounded *Gefreiter* from the 3/23 came running by the headquarters and reported that the British were advancing toward their location with strong forces coming from Beaumont and against the left side of the 2nd trench and in the rear of the position. At the same time British infantry could be seen moving on the right, coming from the direction of the *Geschwind Graben*.

The situation was becoming more critical by the minute and now the staff of the I Battalion went back toward the third trench by leaps and bounds where it was hoped that the men could find a suitable defensive position to occupy. While moving across the open ground, they utilized every scrap of cover possible to remain unobserved by the enemy. The report of wounded *Gefreiter* was soon confirmed, because a dense skirmish line approached the battalion staff from close by and surrounded all of the different groups distributed in the third trench. The enemy approached from half left from the direction of Beaumont and from the rear, from the *Nagel Graben*. The men from IR 23 could also see individual British troops hurrying from the *Beaumont Graben* to east of the *Zwischen Stellung*.

The fourteen man strong staff of the I Battalion held their position only with rifle fire. All of the available hand grenades had already been thrown at the enemy. At this time, the British did not advance any further on the left and on the right of the small group of officers and men. However, strong British forces moved against the front as well as in the rear of the

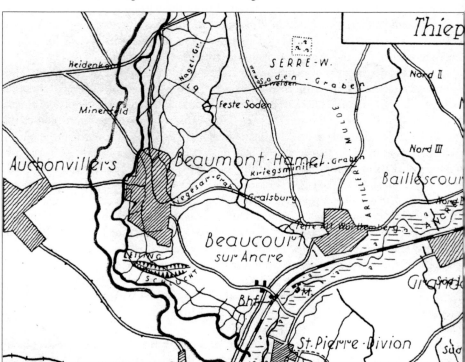

Beaumont-Hamel Sector.

position occupied by the staff.

Now the enemy barrage fire was transferred on to the intermediate terrain and the *Zwischen Stellung* and was maintained with the same intensity as in the early morning. During a short period of time, six men from the staff had were wounded by the heavy fire. *Hauptmann* Eichholz realized the situation was desperate and ordered them to break through the British troops in their rear toward the *Zwischen Stellung* regardless of the dangers presented by the zone of barrage fire.

The staff succeeded in reaching the *Zwischen Stellung* about 9.15 a.m. with the exertion of all of their remaining strength during which time, two further men had become wounded. When the men finally reached the *Zwischen Stellung* they found it was occupied by the 7/23 and a *Schanz Abteilung* from the Recruit Depot, sent there by previous orders from the battalion commander.

Hauptmann Eichholz personally reported to the regimental commander about the events in the left regimental sector. At the same time the regimental battle headquarters observed that the enemy had occupied the *Sommer Graben* and were advancing through L9 in an attempt to penetrate into *Feste Soden*. Bombing parties from the 5th and 7/23 were immediately sent forward to deal with this new threat. The bombers succeeded in clearing the enemy from *Feste Soden* and took 40 prisoners during this counterattack.

At the same time, a bombing party under the leadership of *Hauptmann* Plewig advanced toward L9 and was able to clear 300 meters of this trench from the enemy. All the time that the attacks and counterattacks were taking place, the strongest enemy artillery fire still fell on the *Zwischen Stellung* and the rear terrain.

Because of the unexpected enemy break through into the German lines the regimental staff was ordered to withdraw and move into a new battle headquarters located in the second trench of the *Zwischen Stellung*. During the move, *Major* von Wedelstaedt was wounded at 9.45 a.m. and it was soon evident that the British barrage fire would prevent the staff from ever reaching the new position; to cross the open ground would mean certain death or at the very least severe wounds.

The regimental staff had taken refuge inside one of the numerous shell craters that dotted the landscape up to 12 noon. Finally, the regimental adjutant, *Hauptmann* Meyer (Fritz), persuaded them to return to the old battle headquarters where they could find some protection against the shell fire.

While the regimental staff was cut off from the rest of the regiment, a strong British detachment had made a bombing attack upon the *Nagel Graben* at approximately 10 a.m., approaching from the east. The *Nagel Graben* was vigorously defended by the 1/23 under *Leutnant der Reserve* Welzel but Welzel had far too few men left in his company to be able to stop such a large enemy detachment. The 1/23 slowly withdrew up the *Nagel Graben*, followed closely by British bombing parties until the enemy had captured the *Nagel Graben* all of the way up to the battle headquarters of the III Battalion.

Facing imminent capture, the staff of the III Battalion abandoned their headquarters and moved through L8 into the *Zwischen Stellung* north of *Feste Soden*. No consideration of a counterattack could be thought about, because the regiment had no more reserves in its possession to allow this. In addition, the situation at the I Battalion was still entirely unclear, and the companies of the regimental reserve, already weakened through taskings as bearer troops, had been hastily assembled and used as the garrison of the greatly endangered *Zwischen Stellung*.

The situation at noon

At midday the remnants of the 12/R55 under *Hauptmann* Winkelmann and the half of the 11/R55 under *Leutnant* Stolper had to yield the first two lines of trenches in Sector B7 under intense enemy pressure, while the third trench of B7 and the entire Sector B6 remained in possession of the battalion. The battalion reserve, 40 men from the 11/R55, located in the *Kolonie*, had been surrounded by the unexpected British advance across the Ancre and were taken prisoner after a short fight.

The 10/R55 under *Leutnant* Neise was located in the *Bismarck Stollen*, where a telephone connection to the rear still existed. Neise received orders to clear the *Kolonie* with bombing parties from his company. The 10/R55 attempted to comply with this order but it did not succeed, because the enemy had superior forces. The British then occupied the Telephone Central dugout and all connection to the rear were cut off. Surrounded on all sides, the battalion was limited to defending the last portion of the sector still in its control. The men could only hope for salvation from a counterattack by the reserves.

The III/R55 was unable to provide any assistance for the men trapped in the *Kolonie*. At 2.30 p.m. the British advance from the mill in the direction of Beaumont was prevented through infantry fire. One of the largest concentrations of German troops still left in the forward lines was the connection that existed between *Leutnant* Diekmann, 9/R55, *Leutnant* Neise, 10/R55 and *Leutnant* Nolting, 3/R55.

At 5.30 p.m. all signals, blinker signals, light balls etc. had broken down, all patrols and runners sent out were unsuccessful in making contact with the rear. At 6.30 p.m. *Leutnant* Diekmann, 9/R55, talked with *Leutnant* Neise, 10/R55, and *Leutnant* Nolting, 3/R55, and decided that he would strike through to the *Grallsburg* with four battle orderlies: *Gefreiter* Beller, *Tambour* Zahn, *Wehrmann* Tröster and *Musketier* Strunkmann in order to obtain reinforcements.

Diekmann and his small party left the forward position at 7.30 p.m. and managed to safely work their way to the *Grallsburg* through the communication trench on the left of the *Geologen Weg*, finally reaching their goal. The men arrived in the position of the 8/R55 and found out that *Oberstleutnant* von Laue had been missing since the morning and that the 8/R55 was trying to prevent any further British advance. Diekmann was then guided to the battle headquarters of *Oberstleutnant* von Poser, commander of IR 62, in the *Kriegsminister Graben* by *Leutnant* Feger, 8/R55 and asked him about support for the front line.

Von Poser advised Diekmann that IR 62 was planning to recapture the lost positions by Beaumont at 6 a.m. on 14 November. He added that it would help a great deal if any available men from RIR 55 could also attack the sector from *Feste Alt Württemberg* at the same time. *Leutnant* Diekmann was asked to determine if this would be possible and once he time to discuss this plan with the regimental headquarters, he should send a message back to IR 62.

Leutnant Diekmann and *Leutnant* Feger returned to the 8/R55 where Leutnant Feger offered to go to see *Hauptmann* Minck in the battle headquarters of the II/R55 in the *Artillerie Mulde*, to make his report and to help with the necessary orders for the joint attack. *Leutnant* Diekmann waited by the 8/R55 in vain for his return or a message from him. When Feger had still not returned by 5 a.m. on 14 November and no messages had arrived, *Leutnant* Diekmann accepted the situation that RIR 55 would not be able to attack on the 14th and reported this to IR 62.

Meanwhile, the enemy fire gradually increased more and more throughout the afternoon of 13 November. At 7 p.m. the *Feldwache Kiesgrube* reported that the *Radfahrer* Company had evacuated the *Schloss Stellung* and had moved back to the *Nord Stellung* with part of the company in the *Kiesgrube*. *Hauptmann* Minck immediately sent back orders: the *Radfahrer* Company must hold the *Schloss Stellung*.

Leutnant Lenze also ordered the 7/R55 under *Leutnant* Rödlingshöfer and two platoons from the 5/R55, to immediately hurry forward and assemble in the *Kiesgrube*. They succeeded in accomplishing this task without large losses. *Leutnant* Lenze went to *Hauptmann* Minck in the *Artillery Mulde*, who ordered the 5th and 7/R55 and two machine guns and the *Radfahrer* Company to occupy the *Schloss Stellung* again. *Leutnant* Lenze with one platoon from the 5/R55 and two machine guns were to hold the *Riegel Stellung*. *Leutnant* Lenze did not reach his troops in the *Kiesgrube* until midnight as a result of being detained by the barrage fire.

The fighting at the front continued well into the evening. After 7 p.m. a strong enemy detachment approached from the *Pionier Dorf* through the ground by the *Kolonie* and besieged two battalion dugouts and attacked Sector B6 from the rear. An attempt by *Major* Tauscher, with *Leutnant* Genest, the AVO, two runners and two officer's servants to break out, failed. The two runners were killed in the attempt.

White cloths were stretched out on the ground around the shrinking perimeter of the battalion to show the German pilots the locations of the companies that were still in the position. However, this proved to be unsuccessful in the smoke and fog. Without the exact location of the German troops, once the batteries in the rear finally opened fire on 14 November, many of the shells fell on their own men and caused numerous losses. The fighting in the sector of the III/R55 lasted through the night and into 14 November.

At the right sector of RIR 55 a message arrived at 12 noon that 'the *Leiling Schlucht* was occupied up to the third trench.' It also mentioned that German prisoners were being taken away through the ravine. Now there was no possibility of any connection with the battalion through the *Leiling Stollen,* especially with the third trench and the entrance to the *Leiling Stollen* in British hands. When *Feldwebel Leutnant* Spieker became wounded during the defense of the ravine, *Vizefeldwebel* Hartwig took over the 1st Platoon, who directed the platoon in the position through the night. Two Lewis Guns that had been captured in the fighting were immediately used against the former owners.

Approximately 100 British soldiers were held back in the ravine up to 1 p.m. through machine gun fire. Then, at 3 p.m. the British captured the second trench from behind and it was growing increasingly harder to maintain the position. Now, the first shots from the German batteries began to fall, particularly on the Beaumont-Auchonvillers road.

Until 12 noon the connection with the 1/R55 existed through Dugout No. 3, then, when the British advanced further up the trench, even this last connection was lost and the company was cut off. *Oberleutnant* Graf Matuschka, 4/R55, wanted to hold on to the *Leiling Stollen*. Several attempts by the British to capture the exits of the tunnel in the third trench in the afternoon were successfully repulsed. However, at 3.30 p.m. the British succeeded in occupying the *Minenwerfer* exit in the second trench with strong forces and then penetrated up to the main passage. As the enemy advanced, they threw hand grenades into the dugout entrances and in this manner generated smoke in the narrow, crowded passageways, and thereby endangered the Medical dugout. Dugouts No. 3 and No. 4 were taken in this manner.

The 4/R55 had no more hand grenades left. The few surviving men of the company 22 in total, were distributed at the six exits of the tunnel. Finally, facing overwhelming odds the company leader had to surrender with the rest of his men. The 1/R55 was also facing daunting odds. The company was entirely surrounded by mid-afternoon and there was little hope that it could be rescued. By 4.15 p.m. ammunition was already scarce and the company was pressed back even further into a smaller area. At 5 p.m., *Leutnant* Finkeldey and the remnants of the 3rd Platoon were taken prisoner in his sector. The few defenses still intact were being destroyed one after the other. Machine Gun No. 8 had fired 11,000 cartridges in the fighting before it was finally destroyed.

Of the three machine guns located in Sector B4, Machine Gun No. 1 was in the first trench on the right of the *Leiling Stollen*. It suffered a jam during the fighting so *Leutnant* Lüthgen, 3rd Machine Gun Company, replaced it with Machine Gun No. 5 from out of the second trench, which worked excellently for hours. Then, at 11 a.m. it was destroyed through a direct hit. Machine Gun No. 1, now repaired, moved into its former position again and fired from the second trench to the B Ravine until 3 p.m. Machine Gun No. 2 could provide frontal fire and flanking fire, however, it was finally overwhelmed from the rear and from the left and was captured.

The I/R55 had felt that the main enemy thrust was being directed at its sector. The British line was only 80 meters distant. Parts of the front line trench had already been captured through hand grenade fighting earlier in the morning, where the enemy had broken in to the German lines at the left wing of the 4/R55. The 2/R55 under *Leutnant* Angott was on the left of the 4/R55 in Sector B5. The company leader was located behind the center of the sector in the second trench. During the heavy fighting both *Leutnant* Steffen and *Leutnant* Frerk became wounded; the latter severely.

Leutnant Angott ended up as a prisoner-of-war during the close combat. The left half of the second trench became effectively barricaded to the right by *Leutnant* Schellewald, 3/R55, and he still held his position up to 14 November. By the end of the fighting two thirds of the company were dead or wounded. The battalion staff was forced to surrender when incendiary bombs ignited the dugout frames but not before all papers, maps and other documents had been destroyed.

Both *Priesterwerfer* located by *Leutnant* Schellewald fired until 12 noon, when the ammunition ran out. At 1 p.m. Platoon Schellewald was strongly attacked from the right and a trench piece was lost. During this fighting one captured Lewis Gun became destroyed by hand grenades. *Leutnant* Nolting could not send any support to *Leutnant* Schellewald; he was being threatened from the right and the rear simultaneously; however Sector B4 appeared to be safe at present. Platoon Schellewald managed to hold out until 8 a.m. on 14 November when the small group of survivors were forced to surrender to the enemy.

At 2 p.m. the 9/R55 under *Leutnant* Diekmann held part of the front line of B6 and Platoon Schellewald held parts of the left half of the second trench of B5. *Leutnant* Nolting with 1 ½ platoons held the third trench B5 until to *Zirkus Graben*, exclusive. The 10/R55 held the second and third trenches of B6. From parts of these positions, the men could watch the enemy attack upon Beaucourt and *Feste Alt Württemberg* where the regimental staff should be located. Two British companies were observed standing in reserve at the hillside position. When darkness fell, *Leutnant* Nolting reorganized the defenses and had everyone in the trench stay awake.

At 12 noon *Leutnant* Kracht went to the regimental battle headquarters. When he arrived, he found that British hand grenades had been thrown down into the dugout and the commander and his adjutant had apparently left the dugout, going to the rear. The British having already pressed forward up to the *Ziegesar Graben* were finally stopped in front of the *Grallsburg*. Between 1 and 2 p.m. the enemy barrage fire was falling on the heights of Beaucourt. However, the enemy could still not be seen clearly in the heavy fog. It was not until 5 p.m. when the officers observed dense rows of British troops entrenching in the *Kimmich Graben* up to the *Schloss Stellung*.

The position of the observation detachment under *Leutnant* Dobberke and *Leutnant* Kracht had been held continuously under enemy machine gun fire throughout the day. With the onset of darkness *Leutnant* Kracht went to the regimental headquarters and met *Leutnant* Buchholz, 6/R55. He reported that the connection to IR 62 on the right and to the 2nd *Württemberg Radfahrer* Company on the left had been established by the 8/R55 and one group from the 6/R55. Several orderlies from the 8/R55, had been sent to the rear in order to obtain help, however, no one had returned yet. Under these circumstances, at the onset of darkness, *Leutnant* Feger, 8/R55, following instructions from *Leutnant* Diekmann, 9/R55, left for the II/R55, *Hauptmann* Minck, in the *Nord Stellung* with a report about the situation.

In the growing darkness the burning dugouts in the *Kolonie* could be clearly seen, the fire giving off an odd glow in the smoke and haze. There was still hand grenade fighting audible in Sectors B6 and B7. The officers could see that barrage fire signals were still being fired into the air; unfortunately these apparently went unseen in the rear and no artillery response was forthcoming. The British guns seemed to have no problems firing throughout the day and at night the enemy shells continued to fall on the *Kolonie*, probably on the heads of their own men at this point of the fighting. Finally, some German guns did open fire in the night. Unfortunately, the long awaited support fire came down on top of the dugout being used by the German observers.

At 2 p.m. *Leutnant* Lenze received a message through the *Radfahrer* Company, which had occupied the *Schloss Stellung*. The British were breaking through the line and lay 200 meters in front of the *Schloss Stellung*. Lenze immediately reinforced the defenses of the Beaucourt-Miraumont road and Ancre valley with the 5/R55, one machine gun and a reserve machine gun. He also alarmed the 7/R55 under *Leutnant* Rödlingshöfer in *Nord IV* and brought up one platoon from it as support on his left wing. He then ordered the *Feldwache Kiesgrube* to guard the Ancre crossing and the eastern exit of Beaucourt with one Group each and to take the approaching British under fire immediately from out of the trench.

Reports were sent to battalion headquarters about these actions. It would be a daunting task as the entire terrain as far as the men could see was a sea of erupting earthen geysers as each British shell impacted the soft, wet ground. Small clouds appeared in the sky accompanied by a dull bang as the shrapnel shells spread their cargo of metal balls across the open terrain. Still, there was no shortage of volunteers for this dangerous duty. *Gefreiters* Klinke, Wieners and *Musketier* Hopf 5/R55 voluntarily reported to make the journey to the battalion headquarters through the heaviest fire.

Hauptmann Minck, II/R55, did not learn about the further details of the British attack until 3.20 p.m. *Leutnant* Hollmann, 5/R55, reported: 'The Englishmen are at the railway station Hamel (Station Beaucourt); I secured the *Beaucourt Riegel* and road with one platoon of machine guns. The Englishmen are in the *Kolonie*. The *Schloss Stellung* was held.'

Upon receiving this news, *Hauptmann* Minck issued orders: 'Two platoons of the 7th Company would go into the *Beaucourt Riegel*, the rest to *Nord IV* in reserve', and reported this to the regiment and the brigade at 5.14 p.m. The regimental order sent in reply did not arrive at the II/R55 headquarters until 8 p.m.

Hauptmann Minck issued further orders as the situation unfolded: 'The companies must move further to the right through the *Brée Stellung* to the *Schloss Stellung*, what forces in the *Beaucourt Riegel* that were dispensable, if it was possible, should make a counterattack. Also, to keep an eye on the connection on the right to IR 62.' At 6.35 p.m. the battalion reported to brigade: 'The English have broken through *B-Nord* and *B-Mitte*. The Battalion in *B-Süd* (III/R55) and Battalion in *B-Mitte* (I/ R55) are cut off and surrounded. The enemy lies 150 meters in front of the *Schloss* and *Zwischen Stellung*. Both positions were held by parts of IR 62, 8/R55, *Radfahrer* Company and parts of the 5th, 6th and 7th Companies RIR 55.'

The number of officers continued to shrink in the heavy fighting. *Leutnant* Helmich was one of the latest, he had become wounded during an attempted counterattack at the head of the 6/R55. Finally, in the evening, *Hauptmann* Minck and his staff came to the realization that their position was untenable. The enemy had made major gains along the German front but Minck was determined to remain until he knew of the fate of his men.

> From the battalion battle headquarters (II/R55) we looked at how *Oberstabsarzt* Dr. Brummund was taken away from a dugout 120 meters distant by the Englishmen. In the same manner they cleared the food depot 40-50 meters distant from us, from which however an *Unteroffizier* escaped toward us through a different exit. We held the Englishmen by the neck through rifle fire, and then also heavy artillery fire from our artillery was soon placed upon Beaucourt and forced them to evade it. Since I still suspected at least parts of my battalion were in the position, I did not want to leave the battle-headquarters. At 11.45 p.m. finally one of my orderlies, who had managed to sneak through, brought a copy of a group order, which said Beaucourt was completely in the hands of the Englishmen and would not become taken back; the new line had been indicated, so that nothing further remained for me than to evacuate the dugout with my staff and as the last to leave Beaucourt at midnight. We then reached the new line also happily without losses through the Englishmen, passing close by to an English double sentry that also noticed us, but didn't shoot. *Hauptmann* Minck, II/R55 [13]

Further to the north, by IR 23, the fighting was less severe. About midday the enemy artillery fire had died down somewhat. The companies of the III/23 lying in H1 and H2 did not have any connection with their battalion staff or the regiment after the heavy fighting in the morning. Starting from midday all orders and decisions in the III/23 were being made independently by the leaders of the four companies and the leader of the 1st Machine Gun Company.

The officers in the II/23 were keeping the neighboring IR 169 informed about the situation, as far as it was possible under the trying circumstances. IR 169 placed several Groups with a machine gun into the *Röhrle Graben* and in a communication trench at the left wing of H2 for the protection of the left flank of the regiment and as rear cover.

The enemy attacked the *Zwischen Stellung* and *Feste Soden* in dense columns about p.m. but did not extend his attack to include Sectors H1 and H2 occupied by IR 23. He succeeded in temporarily penetrating into L9 and the *Schmidt Graben* in the *Zwischen stellung*; however he immediately was thrown out again by supporting bombing parties after having suffered heavy losses.

During the intense fighting that had been taking place north of the Ancre the men of RIR 121 were enjoying their time away from the front lines. After months of duty in the trenches, the men could finally sleep well in somewhat comfortable quarters. Surely anything was better than a damp, musty and cold dugout. The men were able to take be deloused, take warm baths, clean their clothes, make repairs to their equipment and finally, parade in front of the division commander who thanked the regiment for its devotion to duty and to acknowledge the bravery of individual men and distribute awards to them.

The regiment had expected to rest at least 14 days, but already after six days, at 4.30 p.m. on 13 November, the regiment became alarmed and a few hours later the men were loaded upon lorries and in dark night paraded again in Gomiecourt before heading toward the front. The disappointment and feelings that the men experienced by having their well-earned rest disrupted was not recorded in the regimental history, probably out of respect for the people who would eventually read the book in the future. Only the people who had actually experienced it at that time could fully understand just how disappointed and angry the men from RIR 121 had become.

What some people might be unaware of were the regional differences within the German Army. Each part of the country had particular idiosyncrasies, different accents, and customs. Not every group liked the other and there were some very strong opinions between the people from the different parts of Germany.

The historians who created the regimental account for RIR 121 mentioned that when the regiment was being relieved from the front lines after such a long tour of duty, the men in the regiment had already suspected that the events currently unfolding would occur. During the relief process, the men who were taking over the position from RIR 121, the men from IR 23, were apparently mostly of Polish descent and this alone gave many men in RIR 121 the impression that they could not hold the position long.

As if this almost self-fulfilling prophecy had come true, the Württemberg regiment was now being called back in order to help restore the situation. It is true that many of the regiments in the 26th Reserve Division had formed an iron clad opinion that they and they alone were able to create and to hold the positions on the Somme as they had successfully done since September 1914.

There was even the thought that when the last Württemberger was finally out of the position, the British also recognized this and who he now had facing him. With this knowledge, the British conducted the attack that was undoubtedly already prepared long before but had not implemented until now. The position had been tenaciously defended for a long time by the men of RIR 121 and now, with 'inferior' troops in place, the enemy had attacked and captured the entire garrison and positions that the Württembergers had created. On 13 November Beaumont was now in British hands, as well as parts of the *Grallsburg* and *Feste Alt Württemberg*. The only conclusion to be drawn from this regional attitude was that if the men of RIR 121 had still been in the trenches, none of this would have happened.

Now, when the men from RIR 121 had fully expected to be sleeping in comfortable beds, they were being deployed behind the front line in order to provide support for the troops holding the newly created positions following the successful enemy advance. These were not happy men to say the least. Over the next days, the companies and battalions of RIR 121 would be moved into the front lines where the men were needed the most.

At 6 p.m., the enemy barrage fire was employed again with particular intensity by Beaumont. Observers in the *Zwischen Stellung* could see groups of British soldiers moving from the heights of the *Sommer Graben* into the wide hollow in front of the *Zwischen Stellung* between L9 and the *Schmidt Graben* and once there, preparing for an attack. Shortly after the attack began, L9 and the *Nagel Graben* were cleared once again of the enemy again through hand grenade fighting by one platoon of the 1/23 and then blocked off with barricades.

After the losses already suffered earlier by the companies in IR 62, the regiment only retained a strength of three companies and the *Bau* Company which represented a battle strength of 280-300 rifles; no other reserves were presently available. As a result of this the 6th and 8/23 located in *Nord I*, which were already badly weakened through losses advanced in support of IR 62 at 7 p.m. on orders from the 24th Brigade. The 6/23 moved across open ground to the *Grallsburg*, the 8/23 moved through the *Soden Graben* and *Zwischen Stellung* to the battle headquarters of IR 62 in the *Kurfürsten Graben*, where they remained until 6 a.m. on 14 November. After arriving, both companies were placed in the *Zwischen Stellung* of IR 62, from which they repulsed a British attack at 7.30 a.m. on the 14th.

About 9 p.m. the rest of IR 23 received orders to recapture the lost terrain. The II/63 was to be placed in under their command for this counterattack. While plans were being made to implement this attack, *Major* von Wedelstaedt finally was transported back to the rear in the evening for treatment of his wounds, and, as *Major* Lemcke could not be reached *Hauptmann* Eichholz took over the leadership of the regiment.

During the night of 13/14 November the enemy maintained a continuous, disconcerting fire on all of the German positions and rear connections north of the Ancre. In addition the enemy infantry behaved in a restless manner; numerous British patrols pushed forward against the *Zwischen Stellung* over and over again without any success.

At 12.15 a.m. on the 14th *Leutnant* Lenze, the leader of the 5/R55 reported to the II Battalion, *Hauptmann* Minck, that the *Radfahrer* Company had still not returned to the *Schloss Stellung* as ordered earlier. *Hauptmann* Minck immediately gave new orders: 'The *Radfahrer* Company absolutely had to hold the *Schloss Stellung*. The 5th Company must maintain the connection to the right, at the very worst under the exposure of the *Beaucourt Riegel*. The rest of the 6th Company with two machine guns was to be placed into the *Schloss Stellung*!' in spite of these orders, the *Radfahrer* Company did not follow Minck's order and did not return to the *Schloss Stellung*. However, RIR 55 did occupy the *Schloss Stellung* until just north of the *Station Graben*.

At 1 a.m. the companies from RIR 55 began to advance through the shattered terrain into the *Schloss Stellung*. On the way to the position a machine gun along with its crew was destroyed by enemy artillery fire. Then, between the head of the column and the subsequent detachments, the men from RIR 55 came upon the III/144 on the same road. The III/144 had orders to occupy the *Schloss Stellung* as well and was in the process of locating the position. Since it appeared that there would be more than enough troops to occupy the *Schloss Stellung*, *Leutnant* Tietse, 6/R55, lead the detachments of the II/R55 back to the *Kiesgrube*.

In the meantime, *Leutnant* Lenze had occupied the *Stich Graben* up to his company leader's dugout with his platoon and two machine guns, which formed the main defensive line of the *Beaucourt Riegel*. From this position, Lenze had a clear field of fire along the road and the valley in front of his men.

At 3 a.m. *Major* von Broesigke arrived with the II/*Ersatz* Reserve Regiment 29 in order to occupy the *Beaucourt Riegel*. With the arrival of fresh troops the position had become very cramped. Large numbers of men in such a small area would only result in unnecessary losses in the constant enemy shell fire. *Leutnant* Lenze then decided moved his men to the *Kiesgrube* and once there, he took over the command of the position. With him was one company from *Ersatz* Reserve Regiment 29 who also came under his orders; in total, Lenze had 150 rifles.

Continuous drum fire lay upon Beaucourt and the *Zwischen Stellung*. Also south of the Ancre in the *Hansa Stellung* up to Grandcourt, heavy fire fell that included gas shells. Infantry fighting stopped finally as a result of darkness as it was impossible to know where the enemy was located.

At 4.30 a.m. *Hauptmann* Becker III/144 arrived by *Hauptmann* Minck and reported, he has the task, with his Battalion to occupy the *Schloss Stellung* and *Feste Alt Württemberg*, and was to report after his companies had accomplished this. Meanwhile *Leutnant* Feger, 8th Company, who had arrived by *Hauptmann* Minck, reported that B6 was still held and, following the instructions of *Leutnant* Diekmann, asked if a counterattack would be made.

From the orders transmitted by *Hauptmann* Becker, it was determined that the division did not intend any counterattack. This conclusion was confirmed when according to messages from IR 95, the entire length of the *Hansa Stellung* on the left Ancre shore had been taken by the British. *Hauptmann* Minck reluctantly agreed with the evaluation of the situation and gave *Leutnant* Feger the order that the men in Sector B6 should break through to the rear.

Leutnant Feger was on the return route from the II/R55 in order to locate *Leutnant* Diekmann when he was reported missing and considered to be dead. Some weeks after this date it was learned that Feger had not been killed, instead he had been captured and sent to a British prisoner-of-war camp.

At 6.10 a.m. on 14 November two runners were sent by *Leutnant* Diekmann, 9/R55, who brought orders to *Leutnant* Neise, 10/R55 in *B-Süd*: '9th and 10th Companies are to be lead back to the *Grallsburg* in order, if by 6.30 a.m. support had not arrived, and it was to be reported through light signals, three yellow light balls fired three times. The 8th Company takes on the flank protection and the reception position.' At 7 a.m. the two runners returned from *Leutnant* Neise with the receipt of the message.

Once it had become light, strong enemy detachments were observed advancing from the hills north of Auchonvillers toward the hollow of Beaumont. At 6.25 a.m. the 12/144 arrived and the company was given instructions that the connection to the right and to *Feste Alt Württemberg* had to be established, furthermore the *Schloss Garten* of Beaucourt had to be searched for British soldiers. RIR 55 had no men available for these tasks. .

Leutnant Brocke, 11/R55, who had taken on the duties as the observation officer of the regiment, was already been located at the extreme left of the regimental sector in the third trench in the *Strassburger Steige* since the regiment had taken over the sector. Several days prior to 14 November he had received a report, reminding him of the danger of a breakthrough from *Feste Schwaben* that was now occupied by the British. This breakthrough was now taking place between the *Strassburger Steige* and *Hansa Stellung*. At 6.50 a.m. the enemy were 'repulsed', however the British had apparently succeeded in breaking through further east of the *Serben Weg* and penetrated further into the Ancre valley. A runner, who *Leutnant* Brocke had sent to the III/95, which was to have secured the Ancre valley, had not come back. The situation on the left flank of RIR 55 was becoming more serious by the hour.

Brigade headquarters had ordered a counterattack that was scheduled for 6 a.m. on 14 November. A number of different regiments were supposed to supply the men required for this attack. As the time drew closer to when the assault should begin, the assigned units were only slowly trickling in to the assembly area. The staff of the II/63 under *Hauptmann* Richter had not arrived until 4 a.m. and approximately 130 men from the 7th and 8/63 as well as one platoon from RIR 99 had not arrived until between 5 and 6 a.m. The planned counterattack had to be postponed as a result. The parts of the 4/63 and RIR 99 that had arrived were then inserted into the *Zwischen Stellung* on both sides of L9.

By 6.30 a.m. it was no longer possible to establish a connection between the *Schloss Stellung* and *Feste Alt Württemberg* because of the heavy drum fire. The 10/144 had pushed up against strong British forces supported by machine guns in their attempt to establish this connection and to reach *Feste Alt Württemberg* through the *Friedhof Beaucourt*.

At 7 a.m. enemy drum fire began to fall upon the *Zwischen Stellung* once again, which continued with the same intensity up to midday. At the same time, enemy drum fire began to fall in the rear positions of RIR 55, especially on *Feste Alt Württemberg*. While the German positions were being bombarded, trench observers by RIR 55 noted that at least two enemy companies located at the hillside position by the Ancre were relieved and fresh troops now occupied the position.

At 7.10 a.m. the enemy had strengthened the drum fire upon the *Zwischen Stellung* and the rear terrain. Despite such heavy fire, *Leutnant* Diekmann had succeeded in reaching *Hauptmann* Leiling, commander of the IV/R99 in the *Artillerie Mulde*. Diekmann was unable to secure any support here, but he did find out that the division would not be making any attacks upon Beaumont. Instead, it was going to give up the positions from Beaumont up to the Ancre.

The British had attacked in dense masses along the front *Schloss Stellung* – left wing of *Feste Alt Württemberg*; however, the *Zwischen Stellung* was not attacked frontally. The British troops suffered heavy losses in the initial assault and the survivors flooded back to their start positions. A second assault would have also been unsuccessful, if it had not been possible for the enemy to attack the rear of the garrison of the *Schloss Stellung* with very strong forces supported by machine guns. Under these circumstances, the position became untenable.

At 8 a.m. the trench sentries in RIR 55 reported, the British had moved into the *Beaucourt-Osthang*. *Leutnant* Lenze had given orders that the northwestern, western and southwestern edges of the *Kiesgrube* be occupied and with the two machine guns brought into position, the garrison effectively fired on any advancing British troops who showed themselves in the ruins of Beaucourt oron the railway embankment. This fire prevented any further advance on the road running along the Ancre. The two machine gun crews behaved in an exemplary manner. The gun being operated by *Landsturmmann* Köstner, 5/R55 steadfastly maintained aimed fire at enemy machine guns despite being in an exposed position above the protection of the trench where he had a better field of fire.

At 8 a.m. four British tanks appeared in front of Sector B6, approaching from half ight. Two of the tanks quickly forced *Leutnant* Schellewald and his men to surrender. *Leutnant* Diekmann, 9/R55, who had been sent to the rear at 7.30 p.m. on 13 November o get help could not locate any men who could be spared and by the time the attacks had)egun on 14 November none had arrived in the position.

The men from RIR 55 had few defenses against the British tanks that were slowly ıpproaching over the rough terrain. The machine guns lacked any K-Ammunition and the ;-Ammunition[14] seemed to just bounce off of the armoured vehicles. There was an attempt o throw a bundled hand grenade charge under one tank; however it missed the target and :xploded harmlessly nearby. In spite of what seemed to be a hopeless situation, the men 'rom RIR 55 continued to fight back as best they could. Finally, after repeated attacks by he British and the penetration of two tanks into B6, the remnants of the battalion were .aken prisoner on the evening of 14 November.

At 8.30 a.m. *Leutnant* Sprenger, 8/R55 sent *Unteroffizier* Rudolf and one other man o find *Leutnant* Goetze, the company leader of the 10/95. They were to obtain any news hey could of the situation facing the III/95 and were also carrying a small supply of hand ;renades for the men of the 10/95. Shortly afterward, the two men returned with the nessage: 'III/95 was surrounded; the 10/95 was entirely cut off by the British.'

While the German position along the Ancre was reported being held by one battalion 'rom RIR 55, the III/R55, in reality there was a serious shortage of men and equipment for ;uch an important sector.

The Englishmen had already taken Thiepval, south of Beaucourt, on 26 September 1916 and that there were material shortages for the construction of the position, at the *T-Stollen* the *Schleusinger Haus* was destroyed; *Leutnant* Schmitz lay sick in the *Kolonie* and *Leutnant* Pegel as trench officer was missing. In the first trench of B7 lay the first platoon (*Leutnant* Weyland) with 30 men in the *T-Stollen*, with 10 men in the *Schleusinger Haus*, a half platoon, *Vizefeldwebel* Potthoff, with 22 men and 4 machine guns in dugouts 4-6, in dugout 5 lay the 3rd platoon under *Leutnant* Harald Haase with 42 men. In the second trench was half of the first platoon (*Vizefeldwebel* Cybulka) with 20 men, the company leader, *Hauptmann* Winkelmann, with 5 orderlies and 3 telephone men. In the front were constant patrols. Report of *Hauptmann* Winkelmann, 12/R55 [15]

Leutnant Brocke, 11/R55, was in a precarious position. He only had four men with him from the 11/R55 and two groups from the 10/95. At 9 a.m. the British attacked the *Strassburger Steige* where *Leutnant* Brocke and his small force defended their position as best they could. However, the overwhelming enemy forces combined with severe machine gun fire forced the few remaining survivors to surrender. The same enemy machine guns later turned their fire onto *Leutnant* Götze, 10/95, and his men sometime after 11 a.m.

There could be no doubt now whatsoever, the British had crossed the Ancre and were firmly established in the first and second trench of the *Strassburger Steige*, which was in the rear of the III/R55.

Until 10 o'clock a.m. there was thick fog. The 11th Company lay behind in B7, Platoon Dreyer (45 men) in the 2nd trench on the right up to the *Junker Graben*,

Platoon Götze with 50 men in the 3rd trench, under the command of *Hauptmann* Winkelmann from the 12th Company. The platoon of *Vizefeldwebel* Crehmer (40 men) were in the *Kolonie* as the battalion reserve. Platoon Dreyer was attacked at 7.15 a.m., Platoon Götze at 7.20 a.m., Platoon Crehmer at 7.20 a.m. was also attacked from behind and from the left. *Leutnant* Dreyer had fallen. When *Leutnant* Götze became attacked at 7.20 a.m. in the flank from the Ancre, it turned into a hand grenade battle three times. Finally the 3rd trench became taken. A new enemy came from the right rear by the 3rd trench. *Leutnant* Götze, contained from two sides, could not help *Hauptmann* Winkelmann, 12th Company. Through a mistake a few ended up as prisoners and were now taken away. Men fired. Enlightenment followed after a short bewilderment. Platoon Crehmer in the 'Kolonie' had an enemy opposite that had previously broken through on the left of Regiment 95 beyond the Ancre in our rear to Beaucourt. *Musketier* Kasner, 11th Company, fell as a sentry during this attack. *Vizefeldwebel* Crehmer fell in the fighting, after he had wounded two Englishmen. His platoon, smoked out of the dugouts, was destroyed at the *Bismarck Stollen*. *Leutnant* Stolper ended up in captivity. The 11th Company, which under *Leutnant* Stolper was the reserve of the III Battalion, lay in the *Kolonie* and should make a counterattack if necessary, also included *Leutnant* Waldemar Haase, the brother of *Leutnant* Harald Haase, 12th Company.

When the English attack took place at 7.00 a.m., there was no counterattack. *Leutnant* Waldemar Haase suddenly noticed how infantry projectiles smashed into the entrance of his dugout. When he wanted to see the cause of this 'mess', the sentry fell dead against the front of the dugout, and *Leutnant* Haase firmly determined that numerous Englishmen blocked the entrance and with that everyone was out. The Englishmen had come across the Ancre, surprising the 'Kolonie', attacked in the fog and overran the reserves and took them prisoner. *Leutnant* Stolper, 11/R55 [16]

Between 9 and 10 a.m. the British were observed occupying Beaucourt and entrenching in and around the village. The enemy also brought additional machine guns forward to reinforce their their position as they had done on the southern bank of the Ancre. *Leutnant* Lenze sent back an urgent request for additional machine guns that he desperately required if he was to continue to hold his position. He received two machine guns from the II/ *Ersatz* Regiment 29, which from 11.30 a.m. worked excellently under an outstanding and proficient *Vizefeldwebel* from Machine Gun Marksman Detachment 4.

At 11 a.m. Beaucourt finally came under German artillery fire, whereas previously, the German barrage fire signals could not be seen by the artillery observers in the rear. It was soon obvious to the defenders occupying the *Beaucourt Riegel* east of Beaucourt that the British were advancing up to the *Osthang* of Beaucourt. It was also obvious that the *Hang Stellung* was completely occupied by the British. Leutnant *Lenze*, the leader of the 5th Company, fired at them with rifles and machine guns with great success. Simultaneously the *Beaucourt Riegel* was being defended against enemy Lewis Guns located south of the Ancre.

Just before noon, a strong enemy attack was made against the right wing of the German position north of Beaumont that was defeated through infantry and machine gun fire. However, the greatest danger to the German line was at the left wing on the northern shore of the Ancre. While the enemy behaved quietly in front of the *Zwischen Stellung*, on the right wing starting at noon on 14 November, he made numerous attempts to advance from Beaucourt into the *Artillerie Mulde* and from there toward the north. It became quite evident that the *Zwischen Stellung* could only be held, if the enemy was prevented in succeeding in his plan.

Limited numbers of reinforcements were available north of the Ancre. Every unit that could be spared was alerted and given orders to move toward the threatened front. In the afternoon one company from RIR 99 was placed under the command of IR 62 and moved into the *Artillerie Mulde*. Soon after this company arrived, it was sent to RIR 55 as a result of a report received from *Hauptmann* Minck. The report advised IR 62 there was a strong possibility that the danger of a British breakthrough of the regimental position existed from Beaucourt.

As a result of the considerable danger that had appeared at the left border of the division sector, IR 62 received orders from brigade that it had to ensure the protection of the left flank of the division between *Feste Alt Württemberg* and Beaucourt. In order to achieve this goal, additional reinforcements had been provided to the regiment to assist it. The 5th and 8/R121, the III/R121 and the 13th and 15/R99 were moved into key positions near the front where they could be available to provide the most assistance.

On 14 November, as the battalions from RIR 121 were moved into the front line the men were bombarded by artillery and fired at by enemy aircraft. As the battalions moved into their assigned positions the different units sent to reinforce the front lines went forward by detachments, man walking behind man with large spacing between the platoons. In such a manner, the companies worked slowly forward through the once well-known position; however, the now devastated terrain was unrecognizable. The battalions from RIR 121 were allotted to the regiments of the 12th Infantry Division and inserted by companies, between parts of Regiments 23, 62, 63, 185 and RIR 99 where there were virtually no connections between these units.

The western part of the *Beaucourt Riegel* and the *Kiesgrube* continued to be defended until 2 p.m. despite heavy and accurate British artillery fire. The British guns were being directed by aircraft observers who flew above the German positions throughout the day. The aircraft were also diving down on known German positions and strafing the defenders with strong machine gun fire as well. At midday parts of *Ersatz* Regiment 29 that had moved into the *Beaucourt Riegel* at night as reinforcements also became involved in the defense of this position.

It was proving to be very difficult for the wounded to leave the *Kiesgrube* or for reinforcements to arrive. Low flying enemy aircraft continued to strafe the men in the *Kiesgrube* or as they crossed open ground when they made their way to the rear; all the while under heavy artillery fire.

Losses were heavy in such fire but could have been even worse were it not for the condition of the ground. The thick mud and churned up earth made the shells less effective than under normal conditions. The high explosive shells penetrated deeper into the ground and the dense clay, mud and chalk lessened the overall effect of the explosion and reduced the danger zone of each impact. It was also not uncommon for a number of the enemy shells to be duds as they burrowed deep into the soft soil without exploding.

Still, while the condition of the ground did help lessen the effectiveness of the shells, there were numerous losses from the enemy fire. While German artillery fired on Beaucourt, heavy artillery fire also fell upon the British located in the *Kolonie*. It was no longer possible to establish a connection with *Hauptmann* Minck who was essentially trapped inside his headquarters. This was because a British machine gun had taken up position just above his battle headquarters and fired at any sign of movement.

At 4 p.m. the British finally made a mass attack against the *Zwischen Stellung* by IR 23 further to the north. It was thanks to the personal efforts of the few remaining officers situated in the *Zwischen Stellung* as well as the self-sacrifice of the men and an effectively employed machine gun by the regimental battle headquarters that the enemy was successfully repulsed with heavy losses. Despite the heavy defensive fire the British troops had advanced to within 100 meters of the *Zwischen Stellung*.

Simultaneously, British bombing parties advanced against the left wing of H2 in the *Röhrlegraben* coming from the east. These too were thrown back, in part by machine gun fire, in part through bloody close combat. By the evening the regimental staff, whose two entrances of the battle headquarters were crushed in, went into the battle headquarters of Battalion Illgner directly north of *Feste Soden*, at the junction of L8 in the *Zwischen Stellung*. *Major* Lemcke was located there, and he now took over the leadership of the regiment.

The 5/23 was then inserted into *Feste Soden* along with the 7/23. The connection with the companies in H1 and H2 that until now had been maintained through patrols could not be maintained during the fighting. The 7/R121 that had arrived during the night, received the task to occupy the *Nagel Graben* and to establish a connection with the companies of *Leutnants der Reserve* Bräuer and Hübner in H1 and H2. The company was unable to establish any connection despite all attempts and when this became known, IR 169 was asked if they could establish a connection to H1 and H2, and to bring supplies of food, water and ammunition to the companies in these sectors. This request would be very difficult to comply with as all of the roads and approach routes leading to the position had been destroyed and were being held under constant enemy fire.

Despite all of the difficulties, IR 169 was able to provide small amounts of supplies of food and ammunition to the troops in and H2 but at a high cost in men lost in the carrying parties. The supplies of ammunition and in particular hand grenades had almost entirely been consumed in the heavy fighting. The men were ordered to search dugouts, trenches and the numerous dead and wounded lying about for any ammunition and hand grenades they could find.

The issue of potable water had also become a serious problem across the entire sector after the recent fighting. The drinking water supply for the troops was completely gone after the destruction of the only well left intact in the *Artillerie Mulde* and after the consumption of the supplies of drinking water stored in the dugouts. The troops were now solely dependent upon drinking rain water out of shell craters. Since almost all of this water was contaminated, in many cases with gas, drinking this water led to many illnesses and degraded the health condition of the men.

The German defensive line north of the Ancre that had stood firm almost since the start of the battle on 1 July was crumbling. Sectors B5 and B6 might have been able to hold out except for the fact that they were being attacked from the rear and the front at the same time. Some men had managed to withdraw from these sectors but for the most part they had become casualties.

It was later determined that Machine Gun No. 7 in the 3rd trench on the right of the *Zirkus Graben* in B5 had apparently been overrun from the rear early in the fighting. Machine Gun No. 6 located in the third trench had been able to hold out longer and by 12 noon had already fired 8,000 cartridges. In the afternoon, the British attacked the third

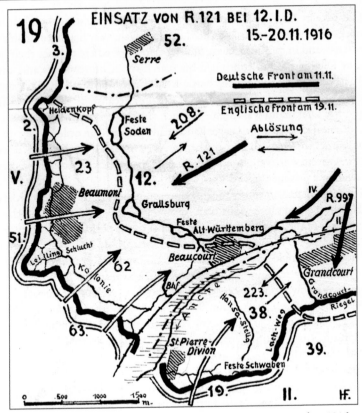

Insertion of RIR 121 with the 12th Division, 15-20 November 1916.

trench and the *Bismarck Stollen*.

At 4 p.m., the remnants of the 9th and 10/R55 had reached the end of their strength and were simply overwhelmed. Enemy fire and the lack of ammunition forced *Leutnant* Nolting, *Leutnant* Neise and *Leutnant* Meyenberg to surrender. There were only 20 men left in the 9/R55, the company had lost 18 men killed, 42 men wounded, while the 10/R55 had lost 14 men killed and 36 men wounded. The losses suffered by the British during these attacks were thought to be much larger.

Leutnant Nolting had done everything that was possible in this situation. With an ever shrinking group of men he held his position on the northern bank of the Ancre until the afternoon of 14 November. The weakness of his position was primarily through the danger coming from the southern shore of the river on his left flank. The first enemy attack had taken place here and had immediately succeeded. The British came from the direction of Beaucourt and station Beaucourt immediately in the rear of the position of RIR 55, the men never stood a chance in such a situation. At 4 p.m. B6 had been evacuated by all surviving troops according to a message from *Leutnant* Sprenger, 8/R55.

Several battalion headquarters were overrun, the officers and men being taken prisoner by enemy troops that had attacked from the southern shore of the Ancre. The existing confusion normally found during heavy fighting was compounded with the capture of the staff of the I and III/R55, and the death of *Oberstleutnant* von Laue and his Adjutant

Leutnant Giesecke by *Feste Alt Württemberg*. All during the fighting there was little or no artillery support fire as the batteries located further in the rear had been unable to see the barrage fire flares and in most instances, did not know just where to place their fire.

Leutnant Diekmann had continued his search for reinforcements and after leaving the IV/R99 he started off toward the battle headquarters of the II/R55, commanded by *Hauptmann* Minck located in the *Artillerie Mulde*. Because of the heavy artillery and machine gun fire Diekmann was unable to reach the II/R55 until about 5.40 p.m. When he arrived, he heard that *Leutnant* Feger had already delivered an order to give up Sector B6 and the companies should withdraw to the *Zwischen Stellung*. By this time, it was all over in Sector B6. Anyone who was going to return had made their way to safety; everyone else was either dead or a prisoner of war.

At 5 p.m. *Oberstleutnant* von Wangenheim, commander of IR 144, sent orders that RIR 55 should be relieved and move to the rear. At 5.30 p.m. *Leutnant* Lenze left the *Kiesgrube* with the remnants of the II/R55, leaving the defense of the position to the men from *Ersatz* Regiment 29 along with two machine guns. *Hauptmann* Minck was still entirely isolated and could not be informed of the rapid changes taking place in the regimental sector. In addition to the enemy machine gun positioned in the rear of his headquarters dugout British troops were now positioned on the right and on the left of his dugout.

At 6.30 p.m. *Leutnant* Diekmann, 9/R55, received a report from the 24th Infantry Brigade that there were plans under way for a counterattack by six companies from the 38th Infantry Division. These troops were supposed attack out of Sectors *Nord III* and *Nord IV* with the goal of recapturing Beaucourt. At 8 p.m. *Hauptmann* Minck gave the order: the 8/R55 should hold the *Zwischen Stellung*. The order never reached the company, it had already moved out of the position. A copy of an order from Army Group A arrived from IR 62 that had been written at 11.45 a.m. that Beaumont would not be taken again. The *Kriegsminister Graben* and *Fischer Graben* would form the new line. *Hauptmann* Minck left the battalion battle headquarters at 11.45 p.m. with his men and reached Courcelles unharmed, after he had made his report to the 83rd Infantry Brigade through the 24th Infantry Brigade about the events of this day.

In the night from 14/15 November the 6/R121, with its company headquarters arrived by groups, and one after the other then became placed into the *Zwischen Stellung* south of L9. This portion of the line was divided into two sectors. *Hauptmann* Illgner II/23, and *Hauptmann* von Raben, II/R121, were in command of the new sectors. The *Sturmabteilung* of the 12th Division now arrived between 2 and 3 a.m. but with only 17 men. Despite the small number of troops, the *Sturmabteilung* was taking up positions in order to clear L8 and L9.

Later in the day the British attacked the *Zwischen Stellung* where the 6th and 8/23 were lying along with men from IR 62 several times, following very strong preparation in each instance. In each attack, the British were repulsed with heavy losses from the defensive fire which often turned into close combat with the 8/23. During one such attack the leader *Leutnant der Reserve* Moldt, was killed, the leader of the 6/23, *Leutnant der Reserve* Lüthke was severely wounded and his company officer *Leutnant* Lummer was slightly wounded.

The British also directed attacks against Sectors H1 and H2. At 8.30 a.m. four tanks accompanied the attacking infantry and slowly rolled forward toward the position of the III/23. It was evident that the British were attempting to roll up the sector as well as cutting it off from the neighboring IR 169 on the right.

The company leaders of the III/23 finally came to a decision, they would need to evacuate their sector and to move their men to the rear to join with IR 169. The orders were given too late for any chance of the move being made safely. The approaching tanks had reached the German lines and had caused a great deal of panic among the men as well as losses from the concentrated machine gun and shell fire. In addition to the threat of the armoured tanks, both British and German artillery began to shell Sectors H1 and H2 because of faulty information about the position of friendly troops.

The largest part of the men who had survived the enemy onslaught and heavy artillery fire used almost their last available strength to move toward Serre in the north. The exhausted garrison was barely able to accomplish this move and many men fell or simply disappeared during the attempt. Some may have only been wounded, some may have ended up being captured but in any case, there was no opportunity to stop and provide assistance to these men. It was acknowledged that it was every man for himself.

Approximately 30 men under *Leutnant der Reserve* Heinrich occupied the right wing of H1 and L5 as flanking protection for IR 169 and became subordinate to the company leader of the 12/R169. The other company leaders of the III/23 also reported to the 12/169. When they arrived at the company headquarters they found a previously written order from the III/169, in which Sectors H1 and H2 were scheduled to be evacuated and through the occupation of L5 and L8 a new switch line should be created. The company leaders of the III/23 remained with IR 169 up to the evening of 15 November; then they went to Béhagnies, where the remnants of their companies were assembled.

The shortage of men was becoming critical. While orders called for the movement of platoons, companies and battalions, in reality the units described bore no resemblance to what they once did in previous months. This shortage meant that in situations where an individual company might once have been sufficient to garrison a portion of the trenches, two or more were now required and even these did not have the strength that was sufficient for the task at hand.

IR 62 had received a number of companies from different regiments as reinforcements. Two of them, 5th and 8/R121 together had only 70 rifles, every man of these two companies immediately became inserted into the *Zwischen Stellung*, the III/R121 was moved into the *Kriegsminister Graben*, the *Artillerie Mulde* and in the *Zwischen Stellung* between *Feste Soden* and the *Grallsburg*, which was now the forward position. The 13th and 15/R99 into the *Fischer Graben* and sometime later the weak III/121 became reinforced through an additional platoon. In the evening of the 15th additional companies from the I/R121 also became placed into the front at the *Grallsburg* and in the *Kriegsminister Graben*. Until the evening of 15 November the II/R121 was in *Feste Soden* and in the *Grallsburg*. The I/R121 was in the old second position *Nord I, II* and *III*. The companies found some shelter, partly in the already overcrowded dugouts; in part they were in the open in shell holes and trench pieces and destroyed battery positions. The weather was rainy and after some frost and snowfall, the ground was completely soaked through as were the exposed men.

When the 7/R121 arrived from *Feste Soden*, it had been immediately sent forward to the *Nagel Graben*. The southern portion of this trench was found to be occupied by the British, and as a result, the 7/R121 became involved in a bitter hand grenade battle at the barricades separating the two sides on 16 November.

Even these weak forces were a welcome addition to the German defenses. After active artillery preparation fire the British attacked the *Zwischen Stellung, Feste Soden* and the

Grallsburg once more. The enemy was successful in penetrating into the German position by the *Grallsburg*; however he quickly was thrown out again in a hand grenade battle. While the German lines had been held, the losses continued to grow with each attack.

Especially heavy fire lay upon the *Zwischen Stellung* and the rear terrain on 16 and 17 November. Further losses were inevitable under the weight of fire, because the dugouts, as far as they had not been crushed in, were overcrowded with wounded. The men were forced to find cover inside the shallow trenches and shell craters as best they could under the circumstances.

The parts of IR 23 still occupying the trenches were exhausted and the men found it difficult to stay awake. This was a direct result of the intense physical activity of the previous days as well as a growing shortage of food. The 8/23 moved back to Noreuil, taking the severely wounded men of the company with them after receiving permission to withdraw from the front line from RIR 121, who they were subordinate to. The 8/23 only had a battle-strength of 3 *Unteroffiziere* and 8 men at this time. In their place came several companies from IR 173 and IR 169 which were placed in the *Nagel Graben* and L9.

Communications between the units in the front lines and with headquarters in the rear were still almost non-existent, all telephone lines had been destroyed and there was no way of knowing if or when they might be in working order once more. Not even runners could be relied upon to make the dangerous journey and return safely.

The headquarters of IR 23 had not received any orders about the reorganization of the sector. In the night from 16/17 November officers from the regimental staff went to the regimental battle headquarters of IR 169 in order to obtain any information or explanation about a possible new division of the sector here. They did find out that IR 23 was now subordinate to the 208th Infantry Division. A command was transmitted by one of the few working telephone connections from the 24th Brigade, ordering the regimental headquarters to move into a dugout in the second position in the vicinity of the *Nordweiche*.

At 3.30 a.m. the staff of the I/23 proceeded to Béhagnies on orders from the regiment where the remnants of the battalion would be assembled. At the onset of darkness parts of the 5th and 7/23 were relieved in the *Zwischen Stellung* by the 10th and 11/185 as well as one machine gun platoon, and then also moved to Béhagnies. The staff of the II/23 and one platoon from the 7/23 continued to remain in the position. The leadership of the III/23 was transferred to one of the few remaining officers in the battalion, *Leutnant der Reserve* Alfons Heide.

In the night of 15/16 November three additional companies from RIR 121 were made subordinate to IR 62 because of the increasing number of losses suffered by the regiment, both in killed and wounded as well as from men reporting sick. The companies from RIR 121 were placed into the *Grallsburg* and the western part of the *Kriegsminister Graben*. One company remained in the *Artillerie Mulde* where the regimental command post had been located since 14 November.

The men had to withstand constant enemy shell fire that fell along the entire sector, no area was spared. The eastern part of the *Kriegsminister Graben* and the *Fischer Graben* suffered especially from flanking fire and considerable losses occurred.

On 16 and 17 November the British continued their efforts to enlarge their success of a few days earlier. British reconnaissance detachments pushed forward against the German lines at numerous locations in an attempt to determine just what opposition they faced. In each instance, heavy fighting flared up in the sectors, especially between the *Grallsburg* and he *Artillerie Mulde*. All of the British probes failed in the heavy defensive fire and all parts of the position continued to remain in German hands. Once the fighting had died down he British forward sentries were located in shell craters between 100-150 meters in front of he German position. Apart from these small attacks, the enemy infantry behaved quietly.

On 18 November the 185th Infantry Brigade had taken over command of the sector north of the Ancre. On the same day, the British had maintained strong artillery fire on the German positions north of the Ancre throughout the early morning hours. At 6 a.m. the ire increased to a level of drum fire and was accompanied by heavy mine fire. In the hours between 6.30 and 7.30 a.m., the enemy concentrated his fire and pounded the *Zwischen Stellung* once again.

The attack that immediately followed the impact of the last shell on the front line achieved some small success at the right wing of Battalion Illgner, II/23, where the enemy had penetrated into the German forward trench, or in reality, a series of shallow trenches and shell craters that had been joined to form a makeshift defensive line.

This was not an unexpected event as a large gap had previously opened up on the right of Battalion Illgner where the boundary formed with the 52nd Division. Due to a lack of sufficient manpower the forces needed to form a cohesive defensive line were lacking. The advancing British troops had moved through the gap without meeting any German resistance and suddenly found they were in the German rear.

The British had been able to capture a large number of German troops who had suddenly found their positions being rolled up from the right as well as being attacked in the rear. Any further resistance on their part would have been useless and the men laid down their weapons and surrendered, including members of at least two battalion staff.

The British soldiers assigned to escort the German prisoners to the rear were under the impression that they were moving back to their lines behind the rear of the II/23 as orientation was very difficult in the featureless terrain. Everything looked the same, churned up brown earth, craters and no familiar features, as anything taller than a tree stump had been blown to pieces in the weeks of shell fire.

The column of prisoners and their guards were spotted by other companies from the II/23 further to the left of the breakthrough. The trench garrison opened a well-aimed infantry fire against the escort party and forced the men to move further to the German rear in order to evade the rifle fire. Now the prisoners and escorts were completely lost and had no idea in which direction to go. The group continued to wander deeper into the German rear in the hope of finding a familiar landmark or friendly troops.

After walking some time the column suddenly ended up on the far left of the II/23, in the rear of *Feste Soden* that was occupied by Württemberg troops from RIR 121. The British being faced with a much larger enemy force surrendered and were disarmed and their prisoners, 12 officers, 80 men were liberated. During the close fighting that followed later in the day additional British prisoners were taken, altogether 5 officers and 170 men.

Among the men released in this manner was the Orderly Officer of the II/23, *Leutnant der Reserve* Kaminsky, who had been sent to the neighboring sector in the previous night with a special task by *Hauptmann* Illgner. The adjutant of the II/23, *Leutnant* Hahm, was also among the prisoners who had just been released by their comrades.

Once the large group of German prisoners had been freed and the remaining enemy assault troops had been forced to withdraw from the right of the II/23, *Hauptmann* Illgner observed two British soldiers approaching the German trench with a German prisoner. The

British soldiers suddenly realized that they were heading directly toward a German trench and they immediately changed direction, going into a trench that lead toward the enemy trenches, barely 200 meters distant from *Hauptmann* Illgner. The trench being used by the enemy was very badly damaged in the shell fire and afforded only minimal cover as it was almost leveled.

Illgner quickly alerted his men to the presence of the two enemy soldiers and their prisoner. Sergeant Obruschnik, the II Battalion *Tambour*, who had already made a name for himself in the recent fighting, immediately moved to the forward edge of the trench with *Gefreiters* Wingral and Gabor. The three men succeeded in shooting down the British escort and freed their comrade. Sergeant Obruschnik received the Iron Cross I Class for this action and his conduct in the fighting of the last few days while the two *Gefreiten* became recognized with the Iron Cross II Class.

At the same time these events were taking place, a strong enemy detachment had managed to penetrate the German lines on the left of Battalion Illgner at L9 in the *Zwischen Stellung* and *Landwehr Graben*. The platoons of the 7/23 advanced in conjunction with parts of the II/R121 and succeeded in throwing back the enemy who had broken in to the German trenches. They took a number of prisoners during the counterattack and then blocked off the *Zwischen Stellung* in the vicinity of the *Soden Graben* by constructing a barricade.

Further to the south, near the *Grallsburg*, the enemy attacked in three waves with larger columns in the rear. The enemy advanced from the direction Beaumont and was being guided by a tank in an attack upon the *Grallsburg* that since 13 November was half German, the other half was British. The tank slowly moved over the rough terrain to within 150 meter of the German trenches when it stopped. The accompanying British infantry pressed the attack and advanced toward the German positions where a fierce hand grenade battle occurred, especially at the *Grallsburg* where the 2nd and 3/R121 were positioned. Finally, the enemy were thrown back and further partial attacks later in the day also repulsed.

Several attacks by numerically superior enemy forces also advanced against the positions held by IR 62 north of the *Grallsburg*. On several occasions, groups of British soldiers managed to penetrate into the German trenches in the area of the *Rekruten Graben*. Each time the enemy penetrated into the trenches, a quickly mounted counterattack by local troops threw them out once again while capturing a number of British prisoners were captured.

Some of the fiercest fighting of the day occurred where the *Zwischen Stellung* and *Kriegsminister Graben* joined. This portion of the German line was being held by the *Schanz* Company [Entrenching Company] of IR 62 under the command of *Leutnant* Benczek. Benczek and his men managed to hold off every enemy attack at this critical junction. Much of the fighting was at close quarters and both sides were within meters of one another as numerous hand grenades were thrown from one side to the other.

Benczek's men faced the greatest challenge when a British tank rolled up toward their position and came to within 20 meters of the German trenches. The Male Mk IV tank opened fire at the German garrison from point blank range with machine guns and the light 6 Pounder guns causing numerous losses among the German defenders. Finally, German artillery fire falling all around the tank forced it to withdraw. Among the numerous dead and wounded was *Leutnant* Benczek who had been severely wounded in both legs from hand grenade splinters.

The II/23 Battalion under the leadership of the battle proven *Hauptmann* Illgner, had held his position during the heavy fighting on 13 November despite the enemy not only breaking in to the German lines, but also breaking through on the left of his battalion. When the largest part of the division sector had been lost to the enemy, *Hauptmann* Illgner had completely held *Feste Soden* with his weak forces. The personal actions of *Hauptmann* Illgner had contributed significantly to the unwavering opposition of his battalion.

In the following hours, the *Landwehr Graben* north of *Feste Soden* was cleared from the enemy by parts of IR 173. The last parts of the 7/23 were finally relieved in the night by parts of the III/185. The staff of the II/23 then went to Achiet le Petit where the regimental commander sent a message through IR 185 to the 208th Infantry Division that the *Soden Graben* and *Feste Soden* were now under the command of IR 185, and that his regiment now possessed neither troops nor any sector. He inquired about the further use of IR 23 and received orders to move to the rear on the following day and on 19 November the regiment went to Noreuil.

The I/23 had been assembled in Béhagnies and had already marched off from there in the driving rain on the morning of 18 November. The battalion marched northward through Noreuil, Bullecourt, Heudecourt, Fontaine-lez-Croisilles, Vis-en-Artois, Boiry Notre-Dame, Biache St.-Vaast, Vitry-en-Artois where it arrived in Noyelle at 7.30 p.m. and the men received billets.

On 19 November the enemy behaved quieter than usual. There were a number of small patrol attacks against portions of the German lines but nothing that threatened the overall German defensive line. However, strong enemy columns were observed advancing from Auchonvillers toward Beaumont. Orders arrived at the regiment that the remnants of IR 62 were supposed to be relieved in the early morning hours of 20 November by IR 23. However, this was not taking place as expected.

IR 23 was in no condition to replace IR 62 at the front. Instead, this regiment also needed to be withdrawn and sent to a quiet sector where the men could rest and the regimental strength could be restored. On 19 November the regimental staff and II Battalion, without the 6/23, were located in Noreuil, the I Battalion in Noyelle and the 6/23 in the *Zwischen Stellung* south of Serre. The III/23 moved at 8 a.m. from Noreuil to Estrées, where at 5 p.m. the battalion received very deficient and cramped quarters. The regimental staff arrived in Estrées in the course of the day. On 20 November, at 8 a.m., the II/23, without the 6/23, marched from Noreuil to Courchelettes south of Douai, where the 6/23 arrived in the evening hours after being relieved by parts of IR 25.

This latest participation by IR 23 in the Battle of the Somme, or as it was known by the men as the 'Hell of the Somme' was over. It would be the last time the regiment would fight on the Somme. However, this last participation had also been the most severe and had caused the most losses. From 7 November until the day of the relief of the 6/23 on 20 November; four officers (*Leutnant der Reserve* Moldt, *Leutnant der Reserve* Hoefler, *Leutnant der Reserve* Metz, *Leutnant der Reserve* Katscher) and numerous *Unteroffiziere* and Other Ranks were killed. Eight officers (*Major* von Wedelstaedt, *Hauptmann* Plewig, *Leutnant* Vogel, *Leutnant der Reserve* Hübner, *Leutnant der Reserve* Lüthke, *Leutnant* Lummer and *Offizier Stellvertreter* Kowallik) and about 400 *Unteroffiziere* and Other Ranks were wounded, eleven officers (*Leutnant der Reserve* Zimnol, *Leutnant* Bürde, *Leutnant* Wilhelm Schaffranek, *Leutnant* Kollibay, *Leutnant* Rother, *Leutnant der Reserve* Vogt, *Leutnant der Reserve* Richter, *Feldwebel Leutnant* Peisker, *Offizier Stellvertreter* Pniock,

Fahnrich Rusche, *Vizefeldwebel* and *Offizier Aspirant* Randt) and over 500 *Unteroffiziere* and Other Ranks were missing, from the latter, the largest part had ended up in captivity.

Finally, the last remaining regiment from the 26th Reserve Division would be withdrawn from the front lines after serving on the Somme since September 1914. The men of RIR 121 were relieved on 20 November and assembled in Gomiecourt. Departing from the positions north of the Ancre was bittersweet to the men of RIR 121. This regiment had occupied this sector for the last seven months without relief. The men knew every trench, every dugout and the entire terrain intimately.

When the regiment departed, the men left knowing that the positions they had created and had successfully defended for so long were now lost to the enemy. The regiment had prided itself on holding every single part of this outstanding position and everyone in the regiment felt that they had shown the other regiments how to refuse an attack. RIR 121 felt that it had been the backbone of the defenses here for the other regiments. This opinion was supported in the following letter from the 208th Infantry Division:

> To the 26th Reserve Division! RIR 121 has proved brilliant in the fighting on 18 and 19 November 1916 in association with my division. It has demonstrated a high degree of bravery, tenacity and faithfulness of duty. It is thanks to them that the position of the 185th Infantry Brigade could be held on 18 November. Signed: Hesse, *Generalmajor* [17]

General von Soden also added his congratulations to the regiment in which he acknowledged their tenacity and bravery in holding such a critical position for so many months without losing any ground. The overall number of losses suffered by RIR 121 on these seven days amounted to 39 dead, 280 wounded, 24 missing. Amongst the fallen were: *Stabsarzt* Dr. Lindemann, *Leutnants der Reserve* Lustig, Scheu, Gakenheimer; wounded: *Hauptmann* von Holtz, *Leutnants der Reserve* Bilfinger, Conzelmann. The regiment had also brought in a large number of British prisoners amounting to 7 officers and 240 men.

On 20 November the relief of the companies of IR 62 as well as the parts of RIR 99 and RIR 121 went forward starting at 6.30 a.m. Only the machine guns from IR 62 remained in their positions a further 24 hours under the command of *Leutnant der Reserve* Grosser. The regiment assembled in Achiet le Petit, where the men received one of the first hot meals they had enjoyed in some time. Following the meal, the troops were transported by motor lorries to Noreuil.

When the survivors of IR 62 reached rest quarters in Noreuil, the regimental strength was approximately 280 men altogether. The regiment had remained in the position without relief from 25 October until 13 November, 18 days long. Even before the men had to face enemy infantry attacks, the artillery bombardments with high explosive shells as well as gas shells had sorely tested the strength of the regiment.

Despite the setbacks and loss of key positions, the regiment looked back at this time at Beaumont-Hamel with pride in that it had succeeded in preventing an enemy breakthrough and caused heavy losses to the enemy ranks. The cost of this success had been high, especially among the officers. In part, companies were being led by *Feldwebels*. The leadership of the I/62 was undertaken by *Leutnant der Reserve* Janocha, the III/62, by *Hauptmann* Richter from IR 23.

On 21 November the regiment was accommodated with the I and II/62 in Biaches

Scheu
Leutn. d. R. im Ref.-Inf.-Regt. 121,
gefallen bei Beaumont-Hamel
am 15. November 1916

Luftig
Leutn. d. R. im Ref.-Inf.-Regt. 121,
gefallen an der Ancre
am 15. November 1916

Gakenheimer
Leutn. d. R. im Ref.-Inf.-Regt. 121,
gefallen bei Beaucourt fur Ancre
am 18. November 1916

(Kriegstagebuch aus Schwaben)

and the III/62 in Pelves. In the course of the morning of 22 November the Machine Gun Company arrived in Biaches and 314 men arrived from the Recruit Depot of the 12th Division, who were allotted to the regiment in order to fill up the companies.

The total losses in the month of November 1916 in IR 62 amounted to: 88 men killed, 260 men wounded, 1,575 men missing. The number of men in these figures that had been buried in the mine explosion on 13 November could not be determined with any certainty. After resting for several days the regiment marched to the railway station in Corbehem and at 12 midnight the regimental staff boarded the first train that would eventually take the entire regiment to Le Catelet.

Perhaps the greatest compliment paid to the men of the different regiments defending the positions north of the Ancre came from Field Marshall Haig, who described the opposition of the Germans at Beaumont-Hamel as the most stubborn on the entire front.

The fighting on the Somme was over. One of greatest battles of the war had finally come to an end after almost six months of constant fighting and with casualties on both sides of the wire exceeding 1,000,000 men. It would still take two more years of fighting before the war came to an end. Until then, the men who had survived the Somme would still face many more challenges, and for many, they would not live to see peace return.

While it had been a difficult day for the Germans holding the line north of the Ancre the threatened breakthrough had not taken place. Confusion still reigned across the German front as the new front line was formed and troop placements became established. Men considered lost appeared out of nowhere while reports came in that provided some information on the men, who had been killed, wounded or captured in the heavy fighting. Accounts from survivors of the 6/R55 indicated that part of the company had managed to hold out in the old artillery position east of Beaucourt, up to 7 p.m. on 15 November; then all of the survivors were taken prisoner.

Reports were also made about men whose actions had made them stand out from their

Machine gun post on the Ancre. (Author's collection)

comrades, men such as *Vizefeldwebel* Kurte and *Unteroffizier* Budde, 5/R55 whose action above and beyond the call of duty were recognized by their officers.

The Battle of the Somme, which officially ended on 25 November 1916, was evaluated as a defensive victory for the Germans. The reasons given for this were simple; the French and British had not succeeded in breaking through the German lines. The machine gun had proven to be an outstanding and very important weapon. Individual machine guns had managed to hold off entire battalions during attacks.

In the old XIV Reserve Corps, the 28th Reserve Division had fought in the Battle of the Somme on two separate occasions while the men of the 26th Reserve Division had fought up to the very last days of the battle. The performances of both divisions in the Somme Battle had acquired the greatest fame and would be considered a bright spot in the histories of these divisions. The Kaiser spoke to the troops of his full appreciation of their actions. In his words, it was only through this victory that the crushing blow became possible against Romania. However, the few remaining men of RIR 55 did not feel as if they had won anything in the recent fighting.

The disaster that befell RIR 55 could be explained from all of the recent fighting combined with the mine explosion by IR 62, the enemy breakthrough at Beaumont, the advance to the *Kolonie* and rolling up the German position from two sides. The troops that had behaved so splendidly at Gommécourt on 1 July felt that they had been sacrificed.

By the morning of 15 November RIR 55 had left the front lines near Beaucourt and assembled in *Bucquoi Nord* where after roll call was held it was determined that there were only 15 officers and 200 men left in the regiment after the fighting. Over the next few days additional men arrived who had become separated from the regiment and on 17 November RIR 55 could report that it had 18 officers and 330 men.

The officers and Other Ranks of RIR 55 were eventually accommodated in Courcelles

Unexploded shell inside the Beaumont Crater. A pen has been placed nearby to gauge size. (Author's collection)

le Comte, northeast of Bucquoi. While this regiment had suffered heavy losses in the latest fighting, the men were not out of danger yet. According to a message from the 38th Infantry Division issued by telephone at 10 a.m., 15 November, the troops were subordinate to this division and must be alarm ready. Additional orders from the 2nd Guard Reserve Division, *Hauptmann* Minck would take over the command of the regiment. By the afternoon the Other Ranks were newly fitted out with equipment and uniforms and on the following day the men had the unheard of luxury of hot baths, delousing and could finally clean their rifles.

Notes

1. Reymann, Oberleutnant a.D. H., *3.Oberschlesische Infanterie-Regiment Nr. 62 im Kriege 1914-1918*, pp. 127-129.
2. Reymann, op. cit., pp. 129-131.
3. Reymann, op. cit., pp. 131-132.
4. Reymann, op. cit., pp. 132-133.
5. Reymann, op. cit., pp. 133-134.
6. The mine crater left behind by this explosion can still be seen today across from the sunken road by Beaumont-Hamel. Many people believe the existing crater was left behind by the mine explosion featured in Malin's film taken on 1 July 1916. However the 13 November mine obliterated the previous crater. Caution should be stressed to all visitors as the crater has steep interior slopes and is overgrown with trees and the bottom is filled with unexploded ordnance. [Shell photo].
7. Reymann, op. cit., p. 120. Report by *Rittmeister* von Dresth, battalion commander III/62 sent from a P.O.W. Camp.
8. Von Wissmann, op. cit. p. 138.

9. *Leutnant* Romberg was a great loss for the regiment. *Leutnant* Romberg had acquired the Iron Cross I Class in September 1916 and proved to be excellent in many positions. (+16.11.16 in captivity).
10. Reymann, op. cit., pp. 134-135.
11. Reymann, op. cit., pp. 135-139.
12. Reymann, op. cit., pp. 120-121.
13. Von Wissmann, op. cit., p. 144.
14. K-Ammunition = Armor piercing ammunition. S-Ammunition= Standard infantry ball cartridge.
15. Von Wissmann, op. cit., p. 137.
16. Von Wissmann, op. cit., pp. 136-137.
17. Holz, op. cit. p. 41.

26th Reserve Division

Withdrawal to the Siegfried Stellung: October 1916 – April 1917

With the Battle of the Somme officially ended, the connection between the 26th Reserve Division and 28th Reserve Division that had lasted from the beginning of the war until late October 1916 was at an end. From the time the 28th Reserve Division left the Somme at the end of October, the two divisions would never fight together again. Each would experience new adventures along different parts of the Western Front until the end of the war on 11 November 1918.

From this point forward in the narrative, I will attempt to provide the reader with the details of the events that befell each division in the last years of the war. While not joined together in a cohesive unit, the experiences of both divisions mirrored one another on many occasions until the Armistice. As such, I have attempted to present the narrative in the best possible manner in order to minimize any confusion in the order of presentation. If I have failed to achieve this goal then you have my apologies. Please understand that this aspect of the third volume was perhaps the most difficult to accomplish.

The new sector occupied by the 26th Reserve Division at the end of 1916 was not

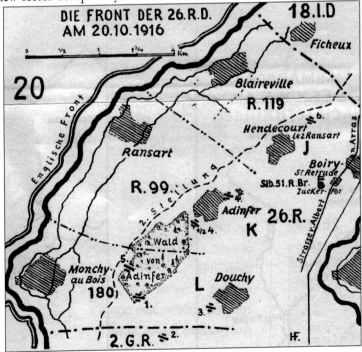

Position of 26th Reserve Division, morning of 20 October 1916.

Leutnant der Reserve Kläger.
(*Kriegstagebuch aus Schwaben*)

Memorial notice for Musketier Max
Altinger, IR 180, his body fell into
enemy hands. (Author's collection)

far from the battlefield of the Somme but for all intents and purposes it could have been hundreds of miles away. The division was now officially part of the I Bavarian Army Corps. The regiments of the 26th Reserve Division had hoped for a period of uninterrupted rest behind the front lines, but the shortage of troops on the Western Front prevented this from happening. The regiments soon returned to the fire trenches following the Battle of the Somme, fortunately in a quiet sector of the front where the division also acted as the army reserve.

From the 51st Reserve Infantry Brigade; the position occupied by RIR 121 lay between Ransart and Monchy-au-Bois. Behind the position was the ruins of Adinfer and south of it Adinfer Wood, from which a splendid long range view of the front was possible. In good weather the city of Arras and both steeples of the Church of Mont St. Eloy could be seen, 20 kilometers distant. A second position lay in front of the wood, occupied at times by individual companies. The regimental battle headquarters, regimental staff and rest battalion were close behind Adinfer Wood and were accommodated in Ayette and the surrounding area. IR 180 occupied the Monchy Sector. From the 52nd Reserve Infantry Brigade; RIR 119 occupied the Blaireville Sector; RIR 99 occupied the Ransart Sector.

Even while occupying the front line, the regiments could moderately recover in the quiet positions from the strains of the past months. Fortunately, while there was the normal random artillery fire from both sides as well as patrol activity and scattered infantry fire, not much else occurred. It was apparent that even the enemy was exhausted after months of fighting and winter was setting in.

Little had changed from the days of trench warfare before the Battle of the Somme had started. Regular patrols were sent out into no man's land as had been the norm. Prisoners were brought in whenever possible in order to obtain intelligence about the enemy formations and troop movements and reports were made of the enemy dispositions. The new positions lacked many of the extensive defenses the men had created further south, but due to the weak strength of the division the only work required of the troops had been confined to only those things that were considered absolutely necessary.

The only construction project being worked on by the men of RIR 121 in the new sector was the regimental command post, as the one that the regiment had taken over was considered to be completely ineffective against artillery fire. Because of the inclement winter weather, the new headquarters dugout was lined with boards to keep out the mud and as much water as possible. The regimental battle headquarters for IR 180 was not considered any better than the one taken over by RIR 121. It was located in a residential house, protected by a light concrete cover. It could withstand field gun shells but it was not secure against medium and heavy artillery fire. To many of the men in IR 180 and RIR 121, this lack of adequate bomb-proof shelters was a clear indication of just how quiet this part of the front had been.

However, even in this quiet sector danger was never far away. The scattered enemy artillery fire all too often would suddenly increase without warning and turn into a fire raid involving light and heavy guns, ball, bottle and torpedo mines, rifle grenades and machine gun fire. All of this activity inevitably produced losses, such as when on the afternoon of 14 October, *Leutnants der Reserve* König, 7/180 and Klager, 9/180, were both killed by shell fire. In order to reduce the chance of being caught out in the open during such fire raids and to provide secure shelters, the men of the 26th Reserve Division slowly began to expand their efforts on new dugout construction.

Following a period of rest, all of the men were eventually put back to work making improvements in the defenses. Each regiment was assigned a sector that was divided into two parts. Work began on each part of the front that required deep mined dugouts, something the veterans of the division were quite familiar with. New construction was started in Adinfer Wood, bomb proof medical dugouts, observation posts, machine gun emplacements, *Minenwerfer* and *Granatwerfer* posts, etc. were all created as quickly as possible. Battle trenches were improved, new communication trenches were created. It was quite similar to the work performed by the men throughout 1915 and early 1916 but in a much shorter amount of time and with fewer men. All of the hard lessons the men had learned about position warfare in the previous two years were applied to the new sector.

There were also many valuable lessons that had been learned during the months of fighting in the Battle of the Somme. Much effort was made to utilize the new information as quickly as possible. A Machine Gun Officer was established in each regiment who would coordinate the deployment and utilization of all three regimental machine gun companies. He would ensure the best way to maximize the power of the weapons, especially in flanking fire. He would also manage ammunition supplies, create multiple posts for each gun and provide full coverage of the regimental front at all times.

In the last month of 1916, *Minenwerfer* Company 226 concentrated on creating new positions which proved to be very difficult to work on in the rain, which came down all too often. Once the *Minenwerfer* had been installed, they were used for fire raids to disturb the enemy working parties and small undertakings were prepared with destructive barrage fire and supported with artillery fire.

Battalion dugout in Ransart, RIR 121. (*Das Württembergische Reserve-Infanterie-Regiment Nr. 121 im Weltkrieg 1914-1918*)

Regimental canteen, IR 180. (Author's collection)

Similar efforts were being utilized into the work required to sustain the division. The Douchy *Ortskommandeur, Vizefeldwebel der Landwehr* Fuchs, supervised field work and the operation of the threshing machines in order obtain as much of the local harvest as possible for use by the division. A large number of bomb proof dugouts were created for the staff, *Ortskommandeur* and troop billets in Douchy in case the village came under bombardment during an enemy fire raid. The rest battalion from RIR 121 made good use of the catacombs that had once been used by local population as a refuge in past centuries during similar conflicts. Even with all of the work required by the men, the regiments were able to hold regular reliefs and rotations during this time.

While the men worked on the positions day and night, they did not neglect the creature comforts. Kitchens, small markets and canteens, were created. A large canteen was established, which was controlled by the battalion headquarters that helped to supply the basic needs of the men, from soap to pencils, stationary and similar items needed to make life in the trenches bearable. Then, before too long, the third Christmas in the field approached, which would be celebrated in a much more subdued manner than in the past; there appeared to be no end of the war in sight.

On 19 December 1916 *General der Infanterie Frhr.* von Soden left the 26th Reserve Division in order to take command of a reserve corps. *Generalleutnant* von Fritsch took over the division in his place. There were many sad faces as the men said goodbye to their former commander, the man who had led the division through some of the toughest times in the war.

During this period of time the division was slowly becoming filled up once again with new recruits, returning wounded from other formations as well as familiar faces of the men returning to the regiments from hospitals after being ill or wounded. Despite all of the efforts in restoring the regiments to full strength, casualties and illnesses restricted the average battalion ration strength at 860 men; the trench strength at 810 men at the end of 1916. This was still considered quite fortunate because all available reserves at this time had already been sent to Romania.

Romania had declared war on the Central Powers on 27 August 1916 and by September the German and Austro-Hungarian armies were on the offensive. While it had been

26th Reserve Division staff saying goodbye to General von Soden. (*Die 26. Reserve Division 1914-1918*)

expected that Germany would be unable to send troops to the Romanian front because of the need for men on the Somme and for the Brusilov Offensive, Germany in fact sent eight infantry divisions as well as the Alpine Corps to the Romanian front.

On 21 December the relatively comfortable lives the men had been enjoying became increasingly difficult as the rain fell in torrents and the mild autumn weather was over. Both sides of the line were affected by the weather and the troops on both sides spent much of their time removing mud and water out of their respective trenches. The men continued to work on the new dugouts despite the heavy rain and they now had to stand in the trenche filled with cold water and mud while on sentry duty, giving rise to an increased number of men reporting sick with trench foot. Neither side was immune from the mud; at the start of the New Year, when the British attempted to break into the division position without artillery preparation, the attempt failed as much due to defensive fire as to the horrible muddy condition of the ground.

During this relatively quiet time training sessions on new means of communication between the infantry and infantry pilots continued whenever the weather permitted. For one officer, *Leutnant* Albert Reihling, 4/R119, the experience proved to be very exciting.

20 December 1916
Dear Johanna!
This time I have seen and experienced many interesting things since my last letter to you. We are just experimenting in the progress on a new means of communication between the infantry and pilots. I was ordered to attend a so-called infantry aviator training course for 8 days and lived through this time at a *Fliegerabteilung* in an old French villa about 30km behind our front to study this matter. We had quite a lot of duties, but it was quite instructive. Most interesting was the mutual living with these most noble Prussian aviator officers who had already been around a long time in this war and the many new things they could tell us about aviation. The local radio operator station was also very clever, where news was taken from the German, French and English reports before you at home had any inkling. And yes, luckily, good news generally came, important successes in Romania. But the best part of the whole command was naturally something else for me: I was able to fly for one half hour. An *Unteroffizier* in the *Abteilung* who was completely unknown to me took me for a ride in the air in a Rumpler Bi-plane. It was wonderful to float freely in the air. We moved over the villages and towns many hundreds of meters below us, in frantic haste, sometimes we were completely surrounded by opaque clouds, or they were even between us and the earth. The incredibly strong wind whipped us, often reinforced by the innumerable revolutions of the propeller. Though I did not know the leader, I got carefree, as if in a tramcar. And I will repeat it as soon as I am provided with an opportunity, but that can wait in line because since the 17th of this month I sit back in the trench indefinitely in the front and wait for Christmas, for New Year's Day, for the upcoming giant English spring offensive and so on. Last year we were able to greet spring with a much lighter heart, because we knew nothing about such huge battles such as they started in the Somme battle for the first time. But we want even more time to build with God's help. That our government's enemies made an offer peace, was very nice and reassuring for us. The German people now know modestly in any case, and will prove to be unanimous and strong in any case. A better leader

than Hindenburg we could not find in this greatest but also most dangerous time for Germany. He directs the military and non-military things of our dear homeland with outstanding spirit. How is Karl's stomach? Please send me his address. I wish you all a quiet, peaceful holiday season and I remain with cordial greetings in love, your faithful Albert.[1]

New *Granatwerfer* or *Priesterwerfer* formations were established in order to concentrate the use of this very effective weapon. While the spigot mortars were served by individual crews, every man in the different regiments was to be trained on their set up and use. All of the men in the regiments would eventually be instructed on the use of close combat weapons. Each man was to become familiar with the handling and working of all infantry weapons to ensure that these would always be ready for action when needed.

Starting in December the infantry were trained in the operation and use of the 7.6cm light *Minenwerfer* by the men of *Minenwerfer* Company 226. In January 1917 the first practices were held firing the light *Minenwerfer* on a flat trajectory carriage which was effective against enemy positions and which could be used as an anti-tank weapon, the latter use becoming increasingly important as the use of tanks increased.

In order for maximum number of men being able to operate the machine guns, a 14 day course was set up that every man was required to attend. IR 180 reported that all of the participants showed great interest in this important weapon and that at the final review of each class of instruction it was a true joy to see the eagerness the men took with the machine guns and how they learned to handle them so very quickly in the comparatively short time provided.

During this time something major was apparently in the works. Rumors had already spread throughout the division at the end of 1916 about a new defensive position being constructed far behind the front. Once the *pioniers,* who had apparently been taken from the division to work on the mysterious defenses, returned to the regiments the rumors only continued to grow.

1916 had been a pivotal year in the history of the XIV Reserve Corps. The months of hard work preparing the Somme defenses had been well worth the effort considering the effect this had on the Battle of the Somme. The positions of the 26th Reserve Division from La Boisselle to Serre had withstood months of heavy fighting and while the trenches were

Certificate for completing a training course on the Light 7.6cm
Minenwerfer, issued to *Sergeant der Reserve* Hermann Klein, 1/R121.
(*Landesarchiv Baden-Württemberg HauptsStaatsarchiv Stuttgart*)

Men of IR 180 in the trenches, December 1916. (Author's collection)

eventually lost, the cost to the enemy had been extremely high. However, losses among the veteran soldiers of the XIV Reserve Corps had also been very high as well and the loss of these trained men would never be fully replaced.

On 1 January 1917 the 26th Reserve Division officially learned of the proposed planned strategic withdrawal from the current positions, where the German line would be shortened considerably and would require fewer men to man the trenches. The withdrawal was being considered by the *Oberste Heeres Leitung* (OHL) in view of the difficulties holding the line in the muddy terrain of the Somme and the Oise. By withdrawing into the new line currently under construction, known as the *Siegfried Stellung*, in the line Arras – La Fère, it would be far beyond the reach of enemy artillery and provided with well-built trenches, protected by wide belts of wire obstacles.

The idea of a strategic withdrawal as well as the events that led to its adoption began in the latter half of 1916. Much of the credit for this concept belongs to *Oberst* von Lossberg, Chief of Staff of the 2nd Army under General von Below. In the second half of 1916 Lossberg called for positioning trenches and artillery on the rear slopes of hills, out of direct enemy observation. Until then, the densely occupied front lines that were visible to the enemy suffered heavily under the enemy's bombardments, but could still usually prevent a breakthrough.

Lossberg felt that the front line should be thinly held, with the defenders supported by machine guns and artillery. The thin line of defenders would stand their ground if possible, but if not, they would blunt the enemy impetus in the attack. This would facilitate the counterattacks that would take place from the rear positions which were occupied in depth, before the enemy was able to concentrate his forces.

The resistance met by the enemy troops would grow the deeper the opponent pressed into the German positions. Instead of a linear defense, it was now a defense in depth. Passive resistance would be replaced with a mobile defense. Much of the overall theory Lossberg used came from parts of captured French documents from May 1915 relating to the idea of a mobile defense. Lossberg made great use of these documents as the outline for his proposals.

During an OHL meeting in September 1916 plans were prepared to construct new defensive positions behind the present front line in five sections from the Belgian coast to Pont-à-Nousson on the Moselle River. The area from Arras to east of Soissons would eliminate the Noyon salient, considered to be the most important of the five proposed sites and also scheduled to be the first one constructed. The official designation was to be known as the *Siegfried Stellung*.

While the idea was based on sound military principles, there had been considerable resistance to the new concept. Ludendorff had serious reservations regarding such a radical change in tactics and the possible negative effects of such a withdrawal on both the army and the civilian population; he would much prefer a more aggressive stance.

He felt that such a massive withdrawal would be difficult to pull off and had inherent risks. There was the possibility of a swift advance by the enemy once they became aware of the plan which could possibly catch the German army in the open. Then there was the issue of demoralization among the troops at the front by voluntarily giving up positions that had been won with so much blood and which had been prominently mentioned in numerous army reports. There was also the issue of demoralizing the people at home, the workers in the factories who might view the withdrawal as a defeat.

Yet, the reality of the situation facing Germany could not be ignored. The German High Command agreed that the old army was gone; the men lost in the fighting could not be replaced with others of the same quality. There were other pressing issues; despite the army controlling the German economy it was still very shaky and showed signs of collapse.

The basic idea and design of the new defensive positions were implemented before the Battle of the Somme had ended. The early stages of construction began in September 1916 and were being kept as secret as possible. Despite all precautions, by late October the British began to learn of a new defensive line being built far behind the front. Statements made by prisoners occasionally made mention of the new defensive system being constructed in the rear, while aerial observation had obtained glimpses of the new work being done. While the enemy had obtained bits and pieces of the puzzle, they did not have enough information to put it all together and as such, little importance was attached to the various reports.

The actual construction of the new positions would involve a massive amount of materials and manpower; both of which were in short supply at the end of 1916. The original *Siegfried Stellung* was planned along traditional lines and would include massive belts of barbed wire, concrete dugouts and trench systems, tunnels, underground barracks, etc. Then, after von Below and Lossberg visited the front and discussed the problems with such an ambitious project, a decision was made that all further construction on the *Siegfried Stellung* was to be completed with the new methods of the defense in depth as outlined by Lossberg.

There had been many logistical issues to consider in the implementation of such a major undertaking. The huge numbers of men required to construct the *Siegfried Stellung* needed housing, food, water, supplies, and anything else that was required to accommodate the workers. In terms of manpower, 50,000 Russian prisoners of war did the rough initial work. 3,000 Belgian workers were employed as well as 12,000 German soldiers and civilians who then worked on completing the project.

In addition to the actual construction of the defenses, a network of light rail was constructed that was needed to transport the machinery and equipment and supplies needed to build the new positions. Workshops, depots, power stations, hospitals and barracks were constructed. From mid-October 1916 to mid-March 1917 approximately 1,250 railway trains were needed to transport the materials needed for the construction of the new position and support facilities.

The planned withdrawal was accompanied by a basic change in how the German soldier was to behave on the battlefield. The details on this change were distributed throughout the army on 1 December 1916. 'No longer will the infantryman have to tell himself here I stay and here I die.' The rigid adherence to duty that had been implemented shortly after 1 July 1916 by von Below had officially been abolished.

The new method of fighting, the new defense in depth would be a major change in how the war was being conducted, especially at the level of the common soldier. Under the new concept of defense in depth the initial line of resistance and early warning would be the double sentry posts directly in front of the enemy. With the reverse slope construction, the first trench line was about 600 meters behind the double sentry posts.

There would be an Outpost Zone – the *Vorpostenfeld*, between the sentry line and main defensive line, defended by a line of pickets placed at intervals. The Outpost zone was thinly held, as outlined in the text book, 'not in a rigid manner by masses of men, but by an elastic defense by means of attacks using artillery, machine guns, rifle and *Minenwerfer* fire to the greatest extent.' Behind the picket line was the support line, small squads of *Stosstrupp* located in small dugouts or shelters made from Ferro-concrete, called 'Group nests', where the men were ready to deliver an immediate counterattack if needed.

A very strong enemy attack could not be assumed to be stopped in the Outpost Zone but its impetus would be greatly reduced. The enemy would meet the second stage of the defenses on the same pattern, in a much larger scale. Now the garrisons of the first and second trenches were the reserve battalions and the battle zone could be extended up to 1,500 meters behind the trenches.

Miniature fortresses were constructed known as '*Widas*' which were placed in a checkerboard manner across the battlefield. Even if these were bypassed during an attack they were designed to hold out for considerable time and harass the enemy advance. The '*Widas*' had concrete machine gun emplacements. The attack would continue to slow when exposed to fire from the second line and artillery protection line and counterattacks by the counterattack division could form close behind the second line.

The Battle Zone located on the reverse slope was concealed from enemy artillery observers. On the other hand, German observation posts 500 meters behind the front could see the entire battle zone and approaches. High quality barbed wire was used in the construction and standardized mass production methods were employed to improve the efficiency and productivity of the workers.

During the period of time when the proposed move was still in doubt, Ludendorff tried to explain the project only as a precaution, not a general retreat in order to suppress any rumors. Crown Prince Ruprecht, the commanding General of the Army Group directly involved with the initial withdrawal, and his Chief of Staff von Kuhl, became the driving force behind the decision to withdraw. They sent a detailed memorandum to the OHL in which they outlined their arguments in favor of the plan on 28 January. The memorandum provided some terse, vivid descriptions of the appalling conditions which prevailed in the positions occupied by the Crown Prince's army group.

Parapets and trench walls were crumbling from the damp weather; the drainage system was badly damaged and failing everywhere and the men in the trenches stood up to their waists in mud and water. Only a few of the deep dugouts at the front were habitable. During the poor weather any attempts at repairs were both ineffective and extremely difficult for the over tired men. The troops were simply miserable and worn out. By taking the front line back it would shorten the trench system by 25 miles. With the new defensive system; fewer men were now required to hold the line and this could all result in a savings of 13 divisions for the general reserve.

While the initial response by many high ranking officers was negative, General Ludendorff and Crown Prince Ruprecht exchanged telephone calls over the next few days during which time the men discussed the issues. There were still arguments over the planned withdrawal of troops. Would it affect civilians at home and the lower rank soldiers? After discussions among the different commands, a decision was arrived at on 4 February 1917 to implement the withdrawal.

On 4 February, the orders to carry out *Alberich Arbeiten* were issued. After a five week preparation period, the withdrawal would take place on 16 March. On 5 February the details of the movement into the *Siegfried Stellung* and the *Alberich Arbeiten* were made known to the 26th Reserve Division and 9 February was designated as the first *Alberichstag*. The withdrawal would hopefully go a long way to resolve the overwhelming enemy manpower superiority and give the German army some breathing room.

What is suspected is that while Ludendorff and Hindenburg were opposed to the withdrawal plan, they simply did not have any viable option to choose from. Perhaps the biggest factor was the ever growing enemy numerical strength. Only 41 German reserve divisions were available which included 13 divisions just formed and which were of questionable value, as well as some divisions withdrawn from the Romanian front. There was no consideration yet of removing any troops from the Russian front. Opposed to this meager force were 75-80 Allied reserve divisions.

The German army was also quite tired and worn out from the heavy fighting. Crown Prince Ruprecht pointed out: 'The army on which we have to rely on now is no longer the old army; it is in urgent need of rest, reanimating and training.' There was also the consideration of the home front and that while the economy had been placed under the full control of the OHL the hoped for improvements had still not materialized.

During the time period when the future of the German army was being discussed, the men at the front saw little change in their daily routine. In January 1917 the cold set in and the New Year began with rain and cloudy bleak skies. By the middle of the month the winter weather had really arrived, heavy fog turned into light frost. On 17 January the first snow fell. The cold stayed and conditions continued to grow colder each week. Then, an old threat made a re-appearance, the danger of mine warfare. Machine gun crews in RIR 119 reported hearing the enemy mining below them in the front line. Counter mines were then started from the German side, something the men were quite familiar with after several years of mine warfare by Beaumont and La Boisselle.

It was also fortunate that so many of the men in the infantry regiments of the 26th Reserve Division had experience in mining as there was a shortage of trained *pioniers*. It was not until 5 November when the 4/*Pionier* Battalion 13 was finally transferred to Monchy after serving on the Somme without relief for many months. During the time spent on the Somme the *pionier* company lost 19 men killed, 56 men wounded and 2 men missing.

„Du haft ihn uns geliehen, o Herr, und er war
unfer Glück; Du haft ihn zurückgefordert und wir
geben ihn dir ohne Murren, aber das Herz voll
Wehmut."   (St. Hieronymus.)

O Herr   Und
    gib   das
        ihm   ewige
            die   Licht
            ewige   leuchte
        Ruhe!   ihm!

Zur frommen Erinnerung im Gebete an
Johannes Riegger,
Schütze im Inf.-Regt. 180, 2. M.-G.-Komp.,
geboren den 11. November 1897 in Hirrlingen,
gestorben den Heldentod fürs Vaterland
am 8. Januar 1917 bei Monchy, beerdigt auf
dem Soldatenfriedhof Moniville südlich Arras.

Laffet uns beten:
Allmächtiger, barmherziger Gott, der Du in
Deiner anbetungswürdigen Vorsehung uns den
Augenblick des Todes bestimmt hast, wir bitten
dich aus vertrauensvollem und ergebenem Herzen:
Siehe gnädig auf die Seele Deines Dieners
Johannes, nimm den in treuer Pflichterfüllung
erlittenen Tod als vollgültige Buße an und führe
sie nach den Schrecknissen des Krieges in Deinen
ewigen Frieden. Vater unser . . .

(Author's collection)

Once in the new sector, the *pioniers* applied their expertise in creating better defensive positions, counter-mining operations and helped in the construction of dugouts. In addition to these services, the 4th Company was also involved in helping to construct the rear position named *Roland*, part of the planned defenses for the strategic withdrawal of the frontline and later participated in the planned destruction carried out in the *Alberich Arbeiten*.

From 9-16 October the 6/*Pionier* Battalion 13 was under the command of the 28th Reserve Division which was then fighting by Grandcourt. From 17 October it belonged to the 52nd Prussian Reserve Infantry Brigade. Finally, the company rejoined the 26th Reserve Division and moved north to the Sector Boiry-St. Martin, where the *pioniers* were put to work.

The stress and dangers of the fighting by Thiepval now became replaced with the stress and difficulties of working in the winter weather. The constant presence of water made it difficult to work in the earth and also had a detrimental effect on the health of the men. In order to provide some relief from the effects of the damp weather, a relatively dry mined dugout in Boiry became furnished for residential use by the *pioniers*. Then, apart from some local undertakings the Boiry Sector remained quiet until the end of the year.

At the end of January 1917 there was a reorganization of the 4/*Pionier* Battalion 13. Formerly in the II Württemberg *Pionier* Battalion 13, it now became part of the Württemberg *Pionier* Battalion 326, which still belonged to the 26th Reserve Division. Under the new organization, the company commander *Hauptmann* Schmidt was transferred to the Headquarters of the XIV Reserve Corps, and *Leutnant der Reserve* Eitel took over command of the company.

Men from the 4/Pionier Battalion 13 in new steel helmets. (Author's collection)

The sector held by the 26th Reserve Division became increasingly active in January 1917 when the enemy artillery, and particularly mine fire, increased. The torpedo mines were quite unpleasant; even the strongest dugouts proved to be defenseless against them.

January 1917 was also a period of time when the German army became reorganized by removing the fourth regiment of any division and combining three of these surplus regiments to form a new division. On 13 January AOK 1 ordered the staff of the 26th Reserve Division to assist in the formation of the new 220th Infantry Division. The new division would include RIR 55 from the 2nd Guard Reserve Division, RIR 207 from the 207th Reserve Division as well as RIR 99 that had been with the 26th Reserve Division since the fighting in the Vosges in 1914.

With the loss of an entire regiment, the 26th Reserve Division had to adjust the occupation of the sector in order to meet the new demands placed on the smaller division. RIR 119 had to take over the sector of the right wing regiment of the neighboring 2nd Guard Reserve Division while the remaining regiments, IR 180 and RIR 121 were also forced to relocate. Once finished, the new division sector had shifted to the south. The sector now stretched from about 2 kilometers south of Ransart until 2 kilometers north of Gommécourt.

With the loss of RIR 99 the division had been reduced to three regiments of infantry

1. Armee.

XIV. Reserve-Korps.

w. 26. Res.-Div.

w. 51. Res.-Inf.-Brig.

w. R. 121 · w. R. 119 · w. J. R. 180
(Reserve-Inf.-Reg. 121) (Reserve-Inf.-Reg. 119) (Inf.-Reg. 180, aktiv)

Jedes Inf.-Reg. zu 3 Batl. und mit 12 leichten Minenwerfern; jedes Batl. mit 8 M.-G.'s.

w. Radfahr-Komp. 2

2. Ul. 20
mit einem Panzerkraftwagen.

w. 26. Res.-Feld-A. Brig.
(später mit der Bezeichnung Artilleriekommandeur Württ. 122, dem die gesamte Artillerie
der Division unterstellt wurde.)

w. II. (Feldhaubitz-Abt.) · w. R.Feld-A. 26
R.Feld-A. 27 · II. Abt I. Abt
3 Batterien zu 4 Geschützen. · jede Abteilung zu 3 Batterien;
jede Batterie zu 4 Geschützen.
(NB. 1½ Batterien zur Zeit bei der 220 J. D.)

w. Sanitäts-Komp. 522 · Fernsprech-Abt. 426

Div.-Kraftwagenkolonne w. 724 · 3 Feldsignaltrupps

Stab w. Pi. B. 326

6. Pi. 13 · 4. Pi. 13 · Scheinwerfertrupp 256
(zur Zeit abkommandiert)

Minenwerfer-Kompagnie
12 schwere
6 mittlere } Werfer
3 leichte
(später 0, 8, 4)

Feldlazarett 505, 502

Pferdelazarett 245

Feldrekruten-Depot
1 Bataillon, 3 M.-G.'s.
(NB. Zur Zeit bei einer andern Division.)

An Artillerie unterstanden der Division zur Zeit noch weiter:
I. Feld-A.-R. 78 (3 Batterien), eine 9 cm Batterie (Fuß-A. 692), eine 10 cm Batterie
(11. 2. G. Fuß-A.), zwei 12 cm Batterien (2. Bayr. Fuß-A. 18, Fuß-A. 338), fünf schwere
Feldhaubitzbatterien (4. Fuß-A. 16, 3. Fuß-A. 93), 6. Bayr. Fuß-A. 18, 3. Fuß-A. 402,
Fuß-A. 215) und zwei Mörser-Batterien (5. Fuß-A. 7, 8. Fuß-A. 12).

New divisional organization. (*Die 26. (Württembergische) Reserve-Division
im Weltkrieg 1914-1918*)

and with this, no longer required two brigades. The staff of the 52nd Reserve Infantry
Brigade under *Oberst* Praefcke was considered dispensable; and it was placed at the disposal
of the Württemberg War Ministry. The 51st Reserve Infantry Brigade under *Oberst* Walther
now consisted of the three remaining infantry regiments. Artillery units were being split up
as well, stretching the capabilities of the divisions to new levels. In the first days of February
the regimental staff and the I/RFAR 27 separated out of the association of the 26th Reserve
Division. RFAR 27 had been formed in June 1916 from parts of RFAR 26 and FAR 13 and

Ersatz troops and it had served the division well during the Somme fighting.

While the final preparations were being made for the unprecedented withdrawal into the *Siegfried Stellung*, life at the front remained normal. On 18 January the 26th Reserve Division moved from the I Bavarian Army Corps and returned to the XIV Reserve Corps control. The Kaiser's birthday was celebrated on 27 January, a bright clear day which helped lift the mood of the men. Then, just a few days later, on 1 February, the 12/R119 managed to shoot down an enemy aircraft, capturing the pilot, a British Captain. Another diversion came with the birthday of his Majesty the King on 25 February that included a church celebration at 9.30 a.m. and a parade at midday followed by speeches by the regimental commanders.

The reality of the withdrawal began to sink in on 8 February when the III/R119 was relieved from the front line and sent to work on the *Siegfried Stellung*. The men worked out in the open air at 10° Celsius. The men from the III/R119 helped to create the *Balkonstellung* [Balcony position] in front of Quéant. *Minenwerfer* Company 226 also received new duties in February in Hamelincourt in preparation of the *Alberich Arbeiten*, as well as by assembling any old equipment that was available that could be evacuated to the rear.

Starting from 9 February the men began to see *pioniers* along with labor soldiers at all crossroads, by all wells in the villages, also by the large buildings, namely in the interior of the churches, performing secretive work. It consisted of digging, mining, drilling and chiseling into the various structures and if anyone asked them what they were doing, they were only answered with a vague shrug. Everything had to become held in strict confidence from the troops until the very last moment, especially about the day of the withdrawal. Every precaution was being taken because it could easily become known by the enemy from an imprudent letter written home giving vital information away unexpectedly or from a talkative prisoner.

Some men, known as 'Connoisseurs of the situation' claimed to know that the mysterious work dealt with the preparations for more extensive destructive work in the near future. As 9 February was the first day of the so-called *Alberichstag*, which would last approximately 35 days, these 'Connoisseurs' were correct, this time. The entire area of land occupied by the Germans from Arras to Laôn would be evacuated and the men, as well as everything not nailed down, would be withdrawn back to the *Siegfried Stellung*. During this time, everything being left behind had to become prepared for destruction.

While the German army was voluntarily abandoning a piece of enemy territory that it had occupied and defended with so much loss of life, the gain being achieved by the withdrawal was so great that giving up this strip of land no longer even came into consideration. The withdrawal would hopefully disrupt all of the enemy's plans. He would have to re-orient his lines, regroup his forces and change artillery positions before being able to even consider an attack.

The enemy would advance into a barren region, with no place for his men to sleep, a 15 kilometer wide zone of destruction where everything of value had been destroyed, and which would severely hamper the enemy advance and make his life that much more miserable. All wells would be destroyed or made unusable and there would be a corresponding shortage of water for the enemy, men and horses. All shell proof dugouts, cellars, catacombs, crossroads and railway lines, all places that offered good observation – church towers, chimneys, windmills, etc. would be destroyed. The buildings would be burned down, large rows of

RIR 121 gun crew 3rd MG Coy, 14 February 1917. (Felix Fregin)

trees and park areas were being cut down.

When the enemy finally advanced into the zone of destruction he would come up against a well-prepared position that was protected by artillery. Also, the time the enemy needed to re-establish contact with the Germans, dig new positions, create artillery emplacements, etc. could be used by the Germans to continue to improve the defensive positions so the time of the withdrawal would be stretched as long as possible.

The mysterious work of the *pioniers* became quite clear when the full details of the *Alberich Arbeiten* became known. Once finished, the mine chambers had become prepared, the explosive charges had been set in place, dammed off and the wires leading to the charges were left exposed, so that at any time the wires could be connected to the detonators. Numerous wire ends could be seen sticking out of all of the interior walls of the churches, about a meter from the floor, just waiting for the moment when they would be used.

The entire area was to be destroyed in Operation Alberich. Barracks were to be torn down, dugouts destroyed, houses and wells blown up. Anything of military value to the enemy was either removed or destroyed. Even old iron scrap was taken back with the army. The designated routes leading to the rear were all marked with special insignia for each battalion during the planned withdrawal.

The men who possessed the skills to work with high explosive charges were accommodated in the dugouts along with the infantrymen and in such close quarters the full details of the destructive work became known to everyone. After the work had been completed all of the uninhabited and lightly-built sheds, stables and barns were destroyed. While the *pioniers* were hard at work preparing the explosive charges the infantry were also hard at work drilling, marksmanship training and perfecting the use of close combat means and the machine guns.

From 10-23 February the Ancre front was systematically evacuated over stages to the hills behind Irles. On 25 February Gommécourt was abandoned, and the British entered the position that had eluded capture on 1 July. All of the positions, dugouts, every

Destruction of buildings during Alberich Arbeiten. (*Das Württembergische Reserve-Infanterie-Regiment Nr. 121 im Weltkrieg 1914-1918*)

facility had been blown up prior to the withdrawal. The British who followed behind the withdrawing Germans were shot up with artillery and infantry fire.

In early March, orders arrived outlining the preparations needed to dismantle the positions. *Minenwerfer* were the first to be broken down and carried back to the new positions by the Other Ranks from the 6/*Pionier* Bn. 13 under the direction of *Leutnant der Reserve* Rehm. Once finished, the old *Minenwerfer* positions were filled in.

Soon the heavy batteries stopped firing and were limbered up and moved to the rear. The field batteries followed a short time later. Individual field guns left behind would represent the fire from entire batteries in order to deceive the enemy, before eventually being withdrawn to the rear as well.

All regimental baggage packed up and moved back by wagon. *Radfahrer* continued to bring new orders regarding the destruction of the positions and stripping the rear areas of all usable items. Kitchens were shut down and driven back. All cooking items were removed and the few men remaining in the position were supplied with small stoves and solidified alcohol so they could cook their meals.

Within a few weeks the war of movement would begin again. All of the fears of the OHL that the withdrawal would adversely affect the men's morale were unfounded. There were no indications of the men being in a depressed mood because of the retreat, it was exactly the opposite, as everyone was looking forward to a change and in some instances on playing a prank on the enemy. Many of the men could just picture the British sitting in front of the abandoned German positions for days and then how angry they would be once it was discovered that they had been deceived so badly.

However, the elated mood of the men became somewhat subdued when the staff came back from a reconnaissance of the new position of the *Siegfried Stellung*. The men had all

Home on leave, soldier from RIR 119, standing second from right. (Author's collection)

heard that the new position had been worked on for months, the stories about the concrete dugouts and complete subterranean barracks that had been constructed. However, when the staff returned they brought back news that the position was far from the ideal that had been expected, especially the position that the division was to occupy. It had barely been started; only the wire obstacles were in place, and the men were expected to move into the new positions in 10 days: 'That was a lovely prospect'.

Everything possible was being done to prevent the enemy from learning of the plan. This would prove to be quite difficult considering the sheer scale of the withdrawal; something was bound to give it away. Enemy observation aircraft were always a concern as they photographed every part of the German defenses. Occasionally, the low flying enemy aircraft fell victim to ground fire as they flew above the trenches. On 2 March two sentries from the 4/R119; Otto König and Finkbeiner, managed to shoot down an enemy observation plane. While it was only a single aircraft, even one less enemy aircraft could make the difference between a successful withdrawal and a potential disaster.

The destruction of even one enemy aircraft was even more important when considering that the foggy weather that had set in since the middle of February had markedly decreased the number of enemy planes seen overhead. The poor weather had reduced the aerial activity by the British pilots considerably, while at the same time the German pilots were exceptionally active hindering possible enemy aerial observation as much as possible.

As March approached, the men thought more and more of the end of the *Alberich Tags*. Instead of being demoralized, the men seemed to be rejuvenated with new life; it was apparently time for something different and new from the monotonous life in the damp, moldy dugouts, even if the new defensive position failed to live up to the rumors.

There was really no time to dwell on personal fears or concerns over the withdrawal.

there was simply too much work to complete if the withdrawal was to be successful. The destruction of the current position included taking all rain gutters and the church bells to the rear, so much material that every available vehicle was constantly under way every night and during the days if the weather was foggy and misty.

On 13 March the regimental and battalion orderly rooms of IR 180 became transferred to Cagnicourt, where the regimental staff and one battalion would be accommodated. In the days from 13 to 15 March no more food came up to the front, instead the troops were issued their rations out of the food reserves located in the position.

The assembly area for the men of IR 180 for the march out of the current position to the rear was located 1 kilometer east of Ayette on the Ayette-Moyenneville road. The route to be used by the regiment was designated with signboards, identified by a round disk for the men of IR 180. The routes assigned to each regiment even avoided the villages because of the expected enemy artillery fire on these locations.

On 15 March the 1MG/R119 was moved to the rear in order to take up new positions where the guns could protect the flank of the regiment during the withdrawal. At the end of the *Alberich Tags*, on 16 March, the village of Douchy presented a bleak picture to the men of RIR 119. Only the church and a number of high trees were still standing upright, until they too were finally destroyed in the following night after the withdrawal of the troops.

Never let it be said that the men of RIR 119 did not have a sense of humor. Before leaving Douchy, a large placard was placed on a ruined house with the inscription: 'Hello Tommy! Headquarters of Sir Douglas Haig, A great pleasure and a hearty welcome, brave conqueror!'

One of the most important aspects of the demolition of the German defenses was the complete destruction of the numerous dugouts found in the positions. This was apparently accomplished with great efficiency and each dugout was prepared in advance so that their destruction became absolutely guaranteed. Four hours before the regiments marched off to

Men from IR 180, February 1917. (Author's collection)

the rear the supports of the cross parts of the dugouts would become pulled out. The first 12 framework in each entrance would then be pulled out and the debris would be thrown down into the dugout. Generally, if the dugout entrances did not collapse as a result of this, it was still quite easy to thoroughly tear them down and make them almost unrecognizable.

No dugout was exempt from this destruction. *Stabsarzt* Dr. Metzger had evacuated his beautifully prepared medical dugout and left it smoldering like a charcoal burner, an intense fire deep inside the earth without the flames becoming visible to the outside. Once all of the wood had been consumed the entire structure collapsed in upon itself.

Oberst Walther was extremely busy on the last day before the withdrawal began. He was in his battle headquarters from 9 a.m. until 11.30 p.m. so he could personally take control over the evacuation and so he could be certain that everyone who was leaving that night managed to get away safely and that everyone was accounted for.

On 16 March regimental orders were distributed stating that the date and time of the withdrawal was fixed for 10.30 p.m. that very night. The troops began to abandon the positions according to the plan in the night from 16/17 March. One of the last acts performed by the men before abandoning the position was the complete destruction of all remaining dugouts. In order to move quickly, the men were only wearing storm packs, everything else had been packed up previously and sent back by wagon. At exactly 10.30 p.m. the position companies left the trenches by Groups and marched back as silently as possible through the communication trenches. They encountered mud and holes at every step, some so deep as to reach over the tops of their boots. The men eventually left the paths and most of them ended up marching in the adjacent plowed fields. Anything that could make noise had been muffled and all smoking had been strictly prohibited. The men slowly moved out of the trenches along the marked route, directly west from Douchy, to the northern end of Ayette.

At 2 a.m. on 17 March, the III/R119 and the 2MG/R119 moved into the rearguard positions under orders from the leader of the rearguard, *Oberst* Walther. By 6 a.m. the guns were distributed into the line: Hamelincourt – Bois leux-St. Marc crossroad until the northwest exit of Hamelincourt – Bois leux-au Mont. The III/R119 occupied a rearguard-position at Boyelles along with the 8/R121 in order to provide protection against any enemy possible advance.

The morning of the 17th was foggy, which would only aid the columns from being observed in the planned evacuation of the positions. The infantry companies left the trenches in order and awaited their turn to move off to the rear, all the while under random enemy artillery fire. When the fog lifted later in the afternoon, enemy aircraft appeared overhead once again making it almost impossible to conceal the massive movement of troops to the rear.

The two officer patrols which had 12 men each that had been left behind in the front lines continued to act as if the full garrison was present. They fired light balls into the night from different locations; they fired randomly into no man's land with rifles and sprayed the terrain with occasional machine gun fire as if it was any other night. At 4 a.m., one hour after the main body of troops had left the trenches the two patrols would also withdraw and followed behind them to the rear. In addition, a few cannons of the field artillery remained behind in position and fired an occasional shell.

The withdrawal by RIR 119 was carried out without any disturbance from the enemy. The routes taken by the infantry came under almost no enemy artillery fire at all so that the

Destructive work, Alberich Arbeiten. (*Das Württembergische Reserve-Infanterie-Regiment Nr. 121 im Weltkrieg 1914-1918*)

Withdrawal to the *Siegfried Stellung*.

regiment, minus the III/R119 and 2MG/R119 moved in an orderly manner and assembled at the designated assembly place where the march via Moyenneville-Hamelincourt-St. Leger to Croisilles began at 2.30 a.m.

While the withdrawal was well planned and was proceeding smoothly, it was still a very dark night. Many of the units became mixed together in the pitch black darkness as all lights had been forbidden. In order to unravel the units, groups of officers with nominal lists were stationed at all crossroads and would provide directions to the marching columns as well as keeping order and re-directing units that had become unattached from their regiments. At 5 a.m. five companies from RIR 119 had reached Croisilles and were billeted in the few houses that were still intact.

The roads were quite muddy and extremely difficult to march on because of the large number of men who were moving toward the rear and also from the heavy road traffic of the last few weeks. Despite these problems the men finally reached their goal, and at 6.30 a.m. on 17 March the regimental staff and the I/R119 with the 1MG/R119 bivouacked in Croisilles. The II/R119 moved into St. Legers, the 3MG/R119 moved into the *Siegfried Stellung* outpost zone.

On the evening of 16 March the battalions of IR 180 also marched to the *Siegfried*

Stellung, where they arrived at 9 a.m. on 17 March. The sector of the *Siegfried Stellung* specified for the 26th Reserve Division became divided between the regiments; RIR 121 occupied the right wing of the sub-sector Bullecourt, RIR 119 prolonged it on the left wing until Quéant and IR 180 received the middle with Riencourt behind it. In the regimental sector the I/180 occupied the right sector with 1st, 2nd, and 3rd Companies the 4th Company was in support in Riencourt, the II/180 occupied the left half of the regimental sector.

Two Machine Gun Companies from IR 180 were distributed across the regimental sector. The inadequacies of the position that concerned the men only a short time earlier had proven to be well founded. There was a lack of accommodations for everyone that was in the position, because sufficient dugouts still did not exist. The men who would otherwise have to remain exposed to the elements became moved back to Riencourt where they would provide support and would only come forward to perform work duty. While in the *Siegfried Stellung*, the 4/*Pionier* Battalion 13 was integrated into IR 180 in Riencourt where it continued to work further on the position. The enemy that followed after did not disrupt the work of the *pioniers* even a little. The regimental staff, as well as the battle echelon of the battalions and machine gun companies moved into quarters in Cagnicourt.

Once the rearguard patrols had moved to the rear the enemy apparently noticed that the light balls suddenly ceased as did the random fire until the front grew oddly silent but did not follow closely after. When the fog lifted later in the day the British saw no sign of the Germans. When they did follow up all they met was a barren landscape, no trees, no buildings, no brush; everything had been destroyed.

In the 35 *Alberich Tagen* everything of value had been removed or destroyed. *Pionier* units followed the infantry withdrawal, blowing up the last remaining items and setting fire to all intact structures. The men could see the red flames mixed together with the red and black smoke as the dense clouds rose up into the air everywhere they looked. Not a single church steeple could be seen anywhere. The success of all this effort was greatly aided by 14 days straight of foggy weather.[2]

By midday on 17 March, enemy patrols arrived near the new position. At 3 p.m. strong enemy reconnaissance battalions moved north from Bucquoy and were taken under fire from artillery pieces located in the outpost line and were forced back. Enemy infantry and cavalry advanced in skirmish lines at Mory and the *Ulans* forced them back to Ecoust-St Mein. Patrol fire flickered all across the front lines. Australians pilots joined in the fighting with their machine guns, strafing the German positions.

The men of RIR 119 wanted to get back at the enemy. A patrol detachment from the 12/R119 under *Reservist* Adolf Kromer who had already been severely wounded three times, and who had volunteered to report to the front despite his latest injuries, and one other patrol from the 11/R119 shot down an enemy single seat aircraft. The aircraft crashed into the ground nearby, the occupant was dead. Two members of the patrols, ignoring the fire from nearby enemy troops, salvaged letters, maps and the machine gun from the plane and brought it all back with them.

In the afternoon enemy cavalry and infantry detachments with machine guns advanced from Frémicourt toward Beugny and in the evening an enemy company occupied Vaulx Vraucourt. The enemy continued to move closer to the new German positions far more rapidly than had been originally hoped for.

At 1 a.m. on 17 March the I and II/R121 began the march to St. Léger, where bivouacs

The final withdrawal, Croisilles, March 1917. (*Die 26. Reserve Division 1914-1918*)

were supposed to be made available to the men. The march was extremely exhausting, the route was literally bottomless. For the past weeks the roads had been used night and day by supply wagons that were transporting all useful materials to the new position. The weather was quite poor, with numerous rain storms and the roads were no longer being repaired as they once were. The result of the heavy traffic and wet weather had turned the roads into muddy swamps. Fortunately the troops were able to still find stretches of where there was comparatively good marching alongside the road, however the vehicles on the road sank up to their axles. It took great effort to get them moving once they had sunk down into the muck.

Towards morning on 17 March the battalions arrived in St. Léger, the division Headquarters of the 2nd Guard Reserve Division, and slipped among the guard units there in a makeshift manner. After a short period of sleep the *pioniers* asked the men to leave the village immediately, because it was to be blown up. The tired men of RIR 121 did not act as hastily as the *pioniers* had hoped for and the men had a leisurely morning wash and then rested while they prepared and drank their coffee without seeing the need for haste.

Finally, the men of the I and II/R121 were assembled outside of the village limits in the course of the morning, at a safe distance from the expected demolition. During the clear, warm spring weather, eating good food and with all sorts of jokes, the battalions spent the day by the village and witnessed the destruction of the villages of St. Léger and Croisilles. One house after the other collapsed as the charges were set off. Croisilles burned at several places and it was especially impressive when the highly situated Château or what the men would call a villa, in St. Léger was suddenly shrouded in a dense cloud of smoke, and after a few seconds when the smoke had cleared, the Château was gone.

Destructive work during Alberich Arbeiten. (*Das Württembergische Reserve-Infanterie-Regiment Nr. 119 im Weltkrieg 1914-1918*)

Following the spectacle of destruction, the battalions continued to march back to the new position. In the evening the battalions arrived at their new sector by Bullecourt. This march was unforgettable by the men who participated. While on the roads and during what appeared to be random meandering the marching columns were all pointed eastward and generally the men could see all of the villages burning as fat columns of smoke climbed towards the sky.

While the previous efforts at destruction had been managed without attracting the enemy's suspicions, the tall columns of smoke and flames that stretched as far as the eye could see could not remain concealed from the enemy. On the evening of 17 March when the German outposts left behind at Ayette were exiting the village, the first British troops were already entering the other side of the village. However, the enemy then followed only hesitantly, so that the III/R121 arrived in Cagnicourt on the morning of 18 March without being molested by the enemy.

The withdrawal to the *Siegfried Stellung* had been completed and had proved to be a success. The enemy was following behind the troops, but they were not being aggressive and only moved forward slowly and then only with patrols at first. This was probably fortunate for the men of the 26th Reserve Division.

While the new defense in depth might be good in theory, the real test was about to come when the *Siegfried Stellung* was occupied for the first time. The men of RIR 121 found the position by Bullecourt was not what they had originally been led to believe. It did not contain the well-developed, massive defensive position that would prove to be impregnable as many had still hoped for. Instead, it consisted of some obstacles, a few trench pieces and some sentry positions. There were no available dugouts but one located by the right border of the regimental sector. Since the exact location of the regimental border was not entirely clear, a dispute quickly arose with the neighboring regiment on the right over which unit

Bröſamle

Leutnant d. R. im Inf.-Regt. 180,
geſt. am 20. Juni 1917 an den bei
Bullecourt erhaltenen Wunden

(Kriegstagebuch aus Schwaben)

had the right to use the dugout. The dispute was over quickly when a compromise was reached, allowing both regiments to share this dugout.

The companies further in the rear received quarters in the small village of Bullecourt which had a population of 396 inhabitants who had still occupied the village until a short time before the troops arrived. The civilians were removed and taken to the rear for safety as Bullecourt would form part of the front line defenses. Only sentries remained in the position. Pickets occupied the outpost zone in front of the position by Ecoust-St. Mein and Noreuil from the III/R119 and IR 180, to which the 3MG/R121 and two officer patrols of the regiment were allotted.

Holding the regimental position on the right was the II/R121, on the left the I/R121, and in front of each battalion was one company in reserve in Hendecourt. The position companies occupied the houses and other buildings of Bullecourt. The regimental staff and III/R121 were in Cagnicourt, as well as the First Line Transport, with exception of the Machine Gun Companies, which were accommodated in Saudemont. The Regimental Transport lay in Aubencheul-au-Bac.

Minenwerfer Company 226 was also quartered in Saudemont and the throwers became placed in the *Siegfried Stellung* by Riencourt and in the vicinity of Bullecourt and Quéant.

In the sector held by RIR 119 the village of Quéant which was in front of the *Siegfried Stellung* had been joined with the main line by a *Balkon Stellung* in the last few hours. The new position contained two trenches which had suffered greatly under the winter weather from rain and frost. The trench walls were sliding in and the floor of the trench was covered in mud.

The only physical sign of the original impregnable position that was visible were the iron frameworks of deep shelters that had been started, which looked like enormous hedgehogs rising into the air. Mined dugouts built in the traditional manner had hardly been started and only a few had been completed. Of the 2,000 men in RIR 119, barely more than 500 of them could find shelter inside them.

The battle troops immediately observed that the dugouts were incorrectly positioned. The entrances were formed at sharp angles, too close to one another. The upper chambers were positioned too high and the protective earthen cover above the developed mined dugouts proved to be a little more than three meters thick so they offered no protection against even medium caliber shells.

The condition of the *Siegfried Stellung* located in the sector occupied by IR 180 was far better than what the men of RIR 119 had found and the regiment took stock of what they had and what needed to be corrected.

a) Trenches: 1st and 2nd trenches as well as in each company sector a communication trench has been completely dug out. The trenches are deep; the trench walls are very steep. In the right battalion sector a communication trench to the rear has begun to be dug out. The artillery protection-line on the Hill of Riencourt is in part dug out.

b) Obstacles: In front of the 1st trench ran 2 rows of 15 meter wide, partially 3 and 4 strips.

Well-constructed obstacle posts. The obstacles are shoved too far forward. The forward edge lies partly up to 120 meters distant from the 1st trench, so that a hand grenade that was thrown from out of the trench could not reach the front edge.

The wire entanglements in front of the 2nd trench are in a strip 5 meters wide.

In front of the artillery protection-line is such only partially existing and weakly built.

c) Dugouts: Of reinforced concrete dugouts, how they in part numerously exist at other parts of the *Siegfried Stellung*, there is not a single one in the entire regimental sector.

Construction type: Inclined galleries, to the large part were positioned too shallow. 11 started dugouts were found in the artillery protection-line. The mine (chalk cave) in Riencourt could contain 300 men however the construction of the entrance had only just begun. Latrines, drainage facilities, etc. did not exist. (180 or Appendix 39?)[3]

By far, the most important shortcoming of the new position was that only nine completed dugouts were located in the first trench, all without built-in recesses for sleeping quarters. Still, 115 men could be accommodated in the dugouts and become safe against enemy artillery fire if the dugout corridors were used.

In the second trench there were five completed dugouts with room for 100 men. In addition, there were a number of dugouts that were in various stages of being completed, nine in the first trench and fifteen in the second trench. Despite all of the work ahead of the men, 18 March was mainly used by the Other Ranks in IR 180 to rest and to allow the men to make repairs to their equipment and uniforms.

After the successful withdrawal, the British followed quicker than had been hoped for or expected. Their supply wagons and artillery came right up to the German lines using all means available. IR 180 determined that entire battalions of Chinese Coolies had been

Evacuating civilians before the withdrawal. (*Das Württembergische Reserve-Infanterie-Regiment Nr. 121 im Weltkrieg 1914-1918*)

put to work on restoring the roads and railways. Drinking water was carried up by wagons; new wells were drilled, entire tin roofed barrack camps were erected everywhere, apparently using all of the lessons learned in British Colonial Wars. Everything needed by the enemy army was brought up through the wasteland created by the German Army.

Already by 17 March the enemy occupied Ablainzeville, Achiet le Grand and Biefvillers. The British advanced on 18 March, with numerous patrols at first, which were often accompanied by infantry flights or cavalry; all of these patrols were driven back. The III/R119, 3MG/R119, half of the 2nd Squadron *Ulan* Regiment 20 and the II/RFAR 26 protected the division sector from positions in the forward zone. They were able to drive off the enemy patrols without the need of stronger forces from out of the main *Siegfried Stellung*, as had been the intent of the new defense in depth.

The villages of Ecoust-St. Mein and Noreuil were strongpoints in the outpost line. The two villages stood like two barricades in front of the main position. In the event of an enemy attack, 'the opposing waves of infantry would break against them like waves against a rock.' As of the morning of 18 March there were no more German troops in front of the outpost line. Only patrols were being sent out to keep an eye on the enemy and his movements.

18 March was a clear, sunny day and RIR 121 was going to put the weather to good use by immediately beginning the extension of the position. For the leaders and Other Ranks of the regiment there was an extraordinary amount of work to perform in a sector they had expected to already be complete. The new position had to become divided into sectors, the terrain in front, in and behind the position had to be accurately explored, including the placement of the sentry holes before or in the wire obstacles, the creation of dugouts, sentry posts, machine gun stands, *Minenwerfer* stands, battle-headquarters, medical dugouts, connection trenches and communication trenches, signal stations, telephone wires, runner

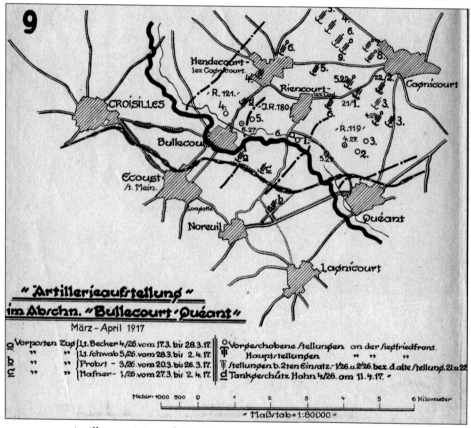

Artillery positions of the 26th Reserve Division, March-April 1917.

posts, intermediate signal posts, repeater posts, ammunition and food depots and many other necessary items had to be carefully positioned and constructed.

One of the very first projects was the construction of mined dugouts. It was a joy to be able to work during the day, completely undisturbed by the enemy. The men could apply their experiences of 2 ½ years of trench warfare and construct a position that suited their needs. Everything that had formerly been created was considered a patchwork, the rebuilding of a position with insufficient materials and little new construction. Here, they could build whatever they felt was best under the conditions. While the British did not bother the work at first, enemy aerial and artillery activity increased quickly.

The beautiful days did not last very long. By IR 180 the adversary began to probe slowly forward in the course of the afternoon of 18 March until reaching the Grande farm Adinfer, according to reports from officer's patrols. The III/180 with the 2MG/180 arrived at the main opposition line in the course of the afternoon from the rearguard position and was accommodated in Cagnicourt as the reserve. Patrols from RIR 121 also came up against enemy detachments by Croisilles. At dawn on 19 March enemy cavalry was performing reconnaissance patrols. The *Ulans* engaged the opposing cavalry and reported the capture of an Indian trooper.

The men had hoped to be able to rest, preferably for a long time before the enemy made in appearance so that they could also fix the shortcomings of the *Siegfried Stellung*, but this was not to be. It had been hoped that the British would have difficulty bringing up his artillery through the devastated zone. Now, despite all of the destruction of roads, trees, villages, bridges etc. he had succeeded in bringing his guns forward to where they were in range of the *Siegfried Stellung*. On 20 March the first 12cm shells fell on Bullecourt. The artillery fire was slow at first, the guns apparently firing from quite a long distance. There were too few shells for the men to become overly concerned by the fire and the Other Ranks took little notice of them at first.

On 20 March, the men of RIR 119 not only had to contend with the artillery fire but also an attempt by the enemy to capture Ecoust-St. Mein and Noreuil. In order to prevent an enemy surprise attack, numerous patrols had been sent forward in order to ensure the timely recognition of any enemy infantry advance. Toward 5 a.m., when it was still dark, a patrol from the 7/R121 under *Leutnant der Reserve* Bittlingmeier on the Ecoust-St. Mein-Beugnâtre road ran into a half platoon of enemy infantry who were also moving along the same road. Bittlingmeier and his men were protected from view by fallen trees along the side of the roadway. They laid down in a mine crater on Hill 111 and opened fire on the unsuspecting enemy troops.

During the fighting, the patrol observed a skirmish line approaching from the direction of Vaulx. When Bittlingmeier and his men fired at the skirmish line the enemy quickly placed a machine gun in action and the patrol was forced to withdraw to the picket detachment of the 12/R119. During this time, it had become daylight and it was not the British who opposed the men of the 26th Reserve Division; they were identified as Australian troops. The Australians attacked in four to five waves and the sentries of the 12/R119 opened a murderous fire on them with rifles and a machine gun that quickly stopped the attackers.

Whether it was part of the new tactics or simply lack of foresight the machine gun only had 2,000 rounds of ammunition available with it, and had already fired all of it after a short time. Armed only with rifles the sentries felt obligated to go back to the battle ready pickets.

The entire area of the fighting could be observed from Ecoust-St. Mein. Battery Platoon Becker, RFAR 26 stood on the railway cut behind the village and covered the Australians with shrapnel and shells which caused some confusion in their lines, but without being able to stop them. The Australians soon reached Hill 111 and occupied the crater located there. The Australians now sat barely 500 meters from the fortified village lying down in the valley.

Then, enemy cavalry and infantry patrols advanced from St. Leger which, if left unmolested would encompass the German position from the right; the situation was becoming critical. The approaching enemy was not being stopped as no infantry fire was being directed against them. While this was taking place, the observer from a different battery arrived with the leader of the 12/R119, *Leutnant der Reserve* Seytter. The officers discussed the situation and took quick action. The target information was distributed to the battery and in a short time effective artillery fire was opened against the advancing Australians with evident success.

The Australian troops moved behind the edge of a hill and into a hollow where they could not be seen from the German lines. At 9 a.m. it became quiet once more. Ammunition was brought up to the front and a patrol occupied the *Unteroffizier* Sentry position once

Incomplete reinforced concrete shelter in the Siegfried Stellung. (*Das Württembergische Reserve-Infanterie-Regiment Nr. 119 im Weltkrieg 1914-1918*)

again on the road to Beugnâtre and reported that the crater on Hill 111 was strongly occupied by the enemy.

At 10 a.m. the Australians attacked once more in strong waves, however they quickly flooded back in the well placed fire from the German batteries. Now it was decided to drive the enemy out of the crater. The artillery was contacted and strong fire was directed against the crater and the section of road behind it. At the same time a 20 man strong *Sturmtrupp* advanced toward the crater under the protection of the artillery fire.

The *Sturmtrupp* was forced to withdraw twice as a result of flanking fire from the right and the left coming mainly from Lewis Guns. *Leutnant* Seytter continued his efforts and contacted the heavy artillery further in the rear. He asked if they could take the crater area under fire with their guns. The artillery willingly went along with his request and opened fire with a 21cm heavy mortar.

The first shell struck near the crater, the second shell even closer and this apparently produced some excitement by the crater garrison and caused them great distress as the massive explosions of the 21cm shook the ground and sent plumes of earth and black smoke high into the air. By the third explosion the largest part of the crater garrison abandoned the position and fled toward the rear; only a strong group of courageous men still held out. The fourth shell exploded in the middle of the crater and killed the entire garrison of ten men. After this, the *Sturmtrupp* took possession of the crater and fired into the parts of the hollow they could observe.

Toward 3 p.m. the enemy withdrew along the entire line, partly in lines of riflemen partly in small groups, and left over 100 dead in front of Ecoust-St. Mein. Platoon Becker from RFAR 26 had used up all of their ammunition on hand so that the enemy could withdraw unmolested. Australian stretcher bearers carrying white flags searched the terrain for their dead and wounded, until they were forced to avoid the patrols from RIR 119 that

Australian troops captured during Ecoust-St. Mein and Noreuil,
March 1917. (*Die 26. Reserve Division 1914-1918*)

had been sent forward.

At 5.45 a.m. the 11/R119 in Noreuil was jolted out of its rest from shots fired by the sentries positioned far out in front. In the darkness, the sentries located on the field railway that lead to Morchies saw a nearby enemy detachment moving forward against the village entrance of Lagnicourt. The sentries fired alarm shots and quickly moved their small picket back to the edge of the village.

An *Unteroffizier* sentry post on the road to Vaulx-Vraucourt was soon encompassed from the south, however, the men still managed to make it safely back to the pickets with both machine guns in their possession under the cover of darkness. The advancing enemy infantry was quickly brought to a stop through machine gun fire and they evaded the heavy fire by moving off to the flank. An enemy company that was advancing in the hollow between Ecoust-St. Mein and Noreuil ended up in barrage fire from the batteries and went back into the copse southwest of Noreuil with heavy losses. The *Unteroffizier* sentry post on the road to Vaulx was also abandoned by the enemy, while two Australian soldiers, who had ventured too far forward, were taken prisoner. There was a pause in the fire following the last skirmish and this was used to obtain fresh ammunition, food and water and one platoon from the 9/R119, which was in Lagnicourt, arrived as reinforcements.

The second strong enemy attack came at 10 a.m., most of which was forced to withdraw toward Vaulx in the concentrated artillery fire. A part continued to advance until it was by the *Unteroffizier* sentry post in which now 150 Australians were firmly seated.

Once the situation became clear, the leader of the 11/R119, *Leutnant der Reserve* Löckle, wanted to retake the sentry post that had been lost. At 2 p.m. the artillery would provide three minutes of effective fire, whereupon a strong patrol would storm the post. Meanwhile

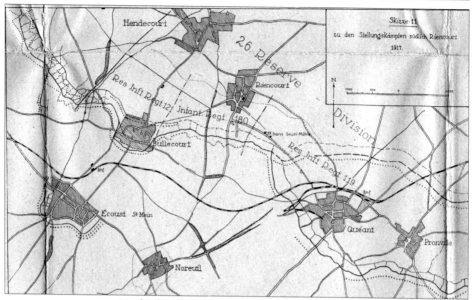

Siegfried Stellung and *Vorpostenfeld* by Bullecourt.

however, the 5/RFAR 26 had fired on the sentry post so successfully that approximately 120 Australians were observed withdrawing, carrying away numerous Lewis Guns.

At 2 p.m. the artillery opened fire as planned, then *Feldwebel Leutnant* Wolf and *Vizefeldwebel* Maier with 20 men from the 11/R119 and *Unteroffizier* Schrödel with eight men from the 9/R119 went forward. One Australian sentry prepared to fire his Lewis Gun when Patrol Maier saw the danger. Maier quickly threw a hand grenade at the gunner, which severely wounded him. The other sentries in the position were dazed and raised their hands in the air and gave up, the Australian outpost was overrun.

The storming party returned with 25 unwounded, six wounded prisoners and three Lewis Guns. At 2.15 p.m. the 11/R119 was able to report that it was in possession of its entire position. They also counted over 100 dead 'Englishmen' before their front that had been attacked, without having lost a single man. The men from RIR 119 reported that the Australians had attacked with four battalions and that they were bitter by the absence of their own artillery.[4]

Following this series of assaults, the enemy did not attack any more in large numbers. Only patrols attempted to overrun the sentries, however they were easily repulsed. Two Australian sappers were observed sneaking about in front of Ecoust-St. Mein, apparently in order to firmly establish the condition of the road and the destruction in the vicinity of Vaulx and Ecoust. They were stalked by the sentries of the 12/R119 and taken prisoner.

The Australians now began to dig in and soon their batteries opened effective fire upon Noreuil, while Ecoust had only been cautiously covered with occasional searching fire. The garrison of Noreuil hung on, suffering the most from a shortage of water. In the excitement of the fighting on 20 March one *pionier* who had been assigned the task of destroying the German wells in the event of capture, apparently panicked and destroyed the upper portion of a well too soon, making the water undrinkable so that now all drinking water had to be carried up from the rear.

While these events were taking place by the 26th Reserve Division, the enemy had pressed back the outpost line of the 2nd Guard Reserve Division to the south and repeatedly attacked the 220th Infantry Division standing north of St. Mein. The Australians were also constructing a new trench in front of the 26th Reserve Division in a hollow that could not be observed from the German lines. The Australians were eventually forced to withdraw from the new trench by the effective fire of the German artillery batteries.

The next few days became quiet once more with little enemy activity to report along the front of the 26th Reserve Division. Perhaps the only excitement came on 24 March when an 'English' aircraft was shot down in aerial combat by RIR 121 and landed close to the position. Still, the enemy infantry continued to move closer to Ecoust and Noreuil, while Bullecourt received 12cm shells daily.

The restrictions placed on the troops about giving away any information on their location was still in effect, however, there were ways to get around them. One soldier in RIR 119 wrote home during this time in which he used the simple method of directing his friends to watch for certain information in the newspapers and that would give them the details on where he was located. He also provided some insights about recent events.

Absender: Chr. Gerber RIR119, 2 Batl. 8. *Kompagnie*

22 March 1917

Dear Family Gross!

I received your valuable little package which pleased me very much. So far everything goes well. I am alive and kicking, which indeed is still the main thing in our field. The weather is the same at home as it is for us, always wet and cold, windy and snow. We came into position again on Sunday, we marched the whole night from Saturday to Sunday until we got there, it is very strictly forbidden to write where you are in position. The English had heavy losses again, mid-month. You will also read it in the paper; it is calculated at 800 dead at the front where we really are. The move is now being made again. From Bapaume to Arras, a distance of 20 kilometers, there are 187 villages where everything is devastated, every tree has been cut down, houses are all blown up with heavy mines and so also the roads that has since fulfilled what is in the Bible, there will remain no stone unturned, it is horrible. If you had to see this, you would just want to cry. It was done precisely for the reason that they would find no accommodations in their advance. Also to be able to teach them proper losses. The mother has placed the seed with the General Command. Since then it has been approved, but now my company commander will not just let me go. It would have been better if I had come to a *Landwehr* regiment. With us always being at the front leave is still scarce. I pray and ask our dear Father in heaven every day that he gives the desired peace to us soon. I will now close with the hopes of a healthy early reunion. I greet you all cordially. Chr. Gerber.[5]

German patrols were very active at this time as they explored the new enemy positions and took advantage of any situation where prisoners could be brought in. One patrol from the 12/R119 took two Australians prisoner on the evening of 25 March just before the company was relieved by the 10/180 in the outpost line by Ecourt. An undertaking by the 9th and 11/R119 against the enemy in the copse southwest of Noreuil failed and resulted in a number of losses in the raiding party.

Ecoust St-Mein taken from an altitude of 1,800 meters. (*Die 26. Reserve Division 1914-1918*)

The Australian artillery fire now increased from day to day and also fell in greater strength upon Ecoust. On 25 March the Australian artillery held a fire raid on the western part of Bullecourt, as well as on the Bullecourt-Croisilles road. Between 12 noon and 2 p.m. the enemy fired 15 shots from medium caliber guns on the Mill Hill of Sanssoucie, in the middle of the *Siegfried Stellung*.

The position by Bullecourt was quite shot up on 26 March. On the same day the Australians had attacked the outposts of the neighboring 2nd Guard Reserve Division and pressed them back. The attack had been expected based upon the level of preparation fire being directed against the neighboring division. The Guard Division was successful in holding the first line on the right of the division sector; however, despite every precaution the enemy was able to capture Lagnicourt.

During the fighting, an enemy officer's patrol attempted to sneak through the German lines between the sentry posts by Noreuil in the dark. They were observed and fired at by a German patrol and a machine gun post of the 3MG/R119 and several of the Australians were taken prisoner.

Following the loss of Lagnicourt, the sentries of the 10/R119 under *Leutnant der Reserve* Zutt, observed the enemy moving in large numbers toward the company position from the sunken road which lead from Morchies. The sentry posts were being threatened on their flank and the men quickly moved back on the picket post lying at the southern exit of the village.

The enemy also attacked the line of RIR 119, approaching Noreuil from Vaulx Vraucourt. However he was brought to a stop or forced moved to the rear in the combined fire of the infantry, machine guns and artillery. Shortly before the attack the 1MG/R119

View of the Bullecourt-Hendecourt road. (*Die 26. Reserve Division 1914-1918*)

relieved the 3MG/R119 and had also taken part in the defense.

During this recent attack, the pickets at the southern exit of the village, which had protected the uncovered flank of RIR 119 against a line of enemy skirmishers, had joined with the retreating Guard units by Lagnicourt. The retreating sentries regrouped and then attempted to regain the village, in vain as the enemy artillery fire increased in strength once again. More men were needed so the 11th and 12/R119 were moved forward to Noreuil as reinforcements. After this, the 10/R119 succeeded in capturing an Australian Lieutenant in front of Lagnicourt and also expelled an enemy machine gun that had been installed in the sunken road leading to Morchies, barely 70 meters in front of the barricade.

At 10 a.m. the second Australian attack broke forth against Noreuil from the south, however it was scattered in the defensive infantry and artillery fire. The men from RIR 119 could see the fierce counterattack by the Guard Division against Lagnicourt, which was ultimately unsuccessful and failed to regain control of the village. Then, on 27 March it became quiet once again and the 9th and 12/R119 could return to their quarters.

On 27 March a new organization of the outpost line took place, the entire III/180 with the 1MG/180, two thirds of the 2MG/R121, two platoons from *Sturmbataillon* 1 and six mounted messengers now formed the outpost garrison of Ecourt. The companies were distributed across the sector as well as in support and reserve positions. The machine guns and *Musketen* from the *Sturmbataillon* were distributed across the sector in pairs.

While the infantry attacks had stopped momentarily, the enemy artillery remained very active. The outpost units suffered heavily under the powerful bombardment of Ecourt, especially when a dugout was destroyed; the existing cellars nearby offered only minimal protection. Despite these problems, the outpost garrison held their position uninterrupted and was able to force back the new enemy skirmish lines which attacked the position all

THE OTHER SIDE OF THE WIRE VOLUME 3

during the day with considerable enemy losses.

In the early hours of 28 March the 10th and 11/R119 were relieved by the 5th and 8/R121 and the 2MG/R121 while the 6/R121 was positioned in Riencourt as the outpost reserve. The entire III/R119 now marched back to Villers-lez-Cagnicourt in reserve. Enemy pressure continued tp grow and soon a battery south of the sugar factory fired on Vraucourt. St. Leger was also attacked by the Australians coming from out of Mory and the village was subsequently abandoned by the neighboring division.

On the morning of 30 March the 1st and 3MG/R121 traded positions, similarly the 6th and 7/R121 exchanged positions, so that now the 1MG/R121 was in Ecoust, the 6/R121 was in Noreuil. The outpost positions were heavily bombarded on this day, and an attack on the outposts was expected. By evening nothing had occurred and the only activity was small fire fights with Australian patrols and reconnaissance detachments.

On 31 March the I/R119 relieved the II/R121 in Noreuil and took over the protection of the *Siegfried Stellung*. In the night from 31 March to 1 April the 5th and 8/R121 and 2MG/R121 located in Noreuil were relieved by RIR 119 and the 3MG/R121 became placed in Ecoust again. In its place the 2MG/R121 occupied the position by Bullecourt. One enemy company did attempt an attack against the outpost position of IR 180 in the night of 31 March to 1 April, which was bloodily repulsed, with the Australians leaving behind an estimated 30-40 dead.

1 April proceeded quietly at first; nothing indicated a renewal of the enemy attacks. However, the position of the 26th Reserve Division was made far worse with the loss of Lagnicourt. The 3rd and 4/R119 that stood in Noreuil were in danger of being encompassed from the south as the village projected sharply forward into the Australian lines and where a number of sunken roads could provide cover for any enemy force approaching from that direction.

Then, in the course of the day, the enemy searching fire increased to the strength never before reached, in total about 4,000 shells, coming from light, medium and heavy caliber guns, some up to 21cm, still without any attack following. Then it became conspicuously quiet in the night, which was interpreted as that an attack was very likely, but would not occur immediately.

At 4.55 a.m. on 2 April the strongest drum fire of all calibers suddenly fell on the entire front, especially by Ecoust and Noreuil, and the hill that lay between the two villages. Every man in IR 180 and RIR 121 were alarmed and at 5.05 a.m. the first enemy attack waves were visible and from every indication it was an entire enemy brigade attacking the outpost position. These waves, as well as two following waves were completely broken in the combined fire from the artillery, outpost troops and machine guns which brought heavy losses to the attackers including the loss of a large number of prisoners.

After further heavy fighting the Australians succeeded in breaking through the outpost positions of RIR 121 and attacked the remaining sentries from the rear and the flank. The machine gun *Schützen* fought back desperately, until their ammunition ran out, likewise the patrol squads of RIR 121, which were in Ecoust. Two officers, *Leutnants der Reserve* Seidler and Kaupp, and 19 men were taken prisoner in the fighting; the remaining men were able to force their way through the enemy lines to the rear.

Leutnant der Reserve Eisenhardt, RIR 119, who was in command in Noreuil, reported about the favorable course of the morning fighting as the enemy attack already seemed to falter. Then, at 5.45 a.m., a new enemy skirmish line advanced. The German artillery

Men of RIR 119 in late March early April 1917. (Author's collection)

Steinhilber
Leutn. d. R. im Ref.=Inf.=Regt. 119,
gefallen bei Noreuil
am 2. April 1917

Eilenhardt
Leutn. d. R. im Ref.=Inf.=Regt. 119,
gefallen bei Noreuil
am 2. April 1917

(*Kriegstagebuch aus Schwaben*)

increased its level of barrage fire but within a short time, the connection to the firing line was broken. Shortly after 6 a.m. green light balls were reported being seen south of Noreuil indicating the infantry were in distress.

As the fighting continued the outpost troops from IR 180 finally had to withdraw to

Leutn. d. R. Probst
gef. bei Noreuil 2. 4. 1917

Leutnant der Reserve Probst, RFAR 26 (*Württembergisches Reserve-Feldartillerie-Regiment Nr.26 im Weltkrieg 1914-1918*)

the pickets due to the increased enemy pressure as bitter fighting surged back and forth for a long time. If the enemy had only been able to attack frontally, both companies from the 10th and 12/180 would have been able to still hold the position for a long time. However, the enemy apparently did not find any particular opposition about Noreuil and then proceeded past Croisilles against the flank and rear of the defenders of Ecoust. The Australians appeared on the hill northeast of Ecoust, strongly threatening the 10/180, and also appeared in the terrain between the two roads Ecoust-Bullecourt and Ecoust-Croissiles, which also threatened the 12/180.

The enemy continued to push forward with all possible strength, still the I/R119 held its entire position. Then German infantry suddenly poured back out of Ecoust-St. Mein. The enemy had successfully broken through the German line there and now pressed after the fleeing soldiers. The situation facing the I/R119 was becoming extremely dangerous. The enemy had already penetrated over the hill north of Noreuil. Frenzied, close combat had broken out in the village. *Leutnant der Reserve* Steinhilber fell in the close combat; *Leutnant* Eisenhardt was shot through the head. The village garrison fought back with desperation, but the superior enemy strength proved too much. Whoever was not killed became taken prisoner. The Australians had already pushed forth via Noreuil and they could be seen storming forward from the artillery observation post. At 6.30 a.m. both Ecoust and Noreuil were effectively lost.

Under these circumstances Noreuil had to become evacuated by RIR 119, with the exception of one platoon of the 6/R119 that had become trapped by the enemy drum fire and caught up in the fighting. The platoon still managed to strike through to the rear along with 30 enemy prisoners. The losses in the 6/R119 on this day besides the missing amounted to 4 killed and 18 wounded.

The events by RIR 119 were to prove disastrous to the men of IR 180. There was a

Leutnant Albert Reihling (center) and his men, 4/R119. Reihling was captured at Noreuil on 2 April after being wounded in the forehead by an infantry projectile. (Author's collection)

POW card for *Leutnant* Reihling, captured on 2 April 1917.
(*Landesarchiv Baden-Württemberg Hauptstaatsarchiv Stuttgart*)

POW card for Leutnant Reihling, captured on 2 April 1917.
(*Landesarchiv Baden-Württemberg Hauptstaatsarchiv Stuttgart*)

distance of at least one kilometer between Picket 1 of the 12/180 under *Leutnant* Morasch, which lay at the exit to Croisilles and from Picket 2 of the 12/180 at the southwest exit of the village. These picket posts were attacked frontally at first and then also attacked on the left flank, however, they were able to drive off every attack. It was not until the first enemy columns appeared between Croisilles and Bullecourt, when the situation became serious. The two pickets fought back bravely despite being encompassed and at 6.30 a.m. one could still hear powerful infantry and hand grenade fire coming from the two posts. Then, it became very quiet, and as every connection had been cut off and it had to be accepted that these men had been overrun and had fought to the last.

It became very evident that Ecoust had to be abandoned if a catastrophe was to be avoided. The senior officer of both companies, *Leutnant der Reserve* Teuffel, 12/180, prudently arranged the retreat to the railway embankment, by which all wounded could be taken with them. Once at the embankment it was anticipated that a new front could be formed there, helped with support from the 9th and 11/180 and also powerful support from the platoon of the 5/RFAR 26 that had been positioned on the railway. The 5th Battery did afford excellent support, the gunners using direct fire, aiming over the back sight and front sight, until all of the ammunition on hand had been fired at the strong enemy reserves that were following the withdrawing men from IR 180. Later, the guns were brought back to a safe location by the infantry when the position became untenable.

The Outpost commander for RIR 119 had received conflicting verbal reports from the slightly wounded men that were streaming back. The situation was still completely unclear, and it was not learned until later that the two villages were lost. The 2/R119 under

,eutnant Malblanc with the rest of the 1st, 3rd and 4/R119 on the railway embankment managed to bring the enemy to a halt; however they soon became strongly flanked in the exposed position by machine guns from the south, so that the position had soon become untenable. Then at 9.45 a.m., after strong fire preparation, the 2/R119 arrived for the attack upon the hill north of Noreuil, drove the Australians back and dug in.

Because the railway embankment could not be held and the companies suffered under the strong enemy heavy artillery fire, the men were forced to move back to the *Siegfried Stellung* at 11 a.m. The outpost protection now fell on the troops that were found in the *Siegfried Stellung* from both battalions of IR 180, who tried to clarify the situation through three officer patrols, each supported by 60 men.

At midday the enemy attacks died down and it grew silent. This was fortunate as the ./R119 had been shattered. It had lost almost half of its complement; in the evening it reported 22 killed, 66 wounded and 149 missing to the regimental headquarters. After the loss of both outpost villages the 6/R119 had taken over the protection on the notch of the railway embankment.

Several hundred Australians were reported killed in the first assault at the hands of the 1st and 3/R119 and a large number of prisoners had been taken. During the transport of the prisoners to the rear the detachment ended up in Australian machine gun fire that ruthlessly mowed down their own countrymen. Only 89 prisoners managed to become

Infantrymen of RIR 119. (Author's collection)

Schott

Leutnant d. R. im Inf.=Regt. 180,
geft. am 3. April 1917 an den bei
Ecouft=St.=Mein erhalt. Wunden

(Kriegstagebuch aus Schwaben)

taken to the rear, amongst them 4 officers. In the evening of 2 April the I/R119 was relieved and moved back to the rear for rest and recuperation.

While one battalion of RIR 119 participated in the outpost fighting, the other battalions worked untiringly on the construction of the *Siegfried Stellung*. In order to complete the construction work in the shortest time possible mining shifts became operated day and night in the *Siegfried Graben*. When resting, the construction troop found meager housing in the cellars of Quéant and Bullecourt. Under these conditions the II/R119 reported that it had installed 5,000 frameworks in just a few weeks.

With the work by the men of RIR 119 the regiment had created spacious bomb proof dugouts in the half cavernous *Siegfried Gräben*, which in every sense matched the men's experiences of trench warfare. In other parts of the front, little was taking place other than the ever present enemy artillery fire. Position construction continued despite the enemy fire, then, the fire-raids increased in strength and heavier caliber guns joined in. Finally, the subterranean mine in Riencourt was able to be occupied.

The recent fighting was seen as a small victory by the men of RIR 119. The outposts of the regiment had held the position for fourteen days and had held off and an entire Australian division in stubborn fighting. 2 April was also considered a day of pride for IR 180 and a day of mourning for the men who were lost. The losses in IR 180 on 2 April were: *Leutnant der Reserve* Schott, 9/180, severely wounded; he died several days after 17 *Unteroffiziere* and Other Ranks killed, 54 *Unteroffiziere* and Other Ranks wounded *Leutnant* Morasch, 12/180 and 58 *Unteroffiziere* and Other Ranks missing.

While too late to affect the outcome of the fighting on 2 April, the combat strength of IR 180 received a significant increase on that day through the distribution of four 7.6cm Light *Minenwerfer* per battalion, so that each battalion had more than one *Minenwerfer*

Beckenschloss, Hendecourt, before the British shelling. (*Das Württembergische Reserve-Infanterie-Regiment Nr. 121 im Weltkrieg 1914-1918*)

Abteilung. With the addition of these weapons a new *Leutnant* was trained to command the detachment. Two *Granatwerfer* were also distributed per company, and were combined with the *Minenwerfer Abteilung.*

The relatively quiet times in Bullecourt were over. While the enemy did not advance any further via Ecoust following the fighting on 2 April, the *Siegfried Stellung* was now the forward most line. Artillery fire of all calibers fell on the position, similar to a major day of fighting in the Somme battle. Luckily there were numerous dugouts that had been created so that everyone could be accommodated in shell proof shelters. The village of Bullecourt, still quite intact a few days before the recent fighting, sank into a pile of rubble and ashes and it soon became advisable to furnish the men with secure cellars and mined dugouts in Hendecourt as well.

The enemy started to fire from very long distances with large caliber flat trajectory guns. It was a considered to be an impressive performance by the British, bringing up this heavy material through the fully destroyed terrain. However, it was quickly realized that the enemy did not have any shortages of men or material and had no need to economize on either. As soon as the weather was clear, fierce aerial activity began once more. Numerous aerial battles played out over the position and several enemy aircraft and unfortunately one German aircraft were shot down and fell close by Bullecourt. Fierce pilot fighting developed above the men of the 26th Reserve Division and the men soon saw aircraft being shot down daily. It appeared as if the enemy was attempting to re-establish sovereignty in the air in order to prepare for another major attack.

While there were no further infantry attacks, the activities observed in the opposing trenches in the days following 2 April were also interpreted as preparations for another major assault. Then, on 5 April, two enemy companies attacked the positions of RIR 119

Beckenschloss, Hendecourt, after the British shelling. (*Das Württembergische Reserve-Infanterie-Regiment Nr. 121 im Weltkrieg 1914-1918*)

once again from the south and the north and broke through the garrison of the railway embankment as well as the 11th and 12/R119 and captured five prisoners. Following this raid, all of the security troops were taken back to the main line. Now the enemy stood immediately in front of the *Siegfried Stellung* that they had named the Hindenburg line.

If a major attack was imminent, the 26th Reserve Division would not have to face it as there were plans to relieve the division on 6 April. In part this was due to the losses already suffered by the understrength division and in part it was due to the fact that some regiments, such as RIR 121, had not been relieved from the front line for rest and training since March 1916. These regiments were in no shape to withstand a major enemy assault.

On 6 April, the 26th Reserve Division was relieved by the Württemberg 27th Infantry Division and sent to the area around Valenciennes where it became a training division. At 11 p.m. on 6 April the II/R121 was embarked on a transport train in Marquion. On the night of 7/8 April the I/R121 was relieved by the I/120, and assembled in Cagnicourt and on 8 April it also be loaded onto a train in Marquion. The regimental staff, I and II/R121 were unloaded in Valenciennes and marched to their billets. On 8/9 April the III/R121 was relieved by the III/120 and also assembled in Cagnicourt but it would never reach its final destination.

In the nights from 6-9 April RIR 119 was relieved by Grenadier Regiment 123, and then sent by train in the area of Valenciennes from where the regiment became transported to Solesmes. When the Ulmer Grenadiers took over the position were reportedly filled with great joy and gratification that their battalions were able to be accommodated in bomb proof dugouts and could sleep on wire bunks. They had professed amazement, as they had been told of the poor construction of the *Siegfried Stellung*, and that they had never moved

Zur frommen Erinnerung im Gebete
an den Krieger

Emil Ott
von Roth

beim württbg. Res.-Inf.-Reg. Nr. 119, 12. Komp.,
geboren am 27. Nov. 1889, gefallen am 8. April
1917 bei Arras (Nordfrankreich).

Allmächtiger, barmherziger Gott, der
du in deiner anbetungswürdigen Vorsehung uns den Augenblick des Todes
bestimmt hast, wir bitten dich aus
vertrauensvollem und ergebenem
Herzen: siehe gnädig auf die Seele
Deines Dieners Emil, nimm den
in treuer Pflichterfüllung erlittenen
Tod als vollgültige Busse an und
führe sie nach den Schrecknissen
des Krieges in Deinen ewigen Frieden.

Vater unser . . . .

Volksblatt Messkirch

Struck on both legs and head by artillery projectile at 3.30 pm, relief
came one day too late for Emil Ott. (Author's collection)

into such a well-built position before and swore to repulse every attack while in it.

The relief of the 26th Reserve Division had come just in time when taking into account the events that were about to take place by Bullecourt.

Notes

1. *Feldpost* letters of *Leutnant* Albert Reihling, 4/R119, translation courtesy of Felix Fregin.

2. The destruction was widespread but not complete. Explosives prepared and placed in position and not blown were found in various trenches and cellars in Bapaume and Vaulx-Vraucourt. Wells had been prepared in the same way in the latter village and not blown. Several houses were left with loose shavings and light firewood packed ready to be fired. Walls were tarred and holes were made in ceilings to give draught. A dump (H.14.c) of 1,500 *Minenwerfer* bombs was left intact with preparations for destruction, apparently in the form of explosive charges lying in the vicinity but not set. Large quantities of stores, M.G. belts, boxes, S.A.A., bombs, helmets were left in the vicinity of Malt Trench and Dinkum Spur. Stores of 77mm. ammunition were left in S.W. end of Ravine M.5.c. & d. Immediately north of Bapaume signs of an accelerated evacuation were visible as follows: Steel helmets, greatcoats, food, solidified alcohol, S.A.A. and bombs were found in the rearguard positions. Rifles and carbines had also been abandoned. A M.G. handcart was found near its battle position. Reports taken from various Australian battalion war diaries.

3. Vischer, op. cit., p. 77.

4. Actually three battalions were involved in the attack, the 6th, 21st and 23rd Australian Battalions.

5. *Feldpost leters from* Chr. Gerber 8/R119, translation and letter courtesy of Felix Fregin.

7

28th Reserve Division

Maas Group West, with the 5th Army by

Verdun, October 1916 to April 1917

While the reader has followed the adventures of the 26th Reserve Division in the months following the end of the Battle of the Somme, what had happened to the men of the 28th Reserve Division? Following the intensive fighting by Grandcourt the 28th Reserve Division was sent to an area that had seen intensive fighting earlier in 1916, but which was unlike anything the men had experienced since the start of the war. The division had been sent to Verdun, a foreboding name to any soldier in the German Army.

Following the second deployment in the Battle of the Somme, the 28th Reserve Division desperately needed time to rest and refit. Losses had been high in all three of the regiments in the division and it would take time before they could be brought up to full strength once again. The same situation faced the 28th Reserve Division in October 1916 as it did in July 1916. The greatest problem facing the division was the shortage of trained men on the western front. This problem would never be fully resolved and would only continue to grow worse as the war continued.

Within days of being extracted from the Somme battlefield, the division was once more on the move to a new part of the front. On orders from the OHL, the 28th Reserve Division was being transferred to the 5th Army under the command of Crown Prince Wilhelm. The division would join the VII Reserve Corps, *Maas Gruppe West* and would take up positions near Hill 304 and the Wood of Avocourt, both of which had seen heavy fighting in the Battle of Verdun earlier in the year.

The 28th Reserve Division was transported by train into the area of *Maas Gruppe West* which was under the command of *General der Infanterie Von* Francois. The journey on average lasted 12 hours as the troop trains travelled through Brussels, Sedan and finally ended up near Dun an der Maas where the troops were unloaded. The entire division was eventually transported to the new sector by Verdun between 22 and 28 October.

With the arrival of the badly frayed 28th Reserve Division the regiments currently holding the sector which included Hill 304 and Avocourt Wood could finally be relieved. Even the grossly understrength 28th Reserve Division was a welcome addition to *Maas Gruppe West*. While this portion of the front line was considered to be 'quiet' there were still daily losses, mostly from the ever present artillery and mine fire. The regiments holding the front were in desperate need for relief.

In the few days required before the entire division could be transported and assembled in the new sector, the three regiments of the 28th Reserve Division began to receive the first of many batches of replacement troops. While awaiting orders to take over the new sector, the regiments of the 28th Reserve Division used this time to distribute the new replacements into the units which required them the most. Whatever short amount of time was still available was eagerly used to provide training for the new men. It was accepted that it would take far longer than a few days to turn the replacements into effective soldiers, but anything that could be done would help to prolong their lives, even if only a few days or weeks.

The new replacements that had joined the division were far from being considered combat troops. In part they consisted of older men that had been combed out of the *Etappen* Formations (Line of Communication formations) and Columns as well as *Landsturm* Battalions, who had been re-examined under the new, less rigid requirements for front line service. Many of these soldiers, while being in the army for some months or years had never fired a rifle before now. The men were now rated K.V. (*Kriegsverwendungsfähig* – Fit for Active Service). In part the new recruits consisted of men from the Class of 1897, barely 20 years old and in a few instances even younger. These recruits had received very little training before being sent to the front and would require time to provide them with the necessary skills needed to survive life in the fire trenches.

On 28 October, RIR 109 was one of the last parts of the division to arrive and the men were accommodated at the Farm de la Madeleine and the villages of Dun and Doulcon. Once all regiments had arrived the relief of the front line could begin. The battalions had been unloaded in the right division sector of *Maas Gruppe West* upon the hills on the left of the Maas River. RIR 109 would take over the left wing sector designated 'C', which included Hill 304. IR 13 was on the left of RIR 109 and formed the right wing of the 13th Westphalian Division.

On the right was RIR 111 which took over the sector which ran in an easterly direction south of Malancourt, through Avocourt Wood and east of Hill 304 and the position known as the '*Toten Mann*', a location mentioned often in army reports during the fighting around Verdun. The position had an average depth of some 1,200 meters. The regimental staff took over the headquarters position in Nantillois, took over command of the new sector on 29 October. The battalions took over the sector in night of 30/31 October.

The four companies of the I/R111 occupied the entire front line of the regiment. The I/R111 had replaced the I/102, and the III/R111 replaced *Landsturm* Battalion Heilbronn which had been located in the Intermediate position approximately 1,000 meters to the rear of the front line. The II/R111 was positioned in the rest area named the *Beugholz Lager* which was located in the *Bois de Beugholz*.

RIR 110 took over the positions being held by IR 49 located at the southern edge of the obliterated Avocourt Wood and Malancourt. The regimental battle headquarters was in a headquarters complex called *Mecklenburg*. The position ran along the southern edge of the wooded area south of Montfaucon and was called the Avocourt *Stellung*, although this village was situated on the enemy side. The obstacles before the front were sufficient; and the distance to the enemy position varied between 20 and 80 meters.

The sector was divided into three parts, from the front to the rear, designated A, B and C. The company sectors became numbered from right to left, for example A1 until A4. A large number of saps projected out from the battle trench towards the enemy position. These bore the numbers 1-14 from the right to the left. The dugouts in the trenches were for the most part filled with water; a few in particular were almost completely flooded. Only one communication trench led into the fighting trench, the *Kaiser Graben*, which could only be maintained as passable with the greatest effort.

Due to the shortage of any communication trenches much of the foot traffic in the wooded terrain occurred outside of the communication trench, however without large losses. The enemy did especially scatter prominent individual positions in the wood with artillery fire at certain times, but they could become avoided. On the left wing of the position was strongpoint B, designated the 'Greiner Eck' by the troops. The right wing hung in the air, because the connection trenches to the neighboring regiment LIR 25 in a hollow were filled with mud.

Before each battalion of the 28th Reserve Division was ordered into position, it was reviewed by General von Francois personally. In the case of every battalion in the 28th Reserve Division, the integration of the new, untrained replacement troops with the veterans within the existing company structures had not been completed. This had the unfortunate effect of reducing the overall combat effectiveness of the battalions. Fortunately, the French infantry opposite the 28th Reserve Division continued to behave quietly, thereby allowing the Baden division time to complete this process.

The new sector by Verdun proved to be a great disappointment to the soldiers of the 28th Reserve Division, especially when considering the extensive positions that the division had created on the Somme between 1914 and 1916. The situation was not made any easier with the poor weather conditions and constant rain showers which made life very difficult for the men. The real enemy was not so much the French lying opposite; it was rather the condition of the battlefield and the weather that made life at the front miserable.

The effects of the heavy fighting from the Battle of Verdun were clearly visible everywhere. The terrain was literally pockmarked with shell holes, one next to another, often overlapping. These craters were later used many times during the creation of the new position. Avocourt Wood existed in name only, a few short tree stumps were all that was left of the once dense forest; even the thickest trees had been shattered and splintered like match wood. Pieces of equipment lay scattered around everywhere; and bodies or more often portions of bodies from both armies were scattered throughout the terrain and were often encountered by the men while moving through the battered position, which was covered by the smell of rotting flesh. Everything clearly indicated that the sector had been the focus of horrendous fighting only a short time earlier.

Some new defensive works had been created since the fighting had died down, however, these were mostly unfinished and a large portion had been badly damaged by the constant artillery fire. There were only a few usable dugouts in the front line, too few to house the entire garrison. The largest part of the men had to be content with a few recently started mined dugouts which extended 2-3 meters into the earth or took cover in Karnickelhöhlen, (rabbit holes) with only a thin layer of cover over their heads. The French troops on the opposing side were determined to consist of French Territorial troops which had also been sent to garrison a 'quiet' portion of the front line.

Despite the relative inactivity of the enemy troops, the overall German positions were located on steep slopes and were very exposed to enemy observation and accurate artillery and mine fire. To overcome this disadvantage, the men were set to work immediately upon arrival in the front line in digging new trenches and repairing the damaged defenses. The work was extremely difficult under the current conditions as the men were constantly removing mud and water from the position and despite their efforts they watched much of their hard work simply slide into a thick mass of mud once they had finished. It would prove to be a never ending task as long as the position was occupied.

In addition to the mud, there was a layer of very hard chalk and stone under the surface, and this proved to be very difficult to work and it required a great deal of effort to mine new dugouts. Almost all of the existing dugouts were shallow tunnel stairways with very narrow frameworks 80 centimeters wide and 120 centimeters tall. The openings were so narrow that it made a quick exit in the event of an attack impossible. They had not been sunk very deep into the ground and as such did not offer any real protection against an enemy bombardment and were not even large enough to allow the men to rest comfortably.

The constant rain and lack of materials needed to shore up the trench walls resulted in the men standing in thick mud when on sentry duty or trying to walk through the trenches. Under the current conditions there was no possibility of creating deep drains in the position or in the bottomless communication trenches. Communication trench VII, which despite being worked on by entire companies, collapsed on a regular basis as the clay walls the entire length simply slid into the trench. In the end, nothing had been accomplished with all of the hard labor by the men.

Still, old habits die hard and the veteran soldiers who had served on the Somme since 1914 carried on constructing secure dugouts and trenches as best they could. This proved to be slow work as there were far too few older veterans in the ranks of the regiments who were experienced in construction methods. Fortunately, creating new and reinforcing old wire obstacles was comparatively easy because of the inactivity of the opposing Territorial troops.

Until the housing situation had improved the men were only allowed to enter the forward positions with storm packs that contained the mere basics required to live inside the trenches for short periods of time. The men worked diligently on improving the existing dugouts and creating new ones wherever possible. The mined dugout entrances were expanded to 80 x 180cm. or 120 x 180cm, making it far easier to exit them in case of an emergency. Second and third lines were created in which deep and interconnecting shell proof dugouts were excavated.

New communication trenches leading to the front were created. The hard limestone, which was directly under the clay stratum, required innovative ideas in order to dig down to a sufficient depth where the men would be protected from enemy fire. There were no *pioniers* available to help with the work, so the men improvised. Bundles of hand grenades were wedged in place in the tunnels up against the limestone and detonated by pulling the string on the center hand grenade from a safe distance. While this method of mining was prohibited by higher commands, there was no other option left to the men. Despite the great dangers involved, they succeeded in going deeper into the ground each day. In RIR 109 this method of mining resulted in two to three wooden frameworks being completed by three men in a work shift of eight hours.

Once at a sufficient depth, the issue of ground water pressure was a major problem as the water simply poured through the wall at the end of the dugout. The solution was simple, to make the interior end wall of the dugouts out of concrete. While water continued to seep into the new shelters, it could now be controlled and removed with homemade pumps.

Many of the trenches were also under water much of the time, like the dugouts, and they too required constant pumping so they could be used. Several additional units were brought up to the trenches to assist with this laborious work and to maintain the position. Two reinforcement companies from Landwehr IR 117 were brought in to assist keeping the water out of the trenches of RIR 109 as well as to create new trenches. In the *Erlenbach* ground, through which the only access road existed that lead into the position. A squad

Food carrier stuck in the mud. (*Lehrer im Krieg*)

from Dragoon Regiment 22 was positioned with the regiment along with extensive drainage equipment. Their sole task was to maintain the access route and keep it open at all times.

There were no kitchens located in the positions, which was considered particularly annoying. The men were exhausted following the hard work of each day and the time and effort required in preparing their meals only added to their misery. The men were required to cook their rations by individual Groups in the trenches on small stoves if they existed or ones created from chalk, usually a cooking hole was created next to each dugout entrance in the forward trench wall.

Then, when the field kitchens were able to travel up to the Intermediate position the hot food could be unloaded. Hauling parties would then attempt to bring hot food to the front line but this proved almost impossible in the very dark nights, under constant rain showers which filled the trenches and shell craters with water and mud. When the food did arrive at all, it was very often cold. Then as if to add insult to injury there was also an increasing concern by the men with the quantity and quality of the rations being totally inadequate.

Then there was the associated problem with the shortage of fuel. Despite being located in a forest, there was little wood available; the wood provided, was often green and wet if it came from the destroyed forest. While charcoal was the fuel of choice as it gave off very little smoke which prevented the enemy from locating where the German troops were cooking, it was not available in sufficient quantities.

Despite the constant rain and wet ground, potable water was extremely hard to come by. A water line which ran from the rear into the front lines had once existed, now the pipe could only be found on a map as it had long ago been completely destroyed. Therefore, water would be collected from nearby shell holes or, collected in the dugouts using groundsheets when it rained. Over time the men became accustomed with the unusual flavor the polluted water gave to their coffee.

The weather and the unfavorable water situation were most likely responsible for the medical reports of that time mentioning that the health condition of the troops was bad. A large number of men came down with Typhus as a result of poor sanitation. Similarly there were chest colds, the bladder and kidney ailments as well as stomach and intestinal catarrh that affected the men. As the weather grew colder the number of men reporting frostbite on their feet also increased dramatically. The loss of men who reported to the sick rooms and military hospitals was subsequently quite considerable. The understrength regiments filled with untrained and low quality men grew even smaller as each week passed.

Finally, after a few weeks, there was some good news to report when all of the companies were provided with position kitchens located as the front line communication centers. Until this improvement was made the companies had continued to enter the position only with storm packs. The lack of extra underwear, socks, etc. and the shortage of time needed to properly shave or bathe and change socks and underwear or to wear a warm greatcoat were noticeably unpleasant. Considering the hundreds of unburied dead lying everywhere in the terrain, one would not think that the odor from unwashed bodies would be so unpleasant.

In order to achieve all of the improvements required in the position and supply the men with food and ammunition the materials needed to be carried up to the front lines. Accomplishing this through the mud filled trenches and routes across open terrain, was difficult under the best of circumstances. Even if you were lucky enough to be in the rear areas or the rest battalion it did not mean you would have an easy time of it. Each night hundreds of men were assembled to carry lumber, beams, food containers, boxes of rifle and machine gun ammunition, *Minenwerfer* ammunition, coils of barbed wire, stakes, duckboards and dozens of similar items.

While the older veterans had been familiar with such hard work, it proved to be very trying for the new replacement troops who were unaccustomed to such physical activity. Fortunately, the rotation of the battalions in the front could still be maintained at a 10 day interval; 10 days in the front line, followed by 10 days in the readiness position and then 10 days in the rest areas before being sent back to the front line once again. Besides the constant fatigue duties the men were required to perform the barracks in the *Beugholz* camp offered inadequate housing and required a great deal of repairs if the camp was to be used as winter quarters. With all of the work required at the front and in the rear there was little time remaining for the training and education of the new replacements.

The physical condition of the position occupied by the 28th Reserve Division did not allow for a defense in depth. There were too few approach routes to the front line, the regiments were located too far apart to offer any real mutual support, all as a result of the uneven terrain. This was of great concern to the 5th Army headquarters as the French had demonstrated their ability to conduct local attacks and as such had been able to recapture Fort Douaumont on the other side of the Maas. There was also an urgent need for positioning of the readiness, second and third trenches and to construct communication trenches. Observation posts and patrols in front in the position closely watched the enemy, in order to prevent any surprises, which could quickly become dangerous considering the inadequate defensive facilities.

The general inactivity of the opposing French troops could not be put down solely to the fact that they were Territorial troops. After all, Territorial troops had effectively fought the XIV Reserve Corps to a standstill in the fighting in late September 1914. It was more likely that the enemy's trenches were in no better shape than the German trenches. This conclusion was drawn when the French were frequently seen with water mops and containers as they too tried to keep the mud and water out of their trenches. It became evident that the French suffered from the same weather related troubles when they also needed relief from the water and muck and their traffic also went 'over the bank' at times. Neither side took advantage of this situation by firing on the wretched men as they tried to avoid the morass inside the trenches. This mutual situation provided a small bit of consolation to the men of the 28th Reserve Division.

In addition to the elements the men of the division soon suffered under the opposing artillery fire and especially under the close combat means with the feared winged mines. It was clear that the French would not remain dormant with the increased activity in the opposite trenches and he made every effort to disrupt the work. At one point in the line, by the trenches outside the Wood of Avocourt, disruption of the German working parties was particularly annoying. The French trenches opposite this position were partially raised above the German lines, allowing the enemy good observation into the *Erlenbach Grund* (Forges stream) that moved in a southwestern direction out of the area of Malancourt, which allowed for accurate bombardments.

The French fire caused great damage to the defensive facilities; however the casualties remained within tolerable limits. The greatest threat to the battle strength of the companies was still the health condition of the troops, which from the middle of November increasingly became worse because of the weather and the poor housing. The problems maintaining the trenches under the constant wet weather did not improve when snow started to fall in the middle of November, which alternated with dew. Despite the unpleasant conditions, work on the position was eagerly promoted by the higher commands. The tangible fruits of the hard work could finally be seen on 15 November when two position battalions could be placed next to one another, each with two companies in the front trench, with the other two in the newly created third trench and in the Intermediate position. In RIR 110 the I Battalion moved to the right and the II Battalion to the left sector; the III Battalion rotated in position time from one sector to the other. This situation provided an improved tactical distribution of the regiment in the position.

The defensive installations RIR 110 had become accustomed to by Fricourt still did not exist, and what had been created remained in bad condition because of the continual rain and snowy weather. The time had still not come to introduce the old proven principle of keeping the opponent off balance through lively fire activity. Every measure for the defense against an attack that was necessary was eagerly pursued. New machine gun posts were created, in part in concrete shelters. Light signal stations, barrage fire sentry posts and installation of gas alarms were positioned throughout the line. For the latter the church bell of Malancourt was used which stood upon the hill at the command post of the right battalion.

In the sector occupied by RIR 109 the rainy weather also caused extensive damage to the trenches, especially the previously mentioned *Laufgraben VII*. It had proven to be impossible to maintain *Laufgraben* VII, and at places the men had to wade in the mud until it was above the knees, if they did not want to become exposed to enemy fire through leaving the trench. The hollow at the runner post was considered by many to be the most dangerous position in *Laufgraben* VII, where so many men were severely wounded through head shots or lost their lives.

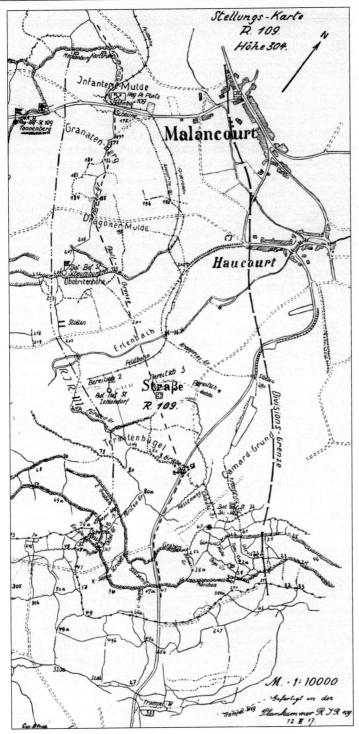

RIR 109 Sector.

One incident characterized this problem the best. The men of RIR 110 worked diligently on the extension of the *Höhenstellung*. At times entire companies from the rest battalion had to be brought up to work on the new position. Finally, after a great deal of effort they could report that the new trench was completed. The position consisted of deep trenches, fire steps, duck boards, traverses and dugouts. It was considered to be a miracle of the fine art of trench construction. Once the position was completed there was a short pause as the men prepared for the Brigade commander to inspect their work.

The Senior Officer appeared punctually at the Battalion command post on the date set for the inspection and accompanied the regimental officers to the *Höhenstellung*. According to the map, the *Höhenstellung* must have been there, however there was nothing of it to be seen. Apparently, in the previous night there was very wet weather and the entire trench had completely collapsed, and had become impassable. Only the dugout entrances had been kept open, but only with great effort. The brigade commander was moderately disappointed by these events, but not any less than the troops which had laboriously worked on the new position for weeks and had to start almost from the beginning once more.

On 10 December the new battalion battle headquarters created by the assembly area was ready and became occupied. Construction was started in the *Erlenbach Grund* and on *Termitenhügel* on a row of large barracks tunnels, so that little by little a reserve position for the Readiness I troops originated. In addition a battalion battle headquarters became created in the left sector of Readiness III and IV. To help out with all of the work required on the position the 1st and 2/143, the 7th and 8/L124 and the 6/106 was placed in possession of the regiment, which helped to create a new intermediate position on *Termitenhügel*.

The rest camp Madeleine farm on the Nantillois-Cunel road consisted of several barracks for each company located in a copse west of the road. They were scattered across the terrain and connected to one another through paths created with wooden slats. The barracks had good air flow that was a benefit during the hot weather, but with the onset of colder weather they needed to be sealed with clay and covered with canvas and roof panels.

Trench raids were quite common events by late 1916. In the two years since raids had become held they had become increasingly effective and deadly. It was still considered one of the best ways to establish the identity of the opposing enemy troops, instill a sense of superiority over the enemy as well as a harsh proving ground for new men who had to quickly learn to survive the type of warfare they faced.

Although the position companies were quite busy with the never ending entrenching the offensive spirit of the men could not be allowed to be diminished. Nightly patrols were sent out across the division sector in order to observe the condition of the enemy positions and the obstacles, sentry posts, wiring parties etc. and at the same time protect the German entrenching activities and wiring parties against a surprise attack.

The enemy was also busy observing the German lines for exactly the same reasons. If any unusual activity was observed, it generally resulted in artillery and mine fire falling on the suspected area. On the night of 8/9 November when the III/R109 relieved the I/R109 in Sector C the commotion caused in the exchange of troops became recognized by the opposing French which then resulted in artillery fire. In the following day, additional artillery and mine fire was directed at Sector C which was particularly heavy on the *K Graben*, the junction of the communication trenches and the hollows. The fire became so heavy that a dugout of the 11/R109 partially collapsed and five men were wounded as a result.

One of the first raids was attempted on 15 November against a position called the 'Entenschnabel', a portion of the French line that projected sharply out into no man's land. The raid was conducted by men from the 12/R109 under the command *Leutnant* Armbruster and was being held to determine the identity of the opposing enemy unit and hopefully to capture a few prisoners. Despite the preparation fire from the artillery and *Minenwerfer* the raiding party advanced toward the French lines and found the wire entanglements in front of the position undamaged. The patrol was discovered by French sentries and forced to withdraw in a hail of French hand grenades and artillery barrage fire.

The enemy also did not remain as quiet as it had been when the 28th Reserve Division took over the sector. In the last half of November there were several enemy attempts to penetrate into the German front line. These rather small patrols were all repulsed such as the one that occurred about 6 p.m. on 20 November when a French patrol came up against Sap 2. The alert sentries from the 2/R110 observed the enemy approaching their position and drove them back with a few well-placed hand grenades. A similar patrol undertaking by *Leutnant der Reserve* Haizmann on the following evening against the enemy position was also unsuccessful.

The regiments of the 28th Reserve Division were still understrength in November 1916 from the losses suffered on the Somme in October. New men arrived periodically such as on 30 November when RIR 110 received a draft of 6 *Unteroffiziere* and 397 men as replacements, which were distributed to the companies of the II/R110. After the battalion had been brought up to strength, it relieved the I/R110 in the front line. The I/R110 then took over the position of *Landsturm* Battalion Reutlingen. With the arrival of the new replacements, patrols and localized undertakings could be held on a regular basis.

However, even simple reconnaissance patrols used to help train the new men could be dangerous if the men were observed by enemy sentries and they could also prove to be embarrassing as well. In the night of 5/6 December a patrol from the 6/R111 came under enemy fire from which one man was wounded. The leader of the patrol wanted to bring him back, however he became disoriented, climbed over the French obstacles by mistake and ended up in captivity along with the wounded man.

The French were probably concerned about the increased frequency of the German patrols examining the front by their trenches and even more suspicious from the increased entrenching activity in the German positions. All of this activity resulted in a noticeable escalation in the fire from the French guns and close combat means in December. At the right wing, in the Wood of Avocourt, where friend and foe lay within a few meters of each other, the construction of wire obstacles and work in the forward most trenches often resulted in hand grenade skirmishes between the opposing sentries.

At the beginning of December larger, well-organized raids began to be held. At this time the undertaking 'Backzahn' was executed by the 13th Infantry Division which was on the left of RIR 109. The raiding party from IR 15 advanced against Points 390 and 391 where the opposing trenches were close to one another. In the following skirmish IR 15 captured 5 French officers and 113 Other Ranks. While not directly involved in the raid, the positions of the 28th Reserve Division came under especially heavy enemy fire in retaliation.

Some of the first enemy prisoners brought in by the 28th Reserve Division were taken in the night of 7/8 December. Patrol Döring, 7/R110 succeeded in capturing two enemy soldiers, from which French *Regiment d' Infanterie* 289 from the 55th Infantry Division was firmly established. Döring received the Iron Cross II Class for his actions.

On 15 December unusually strong artillery and mine fire fell on the positions held by RIR 110. The fire had grown to such an extent that the men were ordered to be alarm ready because everything pointed to an imminent enemy attack. An attack did take place but it was on the eastern bank of the Maas. The heavy fire on RIR 110 was simply an effort to deceive the Germans as to the location of the raid and when no enemy infantry appeared, the alarm readiness was rescinded.

At the end of December, the neighboring 13th Infantry Division was planning another large raid against the French positions opposite it. The undertaking was named 'Leihfeld', and was scheduled to take place at 2.30 p.m. on 28 December. The undertaking would be executed by the front line battalion of IR 13 under the command of Leutnant Leihfeld. At the same time a larger undertaking was being conducted by the 10th Reserve Division which would take place on the right wing of the 13th Infantry Division. RIR 109 was given orders to support this undertaking by a smaller patrol undertaking out of the Unruh Sap. The raid by RIR 109 would act as a diversion for the larger undertakings of the neighboring divisions and would have the full support of the division artillery and Minenwerfer.

The goal of the patrol from RIR 109 was to roll up the French front line trench from the projecting nose just to the west of the division border toward the east up to the juncture with the patrol from IR 13. The patrol, which consisted of 20 men under the command of Leutnant der Reserve A. Ganter II, left Unruh Sap at 2.30 p.m. according to schedule. The men quickly reached the French wire obstacles but quickly discovered that they were intact, the artillery and Minenwerfer fire had not created a breach has had been expected, in fact it was barely disturbed at the point where the patrol had expected to enter the French trench.

After a quick search of the immediate vicinity, a breach was discovered that allowed the raiding party to enter the enemy line in a width of approximately 12 meters. The raiding party quickly came upon 10 French soldiers inside the trench and one of the raiders threw his hand grenade in the middle of them. Following the first explosion, some of the enemy troops attempted to flee down the trench toward safety while several others gave signs they wanted to surrender.

One member of the patrol, Gefreiter Gartner, was standing on the edge of the parapet while holding a hand grenade. He had already pulled the cord to ignite the fuze and was prepared to throw it among the enemy soldiers standing in the trench. When the enemy held their hands high above their heads in surrender and shouted 'Pardon', approximately five to six Frenchmen came toward Gartner already wanting to exit the trench as prisoners. This is where the inexperience of the newer recruits and replacements came into play. Gartner was still holding his hand grenade as the fuze burned, between 5 1/2 and 7 1/2 seconds according to the markings on the hand grenade. The hand grenade exploded in Gartner's hand, killing him instantly, he was barely 18 years old at the time of his death.

The explosion also killed one of the enemy prisoners and wounded several others. The remainder of the patrol penetrated into the trench and escorted five wounded Frenchmen, as well as carrying the body of their fallen Gefreiter. As the appointed time for the patrol undertaking had passed, Leutnant Ganter ordered them to return to the German lines. The final results of the patrol by RIR 109 was five prisoners, with the loss of one man dead, one man missing and six men wounded.

Part of the problem associated with the new recruits at this time was not just the lack of training; it was also the physical condition of the men. While the newer replacements lid often lack sufficient training, matters were made even worse when qualified, trained men were taken away from the 28th Reserve Division. On 21 December RIR 109 was ordered to give up 7 *Unteroffiziere* and 130 Other Ranks who were rated K.V. *Kriegsverwendungsfähig* – Fit for Active Duty] and exchange them for an equal number of men who were rated Gv. (*Garnisonsverwendungsfähig* – Suitable for garrison duty) and Av. *Arbeitsverwendungsfähig* – Suitable for employment as laborers). This was just one more sign that the German Army was having difficulties in finding sufficient replacement troops to fill the ranks, when position divisions began to be combed for men to be used in other divisions with greater needs.

On the day the men were removed the official regimental battle strength of RIR 109 was: 14 officers, 9 *Offizier Stellvertreter*, 2,247 *Unteroffiziere* and Other Ranks consisting of 1,744 rifles and 16 machine guns. The ration strength of the regiment was: 61 officers, 1 *Offizier Stellvertreter*, 2,849 *Unteroffiziere* and Other Ranks, 244 horses. While these numbers indicate a regiment that was nearly at full strength, the quality and experience of many of the men left much to be desired.

It was during all of the activity at the end of December that Christmas suddenly arrived, the third Christmas of the war. Each Christmas since 1914 had become increasingly glum and less joyous as the war dragged on, and this Christmas would prove no different. While the men celebrated Christmas Eve with thoughts of lost friends and loved ones at home, the mood was improved slightly when Christmas gifts were distributed. This year, the packages from home were far fewer than in previous years and held much less than the men were used to. The Crown Prince, the 5th Army Commander, did help the festive mood of the men by distributing a cigarette case to every man in his army.

The Christmas meal was far less appetizing than usual. The Allied hunger blockade of Germany was having a far greater effect from year to year. The scarcity of food at home made itself quite tangible at the front also more and more in the form of severe rationing of food. The fat portion became reduced to 44 grams per day so that more fats could be available for the workers at home. The bread portion too was reduced from 750 to 600 grams per day for the men at the front. The normal allowances of certain foods so loved by the Other Ranks could no longer be issued on a daily basis, but only approximately every third day as supplies were reduced. Potatoes were scarce and in place of potatoes came an increasing number of turnips, also known as 'Entanglements' and 'Hussar Chaff.'

Fortunately the company cooks were able to cope with the every decreasing ration portions and substitutions and were still able to prepare palatable dishes with the raw materials provided to them. One happy note was the increase in the flour issue as a result of the successes achieved in Romania. The increased ration of flour allowed the cooks to prepare dishes the men had not had for some time.

In the case of RIR 111, the majority of the men were unable to fully enjoy the celebrations as two of the three battalions were holding the front line on Christmas Day. Only the II/R111 was able to celebrate the holiday in a modest way in the *Beugholz Lager*.

For RIR 111 the year 1916 came to an uneventful end. The commanding officer, *Oberst* Ley commented that only a few of the men who were now in front of Verdun were in the ranks of the regiment and experienced the fighting at the beginning of the year. While the men had changed, the old spirit of RIR 111 had remained with the firm trust on the ultimate victory. The hope however on a quick end of war had vanished after the enemy had just refused the German peace offer. The watchwords were still: 'With heart and hand for

Christmas 1916. (*Das Reserve-Infanterie-Regiment Nr. 109 im Weltkrieg 1914 bis 1918*)

the Fatherland!'

Then within a few days after the start of the New Year the men of RIR 111 lost their trusted commander, *Oberst* Ley, who had led the regiment since the beginning of the war. Ley had recently been promoted to command an infantry brigade. He spoke to the assembled regiment on the date he left: 'I take with me the proud and solemn memories of all the days that we experienced together since the beginning of the war. I want to thank each officer, *Unteroffizier* and man for their true fulfillment of duty in every situation. Might the dear regiment still be content with glorious days up to the peace agreement! Live well, comrades, do not forget your old commander, even as I will not forget you! *Hoch* RIR 111!' The new regimental commander, *Major* Lentz arrived a short time later.

Other well liked regimental officers left the ranks of the division at this time. The regimental adjutant, *Hauptmann* Edinger-Hodapp, of RIR 111 became recalled to Germany. *Leutnant* Geiger moved into his place. RIR 110 also faced a change in command at this time On 13 January *Major* Gandenberger von Moisy was forced to leave the regiment because of illness. He was replaced by an officer unfamiliar to the men, *Oberst* von Tronchin. The men would not have time to become acquainted with their new commanding officer as he was only with the regiment for three weeks before he was also appointed as a brigade commander. *Oberstleutnant* Bronsart von Schellendorf was the next officer to take command of the regiment.

With the turn of the year 1917 the weather became more severe than ever. The laboriously created facilities collapsed more and more. This finally changed in the middle of January when heavy frost and cold set in. The men now saw the fruits of their labor take root. Wire obstacles, trenches and dugouts were easier to maintain and create once the ground had hardened and this provided greater defensive strength to the position. New battalion command posts had been produced. At the right battalion sector it was christened the *Wartburg*; at the left battalion sector it was called the *Räuberburg*, after the commander of the II/R111, *Hauptmann* Räuber. The dryer surroundings also helped to improve health condition of the troops during this time

New replacement troops continued to arrive at the division in small groups. On 5

January 162 men arrived at RIR 109 from home where they were distributed among the different companies. On 29 January 100 additional recruits arrived from the Field Recruit Depot and were also distributed among the companies of RIR 109.

While new men continued to arrive at the division, in some instances old friends were leaving. The 1st Reserve and 2nd Reserve/*Pionier* Battalion 13 that had been with the 28th Reserve Division since the start of the war was transferred to another formation in the middle of January. In their place came the 1st *Ersatz Pionier* Company 16 which was positioned in Sector '*Strasse*'. RIR 109 noted that the regiment had lost faithful comrades in the 13th Reserve *Pionier* Battalion, who for more than two years had stood at the side of the regiment in all of the heavy fighting and was responsible for the lion's share of the success of the mine fighting at Fricourt and La Boisselle.

With the arrival of the New Year, there was also more time to train the new replacements and introduce new weapons and tactics to the entire division. When the men were fortunate to be located in the rest camps, the time was well spent restoring the worn equipment, performing physical exercise and practices held on training works, with great emphasis on new close combat methods that had been developed in accordance with their experiences from the battle of the Somme.

Part of the new training regimen called for combat training of both officers and Other Ranks in the *Sturm* School of the 5th Army, something that had been placed on hold since the division had left the Champagne the previous October. Once the course was completed, the officers and men would return to their regiments and then pass along their new training to the rest of the men in their companies.

At this time the first orders were issued for training on the newest weapon in the German arsenal, the light machine gun or MG 08/15, which was just about ready to be

MG 08/15 post with well-armed crew, RIR 111. (Author's collection)

introduced to the infantry. While not as light as the enemy's Chaut-Chat or Lewis Gun, the MG 08/15 was an improvement over the much heavier and cumbersome MG 08. At least the new weapon could be used by one man and would provide a great deal of firepower to the infantry companies.

When the new weapon was distributed to the regiments, skilled men were picked from each company for training under the oversight of the Machine Gun Officer of the regimental staff, in the case of RIR 110 it was *Rittmeister der Reserve* Kienitz. Once the men were fully trained on the weapon they were reviewed the division commander. In addition to the training on the light machine gun, all officers had to become familiar with the operation of the heavy machine gun.

One other major change in training was learning the methods of transmitting messages between infantry and infantry pilots using ground signal markers. Apparently the fighting by St. Pierre-Divion had demonstrated the effectiveness of this type of communication and had shown the benefits of the excellent cooperation between the enemy infantry and artillery during all of the British advances there.

Despite all of the changes that had occurred in the war, both in equipment and tactics, some things never seemed to change at all. On the occasion of the Kaiser's Birthday, 27 January 1917, the celebration would be more akin to the old peace time army. For at least one soldier in RIR 111, the day would prove to be most embarrassing.

On 27 January 1917 an orderly delivered a company order commanding me to return to the rest camp *Beugholz* from Nantillois, where I was with a detachment for training on the *Minenwerfer*. When I arrived there I divided the daily duties with *Feldwebel* Martin. Then, at approximately 9.30 a.m. we had to take part in a church service, the Protestants in the church barracks of the camp, the Catholics in the village church in Cierges. Dress: Overcoat, full equipment and the leather helmet from peacetime. The Other Ranks of the company were already virtually ready at the beginning, when we came into the barracks.

I went immediately to the workmen's barracks, where the *Pickelhauben* of the entire company were saved and stored piled up. One had no use for it in the fire trench already for a long time, because there they had been replaced by the steel helmet. However nevertheless the peacetime helmet still was part of the equipment of the German soldier and therefore became carefully provided with names – and entrusted to the care of the workmen. During reviews and parades one remembered the glorious traditions of this helmet again and got it out for a day out of the container.

When I entered into the workshop, all helmets were already gone except for one. It was mine; it was solitary and left in a corner. However its tip had been unscrewed. In vain I started looking in a rush in the barracks, I could find the tip nowhere. Then the time for the church service approached, I ran to the company office and reported the loss of my helmet tip and asked about a replacement point, because an *Unteroffizier* without a helmet tip then was not possible in the German Army. However there was no replacement tip.

Feldwebel Martin smiled ironically, reported to me however that with regard to the considerable cold, on orders of the battalion the *Mütze* should be worn going to the church. Through this additional order alteration I imagined, already to finally be rid of the embarrassment. However I was happy too soon. Feldwebel Martin then told to me, to look that blinking top again for the church service. There remained nothing for me, than I to fit in, although I could not understand the meaning of this order.

After returning from the church service I cleared out around the entire workshop out of annoyance and finally, after half an hour, found the tip in a hole under the floor of the barracks. My joy was great. Satisfied I strode across the rough planks back to the company barracks.

Suddenly I saw through the snow covered trees and hedges a company standing upon the assembly place of the camp, other companies approached; they all wore the peacetime helmet. I was dumbfounded and thought a moment what that signified. The Kaiser parade! went through my mind. Although nobody had said anything about it to me, I quickly ran to the company barracks, to march with the company. However, when I arrived there, the barracks, to my great astonishment, were empty. The company had already gone. The company office was dead.

Through the barracks windows I could observe the battalion. It stood up in an open quadrangle. The company leaders had already reported to the commander, *Hauptmann* Räuber. What should I do? I thought for a moment and came to the decision;

To hobble after would only attract attention! That was an inexcusable clumsiness by an *Unteroffizier* and thoughtlessness against the company and its dashing leader, *Leutnant* Fritzsche. It seemed to me therefore, the cleverest thing was to remain in the barracks. Inwardly I justified my behavior so that my absence doesn't become noticed and that I thereby saved the company any inconvenience. Because in accordance with previous experience on this day, the commander would give a speech for the Kaiser, the *Obersten Kriegsherrn*, and subsequently would confer awards and distinctions to the men. Both could go forward without my personal presence. Finally it was also not my blame that I had found out nothing of the parade. I sat at the table of the barracks and followed the military pageant with suspense. I could see everything well, what went on in front of me, however I understood no words of what was being said. The speech of the commander finished with three cheers for the Kaiser, in which the entire battalion joined in. Then began the bestowing of medals. Officers, *Unteroffiziere* and Other Ranks would be called before the front, and the commander fastened their awards on the chest. Suddenly a pause! The commander stopped to pause. *Leutnant* Fritzsche moved to him here and placed a salute with his hand by the helmet. *Feldwebel* Martin reported standing stalwartly. A short speech followed and a counter speech. Then a runner left the quadrangle and ran toward our company barracks.

What does this have to do with me? I thought and I looked around in the barracks. Quickly I jumped down from the table, grasped a brush and used it on my coat. The runner came in at a rush, hurriedly looked through the room, came to me to and reported: "Orders from *Herrn* Battalion Commander! *Herr Unteroffizier* is to immediately come with him!" When I asked him why I should come, he replied briefly: "you come now and find out." With this explanation he left the barracks.

I quickly threw on the coat, buttoned it up and placed the helmet on, whose tip proudly pointed to the heavens. In two minutes I stood in the middle of the quadrangle in front of the commander. I clicked my heels together and reported in a stalwart posture: "*Unteroffizier* Pflüger in position!" An embarrassing silence prevailed. I sensed that the eyes of the entire battalion were directed upon me. I firmly looked the commander in the eyes, but he looked at me growling. Now the thunder storm broke loose! "What happened to you? Why did you not come here? he asked me. However without allowing me to answer, he went away: "I have only been here three days. Take yourself away!" "As ordered *Herr Hauptmann*!" I mechanically answered, did a short about-face and I hurried, as quickly as possible to join the company. I joined the ranks at the left wing of the *Unteroffiziere*. My helpful man next to me whispered to me: "You should report to the company leader!" Astonished and puzzled as I was, I followed this well-meaning advice almost weak-willed and repeated my report in front of *Leutnant* Fritzsche. He also looked at me sinisterly and thundered at me. "Why did you come here? I arrived here three days ago. Remove yourself!" As ordered, *Herr Leutnant*"! I did an about face and vanished again to the left wing. I had barely taken my place, when the command was given 'Battalion – attention! – route step!' so that the military celebration had reached its conclusion.

At the Company Orderly Room, where I looked for enlightenment over this strange, puzzling incident to me throughout, *Feldwebel* Martin handed over to me the Baden Service medal with the words: "The commander had wanted to present the award to you in front of the assembled Other Ranks, but you were not there." You are not required to sit out the threatened three days arrest." *Unteroffizier* William Pflüger, 7/R111. [1]

With the change of the New Year there were already signs of from the enemy of a possible spring offensive. In consideration of this, the OHL needed to stay informed about the distribution of the enemy forces on a regular basis and track their movements. RIR 11. would be the first in the division to attempt a raid against the enemy lines and to capture prisoners for the purpose of gathering intelligence.

On the evening of 9 January *Unteroffizier* Schmold, 5/R111, along with a *Stosstrupp*

French prisoners clearing snow, RIR 111. (Author's collection)

crawled through no man's land until they were in front of the French wire obstacles. The patrol was most likely betrayed by the tracks it left in the fresh fallen snow and Schmold and his men came under heavy fire and were forced to turn back. Among the casualties suffered in this aborted raid was *Unteroffizier* Schmold who was killed. The French sent out a patrol that apparently was determined to follow Schmold's party back to the German lines but it was also expelled through rifle and machine gun fire.

During the month of January patrols of the 11th and 12/R110 continually went forth against the enemy positions. In each instance the attempts had failed as it was impossible to surprise the French because of the strong enemy wire obstacles. One of the attempts, a patrol lead by *Offizier Stellvertreter* Hippler appeared to have the best chance of success but instead the men became pelted with incendiary bombs while in front of the enemy barbed wire from which Hippler was wounded and one other man from the raiding party was killed.

In addition to capturing prisoners and gathering intelligence, raids were also held to provide greater security to the men holding the trenches. In the hilly terrain along the Maas, it was not unusual that one side or the other had good observation into the opposing trenches in result of holding a prominent point. The *Entenschnabel* and the *Mövchen* sap were considered to be such positions. There had already been a number of bitter patrol fights at both locations but the overall line did not change and the French continued to have excellent observation into the German position.

Under these circumstances, it became critical to advance the left wing of the regimental position until it had taken in part of the French lines. By doing so it would take away all of the outstanding observation posts from which the enemy could dominate the entire left bank of the Maas. The suggestion was forwarded to Division and Corps Headquarter for review. When both gave their approval of the operation, the staff of RIR 109 began to prepare for the undertaking.

In order to ensure success, troops from the neighboring IR 13 would also take part in the attack. The overall command of the operation was given to *Hauptmann* Block, the leader of the II/R109 under the appropriate code name '*Block*'. Simultaneous attacks were also planned at the right wing of the 28th Reserve Division where the large patrol undertaking '*Rattenschwanz*' was being held by RIR 110 on the wood of Avocourt, while further to the east there would be advances by IR 15 subsequently on the left of IR 13 in the *Hecken Grund* and on '*Toten Mann*'.

There was feverish activity in the German lines in order to have everything in place for the attack at the scheduled time. Heavy batteries were moved into position; the field railway brought large quantities of ammunition to the front for the guns and *Minenwerfer*. Entrenching tools were sharpened and explosive devices were constructed in order to destroy existing French dugouts, wire entanglements and traverses where needed. An exact full-scale model of the French positions was created at Madeleine farm, called the '*Blockwerk*' where the *Stosstrupps*, formed from men picked from every company as well as the supporting infantry companies could practice every aspect of the assault until each man could literally perform his duties by memory.

The date chosen for the attack was 25 January 1917 and it was only known by a few officers in order to maintain the element of surprise. Starting on 8 January the regimental sector became divided into 2 Sub sectors '*Strasse* 1 and 2' on the right, '*Strasse* 3 and 4' on the left. The company located in the report center was designated as the reserve company for the

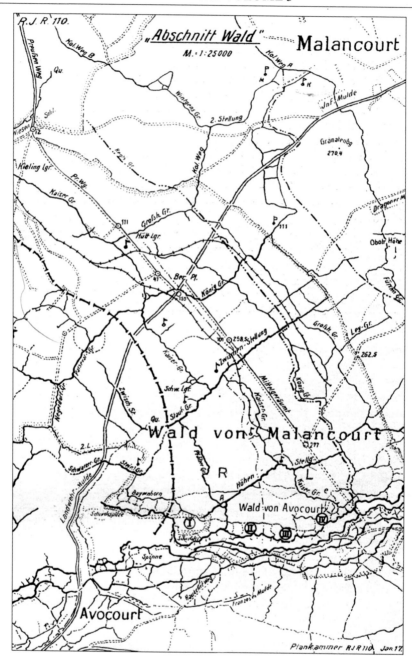

Area of the proposed raid.

left sector, the company in the barracks tunnel was the reserve company for the right sector. In the days before the attack two companies each from two battalions became inserted into the forward most position. The I/R109 was designated as the 'Traveling Battalion'. It must regularly move between both sectors; changing from the left and the right sub sectors on a rotation basis. During the preparations *Hauptmann* Seltsam took over the leadership of the II/R109 in place of *Major* Hennig. *Major* Hennig had been transferred to RIR 365 to become the regimental commander and had left RIR 109 on 13 January.

While the troop dispositions were being worked out, there was additional activity across the front line. New positions were created for the heavy *Minenwerfer* being operated by the men of *Minenwerfer* Company 228. Ammunition columns carried the heavy *Minenwerfer* shells into the trenches day and night and created large stockpiles near each thrower. The infantry worked diligently in the second trench in creating secure dugouts to house the reserve troops for the upcoming attack. As a result of the difficult work, 26 dugout entrances each with six to seven steps into the ground became mined and the *Olga* and *Unruh* Saps had also been extended. A command post named the '*Blockhaus*' and an emergency kitchen for the companies located in the left sector were constructed. The machine guns already in the position would be reinforced through four additional guns from the regimental reserve and six machine guns from the 2nd Company of the Guard Machine Gun Marksman Detachment 30.

In the early morning hours of 18 and 19 January the 9th and 12th Companies moved into the Sector '*Strasse* 1 and 2,' while the 1st and 3rd Company moved into the Readiness barn in '*Strasse* 3.' The 2nd Company moved into the *Kasernen Stollen*. On 23 and 25 January while the 6th Company moved to Sector '*Strasse* 3' and the 4th and 8th Companies took up positions in '*Strasse* 4'. The 11/R109 moved into Support II, the 7/R109 moved on 25 January to Readiness III and IV relieving the 10/R109 located there. The 10/R109 then moved into Sector '*Strasse* 4' behind the 4th and 8/R109 early on 25 January.

The last of the preparations called for the hand-picked *Stosstrupps*, *Flammenwerfer* and *pioniers* under the leadership of *Leutnants* Rüdiger and Richter, *Vizefeldwebels* Leidig and Quitz to move into position from the Madeleine *Lager* where they had been assembled. At the time set for the attack there was intense cold. When the men left the relatively warm quarters in order to take up the assault positions the biting cold quickly expelled any weariness the men may have experienced and some of the men began to softly sing old

Leutnant Richter and Stosstrupp, 11/R109. (*Das Reserve-Infanterie-Regiment Nr. 109 im Weltkrieg 1914 bis 1918*)

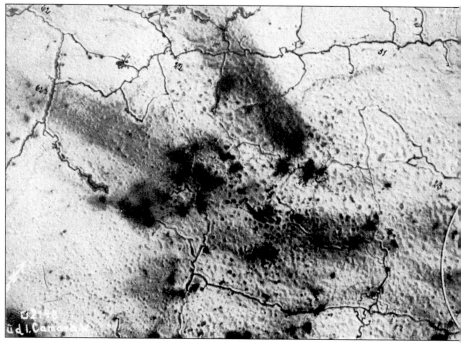

Aerial view of bombardment area for Undertaking Block. (*Das Reserve-Infanterie-Regiment Nr. 109 im Weltkrieg 1914 bis 1918*)

soldiers songs which resounded across the terrain in the early winter morning. This was quickly stopped in order to prevent alerting the enemy sentries.

During the frosty, clear weather the entire Verdun front was peaceful. A dense blanket of fresh snow that had fallen in the night of 24/25 January had put a stop to all local fighting. The final orders for the attack were given out and at 12 noon *Hauptmann* Block received the report that all of the troops participating stood ready at their exit positions. The French were behaving very quietly so it appeared that all of the precautions taken had been successful. The misty, snowy weather had greatly reduced the enemy aerial activity and few French pilots were seen flying overhead.

At precisely 3.20 p.m. the German batteries opened fire and the shells struck the forward most enemy trenches in a massive blow. The *Minenwerfer* simultaneously opened fire against the French wire obstacles. Within a few minutes the enemy batteries near Avocourt as well as the fortress guns of *Fort de Marre* replied to the German fire, especially showering the Camard crest with their shells. However, the German artillery soon effectively silenced the French batteries

The German infantry attack took place exactly as it had been practiced. Shortly before 3.50 p.m. there was a loud explosion that shook the ground under the feet of the men inside the German trenches. The *pioniers* had blown up the wire entanglements at several locations and cleared alleys through the French wire.

Leutnant Richter and *Vizefeldwebel* Leidig hurled forth out of the sap heads '*Unruh* and *Toni*' with their *Stosstrupps*. *Leutnant* Rüdiger and *Vizefeldwebel* Quitz hurled forth out of the sap heads '*Olga* and *Minna*' with their *Stosstrupps*, both quickly reaching the

Grave of *Ersatz Reservist* Heinrich Markheiser, 8/R109,
KIA 27 January 1917. (Author's collection)

enemy wire obstacles under the protection of a sudden snow shower. The men skillfully used the alleys blown through the French wire by the *Minenwerfer* and the *pioniers* and penetrated into the French front line trench, suffering few losses in the process.

The attack quickly turned into bitter close fighting as the French garrison came out of their dugouts and engaged the invading *Stosstrupps*. Closely following the *Stosstrupps* were several skirmish waves, each containing two assault platoons from the 8th and 4/R109 under *Leutnants* Jenne and Unruh. Behind these were two carrying and work platoons from both companies. The 7/R109 formed the reserve; the 10/R109 moved up to the front line and waited with the 5/R109 for further orders. Both the 10th and 7/R109 had been designated as entrenching companies who would consolidate the newly captured enemy trenches and prepare them for defense.

As soon as the German artillery transferred its fire on the enemy rear, everyone pressed into the French trenches following close behind the belt of fire. The terrain presented a picture of the powerful bombardment, the wire obstacles were blown apart and the ground was torn open and churned up from innumerable shell craters. The pure white blanket of snow had been obliterated in the geysers of earth thrown up by each impact, and dense black smoke floated across the landscape. Infantry and artillery projectiles whistled and hissed across the sky, above the heads of the attackers. Countless French shrapnel clouds appeared above the Camard ground without causing any losses among the attacking troops. The French artillery had been completely surprised and the guns still able to fire had set the shrapnel fuzes too high. It was a sign of good luck for the attackers.

To the men holding the German front lines and the officers such as *Hauptmann* Block, these were anxious minutes as they waited nervously for the first reports to come in. They could clearly hear the sound of hand grenades exploding in the first French trench; then the sounds of cheers could be heard through the din of explosions, coming from the second enemy trench.

The attack had been executed like clockwork, exactly as it had been practiced day after day at the *Blockwerk* at Madeleine farm. All opposition in the French front line trench had quickly been overcome and the assault groups advanced through the maze of trenches until they reached the last trench. The actual fighting had lasted only a short time. The French troops were completely surprised and many of the defenders had fled at the first sign of the attack and had ended up in the curtain of German artillery barrage fire which blocked off the sector. Others had simply surrendered with the words *'quelle direction?'* and were directed toward the German lines where they were assembled by the reserve troops and sent back to the rear as prisoners.

The *Stosstrupps* had soon reached the point where they were order to stop and prepared the damaged trenches for defense against the inevitable counterattack. Meanwhile, the partially smashed in dugouts, which were considered far worse than the German dugouts by the men because of the poor construction and depth, were being searched for prisoners, equipment, weapons, etc. by the support detachments. While valuable intelligence materials were being found, by far the most valuable item, according to the infantrymen, was the quantity and quality of the enemy food. Much of the food being found had already become so scarce in the German rations that it was considered extraordinary luck to find it. Food such as white bread, butter, chocolate and similar delicacies were consumed almost as quickly as the attack had been carried out.

Shortly after 5 p.m. *Hauptmann* Block could report to the regimental commander that the goal had been reached and the third French trench in a length of 1,600 meters was occupied by Baden and Westphalian *Sturmtrupps* from the two divisions. However, despite the enemy position being occupied with the assault and support troops, this was only the first part of the larger plan. Now the task at hand was to consolidate the captured position and to incorporate it into the main German defenses.

While the work required to incorporate the enemy position into the German defenses was taking place, the enemy had apparently recovered from their surprise and considerable reinforcements could be observed moving toward the front line from positions by the Village of Esnes. *Hauptmann* Block quickly ordered the German artillery to take them under fire and as the shells exploded they tore huge gaps in the enemy ranks. Unfortunately this fire also caused significant losses in the ranks of the *Stosstrupps* who had inexorably surged toward the approaching enemy reserves.

The total German losses from the infantry assault had been 27 men killed and 53 men wounded, of which a large part had resulted from the German barrage fire. This was a misfortune that was considered to be unavoidable during such undertakings. In a similar manner, a large group of *pioniers* had been blown to pieces at the beginning of the assault while they moved forward out of *Mövchen Sap*, when a 200 pound *Schwere Minenwerfer* shell exploded in the middle of their ranks.

Despite the crushing German barrage fire, the French counterattack lasted until 10 p.m., as the enemy made numerous attempts to recapture the lost terrain. However, all of enemy attacks were met with tough opposition of the assault troops and the support from the work and blocking party companies. Apparently, the support companies had not waited for orders before beginning their advance. They hurried forward upon hearing the news of the successful attack and already after 2 hours they could report that the captured

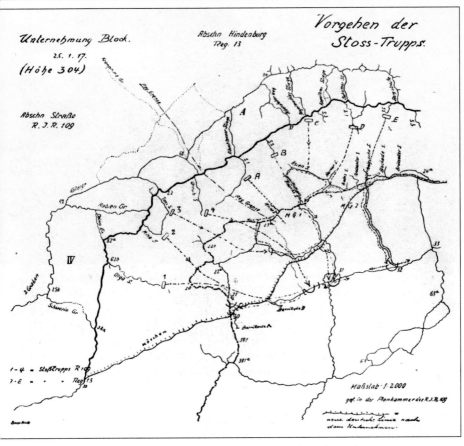

Undertaking Block: RIR 109 *Stosstrupp* plan of attack.

enemy trenches had been cleared and connected with the sap heads of the old German position. In spite of numerous enemy attacks the entrenching and mining work continued uninterrupted until midnight. With the new day on 26 January the support troops were already busy widening the forward most saps.

While the men from RIR 109 and IR 15 had successfully attacked the French lines on Hill 304, the men from RIR 110 had conducted a diversionary undertaking called *Rattenschwanz*', against the enemy position designated as the '*Spinne*'. After effective fire preparation by *Minenwerfer* Company 409 under *Leutnant* Unterdörfer and with artillery support, two patrols led by *Leutnant* Haizmann and *Offizier Stellvertreter* Schwab advanced into the enemy trenches.

During the advance by the men from RIR 110 the fire from a flanking French machine gun became quite disagreeably. Once at the French trenches the wire entanglements and trenches were found to be almost completely destroyed through the preparation fire. Patrol Schwab was able to take three French sentries prisoner. They belonged to the French *Regiment d'Infanterie* 289. One *Fusil Mitraille* and six rifles were also taken. The patrol returned with their prisoners and loot while suffering only two slightly wounded men. *Offizier Stellvertreter* Schwab received the Iron Cross I Class as a result of this successful

French prisoners captured during Undertaking Block. (*Das Reserve-Infanterie-Regiment Nr. 109 im Weltkrieg 1914 bis 1918*)

raid and the patrol participants became presented to His Royal Highness, Crown Prince Wilhelm in the presence of their company commander, *Leutnant* Haizmann, on 16 February in the park of Charmois where Schwab was presented with his award.

In the night of 27 January both assault companies, the 4th and 8/R109, were relieved from the new front line and sent to barracks in the rear for a well-deserved rest. The 2nd and 3/R109 took their place in the defenses. The 2nd and 3/R109 also had to endure heavy fighting over the next days because the French had not given up their attempts to retake Hill 304 and had utilized all of their resources in order to obtain their goal.

The French counterattacks were particularly heavy on 28 January. Shortly before daybreak the French infantry advanced in a surprise attack against the new German position on Hill 304 without artillery preparation. Despite the element of surprise they quickly ended up in the well placed fire of the German support batteries which had been alerted by telephone of the attack. The fire from the guns of the I/RFAR 29 under *Hauptmann* Fröhlich was especially effective due to the close working relationship the artillery had forged with the infantry in nearly three years of fighting in the Vosges, on the Somme and in the Champagne. The projectiles from the guns formed an impassable barrier directly in front of the German trenches, smashing enemy attack completely. Just before midday French drum fire from the heaviest caliber guns fell on the German positions. This fire was followed by three French attacks, all of which broke completely in the fire of the trench garrison and the guns from the I/RFAR 29.

All of the efforts by the French to recapture the lost ground were in vain. The men from RIR 109 were determined to hold on to the new positions and persevered in defending it. Eventually, the French attacks petered out and the enemy began to fortify the new front line they had been left with. Once all of the fighting had died down German defenders were able to improve their position even more. Still, there was always the inevitable enemy artillery fire. The raid had been a complete success; not only had the enemy position been captured, a total of 500 enemy prisoners were brought in as well as numerous machine guns

Crown Prince Wilhelm distributing awards to men of RIR 109. (*Das Reserve-Infanterie-Regiment Nr. 109 im Weltkrieg 1914 bis 1918*)

and other weapons.

The success was a great morale boost for the men, especially the newest members of the regiment. The exploit by RIR 109 was also mentioned in the daily reports by Crown Prince Wilhelm which greatly pleased the men of the regiment. On 10 February General von Francois also praised the regiment for the fighting on Hill 304 and on 16 February Crown Prince Wilhelm awarded *Leutnant der Reserve* Rüdiger and *Vizefeldwebel* Quitz with the Iron Cross I Class and 14 other men with the Iron Cross II Class.

While undertakings of this size and complexity helped to train the new men in trench warfare, it also had a negative effect. With the creation of special *Stosstrupps* consisting of the most daring and physically fit men, many of the casualties from the raid also came from these specialty units. This left the remaining companies slightly weaker every time the best and fittest men were combed out. This method would soon have a negative cumulative impact on the effectiveness of the average infantry company that could not be reversed.

Once the large scale raid had been ended, life returned to normal for the men in the 28th Reserve Division. Patrols were sent out on a daily basis to observe the enemy lines and if possible to take additional prisoners. Following the successful attack by RIR 109 and IR 15 on Hill 304, the enemy became far more observant of any movement in no man's land. The French were determined to prevent a similar German attack from taking place.

On 1 February a patrol sent out by the 5/R109 was discovered by enemy sentries as it approached the French line and became taken under hand grenade fire. As a result of the enemy response *Leutnant der Reserve* Fiederling, one *Unteroffizier* and three men were wounded.

On 7 February, a patrol sent out under *Unteroffizier* Dürr, 7/R109 and *Unteroffizier* Lazniak, 4/RO19, each with ten men and two *pioniers* ended up with similar misfortune as Fiederling. The two patrols had advanced toward Point 31 and Point 32. However, like

Fiederling, they were met in front of the enemy wire obstacles with hand grenades and machine gun fire, so that any further advance was impossible. Also, when no prisoners were brought in by the patrol it was determined that both saps were strongly occupied and protected with heavy machine gun fire.

As the weather continued to be cold and snowy the patrols were growing more dangerous. On the night of 14 February a patrol of the 7/R110 under *Musketier* Morgen attempted to establish the location of the enemy sentries. However, by crawling closer to the French lines through the thick snow their advance became betrayed through the cracking snow blanket and the enemy was alarmed. Although the enemy trench garrison was superior in strength top the patrol, the leader decided to attack and the men rose up and threw a salvo of hand grenade toward the French position.

Almost immediately, the patrol had to quickly drop to the ground when a volley of rifle fire erupted from the French trench. Any hope of surprising the opposing garrison was lost and the patrol moved back without losses. The division acknowledged the leader and the participants of the patrol for their attempt to overwhelm a superior enemy force.

One of the weapons used frequently in preparing for raids was the *Minenwerfer*. Instead of being concentrated into a single unit, the *Minenwerfer* had been positioned with all parts of the regiments. Two *Minenwerfer* platoons under *Leutnant* Bonn and *Offizier Stellvertreter* Gantert, formed a component of RIR 111 starting from the middle of February. The crews of the throwers had previously become trained in a *Minenwerfer* school in the *Beugeholz Lager* by *Feldwebel Leutnant* Kupfermann. Great care had to be taken for the protection of the men while firing the various *Minenwerfer*. The tubes of the *Minenwerfer* were quite thin in comparison to the tubes used by the artillery. In extreme cold weather it was not unusual for the tubes to crack, causing a premature explosion of the mine, so the men would fire them while taking shelter in a nearby bomb proof location.

The *Minenwerfer* were used frequently for the destruction of the enemy wire entanglements as well as providing harassing fire against the enemy infantry. The French did not take this destructive fire lightly and quickly responded by bombarding the German positions with artillery fire; the frequent fire raids caused a great deal of damage. During one such fire raid on 16 February a dugout entrance by the 2/R111 was buried, which set off a sack of hand grenades, killing three occupants of the shelter.

Despite the increased French fire and the intense cold weather, raids continued across the division front. On the evening of 22 February two *Stosstrupps* from the 1/R111 under the command of *Vizefeldwebel* Fischer, successfully penetrated both forward enemy trenches in the Wood of Avocourt following a short period of artillery and *Minenwerfer* fire. The enemy trenches had been considerably damaged by the projectiles, and had apparently been abandoned by the garrison. The raiding party found at least one dugout that had completely collapsed under the weight of the fire. After a brief exploration of the damaged trenches, the *Stosstrupps* returned to the German lines without any prisoners.

Not to be outdone, French patrols began to become more active. This was accompanied by an increase in artillery and mine fire. There was an enemy bombardment in the night from 22/23 February. The men inside the dugouts did not hear many explosions and at first thought the French shells were duds. Then an odd odor began to fill the dugouts and it was immediately recognized as gas. The gas masks were put on and the men set small fires by the dugout entrances and throughout the trenches in order to drive the gas up into the air. Despite these efforts some men had experienced gas poisoning and were taken to the medical dugout for treatment. Further gas shelling in the night caused the carrying parties bringing up food and coffee to wear gas masks as they moved through the trenches, making their journeys that much harder.

It now appeared to the men that the French wanted revenge for the numerous raids and patrols being held by the men of the 28th Reserve Division and became very active along the entire division front. Enemy bombardments with every type of weapon, from light to heavy guns and mines, appeared to become stronger day after day, especially on 23 February in Sector 'Strasse 4.' Five dugout entrances were crushed in by heavy French shells on this day. The dugout where the orderly room for the 1st and 4/R109 was located collapsed due to a direct hit. Rescue efforts were started immediately and the men dug frantically through the tons of collapsed earth. Eventually the rescuers succeeded in digging out *Gefreiter* Göckel of the 4/R109. With this successful rescue, the men redoubled their efforts to locate the other occupants of the dugout. The occupants were eventually found, *Gefreiter* Sutter and *Grenadier* Hartmann, but both men had already died from suffocation.

On 23 February, at 7.50 a.m., a sentry on the right wing of RIR 110 noticed that there was a dark object being pushed along the ground by French soldiers and was eventually placed under the obstacles lying in front of him. Instead of immediately sounding the alarm, the sentry ran to report his observations to the Group leader who also saw the object. The leader went to fetch his rifle in order to shoot at the object when it suddenly exploded. It was later determined that it was an explosive charge which destroyed the obstacles and opened a path into the German trenches. The French raiding party sprang up and rushed through the opening and into the German trench. They threw hand grenades into the nearby dugouts and caused considerable losses to the trench garrison.

A counterattack was prepared by the platoon leader in order to expel the enemy raiding party, which was eventually successful. However, due to the improper behavior of the sentry and his Group leader they allowed the French to penetrate into the trench and to take four men prisoner before returning to their own lines. This was just one more example of the lack of experience of the men who formed the regiments. It was generally accepted that if an old soldier had been present then it is likely the raid would have failed.

Starting at noon on 25 February and throughout the next hours the French bombarded the German lines with shells, mines and gas, resulting in a high state of alert in anticipation that a French attack would follow. At 9.15 p.m. the enemy did attack with small detachments along the entire line of RIR 111, however through the watchfulness of the men and timely barrage fire being ordered all of the attacks failed. On this day the I/R111 suffered four men killed and eleven men wounded from the enemy fire.

On 26 February the right sector of the I/R111 lay under a powerful enemy bombardment. A number of losses occurred in the ranks of the German garrison including two efficient platoon leaders from the 1/R111, *Vizefeldwebel* Stehle and *Vizefeldwebel* Fischer, the latter was the patrol leader from the raid of 22 February. Both men were killed in the bombardment of the German front line through shell splinters. Following the heavy bombardment the situation became calm and everything returned to normal when suddenly, in the afternoon, enemy shock troops broke forth from the eastern edge of the Wood of Avocourt and advanced upon the German front line. The sentries immediately called for barrage fire and an impenetrable wall of fire fell in front of the enemy advance and stopped the assault waves in its tracks. After a short period of time the French troops withdrew.

Trench sentries, RIR 111. (Author's collection)

Later the same evening, while the artillery from both sides actively bombarded the opposing trenches, *Unteroffizier* Gmelin, 4/R111, stood on sentry duty. At about 11 p.m Gmelin observed an enemy skirmish line advancing in the strength of about two groups once again in the eastern part of the wood. He immediately opened rapid fire with the other nearby sentries and the fire alarmed the garrison. The men rushed out of their dugouts and joined in the fight and managed to expel the enemy with rifle fire and hand grenades.

The French raids were quickly followed by additional attempts. Around 10 p.m. on 27 February the sentries from RIR 110 in Sectors A2, A3 and A4 reported that the enemy was clearing his wire entanglements and that there was unusual activity taking place inside the enemy trench. Instead of waiting to see what the French were up to, the sentries called for barrage fire which fell accurately along the opposing trenches. Despite the heavy artillery fire the enemy troops left their trenches at several places and were able to advance up to the German barbed wire entanglements, where they were refused everywhere by rifle fire and hand grenades. In spite of the quick action taken by the sentries RIR 110 still lost three men killed, four men severely wounded and one officer and eleven men slightly wounded.

Despite what the narrative has been portraying, not everything at this time revolved around trench raids and patrols. The regimental band in RIR 109 had slowly recovered from the heavy losses it had suffered in the Somme Battle. It was greeted with great joy when in February, *Vizefeldwebel* Schandert was discharged home and *Vizefeldwebel* Ehrbrecht took over the leadership of the band. In a short time his artistic skill through painstaking practices and rehearsals had restored the band to its former proficiency and the sound of music filled the rear areas once again. It was a welcome relief in the monotonous life by Verdun.

Still, as the weather started to improve, the number of raids continued to increase on both sides of the wire. On the morning of 5 March the French successfully raided the trenches being held by RIR 111. Shortly after the relief of the 1/R111 by the 11/R111 the enemy raiding party suddenly appeared at the German position while the French artillery placed a wall of blocking fire around the targeted trench. The raiding party utilized several gaps in the German wire that had been created several days earlier by artillery fire and which had not been repaired yet.

They French succeeded in penetrating into the first trench and placed two sentries out of action using pistols and hand grenades. The German garrison had been alerted immediately by the dense enemy fire and a counterattack was prepared on the spot by the 11/R111 Company commander, *Leutnant* Diesner. He exited the second trench by climbing over the parapet with his men and advanced toward the threatened sector. In the few minutes it had taken to hold the raid, and before Diesner and his men could arrive, the enemy raiding party had already withdrawn and had taken 1 *Unteroffizier* and 5 men as prisoners from one of the dugouts with them.

The victims of the enemy raid from 5 March had their revenge on 8 March. At 6.45 p.m. two *Stosstrupps* under Sergeant Kienzle, 11/R111 and *Unteroffizier* Zimmermann, 12/R111 broke into the French position at the eastern edge of the Wood of Avocourt after a short but intense period of fire preparation. However the enemy had evacuated his forward line again, which had been badly damaged from the preliminary bombardment.

The assault parties continued to advance toward the second trench where they ran into stiff opposition and it quickly turned into a hand grenade battle at one barricade. The *Stosstrupps* were unable to make any headway against the enemy barricade and *Unteroffizier* Zimmermann also became wounded by a hand grenade splinter. The situation became even more difficult when the French received reinforcements; however they were soon forced to retreat when the *Stosstrupps* pressed forward and captured the barricade. Unfortunately there was no time for a pursuit, because the period set for the undertaking had expired. The *Stosstrupps* returned with all their men, amongst them three slightly wounded, and a few pieces of loot, but without prisoners.

On the afternoon of the same day the men of RIR 109 had successfully refused an enemy infantry attack on a broad front that had been prepared through several hours of severe artillery fire. RIR 109 had not been caught unaware and had been able to repulse the French attack without outside assistance.

A similar attempt by the enemy came in the night of 7/8 March, but this time the results were slightly different. The enemy raiding party became observed by a sentry of the 12/R111 while it was still in no man's land. As a result, the enemy patrol was repulsed in heavy infantry fire in a short period of time and before they could enter the German trenches.

Now it was the turn of the 28th Reserve Division. An undertaking was planned by RIR 110 to be held on 8 March. The target was the enemy trench opposite saps 8, 9 and 10. Two proven patrol leaders, *Vizefeldwebels* Reinecke and Hammer, 7/R110 along with 22 picked men would be divided into two *Stosstrupps* and would prepare for the raid at a practice work located by Robinette farm.

On the date set for the raid the small group of men made their way through the trenches to the starting point. The journey to the front was quite difficult because during the entire afternoon of 8 March the *Kaiser Graben* and the *Pfälzer Graben* as well as the intermediate terrain laid under heavy enemy shell and mine fire. There was another greater disadvantage the men needed to overcome; fresh snow had fallen and the entire countryside was bright as day. As a result of the heavy fire and the bright snow the men were forced to move into the nearby dugouts individually in order to prevent the enemy observers from seeing such a large body of men, which could give the planned raid away.

At 6.42 p.m. the artillery and *Minenwerfer* preparation fire began. At 6.45 p.m., in accordance with orders, the two *Stosstrupps* advanced. *Vizefeldwebel* Reinecke with thirteen men broke forth from Sap 8, *Vizefeldwebel* Hammer with nine men broke out of Sap 10. Reinecke and his men managed to reach the enemy wire obstacles with a few jumps. They quickly overcame the damaged wire and sprang into the enemy trench. The first dugout they encountered was empty and as the men prepared to continue through the French trench they suddenly received hand grenade fire.

Reinecke fired at the enemy with his revolver and shot down two Frenchmen, the others quickly fled back through a communication trench. Three Frenchmen were extracted out of the next dugout the raiders encountered and brought back into the German lines as prisoners by several of the men who had accompanied Reinecke. The *Stosstrupps* continued to advance and Reinecke suddenly saw two additional groups of French soldiers in the trench, which *Stosstrupp* Hammer attempted to hold back through hand grenades.

Vizefeldwebel Hammer and his men proceeded across the open field to circumvent the enemy force however Hammer became severely wounded through several machine gun shots and hand grenade splinters when he and his men threw themselves into nearby shell holes to avoid the French fire. Hammer was forced to relinquish command which was taken over by *Musketier* Heusser.

Meanwhile, *Vizefeldwebel* Reinecke's men attacked the French in the rear and a bitter hand grenade fight broke out. The small French force was slowly pressed back through a communication trench and managed to escape, leaving behind one man dead and several men wounded. The *Stosstrupps* then continued to look for prisoners in nearby dugouts where three additional prisoners were taken and two automatic rifles were captured, probably the M1915 *Chau-Chat*.

All of the events had taken place in a very short period of time and as prisoners had been captured, the two *Stosstrupps* returned to the German lines along with their wounded, the enemy prisoners and captured weapons. The six prisoners, which included one sergeant, belonged to *Régiment d'Infanterie* 143 and *Régiment d'Infanterie* 261. The pluck shown by both leaders and the men who participated in the raid was considered to be exemplary.

The division order on 9 March 1917 stated, among references to all three regiments.

On 8 March ... .. RIR 110 brought back 6 back prisoners from several different regiments and 2 machine guns following a boldly led break-in into the enemy position. I congratulate the three regiments on these striking successes that have provided proof that they have fully matched their duties in defense as well as in the attack. Our division can look forward to coming missions with trust and assertiveness. Signed: Ziethen.[2]

The 5th Army Headquarters also sent a prize of 200 Reich Marks to RIR 110 to be distributed among the patrol participants.

On 8 March the listening post 'Ski Heil' reported unusual enemy activity in front of the post. This was followed almost immediately by enemy artillery, mine and gas fire. An attack did follow by about 60 men who were wearing white snow suits as camouflage, allowing the enemy troops to get close to the German lines. Despite the use of camouflage he raiding party was discovered and a fierce fight broke out at close quarters until the French were finally repulsed without being able to penetrate the German lines.

While small raids and patrols actions managed to bring in enemy prisoners and equipment, a much more ambitious undertaking had been planned for the middle of March by the men of RIR 111. While the troops chosen to participate in the large undertaking were being trained in the rear, life at the front continued in a normal manner in order to deceive the enemy observers. The barbed wire was repaired and reinforced, nightly patrols were sent out and everything appeared to be normal to the casual observer.

What the French did not know was that a model of their trenches had been created at Madeleine farm southeast of Romagne where the assault troops practiced on a daily basis so that when the time came, everyone knew exactly what to do. The undertaking was set for the afternoon of 18 March under the code name '*Lentz*' as it was under the overall command of *Major* Lentz, and actually being executed by *Hauptmann* Bachelin. On the morning of the same day the right connecting regiment, *Landwehr* Infantry Regiment 125, would hold a diversionary undertaking code named '*Wilhelm*' against the enemy position known as the '*Spinne*' in the hopes of confusing the enemy as to the actual location of the main attack.

The goal of the undertaking was the capture of the French trenches in the eastern part of the wood of Avocourt as well as the projecting position connecting to the east and when finished, the captured positions would be integrated into the German lines. If successful and everything went according to plan, the raid would improve the overall German position as well as bring in numerous enemy prisoners. Every aspect of the undertaking had been meticulously planned and practiced until even the smallest details had been accounted for.

The 3rd and 4/R110 became assigned to RIR 111 for the attack and assigned to entrenching work. The 3/R110 under *Leutnant der Reserve* Pommer moved forward on the evening of 17 March from Camp Robinette farm to *Quelle* 1 and accommodated in the 3rd trench where the housing for the men was very cramped. Once the officers and other company leaders had become oriented about the duties assigned to the company, everyone was prepared for the attack.

The 4/R110 under *Leutnant der Reserve* Eggert was accommodated in the 2nd trench at 1.30 a.m. on 18 March in the left battalion sector of RIR 111. While tactically the company was subordinate to *Hauptmann* Räuber, commander of the II/R111, technically they were subordinate to the company commander of the 4/*Pionier* 16. Their task consisted first of all in the installation of a new communication trench, and then manufacturing a new trench-piece in the newly captured enemy trench system.

The preparation bombardment began at 4.10 p.m. on 18 March, which proved to be a total surprise for the enemy. While the guns and *Minenwerfer* began to prepare the break-in location and make it ripe for the attack, at the same time the fire blocked off the target area from receiving any support. The French batteries were also smothered in gas shells in the hope of making them useless for some time to come. The *Stosstrupps*, which were composed of picked men taken from the entire regiment, were ready to spring forth from the fire trench while the *Sturm* Company of the I/R111 waited inside the dugouts of the battle trench. Behind the assault troops stood the 5th and 7/R111 which had been distributed across the width of the attack to be used as hauling troops.

The companies of the II/R111 remained in battle readiness in the left regimental sector and in accordance with the plan they would create a connection to the captured

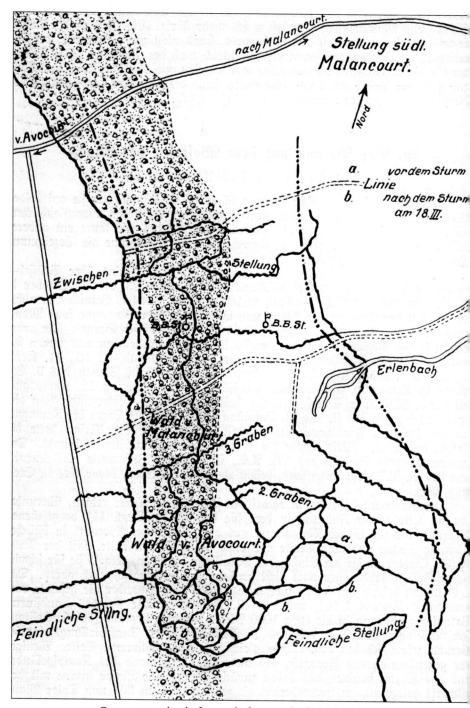

German trenches before and after attack of 18 March 1917.

enemy trenches after the successful attack through the expansion of the saps that had been extended into no man's land. The III/R111 with companies from RIR 109 and RIR 110 served in the second and third lines as security garrisons and as the reserve.

At 4.40 p.m. the artillery and *Minenwerfer* fire was moved to the rear of the enemy trenches and the *Stosstrupps*, each accompanied by *pioniers* and two *Flammenwerfer*, rushed forth. On the right *Leutnants* Scheid and Roth pushed through into the French positions until they reached the southern edge of the wood. They found little opposition and could easily repulse several weak counter thrusts from the right flank while taking cover behind quickly erected barricades.

At 4.35 p.m. the *Stosstrupps* assembled in this misty weather at the break out positions. The artillery battle had reached its highest point at this time. The iron hail came down on the trenches like a hurricane. The Other Ranks waited, trembling with excitement, for the signal to break free. At 4.40 the wire entanglements were cleared and simultaneously the artillery fire was transferred forward. The *Stosstrupps* had broken forth to the attack.

Stosstrupp I, which I commanded, had to break into the enemy line on the right wing and storm against the sap which lay opposite, which was approximately 15 to 20 meters distant. We attempted to cross over the intermediate field at the run. However it was impossible, because we sank into the sticky, soaked earth until up to the ankles. We worked forward at a rapid pace only with great difficulty. There, our own artillery had moved its fire forward and the enemy still fired on our exit position, so we moved into the area free of fire, between the fire belt of our own and that of the enemy's artillery. The French infantry were nowhere to be seen; they still sat in their dugouts. When we arrived close in front of the enemy wire entanglements, we threw two hand grenades into the sap head. The flame-thrower sprayed its 5 meter long stream of flame into it. Then we freely fell upon the sap, however we found it empty and burned out. Down from the embankment we rolled up the communication trench to the rear and reached the first enemy line. This was also empty: nowhere was any opposition shown. *Unteroffizier* Wilhelm Pflüger, 7/R111.[3]

Next to Scheid and Roth the detachment under *Leutnant* Balbach swiftly advanced up to the third enemy trench, where it overran a machine gun and pulled two officers and 30 men out from a dugout. The French, who were occupying a blockhouse at the southeastern edge of the wood, were also soon overpowered. Barricades were quickly erected in each trench section to secure the captured terrain from enemy thrusts from the south. The subsequently following *Stosstrupps* of *Leutnants* Geissinger and Kotthaus immediately received enemy machine gun fire coming from the east just as the men left the German trenches. Despite this fire, the *Stosstrupps* crossed no man's land and entered the French position in the wood. As the *Stosstrupps* came upon a number of French pockets of resistance, each one was systematically destroyed and the advance continued. Once the main opposition had been eliminated, *Leutnant* Geissinger and his men cleared the trench at the eastern edge of the wood which led to the south.

Without being detained, we went in a rapid pace across the ground to the second French trench. When we were still about 15 meters distant from it, the blue-gray enemy suddenly emerged, steel helmet next to steel helmet. It was about 12 to 15 Frenchmen, the entire garrison of a dugout. Standing upon the open field, we closed about the enemy in a semicircle and immediately opened a hand grenade battle. It was an unequal struggle, which was conducted on both sides with considerable obstinacy. However the enemy had almost all of the advantages. He was in fact very surprised, however he was in numbers two to three times superior; furthermore he stood in the trench and was protected through a high wall of earth that had been thrown up, so that he only showed us his helmet. With it he let fly, how I could clearly see a mountain of hand grenades. On the other hand our squad numbered at the moment only 5 men; the *Flammenwerfer* with its entire crew and 2 hand grenade carriers had gotten themselves lost on the way. Our reserve of hand grenades was very limited. Yet before the battle had led to any decision, I was, as the first to expend my last hand grenade. I threw myself on the ground and deliberated on what I should do. Going back was impossible for us, because the successful execution of the undertaking would be strongly threatened on the right wing. Desperately I turned to the rear and looked for help. However the *Sturm* Company still did not come.

Finally the *Flammenwerfer* appeared behind us on the right. The crew immediately recognized our threatened situation and here from the side released a stream of flames upon the enemy, without it however being able to reach them. The impression on the enemy however was so shattering that they all stood up and left, escaping to the rear. I jumped away over the enemy trench and attempted to catch the enemy; however I didn't succeed, because he already had a large lead. There suddenly *Unteroffizier* Schlosser (11th Company?) approached here from the left. At a distance of 20 meters, standing freehand, he placed his rifle site on the rearmost of the fleeing Frenchmen. The enemy recognized the danger that threatened him from two sides; he raised his hands in the air and gave up. However his comrades escaped. *Unteroffizier* Schlosser and the *Flammenwerfer* now looked to obtain a connection to the middle, and vanished forthwith in the tangle of trenches. *Unteroffizier* Wilhelm Pflüger, 7/R111.[4]

The various French access routes which ran through the wood became blocked off through barricades and manned by small groups of German soldiers. With the flank secure, *Leutnant* Kotthaus rolled up the first enemy trench in a length of about 300 meters, continuing to advance until the hand grenades ran out. The deeper Kotthaus and his men advanced, the stiffer the enemy resistance grew as French reinforcements were rushed forward to the threatened sector. *Leutnant* Kotthaus and his men, now without the most critical close combat weapon, the hand grenade, blocked off the captured trench section with a barricade and kept the enemy at bay from behind their makeshift defensive position.

In the meantime my people had taken possession of a French machine gun that the fleeing crew had left behind. The gun was completely set up, a charger strip had been put in, but it had not been able to fire. None of us had any notion of the danger that had threatened us during the hand grenade battle. Only the right wing man of my detachment had been able to see the machine gun. He had also attempted to report his observations to me through shouting during the fighting; however his voice was smothered in the hellish noise of the artillery battle.

Without thinking too long, we carried the machine gun to in the front at the nearby wood edge. With it we now fell into a mine crater because a large German mine had exploded close next to us so that we had been thrown into the crater from the air pressure. There we attempted to bring the captured machine gun into action in order to be able to use it in defense during an enemy counterattack. Despite all efforts it was in vain; the gun appeared to have a jam and was therefore in the moment completely worthless as a fighting method for us.

While we still deliberated about what to do, if to remain defenseless lying at the wood edge or to go back, *Leutnant* Scheidt came running over here from the right. He was completely alone and had apparently dared to go too far to the right. He was happy when he found a connection with us again, however he left to establish the same further to the left to the troops in the middle. Almost in the same moment our infantry company finally came up with fixed bayonets. They created a support behind us and began to dig in. We were given a few sacks of hand grenades from our comrades and could now look forward with confidence at the further development of the battle.

There, as I didn't know exactly if we had already reached the point that were to occupy for the protection of the infantry, I decided to proceed further and roll up the communication trench, which moved from the wood edge up the hill in the direction on the large highway to Avocourt. We left the machine gun in the crater and we worked along to the edge of the wood here through the communication trench. On the way *Unteroffizier* Faller (I Battalion) with one man from his squad called us over to him. Faller, a giant of a man from Gestalt, was an excellent soldier and whose chest was already then decorated with the Iron Cross I Class. We began to roll up this trench together, Faller inside the trench and we down from the embankment.

On the ascent of the bleak and open hill there was no adversary to be seen anywhere. The artillery fire from both sides went away above us. The enemy infantry and their machine guns in the rearward positions first of all were silent; then however fire raids were placed from both sides. We instinctively jumped into the trench. Yet my most skillful and most audacious hand grenade thrower, *Musketier* Schickinger from the 7th Company, received a head shot on the embankment and silently sank down. I considered him to be dead. We left him lying there and rolled up the trench further. *Unteroffizier* Wilhelm Pflüger, 7/R111.[5]

In about 10 minutes from the beginning of the assault, the *Stosstrupps* had completely fulfilled their task and, as it had been drilled at the practice works so many times, occupied the points they had been directed to take. In some cases the *Stosstrupps* had advanced deeper into the enemy lines than had been required under the plan. This was mainly due to the loss of orientation in the badly damaged terrain.

Immediately behind the *Stosstrupps* followed the *Sturm* companies in two to three waves that had been reinforced through additional machine guns. At the right wing the 1/R111 under *Leutnant* Koch had quickly penetrated into the second enemy trench, where they surprised the garrison who were mostly still inside their dugouts and only ran into individual opposition which were quickly overwhelmed.

Going over a dead enemy we reached the next trench position, which ran parallel to the hill crest. We curved to the right, however also here there was no enemy to see. The position was empty. About 30 meters to the left of us stood a small gun without a crew. We held a counsel of war as to what we should do. As with a jolt we firmly determined that we only had about a few hand grenades. Our situation was grave, because we were alone on the hill; our infantry entrenched far behind in the wood. We could easily become isolated. We had dearly wanted to bring the gun with us, but it was impossible, because it was too heavy and placed too deep in the soft ground.

While we still remained and talked, a French hand grenade suddenly flew into the middle of us and remained lying close in front of my left foot. However, there was no enemy to be seen anywhere; presumably he had hidden himself in a shell crater. The hand grenade exploded, a splinter tore my left knee joint in a length of 12 centimeters. All of the remaining comrades remained unwounded.

We clearly recognized now that we had thrust far past the specified goal. Therefore we were immediately determined to go back until by the wood edge. With quiet steps we moved slowly back, without being pursued or becoming taken under fire. On the way we found our comrade Schickinger again. *Musketier* Kilian from my detachment (7th Company) had remained behind with him, and had moved him into the trench and with it determined that he was not dead, but was severely wounded. The bullet had drilled through his temple and smashed his jaw. We took the severely wounded comrade back with us.

Behind the edge of the wood we bumped into our infantry again, which were digging-in under heavy artillery fire. The Other Ranks worked so hard that the sweat poured from their faces. I reported to *Leutnant* Scheidt about our advance and my wound. Then I took leave from him and my good comrades. I should never see *Unteroffizier* Faller again; he already died a hero's death a half hour later when he tried to carry back a captured machine gun. Schickinger entrusted me to the custody of comrades for the further transport to the rear. I made my way to the medical dugout and went back on the same road that we stormed forward on. *Unteroffizier* Wilhelm Pflüger, 7/R111.[6]

At the subsequent 4/R111 under *Leutnant* Beyle the first storm wave consisting of Platoons Krämer and Dahlbeck overpowered several dugouts that had not been damaged or destroyed in hand grenade fighting. The company moved forward via the captured blockhouse until it had reached the southeastern edge of the wood. The 2/R111 under *Leutnant* Holzhauser ran into fierce resistance when penetrating into the enemy trench in the corner of the wood. The first platoon was under the command of *Vizefeldwebels* Müller and Klatte. When Klatte and part of the platoon went to the left to look for the connection to the neighboring troops, he became wounded. However, his men drove the enemy back in an easterly direction and then, as they broke out from the edge of the wood, they reached a line about 50 to 100 meters in front of it.

The left wing company, the 3/R111, under *Leutnant* Beck, pushed forth through the forward most French trench with its right group until they reached the barricade being held by *Stosstrupp* Kotthaus. Suddenly, the French launched a surprise counterattack against the barricade and forced the defenders to evacuate approximately 100 meters of the trench. *Stosstrupp* Kotthaus and the 3/R111 finally managed to stabilize the situation and create a new barricade where the enemy advance was stopped.

About 5 p.m. green light balls went high into the sky, a signal that the overall goal of the raid had been obtained. Numerous French prisoners poured back to the *Wartburg*, where they were assembled near the command post of the III/R111 where they became led to the rear. The *Sturmtrupps* who accompanied the prisoners could not stay with them any longer. It was critical that they immediately return to the new position and help to rebuild the captured line for defense.

While the majority of the fighting was over, there was always the threat of a French counterattack at any moment. Also, the numerous wounded men as well as prisoners still needed to make their way across the shattered terrain that was under heavy shell fire, a daunting task for anyone, especially if they were wounded.

When I tried to climb out of the former French sap head in order to reach our old exit position, a party of French appeared in the intermediate field at a distance of about 20 steps. It was approximately 12 to 14 men that came straight toward me from our exit position. I was so surprised that the blood froze in my veins. I had not expected any help; also I could not call any here, because my voice would be unheard in the noise of the artillery battle. My reserve of hand grenades was depleted. The only weapon remaining to me was a pistol that was being carried hanging about the neck by telephone wire. I had a few shots inside it and was resolved to defend my life to the very last.

I demanded that the French go back into the German trench in their tongue. However they did not heed my shout and came anxiously closer to me. I raised the pistol high and pulled on the trigger; however no shot came out, because I had, as I later determined, forgot to release the safety in the excitement. In desperation I shouted toward the French again and showed the direction to them with the pistol. Thereupon the enemy remained standing, turned around and vanished into the German trench in a few seconds. Now I first saw that my enemy had already given up had and carried behind here a severely wounded Frenchman.

I carefully followed them and I allowed them to bind me in our exit position with an emergency bandage. On the route to the bandaging dugout in the former second German trench I ended up in the communication trench in strong artillery fire and looked for protection in an abandoned tunnel entrance. Six French prisoners, who had been sent back without escorts had also escaped in this dugout in order to find cover. We talked together, they offered me cigarettes and finally, when parting from me, with the words: '*Pour nous la guerre est finie*' (For you the war is over.) *Unteroffizier* Wilhelm Pflüger, 7/R111.[7]

The new line held by the 3/R111 connected with the 2/R111 and then continued to the old German position using a former French sap until the old German line and the captured French position could be joined together; this was being accomplished as the fighting took place. Three minutes after zero hour the platoons of the 3/R110 left their dugouts under strong enemy artillery fire and moved forward through the German trenches until the men were out in the open in front of the old German front line. The men immediately went to work creating three new communication trenches between the position of RIR 111 and the newly captured line taken by the *Stosstrupps*.

The work performed by the 3rd and 4/R110 was hindered greatly by French barrage fire, heavy rain and then darkness. Despite these obstacles, the men persevered in their tasks and completed everything required on time. By daybreak of the following day the companies were taken back into the 2nd 3rd trench. In the following night the three communication trenches started by the 3/R110 were completed and a fourth was started.

Once the fighting had died down, the French dugouts were thoroughly searched for any supplies or hidden enemy troops. The French dugouts were shallow and simply covered with large tree trunks, which offered some protection against light shells and rifle fire but were death traps if struck by medium or heavy shells. The dugouts searched contained large quantities of food, including the rarely seen white bread, a delicacy enjoyed by the raiding party, as well as a large amount of wine and spirits.

When darkness fell, the French forces quickly moved forward toward the captured position in order to determine just what had been lost to the Germans and what still remained in French possession. The French artillery which had been inactive, in part because they were unsure of where friend or foe was located now began to actively bombard the newly captured trenches as well as the approach routes. For the returning wounded men, the night would be long and dangerous.

At 6.15 I came into the medical dugout. At first two or three wounded arrived there. However already about 8.00 p.m. It was overfilled with wounded to such a degree so that all that could still moderately walk had to be evacuated. We formed a squad together in order to go to the Wounded Assembly area situated further in the rear. However the artillery fire already blew our squad apart after a few moments.

For hours I was lost alone in the destroyed woods, falling from one shell crater into the other and finally lost all orientation in the darkness of the night. Toward midnight I finally reached the battle headquarters of the connection officer, *Leutnant* Linnebach. In a comradely manner this officer, who had come from the 7th Company, gave me his orderly, who had formerly belonged to my Group. I hoped that with the support to be able to reach the collection point. However while underway the function of the wounded leg failed completely, so that I could not go one more step. There the physically weaker comrade lugged me on his back by summoning up his entire strength to the large blockhouse dugout, which had been furnished as a wounded assembly area. It was possibly about 1.00 a.m. when we arrived there. Schickinger also became delivered there an hour later; he was conscious but however could not speak. On the next day the transport to the hospital occurred. *Unteroffizier* Wilhelm Pflüger, 7/R111.[8]

The enemy shelling made it difficult for the 7th and 8/R111 to carry the previously prepared construction materials and ammunition to the new front line because the exit positions for the assault soon lay under a strong bombardment. The hauling troops with their heavy loads could find little cover on their journey toward the front but did not allow the heavy shell fire to deter them. Despite suffering losses the majority of the men arrived safely at the new front with the much needed supplies.

The two companies from RIR 110 worked diligently on the connection trenches to the old German position. As the work was completed the commander of the I/R111 gradually obtained an overview of the exact course and the occupation of the new line. It was quickly determined that the connection between the 1st and 4/R111 at the right wing in the wood terrain had been lost. In the evening the 9/R111 became inserted into the gap and the line was continuous once again.

The work on the trenches and the movement of troops was carried out under the protection of safeguards which held and occupied the barricades erected by the blocking troops. Hand grenade fights occurred repeatedly during the night at the barricades with strong enemy patrols which ran up against them in vain. The garrisons at the barricades were effectively supported through artillery fire that could be quickly called up through the newly laid telephone cables. Time after time the French patrols came under well placed barrage fire and were forced to withdraw. The connection Company, the 11/R110, also became involved in the defense against French counterattacks on 18 March and brought in six enemy prisoners.

Organized enemy counterattacks did not take long to appear. On the morning of 19 March the old German position like the newly captured position came under powerful artillery fire and, about 9.30 a.m., approximately three French companies appeared in the Franzosen Mulde, south of Avocourt wood, advancing against the right wing of the new position. The telephone cables that had been laid down during the attack had all been cut in the French artillery fire. The fog was so dense that the light signals used to contact the batteries could not be seen and the defensive barrage fire had to be called up using horn signals.

Despite the delay contacting the batteries the 1/R111 with parts of the 9/R111, supported through flanking machine guns, managed to repulse the enemy attack while it was still in front of the unfinished trench. Additional French attacks on this day were not able to become developed in the accurately placed barrage fire from the German batteries. Once the fog had lifted, the light signals could be seen by the observers and the batteries quickly responded to every request.

In the following night an enemy patrol moving through Avocourt wood toward the 1/R111 was spotted and quickly taken under fire. *Wehrmann* Bailer, *Ersatz Reservist* Schätzle and *Reservist* Boschert went out of their trench and brought back two wounded prisoners, who belonged to a new French division, considered to be a sign that the assault had caused so many losses that new troops had to be utilized to garrison the enemy lines.

With the overall situation returning to normal following the raid some of the troops could be returned to their parent regiments. At midnight on 20 March the 4/R110 was moved back into the camp at Robinette farm and rejoined the I/R110. The losses to the 4/R110 during the raid were extremely small, one man killed and one man wounded. The 3/R110 remained under the control of RIR 111 for a short time longer. In the night from 20/21 March the company was ordered to be alarm ready in the 3rd trench because of an anticipated enemy counterattack. When nothing occurred, the men were allowed to get some rest.

With no sign of any fresh enemy counterattacks the I/R111 which had borne the main weight of the fighting of the last days, could also be extracted in the night of 20/21 March for a well-deserved rest. On 21 March the 3/R110 was taken back into the Intermediate position of RIR 111 and arrived back to the RIR 110 on the morning of 24 March. From the evening of 17 March until early on 20 March the men had been without anything to drink. Despite the hardships and enemy fire, the 3/R110 only lost three men wounded.

With the relief of the I/R111 the forward line of the regiment became divided into six company sectors. On the right was the III/R111, on the left the II/R111. On the morning of 22 March the 7/R111 managed to improve the captured position even further in a surprise coup. Acting on his own, *Leutnant* Fritzsche with a few men from his compan made a rapid advance across the new no man's land and penetrated the French trench abou 100 meters from the intersection of the new German front line with the new French lin Fritzsche and his men captured an automatic rifle and quickly erected barricades on botl sides of the captured position.

While normally such an exploit was restricted to capturing a few prisoners or enem weapons and equipment. In this case, Fritzsche was determined to hold on to his prize. Witl men assigned to protect both barricades, other men quickly began to prepare the trench fo defense as well as create a new communication trench back to the German position. The 7 R111 was able to complete these tasks and before too long the newly captured position wa integrated into the German defenses. By his actions, Fritzsche had advanced the Germar trench to a more favorable situation and had rounded off a sharp projecting corner of the German front line at the southeastern edge of the wood. The men had exerted all of thei strength while digging out this new battle trench in an astonishingly rapid time so that or the morning of 23 March a defensible line existed, complete with wire obstacles.

Fritzsche and his men had received some support in their endeavor once headquarters had learned what happened. In the night from 22/23 March the enemy made attempt to recapture the lost section of trench and attempted to disturb the work of the 7/R11 through hand grenades and machine gun fire. The 4/R110 company was recalled to the front and was assigned to protect the work being performed. Because of the narrow dugout that currently existed, the largest part of the Other Ranks had to sit on the stairways anc were provided with insufficient quantities of uncooked rations which had to be preparec by the Other Ranks as best they could. Fortunately the company was not needed and coulc eventually be returned to the regiment.

The large undertaking by the men of RIR 111 had been completely successful, in part due to the full cooperation between the infantry and artillery as well as the supporting troops. The shortcomings of the former position were eliminated with the capture of the French position. Not only had the men of the 28th Reserve Division gained excellent observation into the enemy rear terrain, the enemy had been denied any observation into the *Erlenbach Grund*. In addition to the improvement of the German position, four French officers and 211 Other Ranks had been captured and brought back as prisoners.

The statements made by many of the French prisoners indicated that the French had already suffered heavy losses in the preparation fire. In addition to the prisoners, 15 machine guns, numerous other weapons, ammunition, equipment as well as important documents were also taken. An artillery piece that was in position at the wood edge was overrun. However, the gun could not be recovered due to French fire, and it therefore had to become blown up.

The losses on the German side had been relatively small, yet with each old soldier lost the regiments and the division grew ever weaker. In the *Stosstrupps* nine men had been killed, one officer, *Leutnant* Roth, and 18 men were wounded. In the *Sturm* Companies 17 men were killed, one officer, *Leutnant* Beyle and 80 men were wounded.

Some of the losses were made up with the arrival of fresh replacement troops, but once again the quality and quantity of the new men left much to be desired. On 30 and 31 March 100 men arrived at RIR 109 each day from the 28th Reserve Division Recruit Depot. The month had come to an end and despite the cold weather, with alternating snow and rain storms, the health of the men was good. At the beginning of April 99 more men arrived at the regiment as replacements from home.

While the undertaking was small by the standards of fighting in the Great War, like the numerous raids held on the Somme, it required an immense amount of planning, resources and determination if it were to succeed. The process began with detailed reconnaissance of the enemy position from the air and from the ground in order to determine the situation of the enemy dugouts, machine guns, *Minenwerfer* and batteries that could become dangerous during the raid.

The target areas for the German batteries, *Minenwerfer* and machine guns had to be determined exactly, and the fire must become regulated to the minute. The routes of the *Stosstrupps* and *Sturm* Companies had to be studied in detail and thoroughly practiced, so that every trench piece becomes clear to the men and the troops would not hinder one another during the attack

Reliable communications were a necessity which included telephones, light signals, horns and other means. Ammunition replacement, secure positioning of food and medical supplies and the stockpiles of necessary construction materials had to be prepared well beforehand. Finally, in the end what remained was the resolve and determination of the men because any undertaking against the enemy was a leap in the dark, where the end result could not be guaranteed. For RIR 111 the undertaking on 18 March had demonstrated that the old attack spirit was still present and it also formed a harsh training ground for the new replacements. In the end, the successful raid was fully acknowledged by all superiors and numerous awards were conferred to the participants.

An experience of the war had taught that the part of capturing an enemy position often placed smaller demands on the troops than the strain of enduring in the revenge fire and the defense against the inevitable counterattacks. The I/R111, which on 25 and 26 March had moved into the captured position once again, was allowed to return to the rear on 28 March under snow and rain storms during a violent bombardment by guns of all calibers and mine throwers. The forward trench, particularly at the eastern edge of the wood was almost leveled, and several mined dugouts were buried.

The French fire was apparently being used to clear a path for a nightly undertaking against the captured position. Following the period of heavy fire, French troops advanced at different positions against the middle and left battalion sector, the 3rd and 4/R111, without being able to penetrate anywhere in the German defenses due to the intense infantry defensive fire. For the most part the enemy troops remained lying in no man's land in the barrage fire of the German batteries. The reciprocal artillery fire continued over the next days and further attempts to attack followed at the beginning of April.

On 5 April the enemy bombardment increased too considerable violence. Movements and troop accumulations were recognized in the enemy trench in the early afternoon which became smashed to pieces through annihilation fire from the German batteries. The enemy's destructive and blocking fire placed on the regimental sector continued in unabated strength throughout 6 April. Losses began to increase under the weight of fire and in addition to other men, *Leutnant* Geissinger, the trusted *Stosstrupp* leader from 18 March, and leader of the 4/R111 became severely wounded.

The defenses created following the successful German raid had already become fully established so when the French infantry attacked three times against the lost trenches, each time on a wider front than the previous attack, between 6 p.m. and 10.30 p.m., they met an unwavering defense. Each enemy attack broke down completely in the rifle and machine

(Author's collection)

gun fire and in the well-placed barrage fire of the artillery. Only at individual places did it come to hand grenade fighting which were all eventually repulsed without the French ever entering the German positions.

After these failures the French finally gave up trying to recapture the lost terrain. The men of RIR 111 could finally hand over the position intact in the nights of 13/14 and 14/15 April to the men of IR 13 that were replacing them. RIR 110 had also been preparing for a large undertaking that was to have taken place in April. Daily assault training and instruction took place in a replica of the attack goal that had been created by Robinette farm, when on 11 April the message arrived that the division was being sent to another location and was being relieved from the position.

The time spent on the Verdun front by the 28th Reserve Division was drawing to a close. On 12 April RIR 109 was relieved from the front line by the men of RIR 55 and in the next few days the 28th Reserve Division moved into the vicinity of Noircourt. The fighting by Verdun in the hard winter of 1916/1917 was considered a serious apprenticeship for the almost newly reformed regiments of the division. The men of the 28th Reserve Division left the 'Hell of Verdun' as battle hardened troops and it had proved to be a training ground for their proficiency in the new style of fighting on the western front.

The new skills acquired by the men had come at a price. RIR 109 had lost 5 officers and 320 *Unteroffiziere* and Other Ranks while in front of Verdun, many of whom were buried on the Maas heights. 12 men from Reserve *Sanitäts* Company 14 were among them, who bravely went out into the open during attacks to selflessly help their comrades and where many had fallen victim to shell fire. *Sanitäts Unteroffizier* Hassler, 7/R109, stood out in particular in his actions until he was wounded by a shell splinter in the Toni sap. RIR 110 and RIR 111 had also lost a considerable number of men during this time, but it could be said that the proficiency of the men in these regiments was far higher than it had been when the men first arrived at Verdun.

What new adventures and experiences faced the men of the 28th Reserve Division was still unknown as was the next destination of the division.

Notes

1. Bachelin, op. cit., pp. 312-315.
2. Greiner & Vulpius, op. cit., pp. 164.
3. Bachelin, op. cit., pp. 315-316.
4. Bachelin, op. cit., p. 316.
5. Bachelin, op. cit., pp. 316-317.
6. Bachelin, op. cit., pp. 317-318.
7. Bachelin, op. cit., p. 318.
8. Bachelin, op. cit., p. 319.

28th Reserve Division
On the Chemin des Dames

Following a short journey by train, the men of the 28th Reserve Division arrived at the new sector located by the Winterberg near Craonne, the scene of a major French offensive. The division was on the Chemin des Dames that was being held by the 7th Army, also called '*das schlafende Armee*' [the sleeping army] by the men on the Western front. The overall trench system that greeted the Baden troops was more reminiscent of what they had known 1914. The area had seen little heavy fighting until this point in the war and was normally occupied by *Landwehr* and *Landsturm* units.

This sector was part of the area attacked by the French on 16 April 1917 in what became called the *Bataille du Chemin des Dames*, under the command of General Robert Nivelle, Commander-in-Chief of the French Army. Nivelle's plan called for a combined Anglo-French offensive that would smash through the German lines within 24 hours. Due to a number of different circumstances, this goal was not achieved and the fighting between the opposing sides continued through the end of April and into May. The portion of the line the 28th Reserve Division had been sent was the focus of the attacks by the French Tenth Army in what became known as the Nivelle Offensive.

RIR 109 being transported by train. (*Das Reserve-Infanterie-Regiment Nr. 109 im Weltkrieg 1914 bis 1918*)

It was easy to see why the French had chosen this location for a major attack. However, while it was a quiet sector with second and third class troops, the terrain was difficult to overcome and provided a serious impediment against an attack from either side of the line. The units holding the sector by the Winterberg had been hard hit in the opening enemy offensive and had suffered huge losses and yet still prevented an enemy breakthrough. It was now critical that the regiments holding the front line become relieved as soon as possible, hence the importance of the arrival of the 28th Reserve Division.

RIR 109 was positioned in the center of the sector assigned to the 28th Reserve Division, on the right was RIR 111 located on the Winterberg next to the 1st Guard Division, and on the left was RIR 110. In the early morning hours of 20 April RIR 110 relieved *Ersatz* Infantry Regiment 28 from the front line. The III/R110 occupied Sector West, the II/R110 occupied Sector East. Despite the constant enemy fire the relief took place without any losses or incidents. During the same night, the I/R110 moved into the two trenches that made up the artillery protection position east of the Corbeny-Berrieux road, up until Corbeny wood. The advance was very difficult because of the darkness and poor condition of the roads, however the I/R110 also arrived in the new position without losses. The companies were then billeted in the open in small woods and trenches as there were no dugouts present.

The greatest part of the front line trench as well as the connection routes had been destroyed by the enemy mine and shell fire at the start of the offensive. Most of the men took cover in any shelter they could find or create in a short amount of time. There were no dugouts located in the support trenches and in the forward line only weak dugouts had existed, however for the most part the entrances had been pressed in under the weight of fire. Even if they had been intact, they were far too shallow to be any protection against even enemy field guns. They were nothing like the deep mined dugouts the men had created on the Somme.

Due to the heavy fire and constant enemy observation no one could leave the holes by day; all traffic inside the trenches and in the approach routes could only take place at night. Almost all the wire obstacles had been destroyed; there were no stockpiles of food or construction materials at all. All in all the men of RIR 110 did not find the position very inviting and did not inspire much trust that it could be held against a determined enemy attack. However, it was pointed out that *Ersatz* Infantry Regiment 28 had not lost a single foot of ground to the enemy assault. The men of RIR 110 were determined that their regiment would also hold the crater position at any price.

During the deployment in the new sector the three battalions of RIR 109 each took over six light machine guns from Bavarian RIR 15. The *Minenwerfer* located in the front lines were under constant artillery fire and as such could not be used. The fighting value of the position was not considered to be very good. On the right flank of the regiment, facing the Winterberg, the French had created new positions at a slightly higher altitude and as such completely dominated the right flank of the regiment.

The French also controlled the area just behind the heights of the Winterberg, and were turning the position into a fortress using the existing defenses. The trenches held by RIR 109 were under fire from enemy 42cm howitzers, a very disagreeable situation under any circumstances. The other parts of the regimental front, while not as exposed as the right wing, also extended out toward the French lines and were considered to be vulnerable to an enemy attack.

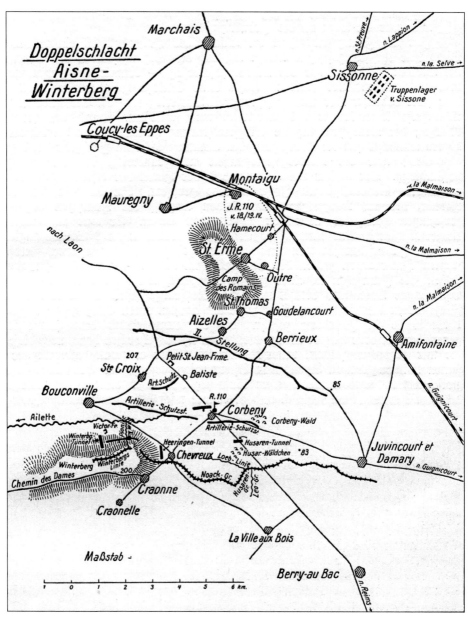

Winterberg: 28th Division positions.

The entire position occupied by the regiment was inadequate in providing any protection against artillery fire. There were no mined dugouts in the left sector, only concrete blockhouses, called mousetraps that offered any protection against the destructive fire of the heavy guns. The blockhouses were not considered any better than if a man sought cover in the open in shell craters. The French occupied the rear slope of the hill in front of the regiment and could accurately direct fire at the German positions. This situation was made worse when numerous short shots fell on the German troops from their own guns when trying to hit the nearby enemy lines.

The second line was also covered by heavy enemy fire and all of the dugouts had been destroyed. The trenches were all very shallow, in part also under water. There were no wire obstacles protecting any of the trenches and there were few traverses, allowing the effect of a single enemy shell to be amplified inside the straight trenches. Almost all of the connections to the rear went over open ground and toward the front were funneled through two useless communication trenches.

The French attacks had even caught the local civilian population unaware. The civilians had only just been evacuated a few days before the 28th Reserve Division arrived. The French artillery continued to cover the rear areas with fire in the hope of inflicting losses on German reserves and troop concentrations. The German guns did what they could to reply to the French fire but they were outnumbered in light, medium and heavy artillery. The Germans did make use of one new weapon, the recently arrived *Gelbkreuzmunition* [Yellow Cross ammunition].[1]

The last regiment of the division to take over a sector in the front line was RIR 111. The regiment was assembled for deployment and moved into the position in the night from 20/21 April where it relieved Bavarian RIR 4 at the Winterberg north of Craonne. The relief required the entire night due to the difficult advance in the hilly and forested terrain and because of the enemy fire that fell on the column as it moved forward. The II/R111 under *Hauptmann* Räuber moved into Sector West, whose battle line moved by the northern edge of Craonne approximately to the heights of the Chemin des dames. Craonne had fallen into enemy hands in the fighting of the previous days, and as a result the 7th and 8/R111 under *Leutnants* Fritzsche and Nerpel occupied the former German second position which was already badly damaged from French shell fire.

The men of RIR 111 found a few, large subterranean tunnels and cellars which were still intact and which offered some protection against the ever-present enemy fire. The distance to the enemy line amounted to 30 to 40 meters in some places, which required the sentries to remain alert in case of any sudden enemy attack.

RIR 111 found itself in an unfavorable position because the line of the right neighboring regiment, *Garde Grenadier* Regiment Kaiser Franz, had been pressed back in the French attack with the exception of the Winterberg plateau, which rose up 60 to 70 meters in the terrain in an expanse of about 500 meters. All connection with *Garde* Grenadier Regiment Kaiser Franz were maintained through patrols only, and the French could overlook the right flank of RIR 111 from their saps that had been driven forward.

The *Wanka Linie* was in the sector of the II/R111, it was located on the Winterberg and existed only out of shell holes with few recently started mined dugouts. It was the 2nd position and was occupied by the 5/R111 under *Leutnant* Meichelt. Behind, on the northern edge of the Winterberg, was the 6/R111 under *Leutnant* Better in the similar looking *Winterberglinie*.

Heavily armed trench sentry wearing body armour for exposed positions.
(*Das Reserve-Infanterie-Regiment Nr. 109 im Weltkrieg 1914 bis 1918*)

There was not enough room to accommodate both companies in the trenches so a portion of the companies were housed in the Winterberg tunnel as the reserve. This tunnel was driven into the mountain approximately 260 meters deep, which, still unfinished, only had two emergency exits at the southern end. An air chute equipped with pumps supplied air for the complex.

The battalion staff of the II/R111 lay in a dugout near the front line. The I/R111 under *Hauptmann* Bachelin defended Sector East. The 1/R111 under *Leutnant* Koch established the connection with the II/R111 at the southeastern slope of the Winterberg in the position called the Bastion; on the left of it was the 3/R111 under *Leutnant* Weissensee which formed the left wing of the regiment, which extended up to the intersection of the trench with the Craonne-Chevreaux road, where a tenuous connection existed to the neighboring RIR 109.

The III/R111 under *Hauptmann* Liehl occupied the positions that reached up to the artillery protection line west of Corbeny in the night of 20/21 April. Some men were fortunate in finding a few still intact dugouts where they spent the night, the rest of the men remained in the open and wet trenches. On 21 April two platoons from the 10/R111 under *Leutnant* Ada moved forward to the right regimental border on the *Winterberglinie* and in the *Münchener Graben* that led to the *Wanka Linie*.

Many of the companies used the fourth platoon as carrying troops to supply the front

Nachrichten troops with heliograph device, RIR 111. (Author's collection)

line. It was very difficult work crossing the swampy ground under enemy fire from high explosive shells, shrapnel and gas and as a result many losses occurred.

In the sector of RIR 109 *Offizier Stellvertreter* Metzner made a number of improvements in the sector communications. He had the destroyed telephone lines replaced by *Nachrichtentrupps* as well as setting up wireless, light signals and earth telegraph stations, runners and messenger pigeon stations. The work by these men would greatly assist the successful defense of the position against enemy attacks. It was quickly determined that messenger pigeons did not perform well under the present conditions and the earth telegraph had no connection to the rear in heavy bombardments. However, a large wireless station in the *Heeringen Stollen* provided good service.

The men of RIR 110 did not have long to wait until they too were the target of an enemy attack. On 20 April the French made the first attacks against the regimental line. Starting from 9.30 a.m. heavy mine and artillery fire lay upon the forward trench, which towards evening increased to the level of drum fire. The right sector battalion command post received so many shells that any traffic in its vicinity was impossible.

Towards 6 p.m. the French attacked the barricade in the vicinity of the old battalion dugout by the *Kabel-Husaren Graben* in the area of the 8/R110 and attempted to roll up the position from there. The attackers succeeded in penetrating into the trench, however they were thrown back again in bitter close combat. At the same time, the enemy attempted a frontal attack against the 6/R110 with about 30 men, supported by two machine guns. This attack was also unsuccessful and the small French force was quickly repulsed in the spirited counterattack by the 6/R110 under *Leutnant der Reserve* Hambrecht.

The French were observed filling up the trenches in front of the III/R110, however no attack developed here because of the promptly deployed barrage fire. Still, the French did have some success by the right neighboring regiment, RIR 15, where French troops managed to penetrate the front line trench. RIR 15 immediately sent over a request for assistance to RIR 110 but before the III/R110 could interfere in the fighting, the trench in the sector of RIR 15 was cleared from the enemy. While the attacks on 20 April were successfully repulsed, the fighting had also resulted in losses in RIR 110: 17 men killed, 2 officers (*Leutnants* Siefert and Senger) and 45 men wounded.

Following the unsuccessful attacks, the French covered the position held by RIR 110 with drum fire, which did not die down until 9 p.m. In the night from 20-21 April the readiness battalion from *Ersatz* Infantry Regiment 28 was relieved through the I/R110, where it was housed in the concrete battery, *Husaren Stollen, Reimser Graben, Strassen Graben* and *Husaren Wäld*. The 2/R110 remained in the artillery protection position, the 3/R110 at the northeastern edge of the village of Corbeny. At 10 p.m. the 1/R110 under *Leutnant der Reserve* Hofheinz was loaned to the II/R110 and took over the *Löblinie* between the *Husaren Graben* and the field railway east of it.

The forward trenches of RIR 110 continued to lay under the heaviest enemy bombardment on 21 April so that not even reports could be carried through the wall of fire. Fortunately the night from 21/22 April proceeded quietly, other than the usual disturbance fire.

22 April began with increased shell and shrapnel fire accompanied by lively aerial activity as the enemy pilots were taking full advantage of the good weather which offered excellent visibility for the observers. In addition, over 30 observation balloons were seen opposite the sector of the 28th Reserve Division. Inevitably, the enemy artillery fire increased during the afternoon as the French fired on the German trench remnants with great accuracy.

The 7.5cm shells crashed there and the sharp ears of the old front fighters could hear the surging and rolling of the 28cm shells here in the general rolling and rumbling. Now everyone holds his breath; now the impact must follow. Where would it hit? Now a dull hit, a crash and burst: Praise God it went right next to them! Earth and stone were thrown as high as a house. Craters 6 meters deep and 12 meters across were torn out. And so it went hours long! Several dugouts were smashed, others were entirely buried with the occupants and even the deepest mined dugouts in part were already pressed in. Finally towards 7.00 p.m. the enemy increased the fire too the greatest intensity, a great whirl of fire lies upon all trenches, now everyone knows, they will now come soon. The trenches in the former Westphalian *Landwehr* and *Braunschweiger* line are filled up. 'Barrage fire!' screams the company leaders, the light balls already climb high, but oh, it is placed too late and doesn't lie on the right position. At 7.30 p.m. the enemy finally pushes forth against our trench, armed with flamethrowers and gas bombs. Now the artillery fire becomes placed to the rear, everyone can exhale now. Our badly frayed, completely exhausted people hurl themselves against the invading enemy with pluck and drive him off with hand grenades in close combat. The *Stosstrupps* of the 6th and 8th Companies could still duly interfere now. The attack is beaten off; the sector is entirely in our hands.

However how the position looks! The entire forward line is leveled; the trench is no longer recognizable. And our brave people! Standing alarm ready at the elevated battle activity for four days, barely having any sleep, they are totally exhausted. Praise is therefore due to the carrying troops. Although the advance route lay under powerful shell and shrapnel fires, undaunted they bring food and ammunition to the front and carried the wounded back. [2]

The I/R110 suffered a bitter loss on 22 April. A former German communication trench, the *Leo Graben*, now belonged to both sides. It lay in the vicinity of the 1/R110, and the trusted leader, *Leutnant* Hofheinz, wanted to personally explore the exact position of the enemy. Hofheinz, along with *Leutnant* Wursthorn and three men from the 1/R110 made their way through the communication trench. An enemy barricade was discovered approximately 400 meters in front of the German *Unteroffiziere* Post. During the advance against the enemy barricade Hofheinz received a stomach shot and his men carried him back to the German position. He died on 23 April in the military hospital at Sissonne, a great loss as he was considered one of the best and bravest officers in the regiment. In addition to *Leutnant* Hofheinz, the regiment suffered 9 men killed, 42 men wounded and 3 men buried on 22 April.

In the night from 22/23 April the battalions received a welcome increase in firepower when the machine gun companies were inserted with their battalions. In the same night the 3/R110 moved forward into the *Reimser Strasse*. At 4 a.m. the 1/R110 reported enemy skirmishers were observed on both sides of the *Leo Graben*; the artillery was quickly alerted to the threat and the enemy attack was unable to develop in the well placed barrage fire. During the entire day of 23 April strong artillery fire of all calibers lay upon all of the trenches. At 7.30 a.m. the enemy attempted an attack against the 6/R110, however the French were thrown back using hand grenades. After a six hour bombardment of the intersection of the *Kabel Graben* and *Husaren Graben* two enemy assault groups advanced against the German barricade at 10 p.m.; they were successfully repulsed in close combat.

In order to determine just what the enemy was up to, several patrols were sent out at night to reconnoiter the enemy lines. One patrol of the III/R110 under the command of *Leutnant* Roser firmly established that the enemy was working on a new trench between the old front line positions and he also brought in a wounded prisoner from *Régiment d'Infanterie* 208. Two patrols held on the following day under the command of *Vizefeldwebel* Albrecht and *Vizefeldwebel* Eisner made the same identification of opposite enemy formation, however because of the German as well as French artillery fire they both returned without any prisoners.

One patrol of the 7/R111 commanded by *Unteroffizier* Menzer succeeded in coming upon a French sentry from behind on 23 April. Menzer surprised a sentry who was coming through a subterranean tunnel which led into a cellar of Craonne. There was a brief struggle with the sentry and one other Frenchman who had appeared, who became shot down. The sentry and the body of the second soldier were brought back into the German trench. With the capture of this prisoner and the insignia from the body of the second man the participation of a new enemy division in the sector was firmly established.

RIR 109 planned a large undertaking in order to also determine if the enemy had

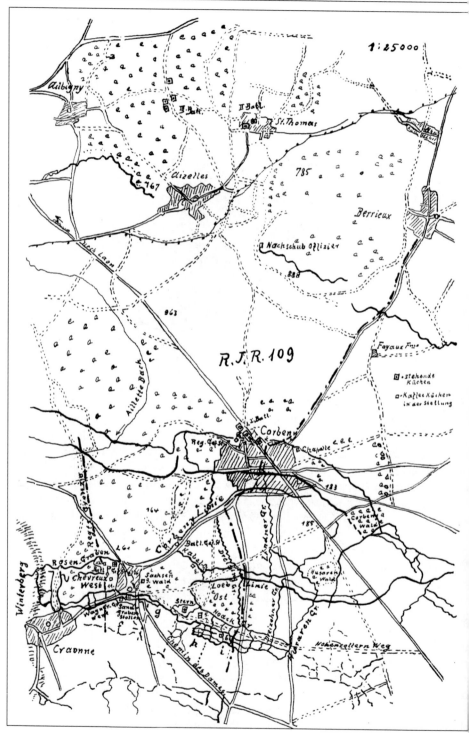

RIR 109 trenches by Corbeny.

brought in fresh assault troops in the regimental sector. Several patrols were sent in the days prior to the planned undertaking in order to determine the exact enemy positions. The patrols from the II and III/R109 established that of the sections of lost trenches, only the Bastion was occupied by the enemy.

The undertaking was scheduled to take place on 24 April under the command of *Hauptmann* Block. The undertaking was prepared through a short but intense bombardment of the Bastion and surrounding areas. Then, *Vizefeldwebel* Quits, 5/R109, advanced against the Bastion with a *Stosstrupp* from his company at 3.30 a.m., however they were unable to reach the position due to severe opposition by the French garrison.

It was decided to make a second attempt against the Bastion and the enemy position was shelled over the course of the day by Group Senden, III/RFAR 29. At 10.30 p.m. Quitz and eight of his men advanced for a second time. This time, Quitz was successful and his small *Stosstrupp* managed to enter the French position and the patrol overcame four enemy soldiers who belonged to the French 66th *Jäger* Battalion, who had only arrived in the position two days before, coming from Alsace. During the withdrawal of the patrol and prisoners *Vizefeldwebel* Quitz was severely wounded by a hand grenade explosion and *Grenadier* Weissenbach was killed. *Grenadiers* Kirrmann and Elsner were singled out for their exemplary behavior during the raid.

During all of this time, the division flank was being protected by several platoons from RIR 111, which formed a regimental border detachment along with one company from Regiment Franz in order to maintain the connection between the two regiments and to block off the position to the right and the left in the event of an enemy break-in. Another platoon lay in the Winterberg tunnel as the sector reserve. The 11/R111 under *Leutnant* Diesner occupied the northern *Pionier Weg* and had assumed the protection of the eastern flank of the regiment. The 12/R111 under *Leutnant* Schweizer was the regimental reserve and was also located in the Winterberg tunnel, where the regimental staff and the staff of the III/R111 had placed their command posts. The 9/R111 under *Leutnant* Stoffler remained in the artillery protection position and was under the control of the commander in charge of the protection position.

The machine guns of the regiment reinforced through the new light MG 08/15 machine guns, which had been taken over in the sector from the previous regiment, were distributed throughout the different trench lines and were considered the mainstay of the defense. The only problem with the machine guns was the lack of sufficient secure positions for the weapons, especially on the Winterberg.

In this distribution, on a front about 1,500 meters wide, RIR 111 expected renewed French assault. There were numerous clues which all pointed to the resumption of the enemy attacks including an increase in enemy aircraft flights, numerous tethered balloons placed opposite the position, new bombardments from batteries, etc. At this time there was also a change in command in RIR 1111 when the regiment received a new commander in place *Major* Lentz who had left the regiment due to illness. *Major* Schüler now took over the full responsibilities of the troops in the regiment.

The men of RIR 111 realized that the successful defense against any enemy attack hinged on remedying the main shortages of the defenses in the shortest possible time. Work on new dugouts proceeded at a feverish rate along with an improvement in the defense in depth by adding new fire trenches. At present, most of the garrison was being housed in a few large mined dugouts which could prove disastrous in the event of a major enemy attack.

The men needed to be distributed evenly across the entire sector if the defensive position was expected to hold.

There were insufficient numbers of communication trenches leading up to the battle line to allow troops to approach unobserved and not become bombarded during daylight hours. In order to correct this shortage, new communication trenches were constructed; earth telegraph positions and pigeon stations were transferred to the control of the staff. A small wireless station was set up inside the Winterberg tunnel and a light signal station was created upon the hill.

The work, which could only be executed at night, became hindered through frequent enemy fire raids, which also impaired supplying the materials needed at the front. Everything, from warm food to ammunition and construction materials needed by the men had to become brought forward along arduous routes, carried forward from St. Erme until St. Croix and from there by hauling troops.

The French had been busily sapping forward against the left wing of Regiment Franz on the right flank of RIR 111 and had finally stopped. The sap was located in a blind spot so that it was difficult to prevent the work through artillery and mine fire. The French had created an excellent exit position for an attack against the German lines, which became increasingly dangerous for the right wing of the II/R111. In order to counter this threat the right wing of the II/R111 became reinforced through additional light and heavy machine guns. Furthermore the regiment formed its own border detachment for the protection of this threatened flank on 24 April under *Leutnant* Diesner consisting of the 10th and 11/R111. The latter company now became moved forward into the Winterberg tunnel. Several machine guns were brought into position on the heights as rear support.

The performance of the troops in the 28th Reserve Division, RIR 110 in particular, was recognized in the division orders of 25 April.

> After the division had been inserted into the position from Craonne-Corbenny after long, hard marches, they succeeded in achieving new successes in short time, under difficult situations.
>
> Repeated enemy attacks broke completely against the position of RIR 110 through the alertness and bravery of the garrison. In bold patrol undertakings all three regiments succeeded in taking prisoners and through the establishment of the enemy force distribution and to demolish the enemy intentions anew.
>
> I am happy that I am able to speak with my infantry of the feeling of the superiority over the enemy in such an outstanding manner. It requires no more indication for the enemy failure than that was denoted through the high expectations of all goals set, insignificant terrain gains; failure of the faith in the tanks, the heaviest losses and no breakthrough.
>
> The realization and the elevated feelings of our successes here as well as on the Aisne as therefore in the Champagne and by Arras would also give us new encouragement. Signed, Ziethen.[3]

Now, after a short period of time in the trenches, the men of RIR 110 were going to be allowed to rest and enjoy a few pleasant days behind the lines. The I and II/R110 remained in the trenches under continuous enemy shelling until the II/R110 could be relieved in the night of 26/27 April by the III/R149. The I/R110 was relieved in the night of 27/28 by the I/R149 as was the III/R110 which was relieved during the night of 27/28 April by he II/R149. The relief of all three battalions went smoothly and without losses because the French artillery and mine fire had diminished significantly since 26 April.

Once out of the trenches the II and III/R110 marched to billets St. Erme and were also billeted in the Wood camp at the foot of the ancient Roman ruins called the *Camp des Romains*. The men were deloused in Sissonne and the equipment became placed in good condition. In the remaining time the men were occupied with the extension of the barracks camp, which became necessary as St. Erme would often be shelled. The total losses to RIR 110 during the time in position from 19 to 27 April during the strongest enemy bombardments and faced with repeated enemy attacks amounted to: 1 Officer, *Leutnant* Hofheinz, 50 men killed, 2 officers, 173 men wounded, 4 men buried.

Not everyone in RIR 110 had a chance to enjoy the brief stay out of the trenches. The I/R110 had arrived in St. Erme between 3 and 4 a.m. on 28 April and became billeted in the cloister, the other Ranks in the rooms and halls of the girls quarters, the officers in the nuns hall. The enjoyment of being able to sleep in real beds with linens did not last very long for the I/R110. At 4 p.m. the I Battalion was alarmed and marched to the 2nd position and occupied the position from the Laon-Reims road until Aizelles inclusive. The I/16 connected to the battalion on the left and became subordinate to *Oberstleutnant* von Bronsart as the commander of the 2nd position. The assignment given to the I/R110 was the extension of the position which barely existed and most importantly the construction of dugouts. The weather was beautiful and therefore there was lively aerial actively on both sides of the line and numerous observation balloons stood in the sky. This resulted in an increase in artillery fire being directed on the men as they worked to create a firm defensive position.

As a result of the relief of RIR 110 from the front line, RIR 111 was forced to extend its front about 250 meters to the left on the night of 26/27 April. With this move the defense of the *Wagnerwerk* fell to the men of the 3/R111. This position consisted of two badly damaged trenches lying very close together, in which few shell proof dugouts existed. The main part of the garrison had to be accommodated behind the position in the southern end of the Heeringen tunnel. One half of the 4/R111 under *Leutnant* Beyle was assigned the Second position, the *Wald Linie*, an extension of the *Wanka Linie* and was given the task of improving and occupying the position. The other half of the 4/R111 was in a readiness position in the vicinity of the battalion command post in the *Pionier Weg*.

The 2/R111 under *Leutnant* Schaber provided the largest part of the men needed for dispatch duty from the relay posts of the regiment up to the command post at Batis farm located on the main Corbeny-Laon road. The runners from the 2/R111 performed their duties under extreme conditions. The terrain the men were required to cross was constantly under enemy fire, however, the runner service never failed to get the messages through. The remainder of the 2/R111 served in the *Pionier Weg* as the reserve.

On 27 April a French patrol attempted to penetrate into the trench of the 7/R111 through the same tunnel by Craonne where the 7th Company had captured several prisoners a few days earlier. The raid was unsuccessful and the French were driven back empty handed. Then, to make sure this did not happen again, the mined dugout was blown up.

On 27 April RIR 109 suffered a great loss when *Hauptmann* Block, the commander of the successful raid held on 24 April, died from wounds he received from the explosion of a *Granatwerfer* that was being fired. Just three days before his adjutant, *Leutnant de Landwehr* Vivell, was also killed, this time from the impact of a high explosive shell. Both men were considered a great loss to the regiment and on 2 May the regiment issued the following order.

> On 24 April 1917, died a hero's death in the true fulfillment of his duty in the forward most line during observation of the enemy: *Leutnant der Landwehr* Vivell, Adjutant of the II Battalion. He belonged to the regiment since July 1916 and had performed excellently in all positions. In his steady courageousness, especially during the storm on Hill 304 on 25 January 1917 and in the following days he afforded excellent service to his battalion. The Iron Cross II Class and the Knight's Cross of the Zähringer Order of the Lion II Class adorned his chest.
>
> He was followed in death on 27 April 1917 by his brave Battalion Commander, *Hauptmann* Block.
>
> *Hauptmann* Block had entered the field with the 28th Reserve Division as the Regimental Adjutant of RIR 110, he was then the leader of our machine gun company and after that a battalion leader in our regiment. He had taken part without interruption in all fighting with distinction in an outstanding performance. *Hauptmann* Block had a proud, cheerful soldier's nature. His outstanding bravery and his fresh daring had become legend. His subordinates, for whose welfare he was always concerned, looked enthusiastically up to him and trusted the intrepid officer, who seemed immune against enemy projectiles. Well-known is his brave defense of Hill 110 in the summer of 1915 with RIR 110, likewise the excellent support that he provided the regimental commander in the great Somme Battle as the leader of the machine gun company, and further in the leadership of the battalion of RIR 111 and RIR 109 in the second Somme battle.
>
> His name will be forever joined with the storm on 304, the 25 January 1917, a day of honour for the regiment, about which His Royal Highness the Grand Duke was personally privileged to tell him a few weeks before. His Majesty the Kaiser had awarded him with the Hohenzollern House medal, the Iron Cross I Class and Iron Cross II Class and His Royal highness the Grand Duke with the Knight's Cross the Zähringer Order of the Lion II Class with Swords and the Military Charles Friedrich Merit medal.[4]

The last days of April passed under very lively aerial activity on both sides. This allowed both the French and the Germans to increase the overall artillery activity along with improved accuracy. This was especially true on the evening of 29 April when St. Thomas Goudelancourt, Aizelles and the roads between these villages were strongly bombarded and gassed.

The sector of RIR 109 also came under particularly heavy fire on 29 April from which several dugouts and blockhouses were completely destroyed. As a result of this bombardment the battle headquarters of the II/R109 had to be transferred to the dugout of Machine Gun No. 10. As there was no space for the battle orderlies inside the small shelter, they had to move back to the position companies in order to find sufficient room. Despite these difficulties the orderlies performed excellent service in the heavy fire, especially *Gefreiter* Dotter who was singled out for his courage and intrepid behavior.

Some chilling news arrived in the evening hours of 30 April when German observation pilots firmly established that enemy tanks were travelling on the road from Pontavert. They apparently had joined other tanks that had been near the front since 16 April. The artillery was notified of this threat and the tanks were taken under bombardment and in part were set on fire. The threat appeared to be postponed at least.

According to statements made by captured officers on 30 April a French attack in a wide expanse was going to take place shortly. The regiments holding the front were quickly notified and elevated battle readiness was ordered for all units. The II and I/R110 were moved from their billets to a hollow east of St. Thomas, where they were placed at the ready on a steep slope. When the expected attack did not take place; the battalions marched back again to St. Erme.

By the end of April many of the French troops holding the former German front line were eventually expelled after several successful counterattacks. All activities such as entrenching, wiring, the construction of dugouts and carrying parties remained under heavy fire and under constant aerial observation during the past 10 days. Many losses occurred when blockhouses were buried or dugouts crushed from the enemy fire. From 19 April to 30 April the II/R109, especially the 5th and 7/R109 suffered 8 dead and 56 wounded. The III/R109 23 dead and 25 wounded.

Moving two battalions from RIR 110 to the hollow east of St. Thomas was repeated on 1 May. The days spent in the second position on this occasion were not especially exhausting for the I/R110 as the enemy fire was bearable, the food was well regulated, and the size of the rations were larger in response to the offensive allowance, and not least of all, the men enjoyed the beautiful spring weather.

At the beginning of May along the front line the enemy fire swelled considerably in intensity on the positions of RIR 111. The heights of the Winterberg and the northern hillside especially became covered with heavy caliber shells. Whatever dugouts that existed or had been started there were soon pressed in. The sandy ground offered little resistance against the heavy shells and many Groups as well as machine gun crews with their weapons were buried. The 5th and 6/R111 positioned in the *Wanka* and *Winterberglinie* suffered heavy losses; among others the company leader of the 5/R111, *Leutnant* Meichelt, was killed

On the night of 1/2 May *Leutnant der Reserve* Jäger and *Unteroffizier* Bleile and eight men from the 10/R109 made a surprise attack against an enemy blockhouse in the French line on the embankment opposite the regimental position and captured two machine guns along with ammunition and returned without suffering any losses. They reported that the enemy garrison had fled at the approach of the patrol.

Enemy pilots continued to be present in large numbers during the day and directed the fire of the French artillery. The artillery targeted a number of key positions in the German lines including the large tunnels created in the position. A 30cm shell impacted the entrance of the *Heeringen* tunnel, fortunately only causing slight damage.

In the night from 2 to 3 May the I/R110 was relieved by the III/R110 and then marched to St. Erme where the battalion was billeted in *Camp des Romains*. In the same night the II/R110 marched to the hill southwest of Petit St. Jean farm and once there it was assigned to protect the right flank of the division artillery.

This proved to be a very unpleasant and dangerous task. The hill occupied by the II/R110 was positioned was clearly seen by the enemy and became strongly bombarded with all calibers because of the numerous German batteries standing in the vicinity. There were no dugouts and the men were forced to take cover in small holes scraped into the ground. Finally, the division commander arrived to view the position and after seeing the conditions he ordered that two companies, the 7th and 8/R110 would return to St. Erme in the evening along with the battalion staff.

RIR 111 also came under increasingly heavy artillery fire and suffered a number of losses. On 3 May two companies had to be replaced by the 12/R111. The men had attempted to create shelters and prepare the shell craters for defense along with parts of the 10th and 11/R111 using every available man. The 5th and 6/R111 became placed into mined dugouts in the *Pionier Weg* where they acted as the regimental reserve while the enemy systematically fired at the northern entrance of the Winterberg tunnel using aircraft and balloon observation.

As a result of this concentrated fire the regimental staff lost two of its best officers who had belonged to the regiment since the beginning of the war. On 3 May *Leutnant* Zwiffelhoffer was killed at the tunnel entrance. He had been the trusted leader of the regimental transport and at the time of his death was the leader of the Communication service. *Offizier Stellvertreter* Knöpfle, a former active *Unteroffizier* in IR 114, an intrepid soldier and the faithful companion of the commanders and adjutants on many dangerous journeys, was also killed.

The French heavy guns were apparently concentrating their fire at the Winterberg tunnel and several direct hits caused the air shaft of the tunnel to collapse. Once that had occurred, staying inside the tunnel became extremely uncomfortable. The air became increasingly close, and the heat was unbearable. The only solution left to supply sufficient air inside the tunnel were two emergency air pumps, but even these did not succeed in improving the situation.

It became so bad inside the tunnel that lingering in the rear parts for any length of time was almost impossible. This meant that the front half of the tunnel had to be exploited under the most cramped conditions. The Other Ranks who occupied the tunnel lay about on the ground and on wooden bunks in the thick dust and haze, many without tunics and shirts in the intense heat despite the ordered battle readiness.

The long awaited enemy attack appeared to be taking place on the afternoon of 3 May when the II/R111 observed troop accumulations in the enemy trench. However, the possible enemy attack was prevented through annihilation and barrage fire that had been requested. A few French advances that did occur were completely repulsed in heavy defensive fire.

The days before the French attack of 4 May were summed up in the diary of *Unteroffizier* Menzer, 7/R111.

> On 2 May heavy French artillery fire. The forward most German position was completely destroyed however on 3 May the French infantry attack was refused under the heaviest enemy losses. Continuation of the heavy enemy bombardment. Mined dugouts were badly damaged over and over and dug out over and over, and after each hit were reinforced with wood beams that were lying around.[5]

After a comparatively quiet night heavy fire began about 10 a.m. on 4 May, directed by enemy aircraft. The main weight of enemy fire appeared to be focused against the location of the tunnel entrance on the Winterberg. The mountain quivered under the powerful impacts of the immense shells and the badly frayed staff and companies breathing the

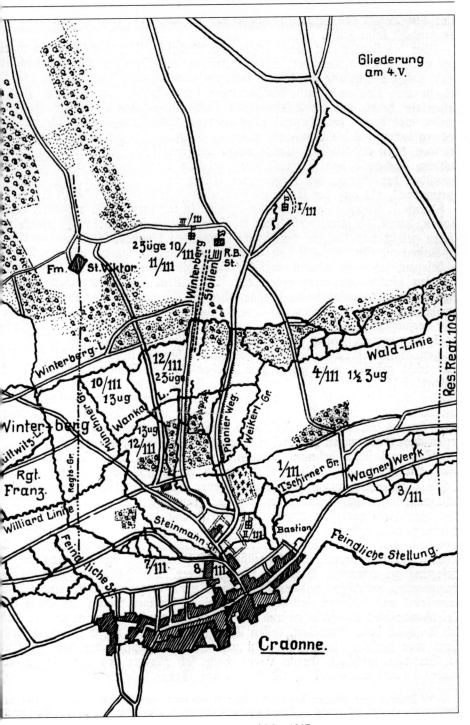

RIR 111, Craonne on 4 May 1917.

noxious air and dust inside the tunnel believed that the musty cave would collapse under the weight of enemy fire at any moment. However, the earth cover of approximately 20 meters was strong enough to prevent the bombardment from penetrating into the tunnel so the men were safe from collapse.

It was 4 May 1917. Today should decide if the expected French came. Comrade *Gefreiter* Karl Viesel and Comrade *Gefreiter* Fritz Denninger, both cyclists with the III Battalion, were also there, and both were being sent back to the regimental staff with the reason there was no message of the situation at the front. It was at 10 o'clock. The French heavy and light artillery had already increased its activity at 9 o'clock. Layer upon layer came down the hillside and their tune was terrible. We heard by the detonation of individual heavy hits coming in close proximity of the tunnel that the sentries had to withdraw. It looked as if they wanted to lay barrage fire on the tunnel. Cyclist *Gefreiter* Viesel and *Gefreiter* Fritz Denninger left the tunnel, in order to come back to the regimental staff. Karl Fisser, 11/R111[6]

On the morning of 4 May 1917 I received the following order: 'Unteroffizier Brinks replaces the platoon leader of the reserve machine gun platoon, *Vizefeldwebel* Wachowski, in the Winterberg tunnel. *Vizefeldwebel* Wachowski is to report to the company orderly room." I started on the path, and luckily arrived at the Winterberg tunnel and I reported to the company leader. Following this I went to the platoon leader and shared with him the instructions I had been given. However, *Vizefeldwebel* Wachowski did not want to go back immediately, but said: 'I will go this evening with the field kitchen.' The French artillery fired strongly on the slope and the hollow. He shared with me the task of the reserve machine gun platoon and wanted to show me where they were camped. We went into the tunnel. An infantry sentry stood in front of the entrance. On the right, behind the entrance stood the two machine guns, one behind the other, so that in case of an attack they were immediately at hand. On the left a signal station had taken up position. On the same side lay a stockpile of cartridges, hand grenades and light rockets. Somewhat behind was the connection tunnel to the regimental battle headquarters. The warehouse was placed behind the mined dugout on the left. The traffic coiled away on the right side. The stay in the tunnel was very uncomfortable. *Vizefeldwebel* Wachowski showed to me the sleeping place. I laid my pack down. There my uneasiness did not become any less, I said to the platoon leader: 'I am going back to the front of the tunnel entrance again.' I went as quickly as possible through the tunnel to the entrance, to breathe some fresh air. Outside I noticed how an enemy pilot circled above the tunnel. The enemy artillery continued to fire upon the tunnel with heavy caliber shells. They were shells with delayed fuzes. The tunnel trembled with each impact. The shells came always closer to the entrance. Ah, I thought, artillery firing with aircraft observation! About 11.30 o'clock the shells struck in close vicinity of the entrance, so that I must shoot back into the tunnel as fast as lightning from each impact. The sentries in front of the tunnel warned me to take cover in good time. Again I stood outside, when a heavy shell came rolling here, suddenly hearing the sound – ran into the tunnel – when the projectile hit the entrance and exploded at exactly the same time. *Vizefeldwebel* Ludwig Brinks, Machine Gun Company RIR 111[7]

However, a tunnel collapse would not prove to be the cause of the disaster about to impact the men inside the Winterberg tunnel. At 11.45 a.m. the northern main entrance of the tunnel was struck by a direct hit from the heaviest caliber shell and collapsed. The ammunition and light rockets stored at the entrance were set on fire, and the vapors, mingled with carbon-monoxide gas, were drawn into the tunnel by the fire and threatened the garrison, particularly the 10th and 11/R111, with death by asphyxiation.

> It might have been 11-12 o'clock. We gave this artillery fire no great attention, because we had become accustomed to such fire raids. There now the 11th Company was here in reserve, so I visited my comrades and went further behind in the vicinity of the wireless room. While we talked and warmed a cup coffee on a fat lamp, the unbelievable happened. A terrible detonation frightened us. What has happened? Other detonations followed, we immediately went to the front, but already black smoke and gas clouds came towards us. North exit 3 was destroyed and smoke and gas clouds already lay over exit 4. We immediately moved ourselves back and began to construct a barricade with knapsacks and overcoats, and the tunics we pulled off from everyone to stack in a pile, but we did not succeed in stopping this cloud of poison gas. Karl Fisser, 11/R111[8]

Several men quickly became unconscious from the poisonous fumes, and an attempt to open the entrance, failed. *Major* Schüler recognized the danger facing his men and he immediately went into the middle of the deep dark tunnel that was so filled with smoke and haze that no light could penetrate, and directed that everyone should leave the tunnel through the emergency exit and should assemble at the battle headquarters of the I/R111.

Under the current conditions the orders had to be passed along, repeated from man to man. The regimental commander as well as the commander of the III/R111 with their staff succeeded in making it through the dense blocking fire as they exited the tunnel.

> Why did you not save us? I still always hear this cry when I think about the catastrophe of the Winterberg tunnel. And from numerous comrades and those related to the victims of the Winterberg I have often heard the same questions: Was there no way to save the many men trapped in the Winterberg tunnel? Had the regiment done everything possible to rescue them? I can honestly answer the last question with a clear conscience, yes.
>
> At that time I was a position clerk with the III Battalion and with the battalion staff and regimental reserve – about two and a half companies – housed in the Winterberg tunnel. I can still see today the then regimental commander, Herrn *Major* Schüler, how he tried to guide us a few minutes after the collapse of the tunnel entrance and the ammunition exploding, where we first of all in the suffocating smoke, and gas crowded at the rear in a panic, yelling over and over towards us: 'By Groups to the emergency exit.' At approximately 12 o'clock I had left the tunnel with the adjutant of the III Battalion, *Leutnant* Schwarz, as well as with my comrades Geier and Emil. *Leutnant der Reserve* Farrenkopf.[9]

There was no doubt that the French attack had started and the first priority of the officers of RIR 111 was to assemble the men quickly and prepare them for further deployment as needed. However the officers waited in vain for their companies to come out of the tunnel. Finally, only about 30 men of the 10th and 11/R111 found their way out of the tunnel into the open. The order to evacuate the tunnel apparently did not penetrate into the smoky darkness due to confusion and panic that had gripped many of the men trapped in this terrifying situation.

> A very heavy shell made a direct hit, going into the ammunition reserves that were piled up at the entrance. Further detonations drove this gas cloud toward us, the air chute aided the penetration, in that it pulled the air to the rear. We moved ourselves quickly back however we did not succeed in constructing a barricade in front of the air chute, because smoke and poisonous clouds came quickly after us. With all of our strength and speed we built a double sandbag barricade behind the air chute in the belief that the gasses would pass down through the air chute, and we could wait here for the rescue, but we still heard the smashing of projectiles above, and how it later turned out, the air chute had become destroyed. We had been cut off from the world, the position was already very bad where we were, the tunnel here was higher than in the front and filled with bad air. And now we waited here in the hope that help would soon come from our comrades; however time passed and already breathing difficulties were noticeable. So we were determined to push through an air chute to the surface, there were *pioniers* with us, who understood how. A couple of comrades placed themselves together, two *pioniers* climbed on our shoulders, in order to create the breakthrough to the surface, but all courage and bravery was smashed by breathing troubles, and so all of our hopes fell completely. Karl Fisser, 11/R111 [10]

The frightened Other Ranks piled up in the constricted emergency exit, it was simply too narrow to allow more than one man to pass at a time. In the growing confusion and panic a young *Minenwerfer* officer believed that the danger of asphyxiation facing the men could be avoided. The officer thought they could all be protected against the clouds of poisonous gas by stacking up sandbags and closing off the tunnel from this threat. Many of the men listened to the officer and rushed back into the tunnel and this became their undoing.

While many of the men inside the tunnel looked for ways to block the spread of the poisonous fumes, others were luckier and had managed to find a way out of the death trap. It all depended upon where they were at the time of the disaster and if they managed to stay calm in all of the panic and confusion.

> What now? I immediately went through the connection tunnel to the regimental battle headquarters and reported to my company leader that the tunnel entrance had been destroyed through artillery fire. We went through the mined dugout to the tunnel. A few officers followed to the place of the disaster. There was no sign of the sentries, ammunition and machine guns situated at the entrance. Officers and Other Ranks contended with each other to set the entrance free. Also *Hauptmann* Boy and I grasped a spade and forcefully helped to get all of our comrades out of this mouse trap. However it would not be. The air was ever worse in the tunnel. The sweat dripped from our bodies. Furthermore the gas penetrated into the tunnel here from the entrance (the ammunition piled up there was exploding). With the effort to free the entrance and through the inhalation of the stifling air and gas clouds I lost

my strength. *Hauptmann* boy grasped me and brought me through the connection tunnels to the regimental battle headquarters. When leaving the tunnel *Hauptmann* Boy said to those standing around: 'Everyone follow me, slowly.' A few officer and Other Ranks had already gone in advance. You could not act quickly, because the tunnels were of small dimensions. The enemy artillery still fired on the tunnel and the hollow. Only a few comrades came from the tunnel into the regimental battle headquarters and from there into the open. How it was possible escapes my knowledge. My opinion was that many more comrades could have been rescued if an unfortunate circumstance had not thwarted this. I was happy to escape death in the Winterberg tunnel. For the comrades remaining in the tunnel it was a terrible death. A mass grave. I think back on it with horror. A black day for the regiment. *Vizefeldwebel* Ludwig Brinks, Machine Gun Company RIR 111 [11]

While these events were taking place, the troops located outside of the Winterberg tunnel desperately tried to save as many men as they could. Despite every effort only a few men could be found near the entrance of the tunnel and carried out of the black, smoke filled cavity, more dead than alive, overcome by the dense fumes. Once these men were revived, they brought news of the terrible hardships and death of the men still inside the tunnel.

All news from the battle front was lacking in the rear. All communication connections were disrupted despite the dedicated efforts by the telephone repair troops. It was quickly determined that the entire position as well as the rear terrain equally lay under powerful enemy fire. There were intervals when the fire let up only to have numerous machine guns spread fire on the trenches and intermediate terrain in the hopes of catching German soldiers taking advantage of the reduction of artillery fire by moving in the open. Enemy pilots flew down low, in order to observe the effect of the bombardment and direct fresh fire on any visible targets. Several times the garrison believed that the French attack was about to occur and were allowed to be tempted out of their modest cover, until the shells fell around them once more with great intensity.

On 4 May, 11.00 a.m., a French feint. Pilots flying very low, to determine the occupation. Further artillery fire. Half of the still remaining companies were buried and repeatedly had to be dug out anew. One resourceful man joined the end of a telephone wire to a strong electricity cable from a previous time, and connected with torch batteries. Suddenly there was a connection with the Battalion, whose dugout was also in the front in a cellar. There the same attempt had been made. However the connection soon ended, the batteries were exhausted. *Unteroffizier* Wilhelm Menzer, 7/R111 [12]

With heavy enemy fire falling on the entire division sector since the early morning it was evident that a major French attack was either about to take place or had already began. The lack of communications with the front made it difficult for the reserves to know just what was going on. In the case of the men of RIR 110 the I Battalion was alerted as a result of the intensity of the French fire and by 11 a.m. the I/R110 was ready to march, however no orders arrived and the men were allowed to wait in place while they waited for further news.

The nerves of the soldiers in RIR 109 were badly frayed from the strain of seemingly

endless enemy artillery and mine fire and the uncertainty of where the enemy would attac
which allowed a bitter fighting mood to rise in the men. Day after day, hour after hour th
fire hurricane continued, losses continued to rise among the men holding the makeshi
positions with so few shell proof shelters. 'They let the blood in their veins boil and though
about the grim reception they would give the attacker when he came.' During this tim
numerous heroic actions occurred that simply went unnoticed as buried men were dug ou
over and over again and where the wounded were rescued and brought to the rear to safet
Many lives were lost in the attempts to help their stricken comrades and still the survivor
waited for the inevitable enemy attack.

After days of heavy French fire it was almost a relief to the men of RIR 109 when o
the early morning of 4 May barrage fire light signals rose up high into the air by the men c
RIR 111 on the Winterberg. German barrage fire initially delayed the French attack, the
with great effort the enemy penetrated the positions in the right neighboring sector of RI
111. The garrison of the trench remnants had been reduced to a small number from days c
shelling. While the few survivors bravely fought back with hand grenades it was a matte
of time before they were overrun by the numerically superior enemy forces. The reserv
company which should restore the situation through a counterattack was blocked off in th
Winterberg tunnel and was unable to interfere in the fighting.

The sector where the French had entered the German position was blocked off o
both sides and flanking attacks were set in motion against the break-in position. Th
advancing French soldiers were recognized by *Leutnant der Reserve* Markwitz and a
artillery observation officer. Markwitz intercepted reports being sent to the II/R109 fron
the regiment and Group Senden was assigned to provide barrage fire and annihilation fir
on enemy positions in Craonne.

While the drama took place inside the Winterberg tunnel, the men holding the fron
line still held their positions in the heavy fire, awaiting the enemy infantry to attack. Th
wait was soon over when in the late afternoon French assault troops poured out of thei
trenches and rushed the German lines.

> On 4 May 1917, 4.00 p.m., the French attacked our position with overwhelming
> strength. Notwithstanding the tenacious defense put up by our comrades, they could
> not resist the superior enemy strength. We suffered heavy losses of wounded and
> fallen comrades in our ranks; six comrades were able to escape the French through a
> side trench; the rest ended up in captivity, mostly wounded. In this hot struggle the
> company leader, *Leutnant der Reserve* Koch from Wald, who had been found in the
> forward most line with all of the battles of the regiment, stood out.
>
> However he also became overpowered from the superior strength and ended up
> in captivity. A German shell, which struck in our prisoner transport, had ripped away
> many more comrades, most of which had taken part in the war from the beginning.
> In a comradely manner *Leutnant* Koch had led the 1st Company with courage and
> energy, benevolence and fairness virtually 3 years and now must bear the fate of
> French captivity. A French officer questioned us, if we still wanted to fight further for
> so long, we all said yes and sat down: 'until to the last man.' He called us crazy chaps.
>
> On the following day we interred our fallen and comrades who died on the
> transportation in a mass grave for the last rest. *Sanitäts Unteroffizier* Maurer, 1/RIR
> 111, had conducted the burial. Honor his memory. *Vizefeldwebel* Henn, *Gefreiter*

Scheidecker, 1/R111.[13]

More long, anxious hours passed until 8.30 p.m. when the French infantry attempted to attack once again, following another period of powerful drum fire. Despite the favorable location for the attack opposite the border of Regiment Franz and RIR 111, the enemy was unable to break through the German defenses. Still, the fighting was intense and the two opposing sides became mixed together in the maze of trenches and shell craters.

The men of the 7th, 8th and 1/R111 were crammed together in a few gassed dugouts, whose entrances were more or less crushed in. These companies, attacked on the flank and rear could barely take part in the fighting. When the Groups rushed out of their dugouts after being alarmed by the sentries in order to occupy the closest crater, they already saw the French hurrying down on them from the left through the trench and down the mountain from behind. The companies fought back as best they could with the small number of men still capable of defending the position.

The companies also attempted to create some breathing room through small counter-thrusts, including one by the 1/R111 that advanced out of the *Greiner Stollen*. The 1/R111 succeeded in bringing a machine gun into action which provided much needed support to the defenders. Despite these efforts, grasped from three sides, they were unable to withstand the overpowering enemy numbers. Of those men not killed, the majority ended up as prisoners of war.

The French at first had not discovered the battalion command post of the II/R111. The staff of the battalion hoped to remain unnoticed and then to become free through the expected German counterattack. However, between 2 and 3 a.m. on 5 May French troops came upon the battalion headquarters and threw hand grenades inside the entrance of the mined dugout. Considering how hopeless the situation had become, *Hauptmann* Räuber ended up in captivity along with his people.

The 3/R111, which had occupied its trench in anticipation of an attack since 7 p.m., could observe the line at the southern slope of the Winterberg being rolled up. Machine guns inserted into the front line effectively fired from the Craonne-Chevreux road against the French troops. The right wing of the company pushed forth from the *Weikert Graben* in the sector of the 1/R111 and blocked it off with a barricade. By doing so, the 3/R111 under *Leutnant* Weissensee succeeded in breaking the enemy advance and held its position with the *Wagnerwerk* firmly in their hands, while at the same time ready to fully support a counterattack that was expected from the north.

The French assault against the Winterberg also soon found serious opposition in the *Wanka Linie* from Groups of the 5th and 12/R111 distributed in shell craters with their machine guns. The first enemy assault against these Groups was stopped in its tracks by the heavy defensive fire. The enemy continued to press its attacks against this small force of men and eventually, after being attacked by superior strength from all sides, especially after the machine guns had been buried or the crews had been killed, the men could no longer hold the position. Eventually the survivors were forced to withdraw toward the *Winterberglinie* while still fighting. Here they were able to bring the enemy attack to a stop with support from the platoons of the 10/R111 lying in the *Münchener Graben*. Part of the 6/R111 came through the *Pionier Weg* in the night and reinforced the handful of defenders of the Winterberg. It was thanks to the intrepid behavior of these troops that the Winterberg did not entirely fall into enemy hands on 4 May.

At 7.19 p.m. the III/R109 erroneously reported to headquarters that the Winterberg was occupied by the French and that patrols had been sent out to exactly determine the situation. Shortly afterward, the enemy sent strong forces against the right sector of RIR 109. Four machine guns were quickly brought into position and took the enemy under fire. Two platoons of the 11/R109 advanced and the French were forced to withdraw under the heavy fire, flooding back to their trenches. The III/R109 suffered numerous losses during the fighting; among them was the company leader of the 11/R109 *Leutnant der Reserve* Ruf and *Leutnant der Reserve* Hoffmann from the 3rd Machine Gun Company, both of whom were wounded.

For the regimental commander and the commander of the I Battalion in the *Pionier Weg* it was difficult to obtain clarity on the evening of 4 May with the commencement of dusk, of what was actually happening in the front and how far the enemy had pierced. For RIR 111 the loss of the companies inside the Winterberg tunnel was almost disastrous in this critical hour. For the regiment, the most important task was to provide support for the threatened right flank once again. The regimental commander sent a message to Brigade headquarters asking about the allocation of reinforcements; and until reinforcements arrived, the remnants of the 5th and 6/R111 would have to form the new seam squad at the right flank. By darkness the two companies were to recover the *Wanka* and *Winterberglinie*, where parts of the 10th and 12/R111 were still expected to be found. However, the bombardment increased towards evening so that only four Groups of the 5/R111 with three machine guns reached the hill position and once there came under the command of *Leutnant* Schweizer, 12/R111. There was no sign of any help coming from the rear.

At about 9 p.m. *Vizefeldwebel* Schmid, 4/R111 observed that the French were advancing from out of the *Wald Linie* against the *Pionier Weg* at the eastern slope of the Winterberg by the heights of the graveyard of Craonne, supported through machine guns that had been brought forward. He immediately took them under fire with his Groups and supporting machine guns and forced them back behind the crest of the hill; at least one enemy machine gun was placed out of action as well. The machine gun of the 3/R111 had also joined in this fighting.

The 4/R111 and the rest of the 2/R111 under *Leutnant* Beyle now occupied the *Wald Linie* and Platoon Göbel, 4/R111, blocked off the *Pionier Weg*. There was no contact with the 6/R111 on the flank on the Winterberg. Patrols were sent out to try and clarify the situation. One patrol under the command of *Leutnant* Heimburger, 2/R111 held at night had firmly determined that the enemy was entrenching in the area of the cemetery of Craonne. Based upon the report from this patrol and other observations RIR 111 came to the conclusion that after the enemy had overrun the trench south of the Winterberg there was still yet to be any fighting about the mountain.

The uncertainty about the fate of the right wing of the 3/R111 continued for a long time. It was only known that the *Wagnerwerk* and the *Wald Linie* were being held by the I/R111. The intention was still to recapture the lost terrain in a counterattack before the French could become firmly established. However, it was also a fact that unless fresh forces were quickly obtained the counterattacks could not take place because the reserves of RIR 111 were either spent or buried in the Winterberg tunnel.

Earlier in the day, attempts had been made to assemble every man possible in order to form a reserve force, without much success. The facts about the disaster in the Winterberg tunnel were still not fully known at this time but as the pieces of the puzzle were put together, the picture proved to be far more dreadful than had been expected.

In the von *Heeringen* tunnel of the R109, where we had been preserved from the heavy shell fire after approximately an hour, I then received the order, to assemble the people out of the Winterberg tunnel. In different dugouts by the *Pionier Weg*, in the artillery protection position and later again in the *Heeringen* tunnel I found in total about 50 men, amongst them numerous wounded. Most however had no rifles and no equipment any more. Because in the Winterberg tunnel it was already well known by one that already for days all of the air had been used up in the middle and rear parts of the tunnel so that even a light could not burn any more – most had been dressed only in shirts and pants.

In spite of further searching of all dugouts until up on the hill of the Winterberg I could only find a few dispersed men. Where were the others? Were they possibly killed after abandoning the tunnel through the heavy fire? Or ... ... did they not all come out of the tunnel? Anxious questions. Further searching. Towards evening I reported the sad result. *Leutnant der Reserve* Farrenkopf, RIR 111 [14]

While the fate of many men in RIR 111 was still unknown, the situation facing the men of the regiment near Craonne became increasingly perilous as the French troops appeared in overwhelming numbers. *Unteroffizier* Wilhelm Menzer, 7/R111 and the few men still with him still held the position as long as they could. Then, towards evening, as the small group of defenders tried to dig out from the collapsing shell crater walls once more there was a shout.

The sentries cried out of shell craters: 'French from the left above!' everyone quickly crawled out in shell holes and demanded barrage and annihilation fire through light signals, however suddenly from the left rear on the hill in close proximity appeared a dense mass of French. *Unteroffizier* Heck now pushed up his machine gun in a nearby shell hole when one officer and 4 men sprang to him placed their revolvers and bayonets on his chest. The leader of the 7th Company, *Leutnant* Fritzsche, now threw hand grenades out of his shell hole toward *Unteroffizier* Menzer and four Other Ranks when a new throng of French appeared in the rear on the hillside; at same time 2 Frenchmen had installed a machine gun on the right in a shell hole in a short distance. Opposition by the six Germans in their current position was hopeless. Therefore 'Up! *Marsch*! *Marsch*!' past the machine gun before it could swing around, then to the right, where the *Garde* was; however the position was further back; on the crest, subsequent to the II/R111 where the French attacked. The mountain rose up in front of our eyes and it was impossible for the 6 Germans. Therefore back again. At the same time we were fired at by a pilot at an altitude of 50 meters. The French machine gun was gone. Therefore a breakthrough attempt, then surrounded and taken captive, approximately one half hour after the start of the attack. *Unteroffizier* Wilhelm Menzer, 7/R111 [15]

The men of RIR 110 were still awaiting orders to move up to the front but evening arrived without anything occurring. By this point many of the men in the regiment believed the earlier alert had been a false alarm; supper was already prepared in the Cloister and a draught of beer had been poured, when a *Radfahrer* appeared who brought the orders that the I/R110 had to be held ready in the hollow east of St. Thomas. When the battalion arrived there at 9.30 p.m. a new order came to the battalion commander, *Hauptmann* Humricht, calling for him and the adjutant to come to the brigade command post.

The situation on the Winterberg held by RIR 111 was still unclear, however from everything found out so far it appeared to be threatening. The I/R110 received orders from the brigade commander that the battalion would be placed in readiness in the Ailette Ground in the vicinity of the artillery protection position. It would then establish a connection with RIR 111 and with the brigade staff and maintain them.

This turned out to be no pleasant task. The advance was horrible; only two guides were available from brigade headquarters, both young cavalrymen who were placed in possession of the battalion. The I/R110 marched by way of the Mill of Aizelles, moving from runner post to runner post and finally on a footpath through dense woods until in the Ailette Ground. The entire route lay under powerful enemy disturbance fire which became especially bad at the hill by the artillery position. The hollows were all gassed, so that on long stretches of the route the men were forced to wear gas masks. Finally, at 2.15 a.m. on 5 May the I/R110 reached the location identified in the orders, with most of the men out of breath.

The Battalion commander and adjutant immediately went to the regimental headquarters of RIR 111 in the *Pionier Weg* for the purpose of establishing the connection to the regiment, while the companies from the I/R110 lay in the wooded terrain without any cover. The III/R110 lying in the second position under *Hauptmann* von Borell du Vernaiy was moved up at 3.25 a.m. on orders from the 56th Brigade into the Artillery protection position behind RIR 111.

The II/R110 under *Hauptmann* Imhoff was moved forward from the flanking protection position without the 7/R110 and the 2nd Machine Gun Company that remained on the hill southwest of Petit St. Jean farm in the artillery protection position. The rest of the II/R110 moved through the difficult wooded terrain under powerful enemy fire to the artillery protection position and occupied it. Despite all attempts, the connection to the right to Regiment Franz could not be established.

The regimental commander of RIR 111, *Major* Schüler, had declared that a counterattack could only be conducted with the support of the I/R110. When this battalion arrived, it became moved under the command of RIR 111 and would be used as follows: The 1st and 3/R110 were placed under the III/R111. The 1/R110 occupied the northern slope of the Winterberg behind the *Winterberglinie* as the counterattack reserve. The 3/R110 lay as the reserve of the battalion in the dugouts by the battalion battle headquarters in the *Pionier Weg*. The 2/R110 stood under the I/R111 and became positioned for the counterattack against the *Weikert Graben*. The 4/R110 remained in the Artillery Protection position as the regimental reserve. Two MG 08 heavy machine guns were attached to each company.

At the same time the troops holding the front line were in a life and death struggle fighting against the French infantry, there was another life and death situation facing many of the men in RIR 111; the fate of those still inside the Winterberg Stollen.

We definitely knew that the oxygen in the air was being used up; the lights went out, the matches flickered. The heat and thirst were unbearable. We had a single bottle of oxygen that we placed by the wall and let it slowly discharge. Our existence became ever more insufferable. It was dark. We only had the torches and meant to save them.

Quite a few comrades were situated by the barricade and listened, whether help would soon not come, but they deceived themselves and all hopes sank in them together. Had we only water and air! However the water was under the gas and smoke cloud, and we could not get the iron rations. Physical and mental convulsions affected us, many lay on the ground, suffering from thirst and the dreadful heat, and so we suffered the breakdown of not being able to make any decisions. The depression among my comrades was terrible, terrible was the darkness filled with requests and pleas for help. In my vicinity one Group had to sit; then I heard them pray with the rosary. A torch flashed on and I definitely believe that I recognized *Unteroffizier* Maier from the battalion staff, and *Gefreiten* Staible, a cyclist with the battalion among them. Karl Fisser, 11/R111 [16]

Actually help was on the way ever since the initial collapse of the tunnel entrance and the fires and explosions set off by the heavy French shells. In spite of the desperate need for every man to defend the position, every effort had been made to locate *pioniers* who would be able to assist in opening the collapsed tunnel and perhaps save some of the trapped men.

The *pioniers* already previously requested from the division now became urgent and repeatedly requested with rescue materials. In spite of the heavy fighting action on the Winterberg hill I was not free of the anxious thoughts about the comrades in the tunnel. And my feelings would be confirmed only too soon. Then suddenly *Vizefeldwebel* Schmidt hurled forth down the *Pionier Weg* with a distressed face, only dressed in a shirt and pants, with the horrible, always repeated cry: 'Why have they not saved us? Where are they then? Must we all suffocate? Most are already unconscious or dead!' Have many people had not left the tunnel at all? What are they doing? If only the *pioniers* came! We could not wait any longer for them. I received the order to immediately look for oxygen apparatus in all of the dugouts. In the next dugout I found none. Now I went across again to the *Heeringen Stollen*, because the pioniers had finally arrived; 25 men however also without oxygen equipment. I reported myself voluntarily to guide them into the Winterberg *Stollen*. It might have been approximately 8 o'clock in the evening. *Leutnant der Reserve* Farrenkopf. [17]

While desperate efforts were underway in order to save the men trapped inside the tunnel the situation deep inside the hill was growing worse by the minute. Under the circumstances that existed inside the Winterberg *Stollen* it is amazing that anyone was still left alive. The men trapped in the inky blackness, suffering from intense thirst and heat and a lack of oxygen tried to remain optimistic that help would arrive but for many, the strain had become too great.

I will never forget the parting of all of my comrades! One called after his wife and his children, the other took leave of his parents and siblings, the same convulsions also came over me, I also took leave of all of my loved ones in sprit. A card will tell you of my absence with the remark: Missing! The fight for life and death was slow and terrible; my tongue stuck to the roof of my mouth, I felt madness when my throat began to close up. Everyone called for water, most had undressed in this hell in order to obtain some relief – however everything was in vain. Death laughed over his harvest and the death held watch at the barricade, so that no one escaped. How long we were enclosed, I do not know. Three or four days? I heard from the edge of the plank bed, leaning on the post, the hollow sounds of the shots in the darkness of our tomb. A few cried for salvation, others for water, it was a place of parting and death. Next to me lay a comrade on the ground; he cried with a cracking voice that we should load his pistol. I also saw this as deliverance so I called to him and groped toward him. He gave me an Army Pistol 08. I pulled the cocking mechanism back with my last strength and gave it to him on his request. A short moment – maybe he was still taking leave from all of his loved ones – and a bang resounded through this tomb – and a rattle came out of his mouth – he was delivered. Others cried after water, water and deliverance. I also wanted to go on that short path, to become delivered, with the left hand I felt my heart beat and thought: soon you will also have peace; I looked for the weapon, which I also found – my dead comrade lay next to me – slowly I succeeded in returning to the old place on the plank bed, I took a short parting from my loved ones, and I placed the weapon against my heart, the barrel was cold, and raised the right hand even higher and? When I awakened, I lay on the ground – a weakness seizure had preserved me from that last move.

Only water, water! In the struggle for life and death I rolled on the ground, I then bumped into an empty canteen, but this canteen was only a joke – and still I guided it to my mouth. Through the rattle of the canteen I therefore heard other comrades crying for water, yes it was insanity that it played with us. My throat and my body ached. Only water, water! Close to insanity, I attempted to kneel, which I also succeeded in, slowly I folded my hands to form a bowl and drank my urine in greedy draughts. New weakness came over me. When I was awake again, I drank my urine once more. I crawled a small piece and bumped into a small hill – it had been sand that had trickled down through the cracks. Here my body could become somewhat cooler. At the same time I found a torch, I attempted to turn it on, which succeeded with my last strength. I lay upon my side, the light burned my eyes, but what I still could see was simply horrible. My dead comrades lay here naked and stiffened in death with outstretched hands! How long I lay here now, I do not know. Karl Fisser, 11/R111 [18]

What Fisser could not have known was that in the midst of a major battle, dozens of men were making every effort possible to free the men inside the tunnel. All of the work performed in the rescue attempts was occurring under constant enemy shell fire as well as a lack of proper equipment that was needed for just such an emergency.

After slowly looking for – meanwhile everything was destroyed through the nonstop fire on the tunnel – I finally found the former emergency exit and penetrated through it with the *pioniers* into the main tunnel. After a few steps the light became very small and in the end went out entirely. Already breathing was very difficult. The perspiration runs out of every pore. The pungent fumes and dense smoke also aggravates to a constant cough. There we stumble over a few bodies. They became brought outside. We go quite slowly along and make attempts by shouting. No answer. Dead silence, only the smashing and throbbing of the shells outside. We stop each other and start to go on again, because one gets air through it more or less. I call the names of my comrades as loudly as I still could: Fleuchaus, Klein etc. No one answers. The smoke grew even thicker, or did we just believe it did? Finally, we can go on no longer and drag ourselves back. We discussed the situation. It was clear: Without oxygen apparatus a further penetration was impossible. We must find oxygen.

First of all I went to the old medical dugout at the upper path with two *pioniers*. It was thoroughly destroyed. Also nothing was found in the remaining dugouts. Our only hope is the *Heeringen Stollen* again. Shortly in front of this one *pionier* became wounded on the thigh. There is also a lack of oxygen in the tunnel. The doctors would not give out the last remaining cylinders, because they have many gas poisoning patients. We finally received an oxygen cylinder from a Medical *Unteroffiziere* 'Saint', only one, small cylinder, containing maybe two to three liters. We go out with new courage and back at the work, although we were dog-tired and almost falling over from thirst. During the opening of the cylinder however the *Pionier Unteroffizier* showed us that the usual valve control on the cylinder was missing. Nevertheless we attempted to open the cylinder with a closed hand and went into the tunnel. When we can go no longer, we attempted, to release the oxygen from the cylinder. However it doesn't succeed. Because the oxygen was under pressure it escaped so strongly that it was not possible to inhale it. We sensed it and had no relief whatever. And before everyone could have a try the small cylinder was already empty after a few minutes. Thus nothing again.

An immense feeling of despair and dejection overwhelmed us. Previously during the hours long search for oxygen it had already become clear to me that my comrades were apparently detained in the rear most parts of the tunnel. However why don't I hear any cough at least, where all the dense smoke and fumes almost broke our windpipes? Therefore however are most already dead? And could we do nothing? It was bleak. Also the *pioniers* have no more suggestions.

... I went back and reported to the battalion and regimental commanders: Without proper rescue personnel complete with respiration appliances provided with oxygen apparatus as well as electric torches a rescue was not possible. All that was already ordered and became urgently requested again. *Leutnant der Reserve* Farrenkopf. [19]

The eastern slope of the Winterberg was now under French control and the enemy had also succeeded in advancing over the *Winterberglinie* until a counterattack by troops from RIR 110 and RIR 111 threw him back. Once the fighting had died down numerous enemy machine guns dug in on the eastern slope of the mountain threatened the right sector of RIR 109 from their elevated positions.

With the arrival of support from RIR 110 precious time had been gained, allowing the reserves to be moved forward. About 2 a.m. on 5 May the 9/R111 arrived from out of the artillery protection position into the *Winterberglinie*. The company had suffered losses when moving through the severe enemy disturbance fire but once in the front line a connection with Regiment Franz could be established once again with patrols.

Following the arrival of the I/R110 at the ordered location the Battalion commander and adjutant immediately went to the battle headquarters of RIR 111 in the *Pionier Weg* for the purpose of establishing the connection to the headquarters staff, while the companies of the I/R110 lay in the wooded terrain without any cover. The III/R110 under *Hauptmann* von Borell du Vernaiy lying in the Second position was moved forward at

3.25 a.m. on orders from the 56th Reserve Infantry Brigade into the Artillery protection position behind RIR 111.

The battalion commander of the III/R111, *Hauptmann* Liehl, ordered the attack to begin at 7.30 a.m. Meanwhile, at this time, powerful enemy artillery fire was placed on the *Winterberglinie* and the hollow located behind the Winterberg, so that the attack was no able to develop. At 11 a.m. the enemy artillery fire increased to the strongest drum fire, the hill and the northern slope of the Winterberg were shrouded in dense smoke and fumes.

Despite all of the best intentions, it had proved to be impossible to coordinate the counterattack given the difficulties in communications between the various regiments as well as the challenging terrain. The II/R110 under *Hauptmann* Imhoff moved forward from the flanking protection position without the 7/R110 and 2nd Machine Gun Company, which remained on the hill southwest of Petit St. Jean farm in the artillery protection position. The II/R110 moved through the badly damaged wooded terrain through powerful enemy artillery fire until it was in the artillery protection position and had occupied it. There was no connection on the right to Regiment Franz with the II/R110 At 3.45 a.m. the II/R110 and parts of RIR 111 counterattacked which were joined by the platoon of *Leutnant der Reserve* Kaiser, 11/R109 who advanced in the *Weikert Graben* and rolled it up and blocked it off at the regimental border.

> However, it was not until about daybreak on 5 May that the I/R110 arrived at the regiment. The readiness position held by two companies of this battalion with parts of the II and III/R111 at the *Winterberglinie* and in the *Pionier Weg* now could no longer remain concealed from the enemy. The moment for the surprise had passed, but with the cooperation of the artillery it still allowed hope for a success. The beginning of the attack under the leadership of *Hauptmann* Liehl became set for 7.30 a.m. The time however was not enough to be able to bring through the orders, and to inform the batteries about the situation and the intent to place it in the picture that our own troops were still on the Winterberg and to bombard it only modestly,. The connection to Regiment Franz was tried in vain, so the attack could be delivered together. The enemy took advantage of this time and started before us. From early morning on he covered the Winterberg and the surrounding terrain with heavy artillery shells and mines so that the breaking forth of the *Stosstrupps* was thwarted. Despite heavy losses the parts of the 5th, 6th, 9th, 10th, 11th and 12th Companies continued to battle French storm troops on the mountain, which must fight from shell crater to shell crater, holding on over and over with rifles and hand grenades, until suddenly the right wing was encompassed and the enemy rolled up the position. *Unteroffizier* William Menzer, 7/R111 [20]

At approximately 10 a.m. the French attacked the *Winterberglinie*. They succeeded in taking only small parts of the position of the 1/R111 and the remnants of the 9/R111 holding the left wing directly behind the brow of the mountain. On the right wing the enemy advanced until he was at the northern slope and immediately brought machine guns into the position. On orders from the I/R110 the 3/R110, the remnants of RIR 111, two machine guns from the 1MG/R110 and a few guns from the 3rd Machine Gun Company occupied the eastern and western Riegel on both sides of the *Pionier Graben* and prevented any further enemy advance through active machine gun and infantry fire. During the fighting *Leutnant* Wursthorn, 1/R111 was killed, *Offizier Stellvertreter* Kloppenburg and five Other Ranks were killed; 21 Other Ranks were wounded. *Leutnant* Haug was taken prisoner along with a number of his men.

He found most of the defenders of the Winterberg dead or wounded in their shell holes. Only 4 men came back from the 9th Company with *Leutnant* Stoffler; *Leutnant* Besser, 6/R111, was killed; *Leutnant* Ada, 12/R111, was buried; *Leutnant* Schweizer, leader of the combined 5th and 12/R111, was severely wounded; all machine guns and *Minenwerfer* had been lost with their Other Rank crews. With every connection to the rear cut off through a dense fire block, the brave handful of men in their individual situations were unable to prevent the dominating heights falling into enemy hands. However the French had also suffered heavily, his thrust strength was exhausted. The further advance could be swiftly brought to a stop at the curtain of the mountain through the fire of a skirmish line that *Leutnant* Schwarz, Adjutant of the III/R111, had formed out of the remnants of the III Battalion and the 3/R110 astride the *Pionier Weg* in the vicinity of the command post of the I/R111. Barricades were erected and equipped with machine guns, and when the French came in such effective flanking fire, they yielded back into the *Winterberglinie*.

The French also attempted to gain terrain from out of the cemetery of Craonne. The attack however was immediately brought to hesitation under the fire of the 2nd and 4/R111 from the *Wald Linie*. Then, when the Winterberg had been taken, the Wald line could be taken under fire from the flank and almost in the rear from machine guns, so that the right wing of the front had to bend back to the north. Soon the fire from their own batteries struck on the Winterberg, and the projectiles of the machine guns of the 3rd Company worked in the area of the cemetery. So the enemy became firmly held. The 3/R111 was not unrestricted in the possession of its position as before. However the utmost demands were placed on the leaders and men through the continuous shelling and the threatening danger from the right flank. The garrison was first reinforced through a platoon from the 11/R109 and later through the 2/R110. All attempts by the French, to remove the barricades at the right wing, failed. However, they did not succeed in gaining a connection to the north through the *Weikert Graben* to the Wald line.

The opening, which gaped here, was only secured through machine guns, so the right wing of the 3rd Company hung in the air, and its position was lost if the enemy thrust forward from out of the Winterberg further to the east and north. Therefore the II and III/R110 were moved forward to support the garrison at the *Pionier Weg* and in the Wald line, and to prevent a breakthrough here in every case. In the evening the commander of RIR 110 took over command of the sector in the new command post in the artillery protection position. The remnants of the III Battalion assembled there, which in the course of the next day were moved off to the camp *Neu Wurzburg* by Sissonne. What was still remaining from the II Battalion became moved back to Ramecourt, in order to likewise find accommodations in the camp *Neu Wurzburg*. *Unteroffizier* William Menzer, 7/R111 [21]

It was at this time that *Leutnant* Farrenkopf had almost given up all hopes of being able to rescue the men trapped inside the *Winterberg Stollen*. The events occurring at the front were consuming all available reserves and equipment and without the proper equipment, there was little that could be done for the trapped men.

It had meanwhile become at 4.00 a.m. – and events occurred that for different reasons further rescue attempts were made impossible. The companies on the Winterberg had been almost entirely worn down. Since daybreak the enemy fire had greatly increased again. At about 5 a.m. I went across to the *Heeringen Stollen* to get a company from R110 as replacements. I brought them at over approximately 6.30 a.m. completely torn apart, after already previously different parts from the first battalion RIR 110 together with the remnants of our companies had arrived for the counterattack. However the R110er already had large losses in the hellish fire, until they had just come upon the hill. There was the further advance by the French with a hugely superior strength already occurring. About 9.00 a.m. the French had penetrated into the *Winterberglinie*. Coming to the tunnel was now no longer possible, even if oxygen apparatus was now still there. On a different day the regiment became relieved. During the rest time following, the thoughts of the dreadful asphyxiation death of so many comrades in the Winterberg Stollen, as well as my sickness because of fatigue and gas poisoning did not allow a joyous mood to arise, although moreover possibly because of my promotion to *Unteroffizier* because of bravery in front of the enemy a certain reason had existed. *Leutnant der Reserve* Farrenkopf. [22]

Following the report of the enemy advance upon the northern edge of the Winterberg the regimental commander of RIR 111 gave orders to the two battalions of RIR 110 in the artillery Protection position to counterattack. The II/R110, without the 5/R110, which remained behind as the protection garrison, would be on the right, the III/R110 would be on the left. The attack goal was given as the plateau of Craonne. At 12.30 p.m. both battalions began the attack and at first the men moved energetically forward. However the attack soon slowed, because the enemy had recognized the movement from the positions on the hill and showered the skirmish line with a hail of shells.

The artillery preparation had been too short; the entire attack had not been prepared adequately and was considered a rash act. The largest obstacle facing the men was formed by the dense, very marshy wood, whereby the formations lost contact with each other. There were no connections with the artillery so that there was no possibility of directing fire where it was needed most.

The counterattack came to a halt on the hill by the battalion battle headquarters at the *Pionier Graben*. On orders from *Hauptmann* Humricht the 9/R110 occupied the *Ost Riegel*, the 3rd, 11th and 12th, as well as parts of the 6/R110 occupied the *West Riegel* on both sides of the *Pionier Weg*. The 10/R110 and the 3rd Machine Gun Company remained in the Artillery Protection Position. The latter companies had both advanced as the reserve companies and had suffered heavy losses including *Leutnant der Reserve* Schäfer who was wounded; five machine guns were also placed out of action.

The 11/R110 had also moved forward until it was by the hill where the battalion battle headquarters was located. However, the connection to the 6/R110 had been lost; similarly no connection had been established to the right with Regiment Franz. Therefore the II/110 went back, leaving the 6/R110 behind with the III/R110 as well as strong patrols in the foreground in the Artillery Protection position. In the course of the afternoon the 2nd

Machine Gun Company moved forward there and into the battle line of the battalion with all of its guns. Despite having to advance in broad daylight and under strong enemy fire, they came forward without losses.

In the night to 6 May the II/R110 moved forward once again according to orders issued from the headquarters of RIR 110 that had taken over command of the sector on the evening of 5 May. The battalion reached the hill by the III/R110 and established the connection to the 6/R110 on the left and on a picket from IR 56 by Victor farm. The 4/R110, which so far had been in the Artillery Protection position, moved forward and occupied the *1st Riegel*. On orders from RIR 111 the attack of 5 May would not be continued, instead, the position would be fortified and held under all circumstances.

The 2/R110 under the leadership of *Leutnant* Carstens, proceeded along the Chevreux-Craonne road in order to establish a connection with a forward shoved picket of the 3/R111, and to clear and occupy the *Weikert Graben*. The outlying picket was successfully reached without losses, then however *Leutnant* Carstens along with two *Stosstrupp* ended up in strong enemy artillery and flanking machine gun fire, and as a result *Leutnant* Hund and a few men were killed. The 2/R110 was unable to establish a connection to any friendly forces the right. The losses in RIR 110 on 5 May amounted to: 2 officers, 46 Other Ranks killed, 5 officers, 154 Other Ranks wounded, 2 officers, 49 Other Ranks missing.

It was hoped that the counterattacks planned for 6 May would have better success. 6 May was a marvelous day, with clear skies and comfortable temperatures. The counterattack commanded by *Generalmajor* Ziethe was launched against the Winterberg by IR 154, IR 19 and IR 56. The leader of the infantry attack was *Generalmajor* Weber, commander of the 9th Infantry Division.

The assault took place at 9.45 a.m. on 6 May, therefore in full daylight with the 11th and III/56 on the right, the I/19 in the middle and the I/154 on the left. This was accompanied by a murderous artillery fire and within minutes the entire area was filled with smoke and gas shells and all visibility disappeared as it grew darker under the clouds of smoke and dust. To add to the hellish scene, enemy aircraft flew over the German trenches and fired at the men.

The attack was supported by eight machine guns from the III/R109, which covered the enemy line with fire, at times up to 4,800 rounds a minute. This attack was also supported from the sector of the 3/R111 through rifle and machine gun fire, which especially impeded the advance of the French reserves. The 2nd and 4/R111, acting as rear support in the *Wald Linie* now lay under active enemy artillery and machine gun fire and the men were forced to look for any cover possible in the storm of shells and bullets.

The attacking troops needed to pass through the lines held by the men of RIR 110. The companies of RIR 110 were ordered to lie down while the assault troops moved through the position and advanced against the Winterberg. For a change, the German artillery fire was very strong while the French response was unusually weak.

IR 154 reached the northern edge of the mountain; however it could not go past the *Winterberglinie* because of an enemy counter-thrust and could not advance because of short lying fire from the German artillery. IR 19 advanced further on to the plateau, thereby capturing much of the Winterberg. After the assault had come to a stop lively enemy aerial activity started once more and with it came strong enemy artillery fire, particularly about the left wing. The *Sturmtrupps* suffered heavy losses and urgent requests for reinforcements came through by written messages.

Zur frommen Erinnerung
an unsern lieben Sohn und Bruder
Bernhard Mülhauser
Schütze, 2. M.-G.-Komp. Res.-Inf.-Regt. Nr. 110
gefallen auf dem Felde der Ehre am 6. Mai 1917
im Alter von 24 Jahren.

Gebet.

Lasset die Kerzen brennen um Gottes Gnade.
aber trocknet die Tränen, denn einen schönern Tod
als ich, findet Ihr alle, die Ihr im Frieden der
Heimat bleibt, nie und nimmer. „Ich habe be-
zahlt, was ich schuldig war, und was ihr alle be-
zahlen müßt — den Tod. Ich bin im Grausen,
aber auch im Jubel der Schlacht gefallen, fröhlich
und stark. Meinen Leib haben sie getötet, meine
Seele haben sie nicht getroffen. Laßt den armen
Leib ruhen in fremder Erde. Gottes Engel hält
bei ihm Wacht.

Vater unser. Gegrüßet seist Du Maria.
Mein Jesus Barmherzigkeit.

Bernhard Mülhauser, KIA by artillery projectile and buried in shell hole. (Author's collection)

At 11.15 a.m. the 3/R110 under *Leutnant* Pommer became inserted at the left wing in support of the *Sturmtruppen*. Luckily, the company reached the *Winterberglinie* without large losses and swarmed into positions by IR 154 and IR 19. Following a request by the company leader, *Leutnant* Pommer, the 9th, 11th and 12/R110 also became pushed into the forward line. At 2.30 p.m. and between 8.40 and 9.40 p.m. enemy counterattacks occurred after substantial artillery preparation fire that were repulsed through infantry fire and hand grenades with heavy losses for the enemy as well as the defending German companies.

The fighting lasted five hours and still RIR 110 had not been drawn into the infantry fighting. Then, when the I/154 urgently requested reinforcements and the readiness troops of IR 154 did not arrive, *Hauptmann* von Borell, decided to send the 11th and 9/R110 in their place as reinforcements for IR 154. Two other companies from the II/R110 were ordered moved out of the Artillery Protection position in the *Pionier Weg*; however they could go back once again, because in the meantime the Readiness companies of IR 154 had arrived and the enemy attack was repulsed.

However, at the 9 p.m. effective fire began from heavy enemy artillery began to fall that lasted until 11 p.m. The remnants of the III/R110 were then moved back again into the Öst *Riegel* and *West Riegel*. Despite the heavy fire that covered the regimental position RIR 110 lost only 3 men killed, 71 men wounded and 1 man missing.

A large number of severely wounded men from IR 154 arrived in the medical dugout of the *Heeringen Stollen* during the fighting where they received their first medical treatment by the *Sanitäts* Company of the 9th Infantry Division that had set up a casualty clearing

Philipp Bunkhofer, KIA, struck in heart by shell splinter at 8.15 am.
Buried at the foot of the Winterberg. (Author's collection)

station inside the tunnel. The slightly wounded men were quickly treated using pressure bandages and then directed to the rear, out of danger, in order to make room for the more severely wounded who could not be moved.

Finally, only weak remnants of the assaulting battalions remained on the mountain. The defense of the recaptured terrain would mainly fall to the companies of RIR 110. In the night the companies of the III/R110 moved back to the *Riegel* Position, the 3/R110 still remained behind on the Winterberg until the morning, when it was also relieved by part of IR 154. The III/R110 returned with a haul of two French machine guns, three light machine guns and two rapid fires guns. *Unteroffizier* Frank, and *Musketier* Mock, both from the 11/R110, were both recognized for their outstanding behavior in the fighting.

The Winterberg Sector would now be taken over by the 9th Infantry Division while RIR 110 occupied the sector from the *Pionier Weg* to the regimental border with RIR 109. On 6 May RIR 110 had lost: 32 Other Ranks killed, 104 Other Ranks wounded, 3 Other Ranks missing, even though it had not been involved in the assault.

In the night from 6/7 May the I/R110 relieved the I/R111. The III/R110 remained in the position in the dugouts of the *Pionier Weg* for the protection of the right flank and for the support of a possible enemy attack. The II/R110 moved into the Artillery Protection position with the battalion command post of the I/R110 inside the *Heeringen Stollen*.

The 2nd, 3rd and 4/R111 eventually became relieved in the night of 6/7 May without enemy interference through parts of RIR 110 and moved into a *Wald Lager* by St. Erme. As the new day dawned, the remnants of the battle tired troops from RIR 111 moved to the rear into the beautiful valley of St. Erme with trees and meadows becoming green and blooming. A picture which stood in glaring contrast to the devastated and shell ravaged battlefield above at the Chemin des Dames, which had become the grave of so many good friends.

The large *Heeringen Stollen* had been created by the *pioniers* and the tunnel was reinforced with gigantic wooden beams. The tunnel offered protection to many men against that continuous artillery fire. Inside of it lay two battalion staff, a few companies from RIR 109, a wireless station, a telephone center, lighting troops, bandaging station, etc. Carrying troops also arrived in the night with materials and ammunition, the food carriers, who brought their fighting comrades food from far in the rear and with it hurried twice each day while risking their lives, the intrepid stretcher bearers who were concerned with transporting the severely wounded to the rear; which was considered more than enough. In the night the temperature in the tunnel climbed so high that the men preferred to undress. There could be no thought of washing as there was no extra water at hand as every drop was needed for the men to drink.

What really tormented the officers and men the most was the sanitary conditions, which were horrible. Regardless of rank, each man had to line up for a shell proof latrine already created for the possibility of the 'tranquil business'. These could not be enlarged in the onrush during the periods of major fighting and the horrible conditions of the latrines meant they could no longer be entered, let alone used.

The alternative was not any better. The so-called 'spade business' was instituted at the tunnel exit. This was apparently well-known by the enemy and the area lay under strong artillery fire day and night. If the situation changed, then one was tempted to try his luck in reaching the open as rapidly as possible. The latter was not a popular choice as many men were caught in the open by the artillery fire and numerous bodies littered the ground by the exit of the tunnel. The stay in the *Heeringen Stollen* was therefore not very pleasant; however there was one benefit, it was shell proof. All of the men who were forced to remain outdoors lay in miserable shelters or in open shell holes.

The I/R109 was the battle battalion and lay with the 4th and 2nd Coy in connection to the *Heeringen Stollen* in the *Wagnerwerk* and *Tschirner Graben*. The *Weikert Graben*, which ran along at the eastern flank of the Winterberg, was not occupied, because it was completely shot up and could be seen by the enemy. In the night would the open right wing of the 2/109 be secured through connection patrols to the 3rd Coy in the *Wald Linie*. Furthermore machine guns from the *Wald Linie* and the *Tschirner Graben* dominated the eastern slope of the mountain. The 3/R110, with the remnants of the 1/R110, lay in the *Wald Linie* and in the *Pionier Weg* and maintained the connection with IR 154 and after its relief with Grenadier Regiment 7.

Towards 11.30 a.m. an enemy patrol of 30 men approached the railway embankment in front of the pickets of the 11/R109 which had been pushed forward in front of Chevreux. The leader of the picket held his fire and allowed the enemy troops to come nearer, and when they were close enough his men opened fire. Two French soldiers who had been sent forward as the point were captured, the others fled back toward the French lines. The prisoners belonged to the 3rd Company, *Régiment d'Infanterie* 32 from the 18th Division, IX French Army Corps. According to statements from the prisoners the patrol was led by an officer and they had been sent out to determine if Chevreux was still occupied by the Germans. Unfortunately for the two prisoners, this was confirmed when the patrol came under fire from the pickets.

On 7 May there was an extraordinary enemy bombardment in Sector i that was being held by the 6/R109. The heavy French shells had collapsed the largest part of the dugouts including the one occupied by *Leutnant der Reserve* Härdle and several of his men. In the heavy bombardment, the collapse of this dugout went unnoticed and it was only with great fortitude that the buried men were able to free themselves alive 24 hours later. The II/R109 suffered losses of 33 Other Ranks from gas shells; the 7/R109 alone had lost 3 Other Ranks killed and 7 Other Ranks gas sick.

The heavy bombardment gave rise to the concern that a new enemy attack was going to take place. *Leutnant der Reserve* Schmidt, 3/R109 with four Groups of carrying troops were sent forward at 3.30 p.m. in the enemy artillery fire to the II/R109 where they were inserted into the weak 5th and 7/R109 as reinforcements. The enemy trench was observed filling up with troops in the evening and annihilation fire was called for. At 9 p.m. the French did attack in Sector West and the Winterberg, and was completely repulsed through heavy barrage fire.

The night to 8 May proceeded quietly until the morning of 8 May when the French artillery became increasingly active. The constant French shelling continued during the day giving rise to the concern that another attack would be taking place in Sector East. At 4 a.m. a platoon of the 1/R109 under *Leutnant* Wiederkehr was moved forward from the artillery protection position as reinforcements into this sector. A platoon of four groups from the carrying party of the II/R109 under *Offizier Stellvertreter* Himmelsbach was also placed in the Corbeny line.

Particularly heavy fire raids lay the entire day long upon the entire sector of RIR 110 and at 5.45 p.m. drum fire from all calibers was placed upon the entire *Winterberglinie* and on the sector of RIR 109. Then infantry attacks followed against the I/154 and RIR 109; RIR 110 would not be attacked. The French fought with great bitterness, and according to statements from prisoners the attacking division had been told that they would not be extracted until the attack goal, Chevreux and the connecting German positions, were taken.

Small local enemy attacks continued on this day, usually followed by a spirited counterattack against a portion of the line the French had captured. One such counterattack conducted by the 7/R109 under the leadership of *Vizefeldwebel* Henk and *Unteroffizier* Albert Ratzel with the *Stosstrupp* men Riexinger, Böttiger, Grau, Braun, Klipfel, Wies, Mutschler and others threw the enemy out of the position in the sector of the 5/R109. Two prisoners from *Régiment d'Infanterie* 32 and three *Musketen*, as well as a number of rifles were captured as a result of the attack.

The 6/R109 also became involved in clearing part of the German trenches lost earlier in the day and threw the enemy out of the first line between the 6th and 5/R109 with support from the *Stosstrupps* of the 1st, 4th, 5th and 7/R109 at about 8.30 p.m. *Vizefeldwebel* Henk, 7/R109 and *Vizefeldwebel* Mayer, the leader of the *Stosstrupps* of the 1/R109 stood out in particular in the fighting here.

The successful actions of 8 May were costly to RIR 109: 18 men were killed, 59 men were wounded and 20 men were missing, including the company leader of the 6/R109 *Leutnant der Landwehr* Herrmann and *Leutnant der Reserve* Wiederkehr who were wounded; *Vizefeldwebel* Pfeiffer, 5/R109, *Vizefeldwebel* Holzach, leader of the *Beute* Machine Gun Platoon and *Leutnant* Ganter II who were all killed during the counterattacks.

Leutnant Ganter II had found that he was unable to use his *Minenwerfer* in the heavy enemy artillery fire, so later in the morning of 8 May he went to his former company, the 6/R109, to act as a platoon leader. When the enemy pressed into the position on the evening of 8 May, he advanced in a counterattack with two Groups from the field position in the

2nd trench. He was severely wounded by an enemy hand grenade and died a short time later. 'With him, a more joyful and faithful comrade would be torn out of our ranks.'

8 May was also the day that the entire RIR 111 was brought together once more when the last parts of the regiment, the relay posts of the 2/R111 and platoons of the Machine gun Companies had found their way to their battalions and the regimental units became reorganized.

The full regiment became assembled on 9 May at the French military camp at Sissonne. The men were provided with housing in large, well-furnished barracks, quite a change from the mud filled shell craters and small trench remnants they had been occupying only a short time earlier. While at Sissonne the men would be able to enjoy a well-deserved rest from the horrors of the Winterberg, something that the previous *Wald Lager* with its huts made out of boughs and foliage or tents could not offer.

Despite being in the rear St. Erme became bombarded daily by long range enemy guns so the men were never far from danger. Also, in spite of the weakened condition of RIR 111 the regiment was required to act as the sector reserve in the event of another enemy attack. Even with the occasional enemy shell or the knowledge of being suddenly sent back to the front, the men were able to relax and recover from the recent experiences.

While the sector held by RIR 110 were not attacked on 9 May the *Heeringen Stollen*, Chevreux and the approach routes lay under the heaviest artillery fire. In the night the enemy gassed the hollows and made relief and transport of food and supplies extremely difficult.

Finally, on the next day, 10 May, after being in the trenches since 18 April; except for a few days when the regiment was moved back and in which the battalions were alarmed each night and were moved forward, orders arrived from Brigade that the regiment was to be relieved. In the first ten days the regiment had endured the utmost powerful artillery fire, beat off separate strong enemy attacks and had considerable losses. Through the further insertion of the regiment in the fighting at the Winterberg very strong losses had occurred. The trench strength of the battalions amounted to an average of 5 officers, 20 Unteroffiziere, 150 men.

The people were without dugouts for the greatest part and were exposed to enemy artillery fire during the entire time in the position. However, while the men still had strong nerves, because of the uninterrupted intense strain that the constant fighting placed on them they could take no more and they were ready to be relieved.

While the intense fighting took place and constant artillery fire continued to fall there were men dedicated to entering the *Winterberg Stollen* in order to save anyone who might still be alive, even after six days had passed since the tunnel had been badly damaged and set on fire. Specialists with the appropriate equipment had finally been located and brought to the tunnel entrances and began the slow, methodical search of the immense tunnel that was still filled with dense smoke and fumes. Finally, on the sixth day trapped inside the Winterberg *Stollen*, was rescue at hand?

> I still lay on the small hill, because I did not trust my ears – did death play games with me? I heard the word: Help! I don't know if it was behind or in front, the darkness of the tomb wrapped around me, and again: Help! Somewhat closer. I rolled around and lifted my head slightly, but it twitched in my eyes like lightning, so that I closed them again. Was it a lamp? Was rescue coming? I attempted to shout with my last

strength and there I heard them: Just be quiet, comrade, we are coming! They made
their way over to me here, my rescuers, and gave me water, water. I could not believe
it, was I being saved? Again the rescuers had to leave me. Then they came with a tent
square and fetched me. Cold air blew toward me and again there is water, water! Then
the rescuers said: today is the sixth day since being buried! Two comrades were still
rescued with me. However I did know who. I believed that my rescuers had dogs with
them, I could not see because my eyes were weak then. I looked forward to be out of
that place of horror, where death held his harvest, to be able to escape death.

Now we went further away from this place, but we would not be happy long,
French artillery fires showered us, and my carriers must take cover, however fate
intended that we would be preserved. Luckily we landed in a medical dugout. Only
a short time to rest, and then we went further to the rear and still one more time
the French artillery sent a salvo after us. Finally we arrived at the dressing station,
an ambulance picked us up. Then we were unloaded and brought into a treatment
room. One put a mask on me, I believe it was oxygen. One attempted to save us, gave
us enough to drink, and then we went further into a military hospital, numerous
comrades stood about our stretchers, after we were unloaded. One bathed us like
small children then we were put into hospital beds. Also here the oxygen mask came
into use. I recognized no one, my eyes were weak, and little hope existed. Not for many
days did I recognize my comrade Viesel, who visited me. Slowly however my condition
improved, only after weeks could I view myself with a hand-mirror, there I first saw
how I looked physically, my chest covered with green and yellow marks – a shadow
of a human being! The doctor said, half a day more, it would have been too late. One
said to me that it looked sorrowful in the tunnel. The other comrades had ended their
misery through shooting, opening their veins etc. we were the only three saved. After
long, careful care, the home military hospital followed, to Altenahr at Bad Neuenahr.
Karl Fisser, 11/R111.[23]

The long awaited rest that was being enjoyed by the men of RIR 111 came to a premature
end on 12 May when the regiment became placed under the control of the 52nd Infantry
Division. The men marched in extreme heat from the camp at Sissonne to the Windmill
camp in a copse about 8 kilometers southeast of Sissonne. While the regiment was at the
new location the first replacements arrived, mostly untrained recruits, some quite young
and others quite old. The new men were given as much training as was possible, especially
in regard to taking cover from aerial observation. Otherwise there was nightly entrenching
work in the artillery protection position to perform.

On 14 May the I/R111, reinforced by the 5th and 6/R111, moved forward into the
second position by Damarcy farm, 3 kilometers southwest of Amifontaine, and once there
came under the command of the active IR 111. The companies occupied a sector on both
sides of the Miette stream, from where the men could see numerous destroyed tanks lying
in the foreground towards Juvincourt. The men of RIR 111 were put to work developing
the trenches and creating dugouts, while under only minor disturbance from enemy fire.
The men from RIR 111 noted that the work performed by active troops was in no way the
same quality as performed by the same number of men in a reserve regiment.

While the men of RIR 111 were occupied in creating new positions for the 52nd
Infantry Division the men of RIR 110 still occupied positions by the Winterberg until

16 May. On this day the entire position, particularly the *Heeringen Stollen*, came under powerful enemy bombardments. However, in the night off 16/17 May the hour of delivery arrived for the I and III/R110. The I/R110 was relieved by the I/154, the III/R110 by parts of Grenadier Regiment 7. The relief of the II/R110 took place in the night of 17/18 May through IR 154. The relief of all parts of the regiment proceeded smoothly and without enemy interference.

The regimental staff of RIR 110 moved to billets in St. Erme, the battalions into the forest camp north of Aubigny, then in the forest camp by Sissonne. The march to the rear through the Ailette valley was a harrowing experience. All of the roads lay under continuous enemy fire with shell impacts on the right and on the left, in front of and behind the columns of men. Finally the men were out of range of the French guns and they could all could take a deep breath once more.

The men of RIR 110 also noted the sudden change from the shattered landscape of the Winterberg into an area covered in green and blooming flowers and trees, spring had arrived in full glory all the while the men sat in Hell. The survivors of the regiment felt as if they had escaped a dreadful fate, they enjoyed the beautiful scenery and 'stretched their chests as they greeted life!' For so many others, not as fortunate as those men marching to the rear, the Aisne-Champagne battles from 18 April to 18 May became their final resting place. The total losses of RIR 110 during the insertion in the Aisne-Champagne was 4 officers, 141 Other Ranks killed; 5 officers, 529 Other Ranks wounded and 1 officer, 61 Other Ranks missing.

In the early morning hours of 17 May the commander of IR 111 spoke of his special appreciation to the battalions of RIR 111 as they moved away again to the Windmill camp. With it the activity of the regiment in the zone of the 7th Army was at an end. In the afternoon the battalions marched with large intervals to Sissonne, where they received billets in and by the church and school. Once there further replacements arrived which were distributed to the companies. So, fairly filled up once again, on 18 May RIR 111 reached Bucy les Pierrepont, 8 kilometers north of St. Preuve with the regimental staff occupying billets in Marle an der Serre. The troops embarked from these villages on the evening of 19 May in Bosmont, east of Marle, as they were transported via Sedan to Brieulles and Vilnes an der Maas. The three machine gun companies travelled on the morning of 20 May from Bosmont, after they had been accommodated the previous night in Cuirieux, 7 kilometers south of Bosmont.

On 19 May the battalions of RIR 110 had reached Bucy les Pierrpont where the entire regiment was billeted in mass quarters. After a rest day on 20 May the battalions marched on 21 May to the railway station at Bosmont where the men were loaded aboard troop trains. The railway journey went to Sedan, where warm food was given out to the men, then on to Vilosnes or Brieulles sue Meuse. The regiments of the 28th Reserve Division belonged to the 5th Army once again at 'Verdun'.

At the conclusion of the time of service in the Aisne-Champagne battles orders still followed that recognized the spirit and worth of our troops.

VII Army AOK from 20 May 1917: To the 28th Reserve Division.
The 28th Reserve Division separates out of the association of the VII Army, and as such I have a need to speak to the leaders and troops of my warmest thanks and my appreciation for their outstanding bravery and good performances.

The division held its position under the most difficult circumstances, broken the onrush of the far superior enemy. The division can look back on the Aisne Battle with pride. My warmest wishes accompany the division on its more distant paths. The commander-in-chief: signed von Boehm, *General der Infanterie.* [24]

Additional recognition was received from *Grossherzog* Friedrich which also praised the regiments of the division for their effort and sacrifices on the Aisne. The men of RIR 111 did look back with pride and sorrow on the battle on the Winterberg, a small episode from the Double Battle on the Aisne and in the Champagne. The regiment had helped stop the massive French offensive that had been designed to break through the German lines within 48 hours of the first attack, something that never occurred.

Judging from the amount of space that this period of fighting occupied in the regimental history, especially the events at the Winterberg tunnel, an event that was described as 'possibly the most terrible experience of the regiment in the war', it even surpassed the events of the Somme in July and October 1916. Along with the memories of the disaster came memories of great heroics and success such as the firm defense by the 3/R111, which successfully repulsed several enemy attacks. The fighting performance of the companies, the 3/R111 in particular, was seen as a page of honor in the history of the regiment. Although the French had already encompassed the right flank of the 3/R111, the men of the company did not yield an inch of ground of their trench to the enemy. The company commander, *Leutnant* Weissensee, became awarded with the Knight's Cross of the House Order of Hohenzollern for his part of the fighting.

The French had expected a great victory, a tangible breakthrough of the German front from this series of attacks, but failed. The disappointment over the failure of the attack was immense; the outcry over the losses suffered by the French army in such a short period of time was even greater. General Nivelle, who had received the epithet '*buveur de sang*' (blood-drinker), was sacked and sent to a post in North Africa. What had not been known by the Germans were the extensive mutinies which erupted in the French army at this time, including at least one regiment from the 18th Division, the same division from which the two prisoners had been captured by Chevreux on 6 May by the men of RIR 109.

The cost for the successful defense of the Winterberg positions for RIR 111 was high: 4 officers, 91 *Unteroffiziere* and Other Ranks were killed; 4 officers, 288 *Unteroffiziere* and Other Ranks were wounded, 10 officers and 585 *Unteroffiziere* and Other Ranks were listed as missing. As the details became known of the fate of the many missing, if they had not been killed they had been taken prisoner in the fighting.

Oberstleutnant Schüler, RIR 111, wrote a brief article at the conclusion of the fighting, titled: 'The Winterberg Tunnel'.

What a profusion of frightfulness, of agony and fate experienced lies in the portrayal shown here. And however also: how splendidly I recall this obvious persistence in the most considerable danger, this soldier's awareness: It is your 'duty'! That is it, what we old R111er proudly rendered in memory of the days at the Winterberg. [25]

Notes

1. *Gelbkreuzmunition*, or Yellow Cross Ammunition was the name given to the new type of gas being used, Dichlorethyl Sulphide, also known as Mustard Gas. It was a vesicant, a blistering agent that would attack

the moist tissue and moist parts of the body (under arms, eyes, nose, crotch, etc.). In sufficient quantities the gas would be lethal.

2. Greiner & Vulpius, op. cit., p. 175.
3. Greiner & Vulpius, op. cit., p. 177.
4. Frisch, Georg, *Das Reserve-Infanterie-Regiment Nr. 109 im Weltkrieg 1914 bis 1918,* p. 191.
5. Bachelin, op. cit., p. 151.
6. Bachelin, op. cit., p. 327.
7. Bachelin, op. cit., pp. 330-331.
8. Bachelin, op. cit., pp. 327-328.
9. Bachelin, op. cit., p. 332.
10. Bachelin, op. cit., p. 328.
11. Bachelin, op. cit., p. 330.
12. Bachelin, op. cit., p. 151.
13. Bachelin, op. cit., pp. 334-335.
14. Bachelin, op. cit., p. 332.
15. Bachelin, op. cit., pp. 151, 153.
16. Bachelin, op. cit., p. 328.
17. Bachelin, op. cit., p. 332.
18. Bachelin, op. cit., pp. 328-329.
19. Bachelin, op. cit., p. 332.
20. Bachelin, op. cit., pp. 154-155.
21. Bachelin, op. cit., p. 155.
22. Bachelin, op. cit., p. 332.
23. Bachelin, op. cit., pp. 329-330.
24. Greiner & Vulpius, op. cit., p. 184.
25. Bachelin, op. cit., p. 323.

9

26th Reserve Division
April-August 1917

During the time the men of the 28th Reserve Division had been engaged in the Nivelle Offensive on the Chemin des Dames, its sister division, the 26th Reserve Division, was also caught up in the same Allied offensive, but against the British further to the north. It was involved in a diversionary attack that was being held to distract the German forces, which was known as the Battle of Arras.

When last discussed, the 26th Reserve Division had just completed the withdrawal to the *Siegfried Stellung* and had experienced the first Allied attacks against the new defensive position before being relieved in the first week of April. The 26th Reserve Division had indeed been relieved from the front lines just in time. Bad weather had apparently postponed an earlier date set for the British attack by Arras. The goal was the capture of Vimy Ridge from which the enemy could see far over the flat terrain up to Douai and the connecting trench systems which would make the German positions untenable. The massive attacks on the German front began on April 9, shortly after the relief of the 26th Reserve Division. The infantry attacks, combined with crushing, overpowering artillery fire created a dangerous situation at the German front. The position divisions holding the line suffered numerous casualties as the British forces advanced and there were no reserves close at hand.

This is the reason why the III/R121 was stopped short of its final destination after being relieved and was then sent to support the 220th Infantry Division near Vis-en-Artois, and later as the reserve for *Gruppe A*. The 3MG/R121 should have accompanied the III/R121 but could not be located as the men were already on the march to their new quarters. It seemed that for part of the 26th Reserve Division, rest and recuperation so longed for would have to wait for the time being.

The III/R121 was among the first troops sent to the threatened front further to the north. The III/R121 marched to Vis-en-Artois where the entire area lay under artillery fire. The companies were assigned to create a new position as well as send out patrols toward the front. After moving to several different places on orders that, because of the ever changing situation, were already out of date before they could be executed, on 10 April the battalion ended up just west of Wancourt between 6 and 8 a.m. with the 9/R121 in the forward most line The battalion staff, 10th, 11th and 12/R121 were located in cellars and dugouts in Guémappe.

On the morning of 9 April the enemy had attacked on both sides of the Scarpe after a short period of fire preparation, with large masses of infantry and tanks. The attack extended south until it had reached Riencourt. On the Scarpe the enemy had overrun the trench divisions and had penetrated 6 kilometers into the German lines on a front 17 kilometers wide. However the attack by Bullecourt, against the 27th Infantry Division was shattered. IR 120 later mentioned that they had RIR 121 to thank that they were able to

Aerial view of Bullecourt and surrounding area. Image taken
from 3,000 meters. (*Die 26. Reserve Division 1914-1918*)

repulse the enemy's attack due to the hard work performed on position construction by the
regiment.

It would also seem that the Ulmer Grenadiers had kept the promise made to the men of
RIR 119 when the regiment was relieved. A few days after being relieved from the position
the men of RIR 119 read the reports of the subsequent fighting around Bullecourt. Six
months later RIR 119 was positioned next to the Ulmer Grenadiers once again, this time
in Flanders, and they were happy, when they were told that it was only the well-constructed
Siegfried Stellung that allowed the success by Bullecourt to be possible; the system of
dugouts built by the regiment had preserved the Grenadiers in the fire-storm of the Arras
Battle. It also preserved the support positions of the *Stosstrupps* and made it possible for the
successful counterattack.

Further troops from the 26th Reserve Division was also destined to become used in
the fighting. After being relieved and sent to the rear the I/180 was next to be placed in
possession of the 220th Infantry Division. While with this division the battalion was sent
to Vis en Artois, Cherisy and Fontaine to perform entrenching duty and used as readiness
troops. The men had little rest while under the new division as the troops were marched
from one location to another. They suffered badly under the poor weather conditions,
which increased the number of men reporting sick, a number which continued to rise even
when the battalion returned to the 26th Reserve Division on 18 April.

While RIR 119 was in rest area on the morning of Easter Monday there was suddenly
strong drum fire in the distance and the battalions were alarmed. The alarm readiness was
increased at midday and the companies of the III/R119 were marched to Aubigny au Bac
and loaded onto rail cars. Sometime after 6 p.m. the trains stopped and the III/R119 was

also placed under the control of the 220th Infantry Division and accommodated in alarm quarters. The men were asking 'what was going on?' it was quickly apparent that the III/R119 had joined the Arras battle. The battalion travelled by motor vehicles on the morning of 10 April to an area south of Vis-en-Artois where they were to dig trenches. The days were dull and cold as snow flurries raced over the flat ground and showered down on the troops as they worked.

The quarters provided to the battalion in Haucourt were overcrowded with troops and the billets were very poor. When evening came, the men were off to dig trenches; the ground was soaking wet and the footwear, already in poor condition from the recent withdrawal from the Somme and the outpost fighting, had not improved. The men were quite blunt about the conditions they faced: 'The quarters were terrible, often there were none. The clothing was soaked through. Man pressed next to man in the open in order to keep warm in the April showers.'

The enemy had apparently broken through the German position west of Wancourt, threatening Vis-en-Artois. In the same night, the 9th and 10/R119 were moved forward and occupied the two villages and sent out reconnaissance patrols in a northwesterly direction. There was active artillery fighting on both sides when at 12 noon the 10/R121 was occupied in entrenching in the second line northwest of Guémappe. The 12/R121 was then positioned by Wancourt in the afternoon and the 11/R121 was placed in the third line north of Guémappe.

The night of 10 April was very restless; artillery fire raids alternated with reconnaissance raids by the British, all during severe snow storms. At 6 a.m. the enemy attacked on both sides of the Cambrai–Arras road with tank support; the attack was repulsed. At 8 a.m. British cavalry rode forward in an attack on the main road and was completely shot up from the flank by the 9th and 10/R121, and from machine guns in the front. All day long and throughout the night there was continuous artillery searching fire and small enemy infantry advances, all of which were repulsed.

On the morning of 11 April, the village of Monchy was lost. An attack accompanied by 15 tanks against Heninel and Wancourt however did not have any success. Despite these local defensive victories, the situation was growing worse all the time. The 11th and 12/R119 were placed in Vis-en-Artois and the battalion received orders to occupy the ridge between Boiry-Notre-Dame and the nearby sugar factory. The 10/R119 marched on the left wing, the 11/R119 on the right wing. The troops dug in creating a zig-zag line and sent reconnaissance patrols forward.

German counterattacks in the afternoon of 11 April failed to recapture Monchy. A skirmish line advanced from the Bois du Vert but the attack was a failure, and the enemy not only retained the village but had also managed to capture Wancourt and Heninel during the night.

The British had attacked the former position of the 26th Reserve Division in force on 11 April and tried to overwhelm Bullecourt with artillery, infantry and tanks. The 27th Infantry Division was in the line at this time and the Australians managed to gain a weak foothold deep into the battle zone. They were eventually thrown back in counterattacks, where 1,100 prisoners were taken. The tanks involved in the attack were destroyed by artillery fire or simply overwhelmed with close combat infantry weapons. The fighting was reported to be extremely heavy and in the end the enemy forces were broken; it became known as 'the Hell of Bullecourt.'

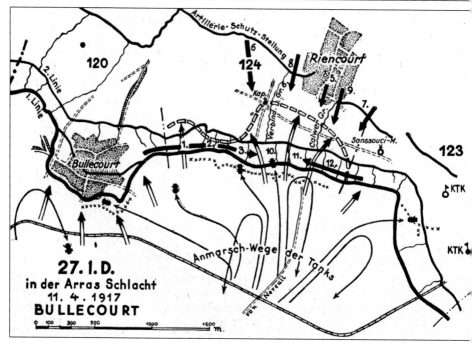

Bullecourt: The attack against the 27th Infantry Division, 11 April 1917.

The companies from RIR 119 spent the next 24 hours in the position. At 4 p.m. on 12 April new British attacks were apparently in preparation, so the battalion was ordered to occupy the nearby hill and was able to repulse the attack from this position. At 7 p.m. the 10th and 11/R119 returned to Vis-en-Artois and found the Alez cave filled with other troops and the men were forced to disperse in order to find shelter. The companies could only be quartered in crowded accommodations with man standing next to man. The next day the battalion moved to Eterpigny into barracks in alarm quarters.

On the morning of 12 April the position by Wancourt was to be evacuated. The III/R121 was supposed to go back into the second line by the fork in the Cambrai-Arras and Boiry-Notre-Dame – Guémappe roads. However, the order arrived too late, and the movement, in which five battalions were involved, was executed in daylight. The enemy knew exactly where the battalions were positioned and took them under fire the entire day. Toward evening the 9th and 12/R121 was ordered to provide support by Guémappe but as the companies arrived, they were dismissed again, because other reinforcements had already arrived.

On 13 April the enemy artillery fire finally stopped, and no attacks took place. Then on 14 April, at 2 a.m. the order arrived; after being relieved by the I/176 the III/R121 would go to the rear by Vis-en-Artois and act as the division reserve. The I/176 arrived too late and this movement was also held in the light of day, in full view of the enemy. It was as if it was a miracle that the battalion managed to reach the Alez cave and the cellars in Vis-en-Artois with only a few losses.

From 14 April on, the II/R119 was located in Vis-en-Artois while the 9/R119 was positioned in a sand mine on the road to Heninel and was to look out for the artillery of the 18th Reserve Division. The British then attacked out of the line Monchy-Wancourt and succeeded in capturing Guémappe, but the III/R119 did not become involved in the fighting.

This was probably for the best as the III Battalion was exhausted by the recent fighting and patrols. There were no dugouts for the men, the trenches were wet, there were swampy shell holes and everyone was soaked to the skin from the rain and snow showers. At best the men had to be content with sunny days but with a cold wind. The troops were housed in cellars and holes with no stoves and the clothes on their backs were soaking wet at all times. The socks on their feet were half rotted; the field kitchens were unable to provide a regular supply of hot food. The men simply lay in their holes, lean and hungry, or out in the open and became completely apathetic. At the same time intestinal illnesses and colds thinned the ranks even more. Finally in the night of 14/15 April the III/R119 was relieved by units from the 220th Infantry Division.

On 15 April the III/R121 moved off via Sailly to Bugnicourt, where it was to receive further orders. Here it became directed to Fressain and spent the night there. On 16 April the battalion was to become loaded on trains in Aubigny-au-Bac. However, when it arrived there, it found out that the transport trains had been postponed for one day; therefore the III/R121 had to march four kilometers to Fressain.

The transport of the III/R121 to Bohain finally happened on 17 April, and from there the men marched Fontaine-Notre Dame, a distance of 16 kilometers after having been sent to another village with the same name by mistake. Once there the men found poor housing in mass quarters. The battalion leader, *Hauptmann* von Raben, reported the following about the condition of the battalion.

> The battalion desperately needed rest after the exhausting days of Bullecourt; no more demands could be made on the strength of the other Ranks. After two nights without any rest, almost five days of rain and snow in open rifleman holes, without straw, lying without the possibility of fires, the battalion had an extremely exhausting sentry duty, which, united with the enemy's artillery fire, made the most extreme demands on the strength of the men. Subsequently, on the day by Guémappe, followed strained marching with full packs, interrupted through quite poor billets and through a twelve hour train journey, a more exhausting night march, that the battalion instead of in the hoped for rest quarters was brought into the cramped and insufficient billets in Fontaine-Notre-Dame.
>
> The battalion had performed outstandingly and exhibited the good reputation of the Württembergers and the 26th Reserve Division again. Losses: 3 dead, 30 wounded.[1]

While part of the division was actively engaged in the fighting around Arras, the remainder was housed in the rear by Valenciennes where the 26th Reserve Division belonged to the Army Group Reserve of the Group of Crown Prince Rupprecht of Bavaria. Here, the men were able to enjoy a quiet life behind the front. Many of the soldiers were able to visit Valenciennes which was described as a beautiful city, filled with art, beautiful scenery and best of all, a place to rest.

The first days in the rear included bathing, both for the men and their uniforms, a parade with weapons, gas masks, and full equipment. Later there were further baths,

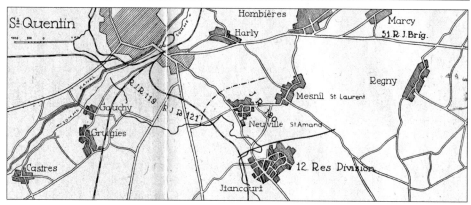

Positions held by the 26th Reserve Division.

delousing and the men were able to attend the local cinemas and other pleasant diversions found in the area. While in Valenciennes the division restored uniforms and equipment and received new equipment and replacement troops.

In addition to being able to rest and relax, there were training courses on defensive battle tactics being held for the officers of the regiment, troop leaders and general staff officers. The division then became designated as a training division while in Valenciennes, holding instructional courses inside a hall in one of the museums located in the city.

The beautiful rest time at Valenciennes came to an abrupt end when at 4 a.m. on 16 April the division was given orders to be ready to move later in the evening. The men marched at 11 p.m. and were loaded aboard transport trains, travelling to the area northeast of St. Quentin. While it was generally recognized that the urgently required recuperation of the men and the training of leaders and Other Ranks in the changes taking place at the front were important. The shortage of troops and the superiority of the adversary in sheer numbers on the Western front was a growing concern, which did not allow the luxury of time needed to accomplish everything that was required.

Many men in the 26th Reserve Division also felt they had especially bad luck being relieved from the front lines and had the feeling as if they were being taken advantage of more than other units. This caused many of the officers and Other Ranks to become disgruntled, especially if they heard that other troops remained at rest for weeks at a time in the Line of Communications zone.

St. Quentin, while once located far behind the front line, was becoming a central area of the fighting once again. The canal had been a busy shipping route before the war, now it was barren and closed to traffic by barges joined together and half sunk. The city offered a desolate picture of destruction; enemy fire had caused a great deal of damage at numerous locations. Despite the devastation, the trolleys still worked, the streets were filled with tables, chairs, beds and other household items that the troops in the rear areas used to furnish their quarters as comfortable as possible.

The men travelled in streaming rain and in pitch black nights in order to reach St. Quentin where the 26th Reserve Division became part of Group St. Quentin. The reason given for the sudden move was a French attack by St. Quentin that had pushed back the outposts along a wide front, captured the front line and had become firmly established in the German position. New attacks were also expected and the trench divisions involved in the fighting so far had suffered greatly and required replacement and support.

The French and British pressed closely behind the German troops withdrawing from the *Siegfried Stellung*, particularly in the direction of St. Quentin, in the expectation of taking the city. The old *Siegfried Stellung* ran behind St. Quentin at this point and if the city was lost, all of the terrain in the rear and the extensive German defensive system could easily be observed from the dominating height of the cathedral.

The latest army news reported that St. Quentin had been joined to the *Siegfried Stellung* by a projecting *Balkon Stellung*. When the withdrawal began in March, the work on this position was not completely finished so that the young, unproven division that was positioned by the city was unable to stand firm against the Allied advance. If the attacks continued with the same weight then the Germans would lose the forward most trenches by St. Quentin.

It was also expected that the enemy, as in the Somme battle, would focus his strength at a single location and break through the *Siegfried Stellung*. Therefore the battle proven 26th Reserve Division was suddenly taken away from its rest and placed into the line before the troops had a chance to recover from the strain of the previous winter, the withdrawal and recent outpost fighting.

Fortunately, no further attacks did occur, allowing the front line troops to be relieved. Most were newly formed regiments which were still being trained and learning the ropes of trench warfare but were prematurely deployed because of the needs at the time. They were young troops without the necessary inner cohesion, toughness and without sufficient experience. These were the reasons specifically mentioned as justification for their relief.

In addition to untrained troops in the front lines, there was a growing concern over ammunition supplies, in particular rifle and machine gun cartridges as a result of an overall copper shortage.

Secret
War Ministry
No. 432/4,17 A2.   20th April 1917
The shortage of copper imposes the necessity of having recourse as rapidly as possible to the partial employment of iron cartridge cases for small arms ammunition. Although the trials ordered in circular letter of the 2nd December, 1916, have not yet been completed, the experience gained on the Western front with cases from the arsenals at Spandau and Dresden have shown that "S" ammunition with iron cases can be introduced without disadvantage.

The employment of this ammunition in machine guns has brought to light instances of cases splitting and fouling the mechanism during continuous fire.

Experiments with a view to obtaining an iron cartridge case equally suitable for the rifle and the machine gun (*Einheitshülse*) will be continued without intermission by the Machine Gun Experimental Committee, in consultation with the Munitions Department.
(Signed) Stein [2]

When entering the new front line, the men from the 26th Reserve Division were not reluctant to voice their opinions. The I/R121 spoke quite badly about Prussian IR 456 when relieving the regiment on 21 April.[3] The battalion found a terrible mess, the French

French trenches at the top, German trenches at the bottom. The communication trench in the center, joining the two lines, was half in French control, half in German control.
(*Das Württembergische Reserve-Infanterie-Regiment Nr. 121 im Weltkrieg 1914-1918*)

occupied the first trench; the second trench was in German hands and formed the new front line. A communication trench between the two lines was blocked off, the French held one side, the Germans held the other. It was currently being used as a listening sap.

There was only one dugout in each company sector, the trench was completely shot up and many men were lying out in the open. The only good thing mentioned was that the position was on a reverse slope and could not be directly observed by the French and received only a small amount of artillery fire. Openly cursing their predecessors, the men from RIR 121 went to work to completely reconstruct the position as it should be. With the main trench located on a reverse slope, the men attempted to create a new forward trench which was eventually accomplished but not without losses.

After a week the position was considered to be in good condition. The hard work did not go unnoticed and when the commander, General Albrecht, toured the position, going as far forward as the listening sap, he spoke of his approval and gratitude in a regimental order. The regimental commander of IR 455, Schmidt, also praised the men of RIR 121 Then, on 26 April the III/R121 was moved to the rear as the reserve where it was still subjected to aircraft bombs.

The time spent by St. Quentin was quite interesting. The *Siegfried Stellung* encircled the city on three sides and lay close to the actual city. At the beginning of March the population of 50,000 men, women and children had been evacuated with their possessions. Even with so much being transported to the rear there was a lot to find in the buildings and houses. In one market place a building was filled with glassware and porcelain ware from the basement to the 4th floor. The men supplemented their kitchen equipment and mess utensils to their hearts content. There were wagons for coachmen, which found new masters, resourceful men found objects concealed in houses and cellars such as clothes, linens, clean wash, food and wine. The Machine Gun Company even found several wagon loads of tires buried in one factory.

The city lay under British and French fire day after day. More buildings burned and one block of houses after another became destroyed in the enemy fire. Under these conditions, whatever men did not save could not be saved and was soon under a pile of debris or burned to ash. Men were seen wearing tails and top hats strolling through the streets with robust women on their arms, a joke by the readiness battalion wearing civilian clothing which they enjoyed despite the constant shell fire. There was a magnificent cathedral where all of the art works had been packed away and brought into cellars for safe keeping. The cathedral was damaged by shells and the interior was filled with debris from the numerous impacts as the enemy apparently assumed it was being used as an observation post despite all protests to the contrary. Despite the bombardment, the *pioniers* made every attempt to save the old stained glass from destruction.

Between 26 and 28 April IR 180 relieved IR 454 from the position south of St. Quentin and took over the left wing of the division sector. The men no longer were deployed as they had once been. Instead of the battalions being placed one next to another and connected on their wings to other units, they were now placed in rows, creating a defense in-depth. With this new formation, the front width of the companies became larger, but this disadvantage supposedly became balanced through the considerable advantages offered by the new system.

The forward battalion was now called the *Kampfbataillon* [Battle Battalion] and its leader was the *Kampf-Truppen-Kommandeur* (K.T.K.) or Battle Troop Commander, who was responsible for the entire garrison in the front line. All auxiliary weapons and close combat means placed in the front line were subordinate to him.

Behind them were found the *Bereitschaftsbataillon* [Readiness Battalion] whose leader was called the *Bereitsschaft-Truppen-Kommandeur* (B.T.K.), Readiness Troop Commander, who was responsible for all activities in the 2nd and 3rd lines. The *Bereitschaftsbataillon* with the auxiliary weapons and close combat means belonging to it formed the immediate reserves for the battle battalion. The last battalion was known as the Rest Battalion

According to the proximity from the enemy, the battalions would be exchanged in shorter or longer periods of time as required with the rest battalion moving forward to relieve the readiness battalion and the readiness battalion then relieving the battle battalion, while the former battle battalion moved into the rest area. The men and machine guns were distributed throughout the various zones, the *Minenwerfer* were also distributed in the same manner. In part the *Minenwerfer* were positioned in cellars in order to conceal their location.

The situation existing in the position taken over by IR 180 was unclear. No maps were available to allow any orientation of the tactical situation. Between the regiment and the neighboring regiment of the 12th Infantry Division was a gap 600 meters wide. The first trench was not constructed in a continuous manner and was very shallow. The rearward trench was only fragmentary and there were no communication trenches. There were no dugouts at the right wing of the regiment, only some concrete shelters with space for only two men lying down. These were actually used to house 1 *Unteroffizier* and 8 men.

Schnorr

Leutn. b. R. im Ref.=Inf.=Regt. 119,
töblich verunglückt bei St. Quentin
am 28. April 1917

(*Kriegstagebuch aus Schwaben*)

Some mined dugouts could be found in the rearward trenches but they were only just started and were connected to individual shallow dugouts. Even with a weak garrison it was not possible to bring all of the *Kampfbataillon* men into bomb proof shelters. The obstacles in front of the first trench were good; they only needed improvement at the left wing. The wire obstacles in front of the rearward trenches were weak, in part just started. The largest part of the *Zwischenstellung* was completely inadequate for defense. There were no signal stations, regimental and battalion observation positions and the telephone connection barely existed.

Fortunately, at this time, IR 180 was positioned in a very quiet battle front, enemy aerial activity was small, the artillery fire was moderate, and the enemy infantry was completely quiet, and positioned about 1 kilometer distant. When the regiment handed over the position to IR 454 the gap to the neighboring regiment had been closed and a well-constructed trench had been created there with covered connections. The wire obstacles had been strengthened and there were numerous mined dugouts that had been completed or still under construction. Signal stations, observation positions, battle headquarters for the staff were all created and occupied and an extensive network of telephone connections with direct connections to every command post was in place.

The warm and sunny weather aided all of the work, and made the stay in the front line pleasant. The men even considered the right wing to be cozy and where a peaceful fondness developed in the very deep railway cut west of Neuville for the shelter it offered. On 19-20 April the I and II/R119 relieved IR 456 out of the position, the III/R119 remained in the rear and eventually moved forward into the suburbs of Isles on 26 April. The regimental headquarters was first located in Marcy, then in Homblieres.

The front taken over by RIR 119 was quiet and there was no battle activity at all,

Prinzing

Leutn. d. R. im Ref.-Inf.-Regt. 119,
gest. am 4. Mai 1917 an den bei
Beaumont-Hamel erhalt. Wunden

(Kriegstagebuch aus Schwaben)

nstead only patrol actions. The regiment was employed more as labor troops than fighting
roops as with the loss of the forward most trenches the entire position was in an unfinished
condition and it lacked everything necessary to be considered a strong position. The two
battalions held the front with two companies each. The remaining two were in reserve. All
available strength was put to use improving the position and to provide accommodations
or the front line troops. The reserves lay in strong cellars in the city where the men were
furnished with very domestic quarters.

While in the position the men learned of some bad news. Their well-liked commander,
Oberst Frhr. Von Ziegesar had been given command of the 27th Infantry Brigade. He left
his regiment with reluctance as he had formed a close bond to his men.

It was probably fortunate that there was so little activity at this time as the rations being
provided to the men had been gradually reduced in size since the end of previous year. This
reduction did not go unnoticed by the Allied Intelligence sections that had been tracking
the changes, mostly through statements made by prisoners and captured documents.

No. 71   Canadian Corps
31st May 1917
Part II.
Information from other sources.
German Army Rations.
From prisoner's statements, it appears that German troops are best fed when in reserve
just behind the fighting line.

The figures given below apply to such troops, and may be regarded as the
maximum ration of the fighting troops.

Bread.- The bread ration was reduced on the 15th April 1917 from 750 grammes to 500 grammes.

Meat.- The daily meat ration has been gradually reduced during the past 18 months. Last October it was officially stated to be 250 grammes (8 3/4 ozs.). to-day it only amounts to 150-200 grammes, with 2 meatless days per week, or an average daily ration of 125 grammes (4 3/8 ozs.).

Vegetables.- The vegetable ration has decreased since October, 1916 from 150 grammes (5 1/3 ozs.) of rice (or its equivalent) to 80 grammes (3 ozs.) of dried turnips.

Groceries,- The ration of 125 grammes (4 3/8 ozs.) of sausage (or its equivalent) has been reduced to 75 grammes (2 2/3 ozs.).

Conclusions.- Since the Spring of 1916, rations have been reduced by the following amounts:

Bread 1/3

Meat 1/2

Vegetables 1/3 (considering the quality as well as the quantity.

Comparison with British ration.

The following table gives a comparison of the principal articles of diet in the British and German field rations:

Article	New British ration		German ration	
	grammes	ozs	grammes	ozs
Bread	453	16	500	16 ⅝
Rice	57	2	– -	– -
Oatmeal	24	6/7	– -	– -
(2 ozs. thrice weekly)				
Flour	– -	– -	20	¾
Meat	453	16	125	4⅜
Dried Vegetables	57	2	80	2¾
Jam	80	3	– -	– -
Cheese	80	3	– -	– -
Bacon	113	4	– -	– -
Sausage	– -	– -	75	2⅔
Total	1317	46 6/7	800	28½ [4]

At first the 26th Reserve Division served as an *Eingreifdivision* (Action Division) for the sector north of the large Cambrai-Arras road. It was also the reserve in the second line and explored the different advance routes leading to the position that had poor fields of fire. The men practiced rapidly assembling, counter attacks and methods to keep enemy attack columns away. Being quite adept at these functions was one reason why IR 180 was assigned the terrain between Epinoy and Sauchy-Cauchy. Despite being adept in the tactics of the time, within the individual companies there was still training in throwing hand grenades and the execution of counterattacks using *Stosstrupps*.

All of the training and practices were about to be put to use in early May when an undertaking was scheduled to take place against the enemy positions. On the morning of 6 May the I/R121 replaced the II/R121. On the same day preparations were being made for the undertaking using seven *Sturmtrupp* and two companies formed from volunteers of men from all of the companies in the regiment. On 8 May the regimental commander held a review of the raiding party at the training location that was an exact copy of the target area of the raid. In just a few seconds 500 live hand grenades were thrown by the men without any accidents worth noting. On 9 May, a review of the raiding party was to take place by the commander of the 2nd Army, however it was cancelled the night before as the division was to move to another location, a 'new pig sty' as the men called it, expecting no better.

Between 9 and 10 May RIR 119 was relieved from its position. The regiment then moved to a beautiful spot by Sensée, where there was good weather and even a chance to swim in the local waters. The 26th Reserve Division was assigned to be an *Eingreifdivision* for Group Quéant under *Generalleutnant* von Moser. However this beautiful existence also did not last long when on 16 May the regiment returned to Bullecourt once more where the division would become a position division in the line Hendecourt-Riencourt.

There had been heavy fighting at Bullecourt since 9 April and there was not much left of the village, only one badly damaged white stone house marked its location. The new front line was the former second line, the K.T.K. position and the reserves were in the artillery protection line halfway between Bullecourt and Hendecourt; both of these villages were also in ruins.

All of the obstacles and trenches had been destroyed in the heavy fighting and the terrain was just a field of craters, like the landscape of the moon. Despite these terrible conditions, the German sentries still occupied the old outpost zone. When the 26th Reserve Division relieved the 3rd Guard Infantry Division the sentries were moved further back. The position now ran on both sides of the village as it made no sense to hold the exposed projecting corner where the sentries were once located. According to RIR 121, 'the British General Staff reported that his troops had captured Bullecourt when in fact it was given to him.'

The exchange of troops in the position without any protective trenches and under artillery fire was very difficult. Only a few dugouts still existed and they were completely filled with men to the very top so that in most men crouched on every step. The good times, when every man had a dugout equipped with stoves, benches and tables was a thing of the past. Because of the overcrowding, the air in the dugouts was suffocating and smoking made the air so bad that many men felt they would pass out from lack of oxygen. Part of the garrison was forced to exist out in the open without protection from artillery fire and the weather, but in their case at least the air was breathable.

On 17 May IR 180 relieved the *Lehr* IR and took over the right wing of the old sector southwest of Riencourt. Since Bullecourt had fallen to the enemy as did the old forward line in the *Siegfried Stellung* the regiment occupied a crater position in front of Bullecourt until southwest of Riencourt. There were no wire obstacles protecting the crater field and because of a shortage of dugouts the larger part of the garrison had to sleep in the craters without any cover.

The line from Riencourt to Cagnicourt was known as *Wotan I*. For communications the following were in place: A light signal station was located in Riencourt and at the regimental battle headquarters located in *Wotan I* as well as a chain of runners from the K.T.K to the regimental battle headquarters to Villers.

The enemy was very active overall, his aircraft were seen in large numbers over the

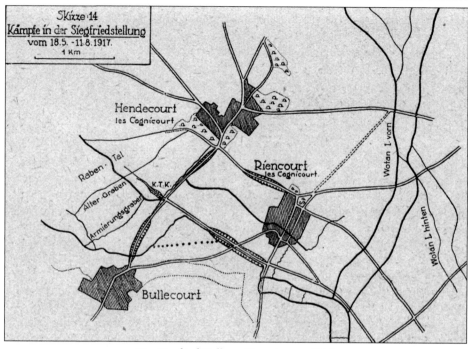

The *Siegfried Stellung*, May–August 1917.

position, powerful disturbance fire and fire raids of medium caliber shells were directed at the front line and over the entire battle zone behind it up to the artillery positions by Cagnicourt and fell on all approach routes. Villers also received artillery fire as well as Brioche farm so that the rest battalion found little peace.

It was extremely difficult to carry up food and water and building materials needed in the front. Wagons could reach the *Wotan* line and from there the supplies were carried forward with great effort under constant enemy searching fire and muddy conditions. While in the rear, a large number of men were housed in the catacombs of Riencourt, a system over 3 kilometers long.

There seemed to be no end to the Battle of Arras by mid-May. On 20 May the British attacked the neighboring division and penetrated into the position. In order to protect the flank of the division the 7/R121 was positioned in a communication trench, the *Alter Graben*, which lead to the right wing. During the entire day strong searching artillery fire swept the sector and there was a great deal of aerial activity with entire squadrons flying over the position firing machine guns at the men in the shell craters and small trench pieces.

At 4 a.m. 21 May drum fire fell on RIR 121 and almost immediately colored light balls climbed high into the air, the signal that the enemy was attacking. The assault waves could be seen in the light from the flares, advancing in dense groups. Artillery, rifle, machine gun and *Minenwerfer* fire initially held them up. While the British worked forward from shell crater to shell crater they were attacked with hand grenades and at individual places with bayonets and daggers and those who could escape fled toward the rear. Only at the border between the left wing of RIR 121 and right wing of IR 180 was the enemy able to break in. Even here, he was thrown out again in bitter close fighting.

Toward 6 a.m. the attack was completely repulsed and the position was held against the far stronger enemy attackers from the British 58th Division. Nine unwounded prisoners and four Lewis Guns were captured in the fighting. The losses in RIR 121 were 12 men killed, 49 men wounded; among which was the well-liked leader of the 6/R121, *Oberleutnant* Rüder who was killed and *Leutnants der Reserve* Frick, Thalheim and Beutel who were wounded. In the coming night still three patrol advances by the enemy were beaten off and two unwounded and three wounded British prisoners were brought in.

During the night of 20/21 May the entire regimental sector and in particular the rearward terrain of IR 180 was also covered with active enemy disturbance fire while the artillery batteries were shelled by heavy caliber guns. At 4 a.m. on 21 May the fire reached a level of drum fire and then at 4.03 a.m. the British advanced in masses in the Bullecourt-Hendecourt sunken road. Red light balls immediately rose up in the darkness, requesting barrage fire.

The 2/180, which was at the right wing of the regiment, met the British attack with well-aimed fire. However, the enemy was too strong, and the 2/180 was slowly forced back, fighting tenaciously from every shell hole. By 4.30 a.m. the British had already penetrated about 300 meters past the German front line when the advance was slowed somewhat.

At this moment, the company leader of the 2/180, *Leutnant* Martis, and his men took advantage of the enemy hesitation and began to move forward in small groups that eventually grew into a full-scale counterattack. The men rushed forward toward the British troops but were met with withering fire and the company was forced to withdraw further to the rear. *Leutnant* Martis assembled the remnants of his company, personally took command of the left wing and turned control over the right wing to *Offizier Stellvertreter* Häussler and *Unteroffizier* Lindenmayer. The counterattack was resumed; no man hesitated and the attack surged forward with the cries of 'Hurrah', as each shell crater was cleared of the enemy troops.

The British defended their positions tenaciously, the men already entrenching under the protection of numerous Lewis Guns they had placed in position. Despite this effort, the British could not withstand the powerful advance by the 2/180, and they slowly yielded to the rear over the former German front line; it was here where *Leutnant* Martis was killed.

The men of the 2/180 were furious about the loss of their company leader and continued to advance on their own until they reached a point about 50 meters in front of the forward line. *Offizier Stellvertreter* Häussler then took command of the company and drove back a second advance by the enemy through another counterattack. At 5.30 a.m. Häussler led the company back and reoccupied the old position. 3 Lewis Guns and 21 prisoners were captured in the fighting and the enemy reportedly suffered extraordinary losses. The 2/180 also suffered heavy casualties in the fighting, losing 40 men killed and wounded.

Offizier Stellvertreter Häussler, *Vizefeldwebel* Kaufmann, *Unteroffizier* Kehrer and Lindenmayer were singled out for their exemplary behavior in the fighting. *Krankenträger Gefreiter* Plitt had performed excellent service bringing in the wounded in the heavy fire despite also being wounded.

Casualties among officers had been high in the war and the loss a good officer such as *Leutnant* Martis was a heavy blow to any company. The younger, newer officers did not have the training or experience of the old officers. The 2/180 was ordered to the rear after the fighting had died down because of the heavy losses it had suffered and was replaced by the 3/180. The night remained restless as the enemy tried two more times to attack the position;

The '*Heldenbilder*'. A derelict tank just outside of the German trenches. (*Das Württembergische Reserve-Infanterie-Regiment Nr. 119 im Weltkrieg 1914-1918*)

each time being repulsed in the heavy defensive fire.

On 25 May, five additional British prisoners were brought in by patrols from RIR 121. The enemy artillery continued to be active for several days, then it died down somewhat. With this, the heavy fighting that had taken place for many weeks had finally ended. Bullecourt had been mentioned in the daily army reports for weeks and the name became connected with the role played by the men from RIR 121. The regiment had successfully defended its position thanks to the hard work the troops had performed in restoring the defenses. With these improvements, the battalions could be rotated from the front line and reserve every three days.

In spite of all of the hard work already performed, the work never seemed to have an end as the men continued to improve the defenses in the rear areas, connecting groups of shell craters into small trench lines and then connecting these into larger defenses, much as they did in October 1914 during the early days on the Somme. With all the work being performed, very little was being changed in the first line so that the enemy aerial photographs would not reveal the exact front line positions. As a result of this effort, or possibly from sheer luck, the forward garrison received the smallest amount of enemy artillery fire of all of the positions. In accordance with the idea of concealing the actual front line there was no traffic in the forward position during the day; only messenger dogs were used to travel back and forth between the forward most line and the K.T.K. and between the K.T.K. and the regimental battle headquarters further in the rear.

Runners would be used to make the dangerous journey only when it was absolutely necessary. The battalion commanders and orderly officers of the higher staff still came up to the front line in the dark, early morning hours so they could obtain personal knowledge

The same tank as in the previous picture. (*Das Württembergische Reserve-Infanterie-Regiment Nr. 121 im Weltkrieg 1914-1918*)

of the overall situation as well as asking the men for their opinions and observations, experiences and requests. They listened to as many men as possible and observed things that many of the officers had never seen before in their time in service.

There were also large numbers of carrying troops who brought up ammunition and food into the position. The carrying parties travelled night after night, through random artillery and machine gun fire and through tremendous difficulties and on poorly defined paths as they struggled to supply all of the needs of the men holding the front line.

The carrying troops wore the new steel helmets, burdened with food packs or baskets strapped to their backs and a large stick in one hand to help the men traverse the difficult terrain. The carriers moved as silently as possible at the quick step, man behind man, through the dark night. The trip to and from the front line was long and exhausting but once finished; the men who had survived the journey were allowed to rest and relax in the rear during the day. Then however, it would all begin once more the next night as soon as darkness fell.

Finally, at the beginning of June the situation at the front had quieted down to the point where the men of IR 180 were allowed to create an actual trench system that replaced

Machine-gun crew, IR 180, June 1917. (Author's collection)

the shell crater line. New barbed wire obstacles were erected; machine gun nests with good flanking effect were created and in a short time the position was turned into a very defensible location.

One thing that was new and disconcerting to many of the older veterans was the lack of a fixed enemy line as there once had been in the fighting from 1915 and 1916. On 1 June a patrol from IR 180 went up to old *Siegfried Stellung* but was prevented from continuing any further by enemy troops who were occupying the numerous shell craters. However, in other parts of the same terrain the patrol found it completely free of the enemy. A half dozen destroyed tanks and several aircraft lay in the foreground, the tanks looked like giant turtles. They were relics of the recent heavy fighting, and represented the newest threat to the infantry. One tank was so close to the trench that it served as a background for the trench photographers as a '*Heldenbilder*'.

On 7 June IR 180 moved to Sauchy-Lestrée where it remained until the beginning of August. While there, many other units were rotated from the front to the rest areas for rest and recuperation. The men held sporting events of all types, which included tree climbing and ring tossing. Concerts were regularly held by the regimental band.

RIR 121 remained in the position in the constant artillery fire and stressful sentry and patrol duty until 12 June. Then, the regiment exchanged positions with RIR 119 and took over a well-constructed position at the left wing of the division by Riencourt.

Once safely in the rear, the men of IR 180 could finally have a chance to relax. The regimental savings fund had grown to a considerable size and was being used to procure very valuable awards to be given out following the sporting activities and also provided ample amounts of beer for the men; something many felt was a good use of the money. In the evenings the battalions would return to the village with the band playing at the head of the column.

Aside from the fun and games, there were also times when serious training occurred. Combat training in the newest forms of defense and attack were held; all weapons and pieces of equipment were restored to good working order. Along with the school for target practice with rifles and pistols, there was target practice while wearing gas masks, instruction on the use of the machine guns sights, installing and removing the *Minenwerfer*, training in hand grenades and *Stosstrupps* tactics, lessons about gas warfare, capturing enemy machine

Hauptm. d. R. Pischel
gef. bei Zandvoorde 9. 6. 1917

(*Das Württembergisches Reserve-Feldartillerie-Regiment Nr. 26 im Weltkrieg 1914-1918*)

gun nests and how to fight against enemy tanks among others. The months of June and July passed in this manner without much else happening.

The men from RIR 119 had been lucky during the first weeks back in the front lines. When the enemy attacked the German lines on 20 and 26 May it was further north of the regimental position each time. The only impact on RIR 119 was during that each attack the regiment came under the enemy preparation fire zone and suffered a number of losses.

Then, starting from 10 June the battle zone of RIR 119 came under artillery fire, which continued for a long period of time and increased in strength that it was believed an attack would follow. At 3 a.m. on 14 June drum fire was placed on the regimental sector, and 20 minutes later two to three British companies attacked on a 600 meter wide front. The main thrust was on the Bullecourt-Hendecourt road where all of the sentries had been killed in the enemy's annihilation fire.

The enemy advanced into the crater field held by the 3/R119. But, before they could become firmly established, the garrison of a neighboring sector, which had repulsed a frontal attack, was able to throw them out at daybreak using hand grenades. The men had often dealt with such strong enemy reconnaissance patrols like this and knew just what they needed to do. The patrols sent out following the fighting were unable to identify the dead British troops as they had no insignia or papers on them. One patrol from the 1/R119 under *Unteroffizier* Schäfer was able to firmly establish that numerous rifles had been thrown away in the attack, which his men found scattered around the terrain. Schäfer was also able to bring in a prisoner that his patrol found hiding out in no man's land.

On 15 June an even stronger enemy attack took place. At 4 a.m. drum fire fell on the positions of RIR 119 and the German guns quickly replied by placing powerful barrage fire

Infantrymen, IR 180, June 1917. (Author's collection)

like a barrier in front of the threatened sector. However, this fire did not deter the enemy who boldly attacked. The enemy line suddenly appeared advancing out of the dense smoke created by the shells. Then, furious rifle and machine gun fire struck into the opposing ranks, forcing them to withdraw. Only a few managed to make it to the German lines where they were destroyed in hand grenade fire. During this attack, *Musketier* Herdtle, 1/ R119, stood out for his actions.

However, while the attack against RIR 119 had failed, the enemy had successfully pressed back the regiment positioned further to the north and forced them back to the second trench where the fighting raged the entire day. The fighting in and around RIR 119 had been so heavy the I/R121 had been sent back to Bullecourt to provide support for the regiment. Considering the successful defense by RIR 119 the I/R121 was not needed and returned to the regiment.

The enemy's success at the neighboring regiment resulted in a new enemy attack on 16 June against the same regiment and the right wing of RIR 119 where the 4/R119 was positioned. In the north, the enemy pressed over the second trench up until the '*Rabental*'. The British now attacked the 4/R119 from the rear, which held firm despite being outflanked. Finally, the British were able to press the 4/R119 into the second trench where they threw hand grenades into the dugout entrances.

The 4/R119 formed a counterattack and managed to throw the invaders out of the trench and took some prisoners in the process. Once again, heavy fighting played out all day by the neighboring regiment. The right wing of RIR 119 now hung in the air and was threatened by being enveloped. The situation did not improve until evening, when the neighboring regiment recaptured its second trench. June finally came to an end with constant artillery fire of varying strength and regular patrol activity against Bullecourt.

New tactics were being used by the British during this recent period of trench warfare; fire raids using gas mines fired from a device called a Livens Projector, named after the inventor Captain William Howard Livens. On 22 June a large number of gas mines were fired at the German lines using this method and within moments the entire area was covered in gas. The men quickly became gas sick if they did not put on their gas masks fast enough.

While the enemy was experimenting with new weapons, the German army was reinforcing the importance of a weapon that had been invaluable in the fighting since August 1914; the machine gun.

No. 84   Canadian Corps
13th June, 1917
Part II
Information from other sources.
Translation of Extracts from captured German documents
Instructions for detached Machine Guns (From 2nd Army Summary)

1. The chief object of detached machine guns is to keep enemy troops, who have broken through the line and reached their objectives, in the positions they have captured and then to annihilate them to the last man.
2. Every man in a detached M.G. position must know that the longer he holds up the enemy, the earlier will reserves come up to relieve him. Any man who is detailed for duty with a detached M.G. must realise that his superiors are conferring a distinction on him and showing great reliance in him. From this it naturally follows that a voluntary iron discipline must be kept among the team of such a M.G. post. The gun crews will be thanked and rewarded.
3. The enemy does not know the location of our detached posts, and everything must therefore to be done to avoid the position being given away, e.g. quantities of smoke, frequent movement, tracks are all to be avoided. When enemy aeroplanes approach, cover is immediately to be sought and men must not stand about to watch the aircraft out of curiosity.
4. The M.G. need not necessarily be fired only from its normal emplacement. It is often far better to make use of a hedge, a shell-hole, or the remains of an old wall, than to stick rather anxiously to the concrete emplacement. Every man must look for and know the alternate positions chosen. This is all the easier as the same gun crews will probably always be sent to the same gun.
5. The main position will always be the concrete emplacement. If the gun crew takes up an alternative position, 1,500 cartridges, water and cleaning materials should be taken to the new position. Alarm practices should be arranged daily by the N.C.O. in charge, including drills for changing positions.
6. Even under the heaviest fire a sentry must be out within calling or signaling distance. This sentry will only be called in by the N.C.O. in charge when the M.G. has started to fire.
7. Every N.C.O. in charge and men of the gun team must make quite certain that he sees the enemy before he starts firing. Ammunition is very valuable and can only be replaced with very great difficulty. Supply of ammunition is to come up with the rations.

8. The following points must be carefully considered by each man: From which direction can Tanks come? On which roads? Across which dry open fields? Where can one check or hold them up? How is one to fight them (a) is one to do it by putting up wire entanglements, filling broad trenches with water, or constructing steep banks? (b) remember to shoot at them with SMK cartridges, which are packed in separate boxes with red stripes down the sides. Aim low down on the side or – if using a telescope sight – aim at the openings.
9. Shoot at aircraft flying below 1,000 metres with SMK ammunition, but do not fire alone; co-operate with flank guns. [5]

Undertakings and patrols continued to be held on a regular basis from which the most important trophy was enemy prisoners. Even if no prisoners were taken all observations of the enemy lines and activities as well as documents, uniform insignia, etc. were considered important in the attempt to determine the enemy order of battle, replacement schedule, sentries and machine gun locations.

One daring patrol from the 12/R121 went out at 1 p.m., in broad daylight, snuck into the enemy trench, overran two enemy soldiers who were boiling coffee and brought them back as prisoners. It was considered almost too simple to succeed, but in this instance it did just that. It was just another example of how fluid the opposing front lines had become. Another patrol from the 9/R121 also overran a position containing two enemy soldiers; however they had to release them when British reinforcements began to approach.

The reserves from RIR 121 were accommodated in the rear in dilapidated quarters, which offered little protection against the wind and rain. A large railway gun located in front of the camp had become very annoying; especially when it fired and everything in the village rattled and shook. The British made numerous attempts to locate and destroy the gun and fired at every location where they thought it might be located; at times all too close to the reserve positions. However, they never did locate it as it moved around constantly; particularly along the western edge of the village. In addition to the railway gun and constant enemy searching fire there was heavy wagon and vehicle traffic at night which disturbed the men's rest a great deal; still, despite everything, the troops were glad to be in the rear.

In the night of 1/2 July the I/R119 attempted a daring patrol under the command of *Vizefeldwebel* Rein. The men in the raiding party left their trench at 11 p.m. and moved forward toward a wood pile located on the Hendecourt-Bullecourt road, which was at the entrance of the village and from there they could see the enemy positions on the right. The raiding party continued to advance and ran into a British trench which they found was empty and which also lead to a large crater.

At that moment, they suddenly they saw a machine gun post with four men behind them, the surprised gun crew ran away shouting the alarm. Rein and his men quickly followed after and caught them. The chase had brought the Germans and their prisoners into the vicinity of a mined dugout in the crater which was found to be occupied by 20-25 British soldiers.

Gefreiter Sauter started to brawl man to man with one enemy soldier, who however broke free and was shot down while trying to escape. From the cries of the sentries and the shot the British soldiers poured out of the dugout. Rein and a couple of his men pressed forth to meet them. Rein emptied his pistol into the entrance and then threw hand grenades into the densely occupied dugout. During the fighting, *Gefreiten* Herdtle and Sauter struggled with three British soldiers around the machine gun, shooting them down and then removed the weapon from the position and eventually brought it back to the German lines, carrying it through machine gun and hand grenade fire.

The noise of the fighting had alarmed the entire British trench garrison and reinforcements poured from out of all dugouts, trenches and from the church, hurrying to the spot in order to punish the 'cheeky invaders'. However the raiding party had already gone back a before the reinforcements could arrive. Herdtle and Sauter were also able to cut and remove two wire cables in the crater, before they had left.

During this patrol action, *Unteroffizier* Bauder with his small detachment had formed the left flank guard and kept back the British who had been approaching the crater from the left. Bauder had become severely wounded and laid on the open ground in the machine gun fire. *Musketier* Biggör saw Bauder lying there, sprang over to him through the heavy fire, threw him on his back and carried him back 50 meters into a shell crater from which Rein, Herdtle and *Musketier* Döttling carried him back along with a stretcher bearer under great difficulty.

Gefreiten Hess and Reichert and *Musketier* Kraus had all been praised for their acts of bravery in the action. When the patrol was counted in the dugout about 30 minutes later, *Musketier* Wölfle, a mechanic from Schwenningen, was missing. It would take some time, but eventually his fate would become known.

During the close fighting with the enemy soldiers who had poured out from the mined dugout, Wölfle had been grabbed by a half dozen strong and powerful hands and made a prisoner. He was questioned in a dugout in the church of Bullecourt and then he was brought back to St. Leger in a transport wagon where he was engaged in a discussion with a Captain who spoke good German. However Wölfle was vague in his responses. He had no insignia or papers on him and so he provided quite extensive responses to all of the questions, none of which had a kernel of truth. Apparently his cooperation greatly pleased his interrogators who were eagerly taking notes.

All of his money had been taken from him except for 17 *Reich Pfennig*. He was then moved to a prisoner of war camp in the park of St. Leger, where he met 80 German soldiers from IR 124 and IR 178, who had to provide labor service. Very quickly, Wölfle became displeased with life in the camp. The men slept in tents on the cold earth, received little food and it was generally bad. On a daily basis the men were given 1/2 pound of bread, a spoon filled with marmalade or butter, a liter of coffee, soup from turnips or bread and one or two times a week 125 grams of horse flesh.

He had handed in his uniform and was given prisoner clothing to wear. While in the camp and at work Wölfle looked around the area, keeping his ears and eyes open. He quickly decided that he was going to attempt an escape and in a few days of being captured he found his opportunity. They say luck favors the bold and on 4 July Wölfle simply decided to take a hike to Croisilles. At 8 a.m. he started his stroll, nobody took any notice of him. Halfway to Croisilles-Bullecourt he hid in a shell hole and waited for darkness. At the western edge of Bullecourt he found a dead British soldier and he pulled off his uniform and wrapped it around him. He then crawled toward the German lines and, after having to wait until a strong bombardment of the German positions had ended, he luckily came into the lines by the 2/R119. For his courageous behavior and the information that he was able to provide regarding the enemy positions and rear areas he was promoted to *Unteroffizier*.

Further bold patrols were undertaken by *Vizefeldwebel* Hörmann of the 2/R119, wh
had already proven his worth at the crater field by Beaumont where he had performe
similar patrols and brought back important information about the enemy position an
distribution of strength. Not every patrol ended in success however. On 6 July a we
prepared patrol undertaking by the III/R119 once again advanced stealthily toward th
wood pile by Bullecourt. Instead of successfully surprising the enemy trench garrison, th
patrol members ended up in severe close fighting and the superior enemy strength was to
great to overcome. Even though the patrol had been forced to withdraw, it had been able t
place an enemy machine gun out of action.

The patrol was forced to withdraw slowly, taking their wounded with them. The Britis
who had apparently also planned an undertaking the same night and at the same locatio
followed after the men of the III/R119 all the way up to the first German trench where th
enemy was driven back by well-placed German barrage fire.

On 12 July, *Leutnant der Reserve* Bohnert with eleven men penetrated into the Britis
line, drove off a double sentry post and occupied the entrance of a former German dugou
Several occupants of the dugout had surrendered when facing the well-armed raiding part
but others refused to come up from below. Bohnert and his men felt they had no othe
choice but to throw hand grenades into the dugout until enemy reinforcements hurryin
toward them forced the patrol back. Still, Bohnert had taken several prisoners and his me
brought back a Lewis Gun as a souvenir. A repeat of a similar undertaking in the followin
night failed as a result of the heavy fire coming from an enemy machine gun emplacement

The German successes irritated the English and forced them to strike a counterblow. A
12.30 a.m. on 15 July powerful preparation fire fell against the regimental sector of RIR 11
one of the first heavy shells hit the only dugout of the 5/R119, located on the Bullecour
Hendecourt road, set fire to a pile of Very light ammunition and set the dugout on fire s
that the garrison were in part burned to death and in part badly injured. In addition to th
losses, two light machine guns without their crews were buried.

The connecting crater garrison soon saw dense masses of British soldiers coming from
the wood pile by Bullecourt in the flickering light of the numerous light balls, breaking forth
along the road. The 5/R119 located to the west of the road held up the attack with rapi
fire. The surprised enemy fought back but apparently forgot to pull the pins on their han
grenades before throwing them, rendering them useless. East of the road however they wer
able to penetrate into the crater field, as the garrison positioned there had been placed ou
of action by the artillery fire or were overrun and shot down. During this time, *Leutnan
der Reserve* Kopf with his small group of men attacked the enemy lying in the craters s
effectively that they soon went back in groups. The retreating enemy soldiers suffered heav
losses from infantry fire as well as well-placed barrage fire and left behind rifles and boxes o
explosives. However, the short fight cost the 5/R119 9 killed and 20 wounded.

The regiment also suffered losses from an increasing number of gas fire raids. On
particularly effective enemy tactic used at this time was to tempt the garrison out of it
shelters in order to defend against a patrol undertaking. Then, the enemy fired gas mine
among the garrison who were hurrying to the firing line. As a result of this tactic, on on
occasion five men were killed and 46 were gas sick including the members of a patrol wh
had fought against the enemy raiding party with hand grenades.

The loss of well proven, trusted men was particularly hard for the regiment. These wer
soldiers with experience and who could be counted upon in every situation. They served a

Regimental dead, IR 180 (Felix Fregin)

good examples for the others and these men were being lost week after week. These officers and men were considered the backbone of the regiment and the units were less effective when these men were gone.

At the end of July RIR 121 was back at the right wing of the division by Bullecourt. The relief of the 1st Guard Reserve Division began on 19/20 July. The situation facing the men of RIR 121 was not very pleasant. They were subjected to heavy artillery and mine fire, patrol attacks, poor quarters and shelters and great difficulty bringing up food and supplies. The heavy work, extreme tension, nerve rendering sentry duty, poor quarters, shortage of support, constant fire and shortage of sleep for long periods of time had a detrimental effect on the men. Intestinal illnesses and stomach troubles further reduced the battle strength of the regiments. The men were shadows of their former selves, gaunt and wan. Uniforms and boots were tattered and thread bare; it was high time the regiments were relieved.

In the days from 19-22 July RIR 119 was relieved by RIR 121 and went to the rear to rest. However, the rest time was short and incomplete. Further training was soon ordered and companies were brought forward to dig trenches. RIR 119 was destined to be thrown back into the Hell of Bullecourt once more when the regiment relieved IR 180 in the time from 2-4 August and the misery started again.

On 7 August orders arrived for the relief of RIR 121, which would start on 9 August The difficult days by Bullecourt were over, and the men were happy to leave. Before the men could be taken out of the front lines there was one more unpleasant day. On 8 August a devastating cloudburst filled the narrow trenches with water, flooded the dugouts and caused the trench walls to collapse.

When on 10-11 August RIR 119 was relieved by RIR 94 and the men were loaded onto trains in Aubigny au Bac, rumors began to circulate that the 26th Reserve Division was being sent to another part of the front and everyone was extremely interested on where they were going. Further news arrived, and as the division was being transported in a northerly direction toward Douai and Lille, finally into Belgium and to Sweveghem, about 5 kilometers east of Kortrijk, the destination became evident, the division was going 'To Flanders' where unending marshy terrain made position warfare very unpleasant.

Notes

1.   Gerster, op. cit., p. 48.
2.   Canadian War diaries.
3.   IR 456 formed part of the 235th Infantry Division that was formed in January 1917. The regiments of the division had been created with 50% of the men coming from the Class of 1918, 50% of the men being returned sick and wounded and some men combed from other divisions. The division was partially trained and then sent into the front lines on 15 March 1917, just before the Allied attacks.
4.   Canadian War Diaries.
5.   Canadian War Diaries.

10

The 28th Reserve Division

May-August 1917

Once the need for the 28th Reserve Division on the Chemin des Dames had ended, the division was being immediately returned to the front lines by Verdun where even such a small division was urgently needed to occupy a portion of the front lines. The journey to the new sector was difficult and uncomfortable as the men of the 28th Reserve Division travelled in pouring rain, thunderstorms and pitch black nights where it would eventually replace the 103rd Infantry Division near Verdun.

The II and III/R111, which had become transported on the morning and early afternoon of 20 May from Vilosne on the Maas, relieved parts of IR 71 on the eastern bank of the Maas on the same evening. The battalions reached a camp by the village of Etraye after a march of about 15 kilometers by way of Reville, south of Damvillers, where a short rest was allowed. Then a field-railway brought the remnants of the companies up to the *Müllerplatz*, south of Flabas. From there guides pointed out the route on a steeply incised road through forested and mountainous terrain to the trenches situated about 4 kilometers to the south. Finally, on 22 May, RIR 110 reached its destination at Vilosne and the skies were finally clear and blue. The II and I/R110 moved into position in the night of 22/23 May. The II/R110 relieved the I/R116 in the outpost position upon Talou ridge while the I/R110 moved into the position of the II/R116, from the Maas Canal bathing area.

These movements apparently did not remain unnoticed by the French. They covered the approach route with disturbance fire that caused losses in both battalions. The sector of the regiment was south of Beaumont and situated opposite the French positions at Louvement. It proceeded on three ridges running from the east to the west, descending to the Maas. Louvement with the southwestern subsequent Pfeffer ridge had remained in the hands of the French in December of 1916 after hard fighting. The wreckage of heavy German guns that had been blown up in their positions at that time, were still in the ravine south of Beaumont. The III/R111 occupied the open left wing in Fosse wood by IR 168, with the 12th and 11/R111 and a support company from *Landsturm* Battalion Heilbronn in the forward line of the Mormont position. This, originally only an outpost position, was barely developed and offered limited possibilities for housing.

It became feared that the companies holding the front line would not have an easy time in the new sector. In the first night the 11/R111 drove back an enemy patrol that had approached the position using an old sap. It was the first time many of the men who had recently joined the regiment had faced actual combat conditions and according to the War Diary of the III/R111 the especially good behavior of the young replacements was prominently mentioned, especially those who had gone into the position for the first time.

The 9th and 10/R111 were located in the second line with the battalion staff in the *Fosses Riegel* and in the *Eck Schlucht* where a few facilities were located. The II/R111 had taken over the protection of the line facing west, on the right of the III/R111. Because

See caption on
following page

Three photographs that, when placed end to end, form a panoramic view of 28th
Division's sector at Verdun. These images depict the extensive trench works with
regard to the defense in depth strategy then in use. (Author's collection)

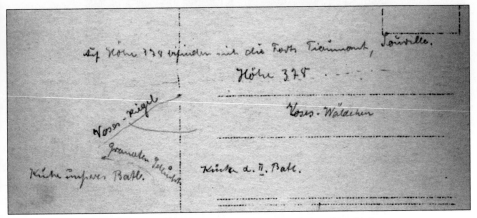

Panoramic photographs legend. Voses Riegel and Wäldchen
should be Fosse. (Author's collection)

the subsequent and to the southwest projection in the Maas arc between Samogneux and
Vacherauville, which ran along the heights of the Talou ridge, was only secured through
outposts, in the event of a strong attack the garrison was to move back upon the main
position.

The 6/R111 was positioned in the *Granat Riegel*, the 5/R111 lay in the *Mormont Riegel*,
both of which turned off in a northern direction from the *Mormont Stellung* and all of
these works required much needed improvements. Behind them, in the *Fosses Riegel* and
in the *Mörser Schlucht*, was the 7/R111 and two platoons of the 8/R111 as the readiness
garrison, in which the battalion battle headquarters was also located.

The *Beaumont Riegel*, as the third line, was protected by 3rd Platoon of the 8/R111
and one company of *Landsturm* Battalion Heilbronn. The right regimental border was
indicated in the forward line by the Vachárauville-Beaumont road which moved in the
Granaten Tal. From here the connection to RIR 109 was maintained through patrols. The
I/R111 was placed in the villages of Vachárauville and Beaumont. The regimental staff had
its command post in Caures Wood, south of the *Müllerplatz*. One company of *Landsturm*
Battalion Heilbronn and part of the Construction Company were also accommodated in
a camp in Caures Wood.

The regiment remained in this position with regular rotations of the battalions until
the beginning of July. Fortunately, the first period of time passed, apart from occasional

Nachrichten troops of RIR 111 who took the previous panoramic photographs.
The position they are occupying is just to the right of the third photograph
where the tree branches are located. (Author's collection)

fire raids, quite peacefully apart from the occasional enemy raid. These circumstances and
the beautiful weather, which had started favored the extension of the defensive facilities
and came as a relief to the numerous replacements as they became adjusted to life in the
fire trench.

> At 8 o'clock in the evening (20 May) we came into a rest camp (Etraye). For the first
> time as newcomers we saw the facilities of a rest camp in the field. However nothing
> would come from our rest, because after receiving the evening rations the *Feldwebel*
> said to us that before we could lie down on our skin, we were going into the position
> at midnight. There one still had no notion, what it actually looked like in a position.
> At exactly 12 midnight we were embarked and transported to the front with a field
> railway. Our company was in possession of only two wagons; it already soon became
> somewhat uncomfortable there. After a rail journey of 2 hours with miscellaneous

stops we came to our destination. Now we thought, here is the position that our company was to occupy, however soon came other lessons. They now called us to take 10 meter spacing from man to man, and then we went away like this in single file for an hour. After a march lasting approximately a quarter of an hour the first shell soon flew away over our heads. Many of the novices looked for cover on the ground, until the older comrades had reassured us and said to us that the shots went further behind us. The Frog had to have noticed however something that a relief was taking place and soon a few impacts found the march route and our company had the first fallen to mourn, still before we were in position. Now it went to the trench into the individual dugouts, where we were relieved. I had, as the first, the luck to now go on guard. The man, who I relieved, said to me that it was a very quiet position, there was nothing going on. I still wanted to inquire how far away the enemy trench was, and soon the man in front of me was missing in the darkness. The French artillery now sent individual greetings across as a reception for us. The 2 hours became like a small eternity to me. After my relief came I would therefore now come once more into a dugout. I was amazed! So I had no dugout available just for me. It was awfully cramped.

That it was not the best place to get into the dugout, I need not probably mention, until one [a shell] arrived 2 hours later. The following day proceeded quietly first of all. It was between Pentecost and splendid weather when I became dedicated to entrenching and placing entanglements. The French were pretty quiet and so we thought that it was not at all so bad in which the war was being conducted. However we soon also learned to know the other side. *Musketier* Lehmann, 9/R111 [1]

Given the large numbers of replacements that were arriving in the division there was a particular need to train the men in the methods of trench warfare. When the battalions were rotated out of the front line they used the rest days in the *Köhlerdorf* by Etraye for training of the replacements in order to make them as proficient as possible. Special attention became placed on target practice training. It had been noticed in the recent fighting that many of the men had relied more upon the hand grenade than the rifle when defending a position and the higher commands wanted to make sure every man was capable of using his rifle correctly.

In addition to normal infantry training, there were courses being held for the new infantry tactics, those used by the *Sturmtrupps*. A training command from *Sturmbataillon Rohr* arrived in the sector and instructed the companies in the new close combat tactics. All officers and *Portepee Unteroffiziere* also completed their training with the heavy and light machine guns. Despite all of the emphasis placed on training, there was still time for the men to enjoy some rest and relaxation. Physical exercise was also considered important in order to keep the men fit and as such open air gymnastic games were promoted heavily.

Along with training came the inevitable nightly patrols and raids needed in order to determine the intentions of the enemy. Because very often patrols were outside the lines from both sides before the front every night there was often small skirmishes with the opposing patrols. This was especially true in front of the sector of the 11/R111 where frequent firefights occurred between both sides. This was most likely because the forward French position north of Louvement was very close to the German line, while further to the west the spacing between the positions of both sides became much wider.

While the overall position was described as being 'quiet', there were still times when

Sturmtrupp training. (Author's collection)

there was some excitement. In the night of 28/29 May a French patrol in the strength of about 30 men attacked a double sentry of the 6/R110 in front of *Talou Mitte*. The enemy troops had apparently crawled through the high grass during a strong wind until they had approached within throwing distance of the sentry post and surprised the two sentries with a salvo of hand grenades. *Musketiers* Bayer and Ulbrich, both men who had come from the most recent group of replacements, fought back with rifles and hand grenades. During the firefight, both men became wounded; Bayer from a splinter in the head, which was assumed to be fatal, Ulbrich received hand grenade fragments on both thighs. *Unteroffizier* Brombacher, 6/R110, hurried with his fellow sentries to help the double sentry post however the enemy had already returned to the French lines, taking the two wounded men with them.

However, while the French were dragging *Musketier* Bayer over the wire entanglements Ulbrich succeeded in escaping his captors. Despite his severe wounds he ran toward the German lines, until he was able to come into a shell hole. On the next day Ulbrich was detected using a stereo telescope and in the night from 29 to 30 May two Groups from the 6/R110 went out into no man's land and brought him back to safety.

The company leader, *Leutnant der Reserve* Hambrecht, tells about this action:

In the last weeks of May the Sixth Company had the middle company sector on the Talou ridge and with it also the protection of the foreground in the Maas valley and towards Vachárauville. A platoon of the company had a picket to occupy in the night at the southern steep slope of the Talou and a chain of double sentry posts in the level foreground until to the Maas canal and to the southeast in the direction of the French position in front of Vachárauville to set up, which was moved into again in the morning.

The platoon of *Vizefeldwebel* Meyer formed the picket, and one of the double posts consisted out of the two young people Ulbrich and Bayer. *Gefreiter* Schwörer with one man had the patrol inside the chain of sentries and they had just left the double post and had reached the vicinity of the picket dugout, when he heard the noise of hand grenades and rifle shots. He immediately alarmed the pickets and hurried with the Half Platoon leader *Unteroffizier* Brombacher, followed by the remaining men with a cheer in the direction of the double sentry post that had been attacked. They still heard screams and the sounds of the French hurrying to run away. The sentry hole was empty. Schwörer fired a light ball up, whereupon the machine gun positioned in the foreground in front of the sentry chain opened fire. At the place of the raid French rifles and pieces of equipment were found as well as the cap of one of the sentries, perforated and bloodstained.

On the early morning of 30 May we looked out into the foreground from Talou hill with binoculars for tracks of the nighttime fighting and saw something lying in the middle of the foreground that resembled a person. Through the stereo telescope in the artillery observation post at the left wing of our sector we then clearly recognized that it was now a German soldier, who was laying in an old shell hole and who moved now and then. At the conspicuous body length it was able to determine that it had to be our right wing man Ulbrich.

The company leader gave *Gefreiten* Schwörer the order to crawl out into the foreground at the onset of darkness with six men, who reported as volunteers, and two stretcher bearers with a stretcher and get Ulbrich before the French did, who had definitely also seen him and had a much easier time to be able to reach him. Schwörer crawled at the head of his men to the position where Ulbrich lay, called the name quietly without getting a reply, he found a position where the grass had been pressed down and feared that the French have come before him. However he crawled a small distance sideways on the left, always quietly calling, until he saw a dark body. He cried: Ulbrich, it is Schwörer, coming to get you. The shape there rose up slightly. Schwörer crawled to him and Ulbrich fell to his neck and kissed him out of joy. He complained he was thirsty, and while he drank one canteen filled with coffee and one with tee, Schwörer directed the stretcher bearers to take him to the rear. *Sanitäter* Greilsheimer and Schwörer placed Ulbrich, who had been severely wounded on the legs by hand grenade splinters, on the stretcher, on which he was quickly brought back to the position.

At first 18 1/2 year old Ulbrich was quite lively despite the wounds and exhaustion. He told how they were overrun in their sentry post, having been showered with hand grenades, and that they had fired and threw hand grenades although both had been wounded, but from the large superiority of about 50 men they were overpowered and had been dragged away. Both lay very still in front of the French obstacles, because the French had very hastily come back to safety. Ulbrich considered his comrade Bayer for dead; however, he was only unconscious because of his head injury. There Ulbrich crawled away to the German position despite his injured legs and remained lying some distance away; later he heard the French who were searching for him, however he had not dared to come far enough forward. Then he crawled further until he was in a shell hole and remained lying there unconscious where he awakened again in the morning. The entire day over he then lay there with shattered legs in the hot sun, almost languishing and filled with despair, because he believed we could not see him and he would die there. It was in the darkness of evening when the French already crawled forth in front of our people and called his name that they had found out from Bayer.

However Ulbrich knew from the voice that he was no comrade and behaved quietly. He therefore did not give Schwörer a reply, until he mentioned his own name. [2]

Ulbrich's conduct was praised in a division order and he was awarded the Iron Cross II Class which was well earned. Bayer and the rescue party also received a commendation on the part of the division. Ulbrich was immediately taken from the Talou and became brought into a military hospital. Unfortunately the wounds Ulbrich suffered in the attack had been too severe and despite all efforts, he succumbed a few days after. After a period of time had passed, Bayer provided some news from the prison camp where he was being held. While his wounds had appeared to be fatal, actually they were not as severe as believed and he had made a full recovery.

On 1 June eleven bandsmen arrived at RIR 109 from the Replacement Battalion. With the arrival of these men there was the opportunity to revive the regimental band. The new men, along with the surviving band members, were allowed to practice and thereby become excused from some of the fatigues and drills the rest of the regiment had to perform. It was a relief to the few existing band members who had long ago given up this profession and instead acted in the capacity as runners and stretcher bearers, not the most enviable of tasks in a battle.

The *Panzerturm*

There was a large concrete dugout in the *Caine Schlucht*, called the *Panzerturm*. In its five rooms were good accommodations for the Other Ranks of the 11/R110. As the *Panzerturm* was one of the few good concrete dugouts located in the outpost position it had been determined that in the event of a strong enemy attack the Talou and the terrain in front of the main position would be given up. As this was the expectation, the *Panzerturm* had been prepared for demolition in the event it had to be abandoned so that it would not

The Panzerturm before the explosion. (*Reserve-Infanterie-Regiment Nr. 110 im Weltkrieg 1914-1918*)

Panzerturm memorial. (*Reserve-Infanterie-Regiment Nr. 110 im Weltkrieg 1914-1918*)

fall into enemy hands intact.

Powerful explosive charges were placed in the individual chambers, which would become set off by a special detonation order from the *pioniers* in the event of an emergency. In order to make sure there was no delay in destroying such a powerful emplacement, the explosive charges and detonation leads had all been prepared in advance with great efficiency.

On 13 June a violent thunderstorm came down over the position, and it rained in streams. The last lightning strike was at 5.25 p.m.; if the lightning had struck the *Panzerturm* directly or had struck the detonator wires, it was not able to be determined afterward. At any event the lightning strike set off the explosive charges in four of the chambers that were occupied. There was an enormous explosion and massive pieces of concrete collapsed into the four chambers, burying every living thing underneath it.

Immediately other men in the vicinity rushed over to set their comrades free; the rescue work was being directed by *Hauptmann* von Borell and *Leutnant der Reserve* Schneevoigt. The entrances of two completely flattened sections were soon uncovered. One severely wounded man and a few dead were recovered. A platoon from the 4/*Pionier* 16 soon arrived, who continued the mining work. Towards morning it became evident that there were still men alive in a room that had apparently still not completely collapsed. The rescuers were able to communicate with them and find out the names of the men still trapped inside. They were eventually recovered after difficult excavation work along with a few of the dead.

The losses had been heavy. Underneath the ruins of the *Panzerturm* rested: 1 *Unteroffizier*, 28 men. 2 *Unteroffiziere* and 8 men were recovered dead, altogether 3 *Unteroffiziere*, 36 men. In total 12 men were rescued. Later, a monument was erected at the *Panzerturm* for those who were buried under the ruins, and which became consecrated by both divisional clergymen in presence of the regimental commander at dawn on the morning of 24 June.

The *Panzerturm* after the explosion. (*Reserve-Infanterie-Regiment Nr. 110 im Weltkrieg 1914-1918*)

A memorial was erected on the spot on which the names were written and the following inscription:

Uncover your head and pray to the memory of the fighters,
In their faithful duty by the enemy, they gave their lives for home,
A thunderbolt has caused their fortresses, to explode,
Struck by the debris, the buried heroes flesh decaying.

Starting from the middle of June the front by the 28th Reserve Division became increasingly active. The artillery fire grew in volume and there was a similar increase in the number of gas projectiles. Enemy pilots frequently flew above the position, and new tethered observation balloons were visible in the rear terrain. The nightly patrols reported that the enemy was eagerly entrenching at night, using old German trenches in order to push his lines closer to the current German positions.

The work being performed by the enemy was disrupted through machine gun, artillery and mine fire, however it could not be stopped permanently. It soon became evident that all of this activity must be considered preparations for an upcoming attack. In order to obtain intelligence concerning the enemy troop dispositions and identities, the army leadership issued directives for nightly patrols to bring in any prisoners, documents or other items that could provide clues to the enemy's intentions.

Early on 16 June a patrol of the 1st and 2/R111 left the trench by the *Granat Riegel* and occupied old dugouts in front of the French position for the entire day in order to be able to intercept enemy patrols or sentries. However, they came back empty handed on 17 June as there had been no enemy soldiers in their vicinity. A squad from the 10/R111 under

Anton Lösch, wounded on lower jaw by shell splinter and captured 4 May 1917.
Died from wounds in French hospital, 16 June 1917. (Author's collection)

Unteroffizier Bauer had better success at the same place in the night from 22/23 June. He allowed a French patrol in the strength of about 15 men to approach close to his hiding place, so that the rifles and hand grenades of the patrol would have good effect.

Once the fighting had started the French received additional support, and when the enemy patrol returned to the French trench Bauer succeeded in seizing a Sergeant and one other man from the opposing patrol and took them prisoner. During the fighting three men from Bauer's patrol had become wounded. One of them remained lying on the ground and thereby escaped captivity by remaining still as death. Upon his return later in the following morning he was able to report that the enemy had a loss of six killed and four severely wounded. Along with award of the Iron Cross II Class to each participant they also received a monetary reward of 10 Marks for each man.

Another prisoner was taken in a different manner in the night of 6/7 July when a French deserter came across to the German lines by RIR 111 and surrendered. In addition to providing the identity of his regiment, the deserter also provided information of a French raid that was being planned in the near future.

RIR 111 was relieved from the position in the following night when the I and III/R111 were relieved through battalions from IR 168. RIR 109 had already been relieved in the previous night when the I and II/R109 were relieved by battalions from RIR 83. The 28th Reserve Division was being moved to the rear once more in order to train the new men and to allow the troops to rest after the difficult times on the Chemin des Dames. That was necessary in order to be able to instruct the troops for the new realities being placed more

As in peacetime: RIR 111 rifle practice. (Author's collection)

and more on the under-leaders and individual men during a major battle, in order to allow them to act independently as the circumstances required.

Concerns had been raised about the battle value of the division following the heavy fighting on the Winterberg. The regiments had barely been filled up once again, and with so few trained men it was questioned if the division should have even been considered to be placed in the fire trench in the comparatively quiet position by Beaumont.

The Grand Duke of Baden had no such doubts and he was convinced that the men of the 28th Reserve Division retained the excellent attitude of fighting troops and whose stalwart parade march demonstrated the old soldier's spirit. The Grand Duke visited the division on 9 July in celebration of his birthday and allowed the veterans of the Winterberg to describe their experiences fighting against the French. However, reviews and parades in the rear areas were not adequate indicators of how effective a division might be in a combat situation. Intensive training and practice was required in order to evaluate the effectiveness of the men of the 28th Reserve Division.

Following the relief of the regiments good housing was provided to the men in the rest camp at Neu Wavrille, where a training field and a shooting range provided opportunities for the much needed training. After the relief from Louvement the field railway then transported the battalions of RIR 111, without the machine gun companies and regimental transport which were marching by road, to the rest area, where all parts of the regiment would assemble in camps located near Montmédy.

Since the rest days by Bapaume from February to March 1916 the men of RIR 111 had not been completely extracted out of the battle front, and now, for the first time in the war RIR 111 was actually outside the range of the guns. The quarters provided were neat and spacious; the food provided was good and prepared well. In addition the nearby situated Montmédy offered much variety and diversions during the men's free time.

7.6cm Minenwerfer course, RIR 109. (*Das Reserve-Infanterie-Regiment Nr. 109 im Weltkrieg 1914 bis 1918*)

RIR 109, like the other regiments, was still understrength following the recent fighting and was in need of new replacements in order to restore the regimental strength to normal. Almost as soon as the regiment had arrived in the rest area 3 *Unteroffiziere* and 35 Other Ranks arrived as replacements from the Field Recruit Depot. These men were quickly distributed in the companies of the I/R109.

On 10 July RIR 109 was moved further north and was placed behind Montmédy in the Ardenne. With the arrival of the latest batch of replacements the battle strength of RIR 109 was: 17 officers, 10 *Offizier Stellvertreter*, 2,468 Other Ranks, 1,986 rifles, 27 machine guns Model 08 and 14 machine guns Model 08/15. The ration strength of the regiment was: 63 officers, 14 *Offizier Stellvertreter*, 2,968 Other Ranks and 234 horses.

The 28th Reserve Division was in the possession of the OHL and was specified as an *Eingreifdivision* on the western or eastern river banks of the Maas. While in the rest area the staff received instructions for the possibility of becoming inserted into the different parts of the sector and explored the approach routes and readiness positions for each part of the front.

Until the end of July the rest time was used to provide the troops with battle training that was designed to provide instruction on the newest forms of warfare, long practice marches, something the men were unaccustomed to, marksmanship, lectures on trench fighting, field-service, by day and by night, hand grenade throwing, lessons on the operation and use of the machine guns and the different methods of close combat means as well as gymnastic games. All of these activities were designed to improve the overall function and effectiveness of the regiments for the future. While this description provides the reader with the outline of the rest period, just how was this time viewed by the men.

The division is extracted! 14 days of rest, far behind the front! 14 days with nothing to hear from battle-troop command and Readiness Troop command, from the outpost and main position, from morning, midday and evening reports, 14 days and 14 nights not to be on sentry duty, not going on patrols, no shells howled and no machine guns could be heard chattering! 14 days in good housing, maybe to sleep in a bed with white sheets, undressed of boots and uniforms and to be able to properly wash with a lot of water and soap! Ah, sleep! Really an entire long night to sleep through for once, without becoming awakened with any trench duty, what bliss! And maybe anywhere behind there are even still regular people, women, girls with laughing lips, even if it is also a French women. 14 days of rest, what pleasures expect the front fighter, what tempting pictures conjure up in front of our eyes in the word 'rest'! [3]

While at rest, RIR 110 was placed in quarters in the valley of the Chiers and its side valleys. It was from this place where German infantry marched off to war in August 1914. The area showed little impact of the war, only the bridges over the Chiers River, blown up by the French, gave any indication that a war was going on. The refreshing waters and warm sun helped to restore the bodies of the men. Daily exercise, training and target practice sharpened the skills of the troops and an instruction command from *Sturm* Battalion Rohr helped train the individual battalions in the new style of warfare.

The old soldiers and veteran combat troops were not very pleased with the schedule of training, but it had to be done. It was critical that the young replacements became proficient in their duties. The companies had to be welded together under the guidance of the leaders, discipline had to be maintained. The exercises and gymnastic games were enjoyed by most of the men, but especially by the young soldiers. Towards the end of the rest time the regiments sponsored amusements for the men with sport festivals with prizes for the winners and free beer for all, a very popular item.

Commanders and adjutants were introduced to the secret new tactics from the First General Staff Officer of the division. Later in the rest period, the officers visited the *Hagenstellung* being occupied by the 6th Reserve Division in order to become familiar with the newest style of the defense-in-depth.

Despite the training duties there remained sufficient time for rest and relaxation. Relaxation included visits to the cinemas and theaters in Montmédy. The simple act of eating without fear of a shell splinter suddenly slicing through a mess kit was enjoyed by all. In regard to food however the fighting allowance was missing, much to the annoyance of the troops. At this stage of the war the food was more varied than abundant. The men naturally looked to improve the portion size through various unconventional means and

Hannover CLII with pilot and observer; these aircraft were
often used as ground support. (Author's collection)

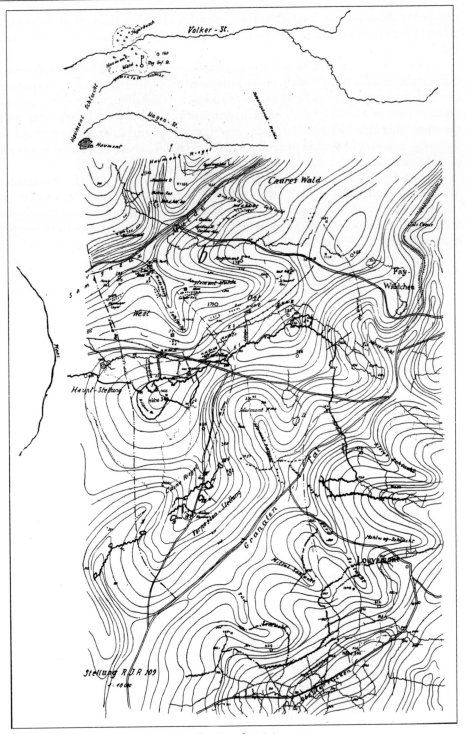

Hill 344 and vicinity.

managed to obtain potatoes, vegetables, fruit, and other delicacies. The methods being used to obtain these food items often brought the men into conflict with the civilian population and the Town Major.

By the end of the month the commanders were convinced through various inspections that real progress was being made in the overall effectiveness of the men. Part of the training involved the new connections between infantry pilots and the fighting troops on the ground. Practices were held using a variety of methods where both sides could communicate with the other using light ball signals from the ground or by the aircraft dropping messages to the troops below, or by ground signals using colored cloth squares. Then, before it seemed possible, the training and rest time had come to an end.

The 14 days at rest passed all too quickly and on 24 July the regimental commander inspected the companies of the II/R110. The viewing of the other battalions had to be canceled, because on higher orders from the division they were being sent to the front again. According to corps orders the 28th Reserve Division was to be inserted on the right wing of *Maas Gruppe Ost* again, actually in the position the division had occupied until 10 July. The division would be brought from Montmédy to Damvillers on a field railway, then the I and II/R109 would be moved to Réville, the III/R109 to Quincy-les Juvigny.

RIR 109 and RIR 110 had taken over a sector west of the old trenches by Beaumont, the main position moved across Hill 344 and pressed up by Samogneux on the Maas; with the outposts being positioned upon Talou ridge. On 26 July the III/R110 relieved the II/R118 in the outpost position upon the Talou and the II/R110 relieved the III/R118 in the main position by Samogneux. The men were in the old position again. At the same time RIR 111 was distributed behind the front as the reserve. The II/R111, whose commander since 19 June was *Major* Höhne, marched on 25 July by way of Marville to Dombras, where the staff was located along with the 5th and 6/R111, while the 7th and 8/R111 and 2nd Machine Gun Company moved into the *Schlesische Lager* located nearby. Eventually the regimental staff took up residence in Solferino farm on 30 July.

On the morning of 26 July the regimental staff of RIR 109 moved to the command post 'Schwarzwald,' formerly called '*Tannenberg*', located in the Bois de Consenvoye, the source of charcoal for the regiments. In the nights from 27/28 July and from 28/29 July RIR 109 relieved the I/R83 in the Sector 1b on the right and the III/R83 and the Machine Gun Coy from *Landsturm* Battalion Reutlingen in sector 1b on the left from the *Samogneux Mulde*. The regimental command post was located quite a distance from the battle battalion, and relied upon a chain of runners and light signal posts in order to maintain a connection. The *Luxdienst* of the regimental staff had the task of keeping a close watch on the enemy.

When the 28th Reserve Division took over their old trenches from a few months earlier very little had apparently changed. The position that had been turned over to the relief troops had not been worked on at all from what the men could see. The men of the 28th Reserve Division were not pleased that all of the hard work they had performed had gone to waste and that they had to work even harder in order to create a firm defensive position. The shell proof dugouts still had to become completed; the front line and communication trenches needed extensive repairs as well as being cleared from mud and debris in order to deepen them.

The sector quickly became quite uncomfortable. The enemy aerial activity was as lively as it was in June; observation balloons in large numbers behind the French line observed every movement inside the German position. The artillery fire from both sides increased aily, however it was still considered to be within tolerable limits. Strong traffic was bserved behind the enemy front, as well as fires and explosions that were caused through he German artillery fire. Even more ominous as an unerring sign of a pending enemy ttack was the French entrenching work northwest of Vachárauville that was encroaching gainst the Talou. Infantry and aircraft observers reported new improvements in the French efenses daily; including trenches several kilometers long that emerged in just one night.

All of the enemy efforts were taken under strong machine gun and artillery fire, but he French continued unperturbed by the additional German fire despite the losses it was reating. In order to protect the work being done on the enemy trench system, strong patrols vere sent out into no man's land against the German pickets. They would all become be epulsed through rifle fire and hand grenades with inevitable losses on both sides.

The army high command expected an attack at any time. The patrols sent out in the irst days following the relief confirmed that the enemy was making preparations for an ssault and had extended his position toward the German lines. The French forward line vas located at the north foot of Pfeffer ridge and had become strongly wired; all patrols sent oward this position encountered very alert enemy sentries. The French artillery increased n strength it methodically bombarded all parts of the German position that the enemy pparently considered to be important.

Everything that could be done in order to meet this threat was being worked on, despite he weakened strength of the division. With the looming threat of an enemy infantry ttack, all of the available reserves had to be positioned in the front lines as a precaution. n the night of 29/30 July the 1MG/R111 under *Leutnant* Brenker reinforced the outpost osition of RIR 110 on the Talou ridge; the company brought eight guns into the position

In order to reach the German front lines the men had to travel on long advance roads n unprotected terrain. In the event of an attack it was to be expected that bringing up resh supplies would be impossible due to the enemy fire. In order to counter this problem, ufficient supplies of ammunition, food and water were placed in depots at different parts of the front line. The readiness companies were entrusted with this task and were einforced through the 8/R111 and half of the construction company of RIR 111. Forty ransport mules were provided to the readiness companies which proved to be quite helpful n completing the strenuous task.

In the rear, replacements continued to arrive almost every day in the different regiments. On 1 August one *Gefreiter* and 22 men arrived from the Field Recruit Depot of the 28th Reserve Division, which were distributed to the machine gun companies of RIR 109.

Starting from 2 August two companies of the I/R111 were positioned in Consenvoye and entrenched in the *Hagen Stellung*, a rearward line that stretched between Brabant and Haumont. The III/R111 assigned two companies to create a cable trench for the division Telephone *Abteilung* that lead from Molleville farm in the wood of Consenvoye in a southerly direction to the front lines; then men had to work in shifts day and night in order to complete it. The two other companies of the III/R111 had to build approach trenches in the sector of the front regiments.

The two companies moved into the position, with one company located by RIR 110 in the *Landwehrkaserne*, a group of dugouts in the Samogneux hollow, the other by RIR 109 in readiness dugouts in the *Hindenburg Schlucht*. RIR 111 sent two companies into a barracks camp in the *Namenlosenschlucht*, 1 1/2 kilometers north of Haumont, from where the men were employed in dugout construction in the *Haumont Riegel*, the extension of the *Hagen*

Stellung southeast of Haumont. One half of the Construction Company took on the *Volker Stellung* north of the *Hagen Stellung* in order to establish food and ammunition depots.

The French made attempts to disturb all of this work through bombardments, and on 9 August a direct hit struck the 9/R111 while it was on the way to the work place from which one *Unteroffizier* and two men were killed. The companies assigned to the front lines exchanged positions as frequently as possible with the companies in the readiness areas. As to reserves, as mentioned earlier, there were none at hand. They were being deployed to work in every aspect of the defense, from positioning supply depots to creating defenses against the expected attack. Matters only became worse with the frequent rainy weather that impeded the work on the defenses and made the stay in the cramped quarters very unpleasant as the water seeped into every corner of the dugouts and camps.

On 5 August *Mormont Schlucht* and Mormont farm lay under heavy artillery fire while four enemy aircraft observed the position. The 2MG/R109 and the rest battalion, II/R109, which was occupied with the construction of dugouts and fire trenches in the wood camp for protection against the enemy bombardments, were moved forward in the night of 7/8 August for the relief of the 1MG/R109 and the I/R109.

There air was already quite 'thick,' and the 1/R109 had to remain in the position to work with the II/R109, while three Groups of the I/R109 were ordered to work on the extension of the runner relay route under the guidance of *Offizier Stellvertreter* Metzner. Three Groups were taken from each company in RIR 109 and were combined as *Schlepptrupps* and used for the creation of intermediate depots and mined kitchen dugouts in the *Kuchen Schlucht*.

Strong French bombardments fell on the positions throughout the entire day on 8 and 9 August. The shelling never ceased during this time and the fire was very accurate as it was being directed under the guidance of several tethered observation balloons. During this time, one of the enemy balloons was shot down in flames by a German pilot, but this still left more than enough French observers in the air so that the bombardment continued unabated.

The enemy fire on these days was systematic and extraordinarily thorough on all parts of the position. The bombardment proved to be very successful as disturbance fire, as all of the French medium and heavy batteries held the narrow strip of German trenches under hellishly accurate fire for hours. This level of attack preparations had never been experienced before by the regiments of the 28th Reserve Division and this alone made it especially ominous; everyone was convinced that an attack was imminent.

The French preparation fire was of great concern for the men of the 28th Reserve Division. When the position had been taken over by the division the brigade had been notified of the poor condition of the position. Also, the covered position strongpoints and machine gun nests had become known to the enemy observers through foot traffic by day and through careless plumes of smoke; as such they had all become systematically destroyed in the preparation fire.

While it was generally accepted that all of the enemy preparations were the precursor of an attack, 'the Frog must be shown one time that we were not doing anything but watching.' RIR 110 was given orders to hold a raid in the night of 9/10 August, which had the code name '*Sonne*' along with two smaller undertakings '*Mond*' and '*Schein*.' These raids would be directed against the enemy trench southeast of the *Steinbruch* on the Vachárauville-Cotelettes Mill road. The patrols were being directed under the watchful eyes of the

Regimental Adjutant for RIR 110, *Leutnant* Reichwald and by *Leutnant* Heizmann at the nearby practice works.

At 2.30 a.m. on 10 August Patrol '*Mond*' was at the readiness position in the area of the left outpost company and consisted of *Leutnant* Glombitza, 3 *Unteroffiziere* and 35 men from RIR 110 and 9 *pioniers* of the 1/Reserve *Pionier* 16. Patrol '*Schein*' was located nearby and consisted of *Leutnant* Recklies from the I/R110, *Leutnant* Brand, Reserve *Pionier* 16, 35 men from RIR 110 and 15 *pioniers* from *Ersatz* Reserve *Pionier* 16.

After an artillery preparation lasting only six minutes the three *Stosstrupps* penetrated into the enemy trench after overcoming strong wire obstacles and then rolled it up. *Stosstrupp* A had particularly good luck and had been able to quickly capture a total of six prisoners. *Leutnant* Brand (*Stosstrupp* A) had advanced along the Champneuville-Vacháruaville field railway. Brand and his men had to overcome an entirely new wire entanglement and had been taken under fire from an enemy protection line, from which a number of French soldiers swarmed out. Despite the appearance of enemy troops, Brand and his men were able to capture two enemy sentries and shot down a third. In the meantime, the main garrison in the French trench opened fire and two additional groups advanced against Brands left flank, forcing *Stosstrupp* A to move back to the exit position, taking along an additional four enemy prisoners.

Stosstrupp B under *Leutnant* Recklies managed to enter the French trench where the patrol encountered approximately a dozen enemy soldiers, who advanced toward the patrol. A hand grenade battle broke out between both sides and within a few minutes most of the Frenchmen had been killed or wounded, the few survivors had been driven back. Soon the trench was only filled with enemy dead, forcing Recklies and his men to continue deeper into the French defenses. Eventually they came across more enemy soldiers of which three were taken prisoner. There was no possibility of advancing any deeper into the French lines because of enemy machine gun fire, so the patrol withdrew to the German lines, taking the prisoners with them.

Stosstrupp C initially found the French trench empty, but eventually came upon several enemy sentries who were taken captive. When it proved impossible to advance any further, the raiding party returned to the German lines. The goal of the undertaking had been achieved: 12 French soldiers from *Regiments d'Infanterie* 102 and 104 remained in German hands. The successful raid was accomplished with the loss of two slightly wounded men in the raiding parties.

Through the interrogation of the prisoners it was firmly established that the French 7th Infantry Division was in front of the division sector. Also, from the statements and the letters of the prisoners it became unquestionable that the enemy had plans to attack in the near future with newly inserted attack divisions. The gratitude of the higher leadership was not lacking.

Extract out of the daily orders of Maas Group Ost from 11 August 1917.

On 10 August 1917, 3.00 a.m. *Stosstrupps* of RIR 110 pressed in a fresh advance, actively supported from artillery and *Minenwerfer*, into the enemy trenches north of Vacháruaville at two places. They brought back 12 prisoners from the Regiments 102 and 104 of the 7th Infantry Division. I speak of my fullest appreciation to RIR 110 and the involved batteries and *Minenwerfer*. Signed: von Garnier. [4]

At the onset of darkness in the night of 10/11 August the French occupied the line south of the Talou that until now had been protected by German sentry outposts. When the commander of the 9/R110, *Leutnant* Ahlhaus, learned of this enemy advance, he gave orders to attack and to drive them back. In the ensuing fight, losses were inflicted on the enemy, while the German sentries and patrols returned with few casualties. Several men, who were not able to come back to the German lines in the night, remained concealed during the day in shell craters and did not return to the main German line until the next night, bringing back the corpse of a fallen comrade. The division acknowledged the prudent and brave behavior of the leaders and all participants of the raid.

Following this skirmish in the Outpost Zone, the outpost line was taken back slightly on orders from the 56th Reserve Brigade and work began on creating new wire obstacles in front of the sentries. On 11 and 12 August the enemy artillery fire took a noticeable increase in strength. A single fire raid consisted of thousands of shells, which bombarded all important points in the defenses; and the number of fire raids continued to grow.

At midday on 12 August it appeared that the enemy was beginning to prepare for his attack on the same day through strong artillery fire upon the forward line and the rear terrain. There was also a great deal of aerial activity overhead, both in enemy observation aircraft as well as single-seat fighters. Heightened battle readiness was ordered for the troops of the 28th Reserve Division, and all entrenching work had to be discontinued. Considering the current situation the 5th and 8/R111, the two companies on detached duty that belonged to the front line garrison, were returned to the II/R111.

Starting from 8 a.m. on 13 August the entire Sector West occupied by RIR 109 along with the outpost position lay under very strong artillery fire that at about 11 a.m. increased to the level of drum fire. At 9.30 a.m. the artillery observer and the crew of Machine Gun No. 7/R109 in Strongpoint 5 were buried in their dugout and could only be saved with great effort. At 3.30 p.m. the new *Pionier Graben* and the *Artillerie Graben* were completely shot up. *Leutnant* Huet and the Other Rank crews of Machine Guns No. 3 and No. 4/R109 also became buried inside their dugout. At 3.30 p.m. the Other Ranks of the Machine Guns No. 1 and 2/R109 suffered the same fate while situated in the old kitchen in the *Caine Riegel*.

> One *Schütze* lost his senses in the intense bombardment and ran toward the enemy in the artillery fire; however he was grabbed in the forward most position and forcibly held down. Then, in an unguarded moment he succeeded in escaping his comrades and he sprinted toward the French lines. Everyone expected that the deluded man would be killed in the frenzied shrapnel and shell fire and never expected that he would succeed in making it through, when suddenly he came running back again and he was grabbed once again by the men in the front line trench. He was restrained until he was transported to the rear later in the night. [5]

When the French bombardment began on 13 August on the position of RIR 110 there were already 15 enemy aircraft flying over the trenches at first light that directed the fire on the Talou. The outpost position and the left wing of the main position were the primary targets of the intense shelling. By midday two medium *Minenwerfer* from *Minenwerfer* Company 228 were placed out of action. Toward 4 p.m. the artillery fire increased in strength upon the Talou, while the entire rear area was shrouded in smoke and fumes.

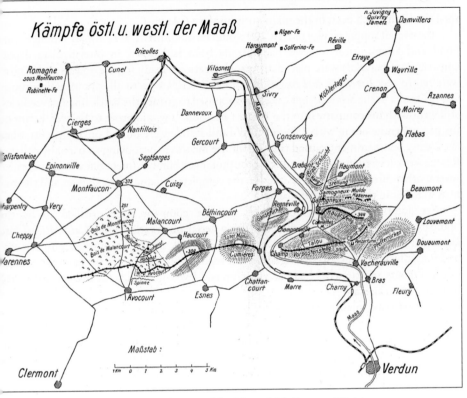

Fighting East and West of the Maas, 28th Reserve Division.

Champneuville and Samogneux were bombarded with medium and heavy caliber guns during the evening hours and the dugouts had suffered considerably in all of the affected positions, especially on the Talou. Strongpoint 5 was completely destroyed, the dugouts were buried and the wireless station was smashed. Now there was no more doubt that the attack was imminent: 'however, when would the enemy infantry break forth? How long would the insane pounding continue?'

All telephone connections had been destroyed in the heavy fire, and all traffic between battalions and companies had to be maintained through runners under these difficult circumstances. The wireless station located in the battle headquarters of RIR 109 had been destroyed, and all artillery observation positions had been rendered useless in the bombardment.

As a result of the elevated battle readiness that had been ordered, the 1st and 2/R109 moved with the battalion staff into the dugouts of the *Völkersammlung* on the southern edge of the Wood of Consenvoye. Four machine guns with two platoon leaders and two light *Minenwerfer* were moved forward into the *Leuder Kaserne* and in the Readiness 'Hindenburg'. *Leutnant der Reserve* Rothfelder, MWO [*Minenwerfer Offizier*] of the regiment, moved to the battalion staff of the II/R109. RIR 110 received Brigade instructions at 12 midnight ordering heightened battle readiness, whereupon the II/R110 with the staff, 7th and 8/R110 and 2MG/R110 moved into the *Brabant Schlucht*, the 5th and 6/R110 remained in *Meininger* and *Cologner* barracks, from where the companies could support the I/R110 that had been in the main position since 6 August.

The overall supply service of RIR 109 would be subordinate to *Leutnant* Kirchenbauer Food and ammunition reserves had already been laid down in intermediate depot construction materials were placed at various locations, ready for use and the relay post were reinforced. *Vizefeldwebel* August Schmidt, 7/R109, who to all extents and purpose was the leader of the *Schlepptrupps*, was not supposed to go into the battle lines, nevertheless still went with his company into the outpost position. It would prove to be a fatal error on his part when he along with *Vizefeldwebel* Emil Raible were buried on 13 August when the enemy bombardment caused the dugout the men were occupying to partially collapse Rescue work started immediately during the prolonged bombardment but was unsuccessful several other direct hits finally resulted in the complete collapse of the dugout and the two men were left in their makeshift tomb.

Six additional dugouts in the left outpost company were crushed in by the bombardment that was being directed using aerial observation. The *Caine Riegel* also lay under uninterrupted heavy fire. A planned attack upon the outpost position was undoubtedly imminent. According to the few reports coming in from the front almost half of the dugouts and trenches had been shot up and leveled from enemy fire being directed by observation aircraft.

The defensive plan of the division had been worked out in the months prior and practiced by the men. The plan called for the outpost companies to detain any enemy advance against the hill through duly ordered barrage fire and the employment of their machine guns, until friendly infantry pilots circulating above the position gave the signal for the withdrawal into the main position through colored light balls. The main position was to be held under all circumstances and if any portions were lost, they were to become taken back by counterattacks.

However, the outpost position was completely lacking any shell proof dugouts and was being entirely inundated from the constant enemy artillery fire and there was a strong possibility that no one in the outpost position would be able to withdraw to the main line Without these men, there would be no chance for any counterattacks if the circumstances called for one.

In light of this possibility, on 13 August the regimental commander of RIR 109 asked to allow the outpost companies to be withdrawn into the main position, and to detain the first enemy attack with only a small number of sentries with light machine guns unfortunately his request was denied and the companies were ordered to remain in the position. The two companies, the 7th and 12/R109, with the allotted machine gun crews remained an additional two days in the hail of enemy fire. The men looked for protection in any cover available while being subjected to the intense bombardment as well as being continuously fired upon by enemy pilots with machine guns.

The French artillery was showering the main position as well as the rearward connections with shrapnel, shells of all calibers and with gas shells. The trench system on Hill 344 gradually disappeared as the terrain took on the appearance of a lunar landscape Then, as if to make matters worse bad weather arrived, turning the churned up ground into a quagmire. There were no German planes to be seen in the air, leaving full control to the enemy pilots, who continued their observation undisturbed.

RIR 111 had been spared from most of the French destructive fire as the regiment was in reserve. The 5th and 8/R111 moved in the night to 14 August into the *Köhlerdorf Lager* by Etraye, where they joined the 1st, 2nd and 1MG/R111 to form the division reserve. The camp was bombarded repeatedly, and on 14 August *Leutnant* Schaulin, 7/R111 was killed by a shell. The companies immediately began to work on dugouts in the vicinity of the barracks in order to find some protection against the enemy artillery fire. The 3rd and 4/R111 remained in Consenvoye along with the 9th and 10/R111 and took up positions in the *Namenlosenschlucht* and were specified as the brigade reserve. These companies were under the commander of the I/R111, who, with his staff were located in an already cramped cellars of Consenvoye.

In the night of 13/14 August the French concentrated their fire on the rearward terrain, in particular on the camps and approach routes. Toward morning the fire let up and between 9 and 10 a.m. almost stopped entirely. There was some confusion among the ranks. Was this a bluff decided to draw out the Germans from their dugouts? Then, at 12 noon the enemy destructive fire began even stronger than on the previous day. The left company sector on the Talou by RIR 110 received the heaviest fire of all calibers up to 38cm, and for the first time the enemy fired on the positions with mines.

One company leader in RIR 110, *Leutnant* Krichau, was wounded on both hands, as the dugouts were systematically being buried; the *Caine Schlucht* was completely shot up. One light machine gun including the crew became buried from a mass of earth. The villages of Champ and Champneuville had to become abandoned, because no shell proof dugouts existed there; the Other Ranks lay in the open fields. All of the entrances to the battalion command post of the outpost position except for one were buried. The main position was no better off as it became covered with very heavy fire, especially the quarry by the right company, the *Hamburg Weg, Reeperbahn* and *Jungfernstieg*. The two battle trenches in the heights of the *Hecken Schlucht* became transformed into a crater field.

The question being asked by everyone was still: 'When would the attack take place?' It was a question that the division headquarters desperately needed to know, in particular if the enemy attack division has already been put in. in order to find the answer, a patrol undertaking on the Talou was planned. Undertaking '*Mond*' from 10 August was to be repeated. Although the men had suffered severely through the prolonged fire and had already been in the position for 18 days, the desired number of volunteers needed for the undertaking reported immediately. At 2.30 a.m. the *Stosstrupp* penetrated the enemy trench after strong fire preparation under the command of *Vizefeldwebel* Schneider. However, the enemy had fled, leaving behind rifles and a knapsack with a letter to a soldier in *Regiment d' Infanterie* 102, 7th Infantry Division. During the withdrawal three men of the raiding party were wounded. Despite the lack of prisoners the raid had been a success. The attack division had not come into the position and therefore the enemy bombardment would continue. It appeared that the French still did not believe that the German position was ripe for the storm and that the German defenders had not been unnerved by the sheer weight of fire.

The bombardment did continue, without any reduction in strength. Losses among the defenders continued to grow as men were killed or wounded in the shell fire. The company leader of the 5/R109, *Leutnant* Ochel, left the position on 15 August because of gas poisoning; *Leutnant* Hainmüller took over the leadership of this company. Machine Guns No. 7 and 9 in the left sector at sap 7 were destroyed by direct hits, the dugouts were crushed in and the gun crews were buried.

While the installation of a new communication trench between the second and first trenches created a safer connection to the rear by the 10/R109; the outpost position had lost all battle value through the effect of the bombardment. All wire obstacles and dugouts were destroyed, and any further occupation signified a further useless sacrifice of the garrison. Following urgent requests by the left sector commander the brigade gave the order at 4.10 a.m. on 15 August to take back both outpost companies and leave the protection of the *Caine* and *Talou Riegels* to weak sentry outposts.

15 August came as an immense relief to the largest part of the III/R110. The brigade order arrived at the regiment at 4.22 a.m.: the outpost positions on the Talou and in the *Caine Riegel* were to be systematically evacuated, and the orders were quickly transmitted to the forward line. Between 5 and 7 a.m. the evacuation that had been carefully planned in the hopes of such an order was carried out. All company and battalion staff of the III/R110 moved back to the *Brabant Schlucht*. Only two Groups from each company; each equipped with a light machine gun and a signal station remained as the outposts on the Talou.

For the Groups left behind, it was truly no easy task to persist in heavy artillery fire for one or more days in the doomed sentry posts. The outpost sentries were still supposed to launch distress signals at the first sign of a major attack and then withdraw to the main position, however, would anyone survive the retreat? The bridges, paths, crossings and roads that had been prepared for demolition were blown up. The companies relieved from the outpost zone reached the reserve position without any significant trouble from the enemy despite the heavy fire.

On 15 August parts of an *Eingreifdivision* provided security in the *Volker Stellung*. The regimental staff of RIR 111 was no longer required in the *Volker Stellung* and became entrusted with the leadership of the division reserve in the *Köhlerhof*, where it was joined by the 3MG/R111. *Hauptmann* Wöhrle, leader of the III/R111, was now the commander of the security garrison at the western exit of Brabant. The village and the knee deep trenches that were provided with only a few recently started mined dugouts was bombarded daily and often gassed.

The observers reported that continuous fire lay upon the German lines east of Samogneux, west of the Maas, and where it moved over *Toten Mann* and included the Wood of Avocourt. RIR 110 continued to lay under the heaviest bombardment during 15 August, with the left wing of the main position suffering in particular; all hollows were also gassed.

On the evening of 15 August RIR 110 ordered a new formation of the regimental sector. The main position would be divided into two battalion sectors. On the right would be the I/R110 with the 3rd and 4/R110 in the forward most line, the 1st and 2/R110 became relieved on the left wing of the main position and moved to the dugouts in the *Landwehr* barracks. Two groups from the 1/R110 and a light machine gun were moved forward into the old battalion dugout in Samogneux and the 3/R110 was placed in possession of the battalion as the counterattack reserve. Two further Groups that were mining in the second battle trench by the 4/R110 remained there and came under the control of the 4/R110. The 7th and 8/R110 occupied the forward line in the left battalion sector, the 5th and 6/R110 lay with the battalion staff in the *Meininger* barracks.

These changes were required as the combat strength of many of the companies had fallen to such a low level that a single battalion was not sufficient to garrison the front line of the regimental sector. It was not any better in RIR 109 where the right battalion sector seemed the most endangered and the companies, already seriously weakened, became divided into

Man from RIR 111 with new Iron Cross II Class. (Author's collection)

three sub sectors on 16 August, and occupied from left to right by the 6th, 8th and 5/R109. In the night of 15/16 August a patrol of the 10/R110 advanced via Champneuville and firmly established that the outpost terrain was free of the enemy, no sign of the attack as yet.

On 16 August the enemy artillery was limited to numerous fire raids. The bombardment and the rainy weather had promoted the destructive work on the position, in which only individual trench pieces still existed. The second trench and the connection trenches were full of water. The entire *Artillerie Graben* and *Pionier Graben*, also the largest part of the K.1 trench were completely leveled. All that remained was a crater area with only a few mined shafts, which were prepared as good as possible for defense and were protected through weak wire obstacles.

In the evening hours of 16 August *Leutnant* Schneevoigt was on the march to the Talou with his company, the 11/R110, equipped with six light machine guns and a signal detachment, in order to relieve the existing outpost sentries. Every individual in his unit knew about the responsibilities that had become placed on them as the advance sentries, each man was aware that this journey could very well be their last yet every man followed *Leutnant* Schneevoigt despite their fear. Finally, the sentries on the Talou were relieved, who happily went to the rear.

On the same evening a patrol from RIR 110 brought in three prisoners; whose statements indicated that three French divisions, the 127th, 69th and 42nd stood opposite the 28th Reserve Division sector. Apparently the latter had just come into the position on the 16th as an attack division. This information was very useful but it also emphasized that the weak Baden division was facing an enemy force more than three times its strength.

At this stage of the fighting RIR 110 had already lost 1 officer and 47 *Unteroffiziere* and Other Ranks killed, 1 officer and 8 Other Ranks wounded and gas poisoned, 2 officers and 100 Other Ranks sick, amongst them numerous men suspected of having typhus. While the numbers do not appear to be high, it should be remembered that the combat strength of the regiments of the 28th Reserve Division were mere shadows of their former selves. These losses were in fact quite severe.

In addition to the losses, the nerves of the Other Ranks were extremely taut from the physical effects of the heavy artillery shells and the numerous fires raids. The III Battalion and parts of the I/R110 had already been in the position for three weeks without relief. While there were no fresh infantry reserves available, the regiment called for the intervention of long-distance artillery fire from the battle reserve; however the weak response did little to improve the situation.

At 12.30 a.m. on 17 August, an enemy patrol came close to Strongpoint 6; however they were successfully expelled by the garrison. Eight *pioniers* from the 4/*Pionier* Battalion 16 were placed in possession of the outpost commander and were distributed in the second squad of the outpost zone. The *pioniers* had the task to blow up the dugouts that still existed in the strongpoint, if a withdrawal of the second squad became necessary. Later on 17 August a patrol from the 11/R110 firmly established that the former location of Picke Station 2 was unoccupied by the enemy, which seemed to signify that the enemy would still continue to pound the position further, try to unnerve the men, but would still not attack.

A particularly painful loss occurred on 17 August when a direct hit on the *Minenwerfer* stand in the right sector of RIR 109, completely pressed in two entrances and a cover of 8 meters of compact earth; whereby 2 *Unteroffiziere* and 20 men, most belonging to the 5th and 6/R109, lost their lives. There were immediate rescue attempts using oxygen apparatus under the direction of the *Minenwerfer Offizier, Leutnant* Rothfelder, which were unsuccessful. It was not until 19 August when the rescuers succeeded in reaching the dugout occupants. However it was too late, the entire garrison was dead. The men lay resting as if they were asleep at the camp. Death appears to have been sudden and painless. The reserve entrance to the dugout was very small and only buried at the top and if the men inside had been conscious they would have undoubtedly made attempts to dig out to the surface using this exit. It was found that the carbon monoxide gas was particularly strong at this entrance and had obviously led to the quick death of the occupants.

By 18 August the fire storm had lasted for three days. At times it became somewhat quieter then suddenly it raged further with twice the strength. One dugout after the other was systematically destroyed with terrible determination with use of aircraft observation. The losses of heavy and light machine guns increased day by day. The trenches no longer existed under the constant pounding; the terrain was smashed and pockmarked by the numerous impacts. Losses continued to rise in the constant shelling. A single heavy shell had collapsed a dugout covered by 8 meters of earth in the left battalion sector of RIR 110. 18 men were killed, 23 men suffered gas poisoning through carbon monoxide gas. The 23 men were only rescued through the self-sacrifice and courageous behavior of *Krankenträger Unteroffizier* Greilsheimer who acted quickly following the shell impact. He created a small opening in one of the entrances and despite the carbon monoxide gas he made numerous trips into the dugout in order to remove the men who were still alive.

The staff of the I/R109 went in to the position in the night of 17 August, where it received billets in the Hamburg barracks and took command over the regimental reserve of which the 2nd and 4/R110 already stood on the right and the 3/R110 in the left sector. In order to improve contact with the battle battalion, the regimental staff moved to a battle headquarters east of Hill 338, Point 5, about 800 meters from the former command post *Kohlerquelle*.

The shelling continued as if the enemy had an unlimited supply of ammunition and guns. On 18 August Machine Guns No. 6 and 8 in RIR 110 were buried by the shell fire. Fortunately, *Leutnant* Losch and the gun crews succeeded in digging them out and brought the guns to a safe location in the night. Machine Guns No. 4 and 5 were also buried; these too could be saved after much digging.

In the afternoon Strongpoint 7 in the Caine Riegel was completely shot up; nevertheless the outpost group posted there under *Unteroffizier* Seufert, 7/R110, undertook a patrol with six men and a machine gun against the *Granaten Tal* at 11.30 p.m. and opened fired on an enemy trench located there, as well as the valley ground, just to let the French know that the Germans were still around.

The extension of a finished deep mined barracks tunnel with numerous exits in the Readiness *Lueder* barracks proved to be very useful at this time. The tunnel contained secure, bomb proof housing for battalion command posts, readiness companies and regimental machine guns. All of the previously inhabited dugouts and kitchen dugouts in the area had become destroyed one after the other resulting in a number of losses.

The systematic destruction of the German defenses had resulted in numerous losses among the infantry companies. As such, the men would have to be relieved on a regular basis or face total destruction under the weight of fire. While it was usually the men located in the forward defenses that suffered the most under such a bombardment, here it did not matter where a man was located, everywhere was considered dangerous. In the night from 18 to 19 August the 10/R110 under the command of *Leutnant der Reserve* Moeser relieved the 11/R110 from the Talou. In the night of 18/19 August the garrisons in Strongpoints 6 and 7 and the machine guns from 7b and 8a were relieved through parts of the 1st, 2nd and 4/R110. With this the entire regimental reserve had been completely inserted into the position. The staff of the I/R110 now went back into the *Völkersamb Stellung*.

On this day the Hamburg barracks in the rear lay under the heaviest fire, from which four entrances were completely buried and four others were badly damaged. Heavy shells with delayed fuzes and torpedo mines wreaked terrible havoc on the barracks, causing so much damage that all of the men located in the rear areas had to go out at night in order to fill up the shell craters lying over the barracks with stones and masses of earth.

The situation facing the men of RIR 109 was no better. Concerns filled the leader of RIR 109 that with the men who had been assigned as *Schlepptrupps*, the men who were absent sick or in some cases simply 'absent', as well as through the increased losses in the enemy fire resulted in a serious weakening of the battle strength of the companies. New arrangements in the occupation of the positions had to be made on a daily basis in order to provide adequate cover of the entire position or to hurry and help buried comrades. The hardest test was on the nerves of the Other Ranks, who worked tirelessly day and night under frightening conditions.

The men avoided staying in one of the few remaining dugouts during the day because of the systematic destructive work of the enemy artillery under aerial direction made these into death traps. Many of the men in the position became violently ill and were barely able to man their positions as a result of the bombardment with gas and phosphorus shells.

The enemy's long-range 28cm flat trajectory railway guns, which apparently stood on the Marre ridge, had an exceptional destructive effect on the position. The counter-battery efforts of the German long-range artillery were not very effective. The counter-battery guns were frequently rotated as there was a critical shortage of these important weapons, and the constant change of batteries helped to reduce their overall effect.

The right wing company of RIR 109 had only one dugout left in its possession, so that barely any fighting strength still existed to oppose the expected attack. The *Caine Riegel* was only being held through officer's posts, and became described in a regimental report to the brigade as a situation that could hardly be expected to detain an attack even for a brief period of time. The withdrawal of this squad that consisted of 60 men during an enemy attack was described as being practically impossible, so long as Hill 344 lay under French artillery fire. Under these circumstances, it was necessary to provide additional rear support for the sector. The II/R266 from the 80th Infantry Division moved forward into the *Volkerstellung* and RIR 111 was placed in position as the security reserve.

The French fire raged throughout the entire night without interruption, 'will the morning of 19 August finally bring the attack?' The answer was no, but the destructive fire continued relentlessly, and the men in the front lines were powerless to do anything about it. Nineteen enemy observation balloons could be seen in the air, French aircraft squadrons hummed in the sky overhead. There were so many enemy aircraft and balloons in the air that even if one was shot down it would make no difference in the situation.

By 19 August there was not a single part of the front line that was not being heavily shelled. Only two dugouts were still intact at the left battalion sector of RIR 109 and these were not shell proof. It was anyone's guess as to how long the two dugouts might survive before a shell destroyed them. The enemy artillery has particularly targeted the barracks in the Samogneux hollow on the 19th. This was probably due to the presence of several heavy batteries that stood in the vicinity that drew the enemy fire. The French fire was very accurate and as the shells fell in and around the German batteries, cartridges burned and ammunition piles exploded. Amidst all of the death and destruction a weak blinker light was observed, it was a message from the Talou from *Leutnant* Moeser: 'Everything is in order!,' it was the last message to be received.

In the late evening hours of 19 August a strong bombardment began on the entire position and Samogneux hollow with gas shells intermingled with the high explosive shells and shrapnel. The gas became so bad that the men were forced to wear gas masks for hours without removing them. Small paper fires were lit in the dugout entrances in order to expel the gas while in the *Lueder* barracks and in the medical dugout the gas clouds were kept away through airtight sealing around the entrances. However it was not possible to avoid losses from the poisonous clouds. The situation grew worse when all of the kitchens were destroyed, and fresh water could no longer be obtained, because the sources in the Anglemont hollow were covered by enemy fire and inaccessible. Starting from 20 August all of the food had to be handled by carrying parties and when these men became missing, new men were taken from the small pool of reserves.

For one group of men who had been lucky enough to be home on leave, they had an unpleasant surprise waiting for them upon their return to RIR 109. Every member of the regimental band in RIR 109, except for three men on baggage watch, had been granted leave. When they came back in the middle of August, they were immediately employed in the extremely dangerous hauling duty.

When the enemy artillery fire raged nonstop over the entire regimental sector of RIR 09, there was no more doubt in the minds of the men that the attack would take place in a few hours. Trying to evade the artillery fire by taking cover in craters to the sides or further to the front did not offer much protection on Hill 344, where the fire of the enemy was particularly concentrated. There was no part of the hill that was not being shelled.

Traffic within the forward most position up to the Samogneux hollow was almost impossible through the fire falling on the northern hillside. Continuous strong fire lay on the rearward connections, particularly on the southern slope of the Haumont ridge and the *Bauernschreck* hollow, so that the carrying parties and transporting the wounded to the rear was almost brought to a complete standstill. The approach of reserves was also greatly impeded in the same manner. The physical and mental strength of the Other Ranks was in a weakened state due to the demands placed on the men, and in it was under these conditions that the enemy finally attacked.

On 20 August heavy drum fire began at 3.30 a.m., which during daylight became increased too the highest intensity. At 6 a.m. barrage fire signals rose up into the sky from the front lines, it was soon learned that the French had finally begun the attack and had penetrated into the German trenches at several locations. Counterattacks were immediately launched in an effort to prevent the enemy from breaching the defensive zone. Within a short time additional reserves were called for and portions of RIR 111 began to be sent forward.

At 5 a.m. specially formed French divisions on the wide front from Fort Vaux until Hill 304, fully rested and prepared for their task moved to the attack. Their hope was to be able to 'march' into the German positions without any opposition; however this was not achieved. When the French assault troops approached the German defenses, numerous hand grenades flew toward them out of shell and mine craters; German machine guns opened fire into the dense storm columns causing heavy losses and soon a bitter fight, man against man began. The enemy assault soon splintered into individual battles, which continued until evening. By the following morning the attacks were still in progress and just as intense as on the previous day.

When the attack began R111 *Hauptmann* Bachelin received orders to move forward from Consenvoye to Brabant and the *Brabant Schlucht* with the 3rd, 4th and 2MG/R111. The route to the front used by the companies was nasty and dangerous, requiring the men to advance in small squads in order to prevent heavy losses. One shell impacted next to another and the hot sun burned down on the tired men, and many felt they would suffocate from wearing their gas masks; so they tore them off in order to breathe and as a result they suffered from gas poisoning.

The 3/R111 under *Leutnant* Winterer moved toward the Maas valley, the 4/R111 under *Leutnant* Beyle was to reach the *Hagen Stellung* east of the village; and the machine guns that had been carried forward with great difficulty were to be distributed to the companies. At 11 a.m. the detachments were officially placed in possession of RIR 110; they were to be held ready in the *Brabant Schlucht* for the position battalion at the right wing, the I/R110.

The *Brabant Schlucht*, in which only a few dugouts of one shattered battery offered any protection for the men, lay under the heaviest fire and it was 2 p.m. before the companies completed their difficult journey and had arrived there. The companies protected *Brabanter Höhe* and the Maas valley through sentries. The enemy had apparently already appeared at

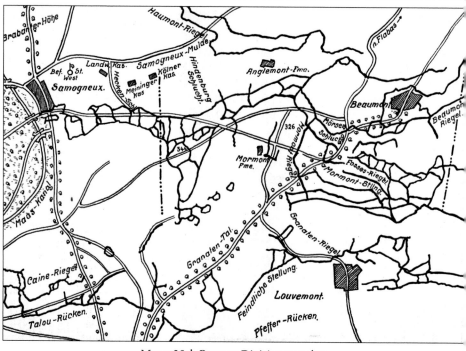

Maas: 28th Reserve Division trenches.

Regneville, west of the river, because soon flanking fire started to come across from the opposite bank.

At first no immediate danger existed for Samogneux. On the other hand the French had thrust forward further east to Hill 344 and in part until in the second trench. The 3rd and 4/R111 were ordered to provide support for this situation and in the course of the evening the two companies reached the II/R110 though the heavily shelled Samogneux hollow to the *Landwehrkaserne*.

No news had come back about the events that occurred in front of the main position in the heavy fighting by RIR 109. According to later reports the few survivors of the outpost zone had surrendered, the *Caine Riegel, Mormont Schlucht*, western, eastern and southern hillsides of Hill 344 were under such strong fire that a withdrawal through these locations was impossible. At the same time the *Mormont Schlucht* was heavily gassed, the *Caine Riegel* as well as the *Caine Schlucht* became covered with smoke bombs. The enemy had pressed unobserved into the *Caine Riegel* between 5 and 6 a.m. under the protection of the smoke and gas and had either killed or captured the surviving sentries, who were supposed to go back once the attack was recognized.

The machine gun at the northern slope of the *Caine Schlucht* had been destroyed by artillery fire. There was apparently no one left to fire the prearranged barrage fire light signals. It was only at the left sector where the barrage fire signal was recognized by the leader who was situated in the crater line with two light machine guns, *Vizefeldwebel* Beuermann, 12/R109, coming from the *Mormont Riegel* and at approximately 5.45 a.m. the signal became repeated. Based upon these signals the German defensive barrage fire was transferred back and directed upon the strongpoint. It was at this time that green light signals were seen in front of the left sector. There was some confusion about which side had fired off the green signals, perhaps it was a French signal for 'transfer fire forward.'

The German barrage fire continued to be directed upon the strongpoints. With the defensive fire being directed on the strongpoints in the outpost zone the enemy attack that followed upon the main position north of the outpost zone was not hindered through the artillery barrage fire. The French advanced through the *Kottelette Schlucht* against the left wing of RIR 110 and the *Artillerie Graben*. Apparently, the sentries and the machine gun crews that were still alive in the crater area of the *Artillerie* and *Pionier Graben* were destroyed through the enemy rolling fire that fell in front of the advancing French storm columns.

A strong enemy attack had developed in front of the left wing about the *Mormont Riegel* against RIR 83. The barrage fire initially held up the attack. However, it then became delivered east of the Mormont farm in the direction of Hill 626. The gassed *Mormont Schlucht* was avoided by the attacking French troops and between this ravine and the *Kottelette Schlucht* the enemy slowly advanced at the southern hillside of Hill 344, also in the *Kottelette Schlucht*. The two forward shoved light machine guns held the left battalion sector in the first crater line, until the French infantry reached their rear on the southern slope of Hill 344. *Vizefeldwebel* Beuermann with a few his men succeeded in reaching the left company in the right sector in the direction of Sap 6. The machine gun he operated had become unserviceable, of the crew of Other Ranks half were dead or buried.

In the right sector of the main position the enemy fire was mainly directed upon the 5th and 6/R109. The last available dugout in this sector had become destroyed and heavy losses had occurred. The leaders of both companies were already in the hospital several days earlier. The new leader of the 5/R109, *Leutnant* Hainmüller, then became wounded, and the last *Unteroffizier* in the company took over the command of the 5/R109, until he was also buried and wounded.

The French assault troops who had attacked the right sector of RIR 109 had encountered almost no resistance and were able to approach the main German position with very few losses. The enemy troops pressed forward, over the *Artillerie Graben* by the right regimental border and by the neighboring RIR 110. *Grenadier* Arnold, who was the only man who escaped out of the *Caine Riegel*, found his way back to the rear through the completely destroyed position of RIR 110.

The enemy rolled up the German defenses to the east from the right regimental border and overpowered the last parts of the companies located there. The French also succeeded in capturing the second trench, from which they advanced upon the southern side of Hill 344 and overran the remnants of the 8/R109. The left wing company of the right sector, the 6/R109 that had not suffered as greatly as the other companies in the regiment and still retained all of its officers, repulsed the French attack under the energetic leadership of *Leutnant* Biegelmaier.

The II/R019 command post lay too far to the rear from the companies, making it very difficult for runners to reach the command post through the heavy enemy fire. As a result the news that the enemy had completely broken in by the right wing company did not reach the II/R109 until 6.50 a.m. Already 20 minutes earlier the men that were lying in the Hamburg barracks, the 7/R109, saw French infantry coming over the hill and alarmed the company, upon which *Leutnant* Markwitz ordered the reserves to counterattack immediately. The *Stosstruppen* stormed up the hillside and suffered heavy losses through well placed French machine gun fire. *Leutnant der Reserve* Sutor and *Leutnant der Reserve* Kasper were both killed, *Leutnant der Reserve* Kaiser was wounded, and *Leutnant* Engert ended up wounded and captured. The survivors were not able to hold the K2 *Graben* and became firmly seated in the craters lying behind this trench.

Meanwhile, the enemy who had captured more ground in the area of RIR 110, advanced with superior strength against the seam detachment that was located in the second trench, of which only a few men escaped complete annihilation. However, the remnants of the *Stosstrupps* continued to hold out in the newly occupied crater line and became reinforced through men that had been assembled in the rear. The situation at the right wing of RIR 109 was very serious and the connection with RIR 110 was completely lost. Meanwhile, the commander of the II/R109 placed the 1/R109 as reinforcements at the right wing when it arrived at the front.

Shortly after 8 a.m. the brigade reserve, the 9th and 10/R111, was placed in possession of the II/R109 and became led forward to the commander of the II Battalion, *Hauptmann* von Heimburg. However the two companies did not arrive until between 11 and 11.30 a.m. with large losses. The largest part of the 9/R111 had become forced back to the left sector of the regiment through artillery fire to the *Lueder* barracks where it came under the command of *Hauptmann* von Wolff. The 10/R111 was placed in possession of the 1/R111 and received orders to roll up the enemy occupied position to the west from out of the second trench at the eastern slope of the *Hindenburg Schlucht*. The counterattack by the 10/R111 initially succeeded during which an enemy machine gun was taken. Then, any further advance came to an abrupt end in the strong German defensive artillery fire that was falling on the K2 *Graben*. Since the company could no longer advance, it arranged an interconnected line between the 1/R111 and the remaining parts of the I and II/R111on the right.

After Picket Beuermann was pressed back to the main position under heavy losses, at 7.30 a.m. the enemy reached the right company sector with strong forces, and in the first onrush took the K1 *Graben* and then advanced toward the K2 *Graben*. The 11/R109 under the leadership of *Leutnant der Reserve* Straub however succeeded in preventing the French from taking this important trench. The commander of the III/R109, *Hauptmann* von Wolff, then sent a message to the 9/R109 under *Leutnant der Reserve* Albrecht to counterattack against the French who had penetrated the line. The *Stosstrupp* under the command of *Leutnant der Reserve* Sauer, first of all hurried along the K2 *Graben* and was able to determine that it was still firmly in the hands of the 10th and11/R109.

However, when Sauer and his men pressed forward from the left wing in the K1 *Graben* to the right, they suddenly saw strong enemy forces opposite them that they held back with rifle fire, until their ammunition ran out. *Grenadiers* Bader and Hiller immediately reported to bring up fresh supplies of ammunition, during which Hiller became wounded. After Bader had returned with ammunition out of the K2 *Graben*, *Leutnant* Sauer was able to roll up the strongly occupied K1 *Graben* with hand grenades. The men under Sauer advanced against the French position with a cheer, moving from crater to crater, and in this manner forced the French to evacuate the K1 *Graben*. *Unteroffizier* Filsinger, 9/R109, was far in front of the rest of the men, 'like a berserk Roland' as he set off with hand grenades against the French nests in the craters, until *Leutnant* Sauer called him back. Once safely back he explained his actions by saying 'The Gaul went through me.'

However the success was short lived as the enemy continued to press forward with new and far superior forces, so that the already extremely weak 11/R109 had to ask for reinforcements. In response to the request, the 12/R109 under *Leutnant* Jenne became positioned for a counterattack. During the counterattack, the companies received several direct hits by French shells; however they were still able to advance, so that the 12/R109 together with the 9th and 11/R109 were able to throw the French out of the K1 *Graben* from the right and could also bring much needed support to the strongly engaged *Stosstrupp* Sauer. Also, the connection with the 6/R109 that was still bravely holding its position on the eastern slope of Hill 344 could be established once again. With this approximately 50 Frenchmen that had become isolated because of the obstacle created by the French artillery fire lying on the position could not be brought in as prisoners due to the same fire. *Leutnant* Sauer had become severely wounded in the head by a rifle shot and remained lying in front of the K1 *Graben*. *Grenadiers* Barth and Bader from the 9/R109 firmly held the French trapped in shell craters through throwing hand grenades in the immediate vicinity of the craters, until they had brought *Leutnant* Sauer safely back to the K1 *Graben* under great peril to their own lives.

By the 10/R109 at the left regimental wing the attacking enemy was detained under heavy losses through light machine guns set up in the outpost zone. It was not until after the insertion of fresh reserves was the enemy able to press forward and at 8.40 a.m. broke through the German line by RIR 83 and at the left wing of the III/R109. One platoon of the 3/R109 armed with a light machine gun that was subordinate to *Hauptmann* von Wolff immediately became sent as reinforcements for the threatened 10/R109 under *Leutnant* Weigele II. With the reinforcements the 10/R109 succeeded in maintaining full possession of the K1 and K2 *Graben* and with it brought in 17 prisoners.

By 11.30 a.m. the enemy was thrown out of all parts of the position of the II/R109. While only small advances followed at the right wing of the regiment that were all refused, the situation at the left wing continued to be very dangerous. No more connection existed with RIR 83, where the enemy sat in the second trench and made attempts over and over to roll up the sector of RIR 109 with the use of flame throwers.

Hauptmann von Wolff, recognizing the threat to the left wing, made arrangements to move the necessary forces needed to secure the position. He placed the parts of the 9/R111, which he had assembled, by the 10/R109 and brought one platoon of the 3/R109 into position to the left rear at Anglemont farm and placed two heavy machine guns in the intermediate terrain in front of the *Lueder* barracks to prevent any enemy breakthrough. The trenches remained firmly in the hands of the III/R109 during the restless night. Numerous small advances made by the enemy were all refused outright. *Hauptmann* von Wolff understood where to place his meager reserves by always quickly recognizing the threatened portions of the line, where the reserves were needed the most. Through his personal intrepidity in the critical situation, he provided his men an excellent example to spur them on.

In the night of 20/21 August, the connection with the left neighboring regiment, RIR 83, was re-established. At 2.30 a.m. on 21 August the extremely exhausted 10/R109 was relieved by the 8/R111 and moved back to the *Lueder Kaserne*. Then, towards 6.45 a.m., it became known that the enemy was also working forward from the right wing of RIR 83, and that the French had also moved up reinforcements at the eastern slope of Hill 344. Destructive and barrage fire immediately became ordered, however without any real effect. The enemy infantry and machine gun fire could not be held back by the weak artillery fire, and the enemy broke forth once again with strong forces.

The French troops penetrated at the left wing company, 8/R111, at the left battalion border, and therefore could reach the K1 *Graben* on the right wing, where a gap between the left and right sector existed. From here, the enemy attempted to roll up the K1 *Graben* with flame throwers once again, forcing the 8/R111 to give up the K1 *Graben*. The parts of the 3/R109 lying directly in front of the trench were encompassed and ended up as prisoners following courageous resistance, but the enemy forces proved to be too powerful. The defenders no longer had any reserves that could throw the enemy out of the K1 *Graben* in a counterattack.

The last paltry reserves had to be put in at the right wing of the sector, in order to prevent the breakthrough of the enemy through the *Hindenburg Schlucht*. At 10 a.m. the enemy was in possession of the entire K1 *Graben*. At the same time the 6/R109 in the right neighboring sector on the eastern slope of Hill 344 became encompassed and pressed back.

The K2 *Graben* held out against repeated French attacks. Then, at 9.15 p.m., the enemy attempted to advance again after a period of lively artillery fire and when parts of the left wing were forced to withdraw, *Hauptmann* von Wolff and the Battalion Adjutant, *Leutnant* Armbruster personally led the scattered forces back into the K2 *Graben* again. In the following three days the small force under Wolff and Armbruster always succeeded in refusing the numerous advances made by the enemy and in doing so, supported both neighboring sectors. The fighting by RIR 110 was no less severe.

The drum fire has already lasted since 13 August; today is the 20th, an eternity! At 1.00 a.m. the brigade shares that the attack is expected in the morning hours. All companies were given increased attention to duty. From 3.00 a.m. on the enemy fire increases to a terrifying drum fire. Hardly anyone has considered this increase to be possible. An iron hail of monstrous intensity rains down on the sector of the regiment. Simultaneously the enemy projectiles used generated smoke and clouds. The hollows were gassed. Observation is out of the question, the signalers could not obtain any connection. At 5.58 a.m. green light balls became fired off at the Talou: 'The Talou becomes attacked.' The remnants of the 1st Coy were placed in possession of the 4th Coy. Anxious minutes! No connection to the front was possible. No orders, no reports came through. Would the 10th Coy be able to move back as scheduled? Would the step by step rear transfer of our barrage fire in front of the main position lift and impede the enemy advance? Finally Battalion Imhoff received a report through *Unteroffizier* Lauber of the 8th Coy that the French sat in the battle trench in dense masses on the right and on the left of Sap 7. Now the situation is clear: the enemy had overrun the Talou and the second crater position under the protection of his drum fire and protected through smoke and fog, our barrage fire lay in his rear. Now he sat on Hill 344 and in the forward battle trench of the left battalion. Only very quick counterattacks can save the situation, the 5th and 6th Coy began immediately. The 6th Coy went forward in the connection to the 8th the widest on the left, *Leutnant der Reserve* Eglin in front. First must the barrage fire that lay on that barracks become overcome. It succeeds, but with heavy losses. Out of the battle trench machine gun fire hits against attackers. One hand grenade salvo after the other forces them into the shell craters. The company leader *Leutnant der Reserve* Eglin and many of his good men fell, but the rest fought back bravely and prevented the enemy forward thrust in the Samogneux hollow. The connection to the left was established. Also the 5th Coy proceeded until it was in the 2nd battle trench of the 7th Coy, where the company leader with a few people fought back against the French. A further advance in the first battle trench was impossible. The company leader of the 5/R110, *Leutnant der Reserve* Schmolling, was wounded. [6]

Simultaneously *Leutnant der Reserve* Carstens, leader of the 2/R110 and parts of the 5/R110 counterattacked on his own initiative with four Groups in support of the II/R110. They went forward through the *Hecken Schlucht* over the 2nd battle trench, but then the 2/R110 returned and was now content with the defense of the second battle trench on both sides of the *Hecken Schlucht*. They were occupying the most important position; if the enemy was able to push through here, then he would be in the Samogneux hollow. The regiment also recognized the danger of this situation and the 9/R110, which had been placed in possession of the I/R110 at 6.40 a.m. was placed at the border of both battalions in the course of the morning by *Hauptmann* Humricht, so that the connection between the battalions was maintained.

The sector of the I/R110 had not become attacked on 20 August. In the morning the French forces sat in the line that ran approximately from Cotelettes Mill until the Maas, and in the evening they were positioned 300 meters in front of the 3/R110 at the southern edge of Samogneux.

RIR 110 desperately needed reinforcements for the weakened II/R110. The 7/266, which attempted to swarm out during daylight hours in order to overcome the hill north of the Samogneux Hollow, was bombarded with machine guns and artillery of all calibers, so that they finally reached the *Landwehr* barracks after taking numerous detours and heavy losses. At 8.30 p.m. the following forces were in possession of *Hauptmann* Imhoff for a potential counterattack: The remnants of the 11/R110, 3rd and 4/R111, 4th and 7/266, 2MG/R110 with five guns, 3MG/R110 with nine guns.

It also had to be considered that when the companies listed above had arrived at the barracks they had already been reduced to about half strength as a result of the French fire, which was about 50 to 60 men each and the men were exhausted. The counterattack was thoroughly discussed with the different leaders: The troops would be in the Readiness position in the barracks line at 12 midnight, then advance to the second battle trench, storming of the first battle trench and finally defending the ground that had been won. RIR 109 then called for barrage fire to fall in front of the readiness position. The counterattack had to be postponed until 2.30 a.m. because of the enemy fire that had been deployed across the sector. Finally, the companies moved forward, however they did not succeed in advancing over the second battle trench due to the strong French defensive fire.

The vulnerability of the Maas valley caused considerable anxiety to the brigade. One battalion from RIR 111 was positioned in the *Brabant Schlucht* in order to block the valley, and in the night of 20/21 August the I/R110 received four machine guns from the 1MG/R111 as reinforcements, also to block off the Maas valley. Two of the guns were to be set up at the sluice at the southern exit of Samogneux, however they did not reach this position, instead they remained with the other two guns by the badly damaged bridge at the northern exit of Samogneux and at 5 a.m. reported to the battalion command post of the I/R110. One platoon from the 2/R110, which was ordered to protect the Maas valley became sent forward to the sluice bridge, however it came under the enemy preparation fire;

the leader was killed and the rest of the men were dispersed.

The morning of 21 August was grey. Since 5 a.m. powerful artillery fire from all calibers lay upon the main position, Samogneux and Samogneux hollow. Again the enemy used smoke bombs and gas shells. With the existing fog any view was impossible, any observation impossible. Shortly after 6 a.m. the attack upon the right battalion took place. Barrage fire was called up and employed immediately. The enemy attacked the 4th and subsequently the 9th, 5th and 7th Coy at several positions out of the front and out of the left flank. The first trench was overrun, the enemy pressed forward on the left with a *Stosstrupp* until up to the barracks, however they became taken under fire and move back in the *Jungfernstieg*. The counter-thrust by the *Stosstrupps* placed at the ready by the 4th Coy in the second battle trench could not begin, because they received fire from the rear. There was no news from the 7th and 5th Companies (*Leutnants der Reserve* Uhrig and Krenz). The people of the 4th Coy moved back to the left under very severe bombardments from three sides. What is the situation at the right wing company? (3/R110). They also become attacked out of the front. After the first battle trench by the 4th Coy was overrun, the enemy pressed forward, aided by the strong fog formation through the hollow on the *Ernst Ludwig Weg* and by the entirely shot up *Minenwerfer* dugout towards the left flank of the 3rd Coy. In the *Steinbruch* and in the *Hessen Stollen* it came to hand grenade fighting: the 3/R110 (*Hauptmann* Pyhrr) was overpowered, the route through the Maas valley via Samogneux seemed open to the adversary. We stand in front of the battalion battle headquarters *Zwingburg* and eagerly observed toward the exit of the Samogneux hollow, the French now curved about the nose of the mountain, a rich prize waved at them: take the Samogneux hollow, all of the terrain south of it would fall into their hands. However everyone, who was still at the place of the Battalion battle headquarters, takes the rifle in his hand, *Leutnant der Reserve* Gerstner brought a machine gun into position, and shortly the shell craters at the entrance of the hollow were full of dead. To be sure the situation of the *Zwingburg* was as comfortable as all others. Hand grenades exploded in front of the entrance, probably thrown from enemy patrols, a Frenchman who was wounded was taken prisoner. 5 men advanced against the battalion battle headquarters in the *Dorfgraben*. We could observe them from above. The battalion cook Haberer can do more than cook; protected by the thrown up ground, he sneaks with a few man behind the patrol and brought back 5 prisoners from *Régiment d' Infanterie* 55. At 7.15 a.m. the regimental reserve in the *Brabant Schlucht* received a written message through a runner that the enemy had overrun the 1st battle trench by the 4th Coy, the situations in the second battle trench however was still not clear. The I Battalion urgently asked about an immediate counterattack. In fact the commander of the regimental placed reserve two platoons of the 1/R111 and three machine guns of the 1st MG Coy/R111 in march. This however did not reach the I/R110. After the fog had cleared the enemy east of Samogneux became fired at with machine guns out from Brabant hill. Our own artillery fired on the village between 9 and 10.00 a.m. and the hill position east of it. Admittedly they had also taken our battalion battle headquarters under well placed fire, in the assumption they are occupied by the enemy. This is quite uncomfortable. The infantry pilot, who in a dashing manner flew at a low altitude, circling above us, understands our signal: 'move the fire forward!' and rescues us out of the uncomfortable situation. [7]

A counterattack under the command of *Hauptmann* von Bissing with the 11/216, 5th, 6th and 8/R266, Machine Gun *Abteilung* 30 and all available parts of RIR 110 at hand to recapture Samogneux and both battle trenches was to be executed at 3 p.m. Then, on orders from the division the counterattack was cancelled. The division then issued orders: 'The regiment will hold the heights north and northwest of Samogneux, where it will afford opposition with all means.' The II/R216 remained as the division reserve in the sector south of the *Volkerstellung,* while the parts of RIR 266 remained as the regimental reserve. Any troops still in the Samogneux hollow that could no longer hold out against the enemy attacks, had to withdraw to the hills north of Samogneux.

The situation by RIR 110 was the following: Samogneux was lost; the enemy sat firmly at the northern exit. The first battle trench was occupied by the enemy along the entire line. About 100 meters behind the second battle trench were a few people of the 4th and 1/R110, the 12/R110 with about 40 men, the 8th and 2/R110 on the right and on the left of the *Hecken Schlucht.* RIR 266 and the 4/R111 sat in the second battle trench connecting on the left. *Hauptmann* Imhoff was forced goes back after the French advance up to the barracks via the Samogneux hollow and had his command post transferred into the *Hangstellung* about 250 meters northeast of the intersection of this position with the *Hessen Weg.* Once in the new position he also encountered the company leaders of the 4th and 1/R110 along with a handful of their men. The staff of the I/R110 still lay in the *Zwingburg.*

In view of the uncertain situation and in accordance with division orders the sector became newly partitioned by RIR 110 at 2 p.m. The sector from the *Maasknie*-Brabant Hill excluding *Haumont Schlucht* was taken on by *Hauptmann* Bachelin, commander of RIR 111. Standing under him were the 2MG/R111, 11/R110, one platoon from the 1MG/R111, 80 men from the hauling troops/R110 and the 5/R266. The left sector from the *Haumont Schlucht* inclusive until the left regimental border was taken on by *Hauptmann* Imhoff. Standing under him were all remnants of RIR 110, the remnants of the 4th and 7/R266, 3MG/R110 and the 6/R266. All parts of the regiment still found south of the Samogneux hollow went back in the twilight at the latest by 10 p.m. to the *Hangstellung* north of the Samogneux hollow. These lines are taken up in the twilight of 21 August.

During the withdrawal into the *Haumont Schlucht* the leader of the 3MG/R110, *Leutnant der Reserve* Siess, was killed. He stood together with *Leutnant der Reserve* Gerstner in front of the battalion dugout while observing the front, when a fist size splinter from an exploding shell struck him on the head and killed him instantly. At 12:45 a.m. the following order arrived from the brigade: 'On higher orders the line of the barracks south of the Samogneux Hollow would still be taken and occupied by RIR 110 again in this night and must be held.'

At 2.30 a.m. on 21 August, when the enemy fire had lessened somewhat, the 4/R111 on the right, the 3/R111 on the left, with three paces spacing between each man, took positions on the hillside above the dugouts of the K2 Graben for an assault. The rows moved as silently as possible and the men soon reached the second trench west of the *Hecken Schlucht.* The French also attacked at this location, and in the ensuing hand grenade battle the two companies from RIR 111 managed to recapture part of the lost terrain, however they were unable to take the first trench back again.

Individual Groups attempted to advance through a communication trench, where they encountered strong French forces that put up a tough fight. The small number of German troops that were attacking were no match for the superior number of enemy troops and were eventually forced to give ground. It did not help the situation that they were also hindered through short lying impacts from several German batteries. In the early morning hours of 21 August the 3rd and 4/R111 prepared their shell craters for defense, as good as possible. The two companies were determined not to yield the newly recaptured ground.

On the evening of 20 August the 1/R111 under *Leutnant* Göbel and the 2/R111 under *Leutnant* Holzhauser with the 1MG/R111 under *Leutnant* Brenker were ordered to move into the *Brabant Schlucht* in place of the 3rd and 4/R111. These companies became moved forward from the division reserve at approximately 7 a.m. from the *Köhlerhof*. From here they should be able to work forward in support of RIR 110 about midday.

Despite being detained through artillery fire, the companies arrived in the *Brabant Schlucht* in a timely manner, in order to take over the protection of the right wing. One platoon from the 2/R111 under *Vizefeldwebel* Müller with four machine guns was placed in position to extend the defenses at the southern exit of Samogneux. During the advance to the new position the platoon ended up in heavy French fire and the men were scattered. *Vizefeldwebel* Müller with a few Groups and two machine guns eventually reached the canal lock directly west of Samogneux and dug in south of this lock.

A different squad from the platoon then became directed to the command post of the I/R110, east of Samogneux. The two remaining machine guns went into position at the bridge north of the village, and later they changed position to the western shore of the canal. In the course of 21 August the guns fired on the French who were observed in Samogneux and drove them back from the Maas. The 1/R111 moved off to the Cologner barracks in the Samogneux hollow while it was still dark because the situation at Hill 344 was still threatened. Once there, they received orders to occupy the second trench at the northwest hillside of the hill. The 1st Company swarmed out and worked forward in the destroyed trench pieces and shell craters up to daylight. The trenches and craters were occupied and a connection to the neighboring unit was established to the right and to the left. With this deployment almost the entire I/R111 was inserted into the battle line of RIR 110 and waited for the renewed enemy attack. Two platoons from the 2/R111, the 2MG/R111 and the rest of the 1MG/R111 were all that remained of the reserves for this portion of the line.

The 9/R111 under *Leutnant* Stoffler and the 10/R111 under *Leutnant* Rothweiler worked through from the *Namenlosenschlucht* for the support of RIR 109. The two companies advanced in rows with large spacing in the early, but already quite warm morning, through a hail of projectiles and gas clouds and reached the *Haumont Riegel*. Returning wounded from RIR 109 reported that the enemy had broken in at the front on Hill 344. As help was urgently needed, the men from the 9th and 10/R111 jumped from shell hole to shell hole, as quickly as the raging fire falling about them permitted, advancing through the Samogneux hollow. The 9/R111 became badly dispersed in the enemy fire and only about four Groups under the *Unteroffizieren* Walz, Canahl (both wounded) and Kornmeier reached the 10/R109 at the left wing of the regiment; they were later reinforced through Group Rothmeier.

Both trenches here were still in German hands, and the men from RIR 111 successfully defended the crater position against several French attacks. Groups from the 8/R111 under *Leutnant* Beck were then pushed into the line being held by the 9/R111 in the early morning hours, and Beck took over command of the position. Other parts of the 9/R111, which had assembled in the *Lüderskaserne*, managed to bring up ammunition, hand grenades and food into the trenches of the III/R109 in the barrage and machine gun fire and brought the wounded back to the rear. When they became alarmed early on 21 August, they supported the ranks of the 12/R109.

The light machine guns of the 9/R111, whose leader, *Unteroffizier* Morath, had already been killed during the advance through a head shot, were brought into position by the 11/R109 by *Schützen* Lehmann and Holz.

> During the advance in a springing manner a *Schützen* from our gun had his right hand shattered through a machine gun shot. I asked a comrade lying beside me named Kaiser, however, to bring two ammunition boxes, so that we not without ammunition when we arrived in the position. He had hardly complied with my request, when he received three shots in the thigh. I believe the Frog has efficiently taken our gun in his sites. I saw only one man from my gun and the entire company. I now took the gun on my shoulder and ran as if I was mad across the shell holes that were full of severely wounded and dead, without taking cover again, towards a dugout that lay at the foot of the mountain, where a white flag was waving. Like a miracle I and my companion Holz, who was already in the field from the beginning in 1914 and still had no wounds, came through this rain of fire. We arrived at a type of tunnel where there were R109er. A *Major* asked me, if our gun was still intact, and was visibly pleased when I responded positively to his question. He entertained us personally and we received a nice drop to drink. We obtained two R109er who would show us the route there. We did not arrive at our destination. There were altogether no more trenches and dugouts. We took up position with the gun on the first traverse, which was still moderately intact, however we did not know if we had any connection on the right or on the left to the enemy or to our own side. Still later four people from our company came to us. The Frogs made individual attacks, but our machine gun accomplished good work, and so we six men could hold the small sector. *Schütze* Lehmann, 9/R111 [8]

The leader of the 9/R111 arrived in the right sector of the II/R109 in the *Hamburg Kaserne* with two Groups, where they formed the rear support for those men still clinging in craters for protection on the northern slope of Hill 344. The French were already in the second trench here, and the Groups that had made contact with men from the 10/R111, filled up the existing gaps in the defensive line. In the night they participated in a counterattack that was held without artillery preparation fire that succeeded through surprise. However, the *Sturmtrupp*, which had come through lively machine gun fire to reach the old second trench, was too weak to hold it against counter thrusts by the French, and were forced back into the old crater position again, where the sentry line became reinforced on the early morning of 21 August through Groups of the 5th and 6/R111 coming out of the Hamburg barracks.

The 10/R111, which had been taken over by *Offizier Stellvertreter* Jockers in place of the wounded *Leutnant* Rothweiler, pushed forward through the *Hindenburg Schlucht* to an unoccupied part of the second trench at the border of the sector between the II and III/R109. *Gefreiter* Bossemeyer, a proven patrol leader, made a reconnaissance patrol that determined that the French were established in the second German trench on the right flank. In spite of powerful artillery fire, *Offizier Stellvertreter* Jockers succeeded in positioning a *Stosstrupp* in order to roll up the enemy occupied trench. The undertaking started at 8 p.m. and the *Stosstrupp* advanced into the trench only to be stopped by friendly artillery fire that was falling too short on this position. The *Stosstrupp* made a number of attempts, all of which were prevented by friendly fire and the attempts only resulted in a partial success. The French, realizing how dangerous their position had become due to the proximity of the German troops, also made an attempt to roll up the German position at the onset of darkness. They too failed due to the opposition from a flanking guard of the 10/R111 and in the short lying artillery fire.

The companies of the II/R111 moved from the *Namenlosenschlucht* through Haumont wood and Caures wood, which were strongly bombarded, arriving at the area of the *Haumont Riegel* about midday on 20 August. The 6/R111 under *Leutnant* Rüttenauer occupied this trench southeast of Haumont, while the three other companies as well as the 3MG/R111 were positioned ready for battle in Caures wood not far from the Anglemont farm.

However, the orders providing instructions for the deployment of the II/R111 had not reached the battalion headquarters; the battle runners, who were to deliver them, had all been killed. For the remainder of the day the companies of the II/R111 acted independently, as the situation dictated. About 5 p.m. the French attempted an attack from Hill 326.1 north of Mormont farm, during which the 7/R111 under *Leutnant* Müller and the 8/R111 under *Leutnant* Beck with four machine guns of the 3MG/R111 participated in the defense. The attack was stopped halfway up the northern slope of the hill. The two companies then became placed into the *Haumont Riegel* on the left of the 6/R111. The *Haumont Riegel* was the target of numerous enemy batteries; because barely any protection existed, considerable losses occurred, and among others *Leutnant* Ley, 5/R111, was killed here.

After 9 p.m. the companies of the II/R111 succeeded in establishing a connection with the battalion commander, *Major* Höhne. New orders now arrived sending the 7th and 8/R111 with four machine guns to a battalion sector of RIR 109. The battalion staff with the 5th and 6/R111 and the rest of the 3MG/R111 had been placed in possession of the right sector. The companies moved along the path in the darkness by squads through the fire block and the gas clouds to the Samogneux hollow and the *Hindenburg Schlucht*. The 5th and 6/R111 were not assembled again until 5 a.m. on 21 August, in the Hamburg barracks and immediately became inserted in the forward line at the northeast slope of Hill 344.

Once in the new position the men found Groups from the 9/R111 under *Leutnant* Beck already in the crater position. The 7/R111, whose leader suffered gas poisoning, became shattered while being pulled out; they could not be reorganized again until 23 August in the *Haumont Riegel* by *Leutnant* Harrer. Parts of the 7th Coy ended up in the *Mörser Schlucht*, west of Beaumont, therefore in the old regimental sector, and participated in a counter attack here by RIR 83 on 22 August. The 3MG/R111 was inserted into the Samogneux hollow.

The security garrison of the *Hagen Stellung*, the 11th and 12/R111, held and occupied their trench on 20 August under considerable enemy fire, ready to defend it against a possible enemy breakthrough. The French advance over Talou ridge and upon Hill 344 could be observed from this position. In the night to 21 August the II/R111 was placed in the regimental sector of RIR 109 as reinforcements in response to the French advance.

On 21 August the terrain was covered in dense fog. At 5.30 a.m. the enemy batteries began to pound the German positions again and between 6 and 7 a.m. the French infantry attacked. From the hill east of Samogneux they penetrated into the village. The leader of the

Verdun: *Mörser Schlucht* with 21cm Mortars. (Author's collection)

platoon from the 2/R111 that was placed with RIR 110 was at the canal lock, *Vizefeldwebel* Müller, had already been killed. The survivors of the company vigorously defended the position against the almost invisible enemy, until they were overpowered by superior strength. Only four men, amongst them two wounded and one machine gun returned to the rear. The other machine gun was rendered unserviceable and was left behind to the enemy.

The other troops of this platoon by the command post of the I/R110 helped to defend the command post after the trenches east of Samogneux were overrun. When the news of the break-through reached *Hauptmann* Bachelin in the *Brabant Schlucht*, he immediately ordered the northern and southern situated hills to be occupied with machine guns, which took the French by Samogneux under heavy fire. The two platoons of the 2/R111 with three machine guns under *Leutnant* Holzhauser advanced in a counter attack, however because of the powerful defensive fire at the southern slope of Brabant hill they were stopped; they did succeed in establishing a connection with the command post of the I/R110.

On the morning of 21 August a counterattack by the 80th Infantry Division took place in the right sector that was occupied by RIR 109, where two battalions of the division attacked Hill 344. The fog had lifted and it was turning into a bright sunny day, when after a short period of fire preparation the counterattack began. The men of RIR 109 watched the counterattack from their position and saw the troops advance over Haumont Hill to the Samogneux hollow.

However the brave men of the 80th Infantry Division had barely been recognized by the French, when a frenzied fire was employed on Haumont Hill. It was a terrible sight on the slopes of Hill 344 for the men of RIR 109. The attack quickly collapsed in the enemy fire and the assaulting troops seemed to simply disappear in the flash of high explosives, plumes of earth and smoke. Only a few men managed to reach the valley and the position of RIR 109. *Major* Höhne with his adjutant and a few men from the II/R111 managed to reach the commander of the II/R109.

Later, at the onset of darkness, units from the 80th Infantry Division arrived in the Samogneux hollow, whereupon one company from the battalion in the right neighboring sector became used for a night counterattack that was primarily being used to retake the

K2 *Graben* in the sector RIR 110.

In the meantime the French had rolled up the second trench east of Samogneux further to the right and several enemy assault groups had overpowered the two right wing platoons of the 4/R111 south of the *Landwehrkaserne*. A large part of the 4/R111 including the company commander ended up in captivity despite courageous opposition. The left wing platoon under *Vizefeldwebel* Esslinger forced the enemy to stop.

The French then renewed their attempts to overpower Esslinger's platoon under the cover of smoke bombs. The French infantry advanced under the protection of machine gun fire, and tried to overwhelm the small platoon with rifles and hand grenades. The platoon, which had already lost many good soldiers, defended their trench against every attack. The platoon was also able to secure the left flank of the position by reinforcing the connection with the neighboring 3/R111.

Enemy patrols were sent out toward the 3rd Coy, in order to determine if the position was ripe for an assault; they became repulsed. *Leutnant* Winterer then directed strong rifle fire on the former first German trench in the thick fog. Three times the enemy attempted to advance; he only advanced until he was by the damaged wire obstacles, where the French soldiers remained hopelessly entangled in the thick barbs. Well placed defensive barrage fire added to the effect of the rifle fire. The enemy now attempted to take the trench from the rear, when a small group of French soldiers advanced through a communication trench until they were near to the *Landwehrkaserne* and then came up through the *Hecken Schlucht* in the rear of the German position.

However flanking fire from Company Winterer and Platoon Esslinger, especially from the light machine guns, forced the French to retreat after suffering numerous casualties. Danger also threatened the left flank of Company Winterer and Platoon Esslinger, which was being protected by only two Groups of men from RIR 110. The French made several attempts to roll up this position after they had covered it with salvos of hand grenades; in each instance they were forced to retreat after losing a number of men. During this fighting, *Offizier Stellvertreter* Röthele, 3/R111, who energetically led the right wing of his platoon, and *Unteroffizier* Schneider, 3/R111, with his Group at the left wing stood out in particular for their actions.

The small group of defenders had become isolated in their position. After a number of additional enemy attacks all connections to the neighboring troops was lost. There was no connection with the command post in the rear; none of the runners sent off with messages had come back. It became ominous that the German batteries, probably in the assumption that the second trench had been lost, took it under fire. *Vizefeldwebel* Esslinger was forced to evacuate his position and posted his Groups fanned out at the upper-half of the *Landwehrkaserne*, in order to further protect the open right flank of the 3/R111.

When a German infantry pilot appeared overhead, white cloths were laid out on the ground for communication. The French believed that the signal cloths were a sign that the defenders wanted to surrender and demanded that the German troops come over to the French lines. In doing so, the French infantry 'only offered a welcome target.' The men from the 3rd and 4/R111 along with a few men from RIR 110, were directed to use all of their strength to retain the trench-piece in their possession, in which they had become established in during the previous night, and make every effort to resist the French attacks. However they could not save the situation.

Because of the unfavorable situation existing in the right sector by RIR 83 and RIR 110, the Senior Command decided that Hill 344 and the ridge east of Samogneux were to be abandoned in the night to 22 August and the line on the plateau north of the Samogneux hollow that included the Haumont ridge, should be taken up as the new main defensive line. The difficult conditions that existed at the time made it difficult to reach every unit in the sector as communication between the front and the rear were spotty at best and the response to such an order was looked at differently by the officers in the front lines who understood the position far better than the headquarters in the rear did.

This order reached the battalions of RIR 110 in the position about 9 p.m., but not *Oberst* von Baumbach, commanding RIR 110, who knew nothing about it. At first strong enemy fire prevented any movement and it was not until between 10 and 11 p.m. that the remnants of the companies could be lead back through the Samogneux Hollow and become assembled in the *Brabant Schlucht*, from which they would withdraw into the *Volker Stellung*.

Baumbach received the first knowledge of the when the II/R110 sent a message to the regimental headquarters pointing out that the *Haumont Riegel* was quite exposed as it was barely 1/2 meters deep and without dugouts. Moreover, the position being so visible on a plateau was an easy target for the enemy artillery. *Oberst* von Baumbach agreed with the assessment and immediately sent the Regimental adjutant *Leutnant* Böhne with *Leutnant* Ganter into the position, to prevent the implementation of this order for the benefit of his troops.

The two officers quickly hurried through the barrage fire and gas into the position and arrived there just as the 7/R110 had reached the *Haumont Riegel*. After a short explanation of the facts the troops moved back to their former position again. *Vizefeldwebel* Frisch, 7/R110, was the first to shout: 'Up, into the old position' and quickly departed with his company. The enemy had apparently not noticed that the position had been abandoned, so that it could become completely occupied again without interference.

Further east on the northwest slope of Hill 344 the men from RIR 111 continued to defend the position against repeated French attacks. The 1/R111 under *Leutnant* Trilling who had taken over command from *Leutnant* Göbel, after he had been badly dazed earlier in the day through a shell exploding close by him, had become isolated during the heavy fighting. The company lacked any connections to the right and the appearance of the French in the *Hecken Schlucht* had caused confusion among the defenders. In spite of uninterrupted artillery fire however every attempt the French, to roll up the position failed, as well as every attack against the front out of the old German first trench was held down.

When this company also received the order to disassemble, the northern slope of Hill 344 and the Samogneux hollow were under such strong bombardment that the evacuation could not begin until after 11 p.m. Towards 5.30 a.m. the company leader and the last of his people left their shell craters. The company then became firmly positioned in the *Hagen Stellung* and was placed in readiness on 23 August east of Brabant as the counterattack reserve. In the night to 24 August they reached the *Volker Stellung*.

The parts of the II/R111 and the 9th and 10/R111 inserted with RIR 109 defended the well-known crater position on 21 August. The French had succeeded in rolling up portions of the first trench from the right, however, the second trench remained firmly in the hands of mixed units of both regiments, regardless of the bombardments and repeated enemy advances. Toward midday *Offizier Stellvertreter* Jockers, 10/R111, became wounded and turned over command of the company to *Vizefeldwebel* Ziser. Before leaving, Jockers made it clear to every individual soldier that under no circumstances could the position be lost. Apparently the men took this directive to heart when on the late afternoon the enemy on the right flank attempted to penetrate into the company sector again, and he became repulsed in severe hand grenade fighting.

Offizier Stellvertreter Jockers advised *Leutnant* Stoffler of the difficult situation of the 10/R111, and Stoffler sent *Vizefeldwebel* Mayer to the 10/R111 with fifteen men as reinforcements. Toward evening the entire sector of RIR 109 was covered with especially heavy destructive fire and heavily gassed. The losses increased almost minute by minute, and numerous gas poisonings occurred. Among the numerous casualties were the leaders of the 5th and 6/R111, *Hauptmann* Illgen and *Leutnant* Rüttenauer, who went to the rear with gas poisoning. The remnants of the companies then became subordinate to *Leutnant* Stoffler and at 9.30 p.m. *Major* Höhne received orders, to go back to the *Haumont Riegel*; he sent these orders on to the different companies.

It was midnight before all of the companies received the orders. The execution of these orders in the night from 21 to 22 August did not fully succeed because of the exceptionally difficult transmission of the orders to all of the different units and the strong fire in the Samogneux hollow. At 1 a.m. on 22 August *Leutnant* Stoffler with the 5th, 6th and 9/R111, which were found behind the battle front, began the evacuation of the position, taking the wounded with them. The 10/R111 was unable to begin its withdrawal until 2.30 a.m. because of severe artillery fire on their line of retreat and while coming out of their craters the men became torn apart on the road to the *Haumont Riegel*.

The commander of the left sector, *Hauptmann* von Wolff, RIR 110, had already come to the conclusion that not only was his current strong position far easier to defend; he also cited the impossibility of transporting his 40 severely wounded men to the rear. As such he had already decided to disobey the order and had reported his decision to headquarters through light signals. Between the actions of *Hauptmann* von Wolff and the cancellation of the order to withdraw from Hill 344, the strategic Hill 344 it remained in German hands and continued to form an important strongpoint of the entire sector for the months to come.

The troops of the II and III/R111 that had gone to the rear had barely laid down to rest when the counter order arrived, sending them back to the front. Again these tired and rolled together detachments went across the strongly bombarded and gassed Samogneux hollow and became assembled by *Leutnant* Stoffler in the Wartburg barracks. He then occupied the old crater position with slightly over 100 rifles, without however being able to produce the connection to the left, where previously the 10/R109 lay. There in the afternoon the enemy attempted to work forward in the direction of the *Hindenburg Schlucht*. *Vizefeldwebel* Sillib pushed forth with two *Stosstrupps* on the left flank and established a connection with the III/R109 here.

Still in the night the 8/R111 at the left wing helped to refuse advances by strong forces in close combat. The battle line at the Samogneux hollow held their shell craters, and shattered enemy attempts to attack. The accompanying artillery fire however weakened the battle-strength more and more. Fortunately *Hauptmann* von Wolff placed the *pionier* company that had arrived on the evening of 22 August on the left wing, which provided some relief to the 8th and 9/R111 in the right neighboring sector.

In the morning hours of 22 August the *Zwingburg* headquarters became occupied by the 2/R111 accompanied by several light machine guns. In the early morning hours the barracks line became occupied again when half of the 2/R266 took over the *Kölner* barracks, another company from R266 occupied the Meininger barracks and one company from R266 occupied the *Landwehr* barracks. In addition there were small groups of men from the *Schlepptrupps* as well as several machine guns from the 1st and 2MG/R111. A line of outposts also became positioned in front of the barracks line for protection and the connection to the neighboring units on the right and on the left was established.

The weak defensive line ran along the Maas Canal west of *Brabant Schlucht* to the west and the southern slope of Brabant hill. The position which was not fully prepared, and where only shell holes offered any protection against enemy fire, was strongly bombarded. The small garrison of the *Hangstellung* northeast of the Samogneux hollow remained in place for the time being. The barracks line came under the command of *Hauptmann* Imhoff.

22 August would also prove to be a difficult day of fighting as the French continued to attack along the entire front.

The Frogs attempted to dig out our machine gun, but our people fought with utter contempt. We had jam after jam with our machine gun, and finally we had no more water in the jacket. After a couple of shots the barrel went neither forward nor back. Now we also grasped our rifles of which enough lay around in the trench and fired until the barrels became glowing. Then still hand grenades became considered here. Comrade Heil slid down beside me. I thought he wanted to pick up cartridges. As I looked at him, his helmet lay on the ground filled with blood. He had received a shot through the left temple across through the head and no more sounds came from him. After being relieved out of the position he was to go on furlough. With the onset of darkness we were determined to look for a connection to our people. I took my machine gun on my back, and as quickly as my legs would carry me, I went away across the destroyed trenches and holes. The entire terrain was covered with artillery and machine gun fire, and one must view it as a miracle that anyone could make it through this fire alive. We met R109er, and I became ordered by an officer to exchange my damaged machine gun. Now my only companion Holz and I stumbled humbly to the rear in the night for three hours; we must bring a new machine gun to the front again in the same night. On the way I suddenly lost my comrade Holz. He had fallen into a quite deep hole and cried out to me that I should come down to him; he had a surprise for me. I allowed myself to glide downward on my rear into a spacious dugout, and we found all sorts of useful things, especially, what was worth a lot, an entire depot of Seltzer water, because on this August day our second enemy was called thirst. After we had nursed our thirst, we packed other bottles in sandbags, and then went further, until luckily we met 12 to 15 people from our company. How happy these were about our bringing water! The joy did not want to end. On the next day, about 2.00 a.m., it became active in our trench, and then we saw that it was *pioniers*, who relieved us. A sigh of relief went through our people. Lead by *Unteroffizier* Kohler, we moved off to the *Namenlosenschlucht*. There lay our former, beautiful barracks squashed like a matchbox on the ground. Our kitchen *Unteroffizier* had cooked a wonderful noodle soup, for which we could properly kneel down. So in the soldier's life seriousness and joyfulness are close to one another. Machine Gun *Schützen* Lehmann, 9/R111 [9]

The security garrison in the *Hagen Stellung* that was occupied by the 11th and 12/R111, continued to suffer under strong French artillery fire throughout the 22nd, which, among others, destroyed the light signal station by the 11th Company through a direct hit. A French pilot, who was shot down by Haumont on this day and who suffered severe burn wounds, was also taken prisoner by the men of the 12/R111. Special attention was being paid to the western Maas bank, where patrols determined that the French had advanced via Regneville. Strong pickets with machine guns became issued for the protection of this sector. Fortunately, in the night of 21/22 August the Maas bridges had been blown up by *pioniers*; effectively preventing the French from being able to cross the river in any strength.

In the early morning hours of 23 August the 11th and 12/R111 under *Hauptmann* Wöhrle moved forward to the *Brabant Schlucht*, to replace a battalion from IR 316 which had previously arrived on the right wing of Sector Bachelin, only to be moved away again, leaving a portion of the line unmanned. The 28th Reserve Division completely lacked any available reserves by this point in the fighting. A makeshift reserve was formed using all available men from the supply service, the transport and store-rooms. The men were assembled to form a weak company under *Offizier Stellvertreter* Schempp that along with similar detachments from the other regiments formed a brigade reserve in Solferino farm. However the enemy also seemed to have exhausted his strength and no further attacks took place.

On 23 August the French behaved comparatively quiet, only *Haumont Schlucht*, *Brabant Schlucht* and the barracks line were taken under artillery fire. This was fortunate as all parts of the 28th Reserve Division were exhausted; the troops were overtired through the constant artillery fire and lack of sleep. Then, the good news spread quickly among the men, relief was at hand. The 28th Reserve Division was being relieved by the 51st Reserve Division, RIR 234, RIR 235 and RIR 236.

In the night of 23/24 August Battalion Bachelin on the right was relieved by the III/ R236 without any difficulties. On the morning of 24 August the survivors of RIR 110 and RIR 111 on Hill 344 were relieved by parts of IR 235, and became reorganized in the *Volkerstellung*. On the morning of 25 August *Hauptmann* Imhoff turned over the left battalion sector to the II/R234.

While in the *Volkerstellung* the 28th Reserve Division remained as an *Eingreifdivision* despite its weakened condition, and was signed to the sector on both sides of the Molleville farm- Samogneux road. Parts of the division regiment that were not required in the position were able to be moved into barracks in the wood of Consenvoye where finally regular meals were available; something the men had missed during the heavy fighting.

On the evening of 25 August and the morning of 26 August the battalions of RIR 111 moved to Lissey, in order to become transported to Montmédy by rail. From this city they marched to Chauvency le Château, where the embarkation for the transport to another front was located. Following this latest period of fighting in the 'Hell of Verdun' an accounting of the losses could finally be made. RIR 111 had lost 2 officers, 64 men killed; 3 officers, 254 men wounded; 1 officer, 95 men missing and 3 officers, 40 men gas sick.

In the night from 24 to 25 August the men of RIR 109 were to be relieved by RIR 235. As was normal, the heavy machine guns of the regiment being relieved would be the last to vacate the position, waiting for the new regiment to set up its own guns. One gun from the 3MG/R109 that had remained behind with RIR 235 would have to wait a bit longer before pulling out. Shortly after the relief had taken place the French attempted a surprise attack against the K2 *Graben* from out of the *Hindenburg Schlucht*. The machine gun was under the leadership of *Unteroffizier* Kübler, who held the French in check for a long time, until all of his gun crew had been killed or wounded. Kübler continued to fire as long as possible against the rapidly approaching French masses and when it became obvious he would be overrun, he attempted to bring his gun back to safety. Sadly, he was killed through a hand grenade and his gun was lost.

In the days from 12 August to 26 August RIR 109 had suffered the following losses: 97 officers and men killed; 385 officers and men wounded; 202 officers and men sick and 229 officers and men missing of which only 89 were known to be prisoners of war.

The survivors from RIR 110 were assembled in the *Köhler Lager*, from where the regiment was also transported from 25 to 27 August into the Champagne once again. In the short time RIR 110 had been at the Verdun front the losses in the regiment had been heavy. 2 officers, 82 men killed; 4 officers, 280 men wounded and 6 officers, 405 men missing.

With the end of August 1917 the period of transition was over. The new methods of warfare were firmly in place and would dominate the fighting that followed. 1917 was almost over and 1918 would prove to be a year of monumental events as each side made desperate attempts to bring the war to a conclusion. For the German Army, 1918 would be the pivotal year where every effort would be made to bring the Allies to the peace table, as every resource at the front and at home were utilized to bring victory and an end to the years of destructive warfare.

Notes

1. Bachelin, op. cit., p. 161.
2. Greiner & Vulpius, op. cit., pp. 189-190.
3. Greiner & Vulpius, op. cit., pp. 192-193.
4. Greiner & Vulpius, op. cit., p. 196.
5. Frisch, Georg, op. cit., p. 208
6. Greiner & Vulpius, op. cit., pp. 199-200.
7. Greiner & Vulpius, op. cit., p. 202.
8. Bachelin, op. cit., p. 168.
9. Bachelin, op. cit., pp. 172-173.

Bibliography

Unpublished sources
Feldpost letters (1916-1919), *Leutnant der Reserve* Albert Reihling, 4 /R
Feldpost letters of Chr. Gerber, 8/R119
Feldpost letters of *Unteroffizier* Otto Nuding, 2/180

Regimental Stammrolle books
Bavarian State Archives. Department IV, War Archive, Munich
Bavarian RIR 8 *Kriegsstammrollen, 1914-1918*
Landesarchiv Baden-Württemberg, Hauptstaatsarchiv Stuttgart
Kriegsstammrollen, 1914-1918, M478 RIR 121
M595, *Vermisstenkartei* I
M596, *Vermisstenkartei* II
M597, *Vermisstenkartei* III

Official War Diaries
On-line Australian War Diaries, Australian War Memorial, Canberra
On-line Canadian War Diaries, Library and Archives Canada, Ottawa

Newspapers
Freiburger Zeitung

Printed sources (books and articles)
Anon, *An der Somme, Erinnerungen der 12. Infanterie Division an die Stellungskämpfe und Schlacht an der Somme Oktober 1915 bis November 1916,* Berlin, 1918
Anon, *Deutsche Verlustlisten,* (1916-1919), Berlin, 1914-1919
Anon, *Die 26. Reserve Division 1914-1918,* Stuttgart, 1920
Anon, *Ehrenbuch der Stadt Karlsruhe 1914-1918*, Karlsruhe, 1930
Anon, *Festschrift zur Wiedersehens-Feier der Angehörigen des ehem. Res. Inf. Regts. 111,* Karlsruhe, 1932
Anon, *Illustrierte Geschichte des Weltkrieges 1914/16,* Band 5-9, Stuttgart, n.d.
Anon, *Kriegstagbuch aus Schwaben,* Stuttgart, 1914-1919
Bachelin, Major Eduard, *Das Reserve-Infanterie-Regiment Nr. 111 im Weltkrieg 1914 bis 1918,* Karlsruhe, 1938
Baumgartner, Richard (Ed.), 'An der Somme, An interview with Soldat Emil Geobelbecker', *Der Angriff, A Journal of World War I History,* 1979, No. 3
Bayerisches Kriegsarchiv, *Die Bayern im Grossen Krieg 1914-1918,* München, 1923
Baynes, John, *Far from a Donkey: The life of General Sir Ivor Maxse Kcb,Cvo, Dso,* London, 1996
Bean, C.E.W., *The Australian Imperial Forces in France, 1917.* Canberra, 1941
Delmensingen, *General der Artillerie* Konrad Kraft von & Feeser, Generalmajor a.D. Friedrichfranz, *Das Bayernbuch vom Weltkriege 1914-1918,* Stuttgart, 1930
Edmonds, Brigadier-General Sir James E., *History of the Great War. Military Operations*

rance and Belgium 1916. 2nd July 1916 to the end of the Battles of the Somme, London, 1938

hrler, Hans Heinrich, Ehrenbuch der Gefallenen Stuttgarts 1914-1918, Stuttgart, 1925

abeck, Hans von, Im Orkan der Sommeschlacht. Ein Abschnitt aus der Kriegsgeschichte des
eserve-Infanterie-Regiment Nr. 99, Berlin, 1930

iedel, Paul, Geschichte des Infanterie Regiments von Winterfeldt (2, Oberschlesisches) Nr.23,
)as Regiment im Weltkriege, Berlin, 1929

orstner, Major a.D. Kurt Freiherr von, Das Königlich-Preussische Reserve-Infanterie-Regiment
Vr. 15, Oldenburg, 1929

rick, Leutnant der Landwehr Albert, Erlebnisse in den Ersten Tagen der Somme-Schlacht (24
uni bis 7 Juli 1916), 1916

risch, Georg, Das Reserve-Infanterie-Regiment Nr. 109 im Weltkrieg 1914 bis 1918, Karlsruhe,
931

'ühren, Franz, Lehrer im Krieg, Berlin, 1932

General Staff, Handbook of the German Army in War, January 1917, Wakefield, 1973

Gerster, Matthäus, Das Württembergische Reserve-Infanterie-Regiment Nr. 119 im Weltkrieg
914-1918, Stuttgart, 1920

Gerster, Matthäus, Die Schwaben an der Ancre, Heilbronn a.N., 1918

Gerster, Matthäus, Treffen der 26.R.D. am 5 Juli 1936, Stuttgart, 1936

[Greiner & Vulpius], Reserve-Infanterie-Regiment Nr. 110 im Weltkrieg 1914-1918, Karlsruhe,
1934

Holtz, Hauptmann Freiherr Georg vom, Das Württembergische Reserve-Infanterie-Regiment Nr.
121 im Weltkrieg 1914-1918, Stuttgart, 1921

Ihlenfeld, Oberst a.D. v. & Engle, Major a.D., Das 9. Badische Infanterie-Regiment Nr.170 im
Weltkrieg, Oldenburg, 1926

Jäger, Herbert, German Artillery of World War One, Marlborough, 2001

Kahn, Leo, Retreat to the Siegfried Line, Purnell's History of the Great War, No. 73, (Volume 5,
No. 9), 1971

Kaiser, Generalmajor a.D. Franz, Das Königlich Preussen Infanterie-Regiment Nr. 63
(4.Oberschlesisches), Berlin, 1940

Kameradschaftsbund, Ehrentafel Res. Inf. Regt. 119, n.d.

Klaus, Major a.D. Justizrat Max, Das Württembergisches Reserve-Feldartillerie-Regiment Nr.
6 im Weltkrieg 1914-1918, Stuttgart, 1929

nies, Oberstleutnant L., Das Württembergishe Pionier Bataillon Nr. 13 im Weltkrieg 1914-
918, Stuttgart, 1937

Kölbig, Kurt Siegfried, Kuhn, Hans-Karl, Gedanken an der Westfront 1914-1917. Das
Tagesbuch des Leutnants der Reserve Karl August Zwiffelhoffer, Nyon, 2007

Korfes, Hauptmann a.D. Dr. Otto, Das 3.Magdeburgische Infanterie-Regiment Nr. 66 im
Weltkriege, Berlin, 1930

Korps Buchhandlung, Der Schützengraben, Feldzeitung des XIV Reservekorps (1915-1917),
Bapaume, 1915-1917

Korpsverlagsbuchhandlung, An der Somme, Bapaume, 1917

Korpsverlagsbuchhandlung, Zwischen Arras und Péronne, Bapaume, 1916

Kühl, Hermann von, Der Weltkrieg 1914-1918, Berlin 1933

Kümmel, Leutnant d.Res. a.D. Studienrat Dr. Phil., Reserve-Infanterie-Regiment Nr. 91 im
Weltkriege 1914-1918, Oldenburg, 1926

Lais, Otto, Die Schlacht an der Somme, Karlsruhe, 1940

Lutz, Ralph Haswell, Fall of the German Empire 1914-1918, Stanford, California, 1932

Lutz, Ralph Haswell, *The Causes of the German Collapse in 1918*, Stanford, California, 1934

Merkatz, Friedrich von, *Unterrichtsbuch für die Maschinengewehr-Kompagnien Gerät 08*, Berlin 1918

Moos, Leutnant d. R. a.D. Ernst, *Das Württembergische Res.-Feld-Artillerie Regiment Nr.27 im Weltkrieg 1916-1918*, Stuttgart, 1925

Moser, Generalleutnant Otto von, *Die Württemberger im Weltkriege*, Stuttgart, 1938

Mücke, Kgl. Preuss. Rittmeister a.D. Kurt von, *Das Grossherzoglich Badische Infanterie-Regiment Nr. 185*, Oldenburg, 1922

Müller, Major d.R. Paul, Fabeck, Oberst a.D. Hans von & Riesel, Oberstleutnant a.D. Richard, *Geschichte des Reserve-Infanterie-Regiment Nr. 99*, Zeulenroda, 1936

Müller-Loebnitz, Oberstleutnant Wilhelm, *Die Badener im Weltkrieg*, Karlsruhe, 1935.

Neubronn, Leutnant Dr. Carl & Pfeffer, Leutnant d. R. Dr. Georg, *Geschichte des Infanterie-Regiments 186*, Oldenburg, 1926

Offiziersverein des I.R. 180, *Totenbuch des 10.Württembergischen Infanterie-Regiment Nr. 180. Namentliches Verzeichnis der im Weltkrieg 1914-1918 gefallenen Offiziere, Unteroffiziere und Mannschaften*, Stuttgart, 1936

Reichskriegsministerium, *Der Weltkrieg 1914 bis 1918. Die Militärischen Operationen zu Lande, Zehnter Band*, Berlin, 1936

Reichskriegsministerium, *Der Weltkrieg 1914 bis 1918. Die Militärischen Operationen zu Lande, Elfter Band*, Berlin, 1938

Reichskriegsministerium, *Der Weltkrieg 1914 bis 1918. Die Militärischen Operationen zu Lande, Zwölfter Band*, Berlin, 1939

Reichskriegsministerium, *Der Weltkrieg 1914 bis 1918. Die Militärischen Operationen zu Lande, Dreizehnter Band*, Berlin, 1942

Reichskriegsministerium, *Der Weltkrieg 1914 bis 1918. Die Militärischen Operationen zu Lande, Vierzehnter Band*, Berlin, 1944

Reymann, Oberleutnant a.D. H., *3.Oberschlesische Infanterie-Regiment Nr. 62 im Kriege 1914-1918*, Zeulenroda, 1930

Riedel, Frieder, *Zwischen Kriegsgericht und Heldentod, Der Grabenkrieg an der Somme 1914-1916*, Echterdingen, 2008

Sheldon, Jack, *The Germans Army on the Somme 1914-1916*, Barnsley, 2005.

Sheldon, Jack, *The Germans at Thiepval*, Barnsley, 2006

Silbereisen, Leutnant der Reserve, Ehrler, Landsturmmann Hans Heinrich, Eisenmann, Landsturmmann Alexander & Schulze-Etzel, Gefreiten Theodor, *Schwäbische Kunde aus den grossen Krieg*, Stuttgart, 1918

Soden, General der Infanterie a.D. Freiherr von, *Die 26.(Württembergische) Reserve-Division im Weltkrieg 1914-1918*, Stuttgart, 1939

Stosch, Oberstleutnant a.D. Albrecht von, *Somme-Nord II.Teil: Die Brennpunkte der Schlacht im Juli 1916*, Oldenburg, 1927

Vischer, Oberstleutnant Alfred, *Das 10. Württembergische Infanterie-Regiment Nr. 180 in der Somme-Schlacht 1916*, Stuttgart, 1917

Vischer, Oberstleutnant Alfred, *Das 10. Württembergische Infanterie-Regiment Nr. 180 im Weltkrieg 1914-1918*, Stuttgart, 1921

Volksbund Deutsche Kriegsgräberfürsorge e.V., *Deutsche Kriegsgräber, Am Rande der Strasse, Frankreich, Belgien, Luxemburg und Niederlande*, Kassel, n.d.

Wissmann, Oberst von, *Das Reserve-Infanterie-Regiment Nr. 55 im Weltkrieg,* Berlin, n.d.
Wohlenberg, Oberleutnant d.R. a.D. Rektor Alfred, *Das Reserve-Infanterie-Regiment Nr. 77 im Weltkriege 1914-18,* Hildesheim, 1931
Wurmb, Herbert Ritter von, *Das K. B. Reserve-Infanterie-Regiment Nr. 8,* München, 1929